GREAT CAMPAIGNS OF WORLD WAR II

GREAT CAMPAIGNS OF WORLD WAR II

BLACK CAT

List of contributors includes:
Major-General R H Barry
C P Campbell
Paul Carell
Peter Elstob
Major-General Sir Francis de Guingand
Guy Hartcup
Col Robert D Heinl Jr
Lt-Cmdr Peter Kemp
Major K J Macksey
Dudley Pope
Denis Richards
Dr Jürgen Rohwer
R W Thompson

Co-ordinating editor: J B Davies

First published by Phoebus Publishing Company/BPC Publishing Limited, London
Reprinted 1988 by Macdonald & Co (Publishers) Ltd under the Black Cat imprint
Macdonald & Co (Publishers) Ltd
3rd Floor, Greater London House,
Hampstead Road, London NW1 7QX

a member of Maxwell Pergamon Publishing Corporation plc

This material first appeared in *Battle of the Atlantic* © 1968 Phoebus Publishing Co/BPC Publishing Ltd; *The Battle of Britain* © 1974 BPC Publishing Ltd; *The Desert War* © 1968 Phoebus Publishing Co/BPC Publishing Ltd; *D-Day: Invasion of Hitler's Europe* © 1968 Phoebus Publishing Co/BPC Publishing Ltd; *Battle of the Pacific* © Phoebus Publishing Co/BPC Publishing Ltd

Printed in Spain

ISBN 0-7481-0151-9

INTRODUCTION

This book is divided into five sections which tell the story of some of the most crucial and bitterly fought contests in the history of warfare. Each one of the campaigns was complete in itself, but together they all had a vital bearing on the outcome of the entire war.

The book opens with the *Battle for the Atlantic* which was, as Churchill said, 'the dominating factor all through the war. Never for one moment could we forget that everything elsewhere depended on its outcome'. The activities of the formidable German Atlantic armoury—the U-boat wolf-packs, pocket-battleships, long-range bombers—and the tactics and technology of the Allied answer, from Asdic and 'Hedgehog' to the armed merchant cruiser and escort carrier, are discussed at great length in this first section.

In July 1940, when Göring promised Hitler he would smash the RAF within a month, Britain stood alone against dictatorship. Invasion was imminent. But, thanks to the tireless heroism of the pilots and ground crews of Fighter Command, the precarious superiority of their Spitfires and Hurricanes, and, ultimately, the morale of the entire country, which are all well documented and photographed in this book, that invasion was 'postponed indefinitely'. By 17 September the real *Battle of Britain* was over.

The Desert War, seemingly self-contained and remote, was fought in the wastes of North Africa, from September 1940 to May 1943. The book describes in detail the constant see-sawing of activity over a 1,500-mile front, the great clashes of men and machinery, but above all, the great generalship that made this war, and its battles, legendary.

While victory in the desert was opening up southern Europe to the Allies, the decision was taken to invade the north. Hitler had boasted to his generals that he was the greatest fortress builder of all time. Buried beneath millions of tons of concrete, behind miles of barbed wire, mines, and guns of every calibre, the 'Atlantic Wall' was the rampart of the Nazis' conquest with the sea as its ditch. Against this mighty bastion the Western Allies pitched their courage, ingenuity, and organizing skill. Operation Overlord, launched on 6 June, 1944—*D-Day*—was the beginning of the end for Hitler. But the book tells not just the story of that one day, but of the months of careful planning and strategic debate that preceded it.

The Battle of the Pacific introduced the Japanese into the fray and was mainly a struggle between them and the United States. Tacitly encouraged by Hitler, the Japanese began a course of economic and territorial expansion in late 1941. They quickly acquired huge land and sea domains, but in six months had overstepped their ability to defend these vast areas. The book takes the reader through Midway, Guadalcanal, Iwo Jima and Okinawa to the eventual and unforgettable climax—the atom bomb explosions at Hiroshima and Nagasaki—and the sudden end of World War II.

Keystone

Left: US Marines crouch behind a rock to avoid the blast as a heavy explosive charge blows up a cave connected to a Japanese blockhouse on Iwo Jima in March 1945

LA MER

CONTENTS

On the road near the town of Carentan, a US doctor is attending to a wounded man who has been hit by a sniper in the aftermath of the D-Day landings in France

THE BATTLE FOR THE ATLANTIC

The outbreak of war found the German navy still in the making but far from unprepared. To the tenuous Allied blockade of the Axis powers came the challenge of the Nazi surface raiders and the deadlier threat of the U-boats.

The war plans of the Royal Navy had been taking shape since 1936, when Hitler's march into the Rhineland had set the pattern of his future path of aggression. Even at that time, it was apparent to the British Chiefs-of-Staff that war would come, and in a memorandum to the Cabinet they assumed it would break out in the latter part of 1939.

As a result of the Rhineland occupation a supplementary naval estimate was introduced into the House of Commons in 1936 to build two new battleships, an aircraft-carrier, five cruisers, and a variety of smaller ships, to be followed in 1937 by estimates which included another three battleships, two more aircraft-carriers, seven cruisers, and a big increase in small craft. And when the nation went to war in 1939, the first of these ships was beginning to join the fleet.

The war plans, which were sent out from the Admiralty on January 30, 1939, represented the adoption of a defensive strategy. That this has to be so in the early stages of a war is a well-proved element in the exercise of sea power. The desire to rush into offensive action has so often been the prelude to local disaster that naval planning in the initial stages of a maritime war must always allow time for a sufficient force to be built up and trained for the offensive. Only when that stage has been reached can the true dividends of an offensive strategy be harvested.

The naval plan in 1939, which was based on the assumption that the war would be fought against both Germany and Italy from the start, fell into three broad parts. The first looked to the defence of trade in home waters and the Atlantic. This was fundamental to any national strategy, for supplies are the vital sinews of war. Second came the defence of trade in the Mediterranean and the Indian Ocean. It was obvious that, if Italy became an energetic enemy, her dominating geographical position in the Mediterranean would force all seaborne trade to use the longer route round the Cape of Good Hope, but it was hoped to contain her ádequately with a strong fleet in the Mediterranean. The third broad part of the naval plan was the imposition of a blockade on Germany and Italy, and with the actual declaration of war was published the list of contraband liable to seizure at sea, even if carried in neutral ships.

To put the plan into operation, the main strength of the Home Fleet was concentrated in Scotland. Far to the north the cruisers of the Northern Patrol kept watch, waiting to intercept any enemy or neutral ship, whether inward or outward bound. From the Shetlands to the coast of Norway a line of search was mounted, partly by air patrols, partly by submarines. The Home Fleet, less a few units stationed elsewhere, lay at Scapa Flow, more than capable of meeting any surface threat which the enemy could mount at sea. At Rosyth lay the aircraft-carrier *Furious* and her attendant destroyers, while submarine flotillas were based at Dundee and Blyth to carry the naval war into German waters. A cruiser squadron and a destroyer flotilla lay in the Humber, while far to the south a force of battleships, aircraft-carriers, cruisers, and destroyers was based at Portland to hold the southern exit into the Atlantic.

In addition to the Home Fleet, the four

Ullstein

Grand Admiral Raeder (centre), Hitler's naval commander until replaced by Dönitz, plans the course of the Atlantic war Germany's U-boats so nearly won

home commands – Plymouth, Portsmouth, the Nore, and Rosyth – each had forces of destroyers, anti-submarine vessels, and minesweepers for convoy duties and local defence, under the command of the local commanders-in-chief. In the light of existing naval knowledge in 1939, all this formed a net strong enough and wide enough to catch any enemy ship attempting to force a way out or in.

In the Mediterranean, the agreement was that the French navy would hold the western basin in force. The British Mediterranean Fleet was therefore based on Alexandria, to operate in and dominate the eastern basin. To implement the blockade, the naval plan called for strong forces in the Gibraltar Straits and the Red Sea, where examination anchorages for all merchant ships entering the Mediterranean were set up.

The German war plans were, of course, tailored to a fleet which was basically unready for war. Shortly after coming to power, Hitler had told Admiral Raeder that he would not precipitate a general war until 1944, and it was on this assumption that Raeder had planned German naval expansion. When the war came in 1939, many of the ships which Raeder had hoped would be ready were still building or in the planning stage. Nevertheless, he still had a useful navy. The three pocket-battleships – nominally of 10,000 tons to keep within treaty limitations but secretly built to 13,000 tons – were immediately available. The battle-cruisers *Scharnhorst* and *Gneisenau,* which also exceeded their treaty limits, by 6,000 tons, were formidable opponents, and the big Hipper-class cruisers, some 4,000 tons overweight, were nearly ready. There were 56 U-boats, of which all but ten were operational, and their crews had been well trained, during the years when no U-boats were permitted, under the pretence that they were undergoing anti-submarine exercises.

The German battle instructions were issued to their fleet in May 1939. The plan envisaged a continuous series of operations in the North Sea to create as much nuisance as possible, mainly by attacks on shipping, and thus tying down large British forces to contain them. All the larger ships were due to cruise in the oceans in a heavy and sustained attack on merchant shipping. The U-boats were to operate against trade in the Atlantic and in the approaches to the main British ports. And to counterbalance the delay in the new heavy ships still under construction, a number of merchant ships were to be taken in hand for conversion into fast, heavily armed raiders.

In the German battle instructions, one ominous phrase was inserted: 'fighting methods will never fail to be employed merely because some international regulations are opposed to them.' It was a foreshadowing of the unrestricted submarine and raider warfare which, it had been hoped in Britain, had by now been outlawed for all time as an instrument of naval warfare.

The German navy made its war dispositions in good time. On August 21, 1939, the pocket-battleship *Graf Spee,* using darkness for her passage of the North Sea, slipped into the Atlantic unobserved. Three days later the *Deutschland,* another pocket-battleship, made a similar move, also undetected. Their supply tankers, *Altmark* and *Westerwald,* joined them there, their passages also being unobserved. Between August 19 and 29, 17 of the ocean-going type of U-boat were sent out to their Atlantic war patrol areas while seven of the smaller coastal type were dispatched to lay mines off the Channel ports. Six more were sent out to patrol the central North Sea.

Under clear skies in mid-Atlantic, a U-boat – safe from sudden aerial attack – finishes off its victim in a surface attack in 1943

Bapty & Co Ltd

The initial task of the Royal Navy was to draw a ring round the enemy, denying him the supplies which could only come over the seas. From the south of Norway, across and down the North Sea, and throughout the length of the Mediterranean, Allied sea power held the ring. Allied land and air power filled the Continental gaps. Only to the east, where Russia enjoyed a breathing space through her non-aggression pact with Germany, was a possible supply line left open. One result of this closing of the ring can be judged by the fact that, from the outbreak of war to the end of 1939, the Royal Navy seized 530,000 tons of supplies destined for Germany.

It was outside this ring, however, that the problems accumulated. Within hours of the declaration of war the Donaldson liner *Athenia* was attacked by U-30 200 miles west of Hebrides, and was sunk with a loss of 112 lives. It is true that the captain of U-30 exceeded his instructions in sinking this ship, but her loss was taken in the British Admiralty as evidence that unrestricted submarine warfare was already in force. The provisional arrangements in the war plan for the defence of ocean trade, which was to have been by the patrol of focal points and the evasive routing of merchant ships, was abandoned, and it was decided to adopt the full convoy system as soon as it could be introduced.

It was at this stage that the Royal Navy began to feel acutely the pre-war lateness of the naval rebuilding programme. Such destroyers and other ships as were available as convoy escorts lacked the endurance to take them far out into the Atlantic, and until the new ships came along, a 'limit of convoy' had to be drawn at about 300 miles to the west. After that point, the ships in convoy dispersed and proceeded independently. Incoming convoys were escorted across the Atlantic by an anti-raider escort, usually an armed merchant cruiser, and then were picked up by the escort forces at the limit of convoy and escorted into British ports. Later, as the new ships became available, the convoy limit was pushed farther out into the Atlantic, but it was not until mid-1941 that the Royal Navy was able to provide an anti-submarine escort all the way across the Atlantic.

But even with these limitations, the shipping loss figures were fairly encouraging. Up to the end of 1939, U-boats had sunk 114

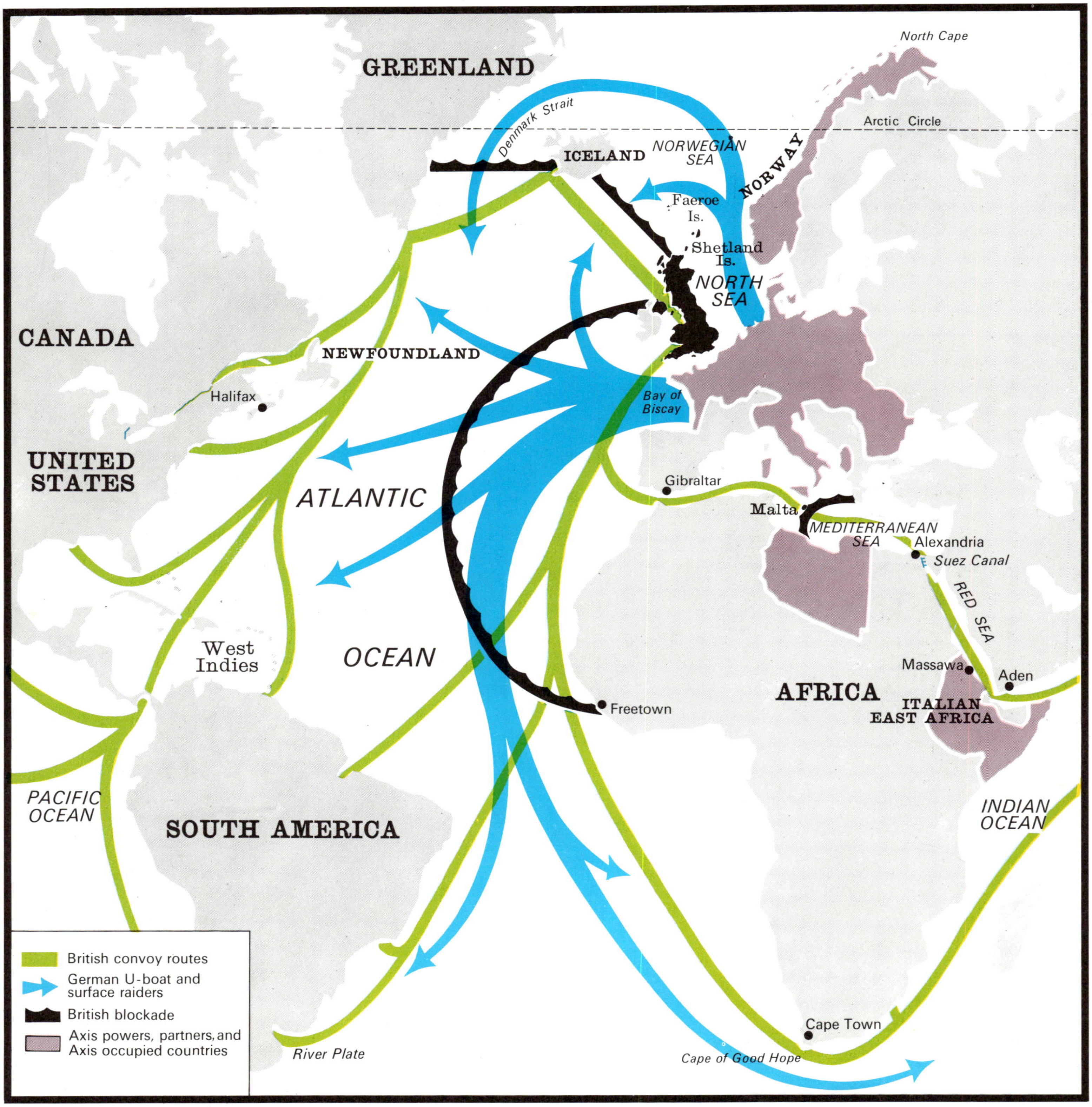

ships with a tonnage of 421,156, but nine U-boats had paid the price. Considering the attenuated strength of the escort forces, these figures were satisfactory. But that these results were ephemeral in the overall picture was always present in the British Admiralty's mind. It was known that Germany was embarking on a very substantial programme of U-boat construction, and that, by 1941 at latest, the number of operational submarines would be doubled or trebled, and that this number would be progressively increased as the war lengthened. There was no blinking the fact that, once the U-boat fleet was at full strength, merchant ship losses would be grievous.

In the meantime, an attempt to take the offensive against the U-boat led to disaster. Two hunting groups were formed, each consisting of an aircraft-carrier and four destroyers, to operate against U-boats in the western approaches. On September 14 the *Ark Royal* was narrowly missed by torpedoes from U-39. The escorting destroyers counterattacked, sank the U-boat, and captured her crew. But it had been a narrow shave.

Three days later the second hunting group was in action. The aircraft-carrier *Courageous* was sighted by U-29, which torpedoed and sank her with a loss of 519 lives, and lived to tell the tale. At that stage of the war aircraft-carriers were particularly valuable ships, since those ordered in 1936 and 1937 were not expected to be operational until 1941 at earliest, and the British Admiralty quickly decided that it was asking for trouble to risk them on that type of warfare. The *Ark Royal* was quickly withdrawn to take her proper place again with the Home Fleet.

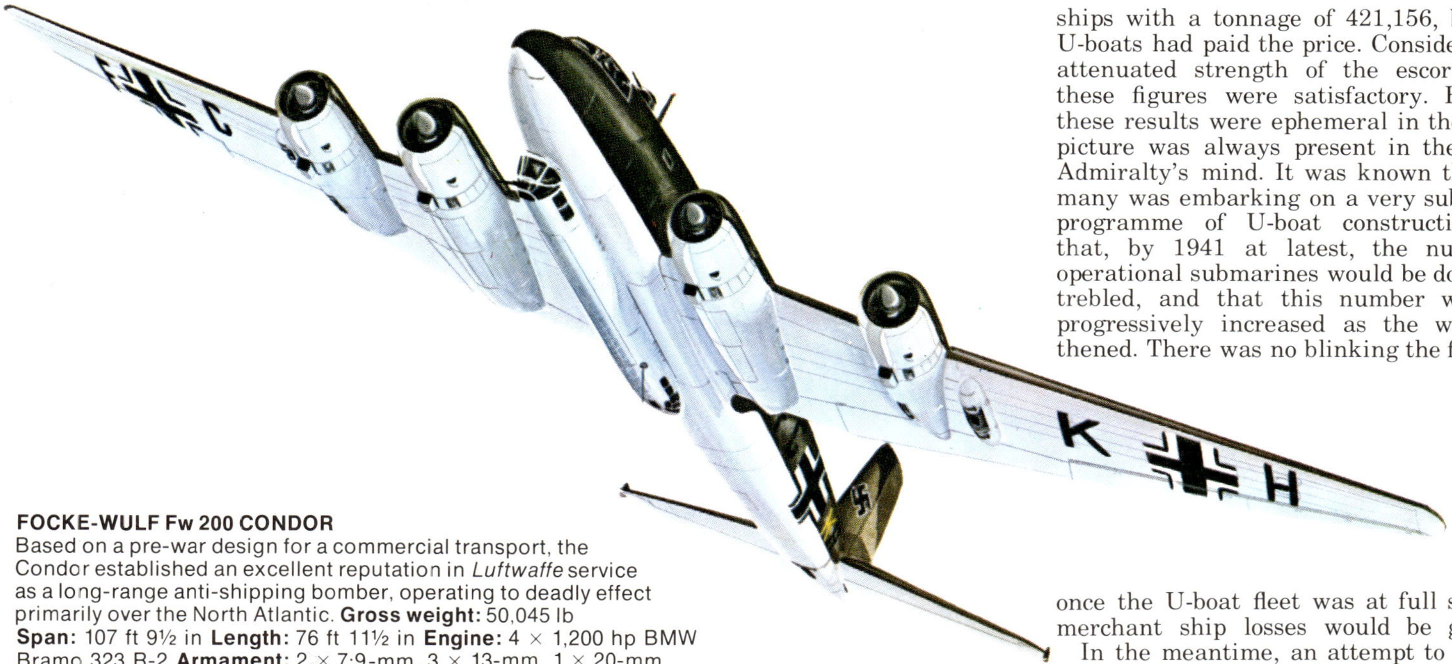

FOCKE-WULF Fw 200 CONDOR
Based on a pre-war design for a commercial transport, the Condor established an excellent reputation in *Luftwaffe* service as a long-range anti-shipping bomber, operating to deadly effect primarily over the North Atlantic. **Gross weight:** 50,045 lb **Span:** 107 ft 9½ in **Length:** 76 ft 11½ in **Engine:** 4 × 1,200 hp BMW Bramo 323 R-2 **Armament:** 2 × 7·9-mm, 3 × 13-mm, 1 × 20-mm machine-guns **Crew:** 7 **Speed:** 224 mph at 15,750 ft **Ceiling:** 19,000 ft **Range:** 2,210 miles **Bomb load:** 4,620 lb

BRISTOL BEAUFORT Mk 11
The RAF's standard Coastal Command torpedo-bomber from 1940 to 1943, when it saw service over the North Sea, English Channel, the Atlantic, Mediterranean and North Africa. **Gross weight:** 21,050 lb **Span:** 57 ft 10 in **Length:** 44 ft 7 in **Engine:** 2 × 1,200 hp Twin Wasp **Armament:** 4 × ·303 machine-guns **Crew:** 4 **Speed:** 268 mph **Ceiling:** 25,000 ft **Range:** 1,054 miles **Bomb load:** 1 × 1,605 lb torpedo or 1,500 lb bomb load

E-BOAT
A serious threat to Allied shipping in the inshore waters of the North Sea, the Channel and the Western Approaches, the German E-boats were larger, more seaworthy, more heavily armed and more reliable mechanically than their British counterparts the MTBs. **Displacement:** 92¼ tons **Armament:** one 37-mm AA, one 20-mm AA; two 21-inch torpedoes

With the horizon clear, crew members sun themselves on the deck of a U-boat

Inside the Admiralty an organisation was growing to co-ordinate the war against the U-boat. Before the war an operational intelligence centre had been set up to deal with all intelligence received of an operational nature, to deduce its value, and to pass it out to the fleet.

On the submarine side a 'tracking room' was established into which came every piece of U-boat intelligence. Reports from agents in enemy countries, giving details of arrivals and departures, U-boat sightings by ships and aircraft, U-boat attacks, and, most prolific source of all, wireless bearings of every message transmitted at sea by a U-boat—all were channelled into the intelligence centre. The tracking room was connected by teleprinters to every wireless direction-finding station in the country, and within minutes of a U-boat using her wireless the bearings were coming in. By plotting the bearings on a chart, the U-boat's position was established.

Alongside the submarine tracking room was the 'trade plot', which showed the position, course, and speed of every convoy and independent ship at sea. By putting these two plots together, the position of any U-boat could be seen in relation to any convoy, and evasive action taken by signalling to the convoy to alter course if it were heading into danger of attack. Both the tracking room and the trade plot were manned day and night, and, as the war developed, a high degree of expertise in forecasting the movement of U-boats was built up. Indeed, so great became the efficiency of the tracking room that by 1943 more U-boats were being sunk at sea than ships sunk by U-boats.

Mine warfare

U-boats, however, by no means constituted the only danger to merchant ships. As early as the first week of war, some ships were being sunk or damaged by mines of a new type, quickly identified as 'magnetic influence' type, for which the British had no minesweeping countermeasure. It was not until November 23 that a German aircraft presented them with the answer. It dropped its mine in the mudflats off Shoeburyness, and at great personal risk it was dismantled by Lieutenant-Commander J. G. D. Ouvry, and revealed its polarity.

With that knowledge it became possible to develop a magnetic sweep which would explode the mines harmlessly and also to provide ships with a 'degaussing mantle' which enabled them to pass over the mines without actuating their firing gear. But by the end of November the magnetic mine had cost the British 46 ships of 180,000 tons, as well as a destroyer sunk and several warships damaged. The total loss by mines up to the end of 1939 was 79 merchant ships totalling 262,697 tons.

Another source of loss, and one much more difficult to counter, was the armed surface raider. It has been mentioned above that the Germans sent two pocket-battleships into the Atlantic, together with their supply tankers, before the outbreak of war. The first hint that they were at sea came to the Admiralty in the form of ships sunk or missing in waters far beyond those where the U-boats lurked. Gradually the picture was built up as more losses were reported, and the reaction of the Admiralty was to form hunting groups to cover the North and South Atlantic Oceans and the Indian Ocean. In addition, battleships and cruisers were sent across the Atlantic to Halifax to act as

A Sea Hurricane about to be launched from a Catapult Armed Merchantman (CAM). With the acute shortage of Royal Navy convoy escort vessels, the CAM ship was vital in Atlantic convoy protection. Unfortunately, each mission for one of these planes meant the loss of the plane as well as a ducking for the pilot who ditched beside his 'mother' ship

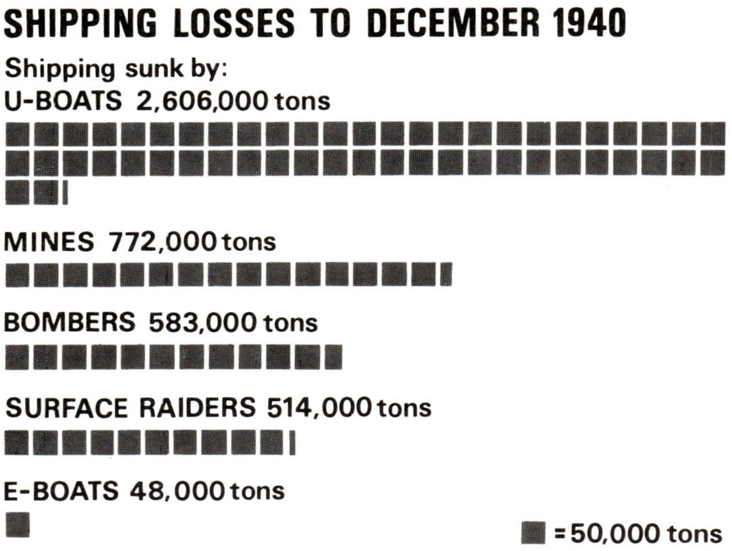

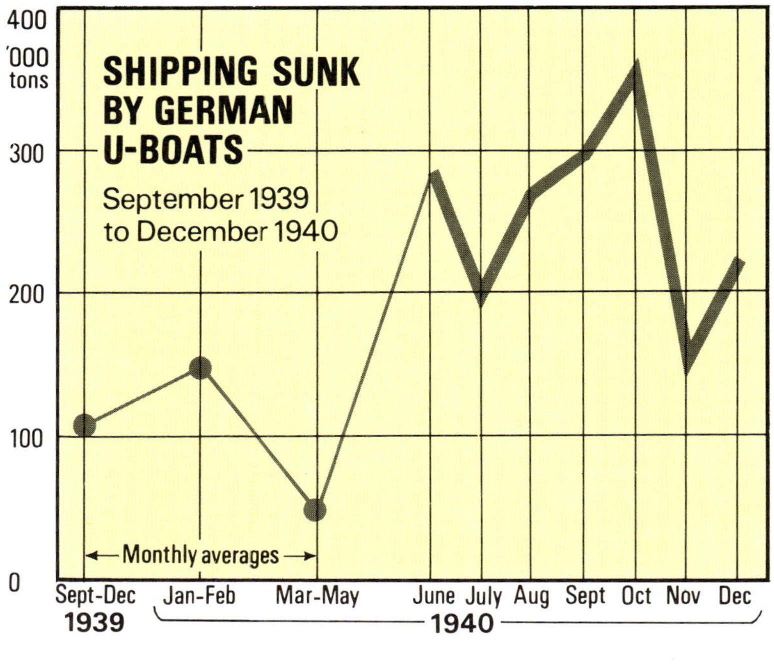

raider escorts to successive convoys sailing to Britain.

The first success, and one that enormously boosted British war morale, was the destruction of the pocket-battleship *Graf Spee* in the estuary of the River Plate. She had been tracked down by the positions of the ships she had sunk, and a brilliant piece of deduction by Commodore Henry Harwood had led to his hunting group being in position to intercept her as she moved towards the South American coast in search of other victims. She had sunk nine ships of some 50,000 tons before she was brought to action, a poor result in comparison with her overwhelming strength and fire-power. The cruise of the *Deutschland* was even less productive. She sank two ships in the North Atlantic before being called home.

The *Deutschland's* efforts in the Atlantic were followed in November by a more ambitious venture on the part of Admiral Raeder, who sent out the battle-cruisers *Scharnhorst* and *Gneisenau* on a combined cruise into the North Atlantic, with the object of dislocating the British patrol lines. It was a preliminary operation to give the two big ships some experience before letting them loose on the main trade routes. They sailed from Germany on November 21, but on the evening of the 23rd, just as they were breaking out into the Atlantic between the Faeroe Islands and Iceland, they were sighted and engaged by the armed merchant cruiser *Rawalpindi*. She, of course, was no match for a battle-cruiser, and was quickly sunk by the *Scharnhorst,* but not before she had sent out two wireless sighting reports.

Admiral Forbes, the Commander-in-Chief, at once sailed from Scapa Flow with the Home Fleet, and HMS *Newcastle,* the next ship to the *Rawalpindi* in the patrol line, closed the position and sighted the two battle-cruisers, but lost them again in a heavy rainstorm. Admiral Marschall, who commanded the two German ships, broke away at high speed and abandoned the operation, returning to Germany. The Home Fleet had little chance of catching the two battle-cruisers, for the distance was too great.

This whole operation raised some doubts in the British Admiralty's mind as to the degree of severity with which these German raiding ventures were to be carried out. It seemed inexplicable that, on sighting the *Newcastle,* these ships should not turn on her and send her to the bottom. Her 6-inch guns were no match for the 11-inch guns carried by the two battle-cruisers, and the fact that they turned back and ran for home hardly made sense in real naval warfare. At the time it was believed by the Admiralty and by Admiral Forbes that the *Rawalpindi* had been sunk by the *Deutschland,* but even this would not explain the sudden disengagement. She also carried 11-inch guns. This was an aspect of German naval warfare that was to recur throughout the war at sea, and one which caused constant surprise.

One other part of the initial German war plan went amiss in the early days. This was the design to employ forces in the North Sea to disrupt British shipping and tie down a sizable portion of the British fleet. On December 12 a force of five destroyers, covered by three cruisers, sailed to lay a minefield off the Northumberland coast. They were sighted on their return by the submarine *Salmon,* which torpedoed the cruisers *Leipzig* and *Nürnberg,* damaging them both. Two days later, as this force approached the Danish coast, it was again attacked, this time by the submarine *Ursula.* The *Leipzig* escaped the torpedoes, but one of her escorting destroyers was hit and sunk.

But the Royal Navy, too, was having its troubles. The biggest blow occurred early in the morning of October 14 when U-47, commanded by Lieutenant Prien, penetrated the defences of Scapa Flow and torpedoed and sank the battleship *Royal Oak.* The loss of the battleship herself was relatively unimportant in the context of the strengths of the opposing navies, but what was of concern was the realisation that the main operational base of the Royal Navy was vulnerable to submarine attack. Until its defences could be made secure by the use of more

THE GRAF SPEE:

Already at sea when war broke out, the fast, heavily-armed pocket-battleship *Graf Spee* was able to wreak havoc in the South Atlantic, where she sank eight ships, as well as one in the Indian Ocean. On December 13, 1939, however, she encountered a vastly inferior Allied cruiser force, joined battle, but—inexplicably—turned and fled to seek refuge in the estuary of the River Plate after an engagement of only 100 minutes

Once safely in the neutral waters of the River Plate, the *Graf Spee* became involved in a diplomatic intrigue resulting in the suicide of her captain and the scuttling of the ship

blockships in the entrances, the Home Fleet was forced to use Loch Ewe on the western coast of Scotland as an anchorage, even though it, too, was open to submarine attack. Indeed, only six weeks later, HMS *Nelson,* the fleet flagship, was damaged by a mine as she was entering Loch Ewe.

A balance sheet drawn up at the end of 1939 would have shown figures favourable to the Royal Navy. The main doubt in the mind of the British Admiralty before the war had begun was whether the threat to British trade poised by surface raiders could be held, and particularly were the three pocket-battleships held in dread. And here there was already a favourable balance, with only 15 British, Allied, and neutral merchant ships sunk and one of the three pocket-battleships lying on the sea bed in Montevideo Roads. The toll by the U-boats had not been unduly heavy: 114 ships of 421,000 tons had been sunk with a loss to the enemy of nine U-boats. Casualties from mines (79 ships of 262,000 tons) were severe, but with the discovery of the polarity of the German magnetic mine, it was believed that the back of this particular problem had been broken. On the debit side could be placed the loss of the *Royal Oak* and *Courageous,* one armed merchant cruiser, three destroyers, and one submarine. Taken as a whole, the picture was reasonably encouraging.

Yet in the longer view there was still much to worry the Admiralty in London. It had been believed before the war—and still was, since no evidence had come in to the contrary—that the British 'asdic' submarine detector, as fitted in all anti-submarine vessels, was a sufficient guarantee against any repetition of such merchant ship losses as had been experienced between 1914 and 1918, particularly when allied to the modern depth-charge, with its multiple depth settings. But evidence was already accumulating within the Admiralty of the size of the German U-boat building programme, and there were those who foresaw a time, judged at around a couple of years, when the defence could well be in danger of being swamped by sheer weight of numbers.

There was one other aspect of the submarine war which caused some uneasiness: a lack of sufficiently 'long-legged' escorts to provide merchant ship convoy for the whole length of passage. As matters stood at the beginning of 1940, there was, on the transatlantic passage alone, a gap of some 1,700 miles across which merchant ships were beyond the range of surface escort. It was an even longer gap on some of the other main trade routes.

As events turned out during the first six months of 1940, these early doubts became real enough. The campaign in Norway in April and May of 1940 and the evacuation of the British Expeditionary Force from the Channel ports in May and early June of the same year are well-known episodes from the history of the war, but a brief reference to them here is necessary to assess their influence on the overall picture of trade defence. During the Norwegian campaign ten destroyers and sloops were sunk and another 14 damaged. The evacuation of the BEF added six more destroyers and sloops sunk and a further 20 damaged.

This was a serious drain of those ships which, by their nature, were the best escorts for the defence of trade—but an even more serious gap in possible escort vessels was caused by the obvious corollary of the fall of France. The Germans were now poised on the Channel coast, and talk of invasion was in the air. This inevitably meant that many naval ships, and particularly destroyers, were tied up to watch for any enemy movement across the Channel, and this duty, which lasted for four months until the danger of invasion began to fade, inevitably led to further and serious shortages in the forces available for merchant ship escort.

Bad as this was, there was worse to follow. In the last months of 1939 the enemy had attempted, though with little success, to organise attacks on convoys by groups of U-boats instead of by single boats. On a convoy being sighted and reported, U-boat headquarters would call in adjacent boats to

RAIDER AT LARGE

Keystone

The burning, scuttled hulk of the ship

Why such a mighty warship—only lightly damaged in her brief encounter with the Allied cruiser force—sought hasty refuge in neutral waters remains a classic maritime mystery. Once there, however, the scuttling of the cornered ship was clearly the only option left open to her captain, Langsdorff

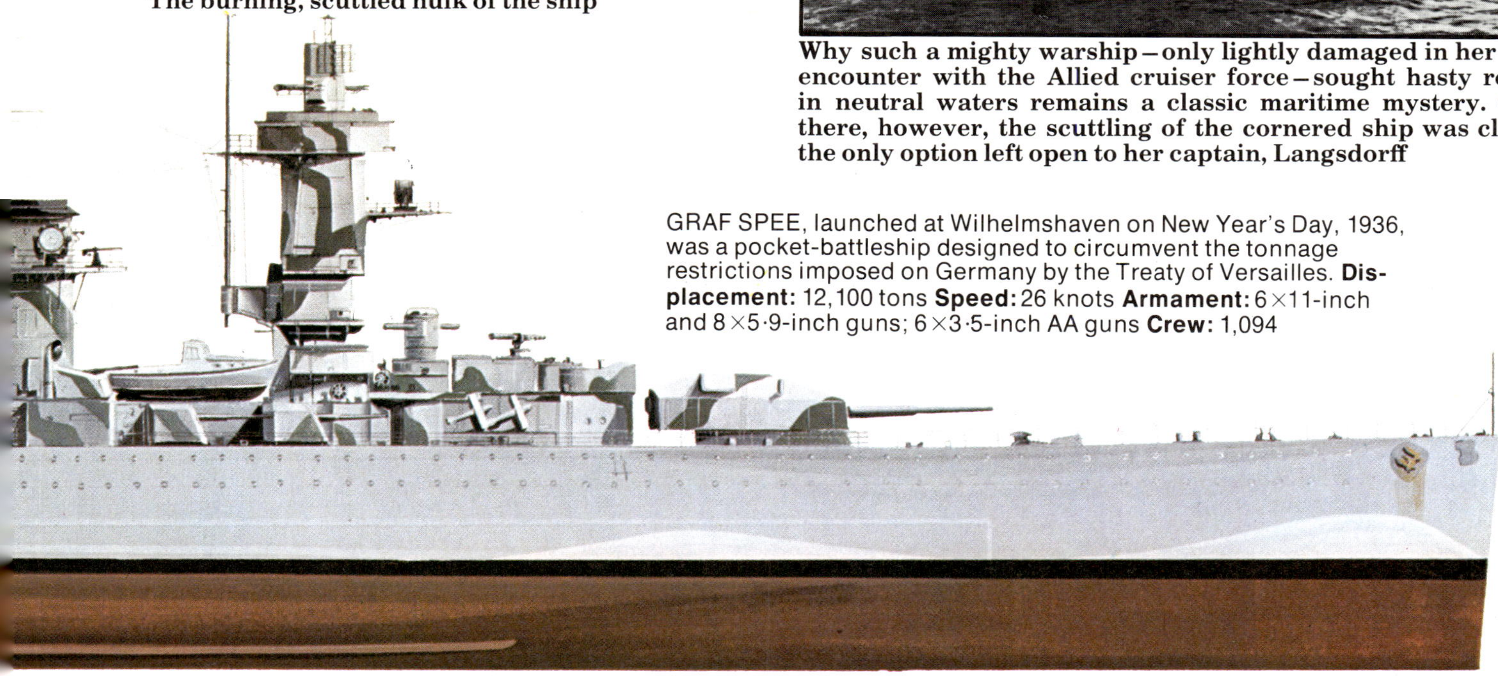

GRAF SPEE, launched at Wilhelmshaven on New Year's Day, 1936, was a pocket-battleship designed to circumvent the tonnage restrictions imposed on Germany by the Treaty of Versailles. **Displacement:** 12,100 tons **Speed:** 26 knots **Armament:** 6×11-inch and 8×5·9-inch guns; 6×3·5-inch AA guns **Crew:** 1,094 press home the attack. From this beginning, it was not difficult to develop a more efficient method of the group attack. The U-boats were organised into operational 'wolf-packs', and when a convoy's course was reasonably well identified, the nearest pack was ordered to the vicinity by the U-boat headquarters. When the convoy was sighted, the U-boat concerned 'homed' the rest of the pack to the convoy by directional wireless signals. No attack developed until the whole pack had arrived.

With this tactic there was added the surface attack by night. A surfaced submarine presents only a tiny silhouette and is difficult to see even in the best conditions of visibility. They are also able to use their diesel engines on the surface and so are much faster than when submerged – indeed, their surface speed exceeded that of most British escort vessels. There was, therefore, very little hope of catching them even if they were sighted during the attack. Even more disastrous from the British point of view was the fact that a U-boat on the surface was virtually immune from discovery by 'asdic' detection.

This completely reversed the confidence with which, before the war, the Admiralty had contemplated an enemy attack on seaborne trade. The 'asdic' and the depth-charge were the twin foundations on which the whole theory of anti-submarine warfare had been firmly based, and these new German tactics completely outmanoeuvred them. The fitting of radar sets in escort vessels was the immediate and obvious answer, since radar would indicate the presence of a surfaced U-boat, but as yet there were no sets available, and another year was to elapse before enough became available to equip the escort fleet.

In the meantime, another duty lay before the Royal Navy. Almost as the evacuation of

Carelessness could easily lead a convoy into the jaws of a U-boat wolf-pack

the BEF from Dunkirk and the Channel ports was taking place, other British troops were being landed in France in an attempt to form a line on which the advancing Germans could be successfully held. But in the rapidly crumbling situation ashore, any hope of stopping the German advance was slim indeed. It became even slimmer when it became apparent that the defeatist element in the French government was strongly in favour of negotiating with the Germans for an armistice.

The decision to bring home the remaining British troops in France, many of them landed only a few days earlier, was taken on June 15, using the ports of Cherbourg, St Malo, Brest, St Nazaire, and La Pallice. In the few days during which this operation was carried out, another 136,963 British troops were brought safely home, as well as some 38,500 Allies, of whom the majority were Polish.

The whole operation was carried out with only one loss, but that was a grievous one. Among other ships sent to carry troops home from St Nazaire was the liner *Lancastria*. She was lying out in the anchorage and had already taken more than 5,300 soldiers on board when she was hit during a heavy German air raid. Although she took some little time to sink, more than 3,000 of those on board lost their lives – mainly because, in the urgency of evacuation, there were insufficient lifebelts in the ship for all the extra men she was carrying.

With this final evacuation of British forces from France, coupled with the armistice which the French government signed with Germany, a completely new problem faced the Admiralty. The situation on which the original war plans had been drawn had now been shattered beyond recognition.

Taking stock, the Royal Navy had to face a situation in which the whole of the western coast of Europe, from the North Cape in Norway to the Spanish frontier in the Bay of Biscay, lay in the hands of the enemy. With the Norwegian ports and bases in his hands, Hitler could now command the eastern North Sea right up to the Arctic Circle. This gave him a wide corridor through which to pass his U-boats, his armed merchant raiders, and his blockade runners in the Atlantic. With similar facilities in the Bay

PRINZ EUGEN
She was the third German heavy cruiser to be built in defiance of the Versailles naval restrictions on the German navy, following the *Hipper* and the *Blücher*.
Displacement: 13,900 tons
Max speed: 32 knots
Armament: eight 8-inch; 12 4·1-inch AA, 12 37-mm AA, eight (later 28) 20-mm AA; 12 21-inch torpedo-tubes; three aircraft.
(Complement: 1,600)

of Biscay, U-boats could reach farther out into the Atlantic, and raiders and blockade runners could penetrate deep into ocean waters before they reached areas where British ships could seize them. This made the British Admiralty's task infinitely more difficult, for a ship is easily concealed in the immensity of the oceans.

A yet more potent threat to the nation's seaborne trade lay in German occupation of the airfields of western France, from which long-range Focke-Wulf 'Condor' aircraft could search the Atlantic for British convoys and report their positions to the waiting U-boats.

This particular problem was solved in a typically extempore fashion. A few merchant ships were fitted with catapults which could launch a Hurricane fighter, and one of these accompanied the more important convoys as they sailed within range of the Condors. When one of them was sighted, the Hurricane was catapulted into flight, shot down or drove off the intruder, and then ditched itself alongside a merchant ship so that the pilot could be picked up.

These catapult-armed-merchant ships or CAM-ships, as they were known, gave way in time to the MAC-ship (merchant-aircraft-carrier), in which a full flight deck was built over the top of a merchant ship, usually a tanker because of her length. The MAC-ships could carry up to about six fighters, which of course could land on again after operations and did not have to ditch alongside. And as time went on, the MAC-ships were replaced by auxiliary (or 'Woolworth') carriers, which embodied merchant ship hulls converted into full aircraft-carriers.

Strangulation of trade

While the battle of the skies was being fought by the Royal Air Force against German bombers and fighters intent on hammering Britain into submission, another battle was being fought in the coastal waters around Britain. Hitler's plan to defeat Britain lay not so much in invasion across the Channel, which was in fact to be his last resort if all else failed, but in the strangulation of trade.

In the wake of the advancing German armies came his motor torpedo-boats, known as E-boats, pushing their bases westward until they reached Cherbourg during the second half of June 1940. Their targets were the coastal convoys, combined with offensive minelaying before the ports of Britain. Heavy air attacks on convoys and ports also took their toll of ships. Although all these were hit-and-run attacks, they tied down a large number of British naval vessels, and it was to take some months of hard and incessant skirmishing before the enemy was held and the coastal trade could pass in comparative security.

Another naval task was the defence against seaborne invasion, which everyone in Britain expected during the summer and autumn of 1940. But this was nothing new; and the Royal Navy swung into its traditional defence, tried and proved through centuries of experience. It was based on the close watch of the invasion forces by flotilla vessels: in the old days by sloops, cutters, and gun-vessels; in 1940 by destroyers, motor torpedo-boats, and gunboats. Behind them, in the east and west coast ports, lay the immediate stiffening of the defence by ships of greater power: in the old days by frigates; in 1940 by cruisers. And behind them again lay the final safeguard of all—the immense strength of the battle fleet, which would be called south to action when the forces of invasion actually sailed.

Here, in 1940, across the waters of the English Channel stood the army of Hitler, as before it had stood the armies of Napoleon, of Louis XIV, of Philip II of Spain. Between them all and their dreams of conquest had stood the British navy. Between Hitler and his dreams it still stood. As the days and the weeks passed, as the invasion barges and the transports which had been taken from the inland waterways with so much dislocation of local trade still lay stationary at their moorings in the Channel ports, the Lords of the Admiralty could echo the words of the Earl of St Vincent, a First Lord of 150 years ago, that 'being a military question they must hesitate to express an opinion about invasion as such'. All they knew was that an invasion 'could not come by sea'.

In all the major fighting which had fallen to the Royal Navy so far—in the Norwegian campaign and in the evacuation from Dunkirk—one unmistakable new lesson had emerged: that ships at sea could not operate in waters dominated by enemy air power. The major naval weapon against the Axis powers—for Italy had joined the conflict on the fall of France—was still the blockade, and to keep this weapon in operation the ring of sea power around Europe still needed to be held. Now, however, it had to be drawn beyond the range of aircraft using the newly won airfields of Norway, Denmark, Holland, Belgium, and France. Britain, outflanked now to the south and east,

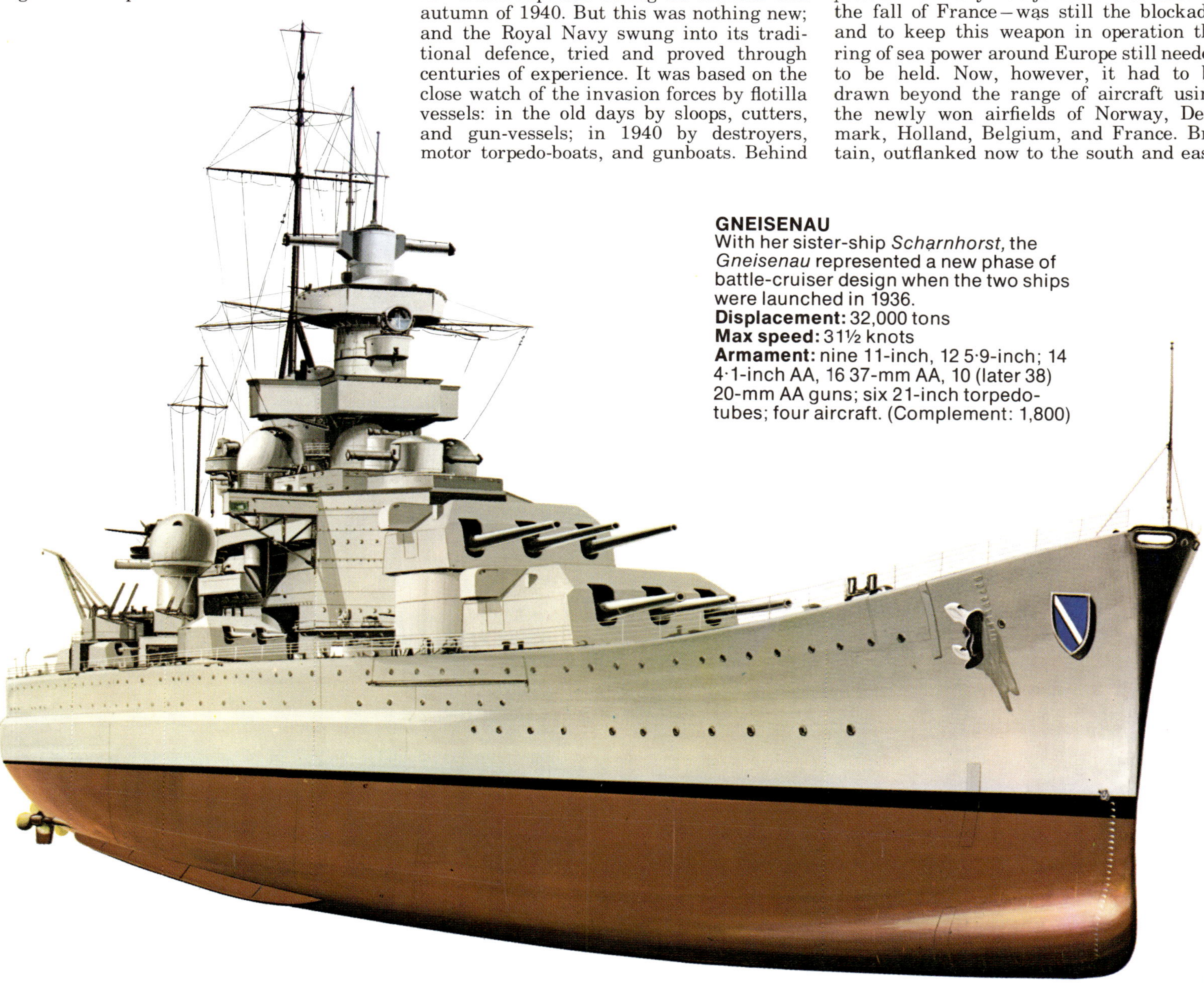

GNEISENAU
With her sister-ship *Scharnhorst,* the *Gneisenau* represented a new phase of battle-cruiser design when the two ships were launched in 1936.
Displacement: 32,000 tons
Max speed: 31½ knots
Armament: nine 11-inch, 12 5·9-inch; 14 4·1-inch AA, 16 37-mm AA, 10 (later 38) 20-mm AA guns; six 21-inch torpedo-tubes; four aircraft. (Complement: 1,800)

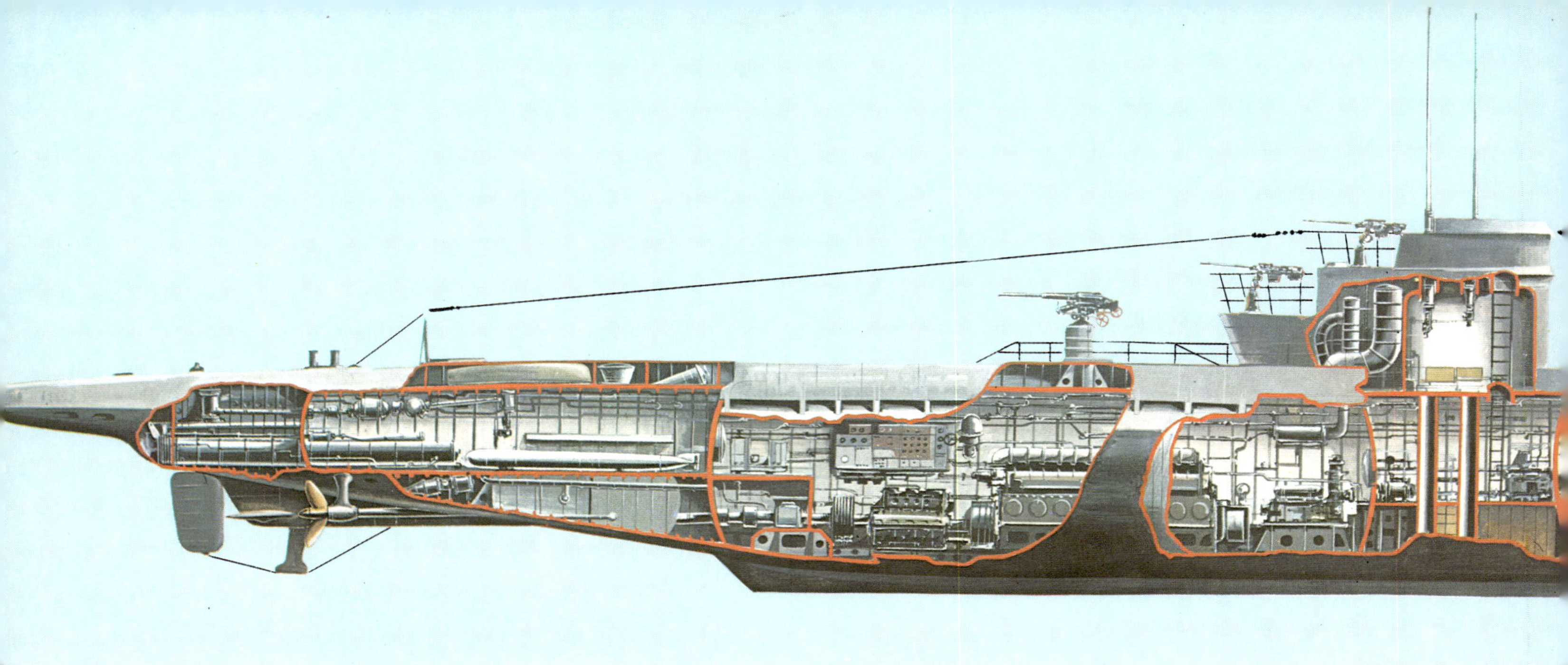

had to guard well the north and west if she were not to be herself defeated. So, to the north, British sea power stretched out to Iceland and across the Denmark Straits to the coast of Greenland. In the west it reached from Northern Ireland out into the Atlantic, sweeping down in a wide arc to the south, to Gibraltar and Freetown. To complete the circle, the Mediterranean Fleet held the eastern waters of the Mediterranean from Malta to the western coast of Greece.

Within this tenuous circle were held the Axis powers. This was the barrier through which they had to break if they were to reach the raw materials of the rest of the world. It could not as yet be held strongly enough to prevent the surface raiders slipping through, nor could it ever stop the U-boats from reaching the outer oceans. But it could, and did, effectively stifle almost the whole of that seaborne trade without which the two dictators could not win their war.

This was a barrier which had to be held at all costs, for if final victory were to be won, the barrier had to serve a dual purpose. There was more to it than stopping the seaborne trade of Germany and Italy; while containing them in isolation, it had also to safeguard the slow build-up of British power and resources against the day when the national strategy could turn from the defensive to the offensive.

Behind its strength had to come the huge imports of oil, steel, tanks, guns, aircraft, and food without which the only future for Britain was defeat. And behind its strength, too, had to come the men, from the Dominions and colonies and, later, from the United States, who would add their strength to the armies which, one day, would carry the war back into Europe. And behind its strength must sail all those troops, weapons, and stores to hold the other vital theatres of war in the Middle East and, a year later, the Far East.

The task, in those summer months of 1940, appeared stupendous – and it was aggravated both by the loss of ships during the operations in Norway and at Dunkirk and by those which were now tied up in the anti-invasion duties. Where, in 1939, it had been possible to provide an average of two escort vessels for each convoy that sailed, now, in the summer of 1940, the average escort strength was down to 1·8 per convoy. The U-boats, now beginning to use French and Norwegian bases, were saving 1,000 miles or more on their passage to their patrol areas, and so were able to operate considerably farther out into the Atlantic, and well beyond the limit to which convoys could be escorted.

Two gleams of light shone fitfully into this dark prospect. The first was produced by the occupation by British troops of the Faeroe Islands and Iceland. Both were dependencies of Denmark, and on the invasion of that country by Germany in April 1940 had been quickly taken over by Britain to deny them to Hitler.

Iceland was notably well placed to act as a base on the Atlantic convoy routes, a base from which escorts could operate to lengthen substantially the limit of convoy both from Britain and from the Canadian ports. There was no question of using it at once, for it takes time to develop the essential facilities of a naval base, but it would unquestionably pay substantial dividends in the future.

The other gleam of light came from the negotiations between Churchill and Roosevelt over the release by the United States of 50 over-age destroyers in exchange for the lease of bases in Newfoundland and the West Indies. These destroyers, of the old 'flush deck and four-pipe' class, were hurriedly overhauled and re-equipped in US bases and taken into the British and Canadian navies. There they served to augment the already over-stretched escort force, at least temporarily until the new construction escort vessels began to join the fleet.

Return of the U-boats

The first six months of 1940 had been a relatively quiet time in the Atlantic on the U-boat front, due partly to the wild weather of January, in which U-boats found it very difficult to operate, and partly to the large-scale withdrawal of U-boats from the Atlantic to take part in the Norwegian campaign. But by June 1940 they were back on the Atlantic trade routes, not in any great strength as yet, as the building programme was only just beginning to bear fruit, but with a steadily increasing monthly total.

From their new Biscay bases, even the small 500-ton U-boats could now operate in areas as much as 600 miles out into the Atlantic, well beyond the limit of surface anti-submarine escort from Britain. There was little opposition to them out there, and the incoming and outgoing merchant ships were sitting ducks to their torpedoes. Closer in, they chose as their targets ships which – because of their speed – sailed independent of convoys, or ships which straggled from the convoys. These, too, were sitting ducks.

During September the U-boat command introduced the first serious wolf-pack attacks against British convoys. Two successive Atlantic convoys, SC-2 and HX-72, were attacked by a pack of ten U-boats north-west of Iceland, and 16 ships were sunk out of them. A month later an even more savage wolf-pack attack was launched. Again the victims were two successive Atlantic convoys, SC-7 and HX-79, and a wolf-pack of eight U-boats, attacking them on four successive nights, sank 32 ships.

It was not unduly difficult to discover the answers to this form of attack. One of them, as mentioned above, was the fitting of radar in the escorts. Another was to discover a method of turning night into day more efficiently than by starshell from the escorts' guns. This was eventually provided by the scientists with the invention of 'Snowflake', a flare which lit up a large area of the ocean at once. But, like radar, this answer also lay in the future.

Another answer was the provision of air escort of convoys. This was a powerful deterrent to the U-boat, for aircraft ranging over the convoy area forced the shadowing U-boat to submerge and thus lose touch. And when fitted with ASV (airborne radar), escorting aircraft had an even wider range of effectiveness, for their sets could detect a surfaced U-boat in thick weather, and at a greater range, where the human eye would fail. But here again, at this stage of the battle, the necessary numbers of long-range aircraft did not exist in Coastal Command, and the protection from attack which they could provide was not available.

Yet another source of protection was deduced from the habits of the shadowing U-boat. In order to 'home' the remainder of the pack on to the convoy, the shadowing U-boat had to make a succession of wireless signals. While these might not be heard by the shore wireless direction-finding stations, because they were made on low power, they

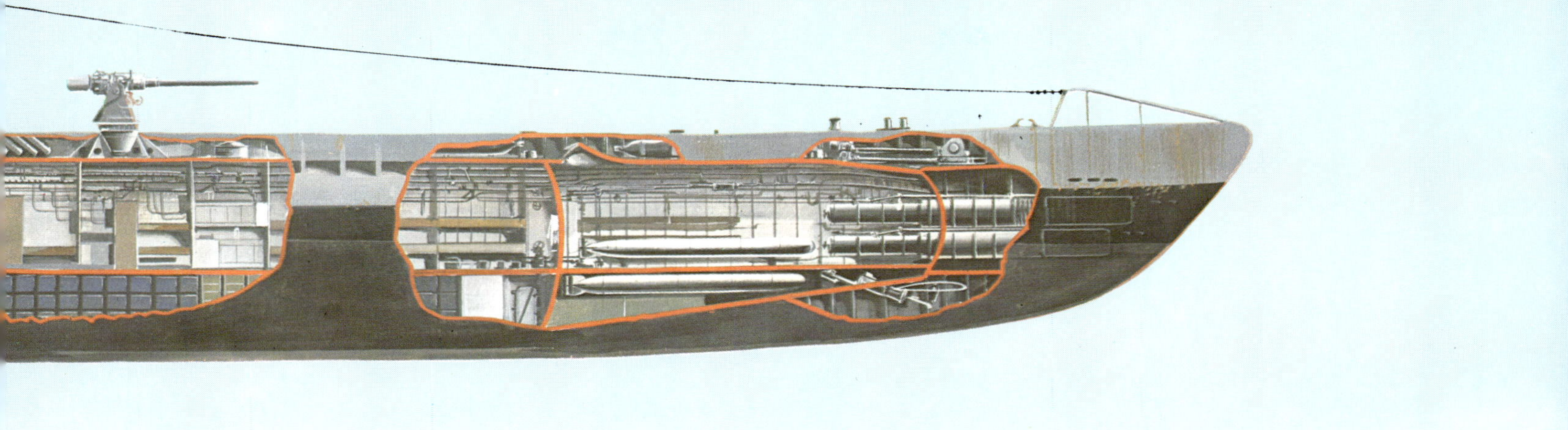

German **Type IXB** U-boat. These ocean-going boats were developed from the UEII Type of the First World War, with more endurance than the Type VII series. They proved less than suitable for the Western Approaches and were used instead in distant waters. Nonetheless, their average of tonnage sunk was as high as any other group of U-boats. Their main drawback was that they took too long to build, and only 14 were ever finished. **Displacement:** 1,051 tons (surfaced) **Armament:** Six 21-inch torpedo-tubes; 22 torpedoes carried; one 37-mm gun; one 20-mm gun **Speed:** 18¼ knots (surfaced) 7¼ knots (submerged)

would normally appear as strong signals on board the escorts. If these ships, therefore, carried a direction-finding receiver, they could run down the bearing of the shadowing U-boat and expect to find her at the other end. This aid to U-boat destruction was, again, only embryonic in 1940, but it was from this date that steps were taken to produce suitable ship-borne direction-finding receivers. They eventually came into the escort fleet in July 1941.

All that remained, therefore, was to strive to extend the range of surface escort farther out into the Atlantic, and to try to divert the convoys, by evasive routing, clear of those areas where the U-boat packs were thought to be lurking. This was the task of the U-boat tracking room in the Admiralty, using every piece of intelligence information that came in. The most prolific source of this intelligence was found to be the wireless bearings taken from shore stations of every signal made by the U-boats at sea.

Actual sighting reports made by the U-boats were quickly recognised as such from the form of the message itself, and convoys could be immediately warned that they were in danger. Sometimes a drastic alteration of course away from the U-boat would shake the shadower off. But although some of the best brains in the Navy were concentrated in the tracking room, the volume of intelligence coming in was not sufficient to enable them to do much more than grope in the dark. Later, as the raw material of intelligence improved both in quantity and quality, the tracking room was to achieve some spectacular successes. But that time was not yet.

Merchant ship sinkings

The losses of merchant ships caused by the U-boats through 1940 tell their own story. The two months of January and February had seen the loss of 85 ships totalling 290,000 tons. During March, April, and May, the U-boats had been largely withdrawn from the Atlantic to play their part in the Norwegian campaign, and during those three months only 43 ships of an aggregate of 140,000 tons were lost. But in June the U-boats were coming back and, moreover, beginning to operate farther afield in the Atlantic, and beyond the reach of the convoy escorts. June saw the loss to the U-boats rise to a figure of 58 ships with a total tonnage of 284,000. And the figures for the remainder of the year were equally grievous.

Losses such as these were beyond the replacement capacity of the British building yards, and although there was still as yet plenty of 'fat' in the total of pre-war tonnage afloat under the British flag, these figures clearly showed the writing on the wall. A fair amount of merchant ship tonnage – particularly Norwegian and Dutch – had accrued to Britain with the German invasion of the western European countries in April and May, but even that could not allow anyone to contemplate the loss figure with anything but a feeling of apprehension. And as yet the peak of U-boat strength had not been even approached.

U-boats in profusion

It was known in the British Admiralty that several hundred new U-boats were on order, and the existing operational strength was but a shadow of what was inevitably to come. Before the war, in his book on submarine warfare, Admiral Dönitz had put forward the estimate that 300 operational U-boats would be required to win a war against Britain. That meant a total force of some 900 submarines, to allow for losses, training, rest periods for crews, refits, and so on. This book had, of course, been read by many British naval officers, and none doubted the German capacity to build up to this figure. Moreover, the declaration by Hitler on August 17 of a total blockade of the British Isles, giving warning that neutral shipping would be sunk at sight, gave an added indication that the U-boat campaign was to be the means by which Germany expected to win her victory.

The loss to the enemy during 1940 was 22 U-boats, although the Admiralty at the time only knew of 16 confirmed cases; the remaining six were sunk by accident or unknown causes. But in view of the German building programme, this was not a satisfactory exchange rate. Taken over the whole year, it meant that for each U-boat lost, very nearly 100,000 tons of Allied shipping were sent to the bottom. Great Britain and her allies would need to do much better than that if the Atlantic battle, on which the outcome of the war depended, was to be won.

There was one great hope. During the year the limit of escorts had been pushed farther out into the Atlantic. As soon as the Iceland base became operational, an even larger step outwards could be made. And with the new construction of escort vessels now beginning to come forward, the time was not far distant when convoy could be established right across the Atlantic from coast to coast. Convoys, the Royal Navy knew, had beaten the U-boat in 1917 and 1918. The Admiralty in London hoped, and expected, that they would do so again.

If U-boats had been the only cause of merchant ship losses, the problem of containment would not have been too great a

1939 September 3: The SS *Athenia* is torpedoed off north-west Ireland.
September 4: The RAF raids warships in Heligoland Bight.
October 14: HMS *Royal Oak* is torpedoed in Scapa Flow by U-47.
November 18: New German magnetic mines are sown from the air.
November 23: The armed merchant cruiser *Rawalpindi* is sunk by the *Scharnhorst* and *Gneisenau* south-east of Iceland.
December 13: Battle of the River Plate.
December 14: The RAF raids warships in Schillig Roads.

1940 January: The British begin to use protective 'de-gaussing' of ships to meet the threat of the magnetic mine.
February 15: Germany announces that all British merchant ships will be treated as warships.
March 1: Germany announces 750,000 BRT sunk by U-boats, 63,000 BRT sunk by surface ships, 36,000 BRT sunk by Luftwaffe, and 281,000 BRT sunk by mines.
March 19: The RAF bombs German installations at Hörnum.
May 11: Churchill gives Bomber Command authority to attack Germany.
May 15: The RAF raids the Ruhr.
June 18: The RAF raids Hamburg and Bremen.
August 24: Central London is bombed for the first time.
August 25: First RAF raid on Berlin.
September 3: The Anglo-American 'Lend-Lease' agreement is signed. Fifty US destroyers are traded for certain British bases in the West Indies and Newfoundland.
October 29: Allied weekly tonnage losses: 88,000.
November 5: The German pocket-battleship *Admiral Scheer* attacks an Atlantic convoy, sinking the *Jervis Bay*.
November 7: The RAF raids the Krupp munition works, Essen.
December 18/19: The RAF raids Mannheim.

task. But at the same time there were serious losses from other causes. German aircraft, operating mainly against the East Coast and English Channel coastal convoys, sank, during 1940, 192 ships of 580,000 tons. Mines throughout the year accounted for 201 ships of 510,000 tons, while the German E-boats claimed a further 23 ships of 48,000 tons. Although the great majority of these were comparatively small ships engaged in coastal trade, and thus more easily and quickly replaced by new construction, the total tonnage added to the overall loss was in excess of 1,000,000.

Return of the raiders

One other cause of loss gave an even greater degree of anxiety and apprehension to the Admiralty: the losses caused by armed merchant raiders – fast and heavily armed merchant ships sent out from Germany to operate individually in the distant oceans. The difficulty was to find them. It had been appreciated, when the raider hunting groups had been formed at the beginning of the war to deal with the pocket-battleships, that this was a most uneconomic use of ships. These groups had steamed many hundreds of thousands of miles, mostly to no avail, for by the time a hunting group could arrive in the vicinity of the last sinking report, the raider herself was by then many hundreds of miles away. And what was, perhaps, even worse than the actual merchant ship sinkings which the raiders achieved was the dislocation and disorganisation which their presence caused to the normal flow of seaborne trade.

What the Germans called the 'first wave' of the armed merchant raiders put to sea during the first half of 1940. The first out was the *Atlantis,* which left Germany on March 31. She was followed by the *Orion* (April 6), and the *Widder* (May 5). Two more, the *Thor* and *Pinguin,* broke through the Atlantic defences, such as they were, in June, and a sixth (the *Komet*), assisted by the Russians, made the Arctic passage to the north of Siberia to the Pacific in July and August. To prolong their periods of activity, a number of supply ships were also sent out, with which they could rendezvous when required.

Only on two occasions – and each time it was the same raider – was any contact made with them by a British warship. On July 28 the armed merchant cruiser *Alcantara* encountered the *Thor* in the West Indies, off Trinidad. The British ship was outsteamed, outgunned, and outfought by the enemy, and as the *Alcantara* limped into port with serious damage, the *Thor* moved down into the South Atlantic to repair her damage and be replenished from a convenient supply ship.

A little over four months later, off the coast of South America, the *Thor* ran into another armed merchant cruiser, the *Carnarvon Castle*. The story was the same, and while the British ship was seriously damaged, the enemy suffered no injury and, after the action, made off into the blue. These two encounters were, in fact, the nearest the Royal Navy ever came during 1940 to sinking one of these elusive and dangerous ships. The damage they caused was widespread and serious. During the year, in the North and South Atlantic, Indian, and Pacific Oceans, these six ships sank 54 ships of an aggregate of 367,000 tons, but in addition they caused a considerable upheaval in the pattern of British seaborne trade through the delays in sailings and rerouting of merchant ships in the vicinity of their attacks. Some, too, were fitted as minelayers in addition to their usual gun and torpedo armament, and the minefields they laid were another cause of loss and delay.

It was not to be expected that the limited success of the first cruises of the *Deutschland* and *Graf Spee,* and the abortive attempt of the *Scharnhorst* and *Gneisenau* to break out in November 1939, would deter the enemy from further attacks on trade by warship raiders. In September 1940 the cruiser *Hipper* made an attempt to reach the Atlantic, but trouble in her engine-room caused her to abandon her planned sortie, and return home.

The next warship to make the attempt was the pocket-battleship *Scheer.* She left Germany on October 27, was not sighted by any British air patrols as she made her way up the Norwegian coast, and reached the Atlantic through the Denmark Straits undetected. On November 5 she sank a British merchant ship, which unfortunately failed to send a wireless report of the attack. Had she done so, it would have been possible to reroute a homeward-bound convoy from Halifax, which was steaming towards the position where the *Scheer's* attack had been made.

The convoy was HX-84, escorted by HMS *Jervis Bay,* an armed merchant cruiser which carried six 6-inch guns mounted on her upper deck. On the evening of November 5, only a few hours after the *Scheer's* earlier attack, the *Jervis Bay* sighted the pocket-battleship approaching the convoy at high speed from the northward. The result, even before the first gun was fired, was a foregone conclusion, for the armed merchant cruiser was not only outgunned, but also outranged by some 10,000 yards.

To save as many of the ships in the convoy as possible, Captain Fegen of the *Jervis Bay* ordered them to scatter to the south under cover of smoke. This they did, using the smoke-making apparatus with which they were all fitted, while Captain Fegen took the *Jervis Bay* into action with her huge adversary to provide as much time as possible for the ships in the convoy to get away. The *Scheer,* naturally, was undamaged during the action – the shells of the *Jervis Bay* could not even reach her – but the delay caused by Captain Fegen's defiance of the raider gave the convoy the chance it needed. By the time the *Jervis Bay* was sunk, the convoy was so scattered that the *Scheer* was unable to find more than five ships to sink, and one more to damage. The remainder escaped. For his gallantry and self-sacrifice on this occasion, Captain Fegen was awarded a posthumous Victoria Cross.

The epic of the *Jervis Bay* gave rise to another epic of skill and endurance, one which has few parallels in nautical history. The ship damaged by the *Scheer* after the sinking of the *Jervis Bay* was the tanker *San Demetrio.* She was hit and set on fire, and abandoned by her crew.

On the following day, some 18 hours after the attack, a handful of her crew, in an open boat under the command of her second officer, sighted her, still alight. They rowed alongside and climbed on board. Her decks were still hot from the fire on board, but they managed to rig some hoses and gradually got the fire under control. After working for several hours on the engines, they succeeded in getting one of them to function, and the ship began her long, slow journey

Depth-charges

Depth-charge mounted on a 'carrier' ready to be fired out in a wide arc from the ship's side, to port or starboard

The detonator hurls the depth-charge away from the ship; the 'carrier' drops away from the charge and is abandoned

A charge is dropped over a ship's stern from a chute where another charge is in place, ready to follow in a close pattern

Underwater explosions have a tremendous effect, due to the concentrated shock-waves. A near-miss could crack a U-boat's hull

A hunting escort-ship could fire wide or close patterns of charges, as the 'asdic' groped for the elusive 'ping' of a U-boat

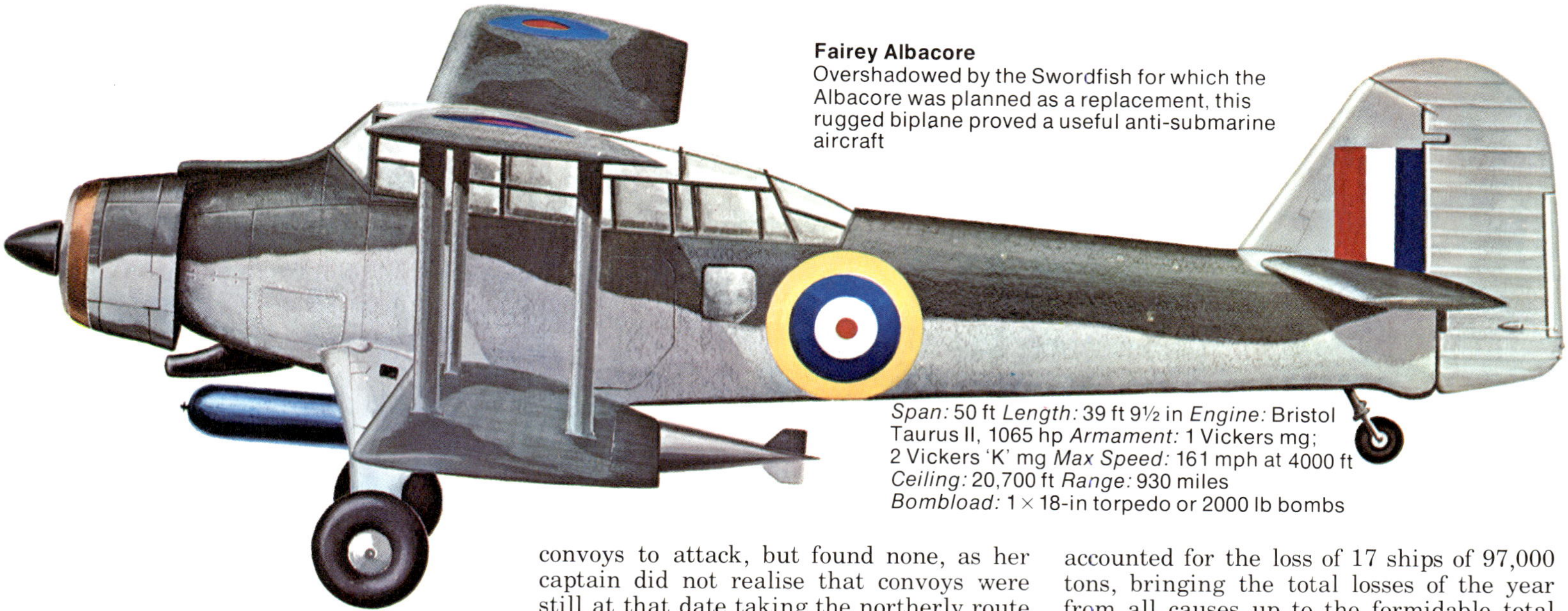

Fairey Albacore
Overshadowed by the Swordfish for which the Albacore was planned as a replacement, this rugged biplane proved a useful anti-submarine aircraft

Span: 50 ft *Length:* 39 ft 9½ in *Engine:* Bristol Taurus II, 1065 hp *Armament:* 1 Vickers mg; 2 Vickers 'K' mg *Max Speed:* 161 mph at 4000 ft *Ceiling:* 20,700 ft *Range:* 930 miles *Bombload:* 1 × 18-in torpedo or 2000 lb bombs

to Britain. Without charts beyond a school atlas found on board, with no other navigational aid, and averaging a little less than 5 knots, these few men succeeded in bringing the *San Demetrio* home together with the greater part of her valuable cargo of oil.

After her attack on HX-84 the *Scheer* steamed south, away from the area in which she had so recently operated. She replenished her oil and ammunition from a supply ship and, after operating off the Azores, moved into the South Atlantic. Here she captured a British merchant ship loaded with foodstuffs, and deliberately allowed her to broadcast a raider report before sending a prize crew on board. The reason for this was to draw attention to her position in the South Atlantic and thus attract to the area any British hunting forces which might be engaged in anti-raider operations. This was to leave the coast clear in the north, where the cruiser *Hipper* was trying to make her second attempt to break out into the Atlantic.

The *Hipper* sailed from Germany on November 30, like the *Scheer* evaded the North Sea air patrols, and successfully broke through the Denmark Straits into the North Atlantic on December 7. She spent a few days in the North Atlantic searching for convoys to attack, but found none, as her captain did not realise that convoys were still at that date taking the northerly route across the Atlantic. As a result of her lack of success she proceeded south to investigate the Sierra Leone route, and in the evening of December 24 gained touch with a convoy. She shadowed it throughout the night, hoping for fat pickings on the following day.

The convoy she was shadowing was, in fact, a troop convoy bound for the Middle East. These were always heavily guarded when at sea. As the *Hipper* approached on Christmas Day to attack, she was disconcerted to find it escorted by an aircraft-carrier and three cruisers. They had no difficulty in driving her off, but unfortunately lost sight of her in the low visibility. The *Hipper* was, in fact, slightly damaged during the exchange of gunfire. She decided to cut short her raiding cruise, and two days later arrived at Brest, on the French Biscay coast.

Next came the turn of the *Scharnhorst* and *Gneisenau,* acting as a squadron. Both had been fairly extensively damaged during the Norwegian campaign, and this was to be their first action since those days, having spent the intervening seven months in dockyard hands. Their effort was abortive. The *Gneisenau* was damaged in heavy seas while steaming up the coast of Norway, and both ships thereupon reversed their course and returned to Kiel.

This 'second wave' of the warship raiders accounted for the loss of 17 ships of 97,000 tons, bringing the total losses of the year from all causes up to the formidable total of 1,059 ships of 3,991,641 tons. Of these, nearly 60% had been sunk by U-boats, the majority of them on the vital North Atlantic trade route.

It is necessary for a moment to leave the Atlantic and take a quick look at the last link of the circle of sea power drawn around the Axis nations. When Italy joined Germany in hostilities during the last days of the fighting ashore in Europe, the naval position in the Red Sea at once gave some cause for alarm. Here, based on Massawa, the Italians had a force of nine destroyers, eight submarines, and an armed merchant raider.

The Red Sea was an essential link with British forces operating in the Middle East, and it was essential to hold this sea area if Germany and Italy were to be effectively denied access to the trade of the outside world and if British forces were to receive the replenishment in men, weapons, and stores they would need to conduct active operations.

As it turned out, the Italian naval threat never materialised. Three of the submarines were sunk and another captured intact within the first month of Italy joining the war; the destroyers took no action to attempt to harass British convoys in the Red Sea; and the spasmodic efforts of Italian aircraft to interfere with British shipping were un-

Magnetic mine

Lowered by parachute, the magnetic mine also had a contact fuse: if it hit a solid surface it was meant to explode like a bomb

As the mine sank, the rear parachute attachment was released: freed from the parachute, the mine would then rest on the sea bed

As a ship approached, the weak magnetic field set up would finally detonate the mine by closing the circuit with the magnetic needle

In shallow water, the explosion, directly below the ship's hull, was devastating. These mines caused heavy tonnage losses

1. 'Chute case (two halves) **2.** Folded 'chute **3.** Needle **4.** Case join **5.** Detonator **6.** High explosive (approx 650 lb) **7.** Anti-roll horns availing. The Red Sea route remained firmly in British hands, and the circle of sea power remained unbroken.

The end of 1940 saw the situation at sea more or less in a state of balance. The Allies had been defeated on the land, both in Norway and France, but the sea defence still held, even if stretched thin in some places. Against the enemy occupation of naval bases in Norway and France, with all that they meant in extending the range of operations of the U-boats, Britain had occupied Iceland and was equipping a naval and air base there which, in the end, would prove decisive to the ultimate outcome of the U-boat war. Against the rapid build-up in numbers of the U-boat fleet, which was to rise at one period to over 360 operational boats, there was the certainty that, during 1941, end-to-end Atlantic convoy of merchant ships would be achieved, and the task of the U-boats would be made much more difficult and dangerous.

German 'Milch Cow' Type XIV
To extend the range of the Type VII U-Boats, the German Navy built ten submarine tankers in 1941. With a fatter and shorter hull than the Type IX boats, and less power, they could carry sufficient fuel to keep four or five U-Boats at sea for twice as long as usual, and they also carried four spare torpedoes in external stowage. They were made top priority targets for Allied ships and all ten were sunk. *Displacement:* 1,688 tons (surfaced) *Armament:* Two 37-mm AA guns one 20-mm AA gun; no torpedo-tubes

Only in one aspect of convoy warfare was there some distress. It had been apparent even in the First World War that submarines hesitated to attack convoys which had air as well as surface escort, even though at that time there was no airborne weapon capable of sinking a submarine. The same hesitation was being experienced in 1940.

But air escort of convoys at sea called for aircraft of long range and endurance – the same aircraft particularly in demand for the bombing offensive on Germany. RAF Coastal Command, which under naval direction provided the convoy air escort, was starved of long-range aircraft, and the convoys suffered severe losses as a result. This was a problem which was not solved until 1943, by which time the navy had acquired enough auxiliary aircraft-carriers to operate their own aircraft on the convoy routes. Later still, American production of long-range aircraft filled the gap, and released the aircraft-carriers for other duties.

As the year ended, there were hopeful signs in a situation which still remained dark from the British military defeats on the Continent. Although now thrust far out into the Atlantic, the sea defence of the nation still held, and behind it the blockade of Germany and Italy was virtually intact. This was still the fundamental weapon which, if it could be maintained, would in the end lead to victory. The great danger which now faced Britain was no longer invasion from the Continent – the chance of that had gone (if it ever really existed) – but defeat in the war against the U-boats.

The whole future of the war now hung upon that groping battle being fought in the vastness of the oceans. It was to be a race between the German U-boat building programme and the time when it would be possible to bring into operation a fully integrated system of end-to-end surface and air escort of convoys. Once that was in operation, the defeat of the U-boats was certain, although there was a long and painful road still to travel.

Bomb-proof U-boat pens on the coast of France

German Type VII (*U236*)
The Type VII U-Boat was the standard design for the U-Boat in the Second World War. It was developed from the Finnish *Vetehinen* design before the expiry of the Versailles Treaty, and many improvements were effected as a result of war experience. *U236* was one of the Type VIIC, the third version, and she came into service in January 1943. She was scuttled in 1945 after suffering damage by air attack.
Displacement: 769 tons (surfaced)
Armament: Five 21-in torpédo-tubes; 14 torpedoes carried; plus a variety of light AA guns *Speed:* 17 knots (surfaced) $7\frac{1}{2}$ knots (submerged)

BATTLE FOR THE ATLANTIC: THE SECOND PHASE

Fox Photos

By the beginning of 1941 the difficulties and complexities of the Battle of the Atlantic were really starting to make themselves felt. The severe merchant ship losses in 1940–2,186,158 tons were sunk by the U-boats alone–had in part been met by wartime redeployment of peacetime shipping, but from 1941 on there was no hope of meeting further losses by this means. By this time merchant shipping had been stretched to its limit, and future losses could be made good only by new construction.

There were several factors which were to single out 1941 and 1942 as the years of special peril in that swaying, groping battle against the U-boats. The most immediate of them was the rapid build-up in numbers of the U-boats themselves, for the increased building programme put in hand by Germany at the outbreak of war was, by 1941, beginning to take effect. From the beginning of 1941 to the middle of 1943, the rate of building far exceeded the rate of loss, so that each succeeding month saw more and more U-boats in the Atlantic.

There were other factors in this battle which also came to the aid of the U-boats. An important one was the length of time a convoy took to cross the Atlantic. Allowing for diversions, weather, and other delays, the average time of passage of an Atlantic convoy throughout the whole of the war was just over 15 days; convoys to and from Freetown took four days longer. These long passages in effect presented the U-boats with more targets as the merchant ships made their laborious voyages across the ocean.

Another important factor was the short sea endurance of British escort vessels. At the outbreak of war, escort for convoys could only be provided up to a distance of about 500 miles from the British coast; beyond that the merchant ships were on their own. The occupation of Iceland after the disastrous land campaign of 1940 provided the opportunity of increasing the range of escort by the provision of a refuelling base on the island, but it was not until April 1941 that the first base there was fully in commission. Simultaneously the Canadian navy developed bases in Newfoundland and eastern Canada, and by the use of these bases the range of surface escort was pushed even farther out into the Atlantic. By April 1941 it was as far as 35°W, a little more than half-way; two months later the first convoy with end-to-end surface anti-submarine escort sailed across the Atlantic. But because of the shortage of escort vessels, the average strength of escort was, in 1941, no more than two ships per convoy. It was not until the new long-range escorts, laid down just before the war, began to join the fleet that the strength of escort could be increased, in 1942 and 1943, to more adequate numbers.

As important as the surface escorts were those of the air, for of all the enemies of the U-boat the one most feared was the aircraft. Their range of vision and speed of attack were both vastly superior to those of the surface escorts, and an aircraft circling a convoy would force every U-boat within attacking range to submerge, thus condemning them to their low underwater speed and a much reduced range of vision. But here again, as with the surface escorts, the problem was range and endurance. As yet there were no aircraft in Coastal Command with a range or endurance long enough to cover Atlantic convoys for more than a short period of their passage, even using Iceland and Newfoundland as additional bases. To try to fill the gaps with carrier-borne aircraft was out of the question, for the few aircraft-carriers in the fleet were all required for other operational duties. Perhaps even more important, in 1941 efficient airborne radar by which aircraft could locate U-boats on the surface was as yet still in the future, as was an efficient airborne weapon which could kill a submarine.

The odds, then, were still strongly in favour of the U-boat, and they remained in its favour throughout 1941 and 1942. These were the years of building up the Allied anti-submarine escort forces, both surface and air, in numbers, in training, in tactical doctrine, and in the provision of scientific aids to locate U-boats – a long and tedious road to travel, made longer and harder by the rapid increase in numbers of the U-boats and by the development of their pack tactics of attack.

Early in 1941 the first step along this road was taken by the removal of the headquarters of the Western Approaches command from Plymouth to Liverpool, and by the appointment of a commander-in-chief whose sole responsibility was to conduct the campaign against the U-boats. Into this new headquarters was integrated the headquarters of 15 Group, Coastal Command, so that both surface and air escort could be coordinated from one operations room. Duplicates of the U-boat and trade plots in the British Admiralty were set up in the Western Approaches operations room, and the two connected with direct telephone and teleprinter links between Whitehall and Liverpool.

Admiral Sir Percy Noble was appointed as Commander-in-Chief Western Approaches in February 1941. He was, perhaps, the first to appreciate that the key to victory in this campaign lay just as much in the training of the officers and men as in the number of available escorts. Anti-submarine training establishments were set up at Dunoon and Campbeltown, experimental work was carried out at Fairlie, and a sea training organisation was based at Tobermory. To this last establishment went all new escort vessels as they completed their acceptance trials. For a month they were engaged in arduous sea exercises designed to harden crews, who were largely new recruits, to accustom them to normal Atlantic weather conditions, and to give them a reasonably intimate knowledge of their own ship and her capabilities.

Specialist training followed the sea training, so that by the time the new ship became fully operational her complement had not only been toughened by the Tobermory training but had also acquired the necessary professional and technological skills. All this, however, took time, and it was not until mid-1943 that the total overall training could be considered adequate. Until that time, the operational need in the Atlantic for all and every escort had to take precedence.

Another decision by Admiral Noble was to organise all the escorts into groups. By allocating eight escort ships to a group, the C-in-C could count on an effective strength of five or six escorts for each group, leaving a margin for refits of ships, leave periods,

After the first 'Happy Time' of the U-boats, Allied losses fell off – but not for long

Bibliothek für Zeitgeschichte

Bibliothek für Zeitgeschichte

Sado-Opera Mundi

Sado-Opera Mundi

Sado-Opera Mundi

training, and other contingencies. The great value of the group system was that each escort captain quickly became familiar both with the other escorts in the group and with the group commander's methods.

It is in this reorganisation of the escort forces, and the emphasis on proper anti-submarine training, that the seeds of ultimate victory in the Atlantic were sown. Yet if it was one important thing to recognise the correct road to travel in search of victory, Britain's actual journey along that road was a vastly more difficult business. The priorities in naval building in 1940 and 1941 had to be balanced between the needs of the operational fleet for aircraft-carriers, cruisers, destroyers, and landing-craft of various shapes and sizes, and of the anti-submarine fleet for frigates, sloops, and corvettes for purely escort purposes. There could obviously be no absolute priority for escort vessels, and so there was no possibility of keeping even level with the rate of U-boat building in Germany, let alone overtaking it. Two and a half bitter years were to pass before the escort groups finally established their superiority in this vast campaign.

The tribulations of 1941, when Britain was still in the throes of reorganising her anti-submarine forces, were magnified by the establishment of German long-range bomber squadrons on the coasts of France and Norway. These consisted mainly of Focke-Wulf Condors able to operate up to 800 miles into the Atlantic. Their mission was two-fold. Primarily their task was to locate British convoys so that the U-boats could be directed to them, but a secondary role was to sink merchant ships proceeding independently or straggling from their convoys. And in their secondary role alone they came a very close second to the U-boats. While, in January 1941, U-boats sank 21 ships of 126,782 tons, the long-range bombers accounted for 20 of 78,517 tons. The figures for February were similar: 39 ships of 196,783 tons to the U-boats, 27 ships of 89,305 to the bombers.

The answer to the Focke-Wulf bombers came in many ways. One was to route the independently sailed merchant ships far to the north, beyond the range of the bombers based in Norway and France, and to bring in convoys along a narrow route patrolled by long-range fighters. Another was to press ahead with the mounting of anti-aircraft guns in the merchant ships themselves, manned by gun-crews of seamen and marines. A third was to fit catapults in the old seaplane-carrier *Pegasus* and use her, with naval fighters embarked, as an anti-aircraft escort for convoys.

A development of the *Pegasus* idea was to fit catapults in selected merchant ships and embark a Hurricane fighter, which could then be catapulted off whenever an enemy aircraft was sighted. On completion of its mission, the Hurricane was ditched alongside a friendly ship and the pilot rescued. It was through means such as these, and also through the reluctance of the Luftwaffe to work in harmony with the Kriegsmarine, that the attack of the long-range bombers on shipping was eventually beaten.

With the gradual extension of convoy across the Atlantic, the reign of the German U-boat 'aces' came to an end. These were the men who had distinguished themselves in the Atlantic battle by the actual tonnage of merchant shipping they personally had sunk. In the first 18 months of warfare, while the convoy system was still being built up and the ocean still carried a large proportion of independently routed merchant ships, the number of easy targets had presented many opportunities to skilled commanders to amass a considerable tonnage to their personal credit.

The U-boat commanders themselves referred to the first year and a half of the war as 'the happy time'. By February 1941 the three greatest of the U-boat 'aces' were Gunther Prien, who had sunk the *Royal Oak* in Scapa Flow and claimed over 150,000 tons of merchant shipping, and Joachim Schepke and Otto Kretschmer, both of whom claimed over 200,000 tons of Allied shipping sunk. All three of them had been decorated by Hitler with the Knight's Cross with Oakleaves for their outstanding success, and all three were men from whom other U-boat commanders drew their inspiration. But by March all three had been eliminated from the battle. Prien, in U-47, was sunk on March 7 by the corvettes *Arbutus* and *Camellia* and the destroyer *Wolverine*; Schepke, in U-100, was sunk on March 17 by the *Walker* and *Vanoc*; and on the same night these same destroyers sank U-99, taking Kretschmer prisoner as he escaped from his sinking U-boat. It was a heavy blow for Germany, for these three had been widely recognised in Germany as the cream of the U-boat commanders.

March 1941 saw the virtual end of the independent U-boat attack. As more and more merchant ships were brought into the convoy organisation, and as the range of convoy was extended farther across the Atlantic, the day of the individual U-boat was over. The British adoption and extension of convoy forced the U-boat command to work out new tactics, and it was from this situation that the pack attack at night was developed.

There was nothing basically new in this. A rudimentary form of pack attack had been evolved during the last year of the First World War, but had not been very successful because wireless signals, necessary for control of the pack, were still, relatively speaking, in their infancy. Tentative pack tactics had appeared in the Atlantic in 1940, but had not been developed because the individual U-boat operating in a fixed area was still finding sufficient targets to make its presence there well worth while. Those days, however, were now over for good, although in early 1942 the U-boats experienced another brief 'happy time'. This followed the entry of the United States into the war, when a small number of U-boats concentrated on the eastern American seaboard and took a heavy toll of the unescorted shipping there. Six months later, when this shipping, too, was organised into convoys, these U-boats withdrew abruptly.

In the organisation of the pack attack, the U-boat command relied on one U-boat of the pack shadowing a convoy during daylight and homing in the remainder by directional wireless as night approached. All attacks were then made on the surface during the hours of darkness, when the tiny superstructure of the U-boat was well-nigh invisible to the defenders. With her high surface speed and her virtual invisibility, the advantages of night attack to the U-boat were considerable.

Yet the whole system had in it one element of weakness. The shadowing U-boat was forced to make a series of wireless signals reporting the convoy's position, speed, and alterations of course. These signals were invariably picked up by Allied directional-finding stations, and the bearings, when plotted in the British Admiralty's U-boat tracking room, revealed the position of the shadower.

For the Germans, the Battle of the Atlantic had two purposes and two phases. At first the Germans were trying to strangle Britain's lifelines across the Atlantic, but by 1942 the U-boats were fighting to prevent the establishment of an Allied invasion-force in Britain. Both phases were governed by the 'Black Gap' in mid-Atlantic, where Allied escorts could not protect the vital convoys. The occupation of Iceland in 1940 had been the first step towards closing the gap, but no positive counterattack could hurt the U-boats until long-range frigates and escort-carriers could shepherd the convoys all the way across. In the spring of 1943, with the Torch landings safely over, the attack on the U-boats began in earnest. The diagram below shows how the gap was closed, and depicts the major Atlantic convoy routes and U-boat bases

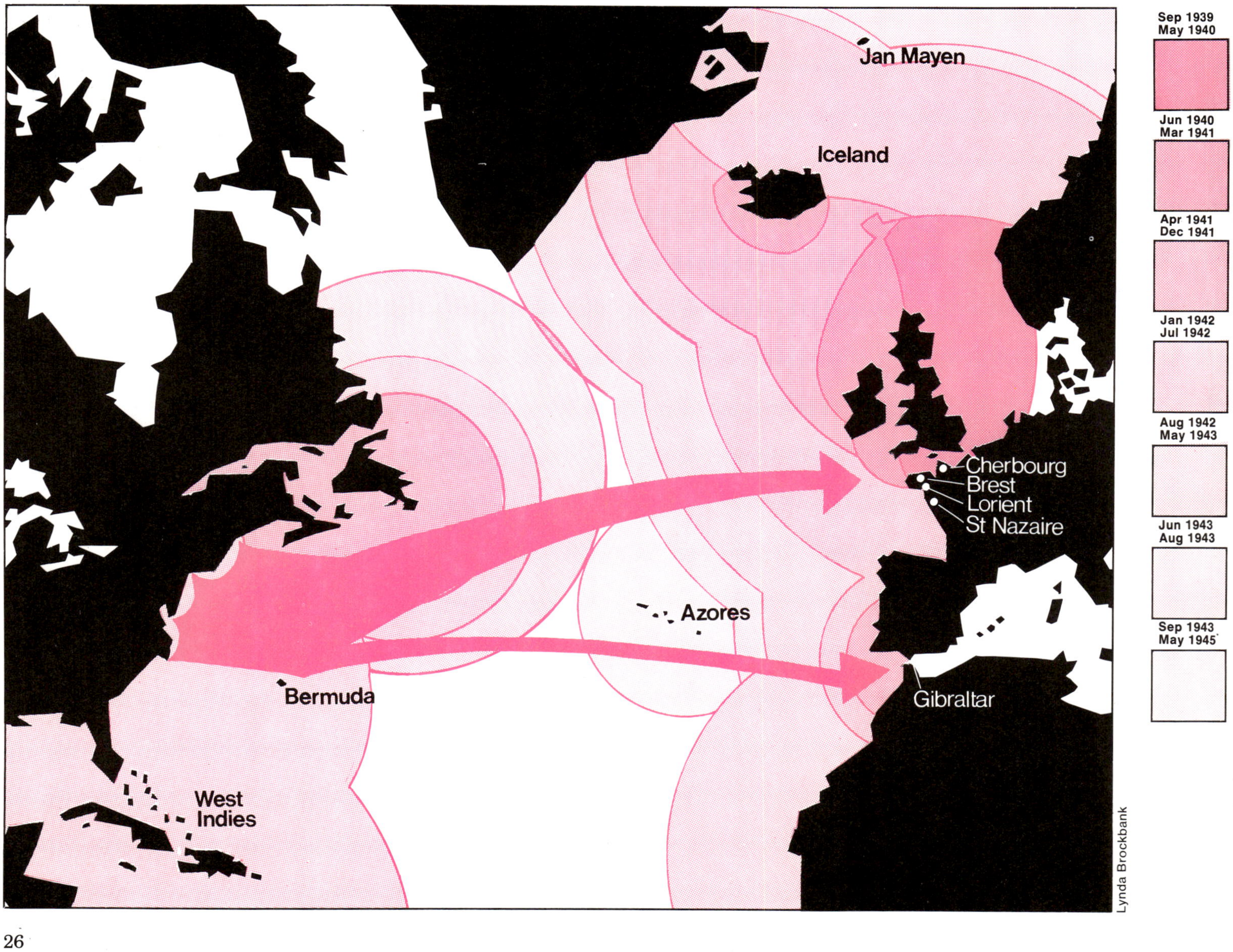

This flotsam of war tells its own tale of another merchantman that failed to get through

'The Battle of the Atlantic was the dominating factor all through the war. Never for one moment could we forget that everything elsewhere depended on its outcome' Churchill

For the Allies, the Battle of the Atlantic was not only a race to develop new and more advanced equipment than the enemy, but it was also a struggle to build even the basic minimum of aircraft and ships to provide an adequate escort for all convoys. Before the war, the escort programme and Coastal Command had been the 'Cinderellas' of the defence budget, and the chronic shortage of ships and aircraft was not something which could be rectified at once, when all other branches of the services were crying out for new equipment. It was not until the middle of 1942 that a massive building programme—much of which was undertaken in Canada—meant that the ships to provide a shore-to-shore escort became available in adequate numbers, and the RAF began to receive aircraft specially designed for the anti-submarine patrol role—instead of having to make do with old equipment which lacked the necessary range and duration. But once the escort forces had received the vital ships and aircraft, equipped with the new anti-submarine weapons, the 'happy time' of the U-boats was quickly ended

HMS *Starling:* an escort sloop of the modified *Black Swan* class. This class, the first of which were laid down before the outbreak of war, proved to be a most efficient escort design, combining good AA and anti-submarine armament with adequate speed and seaworthiness. **Displacement:** 1,350 tons. **Dimensions:** $299\frac{1}{2} \times 38\frac{1}{2} \times 8\frac{3}{4}$ feet. **Speed:** 20 knots. **Armament:** Six 4-inch and 12 20-mm anti-aircraft guns. **Complement:** 192

HMS *Clematis:* a corvette of the *Flower* class. This class was ordered before the war as part of the massive rearmament programme, and the design was based on the whale catcher. The ships proved to be too small to fulfill the ocean escort role adequately, in spite of being excellent sea-boats. **Displacement:** 925 tons. **Dimensions:** $205 \times 33 \times 11\frac{1}{2}$ feet. **Armament:** One 4-inch gun, one multiple pom-pom. **Complement:** 85

HMS *Towey:* a frigate of the *River* class. This was the first of the new ocean escort classes, larger and faster than the corvettes and designed for mass production. The subsequent *Loch* and *Bay* classes were developments of this design. **Displacement:** 1,370 tons. **Dimensions:** $301\frac{1}{4} \times 36\frac{1}{2} \times 9$ feet. **Speed:** 20 knots. **Armament:** Two 4-inch guns, ten 20-mm anti-aircraft guns. **Complement:** 140

HMS *Biter:* one of the escort carriers which were brought into service to bridge the 'mid-Atlantic gap' in land-based air cover. They were built on merchant ship hulls and had wooden flight-decks. **Displacement:** 8,200 tons. **Dimensions:** $492\frac{1}{4} \times 66\frac{1}{4} \times 23\frac{1}{4}$ feet. **Speed:** $16\frac{1}{2}$ knots. **Armament:** Three 4-inch and 15 20-mm anti-aircraft guns, 15 aircraft. **Complement:** 555

Vickers Wellington Mark I: One of the older designs which was modified for use by Coastal Command. This aircraft is fitted with the magnetic ring which was used to destroy magnetic mines in shallow waters. **Length:** 64 feet 7 inches. **Span:** 86 feet. **Speed:** 265 mph maximum. **Range:** 3,200 miles at 180 mph. **Crew:** Five. **Armament:** Four ·303-inch MG. Up to 6,000 lb of bombs

Lockheed Hudson: An American design which was in service with Coastal Command as a training aircraft before the war, and was pressed—very successfully—into front-line service for much of the Battle of the Atlantic. **Length:** 44 feet 2½ inches: **Span:** 65 feet. **Speed:** 292 mph maximum. **Range:** 2,160 miles at 254 mph. **Armament:** Seven ·303-inch MG. Four 500-lb depth charges. **Crew:** Four

Consolidated PBY Catalina: Over 650 of this tough and dependable American design were used by the RAF. **Length:** 65 feet 1¼ inches. **Span:** 104 feet. **Speed:** 185 mph. **Range:** 3,750 miles at 130 mph. **Armament:** Six ·303-inch MG, four depth charges. **Crew:** Up to eight

Short Sunderland: Over 700 were built of this military development of the pre-war 'C' class flying boats. **Length:** 85 feet 4 inches. **Span:** 112 feet 9½ inches. **Speed:** 212 mph. **Range:** 2,980 miles. **Armament:** Two ·50-inch and up to 12 ·303-inch machine-guns. Up to 2,000 lb of bombs or depth charges were carried internally and wound out on racks through panels just below the wing roots

Consolidated B-24 Liberator: Maritime patrol version of the bomber which was built in far greater numbers than any other US aircraft. **Speed:** 300 mph at 30,000 feet. **Length:** 67 feet 2 inches. **Span:** 110 feet. **Range:** 2,100 miles at 215 mph. **Armament:** Up to 14 ·50-inch MG, 5,000 lb of bombs internally—up to 12,800 lb could be carried on wing racks for short distances. **Crew:** 12

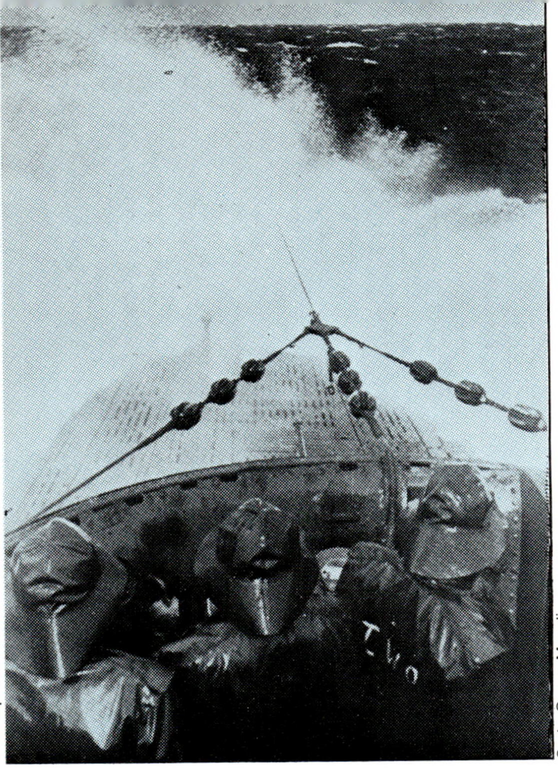

Sado-Opera Mundi

Sado-Opera Mundi

Left: A U-boat tackles heavy weather in the Bay of Biscay. *Right:* A lookout keeps watch from a surfaced U-boat. In this condition U-boats were very vulnerable to air attack

Imperial War Museum

△ Concrete shelters for U-boats were built all along the coast of occupied Europe
▽ A returning U-boat crew is congratulated by the flotilla commander

Sado-Opera Mundi

Yet even with this essential knowledge, there was still a very long road to travel before victory could come to the Allies in the Atlantic. There were, in the years 1941 and 1942, shortages in almost every aspect of the war against the U-boats – shortage of escort vessels, shortage of training time, shortage of adequate weapons, shortage of the technological advances required to deal with the modern German U-boat and her new tactics. But of all the shortages, the most chronic was that of long-range and long-endurance aircraft. It had already become apparent that the convoy which had both air and surface escort to protect it was virtually immune from attack. The problem was to devise a method whereby aircraft could always be on hand throughout the whole of a convoy's Atlantic passage.

To close the mid-Atlantic gap, which was as yet far beyond the range of any shore-based aircraft yet developed, the Admiralty in 1941 placed orders in America for a number of small escort carriers (virtually a Liberty ship hull fitted with a flying deck and hangar space). Yet even with American production methods it would be over a year before they could be expected to become operational. In the meantime, Coastal Command had to rely on a single squadron of very long-range Liberator aircraft which, originally composed of 20 aircraft, was very quickly reduced to a strength of ten by wastage and allotment to Ferry Command and BOAC. All attempts to increase the number, and to obtain long-range Lancaster bombers for the Atlantic battle, failed. The convoys and surface escorts were left to battle it out against the U-boats, handicapped as they were by the lack of one of the most powerful agents for success. Such air escort as did exist (700 miles from Northern Ireland and Western Scotland, 400 miles from Iceland, and 700 miles from Canadian bases) not only left a large gap in mid-Atlantic completely beyond reach of shore-based air escort, but was of itself spasmodic and in any case limited to daylight hours.

The Battle of the Oceans

It is difficult, over so immense a stage as the seas which both divide and join the Commonwealth, to appreciate the vast extent of the Battle of the Atlantic. The term itself is a restriction of the full encounter, for in effect the battle embraced far more than the North and South Atlantic oceans themselves. U-boats and armed raiders operated in the Indian Ocean, across which ran the main sea routes to India, Australia, and New Zealand, as important to global strategy as was the Atlantic. And for a long time the Arctic Ocean was the only available highway for supplies to Russia after the start of her great campaign, though later an alternative route was opened through the Persian Gulf. All of them called for protection from U-boat and raider attack, and what has come to be known as the Battle of the Atlantic was more truly, a battle of the oceans.

In terms of voyages, this vast encounter ran into several hundreds of thousands of miles steamed each week; in terms of ships it could mean as many as 1,000 at sea on any one day throughout the whole of the war, all of them to be protected against attack by an enemy who could operate virtually unseen and unheard. This was the true yardstick against which the battle must be measured, an immense and ceaseless conflict waged over millions of square miles of ocean.

The Huff-Duff, or High Frequency Direction Finder, was developed to locate attacking submarines and destroy them without any prior warning of detection. The device was installed in two of the escort ships, which, by taking a cross-bearing on a U-boat's radio signals, pinpointed its position. This was then transmitted to the 'Hunter Killer' group which could close within Asdic range and destroy the U-boat. This device enabled U-boats to be located at far greater distances, and destroyed or driven off before they could get within range of the convoy

One other aspect of this battle needs to be mentioned. As early as 1941 the Chiefs-of-Staff were already laying their plans to move from the defensive to the offensive. All realised that when this time came, it would call for a vast Allied army based in Britain, with a huge logistic backing, poised for the assault on Europe which alone could lead to complete victory. Most of this great army, and most of its logistic backing, could only come from across the Atlantic, men and materials from the United States and Canada. Security of the Atlantic was vital for this vast movement, and only a clear-cut victory over the U-boats could guarantee such security. This Atlantic battle was the one vital cog in the whole machinery of the war, for failure there would inevitably bring defeat to the whole Allied cause. It was the one and only key which could unlock the door to final victory.

The merchant ship losses in 1941 were grievous. U-boats alone sank 432 ships of 2,171,754 tons, while aircraft claimed another 371 ships of 1,017,422 tons. Merchant and warship raiders added during the year to the total by 84 ships of 428,350 tons, while a further 111 ships of 230,842 tons were lost in enemy minefields laid around the British coasts. From all causes, the final loss for the year was 1,299 ships totalling 4,328,558 tons – an overall loss well beyond Allied building capacity to replace.

These figures give an accurate idea of the severity of the battle, but they were far surpassed by the figures for the following year. The U-boats alone exceeded the total losses for 1941 by very nearly 2,000,000 tons (6,226,215 tons), and the overall loss for the year was 7,790,697 tons, represented by 1,664 ships.

'The U-boat attack of 1942,' wrote Churchill, 'was our worst evil.' Indeed, in no other theatre of the war, save perhaps in the Pacific, was the outlook quite so black. And again it was the same story, the inability of the Allies, in the face of all their maritime commitments, to produce escort vessels and long-range aircraft fast enough to hold the U-boat growth. German ship production facilities were concentrated almost entirely on U-boats to the exclusion of almost every other type of vessel, and the speed with which they were produced can be measured by the steady increase in operational boats. Excluding those used for training and other purposes, the numbers of U-boats available for operations at sea rose from 91 in January 1942 to 196 in October of the same year, to 212 as the year came to its close, and to a peak of 240 in April 1943. And although during 1942 a total of 87 U-boats were sunk, including those lost through accidents in German home waters, the steady production of new boats far outweighed losses.

The entry of the United States into the war brought to the U-boat captains their second 'happy time'. For six months the US relied on sea and air patrols as the means of countering U-boat attacks, in spite of all British experience that convoy was the only method of holding in check the mounting ship losses. Admiral Dönitz, commander-in-chief of the U-boat area, sent five U-boats into the area on the declaration of war against the United States, increasing the number by stages to a total of 21. By June 1942, when the Americans eventually put all their ships into convoy, these U-boats had sunk no less than 505 vessels. This holocaust moved even Dönitz into song. 'Our submarines,' he exulted, 'are operating close inshore along the coast of the United States of America, so that bathers and sometimes entire coastal cities are witnesses to that drama of war, whose visual climaxes are constituted by the red glorioles of blazing tankers.'

Dönitz and the German High Command had calculated that if an average of 800,000 tons of Allied shipping could be sunk each month, an Axis victory was certain. The overall rate of loss throughout 1942 was fractionally below 650,000 tons a month; but optimistic reports on estimated tonnage sunk made by the individual U-boat commanders led Dönitz to believe that his objective of 800,000 tons monthly was being achieved. Yet even 650,000 tons a month was a crippling rate for the Allies, far beyond their capacity for replacement, and it is true enough that, throughout these grim months of 1942, defeat in the Atlantic, and hence in the war as a whole, was a possibility that haunted the thoughts of all the war leaders.

Just as serious as the loss of essential imports which this rate of sinking made inevitable was the unforeseen cutback in the rate of building up forces in Britain for the assault on Europe, without which there could be no final victory over Germany. This build-up of forces had been given the code-word 'Bolero', and the plans hammered out by the Chiefs-of-Staff of Britain and the United States had called for a strength of five divisions of Canadian and United States troops in Britain by the end of 1942. As the year ended, 'Bolero' was so far in arrears that less than one division had arrived, and the overall plan was falling more and more into arrears. The whole future course of the war, every hope, every plan, hung in the balance poised over the Atlantic.

Imperial War Museum

The ideal complement to Asdic, Hedgehog (in action, above) fired a pattern of 24 32-lb bombs. Their contact fuses made the identification of 'kills' easy

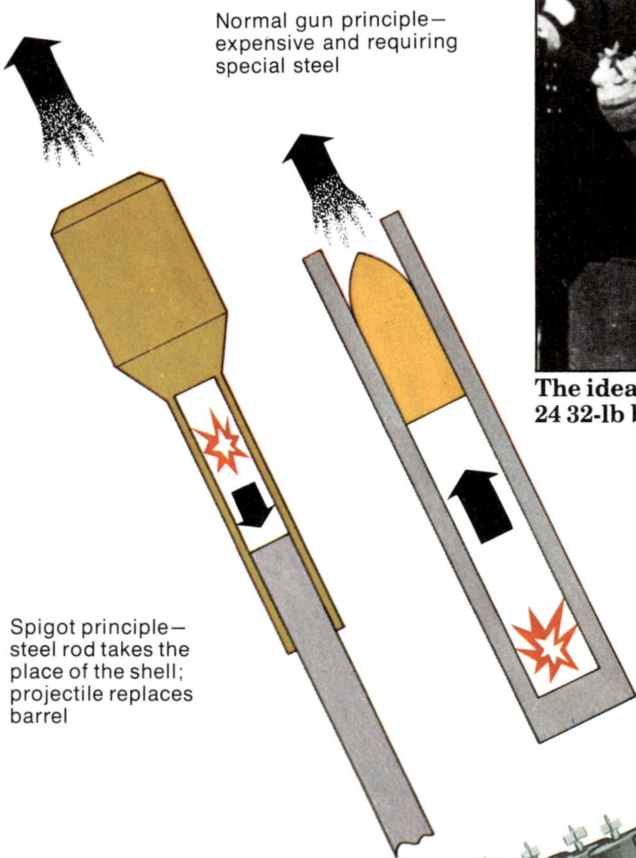

THE NEW TECHNIQUES

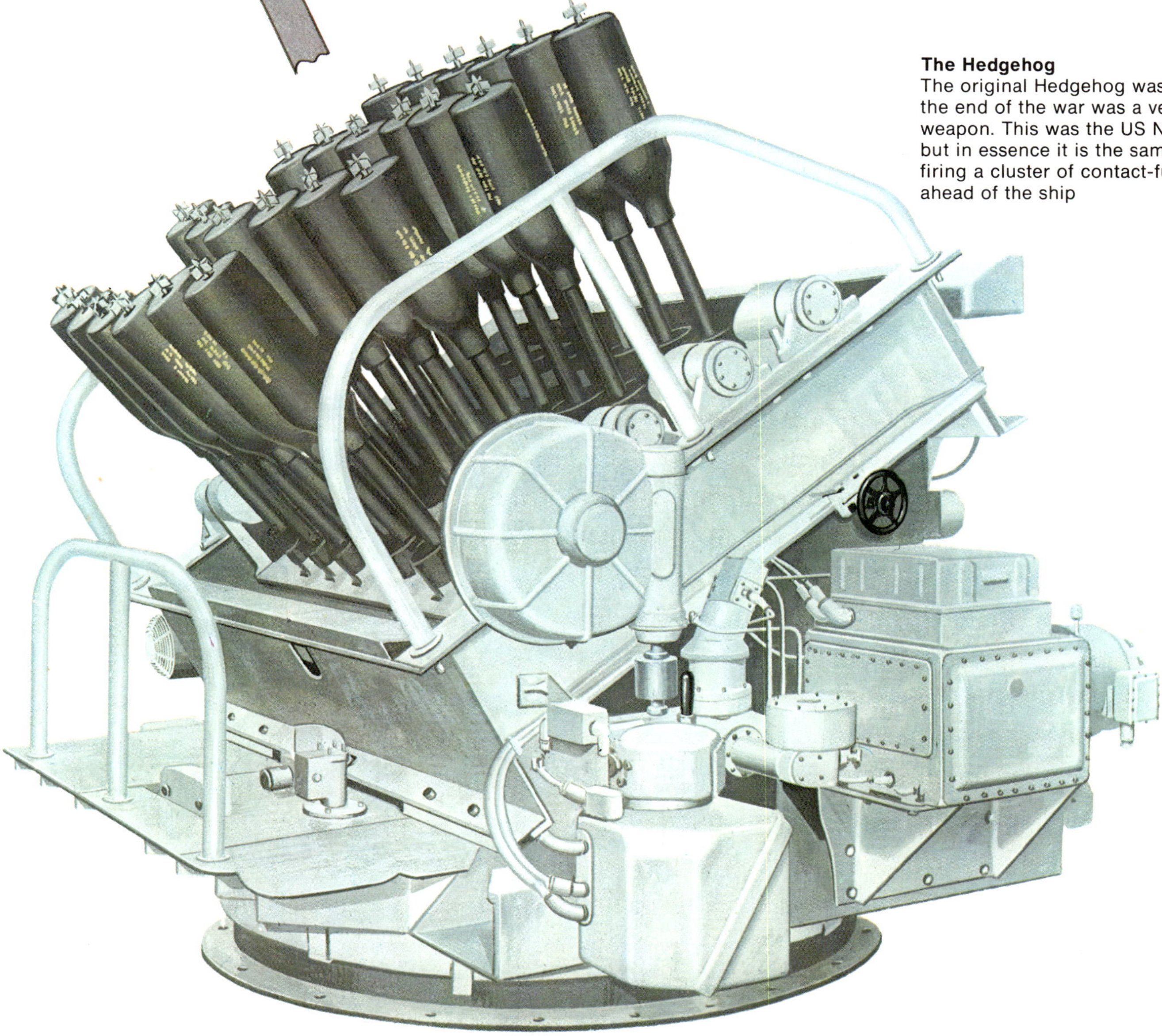

The Hedgehog
The original Hedgehog was refined, and by the end of the war was a very elaborate weapon. This was the US Navy's version, but in essence it is the same spigot mortar firing a cluster of contact-fused bombs ahead of the ship

With new techniques and better tools, now, for the first time in the Atlantic, the Allies had the upper hand

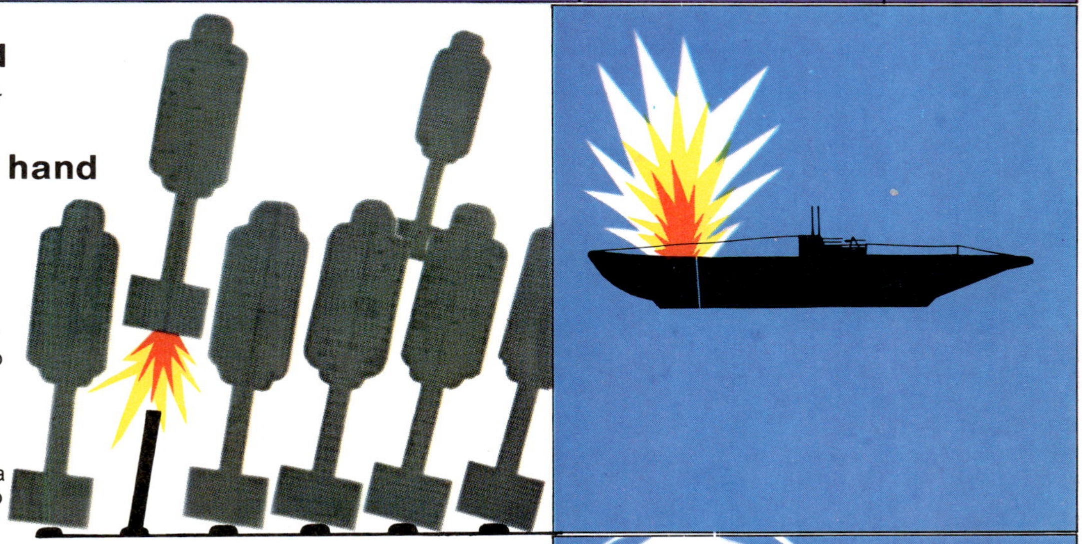

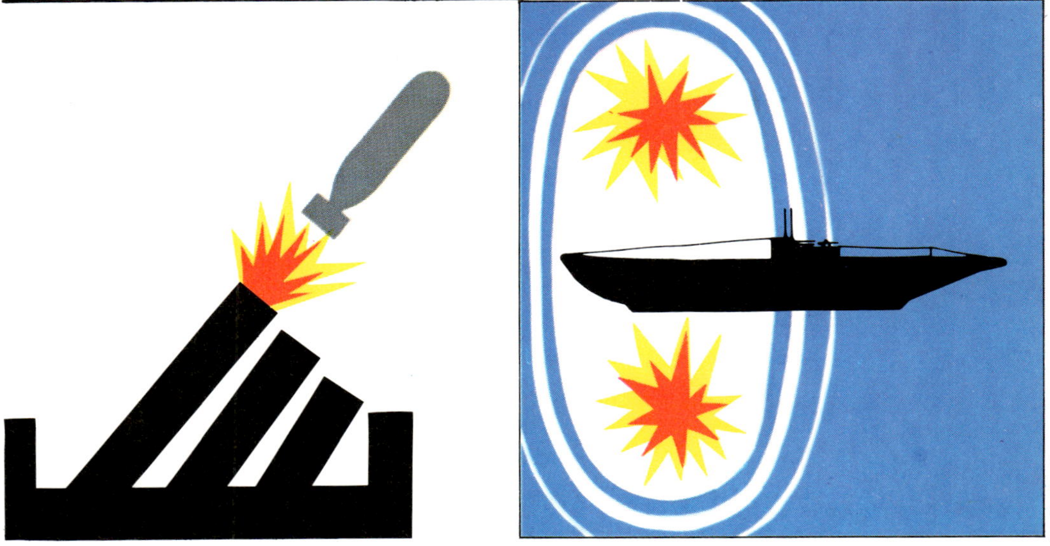

Asdic (top) consisted of a transmitter/receiver which sent out sound impulses, and picked up the echo if an impulse struck an object. By noting the time between transmission and return of the 'ping' the range of the object could be worked out. In its developed form, Asdic used three impulses: one diffused over a wide area (orange) to locate a U-boat, and two others – narrow vertical (pink) and horizontal (green) – to fix its position more accurately. But Asdic had its drawbacks: the receiver picked up echoes from fish, tidal disturbances, and changes in water temperature, and as long as depth-charges had to be dropped astern, the Asdic would lose contact with the U-boat as it passed underneath during the last stages of the run in.

To overcome this, **Hedgehog** and **Squid** were developed. Both threw their bombs ahead of the ship in a pattern designed to straddle a U-boat (above). The charges dropped and exploded at different speeds and depths so as to give maximum coverage of an area. The main difference between the weapons was that Hedgehog (▷ top) fired a pattern of 24 bombs which would explode on contact, while Squid (▷ bottom) fired three bombs intended to explode around a U-boat and crack its hull with concussion. The advantage of Hedgehog was that the Asdic contact would not be disturbed unless there was a hit, but with the Squid it was often possible for a near miss to force a U-boat to the surface

Chris Harrison

During 1942, however, the anti-submarine frigates, ordered in 1939 and 1940, began to come forward from the builders' yards. These were ships which had the speed and endurance so vital in the Atlantic battle. One of the great problems of convoy escort had been the danger of allowing the existing escorts to hunt U-boats to their final destruction, more often than not a long and exacting operation. Their prime duty had always been to protect the merchant ships; but a convoy could not stand still in mid-Atlantic while its escorts were engaged in hunting and destroying. A great number of U-boats, located by radar and asdic, lived to fight again simply because the convoy escorts could not spare the time to hunt them to destruction. The merchant ships always had to come first.

The commissioning of the anti-submarine frigates, however, provided an answer to this problem. The growth in overall force represented by these frigates enabled Admiral Noble to build up support groups of ships, which could be directed to join the defences of any convoy threatened by a pack attack. While the normal escort group could continue with the convoy, providing the necessary close defence, the support group could engage in prolonged hunting operations, holding a detected U-boat with its asdics while the attacks were made. The first support group, under the command of Commander F. J. Walker, was at sea by the third week of September, 1942, but other events were to delay the full implementation of this new contribution to the Atlantic battle.

Almost simultaneously with the arrival of the frigates came the new ahead-throwing anti-submarine weapons; first the 'Hedgehog', a multi-barrelled mortar which threw 24 charges ahead of the attacking ship; and then the 'Squid', which threw a pattern of three full-sized depth-charges. The old method of attack, by dropping depth-charges over the ship's stern, had suffered from the great drawback that asdic contact with the U-boat was lost during the run-in, and the final stages of any attack had to be made by guesswork. The new weapons enabled asdic contact to be held throughout the attack and right up to the moment of depth-charge explosion, resulting in a far greater degree of accuracy.

By the late summer of 1942 the first of the new, small escort carriers, which had been ordered from the United States the previous year, was commissioned for service. She was the *Avenger*, and by the end of the year six more were serving in the fleet. These aircraft-carriers were to provide the final answer to the U-boat threat, their aircraft filling the Atlantic gaps which were still beyond the range of shore-based aircraft. It was in these gaps – in mid-Atlantic, off the north coast of Brazil, and around the hump of Africa – that the U-boats concentrated and continued to find convoys unprotected by air escort. Pack attacks on convoys in these areas were made in such strength as to swamp the surface escorts, and provided a rich harvest for the U-boats.

The stage, then, was set by the late autumn of 1942 to turn to the offensive in the Atlantic. With support groups to augment the surface escorts of threatened convoys, with carrier-borne aircraft to provide the essential air escort across the Atlantic gaps, with the new weapons of attack which enabled the full benefit of asdic contact to be held to the last moment, the prospects of success looked bright. And to Liverpool, in November 1942, came Admiral Sir Max Horton as commander-in-chief. He was a submarine officer of great distinction, and thus brought to his task an intimate knowledge of submarine warfare in all its aspects. He inherited from Admiral Noble an organisation in which most of the essential groundwork had already been done and a command whose forces were growing almost daily as the new ships ordered in 1940 and 1941 reached completion.

One other aspect of this Atlantic battle needs a mention. A part of the difficulties which beset the Allies in 1942, resulting in such heavy losses of shipping, had been caused by the withdrawal from Atlantic duties of the United States escort forces in June of that year. These vessels were needed partly for the Pacific war and partly to escort troop and logistic convoys for the projected assault on North Africa in November 1942.

By the end of the year the division of escort forces in the Atlantic was: Britain providing 50%, Canada 48%, and the United States 2%. Early in 1943, at a convoy conference held in Washington, the United States declared that she would have to withdraw completely from all trade convoy protection in the Atlantic. It was a decision which came at an awkward moment, with the battle at its height and the British and Canadian forces stretched to their uttermost. The American decision, though it represented but a small part of the burden, had to be absorbed equally between Britain and Canada.

As the escort forces were poised, in the late autumn of 1942, to turn to the offensive against the U-boats, a new blow struck the Western Approaches command. Operation 'Torch', the invasion of French North Africa, was mounted in November, and both the escort carriers and the newly formed support groups were detached from the Atlantic convoy routes to provide protection for the troop convoys in which this expeditionary force was transported. This campaign was to last until May 1943, and until the end of March the Atlantic escort forces had to continue the battle still with no air cover over the three 'gaps', and still with no support groups to supplement the escort groups in the battles around the convoys.

Imperial War Museum

Associated Press

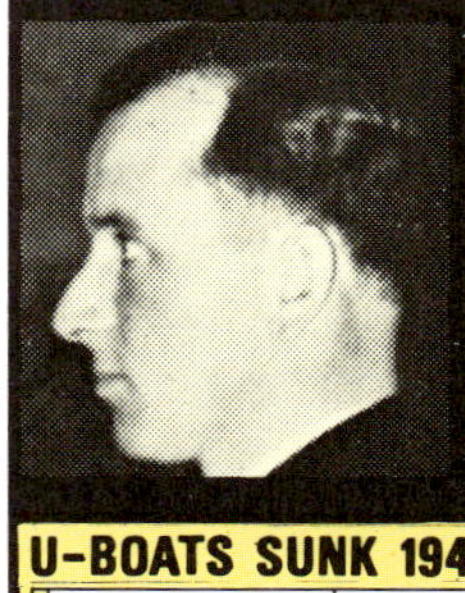

Black Star

These three men were Germany's top scorers in the first 'Happy Time'

◁ Gunther Prien, of U-47, the man who sank the British battleship *Royal Oak* in Scapa Flow – he was lost in action in March 1941

◁ Joachim Schepke, of U-100; he was lost with his ship when he took too many liberties with a convoy's escort

◁ Otto Kretschmer, of U-99. He was Germany's 'top scorer' but was captured when U-99 was depth-charged and forced to the surface – the only one of the trio to survive the Battle of the Atlantic

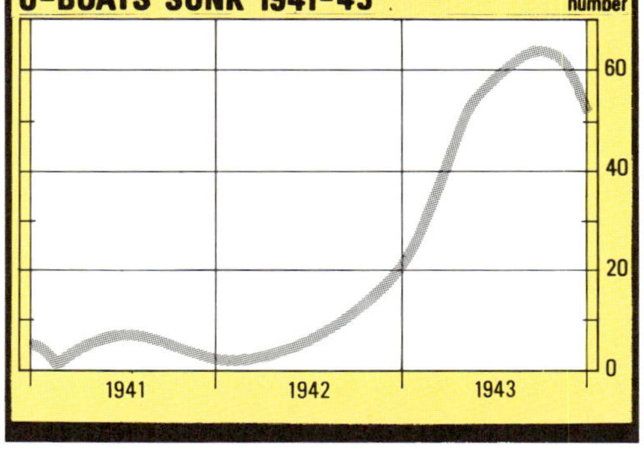

As the year turned, the rate of loss in the Atlantic showed little change from the figures of 1942. Wild weather in the Atlantic during January produced difficulties for the U-boats in their operations, and the loss during the month was 203,000 tons. In February it rose to 359,000 tons; by March it was back to the high average rate of 1942, 627,000 tons of shipping being sunk in that month. It was during this month that the American decision to withdraw completely from the Atlantic was announced at the conference in Washington.

It was, in fact, while this conference was in session that one of the biggest and most disastrous convoy battles of the whole war was fought out in the Atlantic. Two convoys had been sailed from Halifax to Britain, one fast convoy of 25 ships and one slow one of 52. The fast convoy was sighted by a U-boat early in its passage, and before long a pack of eight U-boats was in contact. Over the next three days and nights they sank 12 merchant ships. Some hundred or so miles ahead, the slow convoy was also sighted and reported, and a pack of 12 U-boats concentrated against it. As the two convoys closed up, the two packs merged into one, swamping the defence and causing heavy loss. Out of these two convoys alone 21 ships of 141,000 tons were sunk.

What made this particular convoy battle even harder to bear was that only one U-boat was sunk by the escort forces. It was without question a serious defeat, remarkable even in a period in which there were few gleams of light to encourage the Allies in their desperate struggle.

Climax of the battle

Few could doubt, in March 1943, that the Atlantic battle had reached its climax, and that out of the operations of the next three or four months one side or the other must slide down into defeat. Admiral Dönitz was making his supreme effort, and out of an operational strength of 240 U-boats he concentrated no fewer than 112 in the North Atlantic. Flushed by success, and highly trained, the U-boat commanders were able, by the very nature of submarine warfare, to dictate the conditions in which they fought the battle. Almost without exception the U-boat packs were concentrated in those areas beyond the reach of air escort, and it was here that they reaped almost the whole of their grim harvest.

To the Atlantic, at the end of March, came the escort carriers, released at last from their duties with the Torch convoys. With them, too, came the support groups, so that at long last there existed in the Atlantic the possibility of hunting detected U-boats to their final destruction. And almost simultaneously, two other events made notable contributions to the battle. Using his authority as commander-in-chief of the US forces, President Roosevelt took a hand in the dis-

Hitting back at the U-boats

△ A depth-charge is hurled from an American Coast-Guard cutter in the early stages of a battle with a U-boat (eventually destroyed). ▽ Illustration of the supreme power of the Atlantic air patrols: strafing, bombing, and surface-charge attacks on U-boats in mid-Atlantic

Imperial War Museum

tribution of the very long-range Liberator aircraft being delivered from America. By the end of March, 20 of them were in operation in the North Atlantic; by mid-April the number had grown to 41. It was still far too few to cover the essential needs, but it was at least an earnest promise of better things to come.

The other great contribution came from the scientists. They designed a very short-wave radar set which could reflect from much smaller objects at sea and against which the German radar search receiver, as fitted in the U-boats, was of no avail. These centimetric radars were fitted to many of the surface escorts around the end of 1942 and beginning of 1943, and they led to many more contacts with attacking U-boats, with the added advantage that the U-boats had now no knowledge that they had been detected. The new radar was also being fitted in aircraft, but other priorities in the RAF made it slow to arrive in Coastal Command.

Early in May another considerable convoy battle was fought, providing the first real opportunity of testing out the value of the support group and continuous air escort in anti-submarine warfare. An outward bound convoy was delayed and to some extent scattered by a violent storm south of Greenland, an area which was known to contain a heavy concentration of U-boats. A pack of 12 U-boats concentrated around the convoy. This was the type of situation for which the support groups were formed, and two groups were ordered out from St John's, Nova Scotia, as the convoy approached the area. They were somewhat delayed by the storm which had scattered the convoy, and before they could arrive the U-boats had sunk five ships during night attacks, following this with four more sunk during the following day. One of the convoy's escorts, the corvette *Pink,* attacked and sank U-192.

The two support groups joined the convoy that evening, and for the first time U-boats came up against the full application of the new countermeasures. As the convoy was collected and re-formed after its battering in the storm, the U-boats renewed their attacks, but each one was detected and driven off before damage could be done to the merchant ships. HMS *Loosestrife* detected, chased, and sank U-638; the destroyer *Vidette* held U-125 with her asdic and sent her to the bottom with a hit from her Hedgehog, the *Oribi* rammed and sank U-531, and the sloop *Pelican* detected and held U-438 with her asdic and hunted her to final destruction. Aircraft operating over the convoy accounted for two more, U-710 being destroyed by a Coastal Command aircraft and U-630 by an aircraft of the Royal Canadian Air Force. But the cup of bitterness was not yet full for the U-boats, for U-659 and U-439 collided in the darkness and both were lost.

This was a severe defeat for the U-boats, but one defeat in a campaign does not necessarily mean victory for the other side. Yet the fate of the convoys which followed was to prove that this was, in fact, no flash in the pan. The next fast convoy lost three ships, but the cost to the enemy was three U-boats sunk. The slow convoy which made its passage at the same time had two ships sunk, while two U-boats were sunk by the escorts and others from the attacking pack were seriously damaged. Of the next pair of convoys, the result was even more dramatic. The slow convoy reached Britain with all its merchant ships in company, but in its path lay the sunken hulls of U-954, U-258, U-209, U-273, and U-381. The fast convoy also arrived without loss, with U-752 joining her sisters on the bed of the Atlantic.

Perhaps more impressive still were the overall figures from April to July. In April, when the new and integrated system of surface and air escort was only just getting into its stride, the U-boats sank 245,000 tons of shipping and lost 15 of their number in the process. In May they sank 165,000 tons at a cost to themselves of 40 U-boats. In June the figures were 18,000 tons and 17 U-boats; and in July, 123,000 tons and 37 U-boats.

Nor was this the whole of the Atlantic story, for Coastal Command was conducting a separate offensive over the main U-boat transit areas to and from the Atlantic. Using the new centimetric radar, depth-charges set to explode at a shallow depth, and searchlights to illuminate U-boats detected at night, they sank a further 13 U-boats during April and May, taking full advantage of a tactical mistake made by Admiral Dönitz, who ordered his U-boats to proceed to and from their operational areas on the surface, and fight it out against attacking aircraft. Against the new weapons, they had small chance of success.

Against losses such as these it was hardly surprising that morale in the U-boats cracked. It was a staggering reversal of the trend of the battle in the Atlantic, and even more so in the realisation that it took no more than five weeks from the time the full offensive was mounted to drive the U-boats, at the very height of their power and success, to search for less hazardous waters in which to operate. For nearly three months after the decisive May battles, the Atlantic was empty of U-boats, and even when they did return, though never again in the same numbers, it was very noticeable that the individual U-boat commanders had lost their will to attack.

On the purely analytical plane, one could attribute this victory in the Atlantic battle to the influence of the support groups in anti-submarine warfare, to the provision of continuous air escort over the convoys, to the centimetric radar and the other new weapons provided by the scientists and technologists. A considerable element in the victory must go, too, to the expertise in the interpretation of U-boat Intelligence developed in the Submarine Tracking Room in the British Admiralty. Their handling of all forms of Intelligence, and in particular the directional bearings of U-boat wireless signals, enabled them to predict with considerable accuracy the build-up of U-boat concentrations in the Atlantic and to divert convoys from the main danger areas.

But the real victory went much deeper than this. It lay just as much in the skill and endurance of the men who manned the escort vessels and the merchant ships, in their refusal to acknowledge defeat in the dark years of 1941 and 1942, in their courage which fortified them to return again and again to that vast battlefield where the odds were weighted so heavily against them. Over the centuries there have been, in British naval history, victories which shine like jewels across the years: none can shine more brightly than that achieved in this long, bitter, groping battle fought across the oceans.

In the concept of overall strategy in the European theatre, the winning of the Battle of the Atlantic was always recognised as the essential prerequisite of ultimate victory. When the German armies overran most of Europe in 1940 and 1941, it was British sea power, fortified by the navies of the Dominions and of such allies as had ships to contribute, that alone stood between the Axis and the domination of the world. Sea power, with its flexibility and natural resilience, held the ring around Germany and Italy, denying to the enemy the riches of the world which lay across the oceans. The U-boat campaign was the chosen, indeed the only, weapon of the Axis to break the ring. How nearly it succeeded can be read in the figures of Allied shipping losses in 1941, 1942, and the first three months of 1943. But with the clear-cut victory which emerged in May 1943, not only was the ring still unbroken, but now it could contract, closing in every day until even the coastal waters of Germany became too dangerous for her shipping to use.

With the Atlantic battle won, an endless stream of convoys, securely guarded and virtually immune from loss, crossed the Atlantic, bringing to Britain the troops, the guns, the tanks, the supplies needed to launch in 1944 the direct attack on German-held Europe. With the road now open, the whole future course of the European campaign lay clear and inevitable. To Britain, to North Africa, to Russia, to Malta, an endless stream of men, weapons, and supplies came and gathered against the day of the final assaults. All were carried by sea, and their safe arrival at their destinations proclaimed the planned offensive. The victories which lay so surely in the future, in which the armies and the air forces of the Allies were to shatter the resistance of the enemy, were all made possible by the full opening of the sea routes across the world.

So history repeated itself, for in all war experience it is the winning of the maritime war which precedes the land victory. By mid-1943 the maritime war had been won and the main task of the navies of the Allies had been accomplished; now it was the task of the armies and the air forces to go in and win the final victory.

Winning the maritime war

1941 **February:** Admiral Sir Percy Noble appointed C-in-C Western Approaches.
March: The leading German U-boat aces—Prien, Schepke, and Kretschmer—are eliminated.
April: The Allied refuelling base in Iceland begins operation.
June: First Allied convoy with end-to-end surface escort crosses the Atlantic.
December: The United States enters the war: a second 'happy time' for the U-boats begins.

1942 **June:** US escort forces are withdrawn from Atlantic duties.
September: The first British support group begins operation.
November: Admiral Sir Max Horton takes over as C-in-C Western Approaches.

1943 **March:** In a running battle with the escorts of convoys HX-229 and SC-122, U-boat packs sink 21 ships for the loss of only one submarine. But at the end of the month the escort carriers and support groups return from the Torch operation.
April: U-boats sink 245,000 tons of shipping for the loss of 15 submarines.
May: During attacks on five convoys, 20 U-boats are sunk. During the whole month 165,000 tons of shipping are sunk—for the loss of 40 U-boats.
June: The U-boat toll mounts: for only 18,000 tons sunk, 17 U-boats are destroyed. For the first time, the balance favours the Allies.

Imperial War Museum

The *Bismarck*, spotted by the RAF on May 21 in a Norwegian fjord

THE SINKING OF THE BISMARCK

North Atlantic May 1941 As the battle for Crete moved into its last stages and German victory was assured, the German navy struck at the British Atlantic convoy routes. The *Bismarck*, the strongest modern battleship in the world, slipped out of the Baltic with the heavy cruiser *Prinz Eugen* in company to scourge the Allied convoys. In her first battle, the *Bismarck* sank the British Navy's proudest ship—'the mighty *Hood*'—and one of the greatest dramas of the war at sea began ▷

Behind the planning in Germany which led to the sortie of the *Bismarck* into the Atlantic in May 1941, it is easy to discern the figure of Grand Admiral Raeder. Of all the German war leaders – naval, army, and air – he was the outstanding strategist. He was also an expert on cruiser warfare, and had himself written the volume of the official German naval history on cruiser warfare during the First World War. All this was well enough known inside the British Admiralty; and as soon as it became apparent that the *Bismarck* had completed her trials, it was reasonably certain that Raeder would find some use for her. And in the circumstances of the day, where else but in the Atlantic? All through April and May 1941, the British Admiralty was watching her very carefully, the information of her day-to-day movements coming from photographic reconnaissance and reports from agents.

Admiral Raeder's initial plans, however, went far beyond anything that the British Admiralty contemplated. He had a fairly solid background of experience on which to make his plans, for already during the war

The German occupation of Norway gave Admiral Raeder's High Seas Fleet a relatively secure and defensible base from which to send surface raiders and U-boats out into the sea-lanes of the North Atlantic. Left: A German heavy machine-gun guards the approaches to a Norwegian harbour. Below: A German destroyer patrols a fjord near Narvik

the pocket-battleships *Admiral Scheer*, *Lützow*, and *Graf Spee*, the battle-cruisers *Scharnhorst* and *Gneisenau*, and the cruiser *Hipper*, had been out on raiding cruises in the world's oceans. The Royal Navy knew from experience how difficult it was to find them and bring them to action; and Raeder knew it too.

The one difficulty which had faced these earlier raiders was the organisation of Allied shipping into convoy. To attack a defended convoy invited the risk of damage, which no armed raider could afford when operating so far from her home bases. Many of the Atlantic convoys, moreover, now sailed with an anti-raider escort of a battleship or cruiser, and even the *Scharnhorst* and *Gneisenau*, when operating in company, had not been prepared to risk an encounter with a convoy so defended. In 1940 they had intercepted a homeward-bound convoy from Halifax, and had run away as soon as they had discovered that she was being escorted by HMS *Ramillies*, a ship which normally either of them could, singly, expect to overcome. But in the context of action in mid-Atlantic, with the chance of damage so far from a friendly dockyard, discretion was not only the better part of valour but was also sound strategic sense.

Raeder, when he knew he had the *Bismarck* approaching readiness, decided to try to solve this conundrum of the convoys. If he could concentrate a force of real power in the Atlantic he could then accept battle against the most strongly escorted convoys. In the Baltic he had the *Bismarck* and the *Prinz Eugen* approaching operational readi-

Swordfish – whose torpedoes crippled the *Bismarck* – on board HMS *Victorious*

Fairey Swordfish I
The antiquated 'Stringbag' had the superb handling essential for carrier flying, and delivered cripplingly accurate torpedo attacks in actions from Taranto to the sinking of the *Bismarck*
Span: 45 ft 6 in *Length:* 36 ft 4 in
Engine: Bristol Pegasus 30, 750 hp
Armament: 1 Vickers mg; 1 Lewis mg *Max Speed:* 139 mph at 4750 ft *Ceiling:* 10,700 ft
Range: 546 miles *Bombload:* 1×18-in torpedo or 1500 lb bombs or mines or 8×60-lb bombs

ness. At Brest he had the *Scharnhorst* and *Gneisenau*. A simultaneous break-out from the Baltic and from Brest, and a rendezvous in the Atlantic, could give him the force he needed. In addition, five tankers, two supply ships, and two reconnaissance ships were available to support the force. Raeder gave the code-name *Rheinübung* ('Exercise Rhine') to the operation, and it was planned to take place in the second half of April when the new moon would give dark nights for the two break-outs.

Fate, however, was to step in during April and deal some crushing blows to Raeder's plan. Early in the month it was revealed that repairs and refit to the *Scharnhorst's* machinery would take much longer than originally estimated, and that she could not be ready in time. Then, on April 6, the *Gneisenau* was hit by a torpedo from a Coastal Command aircraft as she lay in Brest Roads, and extensively damaged. Four days later she was again hit by four bombs during a night air raid on the port. And finally, within a day or two of the planned departure, the *Prinz Eugen* was slightly damaged by a magnetic mine in the Baltic, and as a result the whole operation had to be postponed.

Admiral Lütjens, whom Raeder had selected to command the force, advised strongly that the operation should be cancelled, or at least postponed until the Brest ships were again ready to proceed. He was overridden by Raedar. In terms of this operation, on which he had set his heart, the sands were running out. He knew that Hitler was proposing to attack Russia in June, and he suspected that large-scale

Keystone

Admiral Tovey

Imperial War Museum

Admiral Lütjens

naval operations would get no priority once that attack was launched. He decided that *Rheinübung* should go ahead as soon as the two remaining ships were ready, and prevailed upon Hitler to go to Gdynia and address the two ships' companies on the eve of their departure.

The *Bismarck* and *Prinz Eugen* sailed after dark from Gdynia on May 18, and the Baltic was cleared of merchant shipping for their passage. They passed through the Belts at night and at dawn on the 20th were well up the Skagerrak. Here they had their first stroke of bad luck. The Swedish cruiser *Gotland* sighted them while she was out exercising off the coast, and Lütjens was certain that the news of their sailing would be in England in a very short time.

It came to London the same day, sent by the British naval attaché in Sweden. It was the first definite piece of information that the *Bismarck* was at last on her way out, although the British Admiralty had long suspected that Raeder would use her in this way as soon as she was fully operational.

The break-out

The two ships proceeded up the Norwegian coast and anchored in Kors Fjord, near Bergen, at 0900 hours on May 21. There the *Prinz Eugen* topped up with fuel but the *Bismarck,* which had sailed with 9,000 tons in her tanks, still had sufficient on board. The two crews painted out the camouflage on their hulls, and at dusk slipped out to the northward. Looking back after they had left, they saw the flares and bomb explosions of a British air-raid on the port. This encouraged Lütjens to believe that he had given the British the slip, particularly as the weather forecast for the Norwegian coast predicted fog and thick cloud for the next two days.

In Britain, the information from the naval attaché at Stockholm had been followed by considerable activity. On the morning of the 21st an extensive photographic reconnaissance of the Norwegian coast was carried

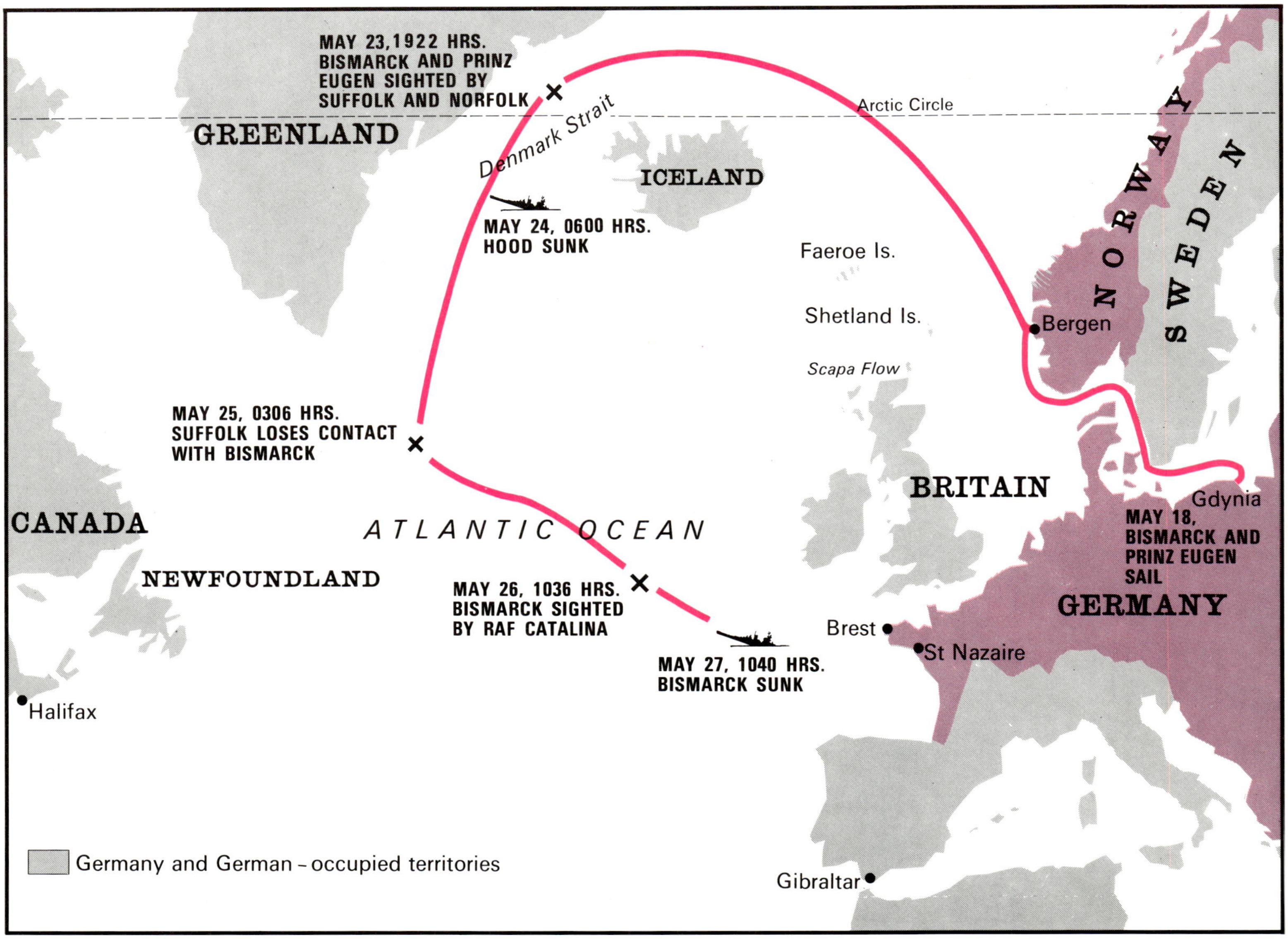

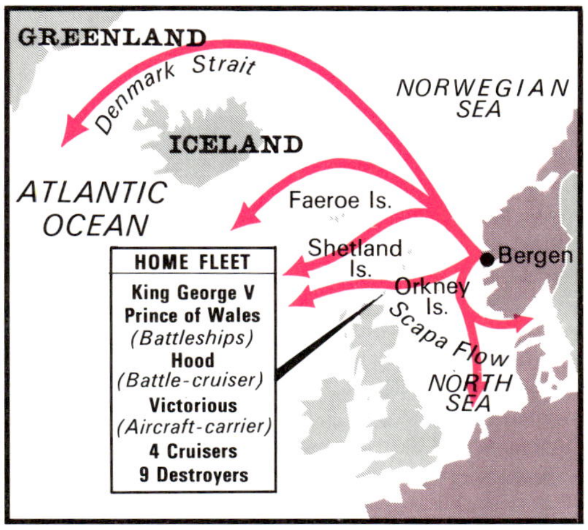

(Right) The break-out routes from German waters, which had to be covered by the Home Fleet. (Below) The battle in the Denmark Strait

out. One of the aircraft, covering the Bergen area, reported seeing two *Hipper*-class cruisers. When the photographs it had taken were examined, they were seen to depict the *Bismarck* and *Prinz Eugen*. The information was passed out at once to the fleet.

Admiral Sir John Tovey, Commander-in-Chief Home Fleet, was at Scapa Flow, flying his flag in the battleship *King George V*. With him were the battleship *Prince of Wales*, newly commissioned and not yet worked up, the battle-cruiser *Hood*, flying the flag of Vice-Admiral L. E. Holland, the aircraft-carrier *Victorious*, the 2nd Cruiser Squadron of four cruisers, and nine destroyers. The *Victorious*, which was under orders to accompany a troop convoy to the Middle East, already had 48 crated Hurricanes on board for delivery in Egypt, and so only had space for nine Swordfish and six Fulmars of her normal complement of aircraft.

At sea were the cruisers *Norfolk* (Rear-Admiral Wake-Walker) and *Suffolk* on patrol in the Denmark Strait, and the cruisers *Manchester* and *Birmingham* covering the Iceland-Faeroes gap. Other Home Fleet ships, including the battleship *Rodney*, were on convoy duty in the Atlantic.

As soon as the news that the *Bismarck* was at Bergen reached the Commander-in-Chief, he ordered Admiral Holland to sail with the *Hood* and *Prince of Wales*, escorted by six destroyers, to cover the *Norfolk* and *Suffolk* in the Denmark Strait. They left Scapa at 0052 hours on May 22. The rest of the fleet in Scapa was brought to short notice for steam. The Admiralty cancelled the sailing of the *Victorious* with the Middle East troop convoy, and also that of the battle-cruiser *Repulse*, which was in the Clyde and under orders to escort the same convoy, and placed both ships under the orders of the Commander-in-Chief.

The day of May 22 was a vital one in the movements of the Home Fleet. A reconnaissance of the Bergen fjords was imperative if the Commander-in-Chief was to know whether the German ships had sailed. But in the North Sea area there were clouds down to 200 feet, and the Norwegian coast was wrapped in fog. All attempts at reconnaissance failed. Finally, on his own initiative, Captain Fancourt of the RN Air Station at Hatston, Orkneys, dispatched a naval aircraft to see what it could do. As observer it carried Commander Rotherham, one of the most experienced observers in the Royal Navy. Flying at times only a few feet above the wavetops, it managed to reach the Bergen fjords and, under a heavy fire, forced home a determined reconnaissance.

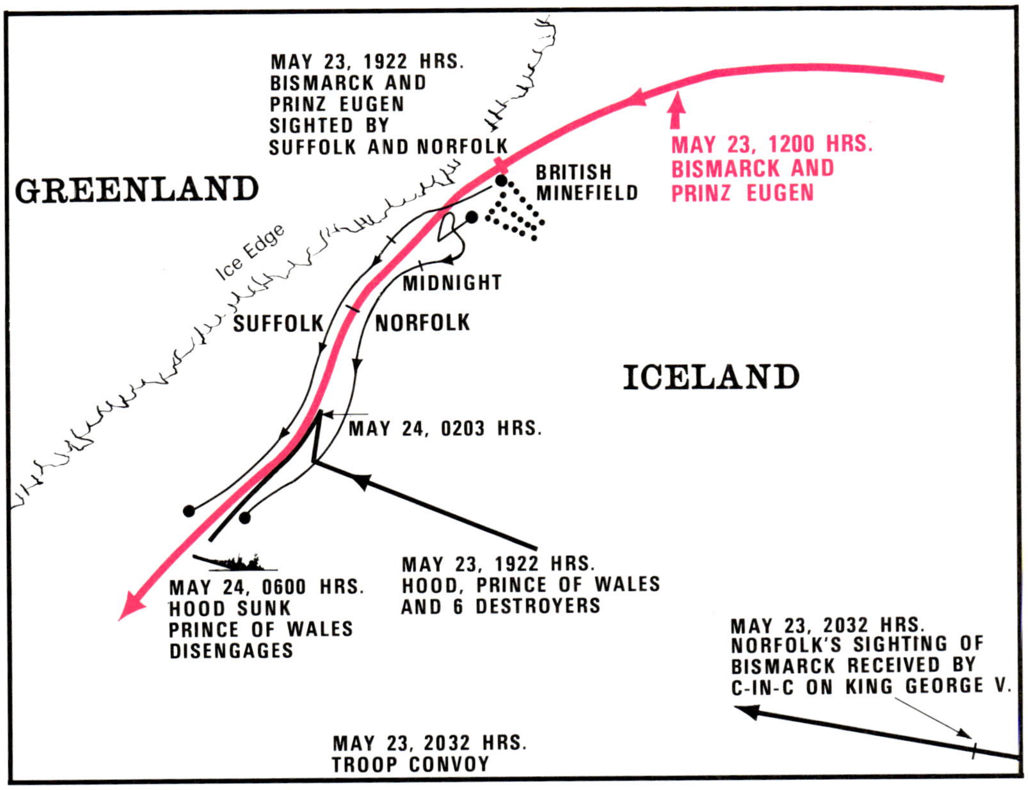

As it turned for home it signalled that the German ships had sailed. The news reached the Commander-in-Chief at 2000 hours that evening.

The German Admiral Lütjens was not quite so fortunate in this matter. A German reconnaissance over Scapa Flow on May 20 had shown quite conclusively that the *King George V*, *Prince of Wales*, *Hood*, *Victorious*, and six cruisers were all there at anchor. The weather on the 21st was too bad for any reconnaissance flights. It was still too bad for photographs on May 22, but a German pilot had flown over the anchorage and made a visual check. He reported that the four big ships were still there. In fact he was mistaken, for the *Hood* and *Prince of Wales* were by then well on their way. This erroneous information was signalled to Admiral Lütjens, and confirmed his belief that he had made a clear getaway. This information, combined with a forecast from his meteorological officers on board that there would be fog in the Denmark Strait, indicated to him that the way into the Atlantic was open. He decided to press ahead instead of going up to the north, where a tanker was waiting for him, and lying low for a few days until the immediate hue and cry had died down.

Meanwhile, the British Commander-in-Chief had put to sea from Scapa Flow. When he received the signal that the *Bismarck* and *Prinz Eugen* had sailed, he began to harbour doubts about the safety of the convoys in the Atlantic. There were eleven of them at sea, six homeward and five outward bound. The most important was the troop convoy which was to have been escorted by the *Repulse*, *Victorious*, and the 4th Destroyer Flotilla. The *Repulse* and *Victorious* had already been placed at Admiral Tovey's disposal, and the *Victorious* sailed from Scapa with him at 2245 hours on the 22nd. The *Repulse*, having escorted her convoy out of the Clyde, left it and joined the C-in-C during the morning of the 23rd.

The *Bismarck* sighted

At noon on May 23 the *Bismarck* and *Prinz Eugen* entered the Denmark Strait. The weather was not quite as propitious for his purpose as Admiral Lütjens had hoped, for instead of the fog forecast by his meteorological officers there was a patchy mist with large clear areas. The ice edge on the Greenland side extended to within about 80 miles of the Iceland coast and the British minefields off the north-west coast of Iceland—whose existence was well known to the German Admiralty—forced the two ships well out into the middle of the strait, where the weather was unusually clear. It was in this area, on the afternoon of May 23, that the British cruiser *Suffolk* was patrolling at a leisurely 18 knots.

As the evening drew on, the *Bismarck* and *Prinz Eugen* closed the edge of the Greenland ice, the shortest route down into the Atlantic. And at 1922 hours, at a range of 7 miles, the two ships were sighted by HMS *Suffolk.* She immediately sent out an enemy report and steered to the south-east towards the mist which enveloped the Iceland side of the strait. The report was picked up by HMS *Norfolk,* which closed to make contact, and one hour later she, too, sighted the two German ships at a range of 6 miles. The *Bismarck,* turning to open her firing arcs, fired about five salvoes at the *Norfolk.* All missed, and the *Norfolk* turned away to open the range.

This was the first intimation to Admiral Lütjens that he had been sighted. He had not seen HMS *Suffolk* during the earlier sighting, and so did not at once know that there were two cruisers in contact with him. However, this soon became apparent when he discovered that two ships were making shadowing signals.

HMS *Suffolk's* first sighting report had been received by Admiral Holland in the *Hood,* and the reported position put the enemy about 300 miles away. Increasing speed to 27 knots, Admiral Holland steered a converging course which would bring him, early next morning, off the exit from the Denmark Strait. At his present speed he expected to meet the enemy at about 0600 hours. The Commander-in-Chief, with *King George V* and *Victorious,* did not receive the *Suffolk's* sighting signal, but picked up that of the *Norfolk* one hour later; the position given placed him about 600 miles from the enemy. He, too, increased speed to 27 knots and steered a converging course, but he was too far away to be able to anticipate action the next morning.

When the *Suffolk's* signal was received in the British Admiralty, the first thought was the safety of the convoys at sea, and especially of the troop convoy which by this time was to the west of Iceland. Its normal escort of the *Repulse* and *Victorious* had, of course, been detached and placed at Admiral Tovey's disposal. To safeguard it, the Admiralty sent a signal to Admiral Somerville's Force H, which was based at Gibraltar, to sail to the northward to meet it. Within an hour of receiving the signal HMS *Renown,* HMS *Ark Royal,* and HMS *Sheffield*—Force H—were passing the Gibraltar breakwater. With them they carried the fate of the *Bismarck.*

The fact that he had been sighted and was being shadowed caused Admiral Lütjens no worry at first. He reckoned that, in the patchy weather, he could give the two cruisers the slip by using bursts of speed to shake them off. It was when this failed to work that he got his first real shock. It had been believed in Germany that the British fleet was not fitted with efficient long-range ship radar, but it became very evident from the *Suffolk's* signals, reporting every alteration of course and speed, that she at least carried it.

This put a very different complexion on *Rheinübung,* and a doubt probably arose in Admiral Lütjens' mind as to whether, in the circumstances, he should not cancel the operation and return to Germany. However, he decided to carry on and continued on his course towards the Atlantic.

Admiral Lütjens ordered Captain Brinckmann of the *Prinz Eugen* to take station

The cruisers *Norfolk* and *Suffolk,* covering the Denmark Strait, shadowed the German ships and gave directions to Admiral Holland in the *Hood*

Associated Press

HMS *Suffolk,* the ship that sighted *Bismarck* and *Prinz Eugen* on May 23

Central Press

One of the last pictures of the *Hood,* taken from the *Prince of Wales*

Associated Press

HMS *Norfolk* in action: she took part in the entire hunt for the *Bismarck* and was in at the kill ahead of the *Bismarck* in order to save any possible damage to her should the two British cruisers open fire. There was very nearly a collision between the two ships as the *Prinz Eugen* was taking up her new station, the *Bismarck's* helm jamming and swinging her out to port as the *Prinz Eugen* passed. The two ships steered in close to the ice as much as possible so that the two British cruisers could not shadow from a position of one on each quarter. The *Prinz Eugen*, in fact, ventured in too close, and her starboard propeller hit the edge of the submerged ice.

Throughout the night Vice-Admiral Holland in *Hood* continued to receive the shadowing reports of *Suffolk*. By midnight the gap had closed to 120 miles, and it looked as though contact would be made

This sequence of photographs showing the final action of HMS *Hood* was taken from *Prinz Eugen* during the battle in the Denmark Strait

1. *Bismarck* (astern) and *Prinz Eugen* engage the *Hood*

2. Into action: *Bismarck* fires a salvo at the *Hood*

3. A salvo from the *Prince of Wales* falls short of *Prinz Eugen*

4. A 15-inch shell-burst (on right) from the *Hood* misses *Bismarck*

5. *Hood* explodes under *Bismarck's* fifth salvo

6. Shells burst near the vanished *Hood* as *Prince of Wales* retires

Imperial War Museum

BISMARCK was the strongest battleship of her time. Her main armament was conventional, but she displaced over 50,000 tons as opposed to *Hood*'s 44,000 tons—and over 40% of *Bismarck*'s displacement was her armour. Yet despite this enormous advantage in protection, *Bismarck* still was capable of a speed of 29 knots. And in comparison with other new battleships of her period, *Bismarck* had formidable secondary and tertiary armaments. Launched in 1939. **Displacement:** 50,000 tons. **Speed:** 29 knots. **Armament:** eight 15-inch, 12 5·9-inch, 16 4·1-inch AA, 16 20-mm AA guns. Two Arado 196 aircraft. **Complement:** 2,200

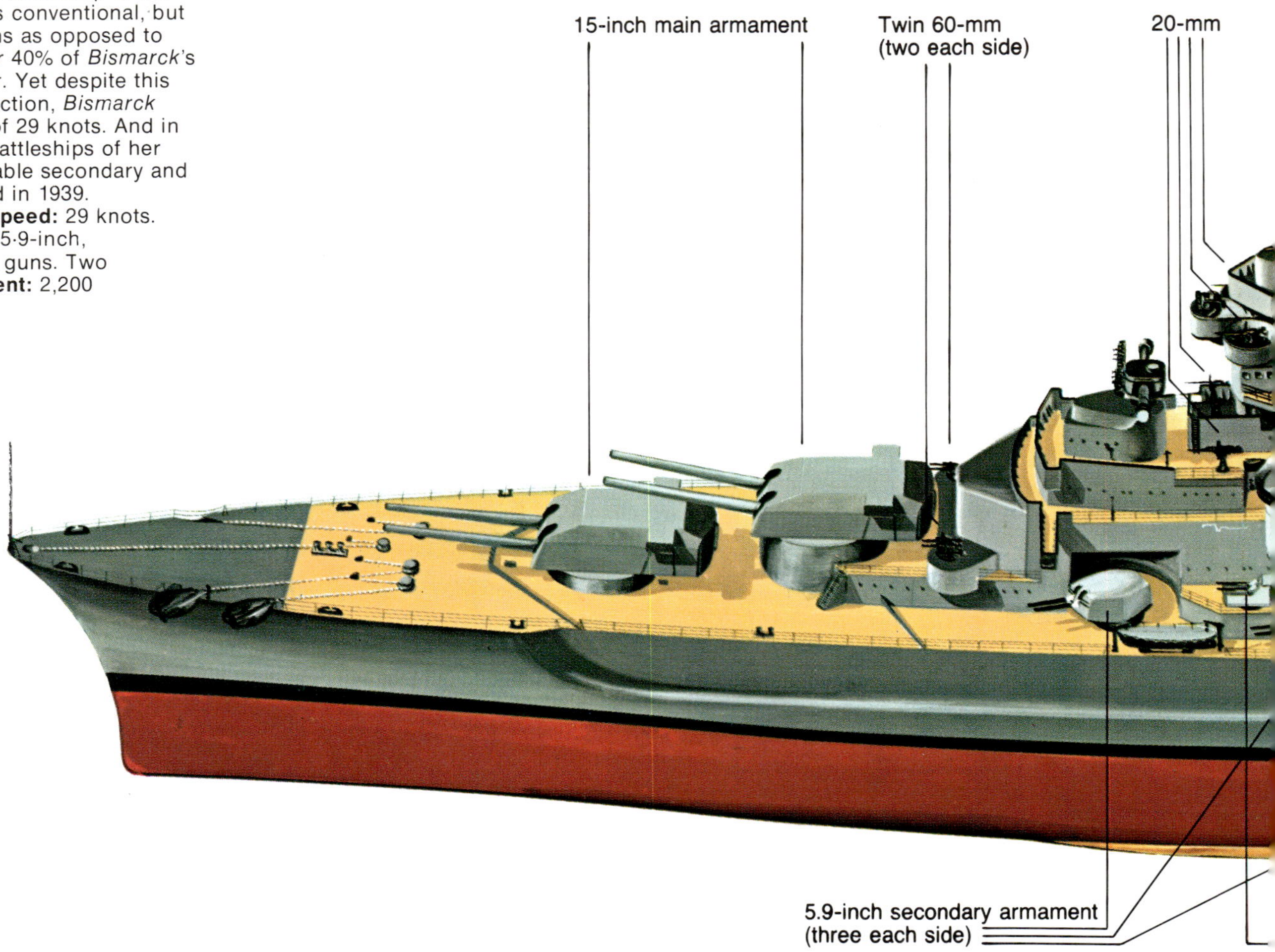

HOOD'S reputation as the pride of the Royal Navy had been established by the 'good-will cruises' of the 1920's and 1930's. She, too, had been the most impressive capital ship of her time when she was launched—20 years before the *Bismarck*—but her fatal weakness was that she had been designed as a battle-cruiser. She could achieve 32 knots, and fire an impressive weight of shell, but these advantages had been bought at a cost in armour. Launched in 1918. **Displacement:** 44,600 tons. **Speed:** 32 knots. **Armament:** eight 15-inch, 12 5·5-inch, eight 4-inch AA, 24 2-pounder guns. Four 21-inch torpedoes. **Complement:** 1,419

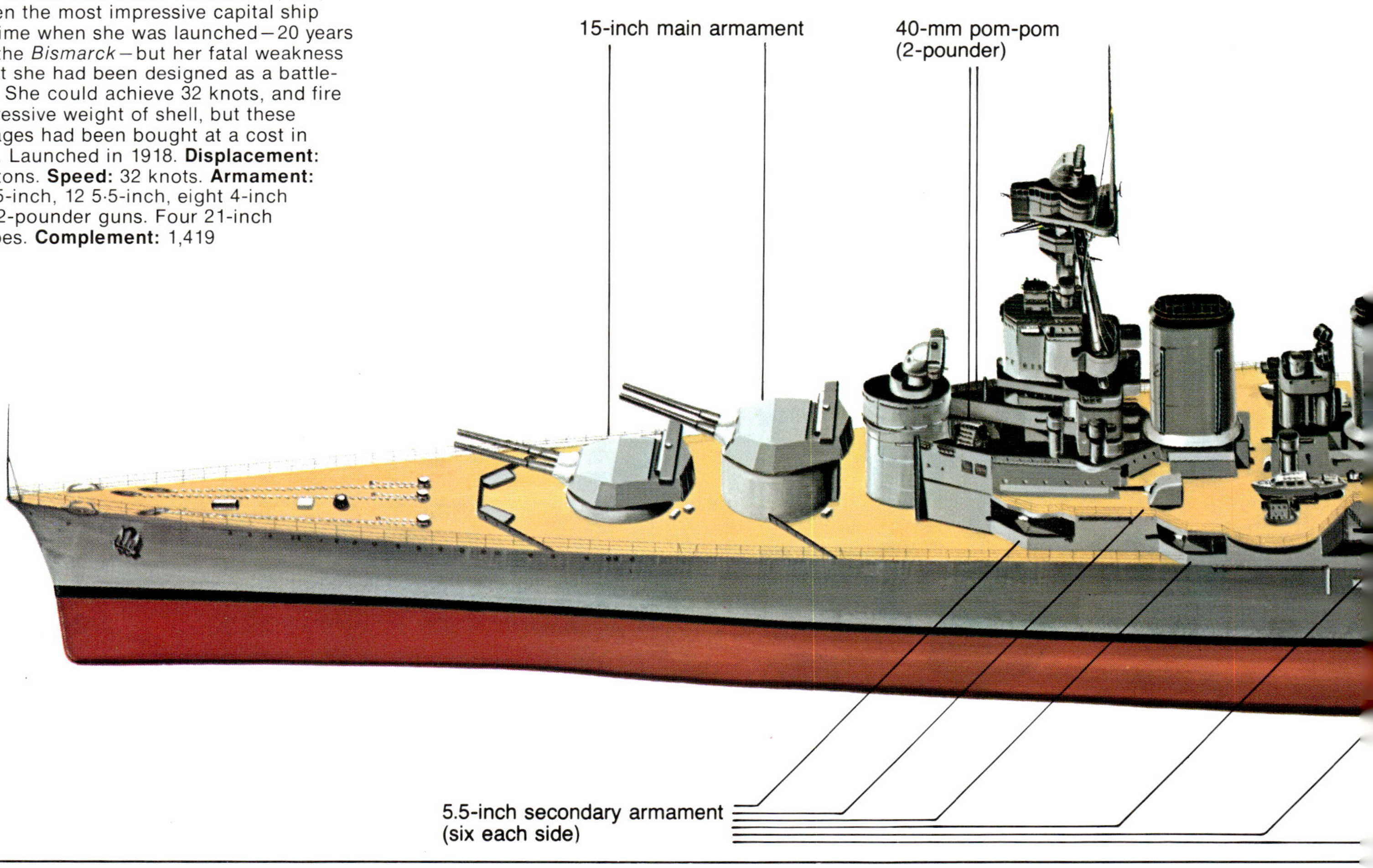

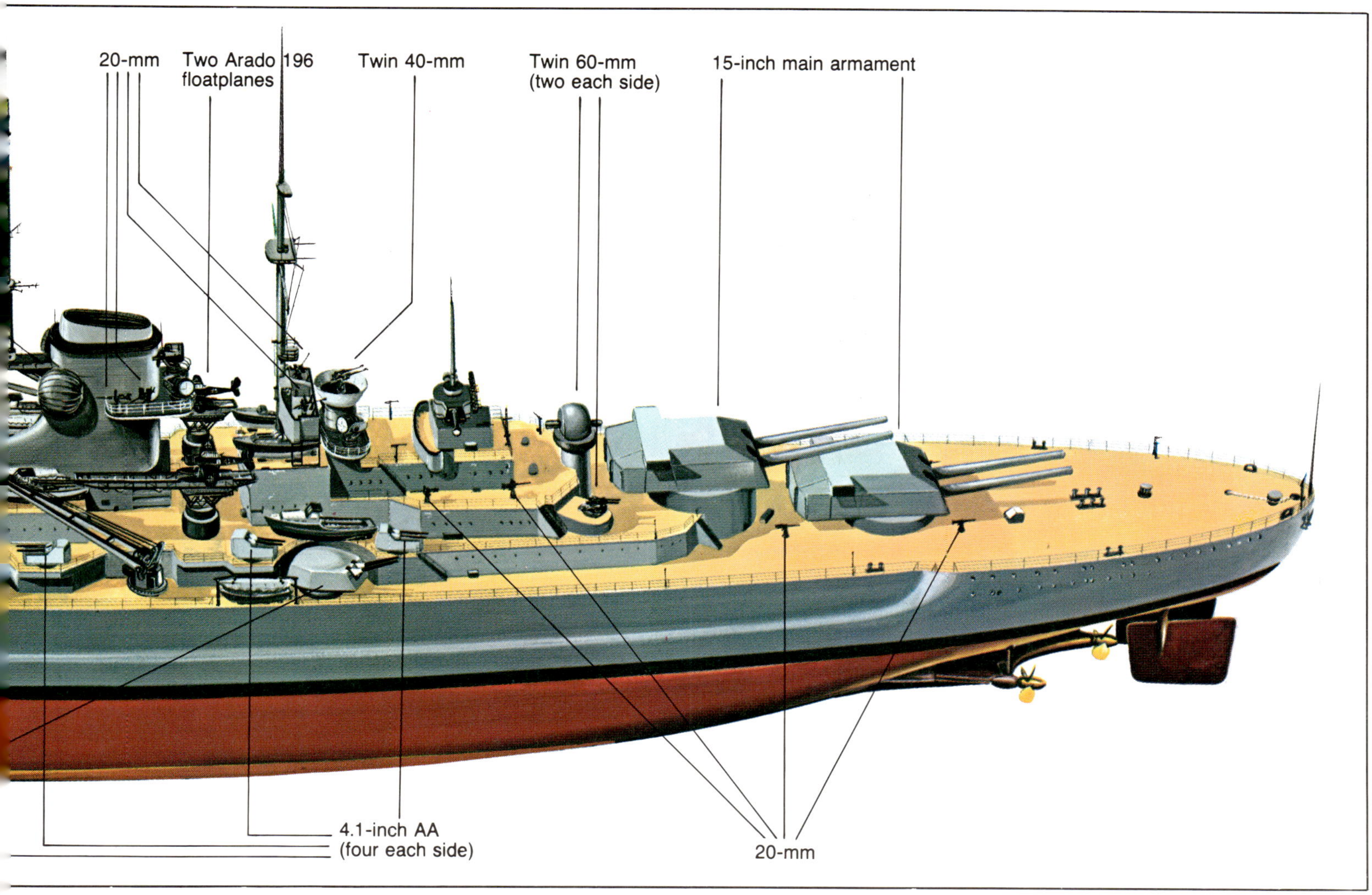
20-mm
Two Arado 196 floatplanes
Twin 40-mm
Twin 60-mm (two each side)
15-inch main armament
4.1-inch AA (four each side)
20-mm

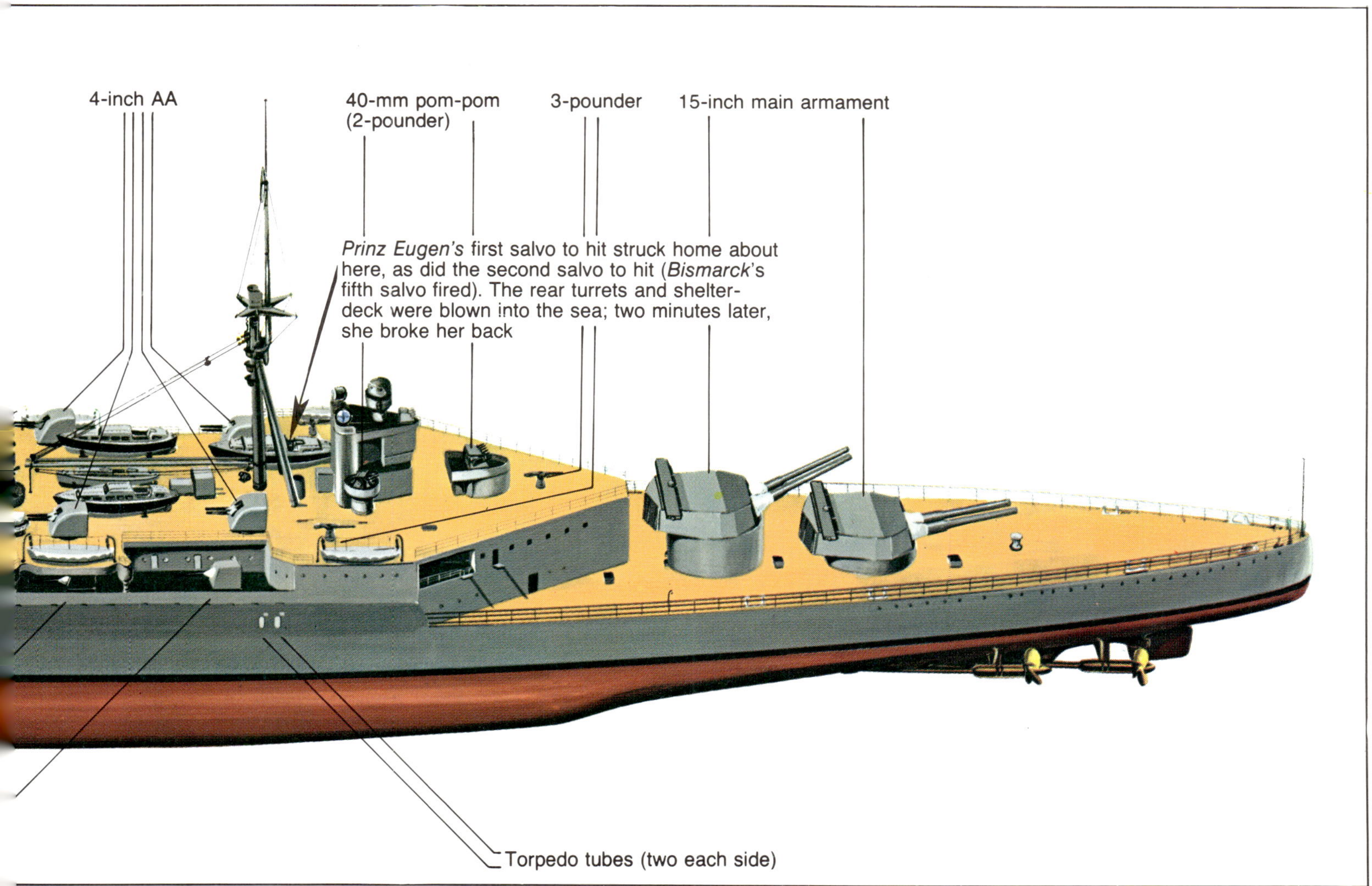
4-inch AA
40-mm pom-pom (2-pounder)
3-pounder
15-inch main armament
Prinz Eugen's first salvo to hit struck home about here, as did the second salvo to hit (*Bismarck*'s fifth salvo fired). The rear turrets and shelter-deck were blown into the sea; two minutes later, she broke her back
Torpedo tubes (two each side)

in about two hours' time. It was just at this moment that, temporarily, the *Norfolk* and *Suffolk* lost touch with the *Bismarck,* and the stream of position signals ceased. At 0203 hours on May 24, still with no further news of the enemy, Admiral Holland hauled round to the south-west to avoid any chance of passing astern of the *Bismarck* and missing her in the darkness. He ordered his destroyers to continue on their north-westerly course on a line of search, and the chase continued.

At 0247 hours the *Suffolk* regained touch with the *Bismarck.* By 0400 hours the *Bismarck's* course would put her 20 miles north-west of the *Hood,* so on their present courses they should meet at about 0530 hours, just as daylight would be breaking through.

Admiral Lütjens, meanwhile, was not unaware that there were more British ships in his vicinity than just the two cruisers. The *Bismarck* had picked up, on her radio receivers, the signals passing between the *Hood* and the shadowing cruisers, and although he could not decipher them, they at least revealed to him that, with the coming of daylight, he might be in action. He was not unprepared.

The wind was blowing from the north, strong, and kicking up a moderate swell. The *Hood* and *Prince of Wales* had hoisted their battle ensigns shortly after midnight; at 0500 hours they were fully 'closed up' at action stations. By 0530 day was breaking out of a grey dawn, and five minutes later the look-outs in both ships could make out the shape of two ships on the north-west horizon. They were the *Bismarck* and *Prinz Eugen,* the latter leading, and the range was 17 miles.

Death of the *Hood*

Admiral Holland turned his ships towards the enemy to close, and ten minutes later the range was down to 25,000 yards. The *Hood* opened fire at 0552 hours, ordered a two-point turn to starboard to open the *Prince of Wales's* firing arcs, and was joined in the firing by the *Prince of Wales.* Two minutes later the *Bismarck* and *Prinz Eugen* replied to the fire, both ships concentrating on the *Hood,* just as the two British ships were concentrating on the *Bismarck.*

On her upper deck the *Hood* was carrying some newly developed anti-aircraft ammunition which had been approved for trial in the fleet. There was no stowage for this below decks, and it was carried in ready-use lockers which were exposed to gunfire. The second salvo from the *Prinz Eugen* hit the *Hood* and a shell burst on the upper deck, setting this ammunition on fire. It spread until the whole midship section of the ship was enveloped in flames under a shroud of dense smoke. From the *Prince of Wales* it looked an awesome sight, although in fact the fire carried with it no immediate danger to the *Hood.*

Eight minutes after the start of the action the *Hood* was hit again, by the fifth salvo fired by the *Bismarck.* The range was now about 19,000 yards, at which the guns fired by both sides were sufficiently elevated to give a high trajectory to the shells, and a correspondingly steep angle of descent. *Hood* was an old ship, designed some 25 years previously, and she lacked the heavy horizontal armour which would protect her from this plunging fire. One of the *Bismarck's* shells, penetrating her deck, reached one of her magazines and burst there. A huge explosion tore the ship in half, the whole bows of the ship rising up out of the sea before the fore part began to sink. A vast cloud of smoke covered the area, and when it had blown away, the sea was empty. One midshipman and two seamen were subsequently picked up out of a total complement of 95 officers and 1,324 men.

As soon as the *Hood* sank, the two German ships shifted their fire to the *Prince of Wales,* which had had to alter course to starboard to avoid the wreckage of the *Hood* and by doing so had brought the range down to within 18,000 yards. She was hit both by the *Bismarck* and the *Prinz Eugen,* and her bridge was wrecked. She was a new ship and had as yet had no chance to work up to full operational efficiency. Her turret machinery, too, was giving trouble. In the circumstances Captain Leach, her commanding officer, decided to break off the action and turned away under cover of smoke. The *Bismarck* made no attempt to follow her. The *Prince of Wales* joined up with the *Norfolk* and *Suffolk,* and the three ships settled down to continue shadowing the enemy.

But the *Bismarck* herself had not escaped from the action unscathed. She had been hit three times, a glancing blow across the deck which did no damage, a shell just forward of the port boiler-room which put one of her main dynamos out of action – and a shell which passed through her bows, piercing two oil tanks. The loss of this oil was insignificant, but what was of far more consequence was that, forward of these two tanks were others which held 1,000 tons of fuel. These 1,000 tons were now inaccessible.

Captain Lindemann, who was flag captain to Lütjens in the *Bismarck,* now strongly advised Lütjens to abandon the operation and return to Germany. In all the circumstances it was wise advice, for not only had a great success been achieved but also all surprise had been completely lost. And in addition there was now a doubt about the *Bismarck's* seaworthiness, and particularly her speed and endurance after the hit on the bows. But Lütjens decided otherwise. It will never be known why he chose the greater danger.

During the early afternoon Lütjens sent a signal to Germany that he would detach the *Prinz Eugen* to carry out cruiser warfare independently in the Atlantic while the *Bismarck* herself shaped a course for one of the Biscay ports. At the same time, through the Commander-in-Chief of U-boats, he arranged for a line of six boats to be formed to the west of his position, over which he proposed to draw his pursuers. He then sent a signal to Captain Brinckmann of the *Prinz Eugen* stating his intentions of breaking away; and ordered Brinckmann to continue his present course for three hours, then to turn to the north and refuel from a tanker south of Greenland, and subsequently to proceed independently into the Atlantic for cruiser warfare. The codeword for this operation was to be 'Hood'.

Brinckmann had no liking at all for this plan. He composed a long signal of protest, but before he could send it, the *Bismarck* signalled the word 'Hood', turned to starboard, and disappeared in a rainstorm. Left on his own, Brinckmann decided to disobey the orders. Instead of turning to the north after three hours, he held on to the south, even though he knew that the nearest tanker in that direction lay at the extreme limit of his fuel.

If, by this manoeuvre, Lütjens hoped to shake off his shadowers, he was disappointed. Letting the *Prinz Eugen* go, they clung grimly to the *Bismarck,* reporting her every movement to the Commander-in-Chief Home Fleet, who at this point was still some 200 miles to the east.

With Admiral Tovey and the *King George V* was the aircraft-carrier *Victorious,* which had on board, in addition to the cased aircraft for delivery in the Middle East, nine Swordfish of No. 825 Squadron. During the afternoon of May 24 the Commander-in-Chief detached her, with the second cruiser squadron, to a position about 100 miles from the *Bismarck,* with the intention of trying to slow the enemy down with a torpedo attack from the air. By 2200 hours that night the *Victorious* was in position, and ten minutes later the Swordfish were airborne.

The squadron was led by Lieutenant-Commander Eugene Esmonde, who was later to win undying fame in an attack on the *Scharnhorst* and *Gneisenau* in their dash up the Channel to Germany. Flying through broken cloud, the squadron sighted the *Bismarck* a few minutes before midnight; but

Fairey Fulmar I
The Royal Navy's first 8-gun fighter, the Fulmar kept the two-seater layout for a navigator/observer and was outmatched by its land-based contemporaries and their naval derivatives.
Span: 46 ft 5 in *Length:* 40 ft 3 in
Engine: Rolls-Royce Merlin VIII, 1080 hp
Max speed: 280 mph *Ceiling:* 26,000 ft
Range: 800 miles *Armament:* 8×·303-in mg

Central Press

Inspection of a Swordfish's torpedo on HMS *Battler*, July 1943

the cloud thickened suddenly and they lost her. Coming round again, they made contact with HMS *Norfolk,* and were directed by her on to the enemy. Still flying in thick cloud, their radar indicated a ship below them; they dived through the cloud to attack —and found themselves above a United States Coast Guard cutter. But she was not alone. Six miles away to the south was the *Bismarck,* and she opened a heavy barrage fire on the aircraft.

It was just midnight. Esmonde pressed home his attack through the fierce gunfire; of the eight torpedoes fired (one Swordfish had lost contact in the cloud), one hit the *Bismarck* amidships. All the Swordfish returned to the *Victorious* and landed-on successfully after the attack, but two Fulmars which had accompanied them for shadowing purposes failed to return. Both of them ditched in the steep Atlantic swell, but their crews were eventually saved after spending many anxious hours in the coldness of the night.

The hit on the *Bismarck* did no damage, though it seems to have been responsible for Lütjens losing some of his nerve. He broadcast a message through the ship to the effect that 27 aircraft had been shot down during the attack, although in fact none had been hit. He also reported to Germany that he was abandoning his plan to lead his pursuers over the line of U-boats, that it was impossible to shake the shadowers off, and that he was proceeding direct to St Nazaire because of shortage of fuel. The *Bismarck* continued her course southward, hoping to find an opportunity during the coming darkness to break the grip of the shadowing cruisers and alter course round to the south-east towards St Nazaire.

The British lose contact

The *Prince of Wales, Norfolk,* and *Suffolk* continued to follow the *Bismarck,* reporting her course and speed at intervals to the Commander-in-Chief. Because of the reliability of her radar set, the duty of shadowing fell upon *Suffolk,* with the *Prince of Wales* and *Norfolk* following astern to act as support should the *Bismarck* attempt to engage. There was a very brief engagement about an hour after midnight when the *Bismarck* exchanged shots with the *Prince of Wales* at a range of about 10 miles, but all shells fell wide.

The *Suffolk* was shadowing at extreme radar range, and at the same time was zig-zagging, as U-boats were believed to be in the vicinity. At 0306 hours on May 25, she obtained a normal radar contact at 20,900 yards. The *Suffolk* then ran out on her outward zig-zag for ten minutes and altered course on her inward run, expecting to find the *Bismarck* again on completion. But the sea was empty, and there was no reassuring echo to her radar impulses.

There were two courses of action open to the *Bismarck*. One was to try to break away to the west, make contact with her supply ships and the *Prinz Eugen,* and open up cruiser warfare in the Atlantic. The other was to break to the east and make for a Biscay port. We know now, of course, that it was the second of these two courses which the *Bismarck* chose, but at the time all the British fleet's dispositions were made on the assumption that the enemy was moving west.

It was natural enough that this should be so, for it was in that sector that all the danger lay. First thought had to be given to the safety of the convoys, and the prospect of an enemy as big and as powerful as the *Bismarck* loose on the convoy routes was one to give considerable alarm to the Royal Navy. Both Admiral Wake-Walker in the *Norfolk* and Admiral Tovey in the *King George V* almost simultaneously reached the decision that search must first be concentrated to the west.

The news of the loss of contact reached the Commander-in-Chief at 0605 hours on May 25. The *King George V* had been steering a closing course, which would have brought her within gun range of the *Bismarck* at about 2100 hours. The hopes—almost the certainty—of an action then in which the loss of the *Hood* might have been avenged were dashed.

At 0810 hours, in good visibility, the Swordfish from the *Victorious* were flown off to search an arc between west and north-east to a depth of 100 miles. They drew a complete blank. At the same time the *Norfolk* and *Suffolk* were searching to the south-west, but they, too, drew blank. There was no sign of the *Bismarck*.

It is just possible that, had he kept silent, Admiral Lütjens might have reached St Nazaire in safety. But instead of maintaining wireless silence and, by doing so, denying to the British a clue to his present movements, he sent a long personal message to Hitler describing his action against the *Hood*—a message so long that it took nearly 30 minutes to transmit. Every Allied direction-finding set was, of course, on the watch for signals from the *Bismarck*; even before the signal had ended, the bearings were beginning to come into the British Admiralty.

As plotted on the British Admiralty chart, they showed the *Bismarck* well to the east of her last known position when the *Suffolk* had lost contact. But in the mistaken belief that the Commander-in-Chief had with him some destroyers fitted with direction-finding sets (enabling them to obtain a cross-bearing), the individual bearings were signalled to the fleet, and not the position which they indicated on the British Admiralty chart. This was, unfortunately, an error of judgement on the part of the British Admiralty, for not only did the Commander-in-Chief have no destroyers with him fitted for wireless direction-finding, but it also placed on him, in the midst of all his operational worries, the onus of interpreting bearings—which in fact gave no clear position, but only an indication of direction.

To this error of judgement by the British Admiralty was added a mistake made in the flagship. The bearings signalled were plotted on a navigational chart and not on the special gnomonic chart used for wireless bearings. Navigational charts distort wireless bearings, and the *Bismarck's* position as plotted in the *King George V* showed her to be nearly 200 miles north of her actual position. This caused the Commander-in-Chief to believe that she was trying to break back to Germany through the Iceland-Faeroes gap, and in consequence he altered the course of the fleet to the north-east. This course, naturally enough, did nothing to close the gap between the *Bismarck* and the British fleet.

It did not take very long for the British Admiralty to puzzle out what had happened in the flagship, and during the forenoon a signal was sent to the Commander-in-Chief that the appreciation in the Admiralty was

RAF Catalina flying-boat

that the *Bismarck* was making for one of the Biscay ports. And at this point yet another mistake was made in the British Admiralty—but, fortunately for them, one which did much to cancel out the previous ones.

At 1320 hours on May 25 a German U-boat made a signal from mid-Atlantic (in fact she was reporting the sighting of HMS *Victorious*). The position as plotted fitted in very well with the presumed course of the *Bismarck* if she were, in fact, making for the Bay of Biscay; and it was assumed in the Admiralty, though against all experience and the known German wireless procedure, that this might be the *Bismarck* giving direct orders to U-boats, using the frequency reserved for them. The position obtained from the bearings was signalled to the Commander-in-Chief, and this was followed a few hours later by another signal from the Admiralty to all units at sea, to act on the assumption that the *Bismarck* was making for the west coast of France. At 1810 hours the Commander-in-Chief turned to the south-east, towards the Bay of Biscay. It was, as we know now, the correct course, but by then the *Bismarck* was about 110 miles ahead of the *King George V*. Nothing much short of a miracle could bring her to action now.

The night drew on in an atmosphere of fading hopes. That dawn it had seemed that nothing could prevent the hoped-for action with the *Bismarck,* so firmly was the German ship in the grip of the *Suffolk's* radar. The *Bismarck* now was lost, and the Commander-in-Chief was following a trail which was, at best, still somewhat uncertain. And, more discouraging still, the problem of fuel oil was becoming increasingly acute. HMS *Repulse* had already had to break away and make for Newfoundland for lack of fuel; *Prince of Wales* was steering towards Iceland to replenish. The fleet's destroyer screen, too, was by now running low, to such an extent that, shortly after midnight, the British Admiralty sent a signal to the 4th Destroyer Flotilla, which was escorting the troop convoy bound for the Middle East, to leave its convoy and join the Commander-in-Chief.

The weather, too, was deteriorating, which mitigated against fast steaming. The wind was blowing half a gale from the north-west, kicking up a heavy sea. Frequent and heavy squalls of rain reduced the visibility, and an abnormally low cloud base cast an unnatural darkness over the waters.

Arrangements had been made in London during the night of May 25/26 between the British Admiralty and RAF Coastal Command for a comprehensive air search to be made in the morning by Catalina flying boats from Loch Erne. They were to be fitted with long-range tanks for extra endurance. Within the scheme of air search were two cross-over patrols to the west of Brest.

At 1036 hours on May 26 one of these Catalinas sighted the *Bismarck* and reported her position; simultaneously, a pattern of air search was being flown by Swordfish from HMS *Ark Royal,* which was coming up with Force H from Gibraltar. Within a few minutes of the Catalina sighting, Swordfish from the *Ark Royal* were also reporting the *Bismarck,* and once they had her, they never let her go. Throughout the day they held her, reporting her position, course, and speed to the Commander-in-Chief and to the Flag Officer Force H in *Renown.*

The position of the *Bismarck* as reported by the Catalina put her 790 miles from Brest and 130 miles ahead of the *King George V* and of the *Rodney,* which was steering a converging course. But it also placed her well to the westward of Force H, which was thus in a favourable position to deny the *Bismarck* an unchallenged run home. Yet the *Renown,* a 25-year-old battle-cruiser, was far too lightly armoured to be any match for the *Bismarck* in a gun duel, and any thoughts Admiral Somerville may have had of a last-resort action to stop the enemy were quickly extinguished by a signal from the Commander-in-Chief that the *Renown* was not to engage.

Air strike from *Ark Royal*

There remained of Force H the aircraft-carrier *Ark Royal* and the cruiser *Sheffield.* Admiral Somerville detached *Sheffield* to make contact with and shadow the *Bismarck,* and with the remainder of his force steered for a position within 50 miles of the enemy from which he could make an air torpedo attack with the *Ark Royal's* Swordfish. At about 1430 hours the *Ark Royal* was in position, with her Swordfish ranged on the flight-deck ready to go.

The weather had been deteriorating rapidly all day, and as the Swordfish took off, the *Ark Royal* was plunging heavily in a rough sea—so much so that her flight-deck

The long-standing partnership of Force H: (top to bottom) *Sheffield, Ark Royal,* and *Renown*

Rear-Admiral Vian on the bridge of HMS *Cossack*

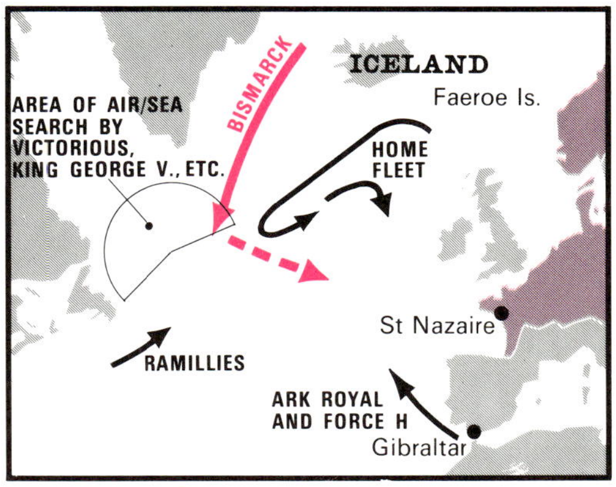

The hunting-groups close in

was rising and falling as much as 56 feet. There was thick cloud, so that reliance by the aircraft on finding the target lay in a radar set fitted in the leader. It located a ship some 20 miles from the estimated position of the *Bismarck* and, diving through the cloud, the 14 Swordfish attacked. Eleven torpedoes were released. But, too late, the aircraft discovered that the supposed enemy was the *Sheffield,* of whose position in the vicinity of the *Bismarck* they had not been told.

Fortunately, the *Sheffield* was not hit. Two torpedoes had exploded prematurely on hitting the water; three others exploded in the *Sheffield's* wake; the remainder were avoided by increasing to full speed. As the strike force returned to the *Ark Royal* one of the aircraft sent a signal to the *Sheffield*: 'Sorry for the kippers!'

The returning aircraft were safely landed-on by 1720. They were refuelled and re-armed at top speed, and the pilots re-briefed, being told to make contact before the attack with *Sheffield,* which would then direct them on to the target.

It was a wild and eerie scene on the flight-deck of *Ark Royal* as the Swordfish lined up for take-off. The deck was being lashed by heavy squalls of rain driven by the north-westerly gale, and the ship herself was pitching furiously in the stormy sea. Choosing their moments as the bows rose, the aircraft made their take-off runs down the flight-deck, and all were safely airborne again by 1910 hours. They formed up into two squadrons of three sub-flights each and, taking their departure from the *Ark Royal,* were homed on to the *Sheffield* by wireless.

Sheffield was sighted by the Swordfish half an hour later. They lost her in the wild weather, but made contact again at 2035 hours, and were directed by visual signal from the ship on to the enemy, then 12 miles away to the south-east. As the Swordfish approached the *Bismarck* they ran into a thick bank of cloud with its base down to about 700 feet. Climbing through it, the striking force got split up, and the planned co-ordinated attack had to be made individually by sub-flights.

From the 15 aircraft which flew off from the *Ark Royal,* 13 torpedoes were fired at the enemy. All the attacking aircraft were met with a fierce and accurate fire from the *Bismarck,* but in spite of it they pressed their attacks home with great determination. One of the Swordfish, after she had landed on the *Ark Royal* with both pilot and air gunner wounded, was found to have been hit more than 100 times by splinters.

Of the 13 torpedoes fired there were two certain and one probable hits. One torpedo hit her amidships on the port side but did no appreciable damage. One exploded on her starboard quarter, and this was the one that sealed her fate: it damaged her starboard propellers, wrecked the steering gear, and jammed her rudders. Two of the shadowing aircraft from the *Ark Royal,* observing the attack, saw the *Bismarck* turn two complete circles and drop her speed down to little more than 8 knots.

As the attacking aircraft, their mission completed, flew back through the wild night to the *Ark Royal,* the harassed *Bismarck* saw a new enemy coming to torment her. Over the darkening north-western horizon could be seen the shapes of five approaching ships — the destroyers of the 4th Flotilla. They were to harry the unfortunate ship throughout the night, and in the morning to deliver her to the avenging guns of the British Commander-in-Chief.

There are times in naval warfare when, in the light of new information, it is right for Commanding Officers to disobey previous orders. Such a time had come to Captain Vian, in command of the 4th Destroyer Flotilla, during the morning of May 26. He had been ordered by the British Admiralty to leave the troop convoy he was escorting and join the Commander-in-Chief to replace those destroyers whose fuel was running short. While on his way he intercepted the signal from the Catalina reporting the sighting of the *Bismarck*. Without hesitation he decided that his proper duty was to intercept the enemy. At 2152 hours HMS *Cossack,* with the destroyers *Maori, Zulu, Sikh,* and the Polish *Piorun* in company, made contact with *Sheffield,* which was able to direct them to the enemy. As the last light of the day

HMS *Zulu,* one of Vian's destroyer-force

was dying the *Piorun,* on the port wing of the line of search, sighted the *Bismarck* 9 miles away to the south-east.

Throughout the night they remained in touch with the stricken enemy, attacking her with torpedoes whenever the opportunity offered. Although disabled by the *Ark Royal's* Swordfish with their hit on her propellers, the *Bismarck* was still well able to defend herself, and her gunfire was still fierce and accurate. Time after time she drove the destroyers off as they closed independently to make their attacks, and although at times individual destroyers lost touch, there was always another there to keep her under observation. She was hit three more times by torpedoes, though it is not known whether they did any appreciable further damage.

At daylight the destroyers were still there, shadowing relentlessly. *Norfolk,* which

The battleship *King George V,* Tovey's flagship

had been in at the start of the operation when the *Bismarck* and *Prinz Eugen* were first sighted in the Denmark Strait nearly four days ago, arrived on the scene at 0753 hours, having been homed to the enemy by the destroyers' wireless signals. A quarter of an hour later the *Norfolk* sighted two large ships to the west at a distance of 12 miles — the *King George V,* flying the flag of Admiral Tovey, the Commander-in-Chief, and the *Rodney,* which had joined the flagship on the previous evening. She passed them the bearing (130 degrees) and the distance (16 miles) of the enemy. The curtain was rising on the final act of the drama.

The *Bismarck's* last fight

On board the *Bismarck,* two days of anxiety, after the successful breakaway from *Suffolk,* had been followed by a night of terror. On May 25 Admiral Lütjens had addressed the crew in an effort to lift their morale, but his words had done little to cheer them. He had told them that they would fight to the last shell, and that if they went to the bottom they would endeavour to take another English ship with them. The *Bismarck's* crew had a high proportion of young and very recently trained seamen, and these were

Seen from *Prinz Eugen:* a direct hit on *Bismarck*

Associated Press

hardly the sentiments to promote confidence in a successful outcome of the adventure.

After the torpedo-hit on the starboard propellers, all on board must have realised that the net was closing on them. Lütjens offered an immediate award of the Iron Cross to anyone who could free the jammed rudders, and although one diver made the attempt in the flooded steering machinery compartment, he was unsuccessful.

All through the night of the destroyer attacks the crew was closed up at action stations. There was no rest for anyone on board. Frequent broadcasts were made over the ship's loudspeaker system giving reports of success against the attacking destroyers. No one kept a count of how many were announced as sunk or set on fire. All that the tired crew knew was that no matter how many were claimed as having been put out of action, there still seemed to be as many as ever still coming in to the attack. In fact, not one of the five British destroyers engaged was even hit, though there were some very near misses. Further announcements during the early morning by Lütjens that German aircraft were on the way to give the *Bismarck* air cover, that German U-boats were assembling in the area to sink British ships which might be approaching, that tugs had been sent from Brest to tow the ship into port, were by now so patently false that no one on board believed them any longer.

With the dawn the gale was blowing as fiercely as ever, and increasing seasickness in the young crew of the *Bismarck* added its torments to those of exhaustion. A last exchange of heroics between Lütjens and Hitler did less than nothing to cheer the men up; it only sickened them the more.

Shortly after 0830 hours the stricken *Bismarck* saw her nemesis approaching over the western horizon. Two British battleships were closing in. To the north, marking the flank, steamed *Norfolk*; to the south, similarly occupied, was *Dorsetshire,* which had left her convoy west of Gibraltar to be in at the kill. East of the *Bismarck,* but under the horizon from her, lay Force H.

At 0847 hours the *Rodney* opened fire. A minute later *King George V* followed suit. Another two minutes, and the *Bismarck* replied to the fire. Her first few salvoes were accurate, the fourth straddling the *Rodney* without actually hitting her. The third salvo from the *Rodney* hit the *Bismarck,* and after that the German ship's gunnery deteriorated rapidly. A salvo from the *Rodney* knocked out both of her forward turrets, and one by one the others ceased firing as they were hit by shells from the two

Crippled by the British torpedo attacks, and with her crew's morale worn low by exhaustion, *Bismarck* struggled on towards Brest—but there was no escape

Imperial War Museum

The erratic, oil-slicked wake of the *Bismarck,* as seen from an RAF reconnaissance aircraft

Imperial War Museum

Shell splashes from the *Rodney* and *King George V,* thrown up around the *Bismarck's* blazing wreck

HMS *Rodney*

Paul Popper

British battleships. Her mast was blown away by a hit, and by 1000 hours all her main armament guns were silenced. For a few more minutes her secondary guns kept up a spasmodic fire; ten minutes later they, too, were silent.

The *Bismarck* lay wallowing in the heavy seas, a black, flaming wreck wreathed in flame and smoke. Her upper deck was crowded with killed and wounded men, powerless to prevent the heavy seas which were surging over her from washing them overboard. At 1015 hours the Commander-in-Chief broke off the battleship action and set a course for home; a few minutes later he signalled to *Dorsetshire* to close the *Bismarck* and sink her with torpedoes. Two were fired into her starboard side and one in her port. It was the final blow. The great battleship heeled over to port, sinking by the stern, then turned over keel up and disappeared. The time was 1040 hours.

The *Dorsetshire* and *Maori* searched the area of the sinking and between them picked up 110 survivors out of an original complement of over 2,300. Another five were picked up later by German and Spanish ships.

It remains only to complete the story of the *Prinz Eugen* and the supply ships. When we last saw Captain Brinckmann he was disobeying his orders from Lütjens and making for one of the southern tankers. The *Prinz Eugen* only just reached her, for the fuel oil with which she had topped up in Kors Fjord was contaminated with sea water. Brinckmann was also worried by a report from his engineer that the starboard propeller, which had hit the edge of the ice in the Denmark Strait, was damaged and causing vibration. The ship's engines, too, needed overhauling after so much high-speed steaming. Then came the final straw: a signal from an Italian submarine reporting five British capital ships in the vicinity was intercepted by the *Prinz Eugen* (the report, incidentally, was false). Brinckmann decided that the Atlantic was no place for him and set a course for France, reaching Brest during the evening of June 1.

Of the supply ships and tankers sent out to sustain the operation, six suffered an ignominious end. The *Gonzenheim*, reconnaissance ship, *Egerland*, supply ship, and *Belchen, Friedrich Breme,* and *Esso Hamburg,* tankers, were all intercepted by British ships and went to the bottom. The tanker *Lothringen* was captured and sent to Bermuda as a prize of war.

Operation *Rheinübung* was over.

The end of Operation *Rheinübung*: the *Friedrich Breme,* sinking (bottom) after being shelled

Imperial War Museum

End of a Leviathan

1941

May 18: *Bismarck* and *Prinz Eugen* sail from Gdynia for Operation *Rheinübung*, Raeder's attempt to concentrate a German naval force against the Allied Atlantic convoys.
May 20: *Bismarck* and *Prinz Eugen* are sighted in the Skagerrak. The British Admiralty is alerted.
May 21/22: *Bismarck* and *Prinz Eugen* reach Kors Fjord near Bergen, Norway. They sail at dusk in thick weather. RAF reconnaissance meanwhile has identified the German ships; the British fleet is alerted; *Hood* and *Prince of Wales* sail to cover the Denmark Strait.
May 22: Foul weather prevents the British from pinpointing the German ships; at 2000 hours the British C-in-C finally learns that *Bismarck* and *Prinz Eugen* have escaped, and he puts to sea from Scapa Flow.
May 23: *Bismarck* and *Prinz Eugen* enter Denmark Strait at noon; as night falls they encounter the British cruisers *Norfolk* and *Suffolk*, who shadow the German ships and report their position to *Hood* and *Prince of Wales*.
May 24: *Hood* and *Prince of Wales* encounter *Bismarck* and *Prinz Eugen* at a range of 17 miles; after an engagement of eight minutes *Hood* blows up; *Prince of Wales*, out-gunned, retires. The German Admiral Lütjens decides to proceed independently of *Prinz Eugen* and heads south in *Bismarck*.
May 24/25: British Swordfish aircraft from *Victorious* attack the *Bismarck* but fail to damage her.
May 25: *Bismarck* heads for France; the British hunting-forces lose contact. The British C-in-C guesses that *Bismarck* will turn in her tracks so he heads away from *Bismarck's* actual position. British Admiralty assumes that *Bismarck* is making for France; at 1810 hours the British C-in-C turns towards France but *Bismarck* has a lead of 110 miles.
May 26: RAF Catalina sights *Bismarck* and alerts the British pursuers. A Swordfish strike from *Ark Royal* nearly sinks HMS *Sheffield* in error. A second strike locates *Bismarck* and a torpedo hit wrecks her steering-gear. During the night of May 26/27, Captain Vian's British destroyers keep in contact with *Bismarck*.
May 27: British battleships *Rodney* and *King George V* close in on the crippled *Bismarck*; hopelessly out-gunned, the German battleship is pounded into a wreck and finished off with torpedoes from the cruiser *Dorsetshire*. At 1040 hours *Bismarck* finally sinks.
June 1: Captain Brinckmann in *Prinz Eugen*, having refused to carry out independent commerce-raiding as ordered by Lütjens, arrives in Brest.

BATTLE OF BARENTS SEA

In the last days of 1942, the heavy German warships *Hipper* and *Lützow* steamed out of their Norwegian base with the aim of sending Convoy JW-51B to the bottom. The ensuing action with the convoy's escort, though seldom publicised, resulted in such a complete and humiliating failure for the German navy that an infuriated Hitler ordered the scrapping of his entire battle fleet

Admiral Hipper, flagship of the German battle squadron which attempted to destroy the convoy

Ullstein

HMS *Onslow*, leader of the flotilla of six destroyers which escorted Convoy JW-51B

Imperial War Museum

By the spring of 1942, the small British Commando raids on the European coast had so alarmed Hitler that he looked for a deeper significance behind them. He guessed that the Allies would counterattack soon, and as early as January 12, 1942, he was convinced that an Allied invasion of Norway was imminent, telling Raeder, Keitel, and Jodl that Sweden was on the point of joining the Allies. Then, he declared, the attack on Norway would become a pincer movement: Britain would attack by sea while the Swedes and the Russians attacked by land, allowing the Western Allies and the USSR to join forces.

Hitler considered that to counter such a threat would be comparatively simple: he was determined not to move troops from the Russian front, so the Luftwaffe and Kriegsmarine must defend Norway by attacking the Allied forces off the coast. For this purpose, *Scharnhorst, Gneisenau,* and *Prinz Eugen* were to move north from Brest. 'If the surprise break-out through the Channel is impossible,' he told Raeder, 'it would be best to pay off the ships and use the guns and crews for reinforcements in Norway.' By January 22, 1942, he had convinced himself that Norway was 'the zone of destiny in this war'—but Raeder disagreed: he thought that the Allied counterattack would be in North Africa.

But it was these preparations against a supposed Allied landing in Norway that enabled the Germans to make a massive attack on Convoy PQ-17 in June, and with the concentration of the heavy ships in northern waters Raeder decided that the fuel situation had improved enough to use the big ships against Convoy PQ-18. Yet—and this was a vital factor in what was to come—the pocket-battleship *Admiral Scheer,* the heavy cruiser *Hipper,* and the cruiser *Köln* did not sail out from Altenfjord. At the last minute, Hitler had warned Raeder that the ships were vitally important for the defence of Norway: he 'must not accept any undue risks'. Not unnaturally, Raeder had cancelled the plan and left it to the Luftwaffe and U-boats to deal with this particular convoy, which lost 13 of its 40 ships.

From PQ-18 in September until the completion of the North African landings in November, when the Home Fleet was strengthened once more, no Allied convoys were sailed to Russia. After the break for Operation Torch, the Russian convoys began again in December 1942 with plans to sail 30 ships in two operations: a 15-ship convoy on the 18th and another of the same size on the 22nd. The designation of the outward-bound convoys was changed from PQ to JW—beginning at 51—so the first half was called JW-51A, and the second JW-51B. At the same time, the homeward-bound convoys were redesignated RA instead of QP; and the first of them—RA-51—was timed to sail from Murmansk on December 30, its escorts being those that arrived there with JW-51A.

Admiral Tovey, C-in-C Home Fleet, decided that in addition to the 'fighting destroyer escort' sailing with the convoys, a separate force of two cruisers—called 'Force R'—would also cover the convoys; but that, because of the danger from U-boats, it would not approach nearer than 50 miles to the convoy unless a surface attack developed. JW-51A sailed as planned and arrived safely, covered by the 6-inch-gun cruisers *Sheffield* and *Jamaica* under the command of Rear-Admiral R. L. Burnett, a veteran of the summer convoy battles.

Although JW-51A was not attacked, the German Naval Staff had drawn up a detailed plan—Operation *Regenbogen* ('Rainbow')—which provided for the pocket-battleship *Lützow* and the heavy cruiser *Hipper,* with an escort of six destroyers, to sail from Altenfjord to attack some unspecified Arctic convoy. Only the choice of convoy remained.

Convoy JW-51B sailed from Scotland on December 22, comprising 14 merchantmen. Some idea of the amount of aid sent to Russia is given by this small convoy's cargo: 202 tanks, 2,046 vehicles, 87 fighters, 33 bombers, 11,500 tons of fuel oil, 12,650 tons of aviation spirit, and 54,321 tons of miscellaneous supplies. Three small destroyers, a minesweeper, two corvettes, and two trawlers escorted it to a position just east of Iceland, where the three destroyers handed over to six larger 'fleet' destroyers.

The 'fleet' destroyers were commanded by Captain R. Sherbrooke in the *Onslow,* who had been Captain (D) of the 17th Destroyer Flotilla (D-17) for only four weeks. The rest of his flotilla comprised the *Oribi, Obedient, Obdurate, Orwell,* and *Achates.* Sherbrooke planned that at the first sign of a surface attack all destroyers except for *Achates* would leave their position around the convoy and join the *Onslow* on the threatened side; the convoy would turn away from that direction, and *Achates* would lay a smokescreen. The remaining escorts—the minesweeper *Bramble,* corvettes *Hyderabad* and *Rhododendron,* and trawlers *Northern Gem* and *Vizalma,* would re-form on the convoy.

By December 28, JW-51B was well to the north of the latitude of the North Cape when it ran into a gale, and was driven far to the

Ullstein

Two of the destroyers which escorted the *Lützow* and *Hipper* move out of Altenfjord: they too failed to press home their attacks adequately south of its intended route. In heavy seas, blinding snow squalls, and with ice forming thick on every ship, the *Oribi* lost contact because of gyro-compass failure and eventually steamed on alone to Russia, while the trawler *Vizalma* and a merchant ship also lost the convoy and, while trying to catch up, actually overtook and passed it. On the 29th, the minesweeper *Bramble* was sent off to make a radar search for the missing ships, and was never seen again by British eyes.

By Wednesday, December 30, the convoy had turned east—and Altenfjord was less than 200 miles away. During the morning, the British Admiralty signalled a warning to Captain Sherbrooke that there was a lot of activity by German radio stations along the Norwegian coast—a tantalising piece of information, which could mean many things. Since the Germans had not attacked JW-51A, had they guessed that a large convoy was being sailed in two sections and planned a major attack on the second half, JW-51B? Or had Force R been sighted? Or was the increased radio traffic unconnected with JW-51B? Sherbrooke could only ensure that the ice covering the ships and their armament was cleared as fast as possible.

'Immediate readiness for attack'

In fact the Germans were preparing a heavy attack: earlier in the day U-354, commanded by Leutnant Herschleb, had sighted the convoy and reported its course and speed. Later she shadowed for nearly eight hours until she was spotted by the *Obdurate,* which tried to ram her.

The chain of command for the German navy in the north ran from the Naval Staff in Berlin (through the Operations Division) to Admiral Carls at Group North in Kiel; to Admiral Kluber, the Flag Officer, Northern Waters, at Narvik; and then—for Operation Rainbow—to Admiral Kummetz, Flag Officer, Cruisers *(B de K)* in the *Hipper* at Altenfjord. As soon as U-354's signal was received, Carls signalled Kluber (who had gone to Altenfjord): *B de K with six destroyers immediate readiness for Rainbow.* The preliminary order to Kummetz contained a significant phrase: *Procedure on meeting the enemy: avoid a superior force, otherwise destroy according to tactical situation.* The phrase seems of no consequence, but it was only to be the first of several cautionary and morale-destroying signals which Kummetz was to receive.

On the same day—December 30—Hitler held a conference at Wolfschanze about a clash between Raeder and Göring over the command of transport ships in the Mediterranean. This had led to Kesselring, the C-in-C South, threatening to arrest any admiral who disobeyed his orders. Such a quarrel was frequent between the services, but earlier Raeder, Admiral Krancke (the navy's representative at OKW HQ), and several staff officers had decided that 'It can be rightly assumed that the Führer had no previous knowledge' of the affair. Krancke was given the task of discussing it with Hitler on December 30; but he immediately found that Göring had also flown in unexpectedly for the conference and had given his version first.

Krancke explained the navy's views; Hitler listened in silence, but then started off an angry monologue—not about the Mediterranean shipping problem, but about the superiority of the British navy, 'which is able to sail through the Mediterranean without paying attention to the Italian navy and the Axis air force'. Krancke, reporting later the violence of Hitler's voice, quoted him as saying: 'Our own navy is but a copy of the British—and a poor one at that. The warships are not in operational readiness; they are lying idle in the fjords, utterly useless like so much old iron.'

When eventually Hitler stopped, someone then reported that there was no British convoy traffic to Murmansk, whereupon Krancke said that he had just received a signal from the Operations Division, which reported U-354's sighting of JW-51B and adding: *Vice-Admiral Krancke* [is to] *inform Führer that C-in-C Navy approves in principle the operational use of* Hipper, Lützow, *and destroyers. Execution is in accordance with the decision of Group North depending on the existing information that the escort with the convoy is not in fact superior.*

Hitler was at once interested, and in the meantime detailed orders were sent by Admiral Carls to Kluber for Kummetz. They contained the following: *There is to be no time wasted in rescuing enemy crews. It would be of value only to take a few captains and other prisoners with a view to interrogation. The rescue of enemy survivors by enemy forces is not desirable.* The implication of the last sentence should not be missed, since there was only one way to prevent it.

Later on December 30, the *Hipper* and destroyers *Friedrich Eckholdt, Richard Beitzen,* and Z-29, and the *Lützow* (commanded by Kapitän Stange), with destroyers *Theodor Riedel,* Z-30, and Z-31, sailed from Altenfjord. Kummetz's plan was simple and potentially

Hitler thought that Norway would be the scene of an Allied invasion: here, units of the High Seas Fleet gather in northern waters

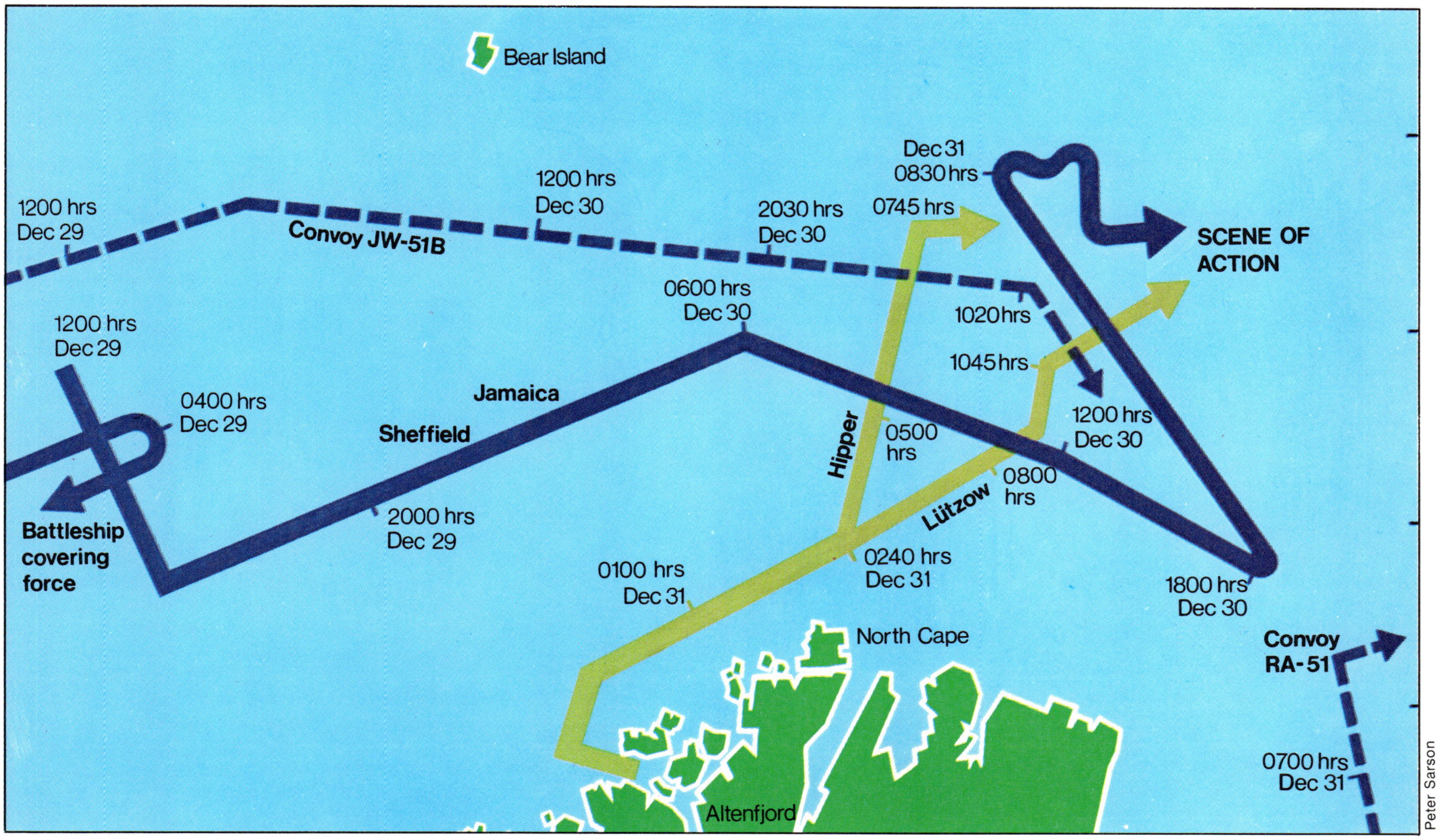

△ It was intended that *Hipper* would attack first from the north to draw off the escorts and turn the ships south towards *Lützow*. But the plan failed because gales forced Convoy JW-51B to the south, *Hipper* was fought off—and *Lützow* hesitated until too late

The Kriegsmarine surface fleet in northern waters: the attack on Convoy JW-51B was its last attempt to justify its existence

effective. The two groups would separate during the night so that the *Lützow* would be 75 miles south of the *Hipper* at 0800 hours next morning, when the two heavy ships would turn eastward to search along the convoy's track, each ship with her three destroyers spread out 15 miles apart and 15 miles ahead. When the convoy was found, the *Hipper* group would attack first from the north, drawing off the escorts and forcing the convoy to turn south towards the approach of the *Lützow.*

But less than an hour after sailing from Altenfjord, Kummetz received a signal from Kluber which said: *Contrary to the operational order regarding contact with the enemy* [you are to] *use caution even against enemy of equal strength because it is undesirable for the cruisers to take any great risks.* Here was the fatal result of the cumulative losses of the German navy: that signal was to have an almost devastating effect on Kummetz's morale. Yet it had only been sent because Raeder, at the last moment, had felt that he must again remind Carls not to take unnecessary risks. Carls had sent a cautionary signal to Kluber at Altenfjord who, in turn, cleared his own yardarm with the signal to Kummetz—who did not know that it originated only because of Hitler's frequently expressed fears for the big ships.

'An enemy of equal strength' could mean anything; there are no tables equating destroyers to cruisers, or cruisers to pocket-battleships. An enemy of equal strength to a heavy cruiser could—in darkness and snow storms—mean three radar-equipped destroyers. In daylight, it could mean six. Much depended on the characters of individual commanding officers—as the Battle of the River Plate had proved, when Langsdorff in the pocket-battleship *Graf Spee* fled from Harwood's three cruisers.

Hitler always failed to realise that a gun, torpedo, or ship is only a piece of apparatus used by men, with or without skill and courage. Different characters, training, and aptitudes always count more in the end than speed or fire-power; and war at sea—more often than most affairs—can be a case of 'nothing venture, nothing gain'. The *Hipper* might have been sunk because she struck a mine off Altenfjord, or she might have been torpedoed by a British submarine lying in wait—but a mine or a submarine could not be regarded as 'an enemy of equal strength'.

Later that evening at Wolfschanze, Krancke told Hitler that the ships had sailed 'and would probably locate the convoy in the early hours of the morning'. He later wrote that 'The Führer emphasised that he wished to have all reports immediately, since—as I well knew—he could not sleep a wink when ships were operating.' In fact, Kummetz's plan and estimate of the convoy's position worked well; next morning—New Year's Eve—he noted in his war diary, '0718: Bearing 060° two silhouettes', and then '0725: signalled to *Eckholdt: Bearing 092° several silhouettes. Investigate.'*

Thus the stage was set for the Battle of the Barents Sea.

By this time, JW-51B was steering east, but had been driven well to the south of the planned route by the gale and was far behind its time schedule. Unknown to Captain Sherbrooke, the minesweeper *Bramble* was about 15 miles to the north-east, while the trawler *Vizalma* was shepherding her merchantmen 40 miles to the north and steaming at 11 knots. The two cruisers *Sheffield* and *Jamaica* were getting into position to steam across the convoy's wake 50 miles astern and then turn eastwards to follow it. Both Burnett and Sherbrooke guessed that New Year's Eve would be the critical day, and both had been warned in the early hours that radio monitoring stations had detected a German destroyer off North Cape, a U-boat ahead of the convoy, and another to the south.

The battle begins

A signal three days earlier saying that Russian aircraft might meet the convoy had been misunderstood by the corvette *Hyderabad,* ahead of the convoy, to refer to destroyers; and when one of her lookouts reported at 0830 hours on New Year's Eve that there were two destroyers bearing due south on the convoy's starboard beam, it was assumed that they were Russian—and Sherbrooke was not warned. Fortunately, the *Obdurate* sighted and reported them as they passed astern of the convoy a few minutes later, and Sherbrooke told her to investigate. Signalling by lamp takes time, and it was not until 0915 that *Obdurate* could reach a position where—having by now sighted *three* destroyers—she made her challenge. There was no reply, but had they been Russians this would not have been unusual—and then one of the German ships revealed her nationality by opening fire, the gun flashes being seen by Sherbrooke, several miles away at the head of the convoy.

All the British ships went to action stations, and at once began to move to the positions ordered by Sherbrooke before the convoy sailed. *Onslow, Obdurate, Obedient,* and *Orwell* steamed for the rear of the convoy, *Achates* got into position to lay smoke, and an 'enemy report' was transmitted on Fleet waves. Then, as Sherbrooke in *Onslow* left the port side of the convoy, he sighted a large black shape among the snow squalls which was certainly larger than a destroyer, and was heading straight for the convoy. Immediately, he ordered *Onslow* to steer straight for it instead of waiting for his other destroyers. The shape was the *Hipper,* approaching from the north, and the three destroyers astern of the convoy were her escort which had been searching ahead, and which had for some time been shadowing the Allied ships.

At first Kummetz had not been at all sure that he had sighted the convoy. 'Probably our own destroyers are in wrong position,' he noted. 'I have the *Hipper* turned towards silhouettes in order to diminish our own silhouette'—and more than ten minutes were to pass before, at 0753, the convoy had been positively identified. Kummetz then wrote: 'Everything depends on making full use of this opportunity. Only speed of action can solve the problem of the danger of torpedo attacks from destroyers, which have to be considered in the light of my directive not to take any serious risks. . . .'

At 0800—while Sherbrooke was still unaware that he was being shadowed—Kummetz had increased speed to 20 knots to catch up with the convoy for an attack at first light, and he was still doing this at 0830 when the *Obdurate* sighted the destroyers. At 0915, as one of them opened fire, Kummetz was far from happy, noting: 'Visibility very poor. Everything seems hazy. Cannot make out whether I am dealing with friend or foe. A total of ten ships now in sight, some of which look like destroyers. It cannot be said for certain whether our shadowing destroyers are not among them . . .'

But as soon as he saw the *Achates* begin to lay a smoke-screen, Kummetz gave permission to open fire on her, and the *Hipper* turned to bring all her 8-inch guns to bear. She had fired several broadsides when suddenly the *Onslow* was seen approaching, followed, in fact, by the *Orwell,* although *Hipper* did not sight her at first.

Although Sherbrooke had previously told his commanding officers that German surface ships would probably be scared of torpedo attacks by destroyers, he also knew that it was extremely unlikely that the British ships would ever get close enough to score hits. But he guessed the threat would be enough—and he was proved right. The *Hipper*'s log records: '0944: a destroyer [*Onslow*] approached from the south-east and then put her helm hard over. She had fired torpedoes.' She had not, but to complete the illusion one of the *Hipper*'s lookouts reported seeing one approaching. The German heavy cruiser swung away, turning her stern to the *Onslow* and presenting a smaller target. This also took her away from the convoy, which was what Sherbrooke had intended, and both British destroyers turned away, keeping between the convoy and the enemy, their torpedoes still in the tubes. As the *Hipper* turned, she opened fire on the *Onslow,* using radar.

Although he had been temporarily driven off, Kummetz was nevertheless full of admiration for Sherbrooke's destroyers, which 'conducted themselves very skilfully. They placed themselves in such a position between the *Hipper* and the convoy that it was impossible to get near the ships. . . . Their relative position forced the *Hipper* to run the risk of a torpedo attack while trying to use her guns on the convoy.' But for all that, the range from the convoy to the *Hipper* was at times down to 6 miles.

At 0957 the *Hipper* again headed for the convoy and opened fire on the *Onslow* and the *Orwell.* Her eight 8-inch guns fired a broadside weighing more than 2,000 pounds, and her 4·1-inch guns another 200 pounds. At that time the *Onslow,* the only destroyer in the flotilla armed with 4·7-inch guns (the others had First World War vintage 4-inch), had two of her four guns frozen up and was firing a 96-pound reply; the *Orwell,* with all four guns firing, 124 pounds. And, of course, the *Hipper* knew that the destroyers' shells could not hurt her.

After three minutes on the new course for his second attempt, Kummetz turned away again, to swing back four minutes later and close on the *Onslow* and *Orwell,* keeping up a high rate of fire which the destroyers managed to avoid by weaving, although still steering eastwards to shield the convoy. Yet again Kummetz turned away, much to the relief and surprise of the two British destroyers.

Sherbrooke then received a radio message from Force R—*Am approaching you on a course of 170*—and, realising that this put Force R to the north, whereas it should have been to the south, began to wonder if the *Hipper* was not luring him round to the north-east while another German force slipped in to attack the convoy from the south. He therefore ordered the *Obedient* and the *Obdurate*—which were still trying to catch him up—to rejoin the convoy.

Kummetz began his fourth approach at 1013, again bringing all his 8-inch, and 4·1-inch armament to bear on the *Onslow* and *Orwell,* and his own three destroyers following astern also opened fire. Both British destroyers dodged salvo after salvo until—at 1019

△ *Lützow:* her 11-inch guns played no part in the battle because her captain vacillated when the convoy was at his mercy

Imperial War Museum

Imperial War Museum

Admiral Kummetz: his fear of a torpedo attack allowed the RN destroyers to hold off the *Hipper* until Force R arrived

—the fifth shell in one of the *Hipper*'s salvos hit the *Onslow* abaft the bridge, ripped open the funnel, blew open the boiler side casing doors, lifted the safety-valve so that high-pressure steam shrieked out, cut radio aerials, and wrecked the radar office. One of the thousands of splinters ricocheted down from a gunnery radar aerial and hit Sherbrooke in the face, smashing his left cheekbone, his nose, and the left side of his forehead, and leaving him with his left eye hanging down his cheek. For the time being, no one else on the bridge knew he had been hit: he continued giving orders without a change in his voice. Eventually another officer, finding himself covered in blood and thinking he was himself hit, looked round to see that Sherbrooke had been badly wounded.

Hipper cripples the *Onslow*

A few moments later, two more of the *Hipper*'s 8-inch shells burst on the foredeck, wrecking both guns and starting fires which soon set cordite charges ablaze. Sherbrooke ordered the ship to be turned to starboard, speed cut to reduce the effect of the wind on the flames, and a smoke-screen to be laid. The *Hipper* then turned her attention to the *Orwell*, which had held to her course, and as her commanding officer was deciding whether to make a solo torpedo attack on *Hipper*—which would have meant certain destruction for *Orwell*—or to cover the stricken *Onslow*, the *Hipper* swung away yet again, to vanish in the obscurity of a snow squall. In the *Onslow*—apart from heavy damage to the ship—40 men had been killed or wounded in less than two minutes. Command of the escort was passed to *Obedient*, and Sherbrooke, finally agreeing to have his wound dressed (he was subsequently awarded the Victoria Cross), ordered the *Onslow* to fall back on the convoy and home Force R by radio.

Imperial War Museum

△ HMS *Jamaica*: with HMS *Sheffield* she formed the covering Force R whose arrival completed the rout of the German squadron

After having dealt the *Onslow* a crippling blow without realising it, and having missed the opportunity of knocking out the *Orwell*—the only other ship between him and the convoy—Kummetz took the *Hipper* away at 31 knots to the east-north-east, hoping that the convoy would soon steam into the arms of the approaching *Lützow*. A ship sighted on the port side proved to be the missing minesweeper *Bramble,* which Kummetz sank before turning towards the convoy again. As he did so he noted: 'I was aware that with the decreasing visibility I was taking a risk. But I was hoping, after maintaining a heavy fire on the destroyers, to find one or more gaps in the defence through which I could attack the merchant ships.'

The *Lützow* had in the meantime come up from the south, sighted silhouettes at 0922 hours, received the *Hipper*'s signal that she was in action, and for the next 50 minutes steamed slowly north-east to intercept the convoy. Soon the pocket-battleship was steaming across its course, and her log noted: 'Several targets sighted through snow squalls.' The nearest was 3 miles away, the farthest 7 miles; the *Lützow*'s guns had a range of 15 miles. Her log then added—despite the reference to 'targets'—'No identification possible.'

At 1050 hours, the *Lützow*'s log recorded: 'Impossible at first to ascertain whether dealing with friend or foe because of the poor light and the smoke and mist on the horizon. To avoid observation from *Lützow* being obscured by the snow squalls and smoke drifting south, I [Kapitän Stange] decided to proceed at slow speed in the vicinity of the convoy, clear of the snow squalls, in order to take advantage of opportunities for attack as visibility improved.'

But Stange had missed his chance: the prize for which Operation Rainbow had been planned was between 2 and 3 miles away. As he passed across the convoy's bows, there was no British escort

Captain Sherbrooke: his gallant handling, even when severely wounded, of the destroyer flotilla won him the VC

whatsoever nearby—yet not one of the *Lützow*'s six 11-inch guns, eight 5·9-inch guns, six 4·1-inch guns, or eight torpedo tubes was fired. Ironically, Admiral Kummetz's plan had worked perfectly: the *Hipper* had drawn off the main escorts, and the comparatively unprotected convoy had run straight towards the *Lützow*. The pocket-battleship then steamed ahead of the convoy, parallel with its course, but Stange wrote: 'Seeing no possibility of approaching the convoy from the east owing to the persistent lack of visibility, I decided to turn west to bring under my fire the enemy engaged with the *Hipper* to the north.' Ten minutes later, destroyers were sighted on the port bow, but Stange increased speed to 24 knots, explaining that 'the intended engagement of these vessels is abandoned due to darkness and extremely poor light.'

At 1106 the *Hipper* made her fifth foray against the convoy, opening a heavy fire on the already badly damaged *Achates,* which was still faithfully laying a smoke-screen, although badly holed forward and with her speed down to 15 knots. Almost at once the *Achates'* bridge was destroyed by an 8-inch shell, leaving a young lieutenant in command of the ship, which was then hit by two more 8-inch shells and began to sink.

The *Hipper* then turned as if to steer across the wake of the convoy, and the *Obedient, Orwell,* and *Obdurate* promptly attacked. The *Hipper* fired back but turned away because—once again—Kummetz was afraid of torpedo attacks. At 1136 hours, he signalled to the *Lützow*: *In action with escorting forces. No cruiser with convoy.* Only a few moments later, 24 6-inch shells burst round the *Hipper*: the *Jamaica* and *Sheffield* had arrived, and had achieved such complete surprise that the German cruiser still had her guns trained in the opposite direction.

At 0830 that morning, when the *Obdurate* had first sighted the three German destroyers, Admiral Burnett's Force R had been steaming north-west, in a good position, he thought, to intercept any attackers from astern, who would be silhouetted against the lighter southern horizon. But because the convoy had been driven so far south by the gale, he was some 60 miles to the north of it. At 0858 hours, the *Sheffield*'s radar picked up two echoes, one larger than the other, $7\frac{1}{2}$ miles ahead, to the north-west and steering eastwards. They could have been stragglers from the convoy, or—more likely—enemy surface ships; and Burnett increased speed and tracked them by radar.

Force R tips the scale

They were in fact the trawler *Vizalma* and her merchantman. Then, at 0932, the reflection of gun flashes—from the German destroyer firing at the *Obdurate*—was seen to the southward. This put Burnett in a perplexing situation—a large and a small ship to the north, and gunfire to the south. Where was the convoy he was charged with protecting? The recent gale meant stragglers, and the gunfire might be from a detached escort. But at 0946 he saw the reflection of what was obviously heavy gunfire to the south—the *Hipper,* opening fire on the *Achates.* A few minutes later, Sherbrooke's 'enemy report' revealed that the convoy was far to the south of its estimated position, and Burnett 'increased speed to 25 knots and steamed towards the sight of the guns'. They were 40 or 50 miles away—between one and one-and-a-half hours' steaming.

For nearly an hour the British cruisers steamed south, the men on their bridges almost frozen stiff by the biting wind, until at 1030 hours *Sheffield*'s radar picked up a large ship 10 miles ahead—the *Hipper*—and a few minutes later a second—the *Lützow*—15 miles on the port bow. Burnett decided to attack the nearest, and both cruisers fired broadsides at a range of 8 miles. A shell from *Sheffield*'s fifth, and one each from *Jamaica*'s fourth and fifth salvos hit the *Hipper*. Her log recorded: '1133: *Hipper* hit on starboard side. . . . Number Three boiler gradually filled with oil and water and had to be shut off. . . . Maximum speed reduced to 23 knots. 1137: *Hipper* received two hits on port side. Fire broke out in the aircraft hangar. . . '

The *Hipper* turned into a smoke-screen being laid by her own destroyers, and one of them—the *Friedrich Eckholdt*—followed by the *Richard Beitzen,* mistook the *Sheffield* for the *Hipper* and steered straight for her. The *Sheffield* hit her with seven salvos and left her smothered in smoke and flame, and sinking fast. The *Jamaica* engaged the *Beitzen,* which managed to escape.

The battle was now virtually over. The *Hipper,* the *Lützow,* and the five German destroyers fled back towards Altenfjord with Force R following long enough to make sure that they did not turn back. The convoy re-formed, but the battered *Achates* finally sank. The Battle of the Barents Sea, as it was subsequently called, was later described by Admiral Tovey, the C-in-C Home Fleet, as 'one of the finest examples in either of the two world wars of how to handle cruisers and destroyers in action with heavier forces'.

1942 Operation Regenbogen fails

December 22: Convoy JW-51B sails from Scotland for Murmansk, escorted by Captain Sherbrooke's six destroyers and the shadowing cruiser escort of Force R.
December 28: The convoy is blown far south of its intended track by a violent gale.
December 30: The convoy is sighted by U-354; German Admiral Kummetz is ordered to take *Hipper, Lützow,* and six destroyers and sink the convoy (Operation 'Rainbow'). Kummetz plans to attack with *Hipper* to the north and *Lützow* to the south.
December 31: 0915 hours: *Hipper*'s attendant destroyers sight the British destroyers and open fire, but Sherbrooke keeps his force between *Hipper* and the convoy.
0944 hours: Two of Sherbrooke's destroyers simulate torpedo attacks and cause the *Hipper* to turn away from the convoy.
1019 hours: On the fourth attempt to get at the convoy, *Hipper* cripples the *Onslow* but wastes the chance to dispose of the last destroyer in her way *(Orwell).*
1050 hours: *Lützow* has closed on the convoy from the south: Kummetz's plan has worked perfectly and all escorts have been drawn off from the convoy, but *Lützow* misses her chance and does not attack.
1106 hours: *Hipper* turns against the convoy for the fifth time but again turns away for fear of torpedoes.
1133 hours: The cruisers *Sheffield* and *Jamaica* of Force R arrive on the scene and open fire on *Hipper,* who retires. *Sheffield* sinks the German destroyer *Eckholdt.*
1137 hours: Kummetz breaks off the action and runs for Altenfjord: 'Rainbow' has been a complete failure, but the battered destroyer *Achates* sinks from damage from *Hipper*'s shells.

United Press

Admiral Raeder, who commanded the Kriegsmarine during its rapid pre-war build-up, and was now sacked by Hitler when he protested against the death sentence on the High Seas Fleet

Keystone

Admiral Dönitz, C-in-C U-boats, who succeeded Raeder as leader of the Kriegsmarine. Although he persuaded Hitler to reverse his decision, the surface fleet never played an important role again

U-boats: scourge of the sealanes

△ **TYPE IX-D2—High Speed and Heavy Armament**
The tactics used by the U-boats during the early years of the war did not differ greatly from those of the First World War: patrolling submerged during the day and on the surface at night, with most attacks being made on the surface. These methods led to a demand for high surface speed and heavy armament, which culminated in the Type IX-D2. Endurance also was increased by storing fuel in the main diving tanks, and reducing accommodation to a minimum. **Displacement:** 1,616 to 1,804 (submerged) tons. **Dimensions:** 287½ × 24½ × 17¾ feet. **Speed:** 19¼ knots (surface), 7 knots (submerged). **Radius:** 23,700 miles at 12 knots (surface), 57 miles at 4 knots (submerged). **Armament:** One 4.1-inch gun; one 37-mm and one 20-mm AA gun; six torpedo tubes, with 24 torpedoes or six torpedoes and 32 mines. **Complement:** 57.

▷ **TYPE VII-B—Germany's Leading Sea Raider**
This was the main sea-going class of submarine in the Kriegsmarine when the war began, and the type which played a leading role in the early part of the Battle of the Atlantic. In 1939 there were only 18 of this type, ten of them the slightly enlarged VII-B. This class had been developed from the Finnish *Vetehinen,* and the B variant had a greater radius and surface speed. **Displacement:** 753 to 857 (submerged) tons. **Dimensions:** 218 × 20¼ × 15½ feet. **Speed:** 17¼ knots (surface) and 8 knots (submerged). **Radius:** 6,500 miles at 12 knots (surface), 80 miles at 4 knots (submerged). **Armament:** one 3.5-inch gun, one 20-mm AA gun; five 21-inch torpedo tubes (four bow, one stern), with 12 torpedoes or 14 mines. **Complement:** 44.

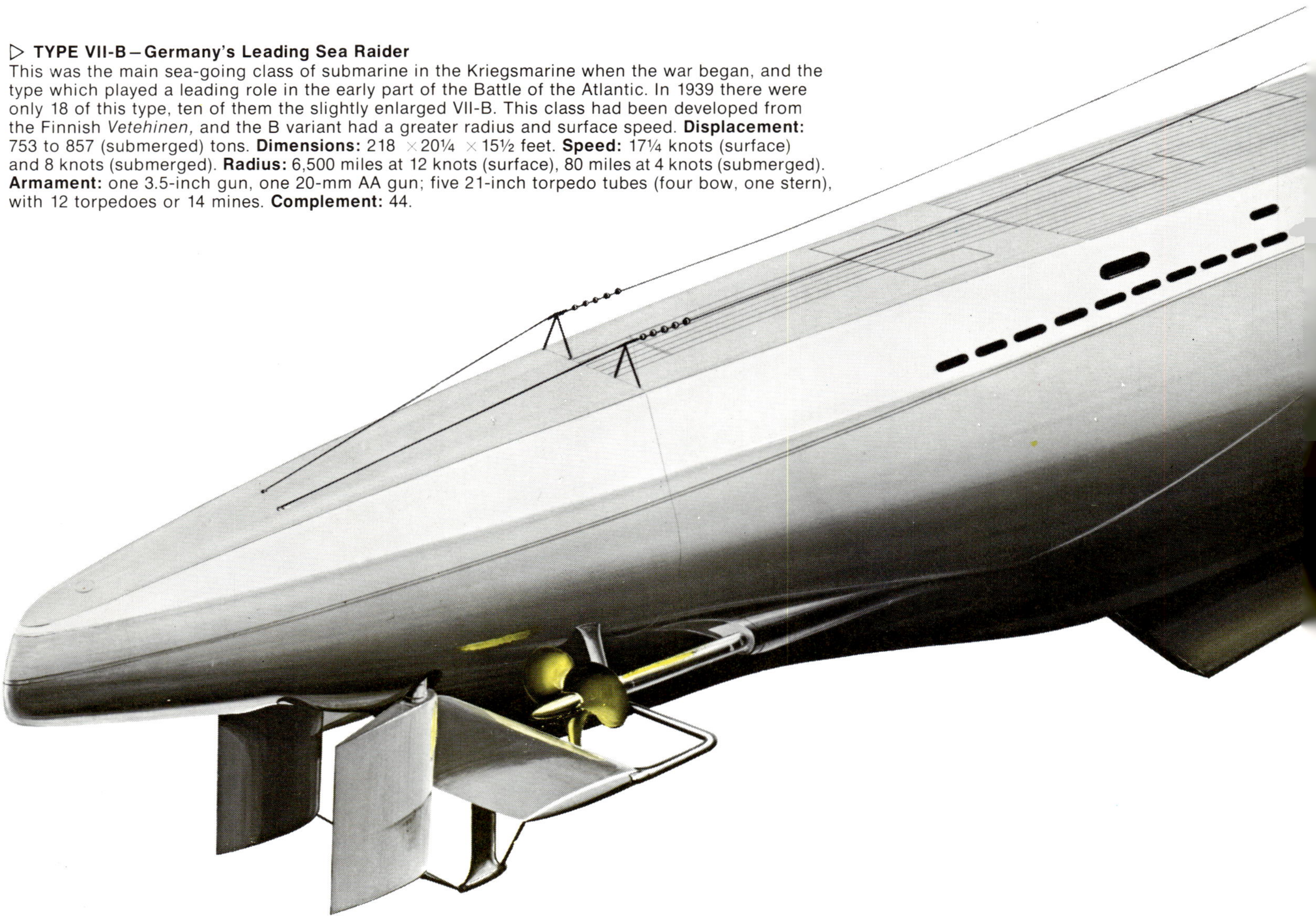

The first 'happy time' for the U-boats had been from late 1940 to May 1941, when they had wreaked havoc on the weakly-protected Atlantic convoys and their under-equipped and inexperienced escorts. But by the summer of 1941 the increasing strength of the escorts, and the wider spread of air cover, forced the U-boat packs to probe further afield to find easier targets—the entry of the United States into the war meant a tempting new source of virtually unescorted victims, and during a second 'happy time' the U-boats again sank thousands of tons with near impunity. But the entry of the United States had also meant that the convoy system would eventually be extended right across the Atlantic, and by May 1942 the U-boats were again being forced to seek new prey in mid-Atlantic. The climax of the battle had come, with the U-boats desperately trying to break the new, tight convoy system and force Britain's surrender before the vital air cover could also be completed across the Atlantic. From July 1942 to May 1943 the battle was fought out: it ended in decisive defeat for the U-boats, whose offensive equipment had failed to keep pace with the Allies' defensive capabilities.

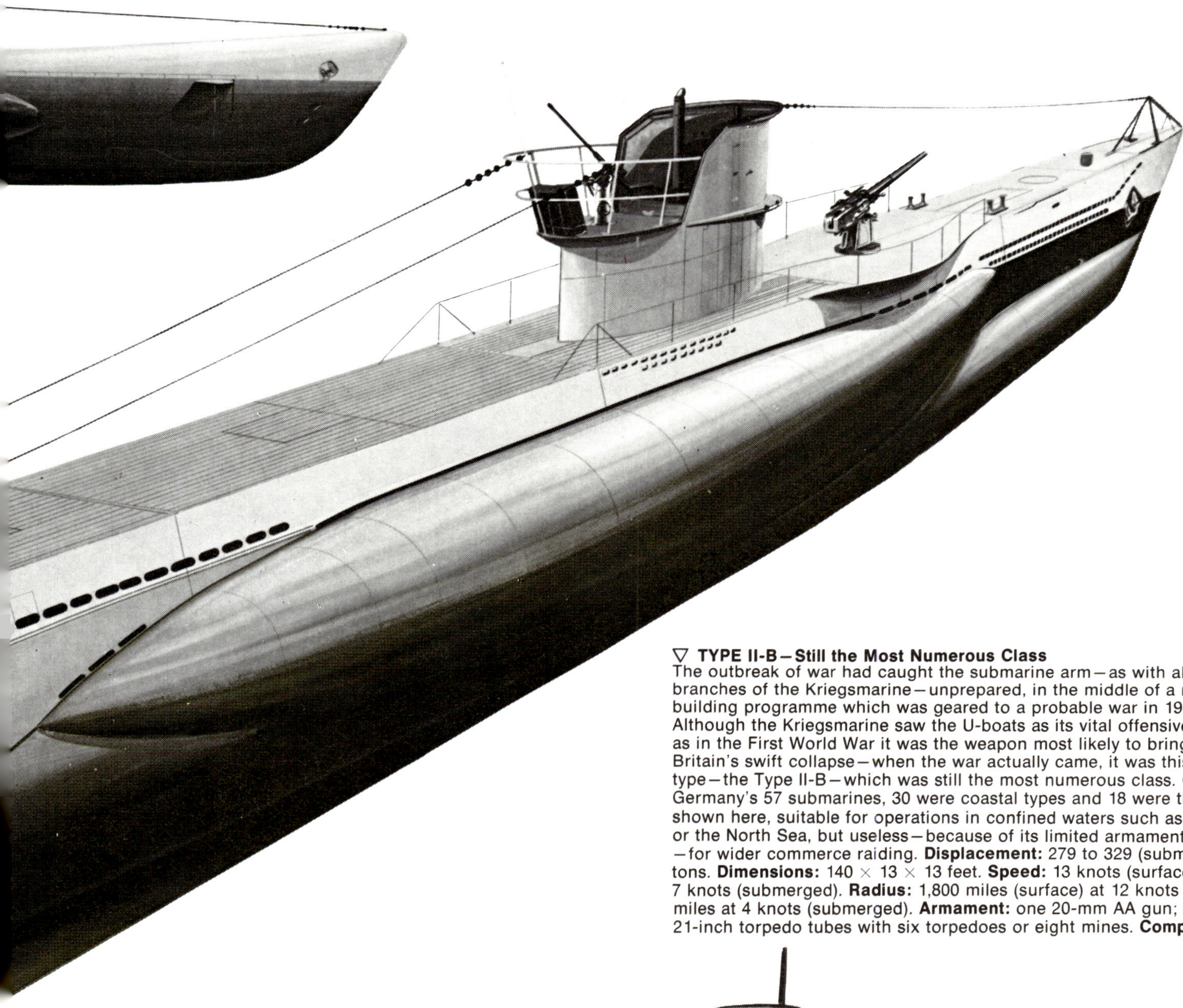

▽ **TYPE II-B—Still the Most Numerous Class**
The outbreak of war had caught the submarine arm—as with all other branches of the Kriegsmarine—unprepared, in the middle of a major building programme which was geared to a probable war in 1944 or 1945. Although the Kriegsmarine saw the U-boats as its vital offensive arm—as in the First World War it was the weapon most likely to bring Britain's swift collapse—when the war actually came, it was this coastal type—the Type II-B—which was still the most numerous class. Of Germany's 57 submarines, 30 were coastal types and 18 were the type shown here, suitable for operations in confined waters such as the Baltic or the North Sea, but useless—because of its limited armament and range—for wider commerce raiding. **Displacement:** 279 to 329 (submerged) tons. **Dimensions:** 140 × 13 × 13 feet. **Speed:** 13 knots (surface), 7 knots (submerged). **Radius:** 1,800 miles (surface) at 12 knots or 43 miles at 4 knots (submerged). **Armament:** one 20-mm AA gun; three 21-inch torpedo tubes with six torpedoes or eight mines. **Complement:** 25.

Atlantic, March 1943

For the U-boat crews, the end came with startling suddenness—but a suddenness which could perhaps have been foreseen. The supply of new offensive weapons to the U-boats failed to keep pace with defensive techniques developed by the Allied navies, who were at last receiving the equipment essential for convoy protection. Here an ex-U-boat officer describes a significant episode in the long, bitter battle for the sealanes

It was during the early part of 1943 that 'B' Service, the German radio monitoring system, succeeded in breaking the naval cipher then being used by the Allies for communication with their convoys crossing the Atlantic.

The German command was quick to put this knowledge to work. Among the signals they intercepted and deciphered were directions to two convoys, some days out of New York, to change course to a southerly route and work around a concentration of U-boats which had been detected on their planned northern route.

Admiral Dönitz, who as Befehlshaber der Unterseeboote (BdU) was in charge of U-boat operations, promptly ordered the U-boats southwards to intercept the first convoy, SC-122, on the course which B Service said it would follow. These U-boats numbered 12, and formed the *Raubgraf* group.

Dönitz also had available, well-fuelled and ready for action, large numbers of other U-boats recently withdrawn from operations against convoys which had reached comparative safety near the eastern Atlantic mainland. Fourteen of these were formed into the *Stürmer* group, and were reinforced by four other U-boats newly out of ports in western France. Nine others became the *Dränger* group, and were reinforced by two more boats from France. This complete force was brought up into a north-south line which coincided with the limit of range of Allied aircraft patrolling from Ireland and Iceland. Once formed up, they were ordered to move forward towards the United States, in the hope of encountering HX-229, the second convoy located by B Service.

To the north, however, the weather was so bad that the *Raubgraf* group was late in taking up its position. By the time it reached the expected course of SC-122, the bleak Atlantic was empty. With a Force 10 wind lashing the wave tops into an almost impenetrable Atlantic spray, and visibility down to a maximum of 500 yards, they continued their search. On the evening of March 15 it appeared that luck was on their side: U-91 sighted a destroyer sailing east, and the submarines converged on the area. When nothing else immediately showed, *Raubgraf* group was split into two. Four of the boats were ordered to search that region and the rest to move east so that they would not be left behind should the convoy have slipped by undetected. But the destroyer, it seemed, was escorting a phantom convoy. Their searching revealed nothing.

Yet luck was still on the side of the Germans. A single U-boat, the U-653, was at the time struggling back to base with a faulty engine after a breakdown on a previous operation. Suddenly it found itself sailing almost as part of a vast convoy of 38 ships, nine of them tankers, in a string of 11 columns. It hastily fell back to keep track of them, and reported the sighting to BdU.

Dönitz signalled straight back to his submarine fleet. He directed the whole *Raubgraf* group, plus two boats which had just refuelled from a submarine tanker, plus the 11 southernmost boats of the *Stürmer* group, to come up at full speed and chase the sighted convoy. Dönitz believed, at the time, that this convoy was SC-122. It was in fact the faster HX-229. When B Service, still busy picking up and deciphering Allied signals, reported that HX-229 was turning to the north, Dönitz directed the remaining six *Stürmer* U-boats and the 11 *Dränger* boats to intercept it. In fact B Service's interpretation of the signal was wrong, and it was thus left to *Raubgraf* group to carry out the attack.

They approached from the starboard side, and with only four escorting destroyers to contend with along the whole front and flanks of the convoy's 11 columns, they were able to penetrate the meagre defences through one gap after another.

U-603 was the first to strike. At 2200 hours her commander, Oberleutnant zur See Bertelsmann, fired three FAT surface-running torpedoes and one normal electro-torpedo. The FATs ran in curves through the convoy along their pre-arranged courses. One struck the Norwegian motor-freighter *Elin K,* at the head of the second column, and she sank within minutes. A second detonation was heard by the elated crew of U-603 but proved to be merely a torpedo exploding at the end of its run.

An hour and a half later U-758, moving abreast of the convoy, fired two FATs, and two electro-torpedoes from starboard into the convoy. One struck the Dutch steamer *Zaanland,* another hit the American steamer *James Oglethorpe,* and both came to a standstill. The escorts immediately dropped depth-charges to drive off the submarine, and the over-optimistic Kapitänleutnant Manseck claimed their explosions as hits on two more vessels.

The damage done in these early attacks was enough to distract almost the entire escort. All but one went astern to pick up survivors, leaving a single destroyer alone to carry out the task of protection. This destroyer could do no more than sweep across the entire front of the convoy, and the flanks were thus left naked. U-435, a submarine

THE LAST TRIUMPHS OF THE U-BOATS

that had been particularly successful in the Barents Sea in 1942, attacked the unprotected port flank. Its first pair of FAT torpedoes struck the American steamer *William Eustis* and brought it to a halt. An escort took off the crew and tried to sink the ship with depth-charges but failed, and at 0300 hours it had to leave.

By 0230 hours U-435, after reloading its bow tube, had regained a firing position on the port side of the convoy, and it discharged two FATs and two E torpedoes with magneto ignition. After a long run its commander, Kapitänleutnant Strelow, heard four detonations which he took to be hits on several ships. In fact, it was the U-91, which had fired a pair of torpedoes at short range into the leading ship in the starboard column, the American freighter *Harry Luckenbach*. The *Harry Luckenbach* emitted a great column of smoke and fire and four minutes later sank to the bottom of the ocean. The escorts tried to foil further attacks with depth-charges, but the U-boats had not been accurately pinpointed and no damage was done. It was another depth-charge explosion that Strelow, with characteristic optimism, mistook for a hit on a tanker in the fourth or fifth column.

Ahead of the convoy U-616 – which for an hour or more had been trying to outwit the defending destroyer and penetrate the convoy from the front – suddenly came face to face with it. Without hesitation Oberleutnant Koitschka ordered a salvo of four torpedoes. At such range it seemed impossible to miss, but at the last moment the destroyer happened to turn away and the torpedoes ran harmlessly on.

Kapitänleutnant Zurmühlen in U-600 was less unlucky. He fired five FATs into the convoy from the starboard bow, without being observed. The first struck the British steamer *Nariva,* two hit the American steamer *Irene Du Pont,* and a fourth set fire to the ship *Southern Princess.*

The last of the *Raubgraf* group, U-228, came into the attack at 0534 that morning, but the range was too great and its three torpedoes missed.

During the night of March 16/17 the *Stürmer* group of 11 submarines, sailing to encounter the reported HX-229 convoy, came by chance upon SC-122. This convoy had a much stronger escort, and around midnight the HF/DF direction-finders picked up signals which showed that at least six U-boats were within 20 sea miles of the convoy. They attacked, but the strong defence was on the alert and most of the U-boats were driven off before they could fire their torpedoes. Only U-338, under Kapitänleutnant Kinzel, succeeded in approaching the convoy. He fired two pairs of torpedoes from immediately in front of the seventh column. After the first pair Kinzel heard two explosions and saw a 300-foot column of smoke rising from one ship, which listed more and more as it burned. In fact, however, not only had the *Kingsbury* been struck, but also the *King Gruffydd* behind it. Both ships sank within the hour. The U-boat's second pair of torpedoes struck the Dutch vessel *Alderamin* whose four masts made her an easy target. As he turned U-338 away, Kinzel fired a stern torpedo at the *Glenapp,* the convoy commodore's ship. This passed beneath the *Glenapp,* crossed the ninth, tenth, and eleventh columns, and finally struck the *Fort Cedar Lake.* This was one of the rare occasions when a U-boat commander badly underestimated his success. Instead of two ships he imagined he had dispatched, Kinzel had in fact accounted for four.

From the radio signals sent out by the U-boats it was clear to their commander-in-chief by the morning of March 17 that his submarines had between them encountered each of the two separate convoys, and that SC-122 was now sailing about 120 sea

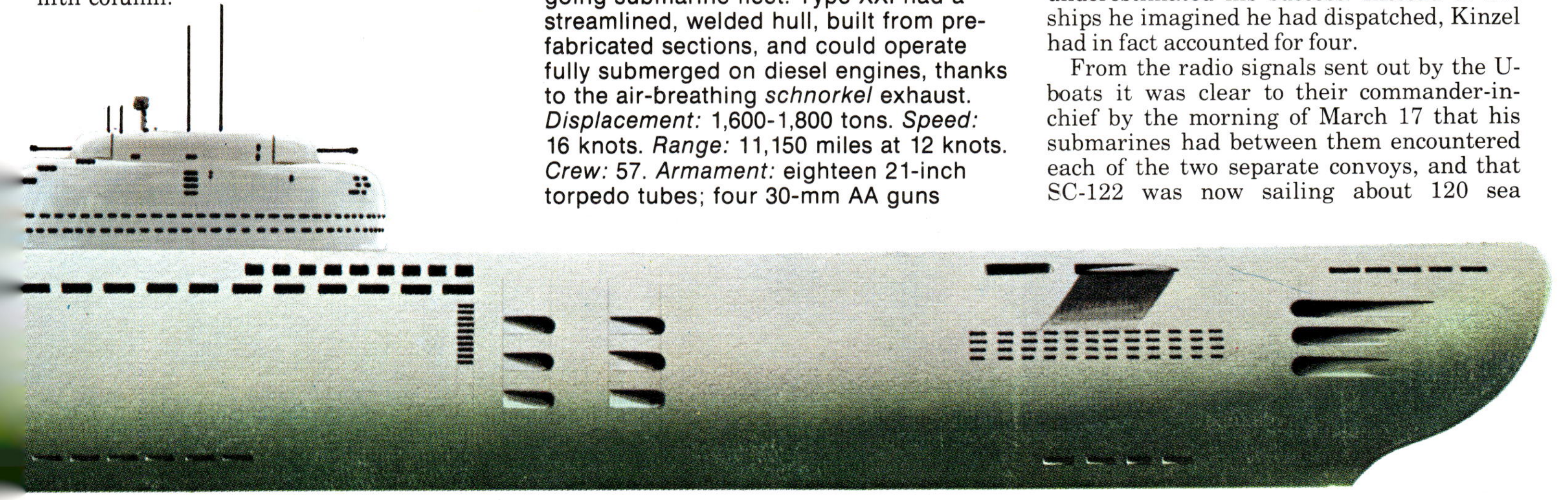

U-Boat Type XXI-C
The last development in Dönitz's ocean-going submarine fleet. Type XXI had a streamlined, welded hull, built from prefabricated sections, and could operate fully submerged on diesel engines, thanks to the air-breathing *schnorkel* exhaust. *Displacement:* 1,600-1,800 tons. *Speed:* 16 knots. *Range:* 11,150 miles at 12 knots. *Crew:* 57. *Armament:* eighteen 21-inch torpedo tubes; four 30-mm AA guns

miles in front of HX-229. At first Dönitz contemplated sending the six northern *Stürmer* U-boats and the favourably situated *Dränger* group to attack SC-122. But the dead reckoning of the U-boats in such heavy weather, day after day, was so inexact that their position reports, often widely separated from each other, introduced an element of real uncertainty as they advanced on their prey over vast distances. The likelihood of their navigating accurately on to a specific convoy was slim, so in the morning permission was given to operate against either convoy. A prospect of great success was building up. Some 28 U-boats could advance to attacking positions before dark, while the *Raubgraf* boats, although some of them were badly shot up, could at least help keep tabs on the convoy with their signals.

But by the morning of March 17, SC-122 had sailed to within range of the aircraft flying escort sorties from Iceland, and all but one submarine was forced, by either the aircraft or the destroyers, to dive or fall astern of the convoy.

Again it was Kinzel in U-338 who alone pushed home an attack. At 1352 hours he fired four single torpedoes in rapid succession. The first struck, and within half an hour sank, the Panamanian steamer *Granville*. Three more detonations were heard, but all proved to be depth charges dropped by the escorts.

The morning attack on HX-229 was more successful. After the devastation of the previous night the convoy had not yet closed its ranks, and most of the escort vessels—there were only five in the first place—had fallen back to rescue survivors.

At 0739 hours U-91, following the convoy, encountered the *James Oglethorpe*, which with its master and a skeleton crew had been restarted and had limped to the aid of the *William Eustis*. U-91 sank both ships with a treble salvo.

U-616, also from astern the convoy, fired a torpedo at one of the escort ships, but missed. An hour and a half later its marksmanship had not improved and a torpedo fired at another vessel also went wide.

Other U-boats now arrived and joined in what amounted to a beanfeast. U-665 from the *Stürmer* group fired a pair of torpedoes at a freighter, but these may have been superfluous shots at the *Fort Cedar Lake* from Convoy SC-122, already damaged by Kinzel during the previous night, and now wallowing in the same sea area into which HX-229 had sailed. Shortly after 1300 hours U-384 and U-631 attacked from the starboard bow and starboard quarter. One of U-384's three torpedoes struck the British steamer *Coracero*, and U-631, with a single well-aimed shot, hit the Dutch steamer *Terkoelei* at the end of the starboard column. U-384 claimed all three explosions as its own and reported three hits. The *Terkoelei* sank at once, and the *Coracero* three hours later.

U-91, after sinking the two damaged ships, continued to follow in the wake of the convoy and soon after 1500 hours caught up with two more drifting ships. Of the three ships torpedoed during the night by U-600, the *Southern Princess* capsized at 1030 hours, before the last escort left at 1230 hours. So these two ships must have been the *Irene Du Pont* and *Nariva*. Kapitänleutnant Walkerling sent them to the bottom.

At 1630 hours air cover for Convoy HX-229 arrived, and U-600, at the time the only submarine in the vicinity, was immediately forced to dive. All contact with the convoy was then broken off—not least because six U-boats were beginning to run out of fuel and had to make for the tanker submarine. Four others had fired all their torpedoes or had fallen so far astern that they too had to withdraw from the action.

As far as SC-122 was concerned, contact was maintained by the U-boats, and after dark U-305 under Kapitänleutnant Bahr came in to attack from the starboard bow. He fired two pairs of torpedoes at long range, but the last failed to leave the tube through a mechanical defect. The first pair struck the *Port Auckland* and the *Zouave*, which sank within five minutes. The third torpedo appeared to hit the *Port Auckland* again as it lay burning. After this attack U-305 was forced to dive by a destroyer. When it surfaced at 2341 hours the wreck of the *Port Auckland* was close by, drifting broadside on to the waves. A single torpedo, fired at point blank range from its stern tube, struck the engine room and sent a cloud of black smoke billowing 600 feet into the air. But still the *Port Auckland* stayed afloat, and Bahr trailed it for two hours in freshening weather. Finally U-338 came up and fired a torpedo at the wreck. But even before it struck home *Port Auckland*, pounded by the waves in what had become a Force 7 or 8 gale, broke up suddenly and sank.

Air cover arrives

That night the skies cleared, and the bright moonlight meant that no submarines could operate. They were invariably detected in time and driven off. The weather continued to improve during the following day (March 18) with a Force 6 wind and normal visibility of up to 5 kilometres, except during the frequent snow showers. Air cover for both convoys arrived during the morning, and around SC-122 several submarines were spotted by the escort vessels, attacked with depth charges, and forced to submerge.

The *schnorkel* device (below) enabled U-boats to run submerged on diesel engines, instead of being forced to run the gauntlet of air attack during regular resurfacing previously necessary in order to re-charge batteries

HX-229 was less effectively protected. At 1552 hours, on the basis of earlier reports and radio signals overheard by other U-boats, Oberleutnant zur See Trojer in U-221 broke through the convoy's defences in a clever underwater attack and fired five torpedoes, including two FATs. Two ships were hit, each by two torpedoes: the American freighter *Walter O. Gresham* and the valuable British refrigerator ship *Canadian Star*. In an earlier daylight attack U-663 claimed to have hit a ship with four torpedoes, but the records fail to bear out his claim, which appears to have been another of those over-optimistic assessments of success by individual U-boat commanders.

During the night of March 18/19 the faster convoy, HX-229, had so far closed up with SC-122 that together they formed one great flotilla. For the U-boats and their commander-in-chief it became more and more difficult to distinguish one from the other, a difficulty enhanced by the uncertain navigation of the U-boats. Even in retrospect it is hard to determine against which of the two convoys any U-boat was operating at a given moment.

With the approach of darkness the aircraft flew home, and many of the U-boats made contact with Allied ships during the evening. But the defending destroyers were still very much alert, and were quick to attack with depth charges any U-boat lurking in the vicinity. Seven were forced to interrupt their operations and dive. U-666 was able to launch five torpedoes, but the range was too great and they all missed. U-441, at 0450 hours, had a similar experience. Kapitänleutnant Hartmann fired three FAT and two E torpedoes one after the other into Convoy HX-229. Hartmann believed that he had hit three ships, but the four detonations on which he based his belief were either depth charges or were torpedoes exploding at the end of their run, for no Allied ship was hit at this stage. At 0506 hours Kapitänleutnant Stuckmeier in U-608 attempted to torpedo HMS *Highlander* with a treble salvo. Five and a half minutes later two detonations were heard, but they too were nothing more than terminal explosions.

U-666 was more fortunate in its second attack on Convoy SC-122. At 0541 hours it fired four torpedoes at short intervals. The first missed, then Oberleutnant Stengel heard three explosions at the correct intervals and saw columns of water shoot into the air. In fact only one torpedo had hit a target, the Greek freighter *Carras*. It remained afloat but was abandoned by its crew.

Dönitz had originally intended to continue the operations until daylight on March 20, but in the early morning of March 19 powerful air cover arrived for both convoys, and it was obvious that more aircraft were available now that the convoys had passed the limit of 600 sea miles from the land bases in Iceland and Northern Ireland. After the attack by U-666, Convoy SC-122 was left undisturbed. The weather had improved, and a west wind of Force 2 with Sea 2 favoured air operations. Many of the U-boats reported aerial bomb attacks and seven had to withdraw damaged. U-338 was hit and so badly damaged that it had to make for base. Others suffered constant attacks from the escorts and had to drop astern.

Among the U-boats following behind the convoy, U-527, at 1000 hours, sighted a lone straggler—the American steamer *Mathew Luckenbach*. An isolated ship away from the safety of the convoy made a sitting

The Hunter

The pattern of attack on a merchant ship by a submarine began when the submarine first sighted the masts of an approaching ship *(inset circle, left).* The speed and course of the ship were calculated, and the submarine set on a course to intercept her. At intervals during the approach the periscope was raised to check the quarry's course *(centre).* When the U-boat reached the firing position *(right),* the angle of fire was determined. The torpedoes were fired to strike the ship at an angle between 90 degrees and 120 degrees. A salvo of torpedoes was fired, all on the same course, at intervals of some seconds. The speed of the target would give 'spread' to the salvo and increase the chances of hitting the target. The importance of the target determined the number of torpedoes fired

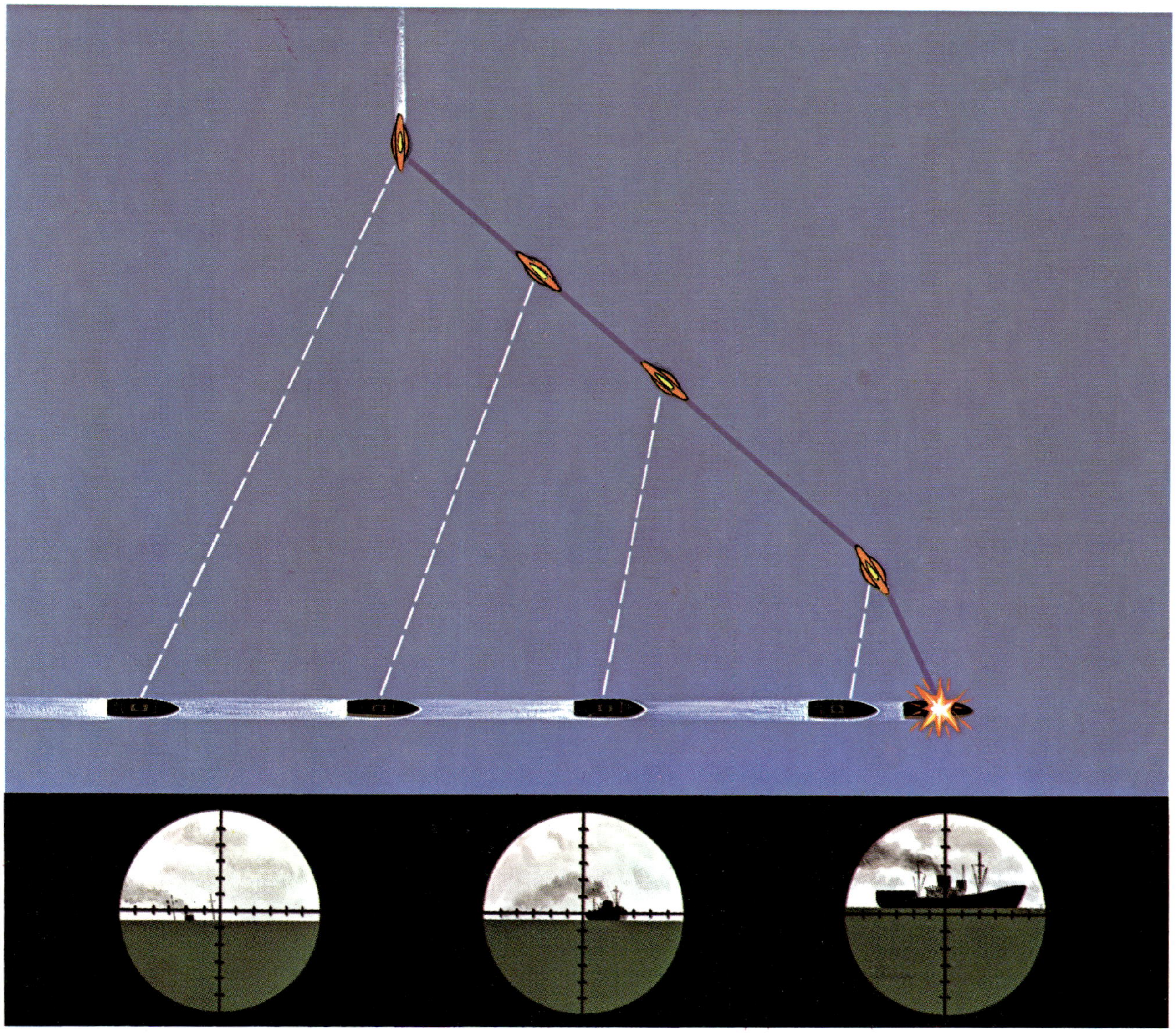

target, and any ship's officers careless enough, or reckless enough, to allow themselves to fall away from even the most meagre destroyer protection, had to be prepared for any fate that came their way. Three torpedoes from U-527 hit the ship aft and brought it to a halt. Escort vessels arrived to take off the crew, and the ship wallowed for ten hours. It was then—just as U-527's commander had decided to deliver the *coup de grâce*—that U-523 came up, took over the honour, and sank the wreck. U-boats were now combing the wake of the convoy like sharks, waiting to pounce on stricken and abandoned vessels. U-333 was among them. At 2128 hours it came across the still floating *Carras,* and with a single well-aimed shot sent it to the bottom.

But the U-boats were by no means having it all their own way. Nine miles away from the convoy an RAF Liberator bomber on escort patrol was engaged in a private battle with a U-boat, probably U-384. The bomber won.

From reports received during the preceding day and night it had become clear by the morning of March 20 that there would be no further chance of a successful U-boat attack. The convoy had now sailed to well within the range of the protecting bombers, and as the morning wore on air cover appeared in greater and greater strength. The submarines were ordered to break off the action and proceed to the south-west. Only chance opportunities of underwater torpedo attacks were to be taken advantage of, should they encounter any more stragglers or damaged ships away from the convoy.

Of the 98 ships which had left New York, 21, with an aggregate tonnage of 140,842 tons, had fallen victim to the U-boats. In addition, out of two previous convoys (HK-228 and SC-121) 18 vessels had been sunk. The whole tally for that late winter amounted to a triumph for the German navy. In the last ten days of February 28 ships were sunk, in the first ten days of March 41 ships, and in the second ten days of March 44 ships—a total tonnage of 695,608 tons. The final figures for March threatened to be even higher than for the previous month of carnage in the Atlantic, November 1942. What was all the more significant was that the U-boats had this time achieved successful operations against ships sailing in convoy—67 out of the 85 sunk during March, compared with only 39 convoy ships out of 139 during the previous November.

Grounds for optimism

On the face of it at least, the German submarine command might well rejoice. Out of 39 U-boats originally assigned to the task, with six always either approaching or leaving the scene of action, they had succeeded in putting no less than 19 in contact with the enemy's merchant fleets, some of which had made more than one attack.

Although it was clear that the best chances of success always occurred during the first night of operations, many U-boats, despite stiffening defensive measures, were able to report continuing success in underwater attacks. Most encouraging of all, the whole of the campaign was conducted successfully with the loss of only a single submarine. At the time, there seemed every reason to go on and exploit the situation by all possible means.

Subsequent appreciation, however, shows that the battle was being evaluated too favourably by the German command. The main reason for the success of the U-boats during the operations on the first night was the weakness of the defence of Convoy HX-229, which consisted of only four (and later five) escort ships, one or two of which were usually astern picking up survivors. The defence was unable to cope with a succession of U-boats attacking at short intervals. The defence of Convoy SC-122 was far stronger, and succeeded in driving off a much larger number of U-boats—almost all, in fact, were forced to keep their distance except the notably successful U-338.

The Allies clearly were quick to profit by this experience. In later battles, with extra destroyers from the Home Fleet (the efficiency of which was increased as much by HF/DF as by radar), and air cover from both bombers and aircraft-carriers, the Allied convoys proved able either to evade the packs of U-boats or to burst straight through them with comparative immunity. It was this strengthened cover which was to lead, within only eight weeks of the HX-229 and SC-122 failures, to a complete reversal of fortunes in the Battle of the Atlantic.

This extraordinary view is taken from a German Air Gunner's position during an attack on a British plane over southern England

BATTLE OF BRITAIN

Keystone

"LET US
GO FORWARD
TOGETHER"

"The gratitude of every home in our Island, in our Empire, and indeed throughout the world, except in the abodes of the guilty, goes out to the British airmen, who, undaunted by odds, unwearied in their constant challenge and mortal danger, are turning the tide of world war by their prowess and devotion. Never in the field of human conflict was so much owed by so many to so few."

Winston Churchill, 20 August 1940

AIR POWER 1939

After the Armistice in November 1918 the greatly expanded armed forces of the Allies were hastily and clumsily demobilized. Improvised war organizations were dismantled, and the watchwords of the British government were economy and retrenchment. The war had been won, there was no visible threat to Allied security, and Great Britain and France were swept by a wave of anti-war feeling, largely induced by the terrible casualties and intolerable conditions of trench warfare.

In 1925 the League of Nations had set up a Preparatory Commission to explore the ground for a general disarmament conference. Progress in this field is never rapid, and for many years the commission was involved in interminable difficulties and arguments. Eventually a Disarmament Conference was convened in Geneva in 1932, at which proposals for outlawing air bombardment and drastically limiting the loaded weight of military aircraft were discussed. Hoping for success in these negotiations, the British government declined to authorize the design and construction of any effective bomber aircraft. In addition, it had introduced in 1924 what became known as the 'Ten-year Rule', which postulated that there would be no major war for ten years. Unfortunately each successive year was deemed to be the starting point of this tranquil epoch, and so the period always remained at ten years.

The Disarmament Conference finally broke up in May 1934 without achieving any result whatsoever. But meanwhile Hitler had come to power in Germany, and was clearly bent on a massive programme of rearmament. In 1933 the British government at last permitted the issue of Air Staff requirements for a high-performance multi-gun fighter, which in due course produced the Hurricane and Spitfire. It is often asserted that these two aircraft, and especially the Spitfire, were forced on a reluctant Air Ministry by a far-sighted aircraft industry and its capable designers. There is not a word of truth in this. Both aircraft were designed, ordered, and built to Air Ministry specifications.

Even after the collapse of the Disarmament Conference in 1934 the British government was reluctant to rearm. Alone among nations the British seem to think that if they rearm it will bring about an arms race. The result of this curious delusion is that they usually start when the other competitors are half-way round the course. The bomber force was therefore given a very low priority, but development of the fighters was allowed to proceed, though without any undue haste.

In 1935 two British ministers, Mr Anthony Eden and Sir John Simon, visited Germany. They reported that Hitler's rearmament in the air had proceeded much farther and faster than the British government had believed possible. This was because the Germans had made a secret agreement to train the Soviet air force, which enabled them to keep in being a sizeable corps of expert pilots and technicians. The government was alarmed, and ordered quantity production of the Hurricanes and Spitfires before the prototype had even flown—the so-called 'ordering off the drawing-board'.

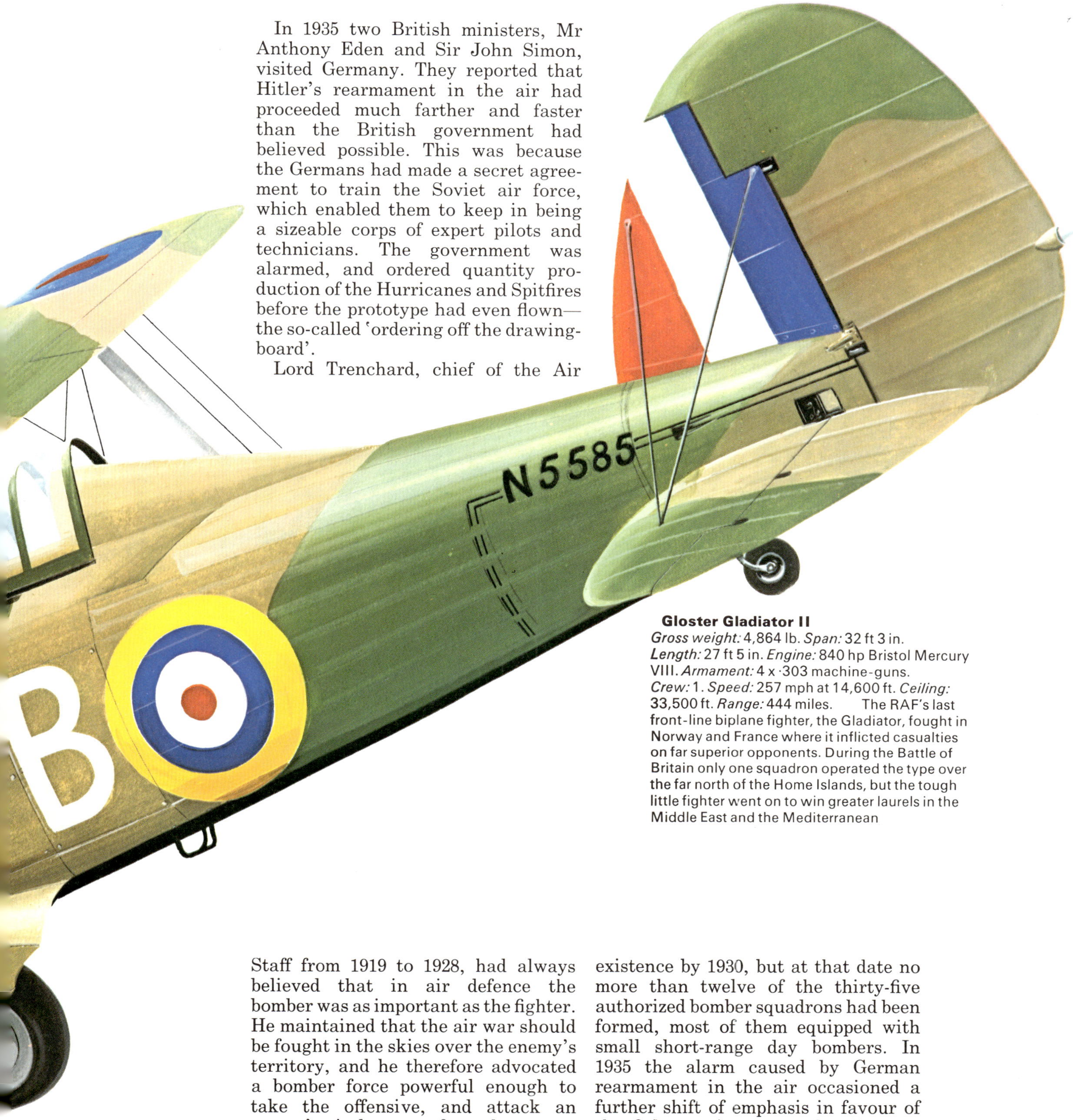

Gloster Gladiator II
Gross weight: 4,864 lb. *Span:* 32 ft 3 in. *Length:* 27 ft 5 in. *Engine:* 840 hp Bristol Mercury VIII. *Armament:* 4 x ·303 machine-guns. *Crew:* 1. *Speed:* 257 mph at 14,600 ft. *Ceiling:* 33,500 ft. *Range:* 444 miles. The RAF's last front-line biplane fighter, the Gladiator, fought in Norway and France where it inflicted casualties on far superior opponents. During the Battle of Britain only one squadron operated the type over the far north of the Home Islands, but the tough little fighter went on to win greater laurels in the Middle East and the Mediterranean

Lord Trenchard, chief of the Air Staff from 1919 to 1928, had always believed that in air defence the bomber was as important as the fighter. He maintained that the air war should be fought in the skies over the enemy's territory, and he therefore advocated a bomber force powerful enough to take the offensive, and attack an enemy's vital centres from the outset. He argued that this would rob an enemy of the initiative and throw his air force on to the defensive.

Eventually Trenchard's views were accepted by the British government, and in the air defence of Great Britain two-thirds of the squadrons were to be bombers and one-third fighters. But because it was thought that the bombers were offensive while the fighters were defensive in character, it was judged that the building up of fighter strength would not be liable to trigger off an arms race. The seventeen authorized fighter squadrons were in existence by 1930, but at that date no more than twelve of the thirty-five authorized bomber squadrons had been formed, most of them equipped with small short-range day bombers. In 1935 the alarm caused by German rearmament in the air occasioned a further shift of emphasis in favour of the fighters. A system of radio-location, later called radar, which would provide invaluable early warning and make it possible to track incoming raids, was pioneered by Robert Watson-Watt, and given all possible encouragement.

At the outbreak of war in September 1939 the odds against the RAF, in terms of modern aircraft, were about four to one. Although money had been poured out like water during the years since the Munich crisis, it had been too late to redress the balance. Only time—as much time as possible—could do that.

Photo. EC. Armées

La Panne beach: destroyed AA guns abandoned at Dunkirk by the British Expeditionary Force

IN FRANCE DEFEAT IN BRITAIN PREPARATION

For the children, filling sand bags was all good fun

Evacuees leave London (above) and they still carried their gas masks as they paddled

A woman warden on duty. (Left) Cigarette cards from a series on air raid precautions

LUFTWAFFE: THE FLAWED WEAPON

Heinkel He 111 B2
Gross weight: 22,046 lb. *Span:* 74 ft 2 in. *Length:* 57 ft 5 in. *Engine:* 2 x 950 hp DB 600. *Armament:* 3 x 7·9-mm machine-guns. *Crew:* 4. *Speed:* 186 mph at ground level. *Ceiling:* 22,966 ft. *Range:* 1,030 miles. *Bomb load:* 3,307 lb.
The B2 version of the He 111 served with the Condor Legion in the Spanish Civil War, outpacing all opposing fighters and carrying out unescorted raids at will. But the resulting over-confidence was shattered by opposition from Spitfires and Hurricanes in 1940 and the He 111 was soon relegated to night duties

German Fighter Pilot, 2nd Lieutenant

A German 2nd Lieutenant fighter pilot began training at an elementary flying training school which entailed gliding on Course 1, elementary flying on Course 2, and single-engine fighter training on Course 3. He then went on to advanced training and lastly to his operational training unit: altogether it took seven to eight months and 107 to 112 hours at the controls. He wore the national eagle emblem on his right and pilot's insigne on his lower left breast. On his visored cap, more rakish than others in the army, was the national rosette flanked by oak leaves and spreading wings surmounted by a flying eagle. Yellow piping and a large 'W' decorated his epaulettes; his collar patch was an eagle and oak leaves on a yellow background. He wore jackboots, grey-blue wool-rayon breeches, jacket with patch pockets, grey shirt, black tie and a Sam Browne belt with eagle-emblem buckle. His flying suit had zippered slash pockets and his flying boots were lined. He had passed a rigid physical examination and was eligible for pilot training after the age of 18. Under normal conditions, *Luftwaffe* pilots enjoyed better food than the rest of the army and the pay was higher

Junkers Ju 87 B2 'Stuka' Cockpit

1 Visual dive indicator
2 Gun sight
3 Artificial horizon
4 Compass repeater
5 Speedometer
6 Boost pressure
7 Altimeter
8 Rev counter
9 Flap indicator
10 Intercom connection
11 Crash pad
12 Manual engine pump
13 Engine priming pump
14 Electrics panel (radio)
15 Oil cooler flap control
16 Rudder bar pedal
17 Target view window
18 Control column
19 Target view window flap control
20 Fuel metering hand priming pump
21 Throttle
22 Starter switch
23 Main electrics switch
24 Coolant temperature
25 Fuel contents
26 Oil temperature
27 Oil contents
28 Compass
29 Oil pressure gauge
30 Clock
31 Dive pre-set indicator
32 Fuel pressure gauge
33 Radio altimeter
34 Rate of climb indicator
35 Water cooler flap indicator

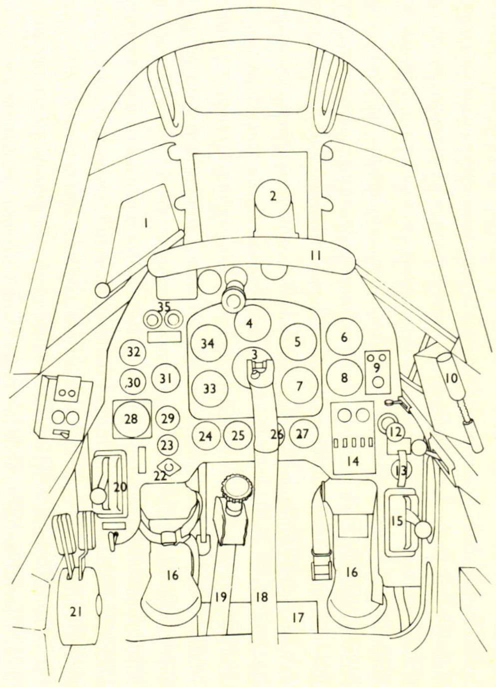

AUF ZU

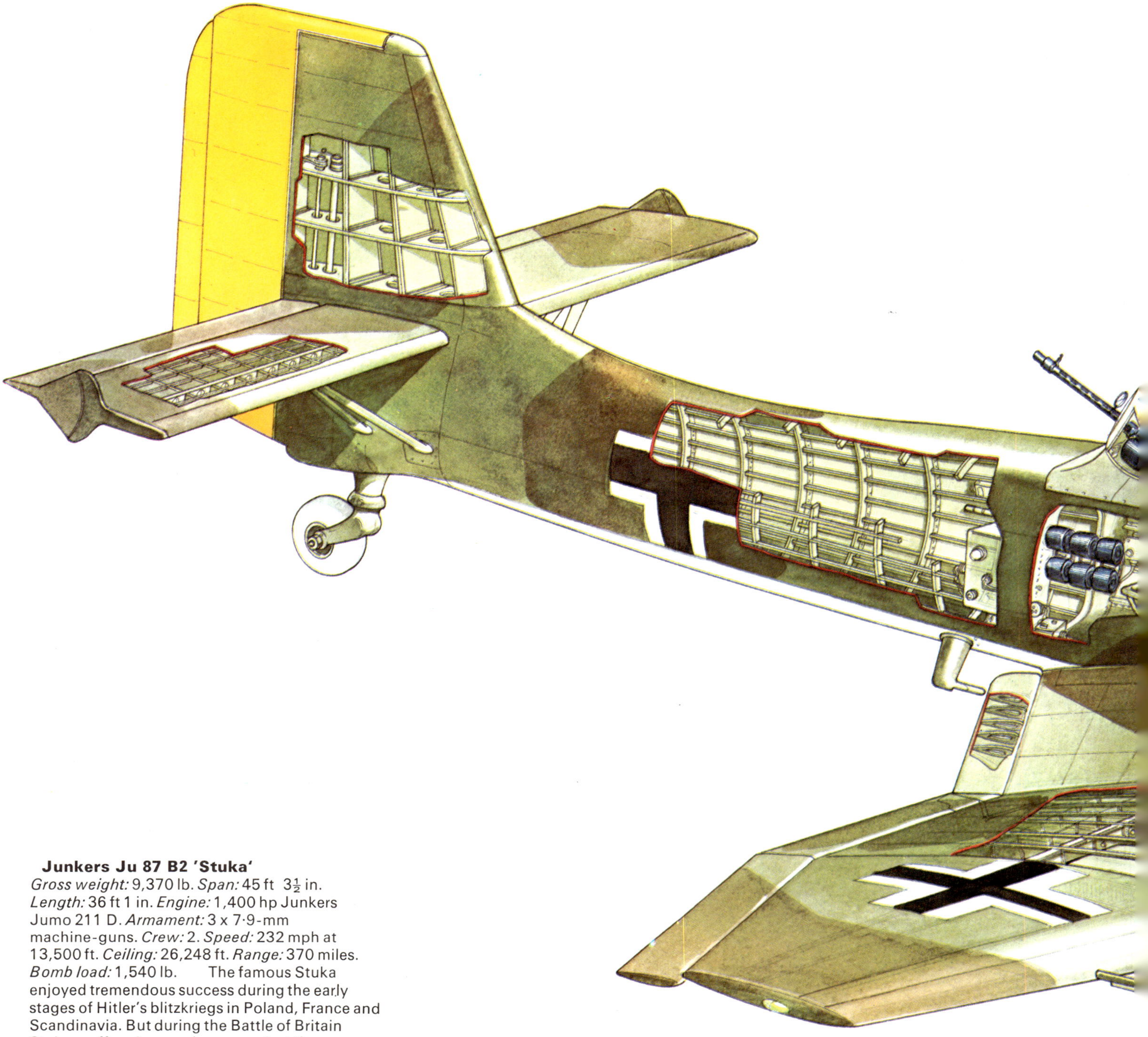

Junkers Ju 87 B2 'Stuka'
Gross weight: 9,370 lb. *Span:* 45 ft $3\frac{1}{2}$ in. *Length:* 36 ft 1 in. *Engine:* 1,400 hp Junkers Jumo 211 D. *Armament:* 3 x 7·9-mm machine-guns. *Crew:* 2. *Speed:* 232 mph at 13,500 ft. *Ceiling:* 26,248 ft. *Range:* 370 miles. *Bomb load:* 1,540 lb. The famous Stuka enjoyed tremendous success during the early stages of Hitler's blitzkriegs in Poland, France and Scandinavia. But during the Battle of Britain Stukas suffered severe losses against the superior Spitfires and Hurricanes, and were withdrawn from the spearhead of the attack

Messerschmitt Bf 109 E-4
Gross Weight: 5,530 lb. *Span:* 32 ft $4\frac{1}{2}$ in. *Length:* 28 ft. 8 in. *Engine:* 1,150 hp DB 601A. *Armament:* 2 x 7·92-mm machine-guns; 2 x 20-mm cannon. *Speed:* 357 mph at 12,300 ft. *Ceiling:* 36,000 ft. *Range:* 412 miles. This was the aircraft of Adjutant of J.G.3 'Udet' Franz von Werra, which crashed in Kent on 5 September 1940. Von Werra was the only German officer to escape his captors and return to Germany during the Second World War

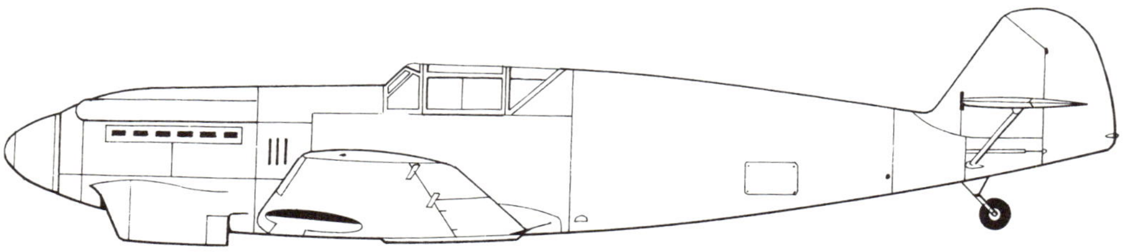

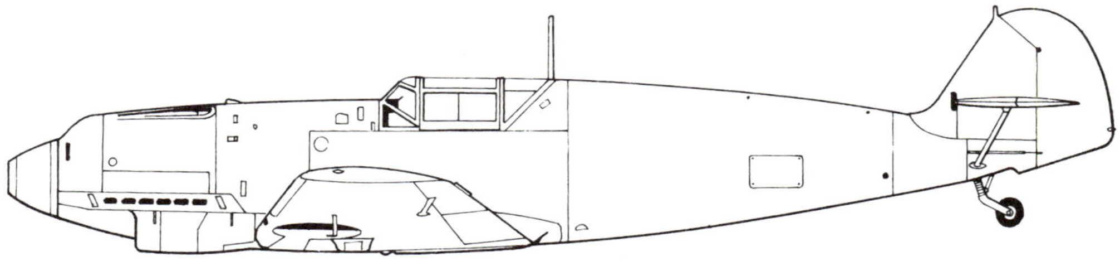

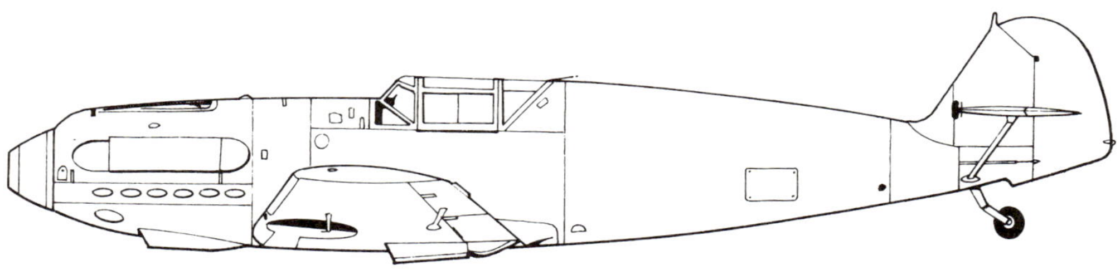

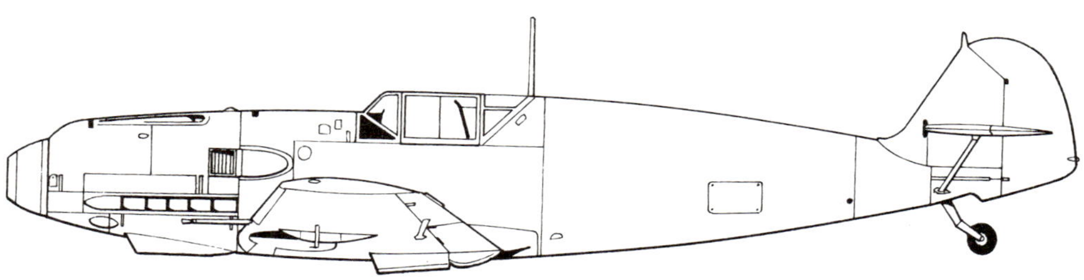

MESSERSCHMITT Bf 109

Bf 109 V-1 (top)
Prototype of the Bf 109 which first flew in September 1935, powered by a 695 hp Rolls-Royce Kestrel V engine because of the shortage of Jumo 210 units

Bf 109 B-1 (second)
Span: 32 ft 4½ in. *Length:* 28 ft. 6½ in. *Engine:* 635 hp Jumo 210D. *Armament:* 1 x 20-mm cannon; 2 x 7·9-mm machine-guns. *Speed:* 292 mph at 13,100 ft. *Ceiling:* 26,575 ft. One of the fighter types which equipped the Condor Legion during the Spanish Civil War

Bf 109 D-1 (third)
Powered by the 960 hp DB 600 engine which gave an increased speed of 323 mph

Bf 109 E-3 (bottom)
Span: 32 ft 4¼ in. *Length:* 28 ft 3¾ in. *Engine:* 1,100 hp DB 601A. *Armament:* 3 x 20-mm cannon; 2 x 7·92-mm machine-guns. *Speed:* 354 mph at 12,300 ft. *Ceiling:* 36,000 ft. Known throughout the Luftwaffe as 'Emil', this was the principal fighter type used during the Battle of Britain

Boulton Paul Defiant Mk I
Span: 39 ft 4 in. *Length:* 35 ft 4 in. *Engine:* 1,030 hp Rolls-Royce Merlin III. *Armament:* 4 x ·303 in. machine-guns in power-operated turret. *Speed:* 303 mph at 16,500 ft. *Ceiling:* 30,350 ft. A modernised version of the two-seat patrol fighter concept of 1918, the Defiant was an easy target for German single-seaters

RAF Fighter Pilot, Pilot Officer
A Pilot Officer, lowest commissioned rank in the RAF, began training as an Aircraftsman II at an initial training school and first flew on his two-month elementary course, soloing after about seven hours' instruction on a Tiger Moth. After another four months, on Proctors, he qualified for his wings and commission, then went to an operational training unit to fly fighters with experienced instructors. Altogether he would have spent over a year in training and up to 200 hours in the air as well as 'blind flying' time in a Link trainer. His minimum age was 18, maximum 35; average height was 5 ft 8½ in. He had passed a written entrance examination, a physical examination, and a colour blindness test. He wore either a serge woollen blue-grey uniform or a four patch-pocket barathea with blue shirt, black tie and black shoes. His rank insigne was a 'half-narrow' blue and grey ring around both sleeves; his wings were white-drab silk with a crown over the RAF monogram and brown silk laurel wreath. He was paid 11 shillings a day, plus £25 a year flying pay and dependents' allowance

ROYAL AIR FORCE: BATTLE AGAINST TIME

Cockpit of a Spitfire Mk II
Pilot's eye-view of the Spitfire's business end. With an eight-gun armament, constant speed propeller, retracting undercarriage, and 1,175 horsepower engine, a complex array of controls had to be shoehorned into a small space. The bucket seat took the pilot's parachute

UP
UP
DOWN
ARTIFICIAL HORIZON
CLIMB
DESCENT
RPM
BOOST
DIRECTION INDICATOR
OIL TEMP
GALLONS FUEL
ON
FUEL
OFF

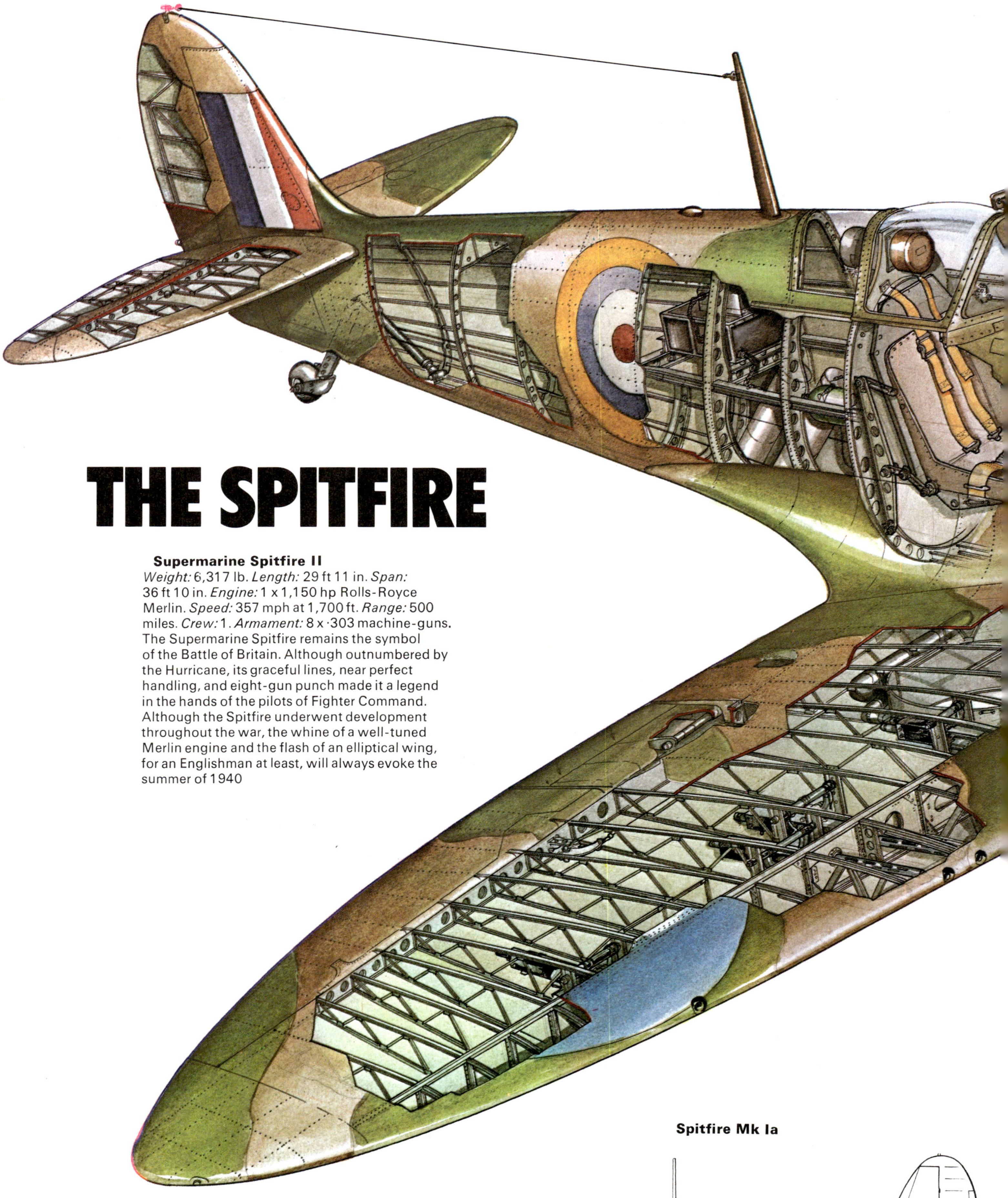

THE SPITFIRE

Supermarine Spitfire II
Weight: 6,317 lb. *Length:* 29 ft 11 in. *Span:* 36 ft 10 in. *Engine:* 1 x 1,150 hp Rolls-Royce Merlin. *Speed:* 357 mph at 1,700 ft. *Range:* 500 miles. *Crew:* 1. *Armament:* 8 x ·303 machine-guns.
The Supermarine Spitfire remains the symbol of the Battle of Britain. Although outnumbered by the Hurricane, its graceful lines, near perfect handling, and eight-gun punch made it a legend in the hands of the pilots of Fighter Command. Although the Spitfire underwent development throughout the war, the whine of a well-tuned Merlin engine and the flash of an elliptical wing, for an Englishman at least, will always evoke the summer of 1940

Spitfire Mk Ia

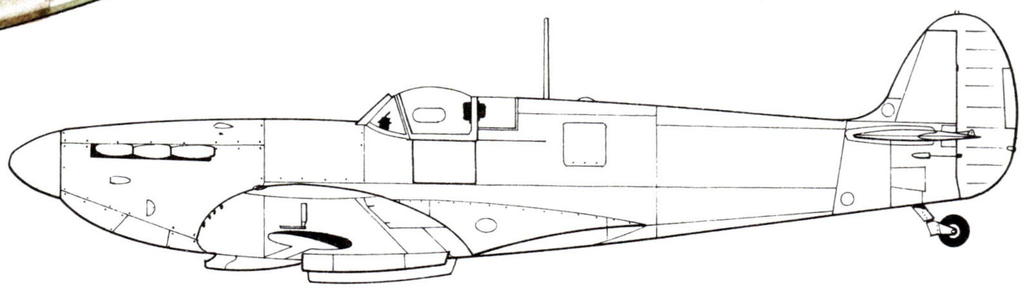

Spitfire Mk II

Spitfire Mk IIa

TH

1

1. Messerschmitt 109E
Known to Luftwaffe pilots as the 'Emil', the 109E was at least as fast as the Spitfire but was found to be less manœuvrable, though more so than the Hurricane. Always handicapped by its short range, its performance as a fighter was further restricted by a bomb load later in the battle, when pressed into service in a fighter/bomber role.
Armament: Two 7·9-mm machine-guns and two 20-mm cannons.
Max speed: 357 mph

2

2. Messerschmitt 110
Göring's folly: the cream of the Luftwaffe fighter strength was deployed in 'destroyer' units, intended to smash through the fighter defences and provide long-range escort for the bombers. Against the Spitfire and Hurricane, however, the Me-110s had finally to be provided with escorts themselves, for their lack of manœuvrability meant that their powerful armament was all too often useless.
Armament: Two 20-mm cannons, four 7·9-mm machine-guns, one free-mounted 7·9-mm gun.
Max speed: 349 mph

3

4

5

INE-UP

8

9

8. Supermarine Spitfire
The Spitfire fighter was the most agile machine in the battle—it could out-manœuvre even the Me-109E. Another vital superiority was its fire-power: eight wing-mounted Brownings which, though out-ranged by the German cannon, held a decisive concentration of rounds per second. In the Battle of Britain the Spitfire also held the advantage of fighting on home ground, unfettered by the range handicap of the 109E.
Armament: Eight ·303-inch machine-guns.
Max speed: 361 mph

9. Hawker Hurricane
Britain's first monoplane fighter was the numerical mainstay of RAF Fighter Command in the Battle of Britain. The Hurricane's ideal role was that of bomber-interceptor; as a rule, only the Spitfire could tackle the Me-109 on level terms, though the Hurricane scored notable successes against the Me-110. During the battle the Hurricane was already being replaced by the Spitfire as the standard RAF fighter.
Armament: Eight ·303-inch machine-guns.
Max speed: 328 mph

3. Junkers 87
The famous gull-winged Stuka was the main weapon which Göring turned against the RAF fighter bases. But the easy victories of past campaigns had been won in the absence of adequate fighter opposition, and RAF pilots found the Stuka an easy prey. Severe losses in operations throughout August destroyed its reputation as the all-conquering weapon of the Luftwaffe, and the Ju-87 was withdrawn from the spearhead of the attack.
Bomb load: One 1,102-lb, four 110-lb bombs.
Max speed: 217 mph

4. Junkers 88
The Ju-88 was the most versatile aircraft in the Luftwaffe's armoury for the entire war, serving as level bomber, dive-bomber, and night-fighter, as well as carrying out valuable reconnaissance duties. It was used by the Luftwaffe as a medium bomber in the Battle of Britain; but neither speed nor its comparatively high number of defending machine-guns was adequate protection from the fire-power of Spitfires and Hurricanes.
Bomb load: 5,510 lb
Max speed: 292 mph

5. Heinkel 111
The standard level bomber of the Luftwaffe at the time of the Battle of Britain, the He-111 suffered from its design as a medium bomber ideal for Continental operations but handicapped—as were all German twin-engined bombers—by the distances to targets in the north of England. Göring was convinced that its use in mass would prove decisive; but the He-111, it was found, was unable to beat off determined RAF fighter attacks.
Bomb load: 5,510 lb
Max speed: 258 mph

6. Dornier 17
The Do-17 was the Luftwaffe's veteran bomber: the type first saw service in the Spanish Civil War. Despite subsequent modifications, it was very weak in defensive fire, especially to attacks from below and to the rear. Known as the 'Flying Pencil' from its slim fuselage, the Do-17 was often confused with the British Hampden bomber, many of which were fired at by their own anti-aircraft guns. Its slender lines dictated a light bomb load.
Bomb load: 2,210 lb
Max speed: 270 mph

7. Dornier 215
This variant was a development of the basic design of the Do-17 with the installation of more powerful Daimler-Benz engines. The Do-215 was faster than the Do-17—fast enough to tax the lower-rated British engines of the early Spitfires and Hurricanes in a chase. In its light bomb-load and weak defence armament, however, the Do-215 was as handicapped as the Do-17.
Bomb load: 2,215 lb
Max speed: 311 mph

6

7

Rolls Royce Ltd

THE BATTLE

Hitler's plan was to soften up Britain for the proposed invasion. But he was not dealing with the same Britain that signed away Czechoslovakia at Munich. Fortified and inspired by their war leader, the British knew that the fate of the West could very well hinge on their courage on land, and on their aggressive spirit in the skies. DENIS RICHARDS

A. W. Gatrell & Co Ltd

The moment drew near for the Luftwaffe's great assault

From the very outset of the war a great German air assault had been expected in Britain. It was for fear of this that mothers and children had been evacuated from the big cities, the blackout enforced, gas masks and Anderson shelters distributed, thousands of beds held vacant in the hospitals. But no 'knock-out blow' from the air, or indeed any kind of blow at all – other than minelaying and raids on Scottish naval bases and east coast convoys – had disturbed the uncanny peace of the British Isles during the autumn and winter of 1939-40.

This quiet remained unbroken even when, in the spring of 1940, the war in the west came abruptly to the boil. Strange as it seemed at the time, there were in fact good reasons for Britain's unexpected immunity. Britain herself had not launched a strategic bombing offensive against Germany during the 'Phoney War' for fear of retaliation while the Allies were still the weaker side in the air. Germany had not launched any such offensive against Britain because she did not think she could achieve decisive results from German bases and because the Luftwaffe was largely cast for the role of military support. This support the Luftwaffe had given, with exemplary effectiveness, during the campaign in Poland; and now, as the Germans struck in the west, it operated in similar fashion in Norway, the Low Countries, and France. Meanwhile, it did not waste its strength in irrelevant activity against England.

This self-imposed restriction lasted until the German army entered the smoking ruins of Dunkirk. Within less than 48 hours, on the night of June 5/6, the Luftwaffe began to show a more lively interest in the British homeland. Some 30 German bombers – far more than on any previous occasion – crossed the east coast to attack airfields and other objectives; and the following night similar forces repeated the experiment. Then came a lull while the German armies in France struck southwards, again supported by the Luftwaffe. It lasted until the French sought an armistice, whereupon within a few hours German aircraft resumed night operations over Britain. From then on until the opening of their full daylight air offensive in August, the Germans repeatedly dispatched bombers – 70 of them on the busiest night – against widely separated targets in England. Their intention was to give their crews experience in night operations and the use of radio navigational aids, to reconnoitre, and to maintain pressure inexpensively (their usual losses were one or two aircraft each night) until captured airfields in France and the Low Countries could be made ready for operations of a more intensive kind.

Meanwhile there was always the chance – or so it seemed to Hitler – that such operations might not be necessary. The Führer accordingly put out 'peace-feelers', at the same time encouraging preparations for the next stage of hostilities. This next stage, the invasion or occupation of Britain, was not one to which the Germans had already devoted long thought. The speed and completeness of the German victory in France had taken even the optimistic Hitler by surprise; and though his armed forces had given some casual attention in the autumn of 1939 to the general problems of invading Britain, it was not until German troops actually reached the Channel coast on May 20, 1940, that the project really came to life. From then on the German navy, anxious not to be caught out by Hitler, began serious planning; but the German army showed comparable interest only after the total defeat of France. On July 2 Hitler formally directed his services to proceed with this invasion planning, though on a purely provisional basis. On July 19 came his public peace offer; on the 22nd, its rejection.

The Luftwaffe was able to use the entire coastline of occupied Europe: the British resources were to be strained to their furthest limits ◁

If the Germans were to take advantage of the 'invasion season' in the Channel that year, their three services would now have to formulate and agree plans with extraordinary speed. This difficulty struck the German naval and military chiefs more forcibly than it did Hitler, who declared to his paladins that only the rapid elimination of Britain would enable him to complete his life's work by turning against Russia. On July 31 he accordingly disregarded the fast-waning enthusiasm of the German navy and army and ordered that an attempt must be made to prepare the invasion operation, to which the code-name *'Seelöwe'* ('Sea Lion') was given, for September 15. The following day, August 1, he issued a directive concerning the only part of the venture on which all three German services were thus far agreed. It was for the preliminary stage, which must consist of the subjugation of the RAF. 'The German air force is to overcome the British air force with all means at its disposal, and as soon as possible.' With these words, Hitler finally decreed the Battle of Britain.

600 RAF sorties a day

While the plans for Sea Lion and the preliminary air battle were taking shape, the Luftwaffe was not of course idle. From its captured airfields it continued to harass Britain by night, and from July 10 onwards it waged increasing war by day against British shipping in the Channel. The German bombers were usually detected by the British radar stations, but since the attacks were delivered at the periphery of the British defensive system they set the Fighter Command a difficult problem. In such circumstances it was highly creditable to the command that the British fighters inflicted more casualties than they themselves suffered: between July 10 and August 10, as we now know, the Germans lost 217 aircraft, Fighter Command 96. On the other hand the German attacks, though sinking only a modest tonnage of British shipping, imposed a severe strain on Fighter Command, which was compelled to fly some 600 sorties a day at extended range at a time when it was trying to build up resources for the greater trials clearly soon to come. As Air Chief Marshal Sir Hugh Dowding, Air Officer C-in-C of the Fighter Command, pointed out to the Air Ministry and the Admiralty, if constant air protection was to be given to all British shipping in home waters, the entire British fighter force could be kept fully employed on that task alone.

These German attacks on shipping, however, were only a prelude to the air battle which the Luftwaffe had now to induce. The prerequisite of Sea Lion was that the Germans should gain air supremacy over the Channel and southern Britain. Only if the RAF were put out of business could the Germans hope to cross, land, and maintain communications without an unacceptable rate of casualties; for the destruction of the RAF would not only obviate British bombing attacks, but would also enable the Luftwaffe to deal, uninterrupted from the air, with the Royal Navy. And beyond this there was always the hope, ever present in the minds of Hitler and his service chiefs alike, that the Luftwaffe's success alone might be so great as to bring Britain to submission, or very near it. In that case, an invasion about which neither the German navy nor army was really happy could become something much more to their liking – a virtually unresisted occupation.

As the moment drew near for the Luftwaffe's great assault, the forces arrayed stood as follows. On the German side there were three *Luftflotten,* or air fleets. The main ones were Luftflotte II, under Field-Marshal Kesselring, in northern Germany, Holland, Belgium, and in north-eastern France; and Luftflotte III, under Field-Marshal Sperrle, in northern and western France. By day, these two air fleets threatened the entire southern half of England, up to and including the Midlands; and by night they could range still farther afield. In addition, to disperse the British defences and to threaten Scotland and north-eastern England there was also a smaller force, Luftflotte V, under General Stumpff, based in Denmark and Norway. Between them, the three air fleets on August 10 comprised over 3,000 aircraft, of which about three-quarters were normally serviceable at any one time. Roughly 1,100 of the 3,000 were fighters – for the most part Messerschmitt 109E's, virtually the equal of the opposing Spitfires of that date, but handicapped in a protective role by their limited range.

To escort bombers to the more distant targets, including those to be reached across the North Sea from Norway, there were some 300 Messerschmitt 110s; but these twin-engined fighters, though sturdy, could not compare in manoeuvrability with the single-engined Spitfire or Hurricane. The remaining 1,900 German aircraft were almost entirely bombers, mainly the well-tried if slow Heinkel 111, the slim, pencil-like Dornier 17, and the fast and more recent Junkers 88, but including also about 400 Junkers 87s – the Stukas, or dive-bombers. These had established a legendary reputation on the battlefields of Poland and France, but their range was very short and they had yet to face powerful opposition.

On the British side, the situation was a great deal better than it had been a few weeks earlier. On June 4, following the heavy losses of Hurricanes in France, Fighter Command had been able to muster only 446 modern single-engined fighters – Spitfires and Hurricanes – with another 36 ready in the Aircraft Storage Units (ASUs) as replacements. But on August 11, on the eve of the main air battle, Fighter Command had 704 of these aircraft in the squadrons and 289 in the ASUs. Its fighting strength had been virtually doubled during those ten critical weeks since Dunkirk, thanks to the fruition of earlier Air Ministry plans and the tremendous efforts of the air-

2
A L

craft industry under the stimulus of the newly appointed Minister of Aircraft Production, Lord Beaverbrook.

Strengthening the shield

During those same ten weeks the British air defence system, built up against an enemy operating from Germany and possibly the Low Countries, had also been extended, thanks to schemes already worked out and in progress, to deal with forces operating from France and Norway. To the existing groups within Fighter Command – No. 11 Group, guarding the south-east, No. 12 Group, guarding the east and Midlands, and No. 13 Group, guarding the north-east up to the Forth – had been added another: No. 10 Group, guarding the south-west. The intermittent defences of the north-west, including Northern Ireland, had been thickened, as had those of Scotland.

This was not only a matter of providing more fighter aircraft and the pilots to fly them. It was also a matter of extending the main coastal radar chain, adding special radar stations to detect low-flying aircraft, extending Observer Corps posts for inland tracking over the south-western counties and western Wales, adapting more airfields for fighter operations, installing guns, searchlights, balloon barrages. All this was the concomitant, on the air defence side, of the gun-posts and the pill-boxes, the barbed wire and the dragon's teeth, that the inhabitant of southern England, enrolled perhaps in the newly formed Local Defence Volunteers and on watch at dawn and dusk for the arrival of German paratroops, saw springing up before his eyes along his familiar coasts and downlands.

The island's air defences had grown stronger and more extensive, but many grave deficiencies remained. Of the 120 fighter squadrons which the Director of Home Operations at the Air Ministry considered desirable in the new situation created by the German conquests, Dowding had less than 60 – and eight of these flew Blenheims or Defiants, no match for the Me-109s. Of the 4,000 anti-aircraft guns deemed necessary even before the German conquests, Anti-Aircraft Command still had less than 2,000. The early warning and inland tracking systems were still incomplete in the west and over parts of Scotland. There was a shortage of fighter pilots: new planes could be produced quicker than new skilled men to fly them. But whatever the deficiencies of the air defence system by day, they were as nothing compared with its alarming weaknesses by night, when ordinary fighters were useful only in the brightest moonlight, and when the men of the Observer Corps had to rely on ineffective acoustical detectors instead of their clear eyesight and a pair of binoculars.

Britain, however, had assets not yet mentioned. Among others, there was RAF Coastal Command, prepared both to carry out reconnaissance and to help in offensive operations; and there was RAF Bomber Command. Most of the latter's aircraft could operate safely only by night, and by night it was by no means certain that they could find and hit the more distant targets. The daylight bombers – about 100 Blenheims – were capable of much greater accuracy; but they needed fighter support, which could be supplied only at short range (assuming the Hurricanes or Spitfires could be spared). Against targets near at hand – airfields, ports, and shipping just across the Channel – the British bombing force was capable of playing a vital part. Against distant objectives, its effectiveness at that date was more problematical.

In sum, the opposing forces, disregarding reconnaissance aircraft and units still stationed in Germany, consisted of about 1,900 bombers assisted by 1,100 fighters on the German side, and of about 700 fighters assisted to a limited extent by 350 bombers on the British side. The Germans had the advantage not only of numbers but of the tactical initiative – of the fact that they could strike anywhere within their range – while the British defences could react only to the German moves.

The British air defence system, however, though incomplete, was the most technically advanced in the world. The early warning supplied by the radar stations (which in the south-east could pick up enemy formations before they crossed the French coast), the inland tracking by the Observer Corps, the control of the British fighters from the ground in the light of this information and the continuous reporting of the fighters' own position – all this, designed to obviate the need for wasteful standing patrols, meant that the British fighters could be used with economy and could take off with a good chance of making interception.

One other factor, too, helped the British: the Luftwaffe's offensive against Britain was largely an improvised one; and Luftwaffe C-in-C Göring, though an able man, was also a vainglorious boaster who in technical proficiency was not in the same class as the opposing commander. The single-minded Dowding, in charge of Fighter Command since its formation in 1936 – the man whose obduracy had preserved Britain's fighter resources against the clamour to squander them in France – knew his job. Göring, as much politician as airman, scarcely knew his; while theoretically controlling and co-ordinating the entire offensive, in practice he was incapable of more than occasional acts of intervention. On the next level of command, Kesselring, in charge of the main attacking force – Luftflotte II – was for all his successes in Poland and France a novice in the forthcoming type of operation; while Air Vice-Marshal Keith Park, commanding the main defending force – Group 11 – had earlier been Dowding's right-hand man at Headquarters, Fighter Command. Unlike their opposite numbers, the two principal British commanders had lived with their problem for years. Their skill, experience, and devotion, like those of their pilots, offset some of the British inferiority in numbers.

Operation Eagle

By August 10 the three Luftflotten stood ready to launch the major assault – Operation Eagle *('Adler')* – which would drive the RAF from the skies of southern Britain. Four days, in the opinion of the German Air Staff, would see the shattering of the fighter defences south of the line London-Gloucester, four weeks the elimination of the entire RAF. Allowing for the ten days' notice required by the German navy for minelaying and other final preparations before the actual D-Day, the date of the invasion could thus be set for mid-September.

August 11 was a very cloudy day, and the Germans confined their activity to bombing Portland and some east coast shipping. On the following day came what seemed to the British to be the beginning of the main attack: five or six major raids and many minor ones, involving several hundred aircraft, including escorted Ju-87s, struck at airfields and radar stations along the south coast and at shipping in the Thames Estuary. Of the six radar stations they attacked, the raiders damaged five but knocked out only one – that at Ventnor on the Isle of Wight. It could not be replaced until August 23 – a sharp blow. Among the airfields, they hit Lympne, a forward landing ground, and Manston and Hawkinge, two important fighter stations in Kent, but all were back in action within 24 hours. Fighters from No. 11 Group challenged all the major raids, and frustrated completely one aimed at Manston. In the course of the fighting the Germans lost 31 aircraft, the British 22.

According to the German records, the next day, August 13, was Eagle Day itself – the opening of the Eagle offensive proper. The attack went off at half-cock in the morning, when a message postponing operations till later in the day failed to get through to some of the German squadrons. In the afternoon the main assault developed with a two-pronged thrust, Luftflotte II attacking over Kent and the Thames Estuary, while Luftflotte III, challenged by No. 10 Group, attacked over Hampshire, Dorset, and Wiltshire. The raiders hit three airfields severely – Eastchurch, Detling, and Andover – but none of these belonged to Fighter Command; their attacks on fighter stations such as Rochford were beaten off.

In the whole day's operations – which witnessed 1,485 German sorties and ended with a successful night attack on a Spitfire factory at Castle Bromwich, near Birmingham – the Germans lost 45 aircraft, Fighter Command only 13 (with six of the British pilots saved). This was a poor sort of Eagle Day for the Germans, but they were nevertheless well satisfied with their progress. They calculated that between August 8 and 14, in addition to successful attacks on some 30 airfields and aircraft factories, they had destroyed more than 300 British fighters in combat. In fact, they had destroyed less than 100.

After lesser activity on August 14 – a matter of some 500 German sorties, directed mainly against railways near the coast and against RAF stations – the Luftwaffe on August 15 attempted the great blow with which it had hoped to open the battle some days earlier. In clear skies the Germans sent over during the day no less than seven major raids, using all three Luftflotten in a series of co-ordinated attacks on widely separated areas. The first clash came at about 1130 hours, when some 40 escorted Ju-87s of Luftflotte II struck at Lympne and Hawkinge airfields in Kent. Then, about 1230 hours some 65 He-111s escorted by 35 Me-110s of Luftflotte V, operating from Stavanger in Norway, headed in to the Northumberland coast in an attempt to bomb airfields in the north-east. These formations were barely retiring when at 1315 hours another force of Luftflotte V, consisting of about 50 unescorted Ju-88s operating from Aalborg in Denmark, approached the Yorkshire coast on a similar mission. Little more than an hour later at 1430 hours, and once more at 1500, Luftflotte II struck again, on the first occasion north of the Thames Estuary against Martlesham airfield and on the second against Hawkinge and Eastchurch

▷ Seen through German eyes: a British fighter pilot bales out of his stricken Hurricane; his parachute canopy is about to open (top)

Imperial War Museum

A seat in the sun—but both sides are at instant readiness for take-off. On RAF and Luftwaffe bases, the youth, the pipes, and the flying-kit were much the same. There is little to distinguish these pilots except the national markings on their aircraft

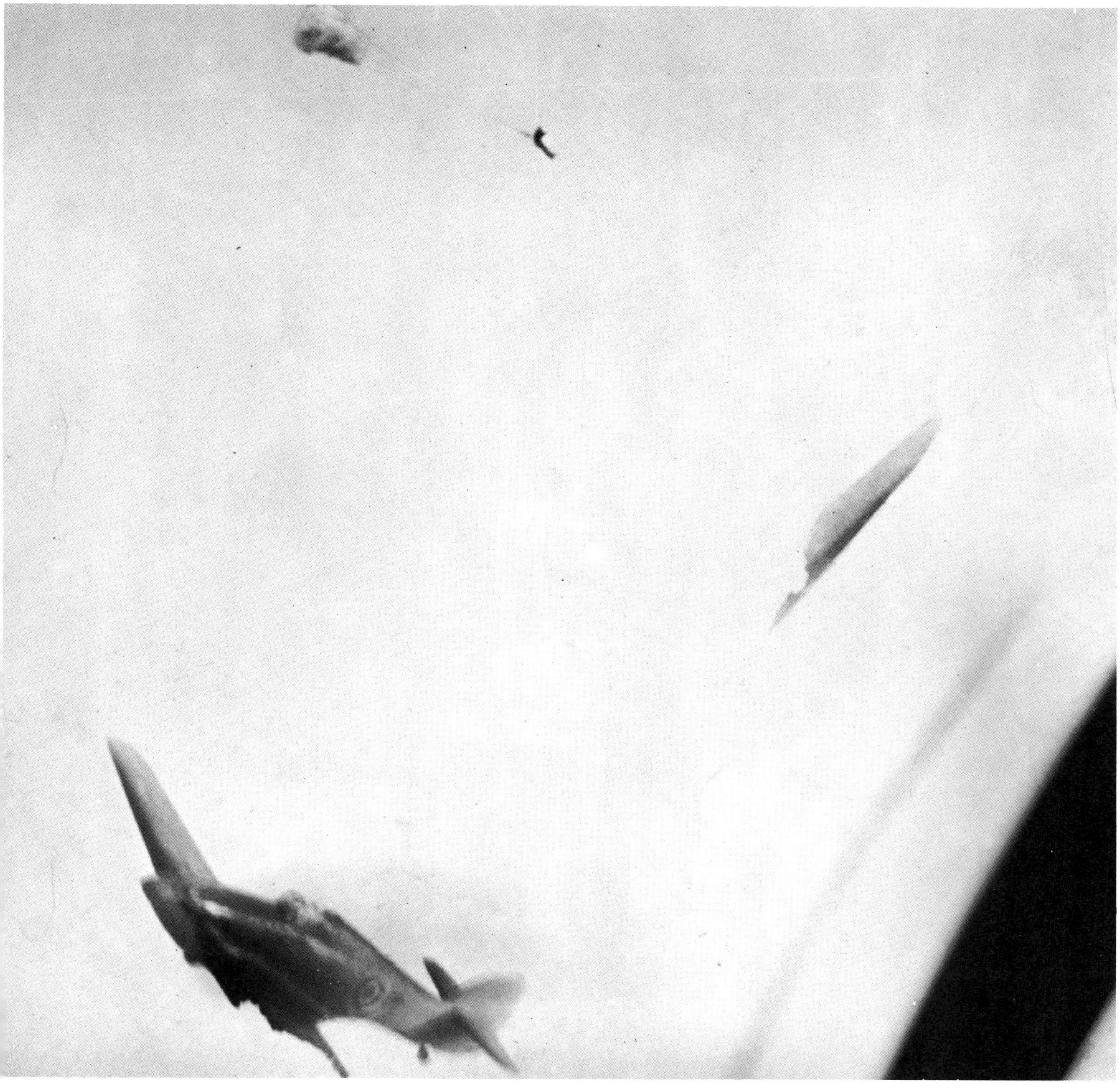

airfields and aircraft factories at Rochester.

Next it was the turn of Luftflotte III: at 1720 hours some 80 bombers, heavily escorted, came in to the south coast at Portland, bombed the harbour, and then attacked airfields at Middle Wallop and Worthy Down. Finally, at 1830 hours, 60 or 70 aircraft of Luftflotte II again penetrated over Kent, hitting West Malling airfields and the airfield and aircraft factories at Croydon. To round off the day's work, another 60 or 70 bombers made sporadic attacks during the hours of darkness.

All this German effort was fiercely challenged. Though the bombing had its successes, notably at Middle Wallop, Martlesham, and Driffield (Yorkshire) airfields and at Croydon, in no case did the British fighters allow the raiders to operate unmolested, and in many cases the primary objectives escaped unscathed. Especially significant was the fighting in the north-east, where No. 13 Group, involved for the first time in the battle, intercepted the formations from Norway well out to sea, and with the help of the anti-aircraft guns on Tyne and Tees destroyed eight He-111s and seven Me-110s, with no British losses. A little farther south, too, No. 12 Group and the local guns, tackling the formations from Denmark, brought down eight of the enemy with no loss on the British side. The Germans thus failed in their main hope – that Dowding, in his anxiety to protect the vital and heavily threatened south-east, would have left the north almost undefended. Instead, they discovered, to their cost, that their attacks across the North Sea were met before they reached the British coast, and that the Me-110s in a long-range escorting role were useless against Spitfires and Hurricanes. The lesson was sufficiently expensive to convince the Germans not to launch any further daylight attacks from this area.

The fighting on August 15 was the most extensive in the whole Battle of Britain. With 520 bomber and 1,270 fighter sorties, and attacks stretching from Northumberland to Dorset, the German effort was at its maximum. But so too was the German loss – 75 aircraft as against 34 British fighters. This did not prevent an effort of almost equal magnitude on the following day, when the Germans sent across some 1,700 sorties, attacked a number of airfields (with particular success at Tangmere), and lost 45 aircraft in the process. With Fighter Command losing 21, the balance remained in the British favour.

The Luftwaffe switches strategy

The four days of intensive attack calculated to clear the skies of southern England were now over, and the Germans took stock. In the opinion of their Intelligence, Fighter Command, if not exhausted, was down to its last 300 aircraft. This appreciation was very wide of the mark, for Dowding still had nearly twice that number of Hurricanes and Spitfires in the front line, in addition to another 120 or so Blenheims, Defiants, and Gladiators. However, it encouraged the Germans to believe that another day or two of major effort might see the end of British opposition. On August 18 the Luftwaffe accordingly struck again in full force, chiefly against airfields in Kent, Surrey, and Sussex; but in doing so they lost 71 aircraft while the British lost no more than 27. Clearly Fighter Command was still unsubdued. After a few days of minor activity owing to bad weather, the Germans therefore made their first great change of plan.

A Ju-87: the legendary Stuka, the terror of Europe – now, matched at last by comparable fighter opposition, now the hunted and not the hunter ◁

Up till then, the main German objectives had been airfields fairly near to the coast; after August 12 they had given up intensive attacks on radar stations – fortunately for Fighter Command – because they found them difficult to destroy. The airfields and other coastal targets they had continued to attack, partly to deny the airfields to the British during the proposed invasion period, but still more to force Fighter Command to join battle in their defence. The German theory was that by such attacks they might, without severe losses to themselves, inflict heavy losses on the RAF – for raids on coastal targets or those not far inland did not involve prolonged exposure to the British defences – while at the same time the Me-109s would be free from worries on the score of endurance and accordingly able to give maximum protection to the German bombers. Such was the German strategy when the battle began. It had not disposed of Fighter Command, so it was now changed in favour of attacks farther inland.

The first phase of the battle was thus over. So far, Fighter Command had more than held its own: 363 German aircraft had been destroyed between August 8 and 18, as against 181 British fighters lost in the air and another 30 on the ground. The period had also seen what proved to be the last daylight attack by Luftflotte V, and the last attempt by Luftflotte II to make regular use of its Ju-87s – both notable successes for the British defences.

At the same time, however, there was one aspect of the struggle which gave Dowding and the Air Ministry acute anxiety. During the same ten days, when Fighter Command had lost 211 Spitfires and Hurricanes, the number of replacements forthcoming from the aircraft industry had fallen short of this total by at least 40. In the same period, Fighter Command had lost 154 experienced fighter pilots: but the output of the training schools had been only 63 – and those less skilled than the men they replaced. Fighter Command, while inflicting nearly twice as many casualties as it was suffering, was thus in fact being weakened – though not, as yet, at anything like the speed desired by the enemy.

It was to increase the rate of destruction of the British fighter force – which unchanged would have left Fighter Command still in existence in mid-September – that the Germans now switched to targets farther inland. They reckoned that by making their prime objective the fighter airfields, and in particular the sector airfields of No. 11 Group from which the British fighters in the south-east were controlled, they would not only strike at the heart of the British defences, but would also compel Fighter Command to meet their challenge with all its remaining forces. In the resulting air battles, they hoped to achieve a rate of attrition that would knock out Fighter Command within their scheduled time: though they also knew that in penetrating farther inland they were likely to suffer greater losses themselves. To guard against this, and to destroy as many Hurricanes and Spitfires as possible, they decided to send over a still higher proportion of fighters with their bombers.

The sector stations of No. 11 Group stood in a ring guarding London. To the south-west, in a forward position near Chichester, lay Tangmere. Nearer the capital and south of it there were Kenley in Surrey and Biggin Hill in Kent, both on the North Downs. Close to London in the east lay Hornchurch, near the factories of Dagenham; and round to the north-east was North Weald, in metropolitan Essex. Farther out there was Debden, near Saffron Walden. The ring was completed to the west by Northolt, on the road to Uxbridge, where No. 11 Group itself had its headquarters – which in turn was only a few minutes' drive from that of Fighter Command at Stanmore. All the sector stations normally controlled three fighter squadrons, based either on the sector station itself or on satellite airfields.

Strikes at the source

The Germans had already severely damaged two of the sector stations – Kenley and Biggin Hill – on August 18. Now, on August 24, they struck hard at North Weald and Hornchurch. On August 26 they attempted to bomb Biggin Hill, Kenley, North Weald, and Hornchurch, were beaten off, but got through to Debden. On August 30 they hit Biggin Hill twice, doing great damage and killing 39 persons. The following day – the most expensive of the whole battle for Fighter Command, with 39 aircraft lost – they wrought great damage at Debden, Biggin Hill, and Hornchurch.

On September 1 Biggin Hill suffered its sixth raid in three days, only to be bombed again less than 24 hours later; and on September 3 the attack once more fell on North Weald. On the 5th the main raids again headed towards Biggin Hill and North Weald, only to be repelled, while on the 4th and 6th the attacks extended also to the Vickers and Hawker factories near Weybridge. The Hawker factory, which produced more than half the total output of Hurricanes, was a particularly vital target. Its selection showed that the Germans, perplexed by the continued resilience of Fighter Command, were also trying to cut off the British fighter supply at its source.

Between August 24 and September 6 the Germans made no less than 33 major raids, of which more than two-thirds were mainly against the sector and other stations of Fighter Command. This assault imposed on the command a still greater strain than the preceding one, against targets in the coastal belt. The fighting was more difficult for the British pilots, in that the proportion of German fighters to bombers became so high, and sections of the fighter escort so close; and over the whole fortnight a daily average of something like 1,000 German aircraft, of which 250 to 400 were bombers, operated over England. Twice, on August 30 and 31, the number of intruders was nearer 1,500.

In the course of the combats and the ensuing night operations the British defences destroyed 380 German aircraft, as against a Fighter Command loss of 286: but many other British fighters were seriously damaged, and no less than 103 fighter pilots were killed and 128 wounded out of a fighting strength of not much more than 1,000. In addition six of the seven sector stations of No. 11 Group sustained heavy damage: and though none was yet out of action, Biggin Hill could control only one squadron instead of its normal three.

So Fighter Command was being steadily worn down. The wastage, both of fighters

Keystone

◁ A Dornier in action: a stick of bombs streams from its bomb-bay

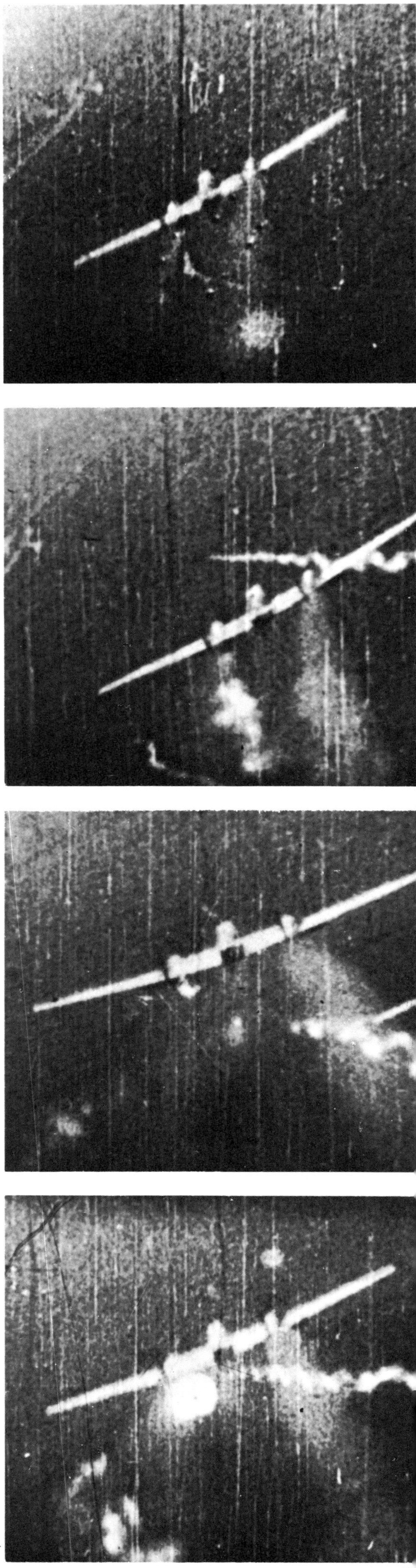

▷ Target and tracer-fire: camera-gun film from a British fighter records the end of a Me-110 fighter. The 110, at full throttle, streams smoke trails from its twin engines (top); tracer fire misses the starboard wing, then the first hit glows on the port engine which explodes (bottom)

Imperial War Museum

Imperial War Museum

◁ Two Dorniers fly over fires started by the first wave

Ullstein

▽ The Luftwaffe strikes at Fighter Command: on an RAF fighter base, a Spitfire in its bomb pen survives a low-level strafing run

The nose-gunner of an He 111 engages a Spitfire at close range ▷

and of pilots, was far exceeding the output. In one sense the command was winning the battle; in another – if the Germans could maintain the pressure long enough – it was losing it.

The Germans, however, were not intending to fight a prolonged battle. They, too, could not afford heavy losses indefinitely – as may be seen from their decision after August 18 to hold back most of the vulnerable Ju-87s for the actual invasion, from their caution in employing Me-110s, and from their increasingly closer and more numerous fighter escort. Their attack, as we have seen, was meant to be a brief one, geared to Operation Sea Lion; and for Sea Lion they were now running short of time. This Hitler recognised at the end of August when he agreed that D-Day, provisionally set for September 15, should be postponed to September 21. For this date to be kept the German navy had to receive the executive order by September 11: and Göring's Luftwaffe had thus to administer the *coup de grâce* to the British fighter forces within the next few days. The attack on sector stations and other inland targets might be doing well, but in itself it was not proving decisive. On September 7 the Germans accordingly switched to another target, farther inland than most of the sector stations and, as they believed, still more vital – London.

Target London

The German decision to attack London was inspired by three beliefs. In the first place, operations against London could be expected to bring about still greater air battles and so – the Germans hoped – still higher wastage in Fighter Command. It was for this reason that Kesselring, though not Sperrle, strongly supported the change of plan. Second, an assault on the capital, if reinforced by attacks during the night against other main cities as well, might paralyse the British machinery of government in the final period before the invasion, or even terrorise the British people into submission. Third, an attack on the British capital would be, as the Germans saw it, an act of retribution. On the night of August 24/25, during the course of the Luftwaffe's usual scattered night operations, some badly aimed or jettisoned bombs had fallen on central London – the first of the war. Churchill and the War Cabinet had immediately ordered retaliation against Berlin; and during the following nights RAF bombers had found and hit the German capital – an occurrence which Göring had assured Hitler could never happen. The enraged Führer promptly vowed revenge and with Göring's eager concurrence unleashed the Luftwaffe against its supreme target.

On the night of September 4 German bombers laid flares over London; on the following two nights small numbers of aircraft dropped bombs on Rotherhithe and other places near the docks. These were the warming-up operations.

In the late afternoon of September 7 some 300 German bombers escorted by 600 fighters crossed the Kent and Sussex coasts or penetrated the Thames Estuary in a series of huge waves. A few bombed the oil installations at Thameshaven, still burning from earlier attacks; the rest, instead of bombing the sector stations, which the British fighters were alert to guard, held on until they reached the outskirts of the capital itself. Though nearly all the British squadrons ordered up eventually made contact, most of the raiders were able to put down their high explosive and incendiaries before they were molested. The attacks fell in full force on London's dockland east of the City. Huge fires sprang up among the dockside warehouses, especially at Silvertown, and these the Germans used as beacons to light their way to further attacks during the ensuing hours of darkness. That night, when 250 German bombers ranged over the capital in a prolonged assault from dusk to dawn, millions of Londoners had their first experience of what they imagined was Blitzkrieg, and what they were soon to call 'The Blitz'.

The climax of the battle was now approaching. Göring took personal charge of operations, and the bombers from Norway and Denmark joined Kesselring's forces for what were meant to be the final and deciding blows. Meanwhile, however, the German invasion preparations had not gone unobserved: since August 31 Spitfires and Hudsons of RAF Coastal Command had been returning with an impressive photographic record of the growing number of barges and other invasion craft in the ports and estuaries across the Channel. On August 31 in Ostend, for instance, there were 18 barges; by September 6 there were 205.

As the concentrations increased, Bomber Command began to attack them, using at first its daylight Blenheims. By September 6 the enemy preparations were sufficiently obvious for the British authorities to order Invasion Alert 2: 'Attack probable within three days.' The following day, when the German bombers turned against London, it seemed that the hour of supreme trial might be at hand. Alert 2 then gave place

Hawker Hurricane Mk I
Span: 40 ft. *Length:* 31 ft 5 in. *Gross weight:* 6,447 lb. *Engine:* 1,030 hp Rolls Royce Merlin II. *Armament:* 8 x ·303 machine-guns. *Speed:* 324 mph at 17,500 ft. *Ceiling:* 34,200 ft.
The Hurricane was developed in 1934 from the Hawker Fury and is best known for its part in the Battle of Britain when it shot down more enemy aircraft than all other air and ground defences combined. The aircraft illustrated was flown by the British ace Squadron Leader Stanford Tuck, whose machine bore 25 victory swastikas beneath the cockpit

to Alert 1: 'Invasion imminent, and probable within twelve hours.'

That night, as the German bombs began to crash down on London, the code-word 'Cromwell' went out to the Southern and Eastern Commands of Britain's Home Forces, bringing them to immediate readiness. In the prevailing excitement a few commanders of Home Guard units rang church bells to call out their men, so spreading the impression that German paratroops had actually landed. Meanwhile, forces of the Royal Navy waited at immediate notice, and the Hampdens of Bomber Command—'heavy' bombers of the time—joined Blenheims, Hudsons, and Battles in intensified attacks on French and Belgian ports.

It was with the British fully alert to what the next few hours or days might bring that the Luftwaffe now strove to repeat the hammer blows of September 7. On September 8 bad weather limited their daylight activity; but at night Luftflotte III was able to send 200 bombers against London in a lengthy procession lasting more than nine hours. The zone of attack now extended from dockland to the capital as a whole, with special attention to railways and power stations, and by the morning every railway line running south of London was for a brief time unserviceable.

On the next day, September 9, clouds again restricted activity in the morning, only for a further assault to develop in the late afternoon. More than 200 bombers with full escort headed for London; but such was the promptness and vigour of the interception that less than half reached even the outskirts of the capital, and the bombs fell widely over the south-eastern counties. No. 12 Group's Duxford wing of four squadrons, led by the legless pilot Squadron Leader Douglas Bader, enjoyed a notable success. All told, the British pilots shot down 28 German aircraft for the loss of 19 of their own.

Very different once more was the story at night. Again nearly 200 aircraft bombed the capital in attacks lasting over eight hours; this time some 400 Londoners were killed and 1,400 injured—all with negligible loss to the Luftwaffe.

Hitler again shifts D-Day

September 10 was a day of cloud, rain, and light German activity—though at night there was the usual raid on London, while other German bombers attacked South Wales and Merseyside. The next afternoon, while the Germans tried to jam some of the British radar stations, Luftflotte III attacked Southampton, and Luftflotte II sent three big raids against London. Many of the bombers got through to the City and the docks; and the balance of losses—25 German ones, against 29 by Fighter Command—for once tilted against the British. On their return, some German pilots reported that British fighter opposition was diminishing. But though the Luftwaffe still hoped to complete its task, the date was now September 11, and Fighter Command was still in existence. With the German navy requiring ten days' notice before D-Day, an invasion on September 21 thus became impossible. Accordingly Hitler now gave the Luftwaffe three more days' grace, till September 14, in the hope that a decision could then be taken to invade on September 24.

As it happened, September 12 and 13 were days of poor visibility, unsuitable for major attacks. Even the nightly efforts against London—which was now enjoying the heartening noise of greatly reinforced gun defences—were on a reduced scale. When September 14 came, Hitler could only postpone the decision for a further three days, till September 17. This set the provisional D-Day for September 27—about the last date on which the tides would be favourable until October 8. The Führer's order was contrary to the advice of his naval chiefs, who urged indefinite postponement—a tactful term for abandonment. Their worries had been sharply increased by the mounting intensity of the RAF's attacks on the invasion barges, large numbers of which had been destroyed the previous evening.

The Luftwaffe now strove to clinch the issue in the short time still at its disposal. Despite unfavourable weather, on the afternoon of September 14 several raids struck at London. Some of the German pilots reported ineffective opposition, and Fighter Command lost as many aircraft as the enemy. The night proved fine, but on this occasion no more than 50 German bombers droned their way towards London. The Luftwaffe was husbanding its efforts for the morrow.

Sunday September 15 was a day of mingled cloud and sunshine. By 11 am the British radar detected mass formations building up over the Pas-de-Calais region. Half an hour later the raiders, stepped up from 15,000 to 26,000 feet, were crossing the coast in waves bent for London. Park's fighters met them before Canterbury, and in successive groups—two, three, then four squadrons—challenged them all the way to the capital, over which No. 12 Group's Duxford wing, now five squadrons strong, joined the conflict. In the face of such opposition, the raiders dropped their bombs

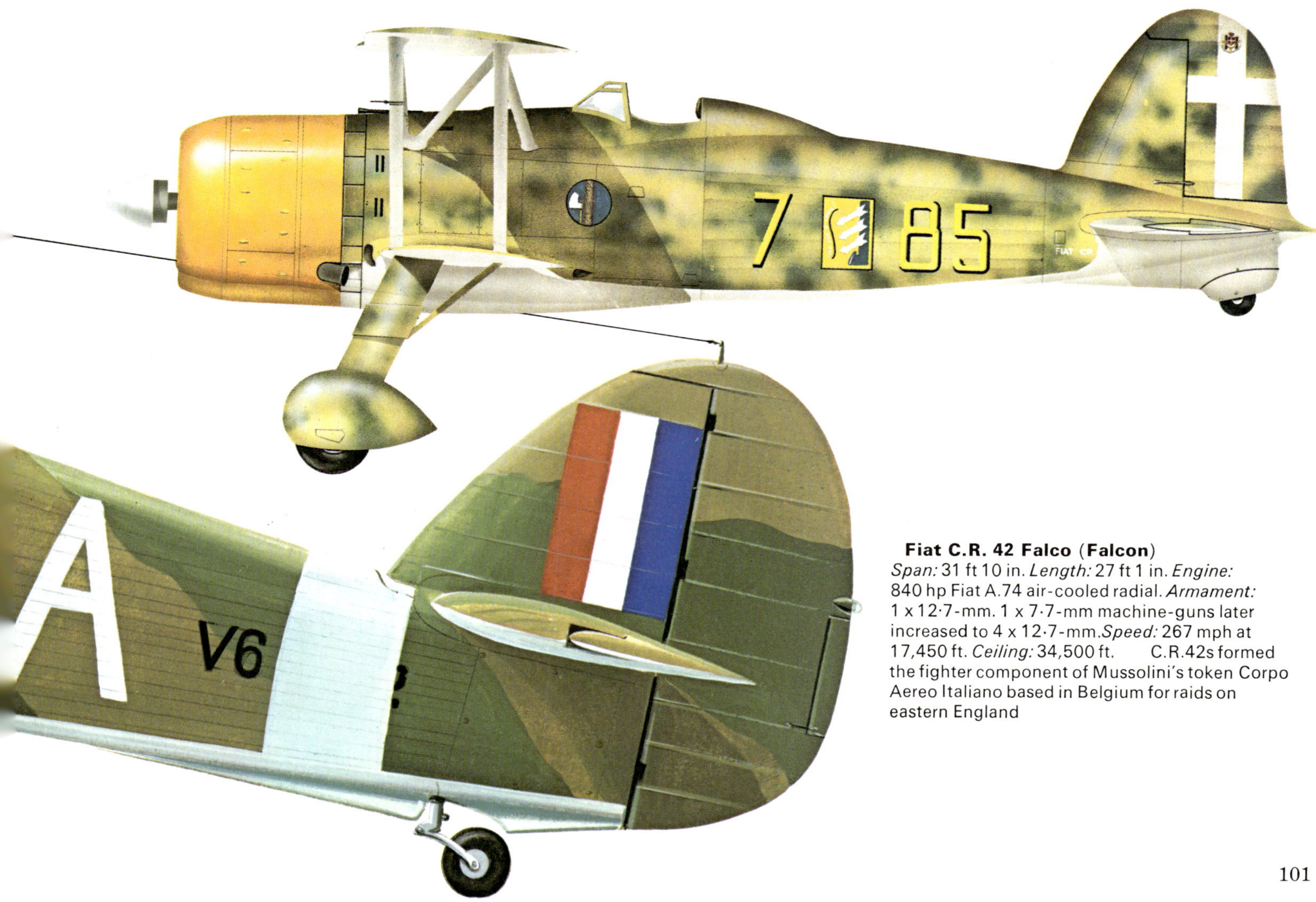

Fiat C.R. 42 Falco (Falcon)
Span: 31 ft 10 in. *Length:* 27 ft 1 in. *Engine:* 840 hp Fiat A.74 air-cooled radial. *Armament:* 1 x 12·7-mm. 1 x 7·7-mm machine-guns later increased to 4 x 12·7-mm. *Speed:* 267 mph at 17,450 ft. *Ceiling:* 34,500 ft. C.R.42s formed the fighter component of Mussolini's token Corpo Aereo Italiano based in Belgium for raids on eastern England

LAND AND SEA SUPPORT

September 1940 : Ack-ack girls practise air raid drill. Women from the Auxiliary Territorial Service worked in anti-aircraft units and performed non-combatant duties, like plotting and ranging enemy aircraft, releasing men for active service

RAF Air-Sea Rescue Launch
The intensity of air operations over the Channel during the early stages of the Battle of Britain focused attention on the need for fast rescue launches co-operating with sea-planes to bring airmen bailing out over the sea back into the battle. The Germans used similar techniques from their side of the Channel

Heinkel He 59
Span: 77 ft 9 in. *Length:* 57 ft 1 in. *Engine:* 2 x 660 hp BMW VI 6·0 ZU. *Armament:* 3 x 7·9-mm machine-guns. *Speed:* 137 mph at sea level. *Range:* 1,087 miles. *Bomb load:* 2,200 lb or one torpedo. Designed as a torpedo bomber, the so-called 'Red Cross' aircraft of the German air-sea rescue service were attacked on sight by the RAF whilst shadowing British convoys

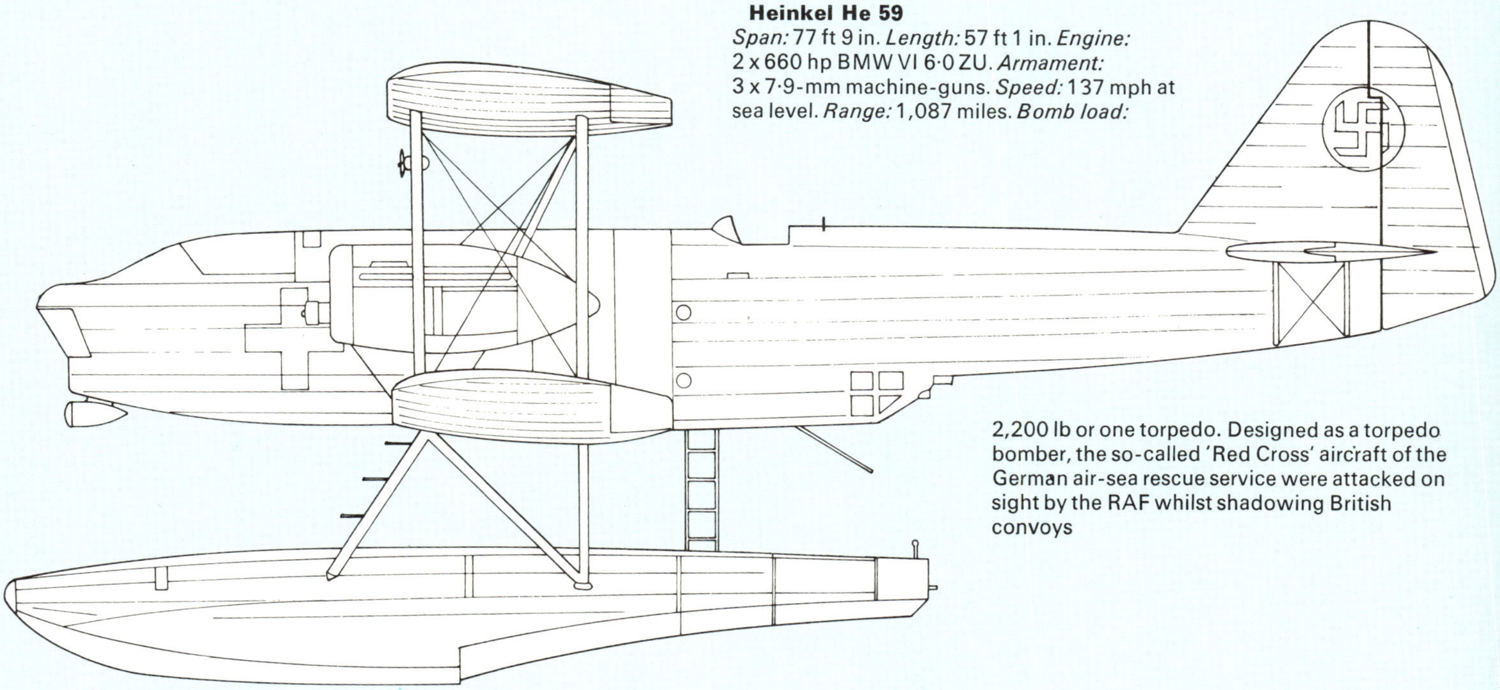

Associated Press

3·7-inch Anti-Aircraft Gun
Crew: 9/11. *Max. effective altitude:* 32,000 ·

Fiat BR 20
Gross weight: 22,266 lb. *Span:* 70 ft 9 in. *Length:* 52 ft 9 in. *Engine:* 2 x 1,000 hp Fiat A80 RC41. *Armament:* 2 x 7·7-mm ; 1 x 12·7-mm machine-guns. *Speed:* 267 mph at 13,120 ft. *Ceiling:* 24,935 ft. *Range:* 1,700 miles. *Bomb load:* 3,500 lb. Based at Melsbroek airfield in Belgium in the autumn of 1940, these Italian bombers were badly mauled in their only daylight raid on eastern England

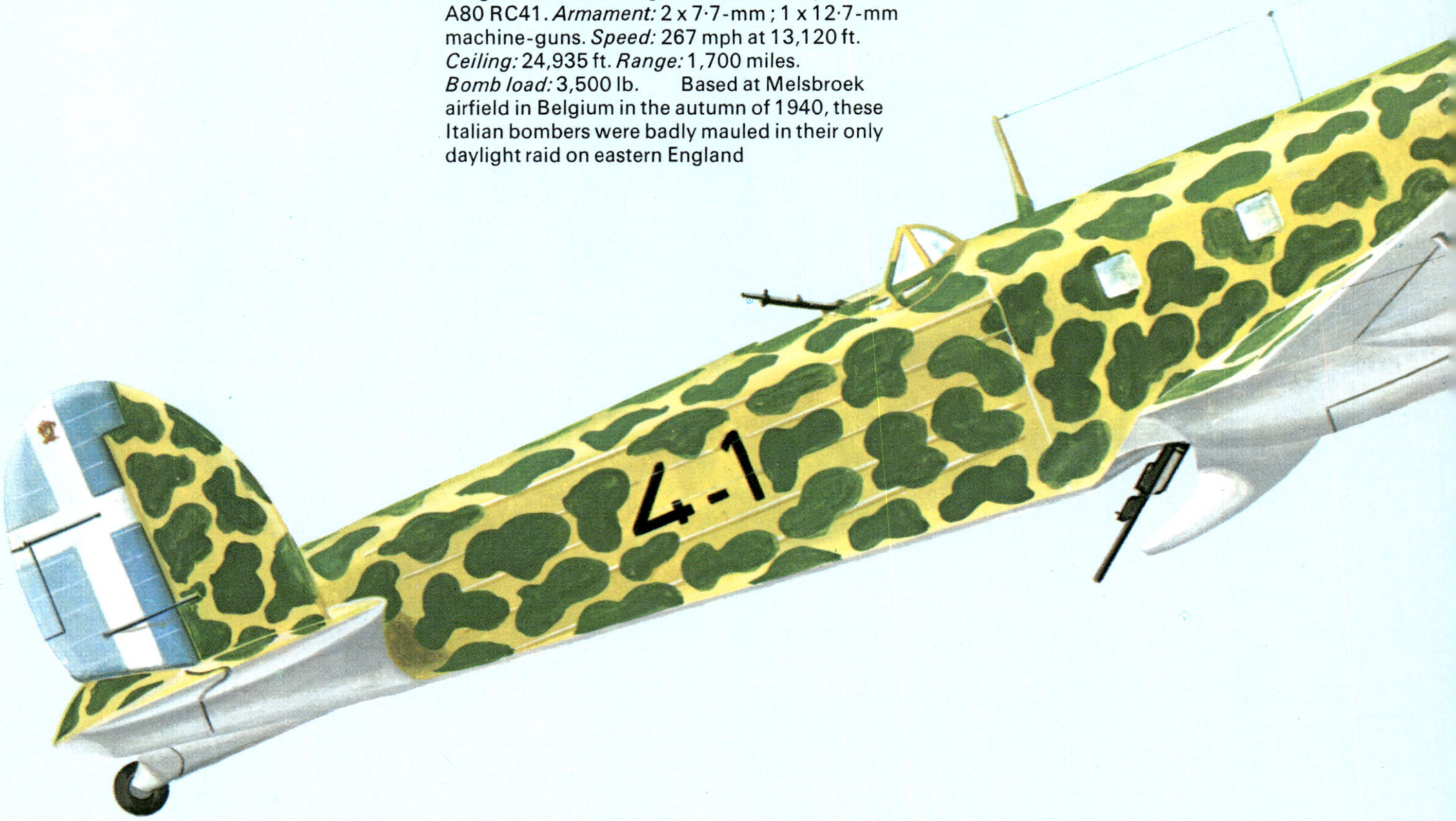

Focke-Wulf Fw 200 'Condor'
Gross weight: 50,045 lb. *Span:* 107 ft. 9½ in. *Length:* 76 ft 11½ in. *Engine:* 4 x 1,200 hp BMW Bramo 323 R-2. *Armament:* 2 x 7·9-mm ; 3 x 13-mm ; 1 x 20-mm machine-guns. *Crew:* 7. *Speed:* 224 mph at 15,750 ft. *Ceiling:* 19,000 ft. *Range:* 2,210 miles. *Bomb load:* 4,620 lb. The Fw 200 'Condor' was designed as a trans-Atlantic airliner for Lufthansa, but during the Battle of Britain, numbers of militarised Condors were encountered in the reconnaissance and anti-shipping role in the Western Approaches and around the British coast

Dornier Do 215 B-1
Gross weight: 19,600 lb. *Span:* 59 ft ⅔ in. *Length:* 51 ft 10 in. *Engine:* 2 x 1,100 hp DB 601A. *Armament:* 6 x 7·92-mm machine-guns. *Crew:* 4. *Speed:* 292 mph at 16,400 ft. *Ceiling:* 31,170 ft. *Range:* 965 miles. *Bomb load:* 2,200 lb. A reconnaissance bomber which carried three cameras as well as twenty 110-lb. bombs

Heinkel He 115K
Gross weight: 20,020 lb. *Span:* 75 ft 10 in. *Length:* 57 ft. *Engine:* 2 x 850 hp BMW. *Armament:* 4 x 7·92-mm machine-guns. *Crew:* 3/4. *Speed:* 217 mph. *Ceiling:* 21,500 ft. *Range:* 1,300 miles. *Bomb load:* 1,760 lb bombs or torpedo. Piloted by mixed Navy and Luftwaffe crews, this adaptable float plane was used for a wide variety of roles

inaccurately or jettisoned them, mainly over south London.

Two hours later a further mass attack developed. Again British radar picked it up well in advance: and again – since they had had time to refuel and rearm – Park's fighters challenged the intruders all the way to, and over, the capital. Once more the Germans jettisoned their bombs or aimed them badly, this time mainly over east London, and, as before, further British formations harassed the raiders on their way back. Meanwhile a smaller German force attacked Portland. Later in the day other raiders – some 20 Me-110s carrying bombs – tried to bomb the Supermarine aircraft works near Southampton, only to meet spirited and effective opposition from local guns. When darkness fell, 180 German bombers continued the damaging but basically ineffectual night assault on London, while others attacked Bristol, Cardiff, Liverpool, and Manchester.

So closed a day on which Göring had hoped to give the death-blow to Fighter Command. In all, the Germans had sent over about 230 bombers and 700 fighters in the daylight raids. Their bombing had been scattered and ineffective, and they had lost the greatest number of aircraft in a single day since August 15 – no less than 60. Fighter Command had lost 26, from which the pilots of 13 had been saved.

This further German defeat on September 15 – combined with the attacks of British bombers against barge concentrations – settled the issue. When September 17 came, Hitler had no alternative but to postpone Sea Lion indefinitely. A few days later, he agreed to the dispersal of the invasion craft in order to avoid attack from the air. The invasion threat was over.

Göring orders more raids

Göring, however, was not yet prepared to admit failure: he still clung to the belief that given a short spell of good weather the Luftwaffe could crush Fighter Command and thereafter compel Britain to submit, even without invasion. Between September 17 and the end of the month his forces strove to attack London by day, whenever weather permitted, in addition to aircraft factories elsewhere. On only three days – September 18, 27, and 30 – was he able to mount a major assault on the capital, and on each occasion British fighters prevented intensive bombing and took a heavy toll of the raiders. The loss of 120 German aircraft during these three days (as against 60 by Fighter Command) was not one which afforded Göring much encouragement to continue.

Had the Luftwaffe's corpulent chief known them, he would not have derived any greater encouragement from the casualty figures during the whole three weeks his air force had been attacking London. Between September 7 and 30 Fighter Command had lost 242 aircraft, the Luftwaffe 433. Equally important, though Dowding was still gravely worried by the continuing loss of pilots (on September 7 his squadrons had only 16 each instead of their proper 26), his anxieties about aircraft were diminishing. From the time the Germans abandoned their attack on sector airfields in favour of an assault on London, the wastage of Hurricanes and Spitfires had been more than counterbalanced by the output of the factories.

The prize of victory had thus eluded Göring's grasp. On October 12 Hitler recognised this by formally postponing Sea Lion until the spring of 1941. In fact, this meant abandonment: Hitler's mind was now fixed on Russia. Until the German war machine could roll east, however, there was everything to be said, from the German point of view, for maintaining pressure on Britain, so long as it could be done inexpensively. During October the Luftwaffe, assisted by a few Italian aircraft, kept Fighter Command at stretch in daylight by sending over fighter and fighter-bombers, which did little damage but were difficult to intercept. At night the German bombers, operating with virtual impunity, continued to drop their loads on London.

The story of the 'Night Blitz' is one of civilian suffering and heroism, of widespread yet indecisive damage – and of slowly increasing success by the British defences. In the battle of wits against the intruders, perhaps the most vital developments were the discovery (and distortion) of the German navigational beams, the provision of dummy airfields and decoy fires, and the advances in radar which made possible accurate tracking overland.

Radar advances resulted in gun-laying radar that gave accurate readings of heights, and so permitted the engagement of the target 'unseen', and in ground-controlled interception (GCI) radar stations which brought night fighters close enough to the enemy for the fighters to use their own airborne radar (A1) for the final location and pursuit. It was only towards the end of the Blitz, however, that the GCI/A1 combination emerged as a real threat to the attackers, who began to lose three or four aircraft in every 100 sorties, instead of merely one.

Meanwhile, the Luftwaffe was able to lay waste the centres of a score or more of British cities. After the early raids in August, the weight of attack by night fell for a time almost entirely on London. Between September 7 and November 13 there was only one night on which London escaped bombing, and the number of German aircraft over the capital each night averaged 163. With the final postponement of Sea Lion, the attack then extended also to longer-term, strategic objectives – the industrial towns, and later mainly the ports, so linking up with the blockading actions of the German submarines.

On November 14 the devastation of Coventry marked the change of policy; thereafter Southampton, Birmingham, Liverpool, Bristol, Plymouth, Portsmouth, Cardiff, Swansea, Belfast, Glasgow, and many other towns felt the full fury of the Blitz. In the course of it all, until Luftflotte II moved east in May 1941 and the attacks died away, the Germans killed about 40,000 British civilians and injured another 46,000, and damaged more than 1,000,000 British homes, at a cost to themselves of some 600 aircraft. On the economic side, they seriously impeded British aircraft production for some months, but in other directions the damage they did was too diffuse to be significant.

Hitler's first setback

The 'Blitz' ceased not because of the increased success of the British defences, but because most of the German aircraft were needed elsewhere. Had Russia collapsed within the eight weeks of the German – and the British – estimate, they would doubtless have returned quickly enough, to clear the way for invasion or to attempt to pulverise Britain into submission. As it was, Russia held, and though the British people were subjected to further bombardments, they were not again called upon to face a serious threat of invasion.

Though the Night Blitz was inconclusive, the daylight Battle of Britain was thus one of the turning points of the war: it was the air fighting of August and September 1940, together with the existence of the Royal Navy and the English Channel, which first halted Hitler's career of conquest. The 1,000 or so pilots of Fighter Command who bore the brunt of that fighting – including the 400 or more who lost their lives – saved more than Britain by their exertions. By earning Britain a great breathing space in which the further progress of events was to bring her the mighty alliance of Russia and the United States, they made possible the final victory and the liberation of Europe from the Nazi terror.

1940

August 1: Hitler decrees the Battle of Britain with the command: 'The German air force is to overcome the British air force with all means at its disposal, and as soon as possible.'
August 13: 'Eagle Day': the Luftwaffe launches its air offensive against Britain, with 1,485 sorties. The Germans lose 45 aircraft, the RAF 13.
August 15: In the most intense attack of the Battle of Britain, the Luftwaffe sends a total of 1,790 sorties over England. They lose 75 aircraft, while Britain loses 34.
August 17: The Germans establish an 'operational area' around Britain; in it, all ships are to be sunk without warning.
August 25: The RAF conducts its first raid on Berlin.
September 3: Britain cedes to the USA bases in the West Indies and elsewhere in exchange for 50 destroyers.
September 7: Some 300 German bombers, escorted by 600 fighters, penetrate the Thames Estuary and bomb London's dockland.
September 13: *Italy invades Egypt.*
September 15: The RAF claims to have shot down 183 German aircraft during daylight Luftwaffe raids on Britain – a figure subsequently found to have been greatly exaggerated.
September 17: Hitler postpones Operation Sea Lion 'until further notice'.
September 23/25: *British and Free French forces attempt to take Dakar.*
October 12: Operation Sea Lion is postponed until 1941.

A formation of the much-vaunted Me-110s; they had long range but rather poor manoeuvrability, and thus they suffered heavy losses in the battle ▷

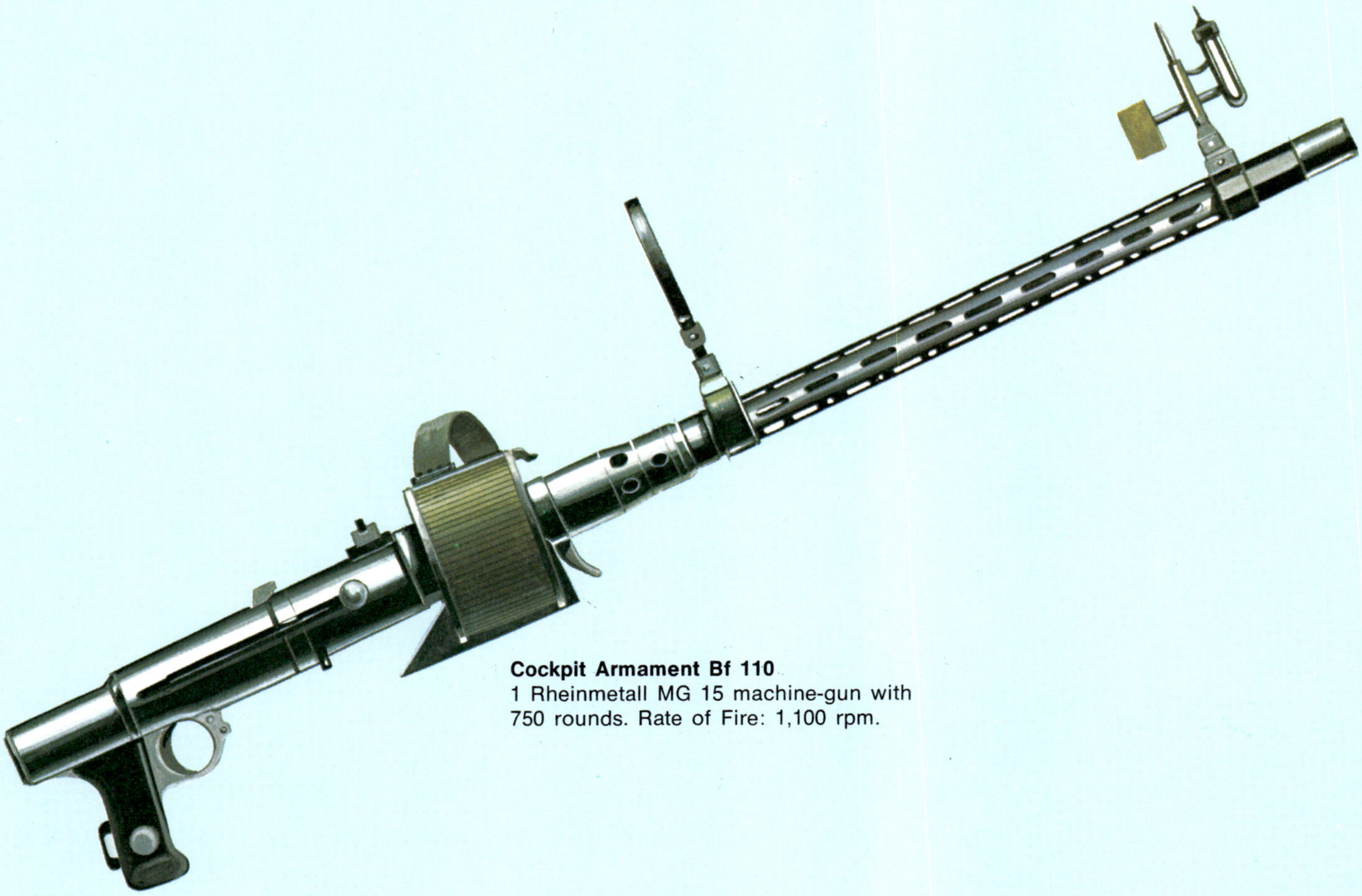

Cockpit Armament Bf 110
1 Rheinmetall MG 15 machine-gun with 750 rounds. Rate of Fire: 1,100 rpm.

Nose Armament Bf 110
4 x 7·92 MG 17 machine-guns with 1,000 rounds per gun

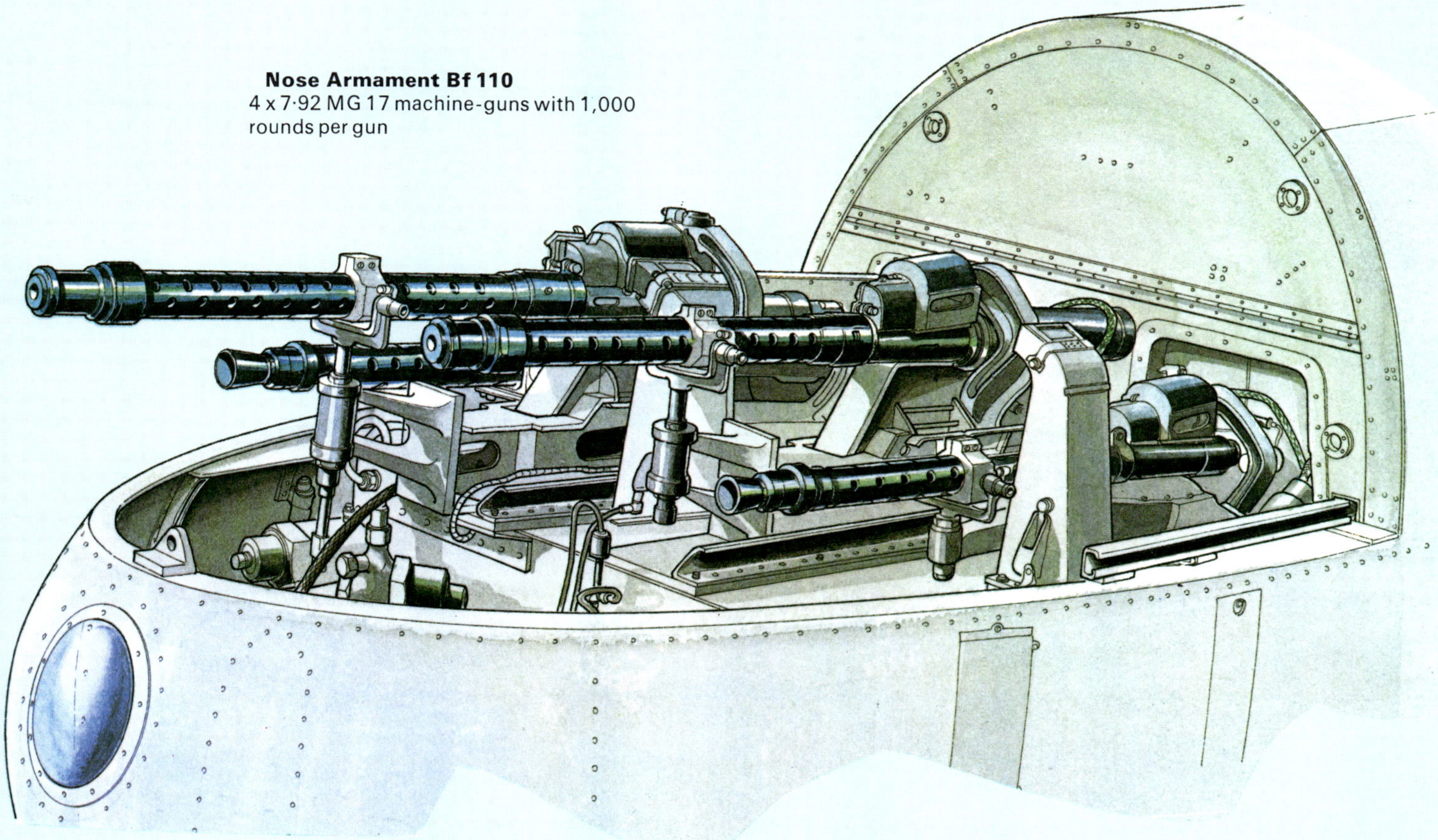

MESSERSCHMITT Bf 110

Span: 53 ft $4\frac{3}{4}$ in. *Length:* 39 ft $8\frac{1}{2}$ in. *Armament:* 4 x 7·9-mm machine-guns; 2 x 20-mm MG FF cannon. *Engine:* 2 x 1,150 hp Daimler-Benz DB 601A. *Crew:* 2. *Speed:* 349 mph. *Range:* 530 miles. The concept of the long-range super-fighter, heavily armed and able to smash through enemy fighter defence, was a major part of Göring's plan of attack. Unfortunately for the Luftwaffe the chosen instrument proved a complete failure. The big Messerschmitt packed a fearsome punch in its nose batteries of cannon and machine-guns but was too sluggish and unwieldly to take on RAF opposition. Indeed their very presence became a major defensive liability for the hard-pressed Bf 109E pilots

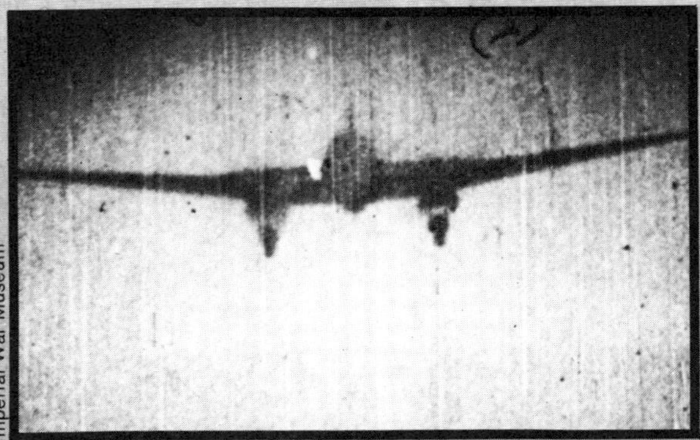

Imperial War Museum

Imperial War Museum

Squadron Leader 'Sailor' Malan, the ex-merchant seaman who became the third highest scoring RAF ace with thirty-five enemy aircraft shot down. The RAF's top scorers were M T St John Pattle with forty-one kills, and Johnny Johnson with thirty eight.

Imperial War Museum

Squadron Leader Stanford Tuck. Between May 1940 and January 1942, he shot down twenty-nine German aircraft making him the eighth highest RAF scorer for the war. In 1942 he was shot down over France and captured.

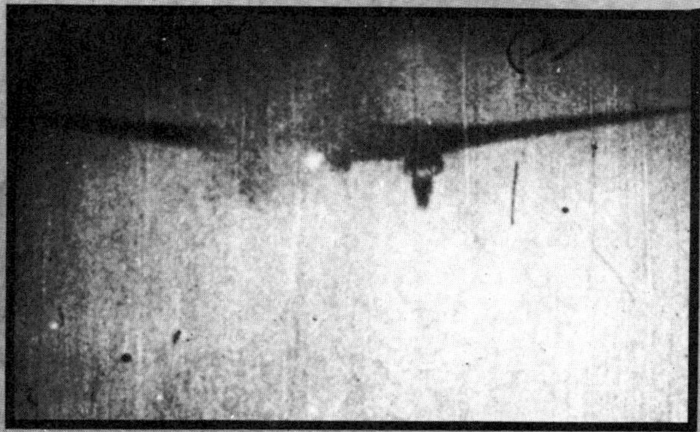

Left: A German Heinkel being shot down. *Main picture:* A formation of Spitfires in flight

THE ACES

Major Adolf Galland, top German scorer in the Battle of Britain. A captain in the Condor Legion fighting for Franco, Galland rose to be chief of the Luftwaffe fighter arm, but ended the war flying combat missions with the Me 262 jet-fighter. Although behind a desk for three years, he shot down 103 aircraft on the Western Front and was the Luftwaffe's fourth highest scorer in that theatre.

Imperial War Museum

Lieutenant Colonel Werner Mölders. Like Galland, Mölders started his combat career in Spain where fourteen victories made him the top-scoring German Ace. In the Battle of Britain he scored fifty-five kills. Flying from the Eastern Front to the funeral of Ernst Udet, the fighter ace of the First World War, Mölders died when his Heinkel transport crashed.

Keystone Press

A formation of Bristol Blenheims, the RAF's maids-of-all-work

RADAR: THE SECRET WAR

Scientists had been aware of the principle of radar many years before they realized that a practical application was possible. Before 1920 it was known that radio waves produced echoes and in 1924 E.V. (later Sir Edward) Appleton used this phenomenon to prove the existence of the ionosphere and to discover the height of its various layers by measuring the time required for a radio echo to return to the ground.

Ten years elapsed before a system for the detection of aircraft in a radio beam was devised.

In June 1934 A.P.Rowe, an Air Ministry scientist uneasy about the way the situation in Germany was developing, on his own initiative leafed through the fifty-three available files on air defence. He found that hardly any effort had been made to tackle the whole problem scientifically. Rowe reported his findings to Wimperis, director of scientific research at the Air Ministry, who then proposed to the secretary of state for air, Lord Londonderry, that a Committee for the Scientific Survey of Air Defence should be set up. This became the celebrated committee under Henry (later Sir Henry) Tizard.

For many years inventors had submitted propositions for a death ray which would immobilize an aircraft or incapacitate the crew. Before the first meeting of the Tizard Committee Wimperis informally asked R.A. (later Sir Robert) Watson-Watt of the Radio Research Station, Slough, whether in fact enough radio energy could conceivably be transmitted to damage an aircraft sufficiently. Watson-Watt passed the problem to one of his staff, A.F.Wilkins, who in half an hour's work showed that, although damage to an aircraft could be dismissed, the detection of radio energy reflected from an aircraft and, therefore, the determination of its distance could be found.

This information was digested by the Tizard Committee when it first met at the end of January 1935. On 26th February the first test of radio detection was held. A van containing suitable radio receivers halted in a field about ten miles from the short-wave transmitters of the Daventry broadcasting station. A pilot was instructed to fly over a course near the radio station. The van's instruments detected the aircraft as it flew through the radio transmissions at a distance of eight miles. It has been written, not without cause, that this simple experiment determined in large measure the fate of Great Britain and even of the world.

The authorities speedily grasped the importance of the experiment and gave permission and funds for research to begin. A small team of scientists under Watson-Watt secretly developed the first practical radar equipment at Orfordness on the Suffolk coast. Rowe had given the cover name RDF to the experiments – R standing for radio (because the tall aerial masts could not be disguised) and DF because direction finding was external to the original proposal. RDF became 'radar' (RAdio Detection And Ranging) later in the war and by then included a number of devices not all of which made use of radio echoes. The radar researchers soon moved to Bawdsey Manor, south of Orfordness and Bawdsey became the prototype of a chain of coastal radar stations.

By the late 'thirties radar had reached a similar state of development in Germany, France, Holland, and the United States. In Germany, although the equipment was technically in advance of the British, the Services, anticipating a short war, made no plans for long term research. They failed, moreover, to discover the purpose of the British radar chain and, when war came, failed to destroy the vital radar stations. In the United States there appeared to be no pressing need for radar. So the US Navy was caught napping at Pearl Harbour. France was the first country to devise a radio navigational system – for the liner *Normandie* – but little attention was paid to military uses.

Two factors were essential to the success of the warning system; one was the speed with which the radar information was despatched to the appropriate quarter by landline or radio; the other was the need to maintain the continuity of a hostile aircraft's track under a permanent reference designation from Command Headquarters downwards to fighter groups and sectors.

The heart of the system was at Headquarters, Fighter Command, at Stanmore, Middlesex, where, in an underground filter room, the radar plots of the position, strength, height, and direction of the raiders were received, sifted, and reported when a track became discernible by specially selected and trained filter officers. In the early stages of the war the height-finding technique was liable to some degree of error and the filter officers had occasionally to resort to simple probability exercises. The tracks provided by the filter officers went to the adjoining operations room where the controller and his assistants sat on a raised dais and watched the airmen and WAAF plotters as they moved the counters on the glass-topped table, representing hostile and friendly aircraft, with their long croupier-like rakes according to the information received through their headphones. From here the air raid warning system was set in motion. The fighter groups and sectors, each equipped with identical operations and filter rooms, also received the raiders' tracks. In the early days of the war all the filtering was done at Stanmore, but after the deployment of German formations along the French coast information went directly to the appropriate groups.

As the coastal radar sets could not 'look' backwards, it was the responsibility of the Observer Corps to provide warning inland, and information on the approach of hostile aircraft was sent to the Observer Corps control rooms.

In the fighter sector operations rooms the controllers directed their squadrons to attack at the right place and time and afterwards brought them safely back to base. The medium of communication was the high frequency radio telephone. High frequency direction finders situated in each sector provided the position of every aircraft and, in addition, every fighter aircraft was provided with an automatic device known as 'Pipsqueak' which switched on the pilot's high frequency transmitter for fourteen seconds in every minute. Each aircraft had IFF (Identification, Friend or Foe) which characterized its radar 'blip'.

***Below left:** Robert Watson-Watt who led the team of scientists which developed the first practical radar equipment, with his wife.* ***Below right:** The original magnetron invented by Randall in 1940 and the copper anode which forms the heart of this device.* ***Bottom:** WAAFs plot raids in operations room, Fighter Command HQ*

Keystone Press

Science Museum

Camera Press

At night, the fighter pilot and his observer had enough to contend with in the business of taking off and landing and of navigating in total darkness and trying to locate an enemy bomber without control from the ground was like looking for a needle in a haystack. It was necessary for the controller to know at one and the same time the position, track, speed, and height of both the night fighter and the bomber. Provided with this information the controller could radio to the pilot the direction and height at which the latter should fly and, if necessary, to reduce speed in order not to overshoot his target. Control by night was made practicable by the Plan Position Indicator (PPI). This device was used in conjunction with a rotating radar beam with which it was possible to estimate an aircraft's range (up to about ninety miles) and direction.

The PPI which next to shortwave radar was the most important radar development during the war, was incorporated in the Ground Controlled Interception equipment. This resembled a domestic TV set with a map of the area imposed on the screen. The controller was able to plot the position of the enemy bomber and the pursuing fighter from the bright spots on the tube face, and by calculating the speed and direction of flight of the enemy was able to direct the night fighter towards it by the shortest route. In the final stages of the pursuit the fighter homed onto its quarry using its own Aircraft Interception set (AI).

But the early AI sets had severe limitations as did the sets for detecting surface vessels, and particularly surfaced submarines. Very narrow radio beams were required which could detect small objects, like a surfaced submarine, from the air, and without interference from ground echoes or from enemy jamming. The Bawdsey scientists had long foreseen the need for microwaves, but at that time there was no valve adequate to generate the high power required. Again, Great Britain made a revolutionary step forward in radar history. Early in 1940, at the instigation of the Admiralty, J.T. (later Sir John) Randall, and his colleagues at Birmingham University, devised the magnetron – a valve no bigger than a child's fist, which eventually provided a reliable output of hundreds of kilowatts in short pulses.

When, in August 1940, it was decided to divulge to the Americans, sixteen months before they entered the war, the latest British scientific achievements, the magnetron was the most important item taken to the USA by the Tizard Mission. The Americans, who had not yet solved the problem of generating microwaves, were now able to produce short wave sets for the detection of night bombers and surface vessels from the air, and for the control of anti-aircraft fire. **Guy Hartcup**

▽ Radar plotted the incoming bomber formations, alerting the AA defences and RAF Headquarters. Fighter Command had to anticipate feints by the incoming bombers in addition to the weight of the German attack itself

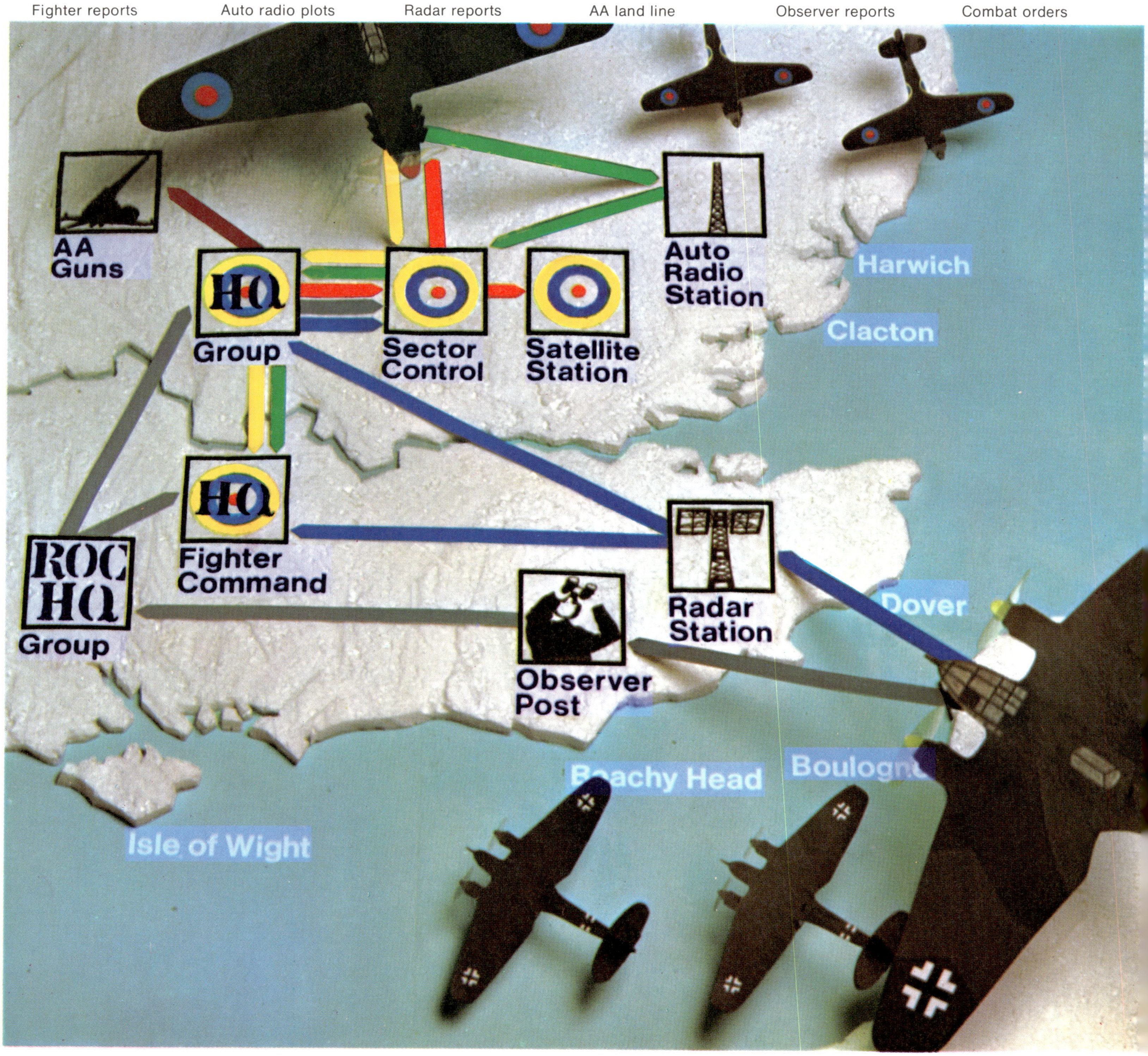

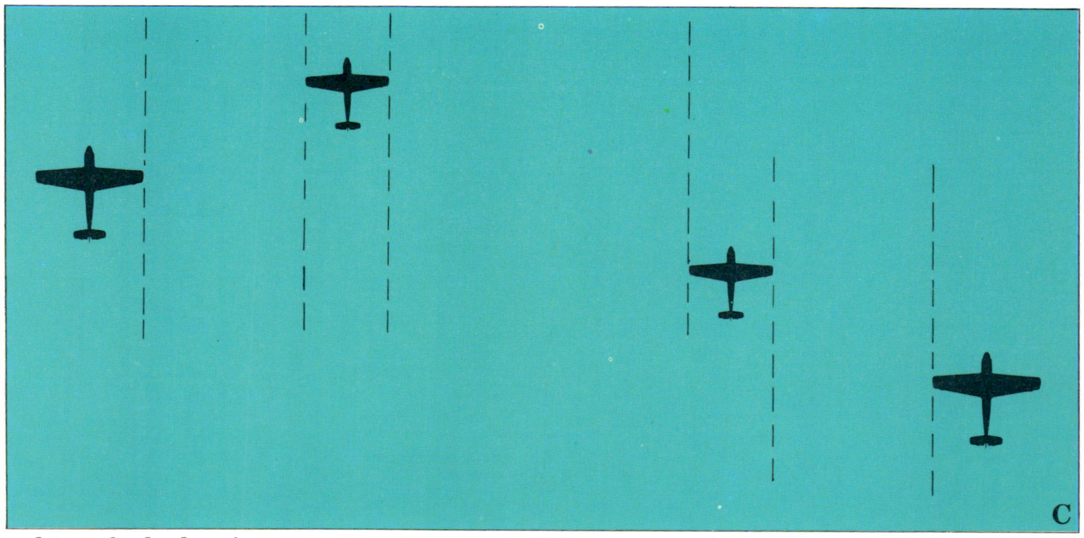

Fighters take off to intercept attack, but land to refuel when it ads for 3. Attack swings away from fighters at 3, returning to 1 d 2, where the fighters are still grounded

B: Parade-ground 'Vic' was rigid and inadequate for the needs of modern air fighting

C: RAF pilots adopted the German 'Schwarm': better known as the 'Finger-four'

RAF Commander (X THEATRE OF WAR)	**Luftflotte** (EQUIVALENT OF ARMY GROUP)
Group	**Fliegerkorps**
Wing Fighter Command Bomber Command Coastal Command	**Geschwader** Kampfgeschwader – Bomber Jagdgeschwader – Fighter Stukageschwader – Dive-bomber
(No Direct Equivalent)	**Gruppe**
Squadron	**Staffel**

Imperial War Museum

Marshal Sir Hugh Dowding

WAAFs plot the battle

Paul Popper

Reichsmarschall Göring (centre), with Luftwaffe officers

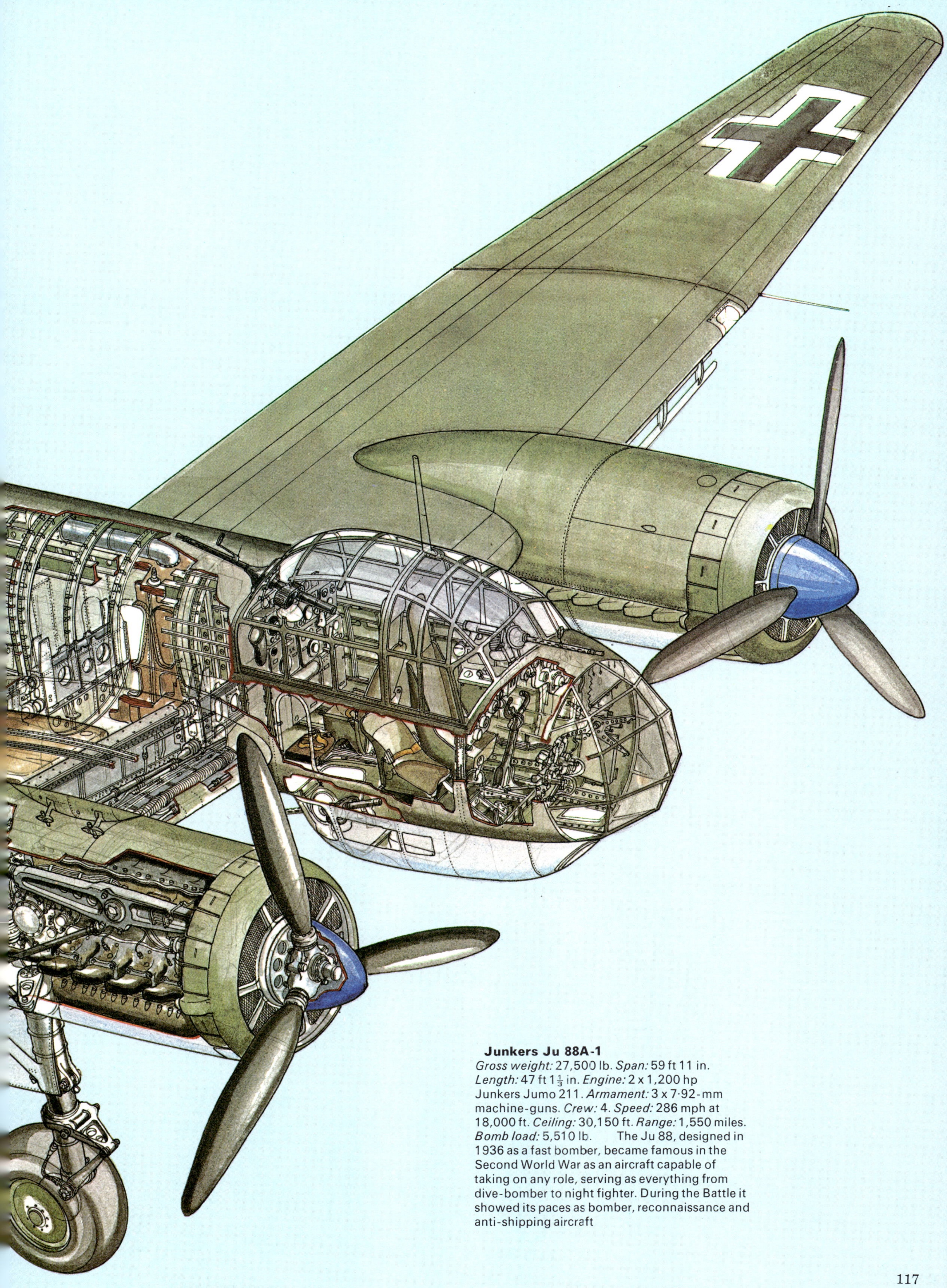

Junkers Ju 88A-1
Gross weight: 27,500 lb. *Span:* 59 ft 11 in. *Length:* 47 ft 1⅓ in. *Engine:* 2 x 1,200 hp Junkers Jumo 211. *Armament:* 3 x 7·92-mm machine-guns. *Crew:* 4. *Speed:* 286 mph at 18,000 ft. *Ceiling:* 30,150 ft. *Range:* 1,550 miles. *Bomb load:* 5,510 lb. The Ju 88, designed in 1936 as a fast bomber, became famous in the Second World War as an aircraft capable of taking on any role, serving as everything from dive-bomber to night fighter. During the Battle it showed its paces as bomber, reconnaissance and anti-shipping aircraft

Searchlights over London: 'the initiative in the air offensive now lay with the Germans'

ONE MAN'S BLITZ

Peter Elstob

ondoners got their first taste of the Blitz on the night of eptember 7, 1940, when 250 German bombers struck hard t the capital. For the rest of that year, and into the next, hey were subjected to relentless pounding from the air

n September 1940 I took a week's holiday owing to me and so missed he first serious night raids. When I got back to London I tried to nd out what it had been like, but the young couple I was living ith seemed unable to describe it. I was, however, made to feel that had missed great goings-on, that not having shared the experience didn't belong to the exclusive club. I almost wished for an air raid - a little one, not too near.

About a week later I got my air raid. The warning went just fter dinner but, apart from checking the blackout curtains, no otice was taken and we sat down to our weekly bridge game. At rst there was quiet outside but slowly the noises which were o become so familiar built up. I wasn't playing very well because I as listening to the noise and trying to sort out what was going on utside. The others didn't seem to notice anything, rubbing their mall experience into the new boy.

Edith dealt and, as an explosion shook the house gently, reminded e that we were vulnerable. I didn't make the obvious joke because didn't feel at all funny.

'One heart,' she bid briskly. Somewhere high above us anti-ircraft shells exploded.

'Pass,' said Roland, her husband. A louder noise as a nearer attery had a go. Surely that was the throb-throb of a bomber's ngine I could hear?

'Your *bid,*' Edith said impatiently.

'Two diamonds.' My words were drowned out by a terrific explo-on. I checked an impulse to dive under the table because no one lse seemed to have noticed it.

'Two diamonds.' I tried again but again there was an enormous xplosion. This time I couldn't help ducking.

'You really *must* try and raise your voice above the bombs,' Roland aid quite seriously.

And, within a fortnight or so, I, like most other Londoners, had lso achieved a certain amount of sang-froid. My initiation came a w nights after the bridge game.

This time the raid started about one in the morning and I was wakened by it. I hadn't remembered to pull aside the blackout ter putting out the light so the room was pitch black. I had awoken ith a start and there was a taste of dust in my mouth, so I realised at one must have fallen close enough to shake my room. There as a series of explosions, as a stick of bombs straddled our neigh-ourhood. The third one seemed to be under my bed for I was lifted raight up and dumped on the floor and sprinkled with dust and aster. The explosion was quite the loudest thing I had ever heard. Reasoning that it was now too late to go down into the shelter I ept back under the blankets and, strangely, fell asleep at once.

In the morning I went to the window but, before pulling aside e blackout, braced myself for the dreadful destruction I was re to see. To my amazement nothing had changed: the back gar-ns with their little sheds and clothes lines were exactly as always d not even a window was cracked. We found out, of course, where e particular bomb had fallen, but there wasn't a great deal to see, r it had gone through the roof of the house nearly opposite ours d had burst deep in the cellar. The casualties had been taken away, the small fire put out, and the road cleared of rubble.

One evening after the sirens had sounded their usual warning and nothing had happened, there was a sound like stones being thrown against the house or a number of slates falling off the roof. We ran to the front door and found an incendiary bomb burning brightly on the mat. Roland dashed upstairs for the bucket of sand he kept for just such an emergency; I ran into the kitchen and snatched up a bowl of washing-up water. The suds doused the bomb, snuffing it like a candle.

From the doorway we could see that there were many other in-cendiaries, some burning out harmlessly in the road or basement areas, some on houses, and one on the back seat of a car, having burned through the roof. Roland dumped his bucket of sand on that one and was pleased that it obediently went out. The bombs were about 9 inches long and burned with a white light for three or four minutes, leaving only the tail fins.

There were many people in the street shouting instructions to each other. Roland, Edith, and I were busy with bucket and stirrup pump when someone ran up shouting that the stables were on fire. These were at the end of a cul-de-sac behind our house and in them were kept a number of milkcart horses. We ran round to find thick smoke rolling out of the large open doors and were told that the terrified animals wouldn't come out.

There didn't seem to be any flames so I thought that probably some wet straw was smouldering. I bent low and felt my way along the wall towards the stalls. The lights were still on and I unlatched a stable door and found myself face to face with a large, very fright-ened horse. I shouted and clapped my hands but he took no notice of me, standing rooted to the spot. I got hold of his mane and tried to pull him out but he tossed his head and showed his yellow teeth. Fortunately someone had had the wit to go for two of the milkmen who lived near by. They quickly got bridles on the animals and were able to lead them out.

The daughter of a trapped woman was standing on her doorstep crying hysterically. Roland asked her which room her mother was in.

'Second floor back, but she's dead. Oh, poor mum, she's dead, I know she's dead.'

Roland gave me a full bucket of water and kept the stirrup pump himself. We soaked handkerchiefs, tied them over our nose and mouth and went up the smoke-filled stairs on our hands and knees. He kicked open the bedroom door. The room was full of smoke but there was a red glow in one corner and he crawled towards this. I pumped and he directed the spray.

The incendiary had crashed through the roof and the bedroom ceiling, landing on the bed. All the smoke in the house was coming from the burning mattress and bedding. The bomb had long since burned itself out and the spray soon had the fire out. As the smoke cleared we could see an old lady in the bed. She was quite dead.

Once outside again we were grabbed by a little old man in a white muffler who begged us to put out some incendiaries lodged in his attic. We got these out fairly quickly but he then pointed to a ladder and an open skylight, saying there were more on the roof. Somehow I found myself edging along the peak of the roof clutching a stirrup pump while Roland came behind with the bucket.

From up there we could see down into the street and away over the rooftops. It was an extraordinary sight: all around the horizon fires glowed, searchlights slowly raked the dark sky, anti-aircraft guns flashed silently, there being no apparent connection between them and the almost continuous noise of the guns. High above us shells burst like fireworks. But the most insistent noise came from the street immediately beneath us. It was the excited sound of many people shouting as they scurried in and out of their houses.

I started to spray the incendiary lodged by the chimney when I heard the sound of more bombs coming down and hugged the peak of the roof. Moments later a stick of small, 50-pound high-explosive bombs fell in a line across houses and street.

The bombers, earlier in the evening, had dropped nothing but hundreds of incendiaries. But this wave, a couple of hours later, came back with instantaneous high-explosive bombs where the fires were brightest and most people were in the streets.

The explosions caused panic; people ran back into burning houses or threw themselves into basement areas. I heard screams above the explosions as I tried to dig myself into the slates of the roof.

The rain of bombs lasted only a few minutes but it was dawn before the fires were all out and the injured had been taken away. We sat in the kitchen of our house drinking cocoa with neighbours who had lived near each other for years but had never spoken. Now they were talking and gesticulating in a most un-English manner as they described the narrow escapes of the night.

From the street shelters came the ones who had been down there during all the excitement. The rest of us looked at them sorrow-fully, knit together by the experience we had shared.

Fox Photos

△ Old Bailey in ruins: many landmarks were hit by the Blitz

Imperial War Museum

△ Rescue workers bring out a man buried by rubble for 14 ho

Mirror Pic

△ Adding to the havoc of the bombing were the fires that raged in the Blitz's wake: firemen work while others hunt for surviv

By May 1941 bombs had killed some 40,000 British civilians

Keystone

△ Street damage like this often cut power and water lines

Ullstein

△ The bombing of Coventry marked a shift to strategic targets

Heinkel He III H3
Weight: 19,130 lb. *Span:* 74 ft $1\frac{3}{4}$ in. *Length:* 53 ft $9\frac{1}{2}$ in. *Armament:* 5 x 7·92-mm machine-guns ; 1 x 20-mm cannon. *Engine:* 2 x 1,200 hp Jumo D-1. *Crew:* 5/6. *Speed:* 258 mph. *Range:* 760 miles. The twin-engined Heinkels were the principal weapon in the German heavy bomber squadrons and had proved their tactical value in campaigns from Spain to the fall of France. As a strategic bomber however, attacking the industries and defences of Britain, the type proved lacking in offensive power and defensive armament

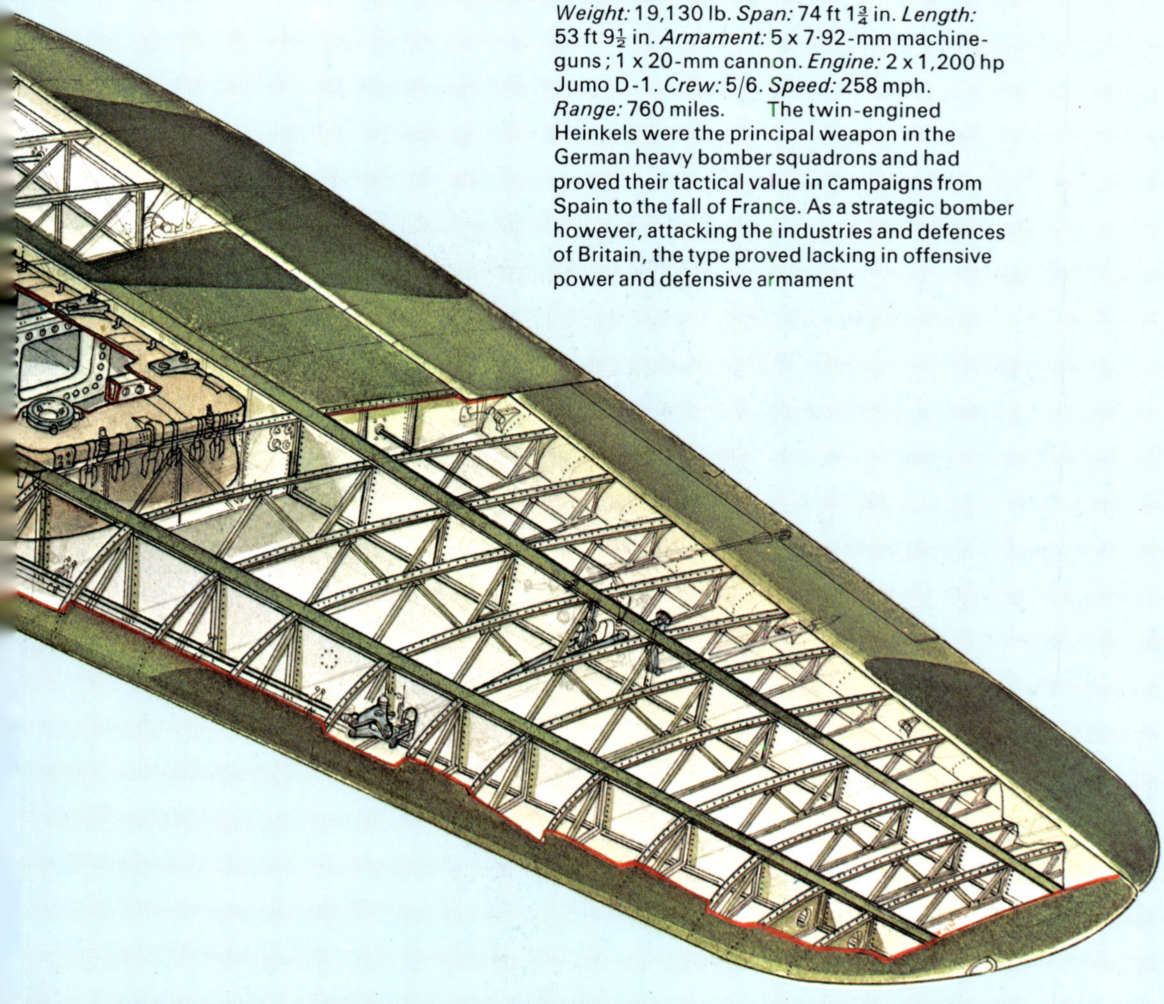

"The defence of Southern England will last four days and the Royal Air Force four weeks. We can guarantee invasion for the Führer within a month."

Reichsmarschall
Göring, 11 July 1940

THE DESERT WAR

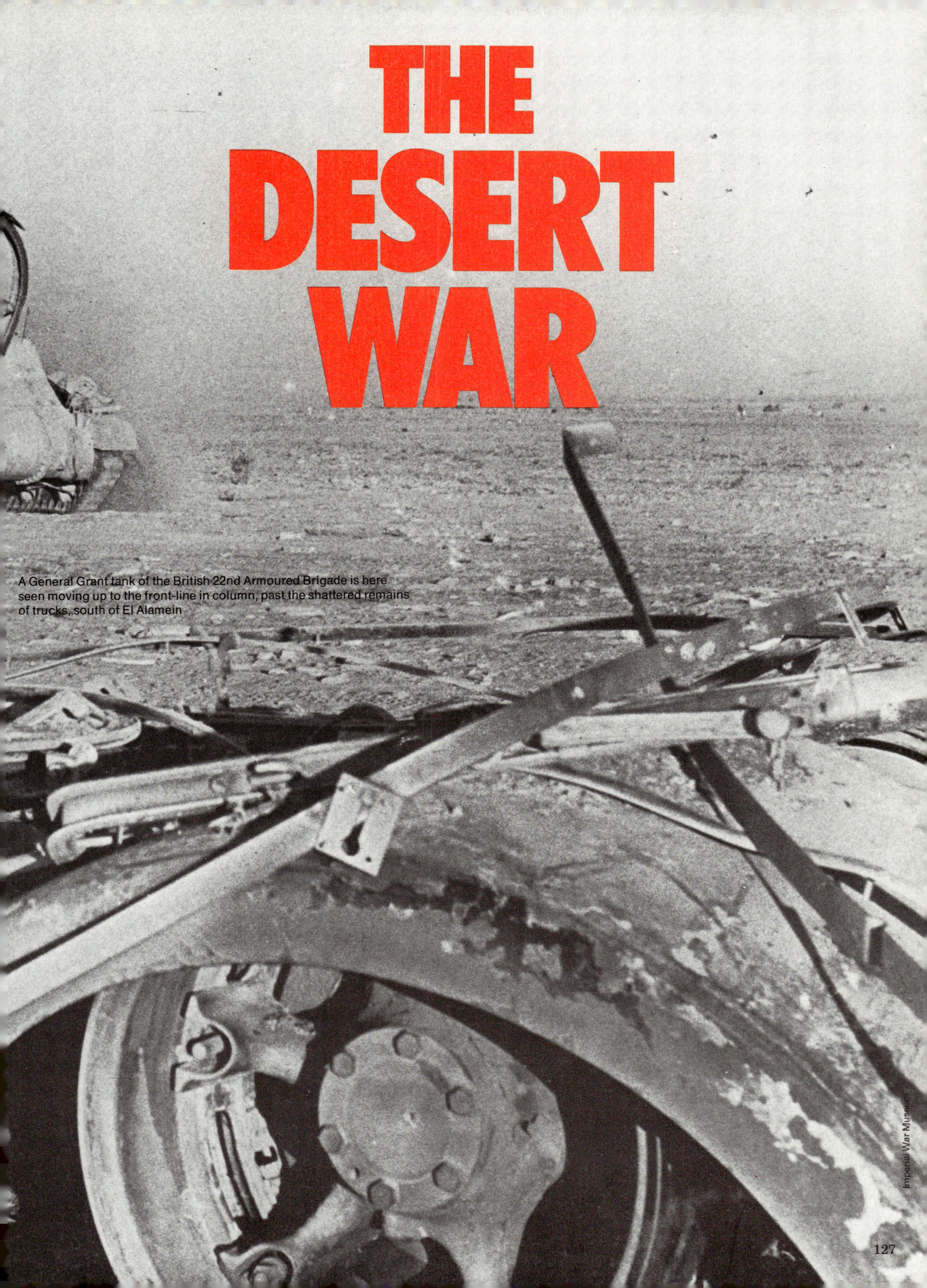

A General Grant tank of the British 22nd Armoured Brigade is here seen moving up to the front-line in column, past the shattered remains of trucks, south of El Alamein

Imperial War Museum

THE FIRST SWING OF THE

Sandwiched between French Algeria and British Egypt, Mussolini's North African colony of Libya represented, at the outset of war, a vulnerable outpost of the Axis Empire. Until the Fall of France in June 1940, that is. Immediately the situation was reversed. Now there was only the British presence in Egypt barring the road to the Nile and the oil-rich states of the Persian Gulf. And against General Wavell's 30,000-strong Western Desert Force, the Italians—under General Graziani—could muster no less than 250,000 men.

From the moment Italy joined the Second World War, on June 10, 1940, Mussolini's ambitions in North Africa were clear. Graziani was to sweep through Egypt, cross the Nile, and raise the Italian flag over the oilfields of the Middle East. Graziani, however, could only make a hesitant advance of 65 miles into Egypt. There, at Sidi Barrani, he dug in and refused to go any further, saying his lack of armour, guns and equipment was such that any further offensive was impossible.

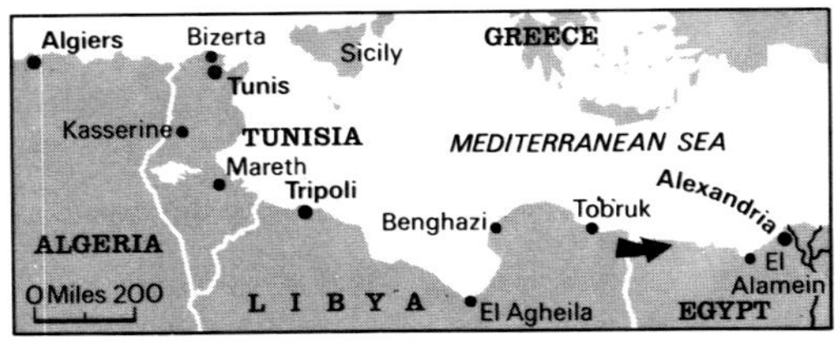

Over the top. Pith-helmeted infantrymen of Graziani's Italian desert army attack during their initial, hesitant thrust of 65 miles to Sidi Barrani in Egypt

Light field-gun support for the advancing Italian troops

PENDULUM

om Rome nonetheless there came a mmuniqué announcing Graziani's vance and making naïve claims that 'all quiet and the trams are again running in e town of Sidi Barrani'. But the grossly tnumbered British Western Desert rce in Egypt harboured no such delusions. e Italian army, static and dug in at li Barrani, presented a target that Gen. avell was not slow to appreciate.

ht: **Autoblinda 40:** medium armoured car of the Italian sert army. Turret gun: 20-mm Machine-gun: 8-mm.

Below and left: Italian M15/42 medium tanks moving across ideal terrain into Egypt. Badly designed and poorly armed, they proved no match for the British Matildas of the day

Paul Popper

The Italian C-in-C: Marshal Graziani

WAVELL'S 30,000

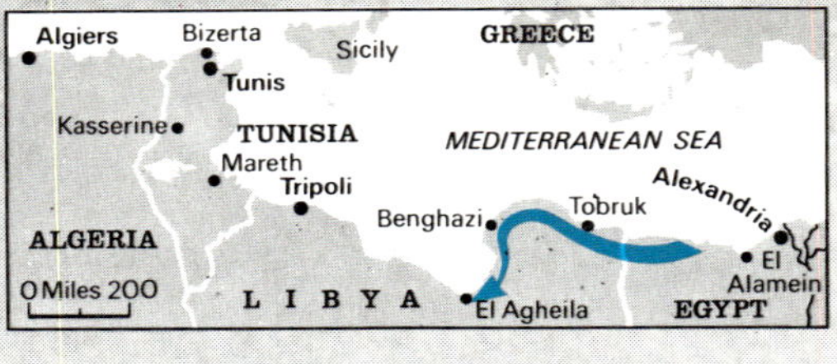

In a short and memorable campaign during the last weeks of 1940 and the beginning of 1941, the British managed to drive the Italians out of Egypt, Libya and Cyrenaica. It was the first British offensive of the Second World War and the first victory on land. Even as it happened it was transformed into a legend—a legend, that is, until other events—victories and defeats—pushed it into the background of men's minds.

On any numerical calculation, the success of Graziani's invasion of Egypt was a certainty, so large was the size of the invading army compared with the British force available to defend Egypt. But its mobility was low, and the handicap that limited mechanisation imposed on manoeuvre—for surprise—was increased by administrative inefficiency. After a 70-mile advance through the Western Desert, the Italians halted at Sidi Barrani, and there stuck for a couple of months.

The British Commander-in-Chief in the Middle East, General Wavell, decided to try the effect of an upsetting stroke by the Western Desert Force—the embryo of the 8th Army—under General

An Italian heavy machine-gun fitted with anti-aircraft sights dug in on the desert front

Fort Capuzzo, captured on December 14, 1940

O'Connor. It was visualised in the nature of a powerful raid rather than an offensive. There were only two divisions available, the 7th Armoured and the 4th Indian; after this stroke the latter was to be brought back to the Nile and sent down to the Sudan, to help in dealing with the threat of the Italian army in Eritrea and Ethiopia.

The 'raid', however, turned into a decisive victory, thanks to the paralysis and dislocation produced by General O'Connor's surprise move through the desert on to the enemy's rear. This sudden blow was delivered on December 9, 1940. A large part of Graziani's army was cut off and 35,000 captured, while the remainder only regained the shelter of their own frontier after a panic retreat that reduced them to a disorderly rabble.

The whole campaign might have ended at this point if Wavell had not insisted on the 4th Indian Division being withdrawn in accordance with the original plan. Deprived of its backing, the 7th Armoured Division was naturally unable to penetrate the Bardia defences, and several weeks elapsed before a fresh infantry division, the 6th Australian, could be brought from Palestine to act as a 'tin-opener'. Then Bardia was captured, on January 3, with 40,000

Imperial War Museum

Wavell (on right) with O'Connor, his architect of victory

British barrage hammers Italian desert fort to the south of Sidi Barrani

Imperial War Museum

British howitzer bombards besieged Bardia

Imperial War Museum

Imperial War Museum

British light tank at speed

Right: The **Gloster Gladiator.** Highly manoeuvrable but outclassed in both speed and firepower by the newer monoplane fighters, this plane last saw active squadron service with the RAF in North Africa, a backwater in the air war for both Axis and Allies alike. **Max speed:** 246 mph **Armament:** four Browning .303 machine-guns

Above: **Fiat CR-42.** This was the last single-seater biplane to be used by any combatant in the Second World War. **Armament:** two 12.7-mm machine-guns **Max speed:** 261 mph

Below: **Breda Ba-65.** This saw service in Ethiopia in 1935 and was basically a ground-attack plane. An observer could be carried for scouting. **Armament:** four 12-mm machine-guns **Max speed:** 267 mph

prisoners. Tobruk fell on the 22nd, with a further 25,000. In both cases the infantry/tank battalion, the 7th Royal Tanks, with its thickly armoured Matildas, proved decisive—as it had at Sidi Barrani.

The surviving part of Graziani's army retreated past Benghazi towards Tripoli, but was intercepted by an indirect pursuit that proved one of the most brilliant and daring strokes of the war. The 7th Armoured Division made a dash through the desert interior to reach the sea south of Benghazi on February 5, 1941. Its leading elements covered 170 miles in 36 hours over difficult and unknown country. While one group under Colonel Combe established a block across the enemy's line of retreat at Beda Fomm, another group—the 4th Armoured Brigade under Brigadier Caunter—pummelled his forces until they surrendered. The two groups combined amounted to only 3,000 men, yet by their audacity in thrusting across the path of a vastly superior enemy they secured a 'bag' of 21,000 prisoners.

Such Italian troops as remained, besides being ill-equipped to meet a tank thrust, were badly shaken by the fate of their main army. O'Connor was eager to exploit his victory at Beda Fomm, and was convinced that he could carry out the fresh bound with little delay for the replenishment of supplies. But a halt was called by the British government in order to provide the means of dispatching the ill-starred expedition to Greece. Wavell was instructed to leave only a minimum to hold Cyrenaica. O'Connor also went back to Egypt, and the control was left in less capable hands.

Italians under RAF attack during their retreat in the desert

Left: **Fiat BR-20 Cicogna.** One of Italy's heaviest bombers, this plane served everywhere in Mussolini's empire except East Africa. **Bomb load:** 3,300 lb **Max speed:** 267 mph

Below: **Savoia SM-79.** Like the Luftwaffe's Do-17, this had been blooded in the Spanish Civil War and was the standard long-range bomber of the Regia Aeronautica.
Bomb load: 2,205 lb **Max speed:** 260 mph

British and Italian Desert Armour

Above: **M13/40** tank. Despite heavy losses this remained the standard Italian medium tank during and after Wavell's campaign. **Armour:** 40-mm **Turret gun:** 47-mm

Above: Italian **CV3/35.** This was the equivalent of the British machine-gun carrier from which it was developed. **Armour:** 14-mm **Machine-guns:** two 8-mm

Above: British **Universal Carrier**. Popularly called **Bren-gun Carrier**, this maid-of-all-work infantry weapon was well-suited to conditions in North Africa. **Armour:** 11-mm

Above: British **Infantry Mk II** tank, the 'Matilda'. Infantry tanks decided the battles for the Italian bases in 1940/41. **Armour:** 78-mm **Turret gun:** 2-pounder

Left: **Rolls-Royce Armoured Car.** A handful of these relics of the First World War saw action in the Libyan campaigns of 1940/41. **Armour:** 7-mm **Machine-gun:** .303-in.

Imperial War Museum

Some of the 40,000-strong army of Italian prisoners taken at a cost of 500 Commonwealth casualties in the fighting for Bardia

Alfredo Zennaro

General Bergonzoli goes into captivity

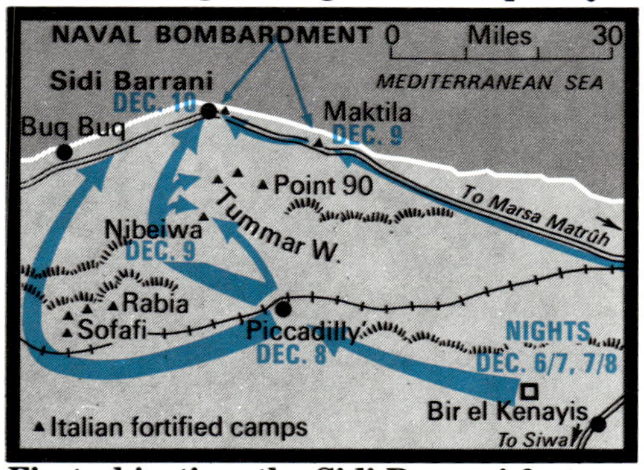

First objective: the Sidi Barrani forts

The threat: in June 1940, Italian Libya menaced Egypt and the Suez Canal

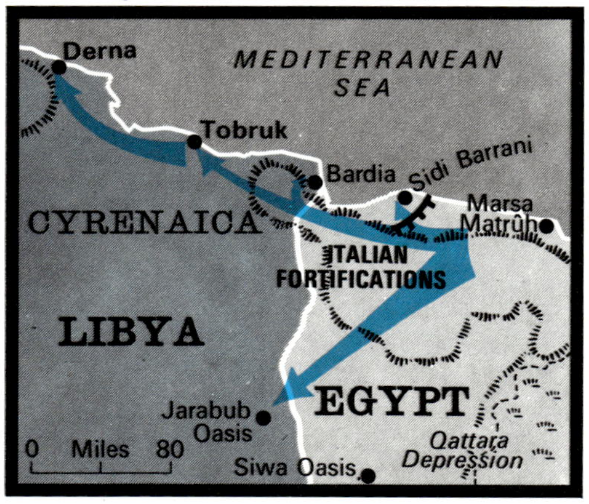

Horizons widen: Bardia/Tobruk/Derna

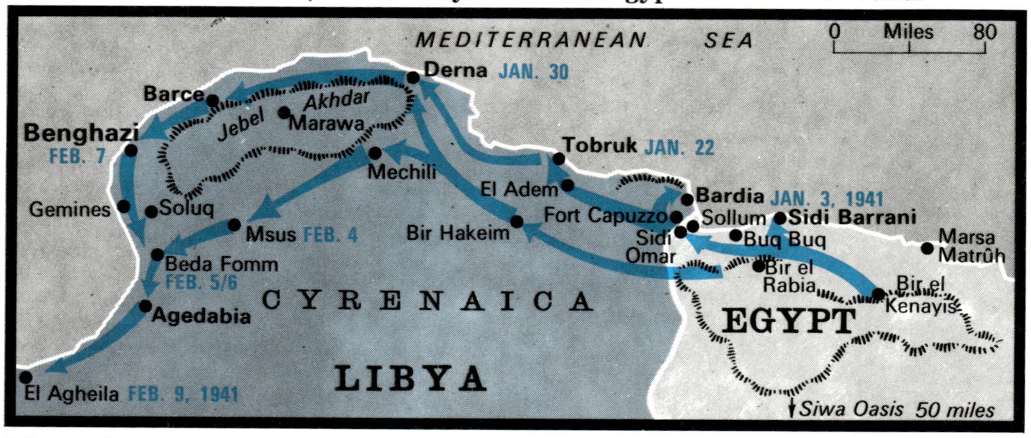

The final achievement: Wavell's original attack became a landslide conquest

ENTER THE AFRIKA KORPS: ROMMEL'S FIRST ATTACK

△ German motorised units on the move in the desert
▽ Axis defences of Tripoli at the end of Wavell's advance

Struggle with the desert: in heavy going, a German heavy tank is given marshalling directions

The scorching pace of the conquest of Cyrenaica had exhausted the men and machines of Wavell's 'Thirty Thousand', some of which were withdrawn for service on other fronts. They were replaced by untried commanders and troops, with nondescript armoured vehicles – and were to receive damaging treatment from Rommel and the Afrika Korps, who used superior tactics and had better fighting vehicles.

Rommel (right) plans his first attack

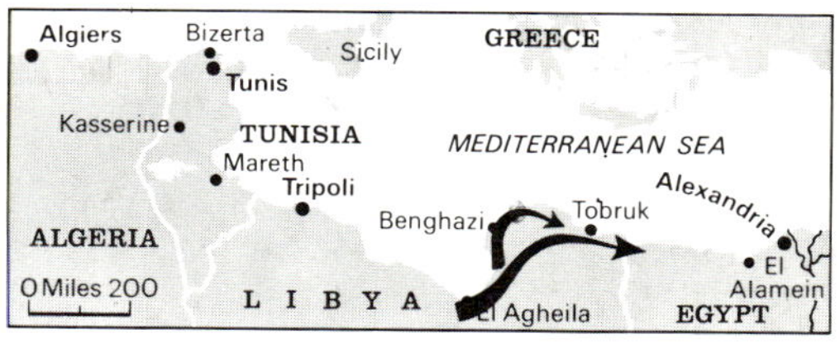

Rommel arrived in Africa on February 12, 1941, followed by the Afrika Korps, which at that time was limited in numbers and supported by a relatively small airforce. The XV Panzer Division did not arrive until the end of May and the leading formation, V Light Division, was not complete until mid-April, although 105 medium and 51 light tanks had landed by March 11. The Italian army had five divisions and 60 light tanks of doubtful value.

Convinced that the British lacked a plan of aggression, Rommel easily captured El Agheila on March 24, and then attacked the British 2nd Armoured Division's positions at Mersa Brega on March 31. When Mersa Brega fell after a day's fierce fighting, Rommel launched a full-scale offensive to recover Cyrenaica. By swift moves round his opponents' flank and into their rear, he disrupted their advanced dispositions, and then by an encircling bluff produced the surrender of their main force at Mechili. The only intact body to survive the net were the two brigades of the Australian 7th Division, which withdrew under fire to join the Australian garrison at Tobruk. Within two weeks Rommel reached the Egyptian frontier, but he had overstretched his supply lines and was compelled to halt.

The only thorn in his side was Tobruk, where the improvised defences held out against the first attacks of his leading units.

Supply and defence for the Germans: Junkers 52 transports and Me 110 fighters

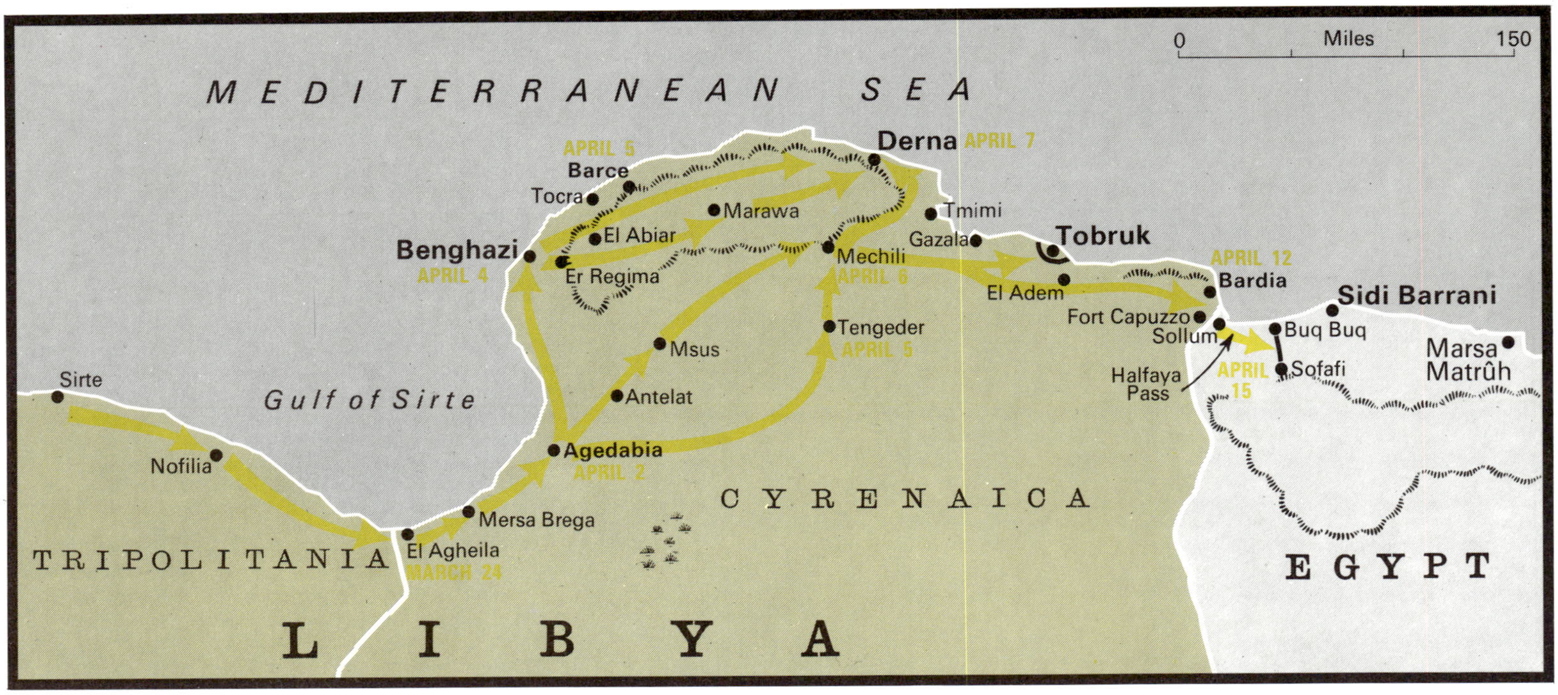

Below: **Panzer III.** This tank was the mainstay of the early German war offensives. In use with the Afrika Korps it was superior to any Allied armour before 1942. **Crew:** 5 **Weight:** 19.5 metric tons **Armament:** MG34 machine-guns, front and co-axial 37-mm or 50-mm main armour-piercing gun **Armour:** 20-57 mm **Range:** 165 km road; 95 km x-country

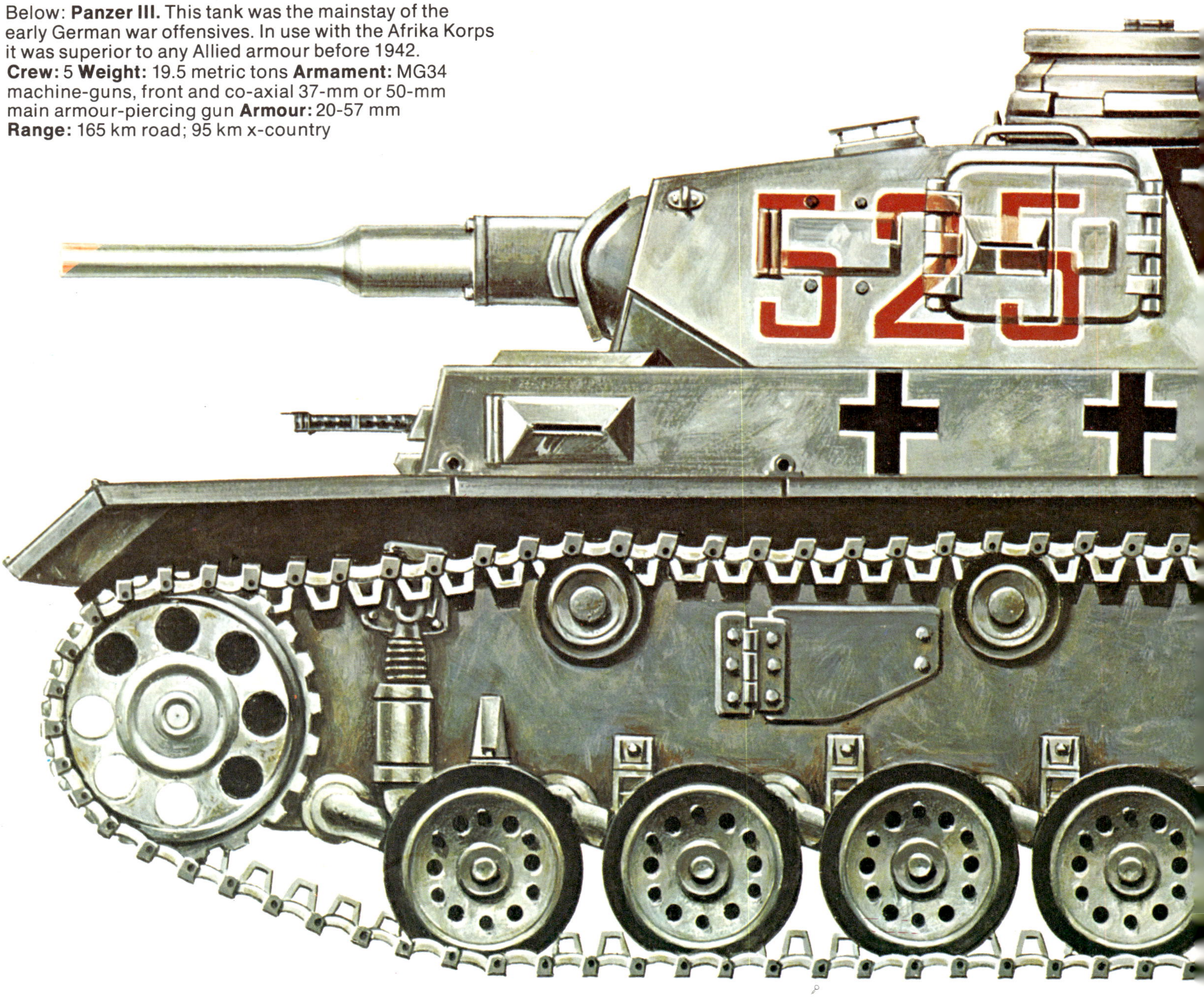

Rommel's next assault was well planned and executed, but although the perimeter was penetrated the attack failed. The Australians at Tobruk were not easily intimidated and calmly allowed the German tanks to over-run their lines so they could tackle the supporting infantry. It was the first time that the Germans had driven their tanks through infantry that did not automatically surrender. It was also the first time in the war that the Germans were defeated: they could not take Tobruk from the Australians.

Setting aside Tobruk, which was to remain in a state of siege for eight months, all that had been achieved by Wavell and O'Connor in four months had been swept away in one month by Rommel. No longer was the war to be one-sided: after this, the battle was to be one of constant movement between forces of roughly equal strength whose success or failure depended on the superior skill or luck one commander might have over the other. For the next two years it was to be the virtuosity of Rommel versus a succession of unhappy contenders.

Above: German **Sd.Kfz-251/7.** In common with the other vehicles illustrated below, this half-track personnel carrier was one of the mainstays of the Afrika Korps' light-armoured force. **Speed:** 31 mph **Range:** 185 miles **Crew:** 2 plus 9 troops

Right: German **Sd.Kfz-222** light armoured car. **Speed:** 50 mph **Range:** 180 miles **Crew:** 3 **Armament:** one 20-mm cannon, one 7.92-mm machine-gun

Right: German **Sd.Kfz-251** half-track reconnaissance vehicle. **Speed:** 31 mph **Range:** 185 miles **Crew:** 2 **Armament:** 7.92-mm machine-guns

Below: German **Sd.Kfz-231** heavy armoured car with drive and steering to all wheels. **Speed:** 53 mph **Range:** 187 miles **Crew:** 4 **Armament:** one 20-mm cannon, one 7.92-mm machine-gun

THE SIEGE OF TOBRUK

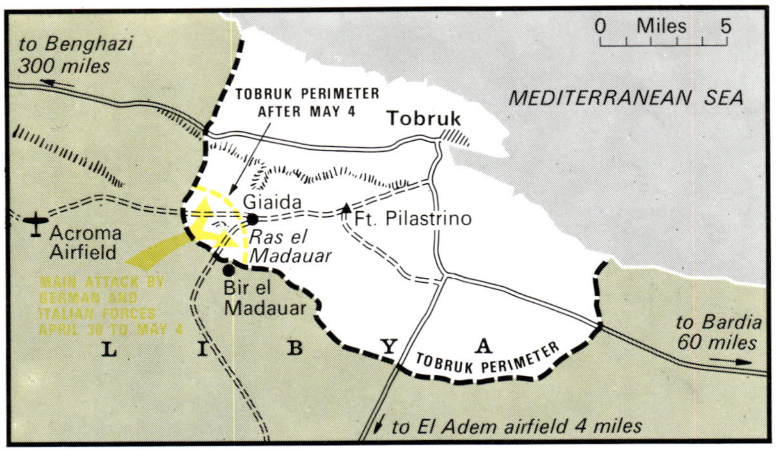

Tobruk was threatened by the German salient at Ras el Madauar, but Rommel had underestimated the strength of the western defences. The perimeter was in fact more vulnerable from the south-east corner, where O'Connor broke through the defence in 1941

Tobruk is a small but important port on the coast of Cyrenaica. Its pre-war population numbered about 4,000 people, living in a few hundred white buildings standing out starkly against the sun-baked, rocky ground sloping down to a tiny quay. The square in the centre of the town boasted a few dusty palm trees; and in times of peace the busiest installation in Tobruk was probably the water distillation plant which, with one or two wells, produced 40,000 gallons a day.

The importance of Tobruk lay in the fact that its harbour was the only safe and accessible port for over 1,000 miles, between Sfax in Tunisia and Alexandria in Egypt, apart from the even tinier harbour at Benghazi. Like Benghazi, Tobruk had been built by the Italians as one of the principal defences of Libya from the east and as a naval base.

In peace, it was important as the main outlet for the products of a vast area of hinterland. But in war, during the struggle for North Africa, its importance was greatly increased because any advance beyond it, either to the east or west, was doubly imperilled. First, the possession of Tobruk was essential as an unloading point for supplies and reinforcements, which otherwise had to be brought along difficult and lengthy lines of communication, either from Alexandria in one direction or Benghazi in the other. Secondly, in the hands of a determined and aggressive garrison, it could represent a serious offensive threat to the flank of any advance which by-passed it.

Winston Churchill himself described it as a 'sally port' and declared: 'Nothing but a raid dare go past Tobruk.'

The original Italian maps of the Tobruk defences show two lines of strong-points, completely sunk into the ground. These covered a perimeter of some 35-40 miles with a radius of about 20 miles (see map). The outer defences consisted of a series of heavily concreted dugouts—many cleverly improvised from natural caves—each holding 30 to 40 men. These dugouts were interconnected by trenches with locations every few hundred yards for machine-guns, mortars, or anti-tank guns. The trenches were roofed in with thin boarding and covered lightly with sand so that they were invisible from even a few yards away. In front of the outer defences barbed wire was laid, varying in some places from a single coil in width to a belt 30 yards wide elsewhere.

In front of the barbed wire the Italians had built an anti-tank ditch, often cleverly adapting an existing natural ravine. Straight-sided, and averaging 7 feet deep and 10 feet wide, the ditch was designed to thwart any attempted crossing by a tracked vehicle. The inner defence line was some 2,000 to 3,000 yards behind the outer line and constructed to the same pattern, but without the anti-tank ditch.

When Rommel launched his forces against the Western Desert Force in April 1941, and the opposition crumbled before him, one of his first thoughts was to capture Tobruk so as to eliminate it as a hazard, and to shorten his lines of communication for his drive into and beyond Egypt.

He did not anticipate any great difficulty. Wavell's forces had captured it from the Italians in two days, and the confident Rommel thought that it would not take much longer—if as long—to wrest it back.

However, the hastily improvised defence by the 9th Australian Division—augmented by 18th Brigade from 7th Australian Divi-

German armoured cars in a night battle for Tobruk: Rommel was becoming impatient, and threw his force into a full assault

sion and the remnants of 3rd Armoured Brigade, with field and anti-aircraft regiments, all under Major-General Leslie Morshead – was more than a match for the dying momentum of Rommel's push.

Siege warfare – modern style

From then on, Tobruk was in a constant state of siege. But it was not a siege in the same sense as those of Ladysmith and Mafeking in the Boer War, or of Lucknow in the Indian Mutiny, where isolated garrisons were surrounded by a numerically superior enemy and completely cut off from friendly forces. Constant contact was maintained between Tobruk and the main Allied forces by the Royal Navy – although it should not be imagined that this was in any way a 'milk run'.

Yet it was certainly a siege in the sense that Tobruk was a fortified position under continuous attack by the enemy. Every inch of the defended area was within range of the German and Italian artillery, and the harbour working-parties came under fire almost as much as the troops in the outer perimeter.

Beyond dispute the survival of Tobruk depended upon the harbour being kept in working order and the continuance of supplies along the tenuous sea-lane leading to it from Egypt. Nothing of use to the survival of an army was indigenous to Tobruk except for the shelter given by the natural caves. Everything had to be brought in from Egypt; and Rommel, realising this, concentrated almost as much on neutralising the harbour and interrupting the sea life-line as he did on planning a landward assault.

Since the days of Wavell's offensive the British army in Cyrenaica had been supported and supplied from the sea by ships of the Inshore Squadron, a heterogeneous armada comprising anything from a destroyer to a monitor, sloop, gunboat, trawler, sponge-fisher, or lighter. In Tobruk's most heated hour, these ships, supported sometimes by the Mediterranean Fleet, as often as possible covered by fighter aircraft, regularly braved the perils of mines, shells, bombs, and torpedoes to run men, machines, and supplies (including water), along the enemy-held coast to the besieged fortress.

Losses among the Inshore Squadron were heavy, particularly by day, and at times it became permissible to voyage only on the moonless nights. Daylight attacks such as those aimed at the anti-aircraft sloops *Auckland* and *Paramatta* on June 24, when they were escorting the valuable petrol-carrier *Pass of Balmaha,* give an indication of the scale of Axis efforts. On this occasion, combined raids by torpedo-bombers and 96 dive-bombers accounted for *Auckland* and stopped *Pass of Balmaha.* At the other end of the scale, a captured Italian fishing schooner *Maria Giovanni,* skippered by an Australian, Lieutenant Alfred Palmer, ran the gauntlet night after night until tricked into disaster by the Germans. In common with others, Palmer guided himself into Tobruk harbour by a shaded green light at the entrance, but he was not to know that one night the Germans had lit a decoy to the east. To his surprise Palmer ran himself hard ashore and was taken prisoner by the Germans as he and his crew were industriously digging a channel through which to refloat the ship.

Against the backcloth of coastal sea and air battle, the fight on land muttered and grumbled amid bombardments and patrol-scuffles while Rommel, chastened by his first rebuffs, raised his strength for a full assault. He was becoming impatient. Any other advance beyond the frontier was out of the question until Tobruk had been taken, but he was not ready until April 30.

The attack on that day began with a continuous pounding from Stuka dive-bombers and artillery, against which the defenders' powers of retaliation were limited. They engaged the dive-bombers with anti-aircraft and small-arms fire, and the British artillery put down counter-fire on the enemy gun-positions. But because the garrison could not expect fresh supplies of ammunition until the next moonless night – a week away – ammunition had to be husbanded and every shot made to count.

The German dive-bombers were unchallenged in the air, for the RAF Hurricane squadron, unable to operate from airstrips under continuous fire – with their runways frequently cratered and with workshops and petrol-dumps shelled every day – had been withdrawn on April 25.

As the dive-bombers drew off from their targets, the attacking infantry and tanks moved in against the western sector of the defences. But the defenders were far from subdued, and the Germans and Italians were met by ferocious fire from the British artillery and tanks and the Australian infantry.

It was a grim and bitter battle. Writing of it later Rommel said: 'The Australians fought with remarkable tenacity. Even their wounded went on defending themselves with small-arms fire, and stayed in the fight to their last breath. They were immensely big and powerful men, who without question represented an élite formation of the British Empire, a fact that was also evident in battle.'

By the end of the day the Germans and Italians had succeeded in penetrating the defences of Tobruk and had established a 2-mile salient into the Australian positions on the western sector of the perimeter. The salient included the important hill of Ras el Madauar, which dominated a large part of the defended area.

Still determined to subdue Tobruk, Rommel next day put in fresh troops, to exploit the Ras el Madauar salient, but although the fighting raged unabated until May 4, the attackers were unable to advance farther.

The salient of Ras el Madauar, however, remained a constant threat to the besieged garrison and – although there was sporadic activity on the other sectors of the defended perimeter – from May 4 onwards the defence of Tobruk was, in essence, the defence of its western sector. Here the hard outer shell of permanent defence works had been breached, and the opposing forces faced one another from hastily improvised foxholes. It was, in a way, the soft under-belly of Tobruk: the Germans and Italians expected that if the breakthrough came anywhere it would come in the western sector, and this was the area to which they devoted most of their attention.

By the time Tobruk had been under siege

The 'Rats of Tobruk' spent much of their time underground in shelters – the ventilators for this one came from the clutter of wrecked ships in Tobruk harbour

for a month the area around the town was littered with burned-out tanks, vehicles, and all the debris of war. The town itself was reduced to a heap of rubble in which only one house remained standing, and in this—despite the fact that it stood out among the flattened buildings like a sore thumb—General Morshead maintained his operational headquarters.

For the defenders of Tobruk each day brought a fresh crop of problems. Problems, that is, in addition to those normally associated with desert fighting—the strange disorientation brought on by a featureless landscape which induced a tendency to walk in circles; and daily temperatures in the hundreds, so that to touch a tank left standing in the sun meant a burned hand. There were problems of food; not a shortage, perhaps, but a monotonous sameness with everything coming out of cans. There was, like elsewhere in the desert, a shortage of water, and what little there was was salty. There was an almost total absence of bread, and a superabundance of fleas, flies, and rats.

Added to these discomforts was a problem rare in the annals of defended strongholds. The Axis airfields from which sorties were made against Tobruk were sufficiently close for the defenders to hear the aircraft starting up prior to take-off. Two of the airfields, El Adem and Acroma, were only about 10 miles away, and some of the defenders swore that in the still, desert night air they could hear the ground crews singing as they worked on the aircraft.

There was only one permanent line of defence against the bombers once the RAF fighters had been withdrawn on April 25, and that was the anti-aircraft guns of the Royal Artillery, supplemented by the guns of ships in harbour. Two regiments of 3·7-inch and captured Italian 102-mm guns, plus three regiments with 40-mm Bofors stayed for the whole siege, pitting their wits against each new variation and combination of attack by high-level and dive-bombers. Throughout countless raids the gunners emulated their colleagues at Malta by maintaining a miniature 'Grand Barrage' in the face of the fierce bravery of German pilots who sometimes swept at less than 500 feet over the gun pits. By July the dive-bombers actually began to let up, and it became possible even to unload ships in daylight. Alone, the anti-aircraft gunners prevented bombing with impunity and so they, above all, enabled the supply vessels to unload and maintain the garrison.

The western sector, around the Ras el Madauar salient, had its own special problems. The rocky nature of the ground made deep digging almost impossible and, on those days when fighting was not actually taking place, both sides lay in their shallow trenches unable to move. A German account of conditions in the salient at the time says: 'The Australians were crack shots. Their sniping was superb. Even the most trivial movement from the foxhole—rump too high—and ping! You'd had it.'

For night patrolling, the Australians wore crêpe-soled shoes, long trousers, pullovers, and berets. They were armed with sub-machine guns and grenades, and their objective in most cases was a single enemy stronghold. They would descend on it silently on a moonless night, throw their grenades and empty the magazines of the sub-machine guns into the enemy emplacement, then disappear back into their own positions as swiftly and silently as they had arrived.

The Germans used much the same technique against the Australians and British, and on occasions a patrol from either side would encounter one another in No-Man's-Land, and a short sharp action would develop, often involving fierce, hand-to-hand fighting

Ju.87 B2 (Tropical). The desert version of the Luftwaffe's infamous dive-bomber, used in North Africa as flying artillery. **Speed:** 233 mph at 13,500 ft **Range:** 375 miles with 1,100-lb bomb load **Crew:** 2 **Ceiling:** 29,500 ft **Armament:** three 7.9-mm machine guns

Conditions worsen

As time went on, conditions in the besieged area became steadily worse, a fact of which Rommel himself was very much aware. Writing home to his wife in June he said: 'Water is very short in Tobruk, the British troops are getting only half-a-litre a day. With our dive-bombers I'm hoping to cut their rations still further. The heat is getting worse every day and . . . one's thirst becomes almost unquenchable.'

Churchill, too, was highly sensitive to the importance of Tobruk, and the role it should and could play in the Middle East campaign. After Tobruk had successfully beaten off one of the many attacks by the Axis forces, he cabled: 'Bravo, Tobruk! We feel it vital that Tobruk should be regarded as a sally port.'

This the Australians and British did, although often their efforts were overshadowed by events elsewhere. The eyes of the world were on the airborne invasion of Crete, the German assault on Russia, and—somewhat nearer to the beleaguered garrison—the abortive Operation 'Battleaxe'. Nevertheless, the Australian and British troops in Tobruk continued to play a decisive part in the tactical moves of both sides in the Western Desert.

Then, in August, Churchill began to receive demands from the Australian government for the withdrawal of their troops from Tobruk. Already, in response to this pressure, Auchinleck had relieved one Australian brigade by the Polish Carpathian Brigade (Lieutenant-General S. Kopanski), but this was not enough. By early September the Prime Minister of Australia (Mr Fadden) had become firmly determined that the Australian troops must be withdrawn from Tobruk. The reason he put forward at the time was: '. . . in order to give them an opportunity for refreshment, restoration of discipline and re-equipment, and to satisfy public opinion in Australia.' The Australian government was also said to be 'anxious about the decline in health resistance of their troops in the fortress and the danger of catastrophe resulting from further decline and inability to withstand a determined attack'.

There seems to be no evidence that the Australian troops were themselves clamouring to be relieved. They had fought with vigour and determination under the most trying conditions for five months, but they would probably have borne the strain longer if called upon to do so. Nevertheless, during September the rest of the Australians were replaced by the 70th British Division (Major-General R. M. Scobie, who also assumed command of the garrison).

It was not an easy change-over. The ships which brought in the 70th Division and took out the Australians were subjected to severe air attack in the process, the minelayer *Latona* being sunk and the destroyer *Hero* damaged.

When the Polish Brigade arrived in mid-August, General Morshead allocated them at first to the comparatively quiet southern sector, but after a few weeks they took over, with the Durham Light Infantry and Black Watch, the western sector with the salient.

By then the sector was showing all the

The Australians at Tobruk showed that the Afrika Korps was not invincible

signs of the four months' siege. The 'No-Man's-Land' between the forward posts was thickly carpeted with mines and booby-traps, and strewn with the unburied bodies of soldiers of both sides. But the defences – if such they could be called – were still in the same primitive condition; narrow and shallow trenches in which there was no room for the occupants to sit or kneel. In some places there was nothing but small, improvised stone breastworks.

The exposed nature of the forward defences in the western sector made any daylight approach to them impossible. Once the sun had risen, the defenders could not move out, nor could their reserves or supplies get up to them. Life would have been impossible had it not been for the fact that, by one of those unspoken mutual arrangements which sometimes come about in war, both sides observed an unofficial two-hour armistice, beginning at dusk. During this period, neither side opened fire on the other and the troops on both sides could emerge safely from their cramped positions. Food, water, and ammunition could be brought up to forward defended positions and life could be made slightly more bearable on both sides.

Each night the Germans signalled the end of the two-hour armistice by a burst of tracer-bullets fired straight up into the air, and from then on it was 'business as usual'.

Another mutually accepted custom was the raising of a Red Cross flag when a man was wounded. Fire immediately switched from that point and stretcher-bearers could safely approach to remove the wounded man. Indeed, on one or two occasions when casualties were heavier than usual, ambulances were allowed to drive up unmolested to the Red Cross flag to remove the wounded.

When the Poles took over the western sector from the Australians, their first instinct was to reject these cease-fire arrangements. They were all men who had, at great risk to themselves, escaped from a Poland occupied by the Germans, who were applying barbarian methods of treatment. There was a powerful emotional barrier inhibiting the Poles' acceptance of anything in the nature of a pact with the Germans.

However, General Kopanski realised that any change in the established customs would alert the Germans to the fact that a change of units had taken place, and this, of course, the defenders wished to keep secret as long as possible. Accordingly he ordered his battalion commanders to continue to observe the armistice and cease-fire arrangements of the Australians and this they did, although with some reluctance. After a few days in the sector, however, they began to appreciate the practical value of the two-hour nightly armistice, realising that without it the forward companies would inevitably have died from thirst and starvation. But they discontinued the hoisting of the Red Cross flag as soon as possible. Each section was equipped with medical supplies and with the aid of these, plus some improvised surgery, it was possible in the majority of cases for the wounded to wait for evacuation until the two-hour armistice at dusk.

Nevertheless, on their side the Germans and Italians continued the custom of hoisting a Red Cross flag and evacuating wounded in daylight, and although the Poles did not fire on the casualty clearing party, the flag – as General Kopanski put it – 'greatly facilitated our pinpointing their strongholds, and destroying them very efficiently and inflicting new casualties later on'.

Tobruk harbour as another German raid explodes on the town and its defences

With the relief of the 9th Australian Division by the 70th British Division complete, there were now in Tobruk three infantry brigades (14th, 16th, and 23rd), a tank brigade (32nd, comprising 1st and 4th Royal Tank Regiments and a squadron each from 7th Royal Tank Regiment and the King's Dragoon Guards), seven artillery regiments, plus an anti-aircraft artillery brigade, a Czech battalion, a machine-gun battalion of the Royal Northumberland Fusiliers, an Australian battalion and – later on – two New Zealand battalions with supporting artillery.

This was the force with which General Scobie intended to break out from Tobruk and link up with a co-ordinated offensive by the 8th Army: Operation 'Crusader'.

Inside the besieged fortress General Scobie decided that the Tobruk garrison should break through the lines of the enemy on the eastern sector, in order to meet the approaching units of the 8th Army. This was to be the task of the 14th Infantry Brigade (Black Watch, Bedfordshire and Hertfordshire Regiment, York and Lancaster Regiment) under its commander Brigadier B. H. Chappel, with the support of the tanks of the 32nd Tank Brigade and the machine-gunners of the Royal Northumberland Fusiliers.

The break-out was planned for dawn on November 22. But three hours before the break-out, the Polish Brigade was to launch a feint break-out from the western sector, preceded by a heavy artillery barrage.

During the hours of darkness on the night November 21/22, the Tobruk troops moved to their arranged jumping-off points. In the distance they could hear the sounds of the fierce battle in the Sidi Rezegh area, where the 8th Army was fighting to reach them.

All those awaiting zero hour – British, Poles, Czechs, New Zealanders, and Australians – were hopeful that the siege was about to be ended. But much hard fighting lay ahead. Operation 'Crusader' was destined to continue for many weeks and the siege of Tobruk was not to end until December 10, when land communications between the garrison and the main body of the 8th Army were once again firmly established. Then the Royal Navy could relax from its task of being the only link between Tobruk and the rest of the Allies – a task which had included delivering to the garrison 34,000 men, 72 tanks, 92 guns, and 34,000 tons of stores over a period of 242 days.

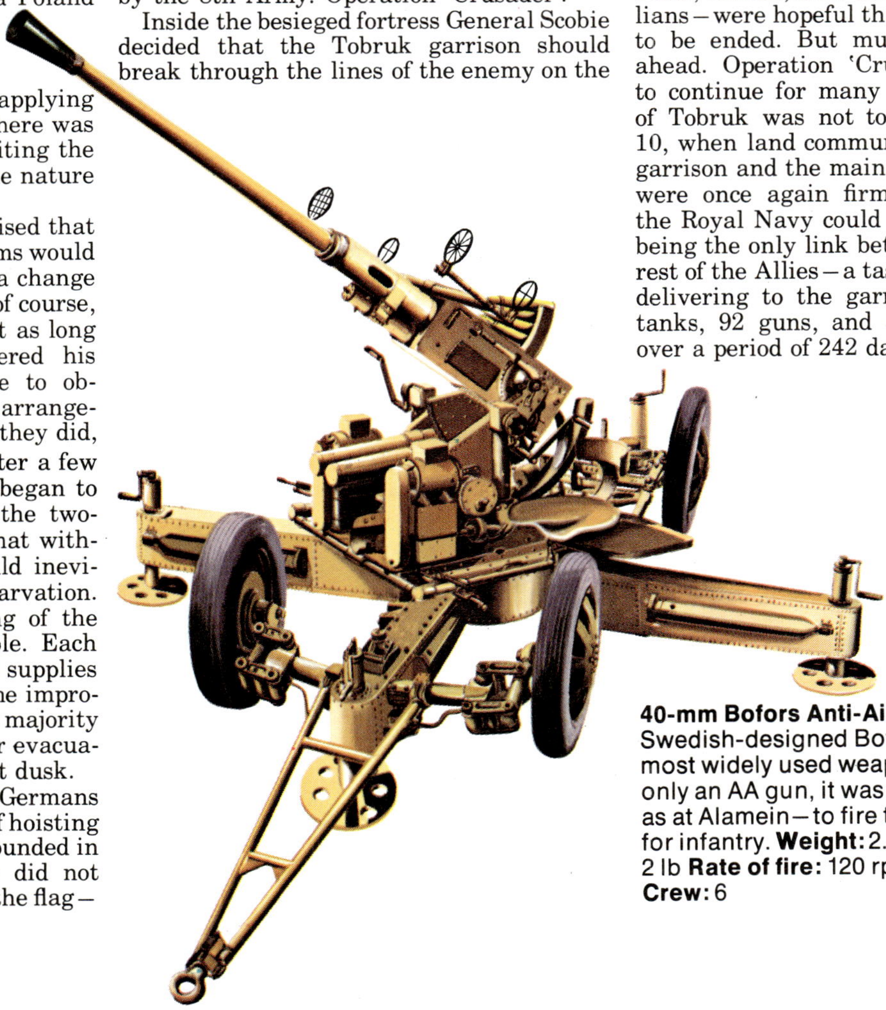
40-mm Bofors Anti-Aircraft Gun. The Swedish-designed Bofors was one of the most widely used weapons of the war. Not only an AA gun, it was also used – as at Alamein – to fire tracer as a guide-line for infantry. **Weight:** 2.4 tons **Weight of shell:** 2 lb **Rate of fire:** 120 rpm **Ceiling:** 12,000 ft **Crew:** 6

DUELS WITH THE AFRIKA KORPS

In one month Rommel's first offensive had taken him all the way from Tripolitania to the border of Egypt; but the British could not allow him to consolidate his hold on the strategically important passes at Sollum and Halfaya. The Allies' high hopes, though, were soon dashed. Rommel proved himself as tenacious and resourceful in defence as he was daring and fluid in attack.

When Wavell received news that a convoy of tanks and aircraft was on its way (the Tiger Convoy) he planned a limited operation—Operation Brevity—to drive the Germans from the frontier. Brigadier Gott's force attacked on May 15 with all available tanks but they were unable to consolidate their gains and retreated when the Germans counterattacked. On May 27 the Germans reoccupied the Halfaya Pass.

The Tiger Convoy docked at Alexandria on May 12 and disgorged 238 tanks and 43 Hurricane fighters. Churchill insisted that his 'Tiger Cubs' be used in an immediate offensive, and although unhappy about the operational readiness of his newly-equipped forces, Wavell launched his last desert offensive—Operation Battleaxe—on June 14. The British attacked with tanks and infantry looking for a decisive battle—tank against tank—which they hoped to win with their superior numbers. But Rommel had other ideas. With calculated deliberation he held his hand, letting the defensive positions break the British tank attacks on their own. Although he had lost a fair proportion of his infantry and guns, his tank force was practically as fresh as it had been at the start of the battle and, as a result of attrition, actually superior in numbers to the British.

Operation Brevity

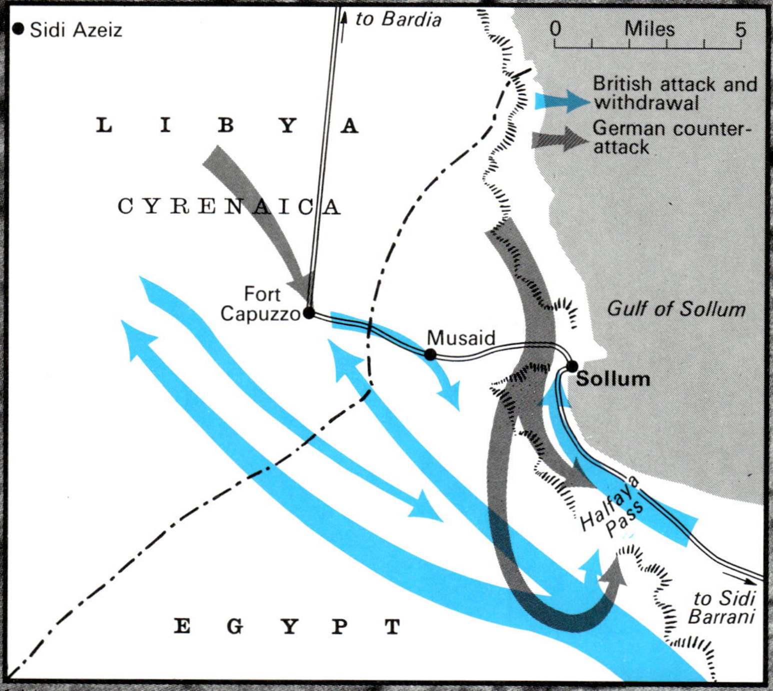

Operation Battleaxe

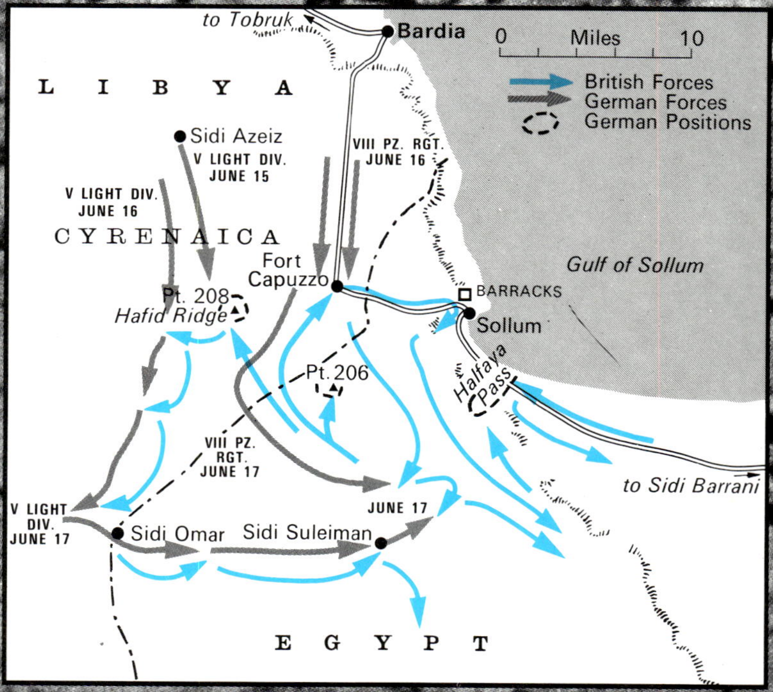

He then launched a well-judged armoured counterstroke wide round his enemy's desert flank, and sent the British scurrying back.

In November 1941 the British mounted a bigger offensive – Operation Crusader. By this time Wavell had been replaced by General Auchinleck as Commander-in-Chief, while the enlarged forces on the Libyan frontier had been constituted as the 8th Army, under General Cunningham. The offensive opened on the 18th, with a desert flank advance which placed the British close to Rommel's rear. In meeting the superior numbers and mobility of the British mechanised forces, the Germans skilfully applied tactics which lured the British tanks into traps that were lined with their own concealed tanks and deadly 88-mm guns. Rommel thus strikingly demonstrated, as already in Operation Battleaxe, the defensive-offensive method and baited gambit in modern mechanised warfare – blunting the edge of his opponent's 'sword' on his own 'shield', preparatory to the delivery of his thrust.

The German '88' flak guns knocked out many British tanks.

Next day Rommel, judging the situation to be ripe for bolder action, launched the mobile part of his forces on a daring swoop round the 8th Army's desert flank and over the frontier on to its communications. As it burst through into the British rear areas it spread confusion and panic. The effect might have settled the issue of the battle if the decision to persist or retreat had remained with Cunningham. But Auchinleck, who flew up at this crucial moment, insisted on a continuance of the battle, and then, on returning to Cairo two days later, appointed Ritchie to command in place of Cunningham. Auchinleck's intervention brought victory out of defeat – yet it was basically more of a gamble than Rommel's strategic raid, because it staked the 8th Army's survival on the maintenance of its far advanced position.

While Rommel's deep thrust failed in its aim only by a narrow margin, the penalty of failure was large. For while he and his three armoured divisions (two German and one Italian) were operating over the frontier, far away from the remainder, the split-up British forces which he had left behind were able to recover their balance, resume their offensive pressure, and link up with the garrison of Tobruk, before he returned to the relief of his non-mobile formations. Although he succeeded in regaining the advantage temporarily after several days' hard fighting and close-quarter manoeuvring, it was a barren success. His losses were much heavier than in the opening phase, and a bigger subtraction from his limited tank strength than he could withstand, particularly in view of the larger reinforcements available to the British. On December 6, 1941, Rommel was forced to break off the battle around Tobruk and retreat, first to Gazala, and then back to the frontier of Tripolitania.

Operation Crusader

Far left: Operation Brevity, which started on May 15, 1941, was the British attempt to throw the Germans back from the frontier and pave the way for future operations in Cyrenaica. The British started well but had soon to withdraw in the face of German counterattacks. *Left:* Operation Battleaxe was more ambitious, but failed because of Rommel's excellent defensive tactics. *Right:* Operation Crusader. After losing the initial battle Rommel immediately fell back to his defensive position at El Agheila

Matildas on the move: the battle for Halfaya ended their reputation as the invulnerable queen of the battlefield, for the 88s, used as anti-tank guns, penetrated their thick armour with ease

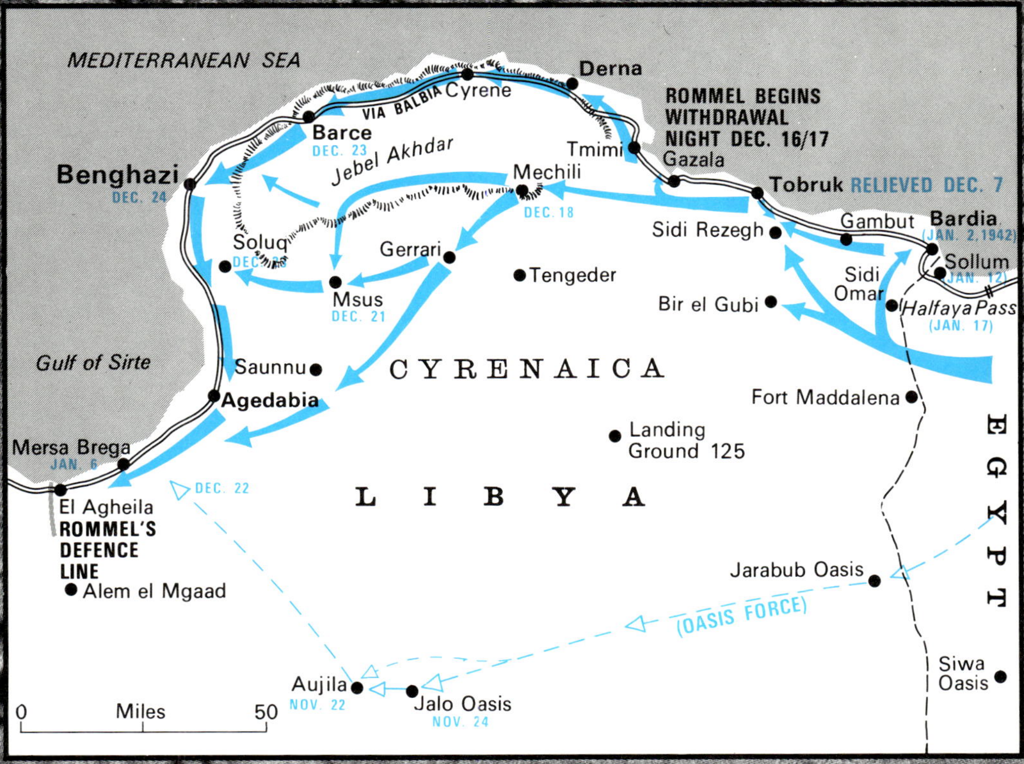

Newcomers to the Desert War

By November 1941 the 'second generation' of British infantry and cruiser tanks, together with the American light Stuart tanks, had reached the desert theatre – but they met with mixed success in 'Crusader'. The Allies were painfully learning the tactics of the German Panzer divisions, but the reliability of the older German designs was still superior

Cruiser Mk 6 – the Crusader, dogged by mechanical failures. *Armament:* one 2-pounder, two 7·92-mm Besa machine-guns. *Armour:* 39-mm (max).

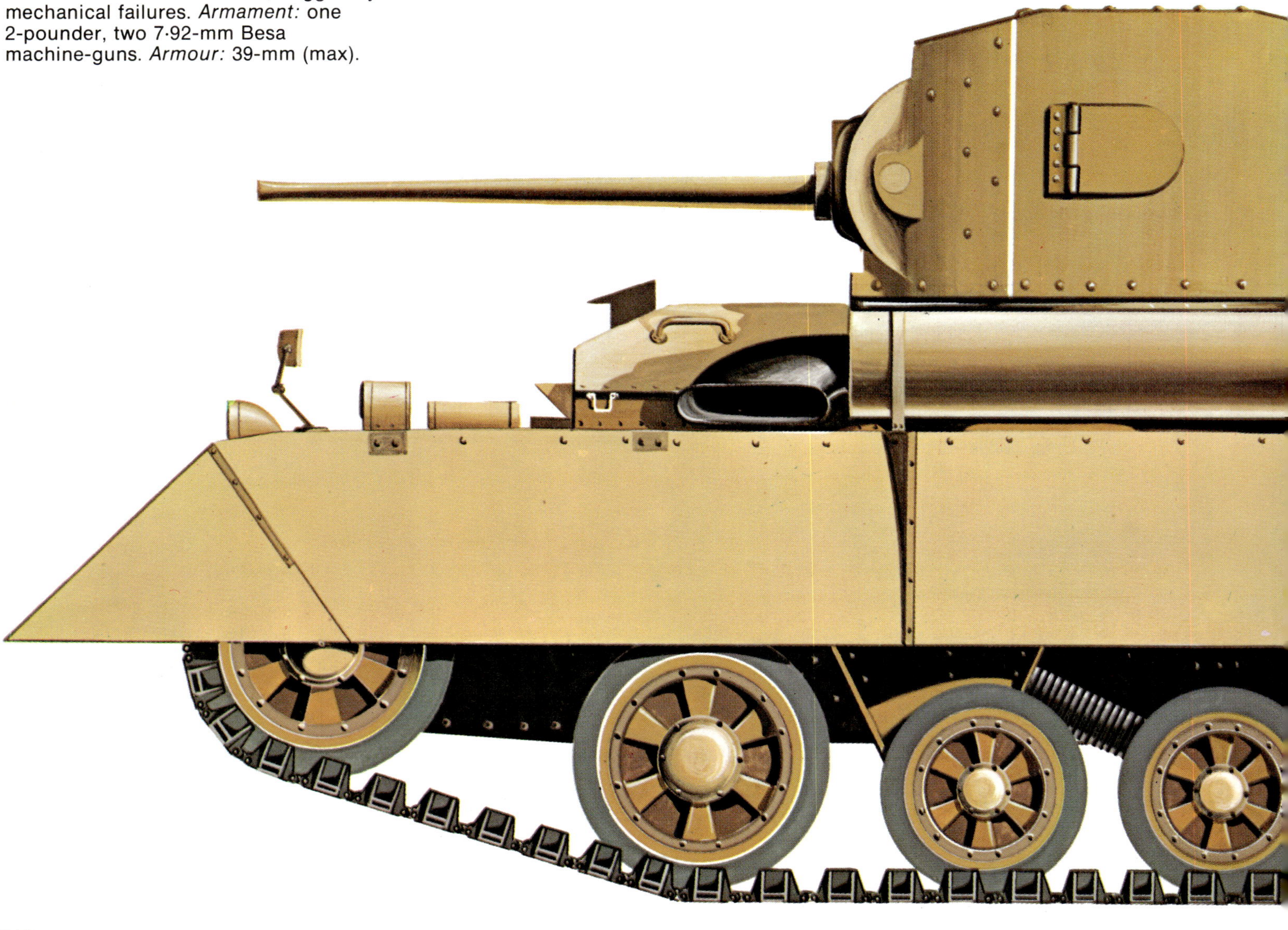

Light Stuart Mk 1 ('Honey'). First American tank used by the British in the war. *Armament:* one 37-mm, two ·30-inch machine-guns; one ·30-inch machine-gun (mounted on cupola). *Armour:* 44-mm (max).

Infantry Mk 3—the Valentine, successor to the Matilda—but still not fast enough to match the speed of the German tanks. *Armament:* one 2-pounder, one 7·92-mm Besa machine-gun. *Armour:* 65-mm (max).

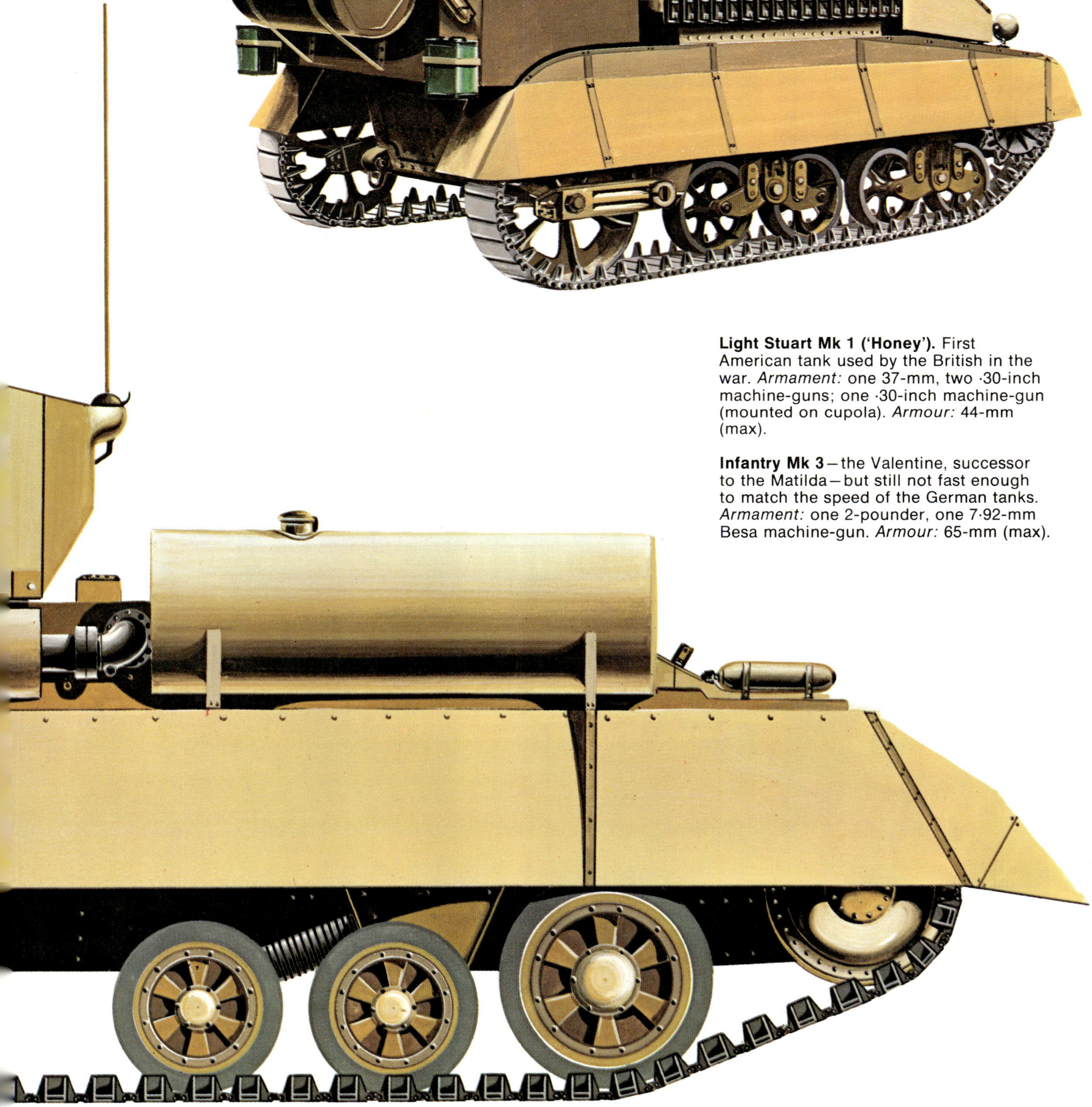

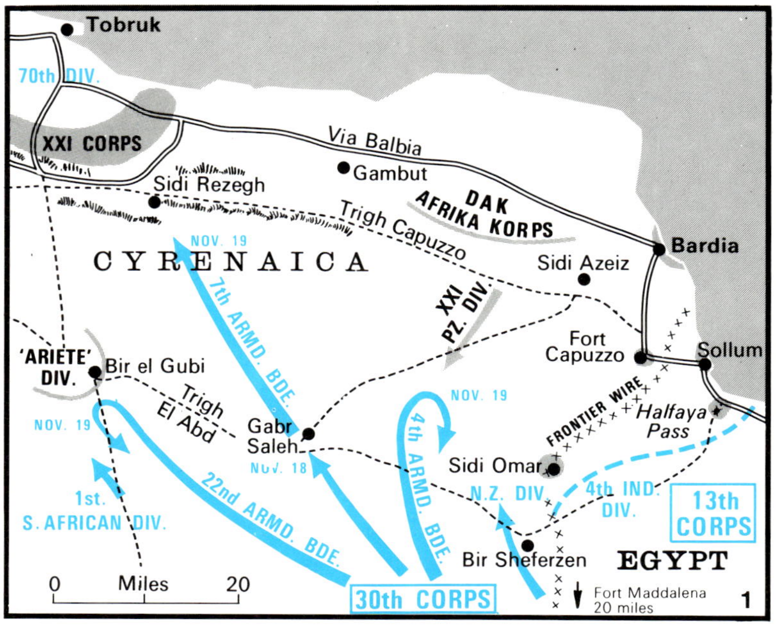

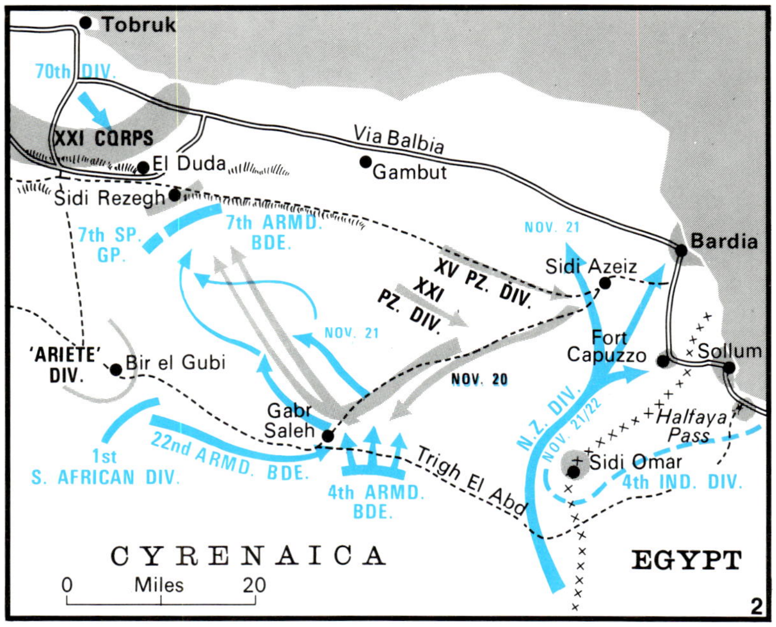

1. **November 18/19: Operation 'Crusader' begins.** The Allied plan is to mask the German frontier positions in the Halfaya/Sollum area with the forces of General Godwin-Austen's 13th Corps, while General Norrie's 30th Corps drives directly for Tobruk to raise the siege. General Scobie's 70th Division—the Tobruk garrison—is prepared to break out of the perimeter through the siege-lines of XXI Corps. The Allied attack starts well: 7th Armoured Brigade pushes to within 10 miles of the Tobruk perimeter, capturing the airfield at Sidi Rezegh. On the flanks, however, 22nd Armoured Brigade is halted by stiff opposition from the Italian 'Ariete' Division, and a counterattack from XXI Panzer Division's Stephan Group halts the advance of 4th Armoured Brigade. The two Panzer divisions of the Afrika Korps (DAK) are deployed between Bardia and Gambut under the overall command of General Cruewell. At this stage, Rommel's main concern is still the attack on Tobruk; and the first German reaction to the British penetration in the centre comes from the initiative of Cruewell, not Rommel. It is Cruewell who sets in motion a positive Axis countermove.

2. **November 20/22: The 'multi-layer battle' develops.** Cruewell has already sent the DAK on a wild-goose chase towards Sidi Azeiz; and now Rommel, realising that a full-scale Allied offensive is in progress, orders Cruewell to move against 7th Armoured Brigade at Sidi Rezegh. And the Tobruk garrison has begun its break-out by driving a salient into the siege-lines against unexpected resistance; but hopes of a link-up between 7th Armoured Brigade and the Tobruk garrison are dashed by the approach of the DAK from the south-east. The most extraordinary and confused battle in the desert war to date has begun. Rommel has started well, with a definite achievement: the 8th Army is forced to halt in the centre. The Tobruk garrison has to suspend the break-out, and the attack by 7th Armoured Brigade against El Duda is checked with heavy loss. Cruewell's attack from the south-east is held, but only after 7th Armoured Brigade has lost 113 out of its original 141 tanks. Heading the advance on the right, Freyberg's New Zealand Division by-passes the German frontier garrisons.

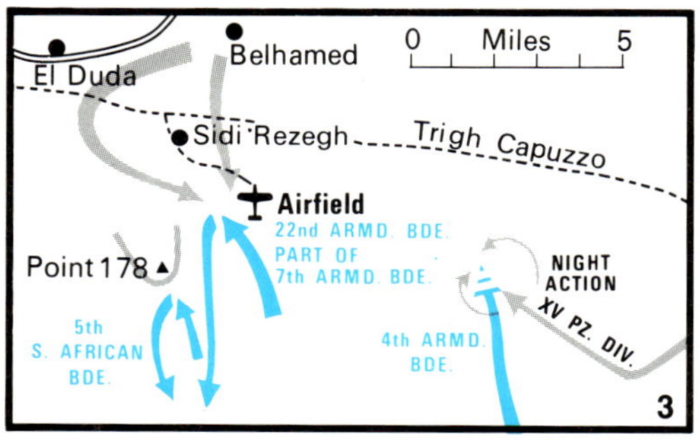

3. **November 22: The British spearhead is blunted.** In the afternoon, 5th South African Brigade is thrown back after its attempt to capture the southern end of the Sidi Rezegh escarpment; and XXI Panzer Division reopens the armoured battle. The German attack forces 22nd Armoured Brigade to fall back on the South Africans' position after 4th Armoured Brigade is unable to help. That night XV Panzer Division surprises 4th Armoured Brigade and shatters it as a fighting entity.

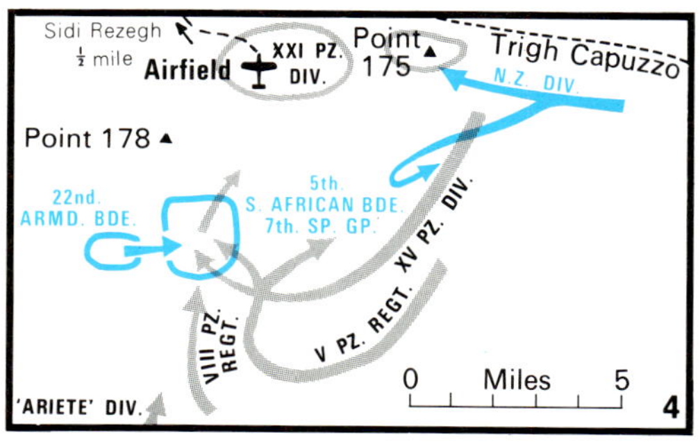

4. **November 23: XV Panzer Division wipes out 5th South African Brigade.** Cruewell continues to act with energy, despite the capture of the whole of his operational HQ. As XV Panzer Division heads south-west to join up with the 'Ariete' Division, it runs into the transport of the 5th South African Brigade and engages it. About noon, the V Panzer Regiment from XXI Panzer Division arrives on the scene to add to the German strength. The 22nd Armoured Brigade gives all the help at its disposal, but to no avail—by nightfall, the 5th South African Brigade has lost two-thirds of its men and all of its equipment, and has ceased to exist as a fighting entity. In the two days' fighting, 30th Corps has suffered heavy loss; but on the eastern flank, 13th Corps has been making good progress. It has taken part of the Sidi Rezegh escarpment and is only 6 miles from the airfield. But now Rommel prepares a plan which seeks to gamble on the complete disruption of the 8th Army's deployment. This is the 'dash to the wire'.

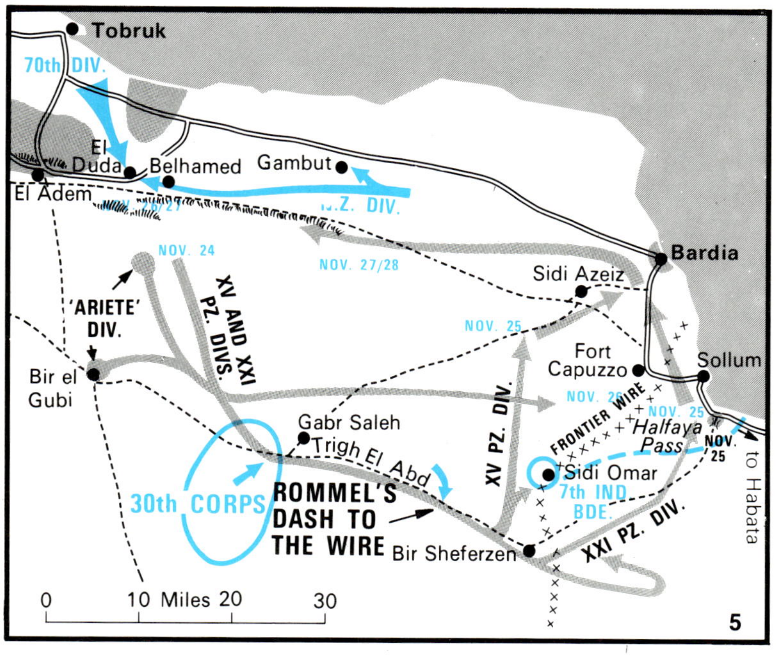

5. **November 24/28: Rommel's gamble does not succeed.** One of the worst results of the 'dash to the wire' is that it disorganises the Axis forces as well as the Allied opposition. But it does not break the Allied offensive: Rommel is unable to prevent the first relief of Tobruk. Violent German counterattacks between November 29 and December 1 reimpose the siege, but this pace is too hot for Rommel—he is forced to abandon the siege and to retreat from Tobruk.

Trump Card of the German Desert Army: The 88mm Flak Gun 18

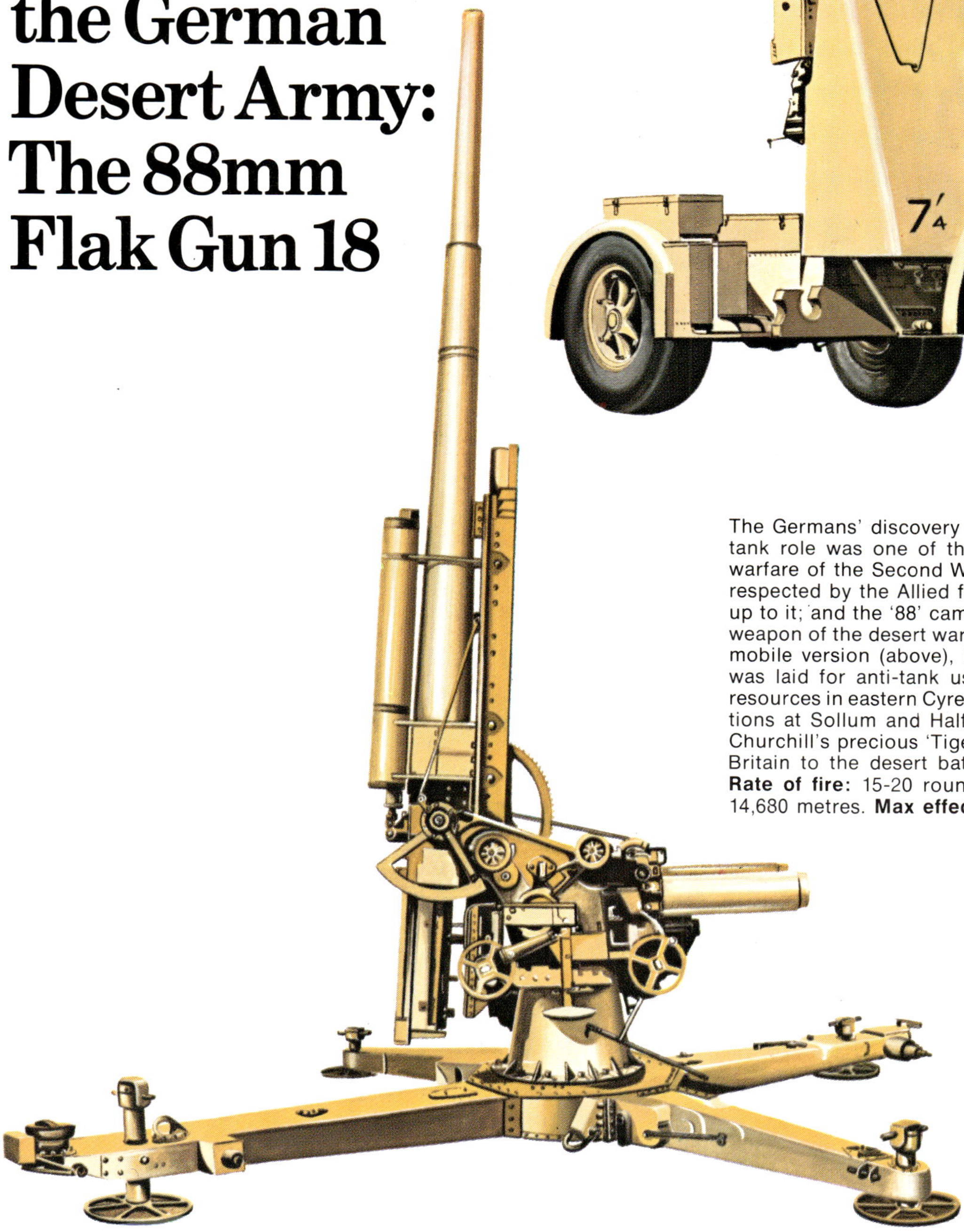

The Germans' discovery of the potency of their heavy flak guns in an anti-tank role was one of their most startling contributions to the armoured warfare of the Second World War. The '88' was a weapon both feared and respected by the Allied forces in the Western Desert; no tank could stand up to it; and the '88' came to be regarded as the ultimate German wonder-weapon of the desert war, with almost mythical powers. It is here seen in its mobile version (above), in its normal anti-aircraft position (left), and as it was laid for anti-tank use (below). Rommel eked out his over-stretched resources in eastern Cyrenaica by digging-in '88s' to hold his front-line positions at Sollum and Halfaya; and these guns reaped a rich harvest when Churchill's precious 'Tiger Cubs' were rushed from the training-grounds of Britain to the desert battlefield. **Calibre:** 8·8-cm. **Overall length:** 25 feet. **Rate of fire:** 15-20 rounds per min. **Crew no:** 6. **Max effective altitude:** 14,680 metres. **Max effective horizontal range:** 10,600 metres

ROMMEL STRIKES BACK

By mid-January 1942, Auchinleck's spearheads had reached the Gulf of Sirte, and Cyrenaica seemed lost for Rommel's exhausted Panzer army. But in fact the pattern of the desert war was repeating itself: as Rommel's forces fell back on their bases in Tripolitania, the 8th Army advanced farther and farther from its bases in Egypt. Both sides had suffered heavy losses in men and equipment and a race was on to bring the opposing armies up to strength. This time, however, the German and Italian armies had the advantage of a shorter supply route from Tripoli and better protection for their convoys—thanks to the attacks on Malta. The Afrika Korps was once again ready to attack.

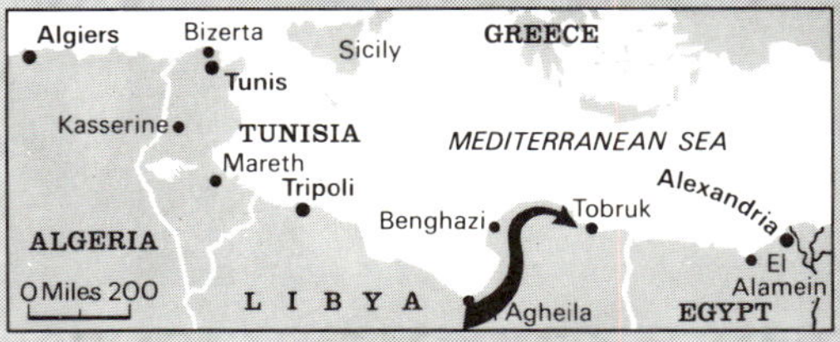

Rommel's Panzers deploy for the attack on the British outposts at El Agheila

Sado-Opera Mundi

Rommel's second offensive in Cyrenaica followed the lines of his debut in March and April 1941. It began with a timely blow against the Allied outposts, at Mersa Brega and Agedabia, which disrupted all hopes of the 8th Army for an invasion of Tripolitania. Rommel had hoped merely to delay the British attack by striking while the 8th Army was off balance and spread over a large area; but when he saw the confusion he had caused, Rommel ignored the orders of Commando Supremo, the Italian High Command in Rome, and fed in his Panzer forces until the strike became a full-scale offensive which kept the 8th Army on the run. This time Rommel was not able to press on to Tobruk, but was halted west of Gazala. In three weeks, nonetheless, he had reconquered western Cyrenaica for the Axis—the 'Desert Fox' had done it again.

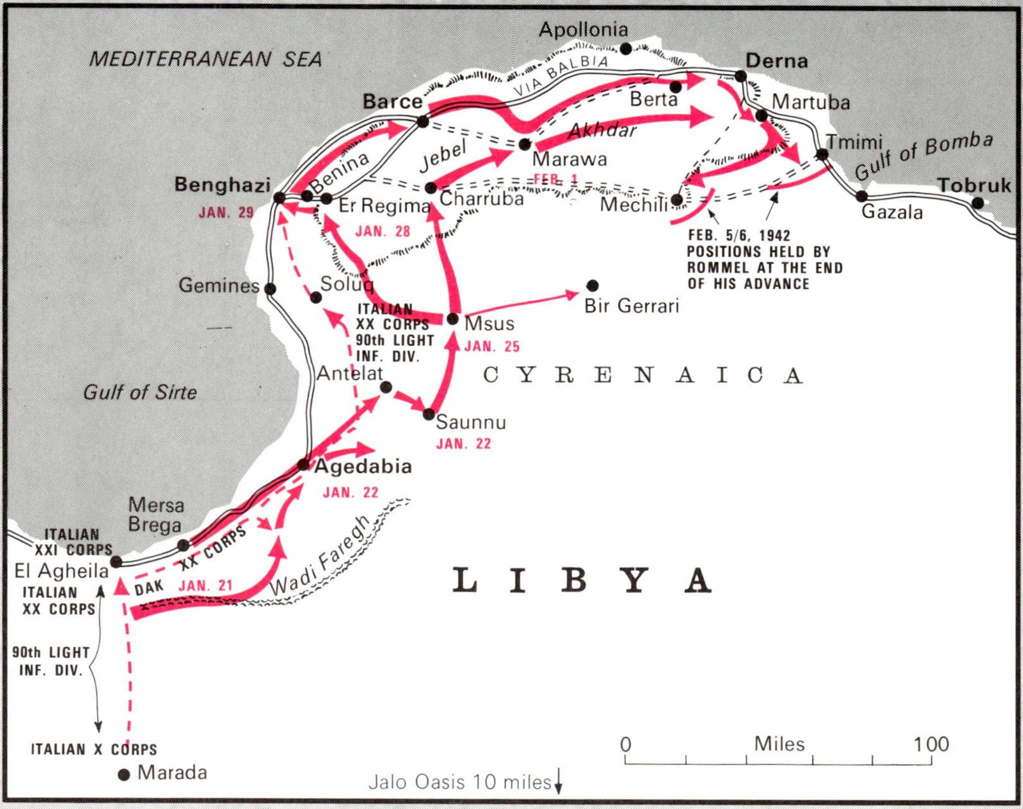

Imperial War Museum

Far left: **A mobile piece of German artillery in action during the advance to Mechili**

Left: **A Mark IV Panzer of the Afrika Korps. This was the best tank in the desert at the time**

Right: **Rommel and his staff. With renewed confidence Panzerarmee Afrika gathered momentum**

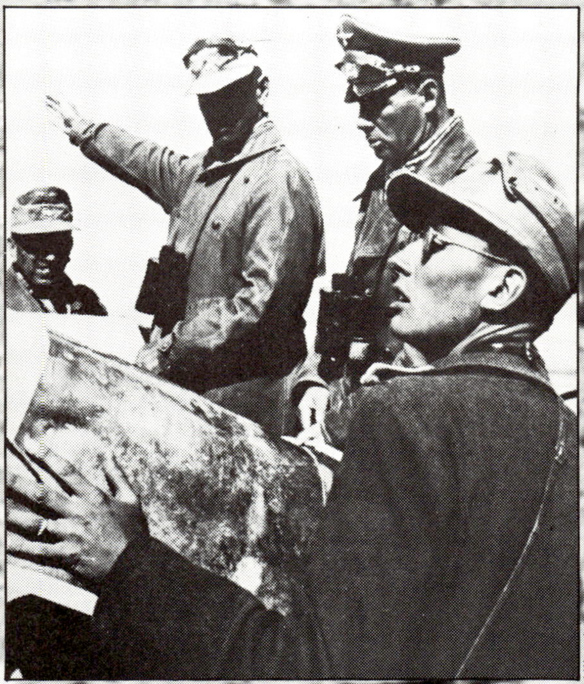

Ullstein

New equipment for the Axis...

Apart from receiving some Mark III Specials (see below) the Germans concentrated mainly upon improving equipment which had already proved reliable and battle-worthy. The Panzer Mark III, with its short-barrelled 5-cm gun, was the most numerous German tank, and its armour was strengthened by bolting plates of face-hardened steel on to various parts of its anatomy. Although the majority of the Italian armoured formations were still equipped with their 'mobile coffins', as Axis soldiers called the M13/40, they had begun to receive some new equipment like the self-propelled gun below

Italian 75/18 Semovente (self-propelled gun): although much Italian equipment during the early years of the war was obsolete and ill-suited to desert warfare, by 1942 they had begun to produce somewhat improved weapons. The 75/18 Semovente first saw action with the Ariete Division early in 1942. **Weight:** 12 tons. **Speed:** 20·5 mph maximum. **Crew:** Four. **Armament:** One 75-mm gun, and one 6·5-mm machine-gun. The main armament had a maximum range of 10,280 yards, and a maximum rate of fire of four rounds a minute. It had an elevation of 22½ degrees and depression of 11 degrees, with a traverse of 17 degrees left, and 20 degrees right

Panzer Mark III Special: by mid-1942 the Afrika Korps had begun to receive a new version of the Mark III. It was equipped with the long-barrelled 5-cm gun, similar to the formidable Pak 38, and was also designed with 'spaced armour'—an extra frontal plate separated from the basic armour by an air space of 4 inches, and intended to break up the armour-piercing cap of an anti-tank shell and thus reduce its power to penetrate the plate behind. **Weight:** 22 tons. **Armour:** 57-mm maximum, with a 20-mm spaced plate. **Speed:** 25 mph road speed. **Radius:** 100 miles maximum. **Crew:** Five. **Armament:** One 5-cm long-barrelled gun, and two 7·9-mm machine-guns

and the Allies

For the Allies the lull before the Battle of Gazala saw the introduction of equipment which went some way toward counteracting the grave deficiencies which had become apparent in the earlier battles. But these new weapons were still in very short supply, and although individual pieces compared well with their enemy counterparts, their performance was jeopardised by serious deficiencies in other equipment—particularly the failure to develop an armour-piercing warhead which could penetrate the new thicker German armour at extreme ranges

M3 General Grant: The first American medium tank received by the British forces. Its arrival was greeted with enthusiasm, for the 8th Army now had a tank with a gun capable of engaging German tanks and anti-tank crews on equal terms—and this could be done from behind the heavier armour of a reasonably fast and very reliable tank. Its major weakness was that the vital 75-mm gun was mounted in one side of the hull and thus had a very restricted arc of fire. **Weight:** 28·5 tons. **Armour:** 57-mm max. **Speed:** 28 mph maximum on roads. **Radius:** 108 miles maximum. **Crew:** Six. **Armament:** One 75-mm (hull) and one 37-mm (turret) gun, and four ·30-inch machine-guns

Six-pounder Anti-Tank Gun. The development of a larger gun to replace the 2-pounder had begun in 1938, but the stress of general rearmament had meant that the gun was not ready for trials for two years. Its delivery was further delayed by the fact that it was decided to use the tried 2-pounder to re-equip the army after Dunkirk. As a result the 8th Army had only 112 of the new guns by mid-1942. **Crew:** Five. **Weight in action:** 2,560 lb. **Range:** Up to 5,000 yards. Could fire either armour-piercing shot or high-explosive shell—but the latter was in limited supply

THE FIGHT AT GAZALA

From February until mid-May 1942 there was a lul in the desert war as both sides renewed their forces But Rommel was anxious to continue his reconques of Cyrenaica, and Churchill was continually urgin his commanders to resume the offensive. Romme attacked first, but it soon seemed that he had mis calculated—that lack of fuel and water woul destroy the Afrika Korps. However, the 'Deser Fox' was saved by his own willingness to improvise

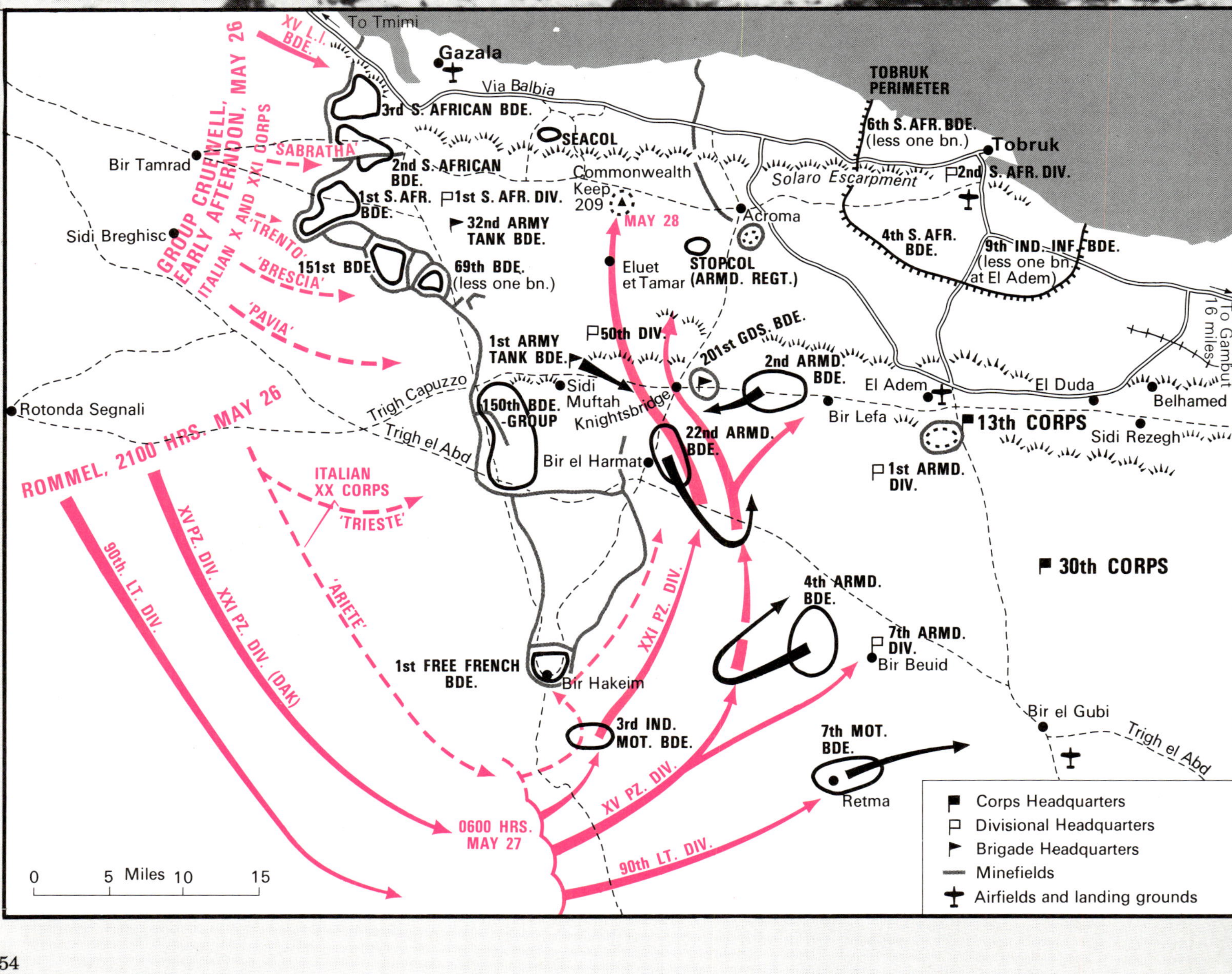

and by the slowness of the British commanders. The result, the fall of Tobruk, was not only a terrific blow to Allied morale but also meant that the road to Egypt and Suez now seemed open – and Rommel urged on his men and tanks towards a spot on the map called Alamein.

Of the opposing forces the British were in greater strength on the ground with 100,000 troops and 849 tanks, as opposed to Rommel's 90,000 troops and 560 tanks. But the Axis had an overwhelming superiority in the air while their tank formations contained a proportion of the best tanks in the desert. Furthermore Rommel possessed a more finely-tempered, though considerably smaller, army. The Italians were hardly outstanding soldiers, but the Afrika Korps embodied a rare degree of experience and skill. Nor can there be anything but admiration for the way in which the enemy commanders handled their armour. With rare exceptions, they kept their tanks concentrated, and wisely protected them behind an effective artillery screen until the moment for the *coup de grâce* had come.

The 8th Army, on the other hand, was at this time a mixture of tired veterans and brash newcomers, who were given scant time to settle in before the blow came. And the much-vaunted Gazala Line

Prelude to Tobruk – German artillery batters the British during fighting in the 'Cauldron'

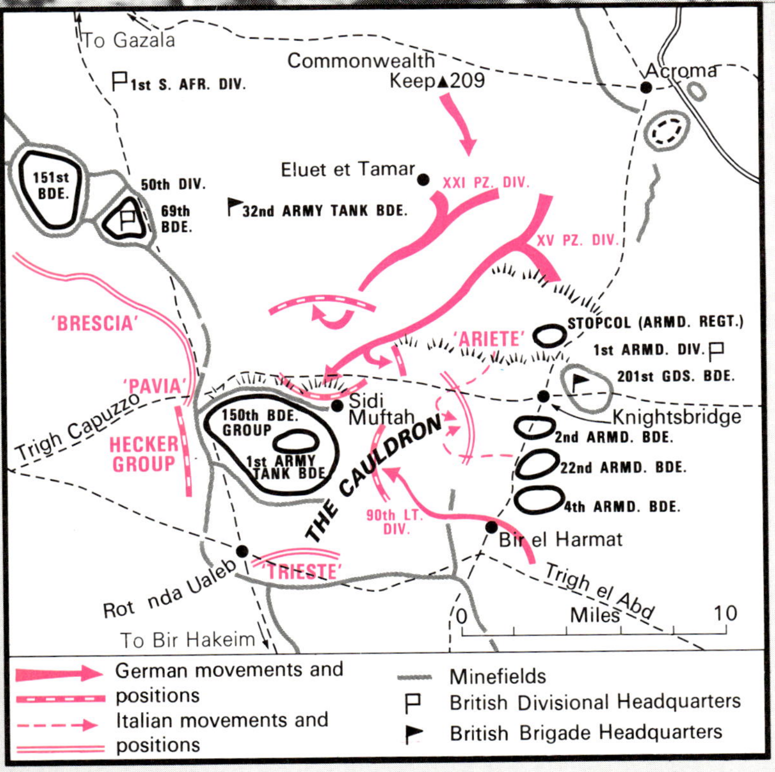

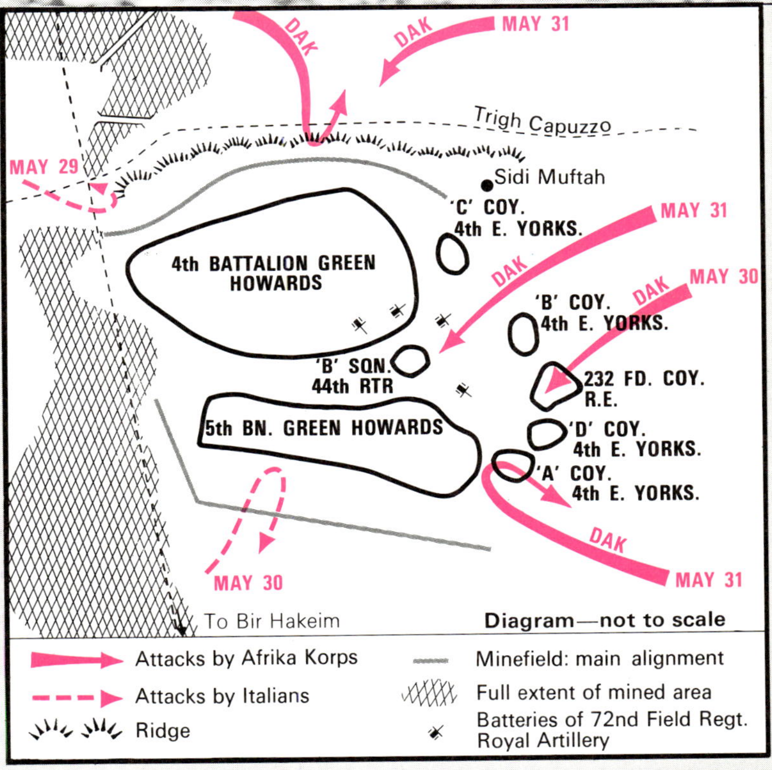

◁ **Phase 1: The Gazala Line is turned.** The front-line brigades of General Ritchie's 8th Army were deployed along the Gazala Line in an inter-connected system of 'brigade boxes' and Ritchie hoped to exhaust Rommel's attacks against these defences. But the Gazala Line had one great weakness: its southern flank at Bir Hakeim extended into empty desert – and Rommel opened the battle with a vast sweep around the Gazala Line with his Afrika Korps, while Cruewell and the Italians pinned down the rest of the line. Within 24 hours, German spearheads were astride the 8th Army's communications. But the Bir Hakeim garrison held out in the German rear.

△ **Phase 2: Rommel turns on 150th Brigade box.** This box nearly wrecked Rommel's attack: General Bayerlein later said: 'We never even knew that it was there; by the evening of the third day we were surrounded and almost out of petrol.' As Rommel's armour moved west into the 'Cauldron', it seemed to Ritchie that all was going well and that Rommel would be trapped against the Gazala minefields with no supplies. The battle now devolved on Rommel's attempt to crush the 150th Brigade box, while his sappers fought to keep open his supply-lines through the British minefields. This was the time for a counterattack by 8th Army – but Ritchie held back and missed his chance

△ **Phase 3: The fight for 150th Brigade box.** For almost 72 hours, Rommel's entire efforts were concentrated on this vital sector – but again the 8th Army missed its chance to throw in a heavy counterattack. This 'battle within a battle' was one of the unsung epics of the desert war, as the box garrison was forced steadily back by the German attacks. Since the battle had opened, the 150th Brigade box had exhausted the supplies calculated to last for 21 days – and the end finally came on June 1, heralded by a crushing Stuka bombardment. Rommel had secured his lifeline through the Gazala Line – but Bir Hakeim still held out at the southern flank of the battle-front was more suited to be the springboard of a fresh offensive than to provide a well-balanced line of in-depth defence fortifications.

In May 1942 Rommel attacked first with a diversion in the north by the Italian infantry, followed by a wide flanking manoeuvre with his armour which, in the night of the 26th, threw the 8th Army off its balance. He was checked, however, before he could reach the coast and cut off the British forces holding the Gazala Line. Thereupon he took up a defensive position with his back against the British minefields—which led the British to feel that he was cornered, and bound to surrender. But their countermoves were too direct and they fell into the defensive traps which Rommel had quickly improvised when he was checked. With its reserves entangled and expended, the 8th Army was unable to meet Rommel's next flanking move, and was beaten piecemeal—once again the 'Desert Fox' had turned the tables of defence into offence.

While one portion was falling back to the frontier, another portion withdrew into Tobruk. Rommel's armoured forces swept past Tobruk, as if heading for the frontier, then suddenly switched round and struck at Tobruk in reverse, before the forces there had settled down. Penetrating the defences at a weak point, the Germans overran the garrison and captured almost the whole of it—together with such an abundance of supplies and transport as to provide the means for a prolonged advance on their own part—an advance that was not long in coming.

Not unnaturally, the news of Rommel's heavy defeat of 8th Army and his capture of Tobruk caused a wave of exhilaration to run through Germany and Italy. Overnight, Erwin Rommel's detractors in high places—and they were not lacking in either Rome or Berlin—became his staunchest champions, and there was widespread approval for the Führer's announcement that he was immediately conferring the rank of Field-Marshal on the brilliant desert commander. It seemed that the war in the Western Desert, already a little over two years old, was on the point of being resolved.

To the east of the Egyptian frontier, the brave but bewildered and exhausted formations of General Ritchie's defeated army began painfully to regroup themselves. In a desperate bid to stop the Axis onrush, General Auchinleck took command of the 8th Army, but the improvised defences at Marsa Matrûh were no match for Rommel's army and the British fell back to El Alamein. For the first time this desert bottleneck was about to become the hinge on which the outcome of the Desert War would swing.

▽ **Phase 4: Rommel's breakthrough.** Ritchie's counterattack came too late: his attempts to smash Rommel's hold on the 'Cauldron' were beaten off, and in a fierce attack Rommel shattered 30th Corps. This time he made no mistake about Tobruk, and broke through in the south-east corner

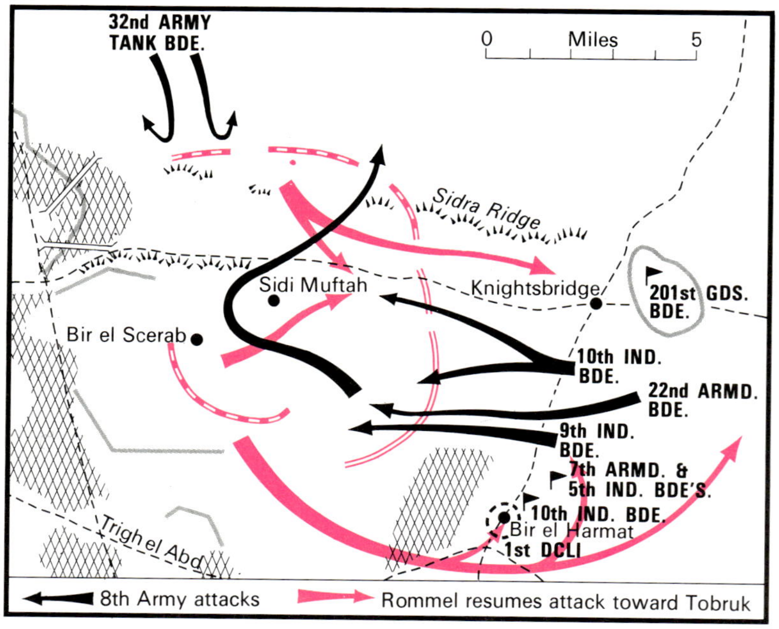

Auchinleck meets Rommel

1942 June 23: The Middle East Defence Committee authorises the withdrawal of 8th Army from the Egyptian frontier to Marsa Matrûh.
June 25: General Auchinleck takes command of 8th Army; General Ritchie is sent on leave. Auchinleck appoints Major-General Dorman-Smith as his acting Chief of the General Staff.
June 26: Auchinleck cancels the order to stand on the Matrûh-Sidi Hamza line—8th Army will withdraw eastwards as the enemy advances. Rommel begins to move his forces forward, with his armoured divisions astride the southern escarpment, and 90th Light Division to the north, aiming to cut the coast road east of Matrûh.
June 27: 1200 hours: The Germans have reached a position from which they threaten the withdrawal of 13th Corps; 10th Corps is ordered to attack to relieve this pressure.
1920 hours: 13th Corps issues the withdrawal codewords. 8th Army HQ orders 10th Corps to withdraw as well, but it does not receive the order until early the next morning.
June 28: 10th Corps is trapped with its back to the sea. At 1200 hours Auchinleck orders 10th Corps to break out that night, but 13th Corps, which is intended to launch a diversionary attack, is not informed of this plan until 2100 hours, by which time 10th Corps is moving out to the south—leaving over 7,000 prisoners.

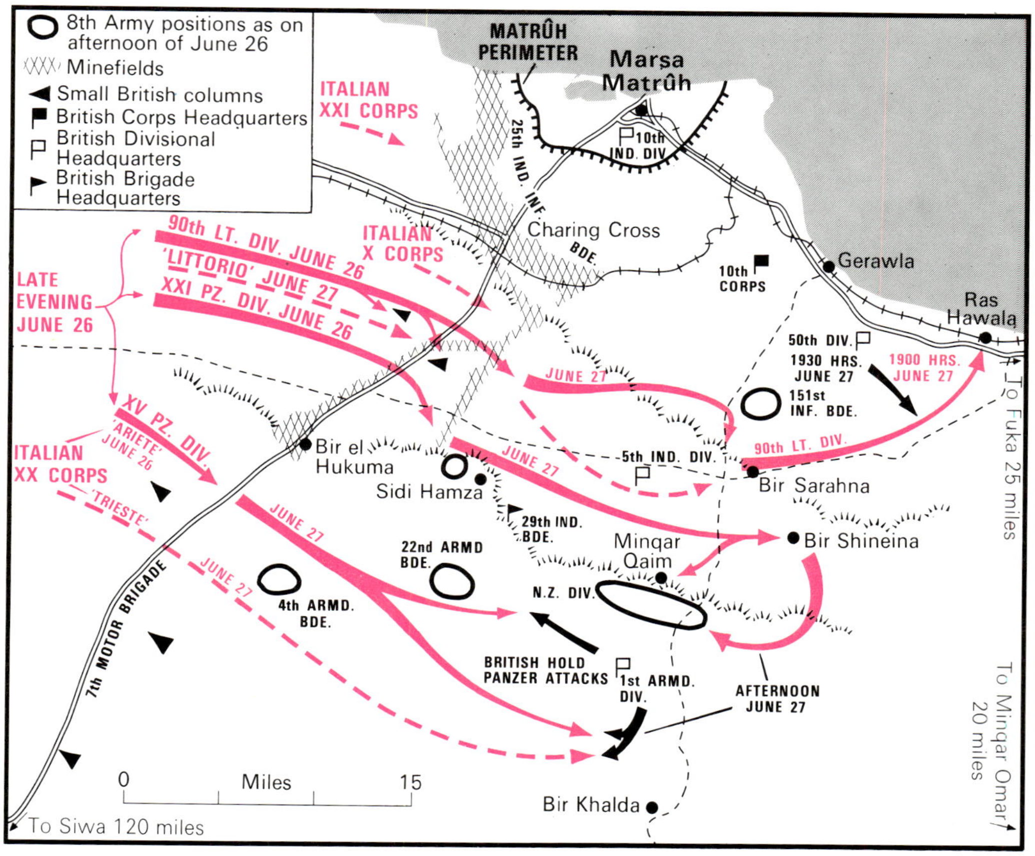

Matrûh was Auchinleck's first battle after ◁ taking over command of 8th Army: his disorganised forces tried to hold the threadbare defences, but Rommel simply repeated his encircling tactics. The next stop was Alamein

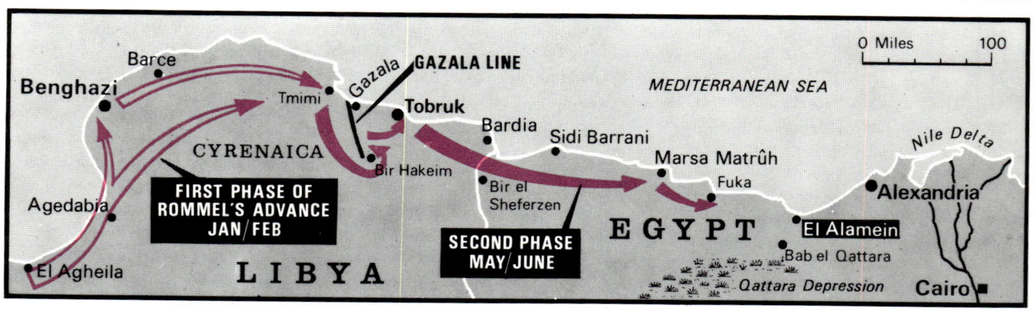

Rommel leads the Axis Panzerarmee to the ▷ height of its success: the invasion of Egypt. His first attack in January had recovered western Cyrenaica for the Axis; the battles of May/June hurled 8th Army back into Egypt

"For you the war is finish!"

Associated Press

We learnt yesterday that we are now definitely cut off here in Tobruk. Jerry has driven along to the south through El Adem and Sidi Rezegh and cut the coast road, probably near Gambut.

We are in a big, wide, flat area which has been used as an aerodrome and lies between the road to Bardia and the sea, and is to the south-east of the town.

9 am–Eric and I are squatting in our new and still unfinished trench. There is a hell of an attack on and it's been going on for the last two hours. A colossal barrage of AA is going up, and dive-bombers, mainly Junkers 87s, are very numerous. We haven't seen one of our planes yet! No 'drome to work from, I suppose. I only hope my luck holds.

Mid-day–Have just snatched a little grub. Things are looking bloody black. Jerry is slowly pushing our tanks and guns back from the eastern edge of the perimeter defences and he is now up on the escarpment to the south-east of us. It has been one long roar of bombs, guns, and shells all morning.

After making the last entry we spent a terrifying afternoon in our dug-outs and trenches. Hour after hour we were cooped up while Jerry's creeping artillery barrage crept nearer and nearer, and beyond that a mass of tanks of all sizes spitting all they had got. Of what use are our puny .303 Lee Enfield rifles against that lot? This morning we could at least bang away at the Stukas and feel we might hit the bastards.

The last two hours were hell indeed. It seems fantastic now that so many of us got through unscathed. Shells were bursting all round, making the sides of the trench crumble in upon us. They were evidently aiming mainly to knock out the Coastal Defence and AA gun emplacements just behind us, and, being in between, the shells were roaring low over our heads, seeming only a foot or two above the ground. They made a whistle and roar like a train, and the shrapnel a horrible tearing sound. Many of them also fell short, exploding on contact with the rocky surface round about. But our big main danger and fear were the AP shells bursting in the air. How we wished our tin helmets were 12 ft in diameter instead of 12 inches!

At last, at about 5 o'clock, and after ten hours of practically continuous shelling, a mass of Jerry tanks and armoured vehicles rumbled into our location, nosing around trenches, dug-outs and wagons, lids down and guns slewing, ready to blast the slightest signs of opposition. So we were taken prisoners.

We scrambled out of our trenches and were soon marched off after being allowed to hurriedly collect a few things together. However, the Germans–Rommel's Afrika Korps–treated us with reasonable consideration and I saw several signs of compassion and nothing of the snarling Nazi we had been led to expect–let's hope it stays that way. As we marched by, a German officer, smiling triumphantly, leant down from the turret of his huge tank and said to me 'For you, the war is finish. Thank God you have got away alive!'

First we were marched here and then there. We must have covered several miles, our numbers constantly swelling as more prisoners were brought in. What a disaster this is for us out here in North Africa. Firing and fighting was still going on a short distance away and we passed very close to a heavy Jerry field gun in action.

The reason for the fall of Tobruk was plain to see, as Jerry had a colossal number of very heavy guns and the perimeter defences did not appear to have been prepared for a second siege at all.

At last they decided where to put us, and, after a short march up to and over the coast road we lay down and slept on the open desert surrounded, of course, by armed guards.

I shall never never forget the heat, thirst, and exhaustion of this day.

[A first-hand account by M. W. Brown.]

FIRST ALAMEIN: 8TH ARMY OUTWITS ROMMEL

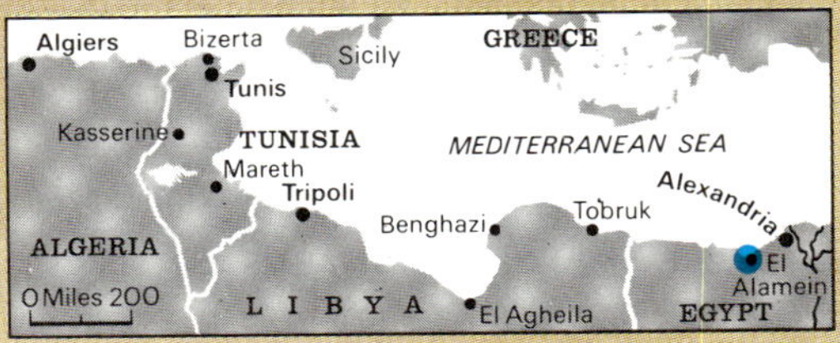

Imperial War Museum

A General Grant tank of the 8th Army moves up to the battle area at El Alamein

If Rommel was to be stopped El Alamein was the place to do it. Although the distance between the impassable Qattara Depression and the sea at El Alamein was only 30 miles, Auchinleck had neither the time nor the forces to construct a static defence line of linked fortified positions. Instead he took a leaf out of Rommel's book and relied on mobility, flexibility and tactical judgment.

Auchinleck reasoned that Rommel would try to by-pass the strong point of El Alamein on the coast and cut the coastal road to Alexandria behind it, so he organised his defences in depth south of the El Alamein perimeter. Rommel's forces were also depleted, although morale was very high. He launched his attack early on July 1 south of the El Alamein perimeter as Auchinleck had expected, and much to his surprise his army was checked. As the battle wore on Rommel was severely hampered by the counterattacks launched on his Italian formations. On July 3 the New Zealand Division destroyed the Ariete Division with a bayonet attack; while on July 11 the Australian 9th Division knocked out the Sabratha and Trieste Divisions in the north. By July 18 Rommel was overextended and on the defensive – he could neither advance nor retreat.

Auchinleck's success at El Alamein had upset the Axis grand strategy for the Mediterranean. Operation Hercules, the proposed airborne assault on Malta, was cancelled and the troops sent to reinforce Rommel's battered army. Mussolini, who flew to North Africa for the victory celebrations, went back to Rome.

First Alamein: The Opening Moves
Few would have banked on 8th Army's power to halt Rommel at El Alamein, but Auchinleck intended to fight a decisive battle there. With only two operative infantry divisions and a still unorganised armoured division, Auchinleck prepared to 'occupy' what has become inaccurately known in history as the 'El Alamein Line'. Indeed, the coming battle was to be one of the most fluid in the entire desert war, for Auchinleck knew that mobility would have to make up for his lack of troops. He was out to fight Rommel to a standstill, and this he did. Allowing Rommel to commit the weight of his attack in the centre, Auchinleck then prepared to strike hard towards Tell el Eisa, thus forcing Rommel to extend the Panzerarmee's line to the sea and dig in. But the prelude was to be Rommel's series of attacks along the Ruweisat Ridge – and his first check since Gazala

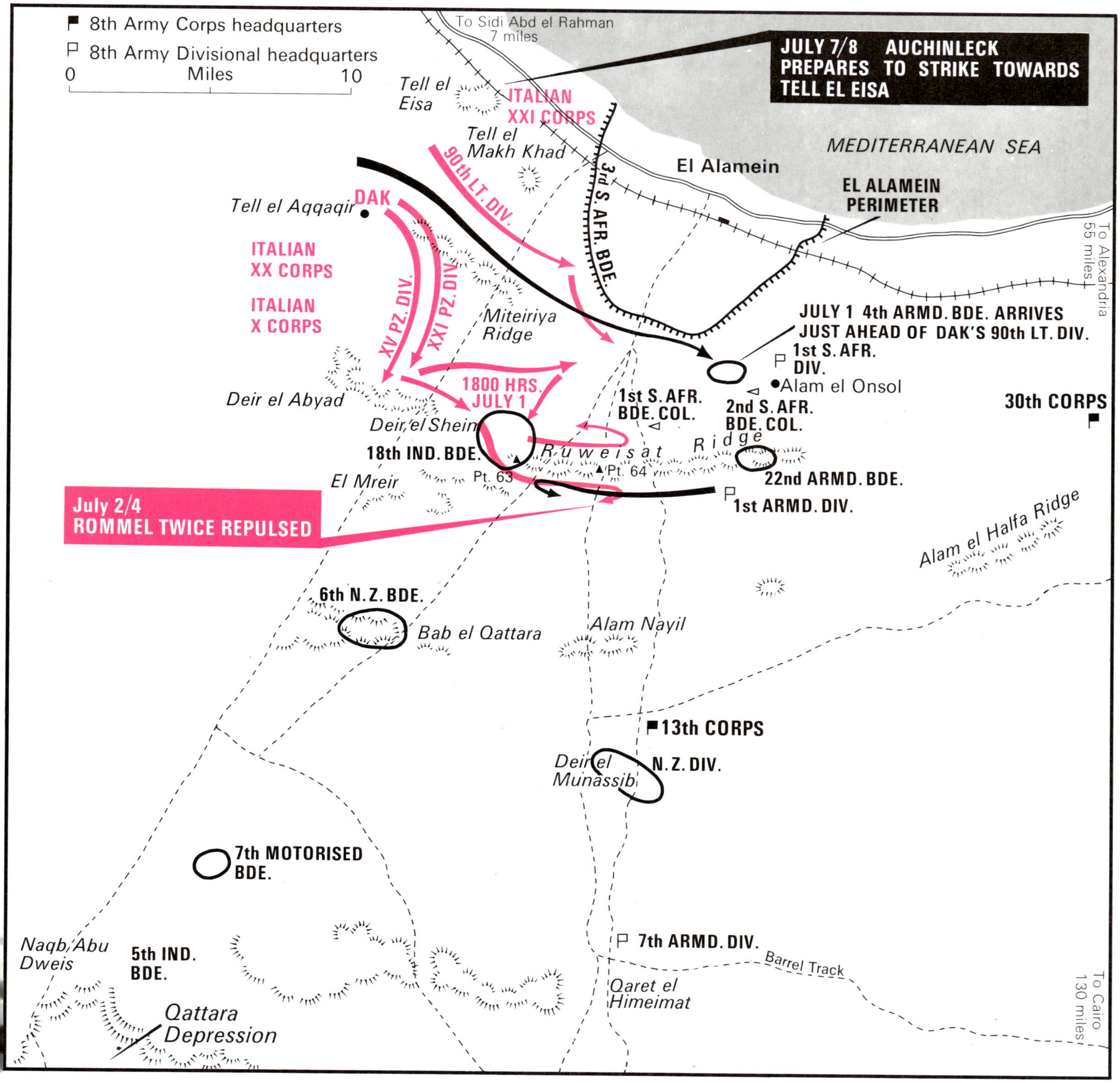

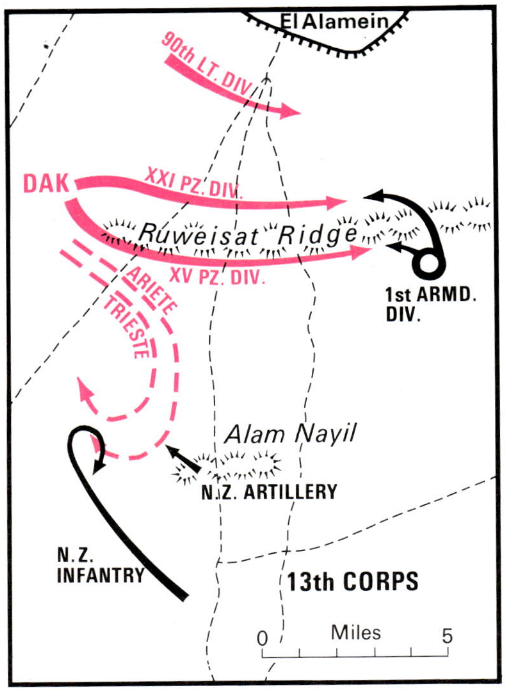

◁ **July 3: Defeat for the DAK and Ariete.** Rommel was then forced to abandon his hopes of by-passing Alamein as he had Matrûh

▷ **July 10/11: Auchinleck crushes the Sabratha Division.** By July 9, Rommel was extended from the Depression to the sea. The Australian attacks on Tell el Eisa in the next two days destroyed 'Sabratha' and mauled 'Trieste'; when Rommel counterattacked with the DAK on July 13/14, he suffered heavy German losses as well. Auchinleck's defence plans were working well—and were inflicting damaging losses on Rommel's Panzerarmee

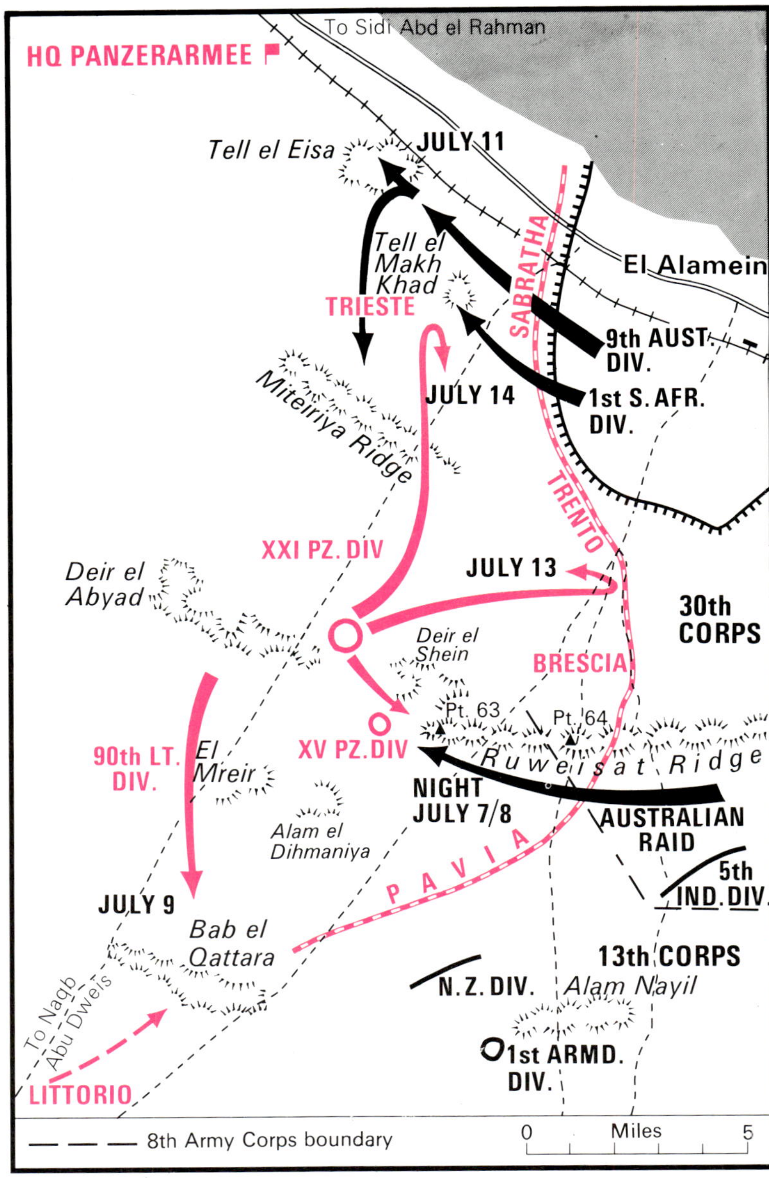

Ullstein

▽ **Left: July 14/15.** Auchinleck strikes at the western Ruweisat Ridge. Although the New Zealanders on the left flank gained their ridge objectives, these could not be consolidated. Rommel's counterattacks on the 15th recaptured Point 63—but the rest of 13th and 30th Corps consolidated on their ordered objective. This was another devastating blow to Rommel's hopes, for the Italian X Corps suffered damaging losses. ▽ **Right: July 21/22.** The second attack on western Ruweisat kept up the pressure on Rommel, but it gained no ground. Now the battle was crystallising: minefields defined the front. ◁ A German sapper lifting British mines—the perilous task which was to be the essential preliminary to all future attacks by both sides on the Alamein front

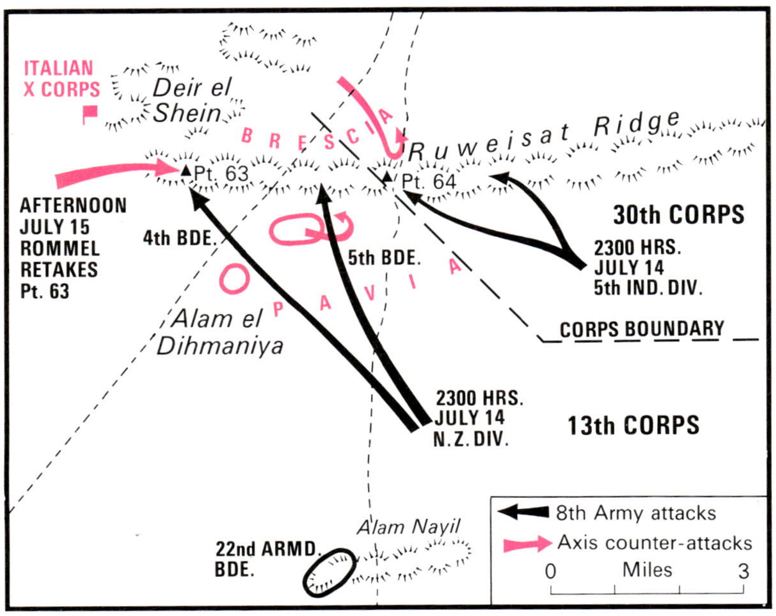

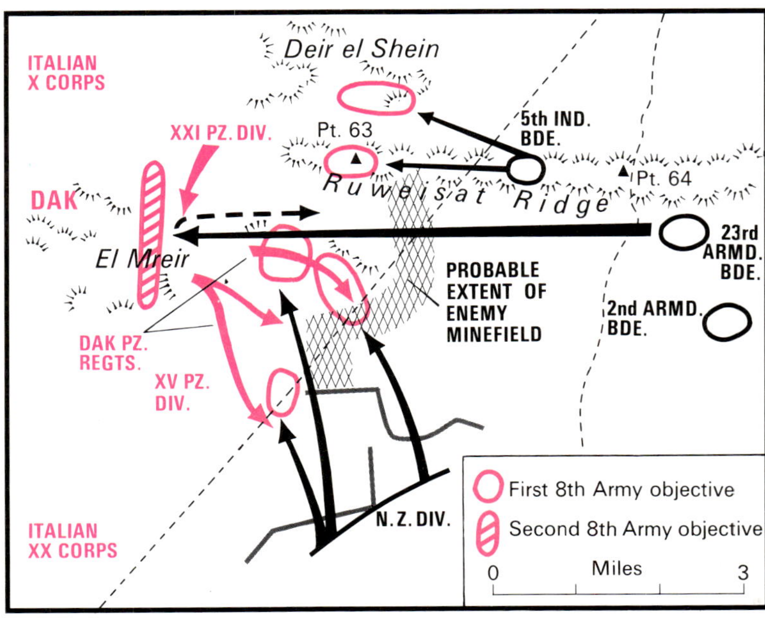

Imperial War Museum

△ 'The strength of the defence came as a complete surprise to me' – *Gen. Bayerlein*

Alfredo Zennaro

△ Vehicles of the Afrika Korps assemble before their vain attempts to break through

▽ British minefields held up the Axis advance so that their infantry made few attacks. Again, it was up to the armour

Alfredo Zennaro

ALAM HALFA

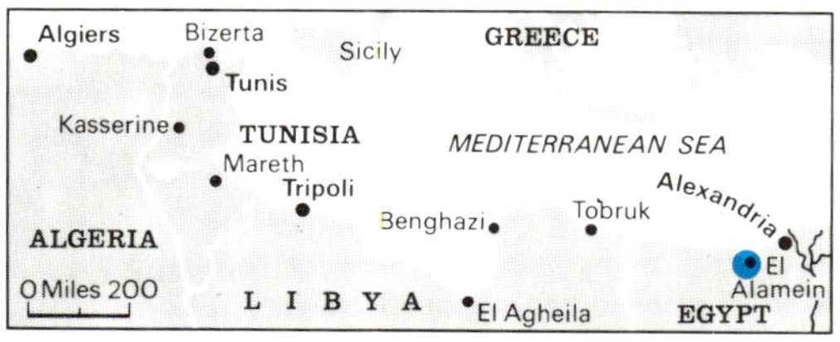

The Battle of Alam Halfa was Rommel's last attempt to break through to the Nile Valley. It was also Lieutenant-General Bernard Montgomery's first battle in the Western Desert after taking command of the 8th Army. Thus both commanders came to grips under conditions of unusual tension, each aware that his personal reputation depended on the outcome – the German feverishly anxious to gain another quick success with dwindling resources if he were not to fail forever; the Briton careful to consolidate his hold upon the hearts and minds of a convalescent army, as a prerequisite to the battle of annihilation he planned to fight at a later date.

Rommel launched his attack on August 31 with a strong armoured thrust along the Qattara Depression, intending to turn north behind Alam Halfa Ridge. However, he was delayed getting through the British minefields, giving Montgomery time to take the necessary counter-measures. With a threat to his flanks developing from 7th Armoured Division in the south and 10th Armoured Division in the north, Rommel turned in early against Alam Halfa Ridge which was heavily defended by the British. There the battle raged until September 2, when the shortage of fuel and supplies, the stubborn Allied resistance, and the incessant air attacks forced the Germans to break off the attack and retreat to their own lines.

Rommel repeated the tactics which had served so well at Gazala – diversionary attacks while the main strength of Panzerarmee swung round to the south to outflank the British and cut their supply lines. But the threat of attack by 7th Armoured Division forced him to shorten the attack, and lack of fuel and stubborn Allied resistance destroyed it

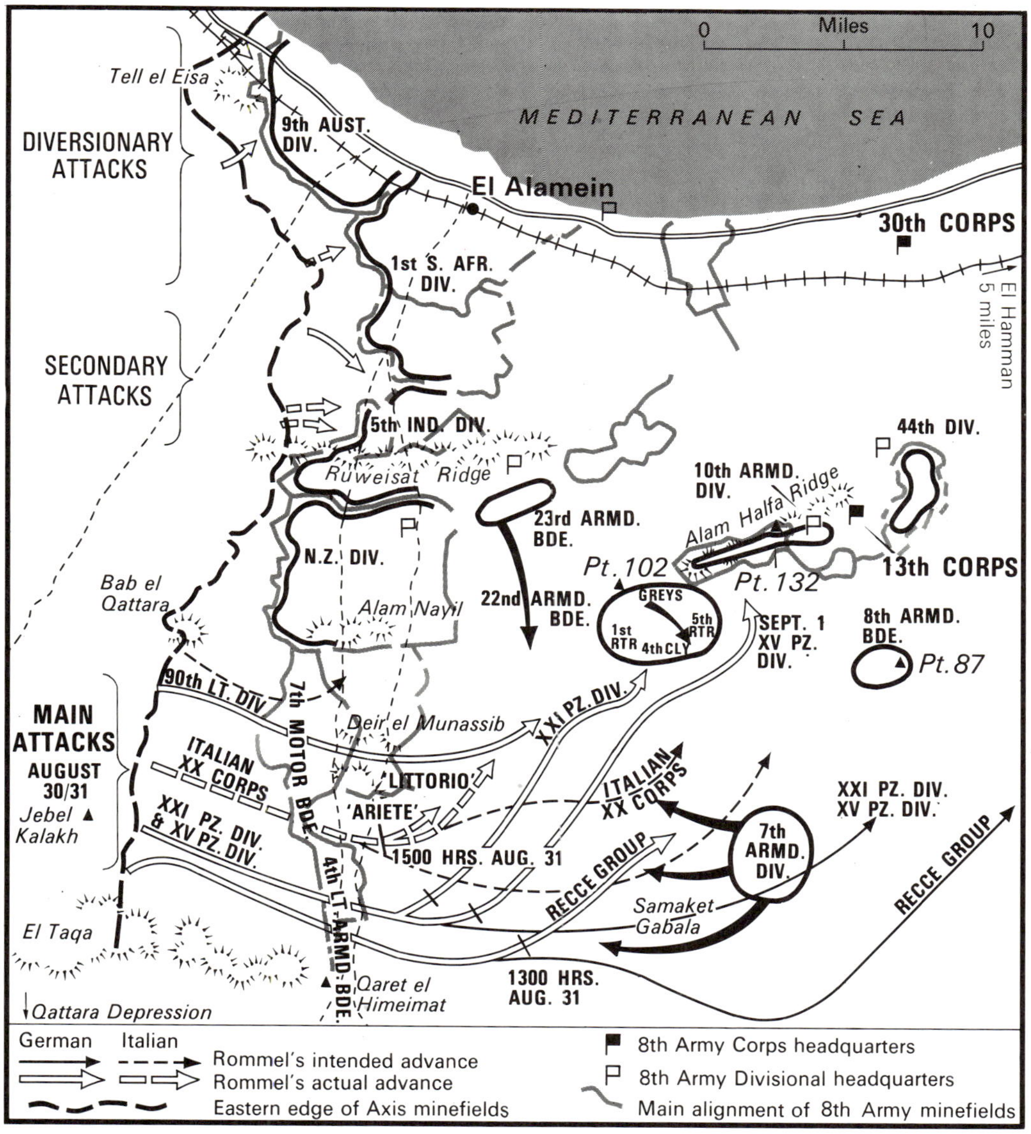

Supply: The Basis of the Battle

Desert supply lines are particularly vulnerable, as all petrol and ammunition, essential requirements for the battle, must pass along them. Hence one should protect one's own by all possible means and seek to confuse, or better still to cut the enemy's. Operations in the opposing supply area will cause the enemy to break off the battle, since *supplies are the basis of the battle, and must be given priority of protection.* [*Rommel*]

Ultimately, the victor in the desert war would be the side which got the most and best supplies in the shortest time. Never before had 8th Army's supply line been so strong: the front line was now only 70 miles from the chief depot at Alexandria (see map). But Rommel's army was at the opposite extreme: it had to haul its supplies all the way from Tripoli (1,420 miles), Benghazi (660 miles), and Tobruk (370 miles). The underlying law of warfare in the Western Desert was once again at work; the farther a victor advanced, the weaker he became—but a beaten army which fell back on its base became stronger in proportion. Rommel stood at the gates of Alexandria, shackled by this law. All his supplies sent by sea were in double danger, from both RAF and Royal Naval attacks. And the Axis transports, struggling eastwards up to the front, were plagued by the roving bands of the Long Range Desert Group and the raids of the Desert Air Force. Meanwhile, the 8th Army's supplies flowed ceaselessly from the rear depots to the front line, bringing reinforcements which blunted all Rommel's attempts to break through—and preparing for 8th Army's resumption of the offensive against Rommel

△ **Fordson (¾ ton)**

▽ **Bedford (3 tons)**

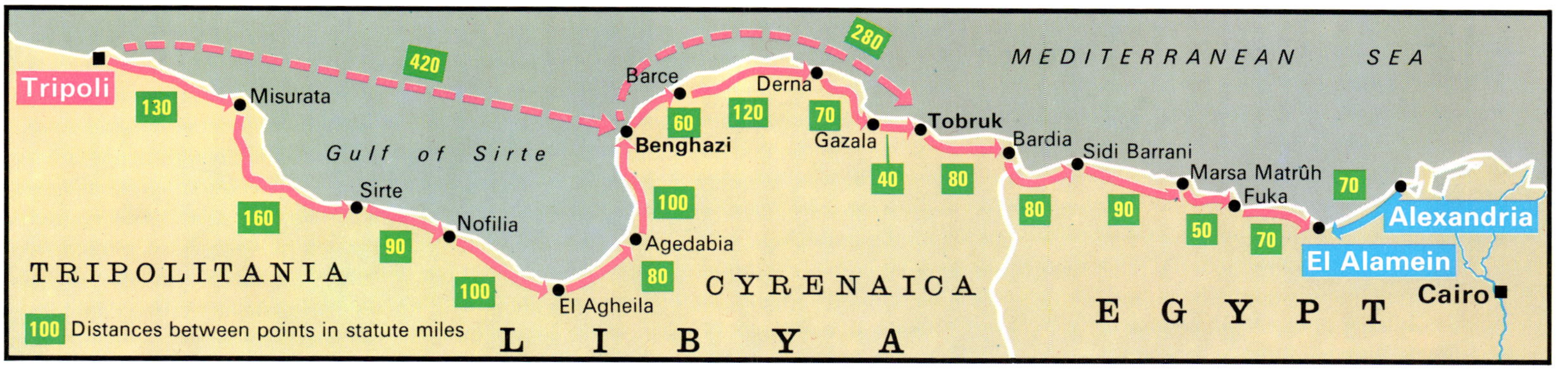

△ Leyland (3 tons)

△ Opel (3 tons)

▽ Isotta-Fraschini (3 tons)

▽ Büssing-NAG (4½ tons)

ALAMEIN: THE

Western Desert, October/November 1942

Major-General Sir Francis de Guingand

Now began what in British eyes has long seemed the most important battle of the war – popularly known as the Battle of Alamein. This title ignores the First Battle of Alamein, fought over virtually the same ground 16 weeks before, at which Rommel's advance was halted and the Afrika Korps given the first inkling of its fate. For now the supply situation favoured the British. Between July and October many changes had been wrought in the 8th Army: the men were rested, conscious of their hard training, aware that for the first time their weapons and equipment were superior in both quality and quantity to the enemy's. And most important of all, they had seen the enemy beaten back at Alam Halfa and knew that he was no Superman. Now it would be demonstrated to the world

When the Axis armies in Africa rose to meet the onslaught of the 8th Army on October 23 they were at a disadvantage in almost every department. Not least of their deficiencies was the absence of their great leader, for Rommel was a sick man and had returned to Germany for rest and treatment on September 23. In his place General Stumme held command – disgruntled in the knowledge that, if an attack came, Rommel would return at once, convinced that he alone was capable of taking the right decisions in an emergency on the Alamein front against the British.

Yet even Rommel regarded a defence against an enemy as strong in material as the British as a 'Battle Without Hope' while, from his masters in Rome and Berlin, he had obtained many promises but little practical help. So, daily, his reserves of men, tanks, guns, ammunition, fuel, and supplies fell lower, making comparison with the British an even gloomier exercise. For instance, Rommel was aware of a British superiority of 2 to 1 in tanks when, in fact, it was nearer $2\frac{1}{2}$ to 1 overall (including 300 Italian tanks) and $5\frac{1}{2}$ to 1 counting Germans alone. And the Royal Air Force now dominated the air, making the Luftwaffe's despairing efforts appear puny by comparison. While in Rome, Rommel told Mussolini that unless the supply position was improved the Axis would have to get out of North Africa, but he sensed his failure to transmit the gravity of the situation and in Berlin he recoiled before a wall of blind optimism and false promises.

At the front, meanwhile, all Panzerarmee could do was prepare an even denser fortified area in the neck between the sea and the Qattara Depression, based on the prime consideration that, if they were driven out into the open, they would be overwhelmed for lack of sufficient vehicles or fuel to withdraw or fight a mobile rearguard action. Thus they planned to hold each piece of ground at all costs, cleaning up each enemy penetration with an immediate counterattack.

The German system of defence which evolved was not unlike that to be found on the Western Front at the end of the First World War – a battle zone spread out in depth behind a screen of outposts, in an effort to acquire time for mobile reserves to assemble and counterattack. One technical feature, in particular, amplified the 1918 concept – anti-tank and anti-personnel mines. Some 500,000 of them, supplemented by buried British bombs and shells, were sown thickly around each defended locality, creating a deep belt along the length of the front.

In each sector Italian troops, well laced with Germans to give stability, waited the impact with mounting anxiety. The pattern they formed contained an invitation to a Battle of Attrition – it only needed the British commander to accept that invitation and a drawn-out battle would be in prospect.

Before the Battle of Alam Halfa was fought, Winston Churchill paid us a visit on his way back from Moscow (August 19) and stayed at our headquarters at Burgh-el-Arab.

General Montgomery took special care to see that the Prime Minister and his party would be comfortable. He gave up his own caravan and sited it within a few yards of the sea, so that our distinguished guest could bathe when he felt so inclined.

TIDE TURNS

Imperial War Museum

Churchill gave us the most vivid description of his visit to Moscow and how he had to talk 'cold turkey' before it was accepted that Great Britain was doing something to win the war, but he had come away with a very deep impression of Stalin's leadership; and enthralled us with details of our gathering war effort, and what we were preparing for the enemy. I well remember him saying: 'Germany has asked for this bombing warfare, and she will rue the day she started it, for her country will be laid in ruins.'

Once Rommel had failed in his last desperate offensive, he was faced with two alternatives. Either to stay and await the attack which he knew would most surely be launched against him, increasing in the meantime the strength of his defences; or to withdraw to some favourable position before we were ready to follow him up in sufficient strength, thereby shortening his lines of communication and so rendering his supply position less precarious.

He chose the first of these courses, no doubt largely because he lacked the necessary transport and petrol for a withdrawal; but in any case a retreat would have been against his character and would certainly have proved very unpopular with the Axis High Command. His decision meant therefore that the longer we waited before launching our offensive, the more formidable his defences would become – particularly with regard to minefields, wire, and the construction of prepared positions.

It was therefore obvious that it was to our advantage to attack as soon as possible and this view was strongly held by Churchill, who started to press General Alexander – Commander-in-Chief Middle East – for an early offensive. He wanted this to take place in September. He had an additional important reason and that was the fact that Operation 'Torch', the Anglo/US landings in North Africa, was due to take place early in November, and therefore hard and prolonged fighting on our front would be of great benefit.

One day Alexander arrived at our headquarters, bringing with him a signal from Churchill saying that he more or less demanded that we should attack in September. After reading the document Montgomery said 'Hand me a pad, Freddie', and seizing it he wrote down these points:

- Rommel's attack had caused some delay in our preparations.
- Moon conditions restricted 'D' day to certain periods in September and October.
- If the September date was insisted upon the troops would be insufficiently equipped and trained, and failure would probably result. But if the attack took place in October then complete victory was assured.

Turning to Alexander, he handed over the pad and said: 'I should make these points in your reply; that should fix it.' A signal was subsequently dispatched on these lines and produced the required result; for what could any Prime Minister do with this clear-cut military opinion before him! Montgomery in his memoirs recalls that he told Alexander 'privately' that if the attack was ordered for September they would have to find someone else to do the job.

Taking all considerations into account, Montgomery decided that we should attack during the October full moon and the exact date fixed was the 23rd. It was essential that we should attack at night owing to the formidable minefield problem.

I now come to the plan itself. There was no way round the enemy positions; the sea and the Qattara Depression saw to that, so a hole had to be punched through their defences. Montgomery had decided to launch the main attack on the right flank with General Leese's 30th Corps, together with a secondary attack on the southern flank by General Horrocks' 13th Corps. The plan was to pass 10th Corps (General Lumsden) through the gap made by 30th Corps to sit astride the enemy's supply line, and so force him to deploy his armour against us, when it would be destroyed. This was in accordance with normal teaching. Having destroyed the enemy's armour, his troops could be dealt with more or less at leisure.

The Army Commander had laid down three basic fundamentals which would govern the preparatory period. These were: leadership – equipment – training. He soon put the first matter in order, and the re-equipment of the army was going well. But early in October he realised that the training of the army was still below what was required, and in view of this weakness made one of his rapid decisions. He would alter the conception of the plan so that instead of first going all out to destroy the enemy's armour, he would eat away the enemy's holding troops – who were for the most part unarmoured – and use our armour to stop the enemy from interfering. Without their infantry divisions to hold the line, providing firm bases for their mobile forces, the enemy's armour would be at a grave disadvantage and their supply routes would be constantly threatened. It was unlikely that they would stand idly by while this 'crumbling' process was going on, and so it was probable that we would force his armour to attack *us,* which, once we were in a position to receive it, would be to our advantage.

The final plan in outline as given out by the Army Commander on October 6 was as follows:

- Main attack by 30th Corps in the north on a front of four divisions [to secure a bridgehead – objective 'Oxalic' – beyond the enemy's main defended zone]. Two corridors were to be cleared through the minefields, and through these lanes 10th Corps was to pass.
- 13th Corps in the south was to stage two attacks. One directed on Himeimat and the Taqa feature. The other into the area of Gebel Kalakh and Qaret el Khadim. These attacks were to be made with the primary object of misleading the enemy and thereby containing forces that might otherwise be used against 30th Corps.
- Both the above corps were to destroy the enemy holding the forward positions.
- 10th Corps was to deploy itself [to a line 'Pierson', just west of 'Oxalic'] so as to prevent 30th Corps' operations from being interfered with. And its final object [by an advance to area 'Skinflint'] was the destruction of the enemy's armour.
- The attack was to start at night during the full moon.

The artillery plan was very carefully prepared. We would go into battle with great gun power and considerable supplies of ammunition. The battle was to open with a very heavy counter-battery bombardment, and then most of our artillery would concentrate on the enemy defences by barrage and concentrations.

The air plan was a good one. Before the battle Air Vice-Marshal Coningham's Desert Air Force had been wearing down the enemy's air effort. On one or two occasions he had shown brilliant leadership by taking advantage of fleeting opportunities when isolated rain storms had grounded portions of the enemy's air force. Low-flying attacks laid on with great rapidity had taken a very heavy toll of the enemy's aircraft and petrol.

During the first night our air forces were to undertake attacks against enemy gun positions, and so help our counter-battery plan. Later they were to switch to the areas where the enemy armoured divisions were located. Our available air strength on 'D' day was 500 fighters and 200 bombers – at that time a considerable force.

The 'going' was one of the matters which gave us a lot of anxiety, and we went to endless trouble to obtain information as to what the ground was like in the area over which we were making our thrusts. Air photos, interrogation of prisoners, questioning of our own troops who had at one time or another traversed the area – these were some of the means employed. We built six tracks leading up to 30th Corps' starting line, and this in itself was a tremendous task, constructed as they were through very soft sand.

Imperial War Museum

Montgomery was determined not to begin his attack until the 8th Army had overwhelming superiority. Time was on his side, for the Allies now controlled the supply lines, and troops and new equipment – like this Sherman – could be delivered in unprecedented quantities. Meanwhile the Afrika Korps was not only starved of equipment but it would go into battle without Rommel, who was ill

Montgomery's dummy army

The deception arrangements were particularly interesting. We had decided quite rightly that strategic surprise was out of the question, for the enemy knew we were going to attack. On the other hand tactical surprise was quite possible. We considered we could delude the enemy as to the weight, the date, the time, and the direction of our attack. Our plans were all made with this in view, and they proved most successful.

The first problem was to try to conceal our concentration as much as possible from the enemy. The staff worked out the complete layout on the day of the attack – the number of guns, tanks, vehicles, and troops. A very large 'operations' map was kept which showed this layout in various denominations. We then arranged to reach the eventual density as early as possible, and to maintain it up to the last moment, so that the enemy's air photography would show no particular change during the last two or three weeks. To achieve this we used spare transport and dummy transport. These were gradually replaced by those belonging to the assault units and formations as they came up to take over their allotted sectors. These changeovers took place at night, and we had special dummy vehicles made under which guns could be concealed. All moves forward were of course rigidly controlled, and slit trenches were dug and camouflaged at night in which the assault infantry could be concealed.

The next task was to make the enemy think that the main attack would be launched in the southern sector. This, I might add, was not very popular with 13th Corps, but they nobly accepted the plan for the common good. Besides various other methods adopted, we built large dummy dumps away to the south, and also a dummy pipe line and water installations. It was so arranged that the work would appear to the enemy to be aimed at completion a week or two *after* the actual date of our attack. Finally on the night of the attack itself the wireless traffic of the headquarters of an armoured division was so employed as to indicate that a large move of armoured forces was taking place in the southern sector.

On the night of the 23rd we arranged for a feint landing to take place behind the enemy's lines. About 4 pm a convoy sailed westwards out of Alexandria. After dark all but a few fast craft put back, but those remaining staged a dummy landing. Shelling of the coast, mortar and machine-gun fire, and light signals were used. It was timed to take place about three hours after our attack had started, and it was hoped that this would tie down enemy reserves. The loading of the ships was no doubt witnessed by enemy agents, who could see tanks being shipped and troops marching aboard. There is no doubt that all these measures helped materially to confuse the enemy and gained us tactical surprise.

On the administrative side there was a great deal to be done. The whole basis of administration had to be altered. Before, when we were on the defensive, the weight of resources was held back; now that we intended to attack they had to be placed as far forward as possible. The consequent carrying forward of supplies and the camouflaging of the dumps was no small task, and preparations were made to construct the railway forward as rapidly as possible. We also made preparations to open ports when they were captured and perfected our organisation for the recovery and repair of tanks and vehicles.

Montgomery's change in plan as regards the use of our armour nearly caused a crisis between himself and General Herbert Lumsden, who had been selected to command the 'Corps d'Elite' – the 10th Army Corps. Lumsden had fought with conspicuous gallantry when commanding an armoured division in the 'bad old days'. He was a cavalryman through and through and not unnaturally thought in terms of the mobile battle and yearned for the day when his armoured formations, equipped with modern tanks, would be launched through a gap made by the infantry, to roam far and wide. The Army Commander's new instructions were therefore not to his liking.

Shortly after this Lumsden held a corps conference at which he explained his plan and views to all the commanders in his corps. Montgomery was temporarily absent from the army on this occasion and I therefore decided to attend this conference myself.

It soon became clear to me that this new conception of the use of armour had not been fully accepted by the corps commander, and at the end of the meeting I had a talk with Lumsden pointing out the Army Commander's determination to fight the coming battle this way. But I could see that he was anything but happy and there appeared to be a recrudescence of the bad old habit of questioning orders.

On the Army Commander's return, I reported fully on what had taken place and he lost little time in making his views crystal clear to the commander of 10th Corps; and Lumsden, being a good soldier, accepted the position and made the necessary changes in his plans.

Large-scale rehearsals for the coming battle were carried out, and the lessons learned gone into very carefully by the various commanders. And by the end of the third week in October we realised that all these vast preparations were successfully reaching their conclusion. From the staff

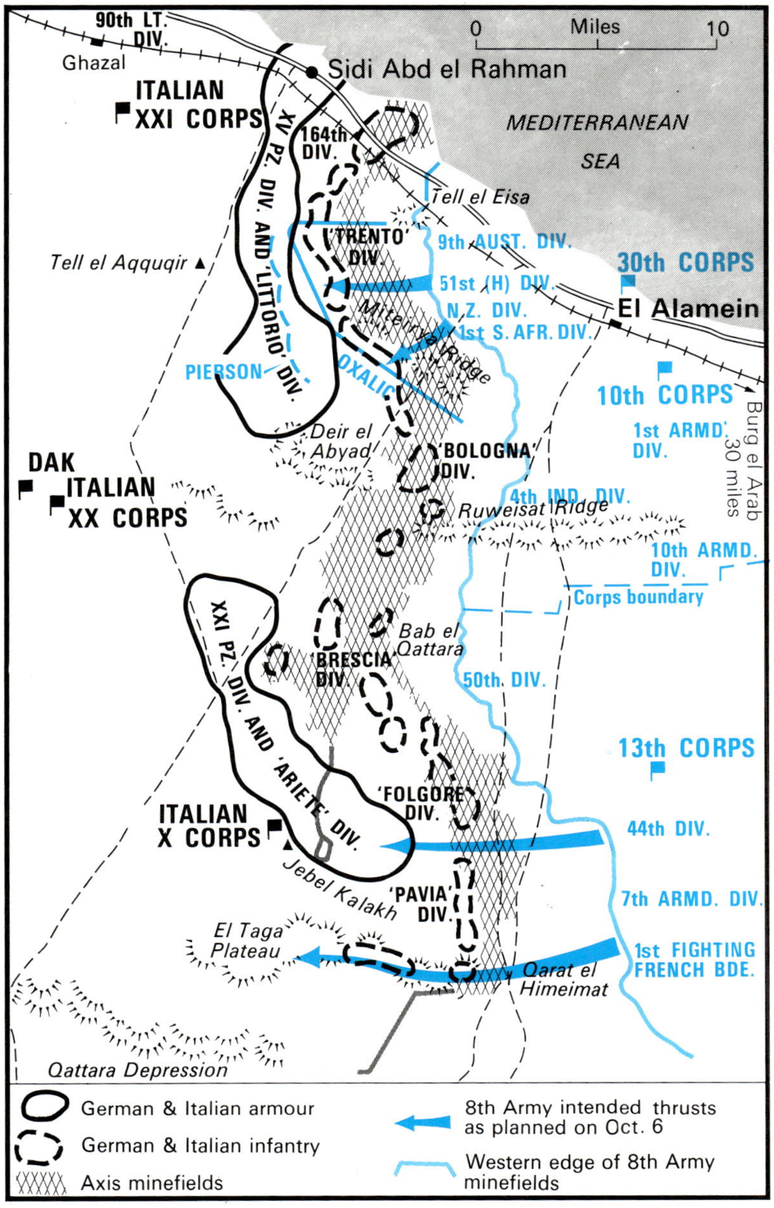

At Alamein in October the 8th Army was faced by an enemy position which could not be turned, but must be breached by direct attack. Montgomery at first intended to use 30th Corps to push two corridors into the enemy lines through which the tanks of 10th Corps would flood to force an armoured battle and cut the Axis supply lines. But weaknesses in his forces' training made him decide to alter this plan: 30th Corps was still to open two corridors through to 'Oxalic', but it was then to concentrate upon 'crumbling' the enemy's holding troops. The tanks were to go no further than 'Pierson', where they would cover the infantry and await the German armoured counterattacks on ground of their own choosing. Further south, diversionary attacks by 4th Indian Division and 13th Corps would hold a large proportion of the Axis armour during the vital opening phase of the battle. On the Axis side, Stumme had split his armour (XV Panzer in the north, XXI Panzer in the south) to cover both possible lines of attack. This unprecedented step weakened his ability to mount a concentrated counterattack, but General Bayerlein believed that it had been approved by Rommel before he left Africa

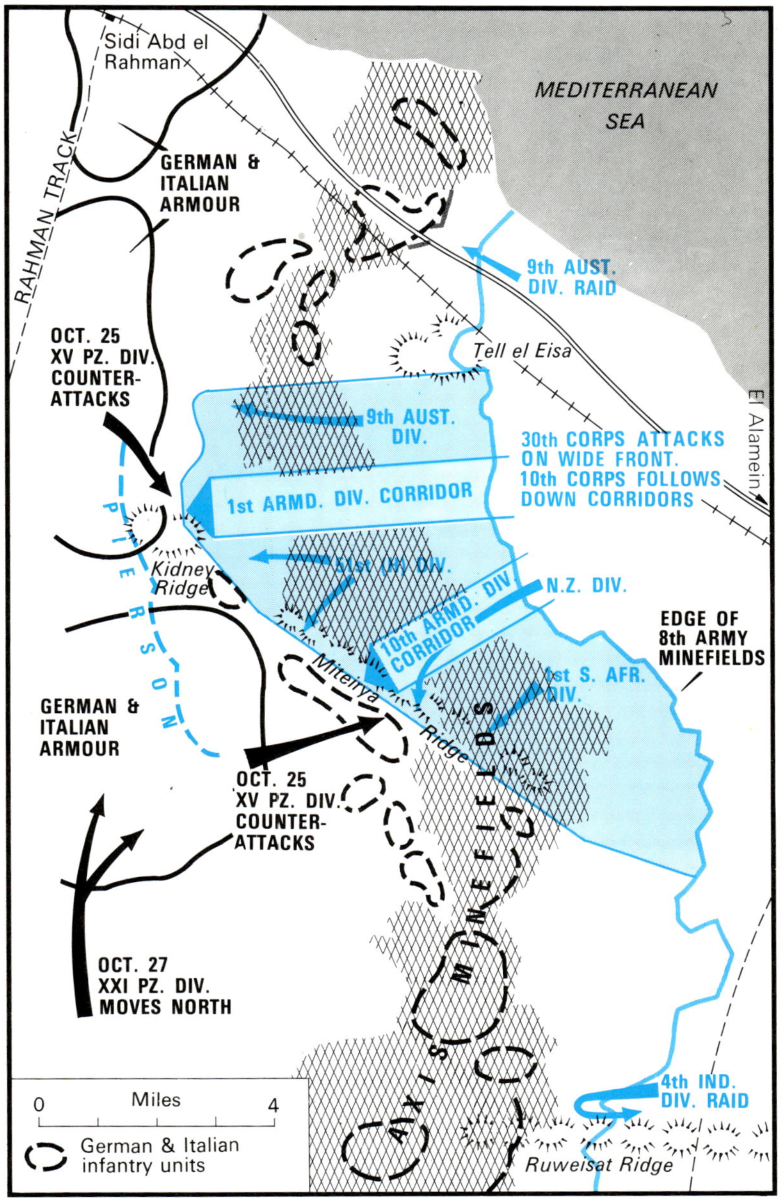

After an extremely heavy artillery barrage, troops of 30th Corps, on a four-division front, advanced into the enemy minefields. By dawn on October 24 the infantry had reached most of the objectives of 'Oxalic', but stubborn enemy resistance and congestion in the corridors prevented the tanks from clearing the minefields. At first German reactions seemed hesitant and unsure – not only were Panzerarmee's commanders still uncertain as to where the real attack would come, but Stumme had died of heart failure on the first day, and for vital hours the Axis forces had no leader until General von Thoma was able to take over. It was not until the third day of the attack that a new Axis certainty about counterattacks showed that Rommel had returned. Throughout the 24th and 25th, 30th Corps inched forward, while 13th Corps successfully held XXI Panzer in the south. But Montgomery had realised that the impetus had gone out of the initial attacks, and, using attacks by 9th Australian Division in the north to cut off enemy forces in the salient and force Rommel to concentrate on their relief, he halted and began to redeploy 8th Army for a new breakout attempt

point of view there was a healthy slackening in the tempo of work, denoting that the stage was now set.

Montgomery had been indefatigable, and had satisfied himself that all was in readiness. He very rightly had decided that in order to get the best out of his troops it was necessary for them to know the whole plan so that they would realise how their particular contribution fitted in with the general scheme of things.

On October 19 and 20 he addressed all officers down to lieutenant-colonel level in 30th, 13th, and 10th Corps. It was a real tour de force. These talks were some of the best he had ever given, clear and full of confidence. He touched on the enemy situation, stressing their weaknesses, and said he was certain a long 'dog-fight' or 'killing match' would take place for several days – 'it might be ten'. He then gave details of our great strength, our tanks, our guns, and the enormous supplies of ammunition available. He drummed in the need never to lose the initiative, and how everyone – *everyone* – must be imbued with the burning desire to 'kill Germans'. 'Even the padres – one per weekday and two on Sundays!' This produced a roar. After explaining how the battle was to be fought, he said that he was entirely confident of the result.

The men were let into the secret on October 21 and 22, from which date no leave was granted, and by the 23rd a tremendous state of enthusiasm had been produced. Those soldiers just knew they would succeed.

On the morning of October 22, Montgomery held a press conference. He explained the plan, his intentions, and his firm conviction of success. Many of the war correspondents were rather shaken by the confidence – this bombastic confidence – which he displayed. They felt there must be a catch in it – how could he be so sure? Some, I think, thought the maze of minefields and deep defences that the enemy had constructed were too difficult a problem to justify such a sanguine attitude.

In the afternoon of the 23rd we drove up to our battle headquarters, tucked away on the coast within a few minutes of 30th and 10th Corps Headquarters. We had well protected buried cables running back to our main headquarters and to the various corps; vehicles

Line-Up for the Battle

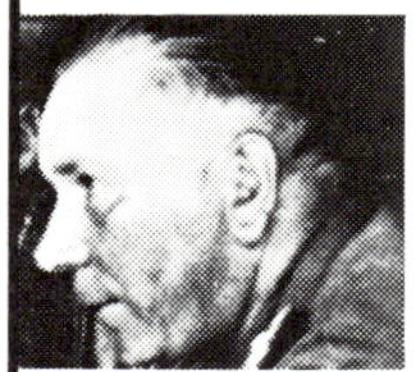

Panzerarmee Afrika

Gen Stumme (until Oct 26) and Fld Mshl Rommel

Reserve
German 90th Light Division
Italian **Trieste** Motorised Division
Luftwaffe XIX Flak Division

North
German XV Panzer Division
German 164th Motorised Division
Italian **Littorio** Armoured Division
Italian XXI Infantry Corps—**Trento** Division

Centre
German XXI Panzer Division
Ramcke Parachute Brigade
Italian XX Infantry Corps—**Brescia** and **Bologna** Divisions

South
Italian **Ariete** Armoured Division
Italian X Infantry Corps—**Pavia** and **Folgore** Divisions

8th Army

Lieut-Gen Montgomery

30th Corps—Lieut-Gen Leese
51st (Highland) Division—Maj-Gen Wimberley
4th Indian Division—Maj-Gen Tuker
9th Australian Division
New Zealand Division—Lieut-Gen Freyberg
1st South African Division—Maj-Gen Pienaar
23rd Armoured Brigade Group
9th (UK) Armoured Brigade

13th Corps—Lieut-Gen Horrocks
7th Armoured Division—Maj-Gen Harding
50th Division—Maj-Gen Nichols
44th Division—Maj-Gen Hughes
1st Free French Brigade Group
2nd Free French Brigade Group
1st Greek Infantry Brigade Group

10th Corps—Lieut-Gen Lumsden
1st Armoured Division—Maj-Gen Briggs
10th Armoured Division—Maj-Gen Gatehouse
8th Armoured Division—Maj-Gen Gairdner

Rommel
Nehring
Thoma
Bayerlein

Montgomery
Leese
Horrocks
Lumsden

Allied leadership was new and backed by great material resources, but Axis command suffered from changes and resultant indecisiveness. When the offensive began, Panzerarmee was led by General Stumme, but after his death on the first day of the attack it was commanded by General von Thoma until Rommel, who had been ill, returned on October 26

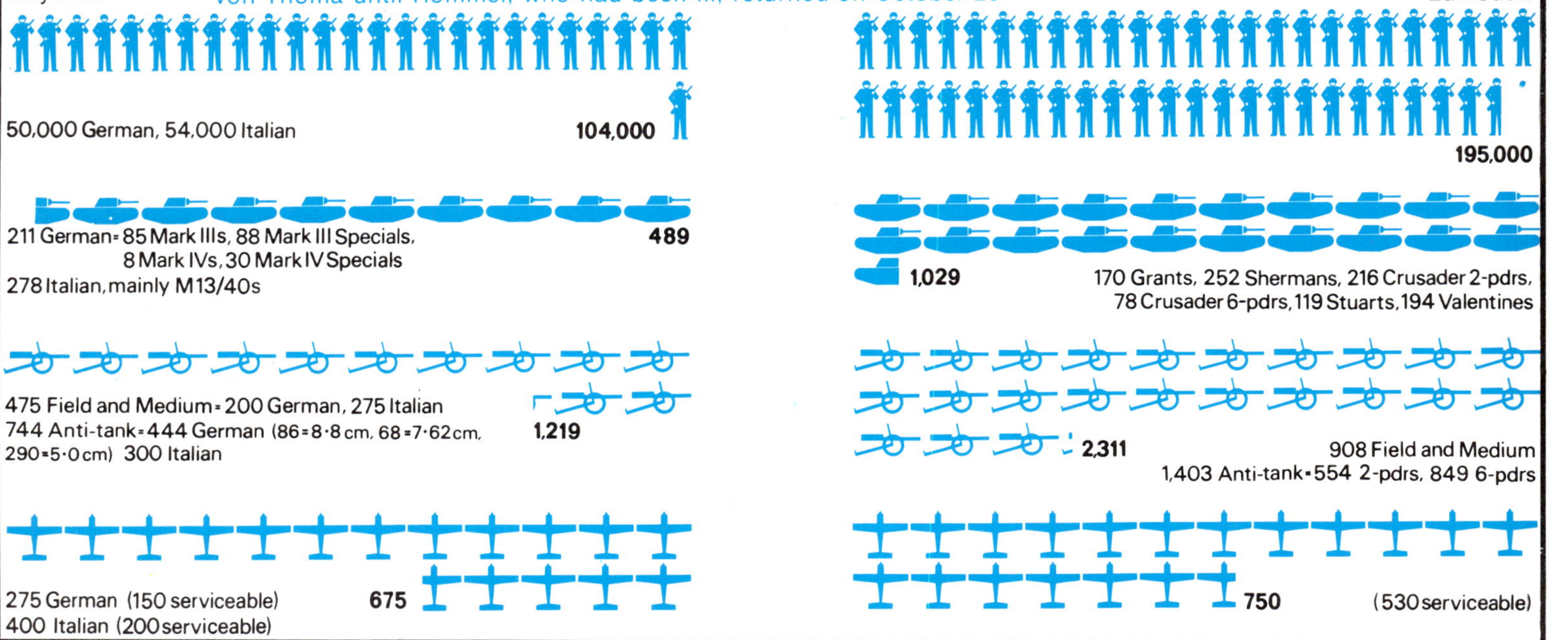

were dug in as we were rather far forward and near the desert road, which would undoubtedly become—as it did—a target for enemy air attack. I decided to make this tactical headquarters my base, and it worked very well. My people could talk to me on direct lines and come up for conferences within the hour.

It was a lovely evening, and I drove out after dark to see by the light of the moon the move forward of some of the troops. All was going well, and everyone looked cheerful. This was the day for which so many of us had been preparing and waiting.

As the time drew near we got into our cars and drove to a good view-point to see the opening of the battle. We passed the never-ending stream of tanks and transport—all moving with clockwork precision. This was 10th Corps moving up to its starting line, with the moon providing sufficient light to drive by, but the night protecting them from the prying eyes of enemy aircraft. We had some of our own machines flying over the enemy's forward positions making distracting noises; otherwise all seemed fairly quiet and normal. An occasional Very light and burst of machine-gun fire, a gun firing here and there, as would happen any night. We looked at our watches, 2130 hours—ten minutes to go. I could hardly wait.

A 1,000-gun barrage begins

The minutes ticked by, and then the whole sky was lit up, and a roar rent the air. Over 1,000 of our guns had opened up. It was a great and heartening sight. I tried to picture what the enemy must be thinking, did he know what was coming? He must do now. How ready was he? Up and down the desert, from north to south, the twinkling of the guns could be seen in an unceasing sequence. Within the enemy's lines we could see an occasional deep red glow light up the western sky. Each time this happened Brigadier Dennis, the commander of 30th Corps artillery, let out a grunt of satisfaction. Another Axis gun position had been blown up. We checked each change in the artillery plan; the pause while the guns switched to new targets. It was gun drill at its best. Now the infantry started forward. We could see the periodic bursts of Bofors guns which, with their tracer shell, demarcated the direction of advance. Behind us great searchlight beams were directed towards the sky, to help the forward troops plot their positions, and so find out when they had reached their objectives, for few landmarks existed in this part of the desert.

About 2300 hours I crept away and drove back to our headquarters. I knew we could expect to hear little of interest for some time yet, and so I snatched an hour or two's rest before being wakened up to hear the first reports come in.

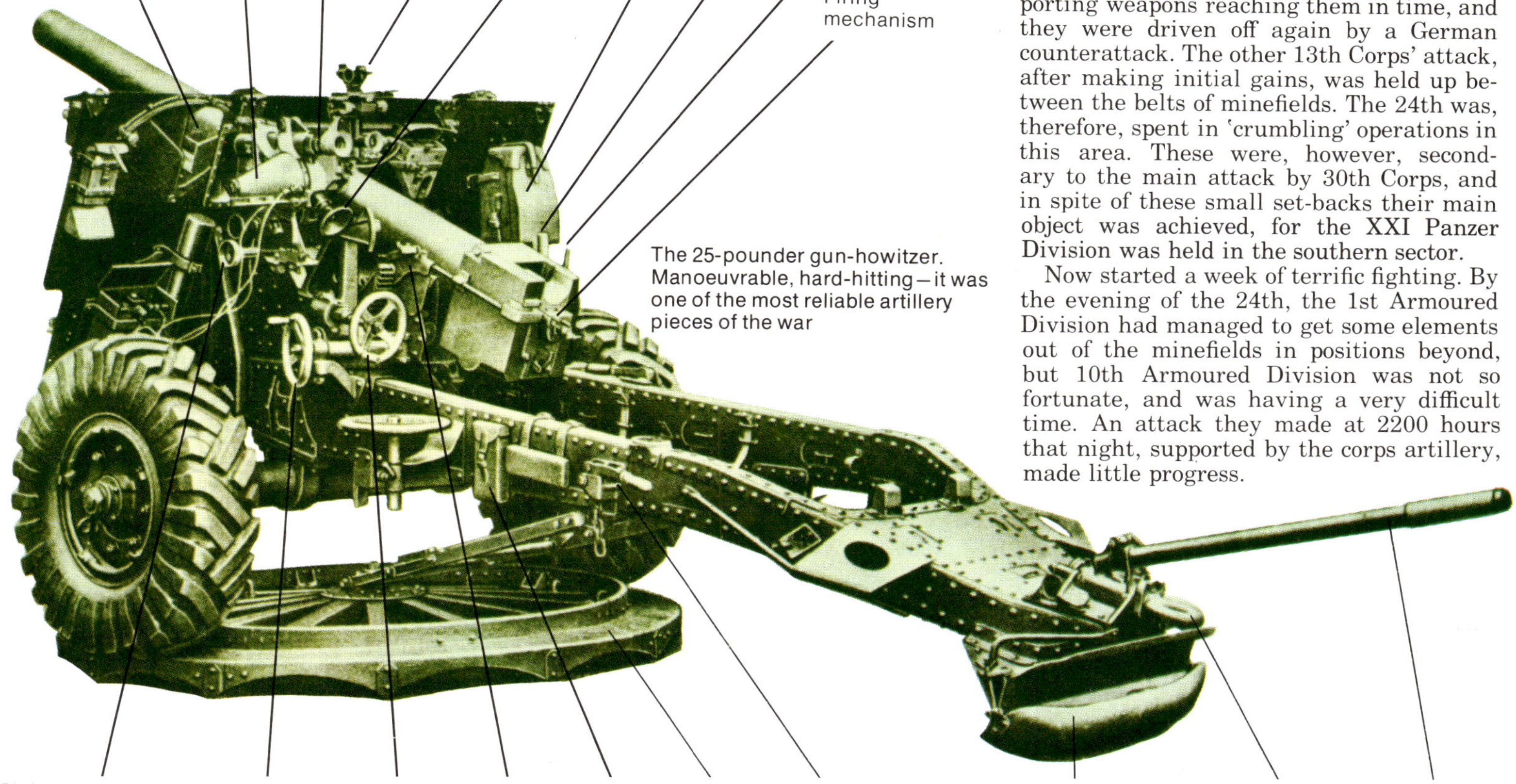

The 25-pounder gun-howitzer. Manoeuvrable, hard-hitting – it was one of the most reliable artillery pieces of the war

As I closed my eyes I felt full of confidence and hope, but never did I think that this was the opening of a campaign that would bring us to the very gates of Carthage.

Although the Battle of El Alamein was a comparatively small affair in relation to later battles fought during the war, for a number of reasons it must rank high in importance. To start with it meant the turn of the tide in Britain's fortunes. In fact the victory stood out as a priceless jewel after a series of depressing defeats. Then it provided a much-wanted stimulus to British morale, for it convinced our armed forces that, given the right leadership and weapons, they could beat the Germans, and it also inspired confidence among the British people in ultimate victory.

By previous standards in the Middle East, however, it was a great offensive and probably some of the bitterest fighting in the whole war took place over those sandy wastes. Our new commander never once lost his confidence or the initiative, while his troops were always convinced that they would win through in the end. I do not propose to give a very detailed description of the operations, but will confine myself to the broad framework of the battle and concentrate upon the highlights.

On that night of October 23/24, 30th Corps attacked with four divisions down two corridors cleared through the minefields. This attack was made on a fairly narrow front of 6 to 7 miles, with the northern flank tied to the Tell el Eisa feature, and the Miteiriya Ridge forming the southern limit.

The enemy's and our own dispositions at the outset of the battle are interesting for three reasons:

- The greater part of the enemy static defences was manned by Italians.
- The German infantry divisions, 164th Division and 90th Light Division, were protecting the vital coastal road sector.
- The German armour (Afrika Korps) was held in reserve and distributed equally between the northern and southern sectors.

Besides 30th Corps' main attack, a brigade of the 9th Australian Division carried out a feint between Tell el Eisa and the sea. This, together with the phoney seaborne operation, had a worrying effect on the enemy, while farther south the 4th Indian Division launched a strong raid from the area of the Ruweisat Ridge.

Then, at 0200 hours on October 24, the leading elements of the 1st and 10th Armoured Divisions crossed their start lines.

The Germans reel . . . and recover

Progress was good, and the task of clearing the lanes through the minefields went on well, but by the morning the armour had not managed to get out beyond them. Throughout the night, the Miteiriya Ridge was a very unpleasant place to be, and fierce fighting took place, for once the enemy had recovered from the initial shock, he concentrated his artillery and mortar fire on the corridors, and XV Panzer Division carried out a counterattack. The Army Commander examined the situation on the morning of the 24th, and decided that although a very good start had been made, it was important that there must be no slackening in the efforts to get the armour through, and that the 'crumbling' operations by the New Zealand Division must start at once.

In the south, 13th Corps had started on schedule. The French had successfully assaulted the high ground about Himeimat, but the soft sand had prevented their supporting weapons reaching them in time, and they were driven off again by a German counterattack. The other 13th Corps' attack, after making initial gains, was held up between the belts of minefields. The 24th was, therefore, spent in 'crumbling' operations in this area. These were, however, secondary to the main attack by 30th Corps, and in spite of these small set-backs their main object was achieved, for the XXI Panzer Division was held in the southern sector.

Now started a week of terrific fighting. By the evening of the 24th, the 1st Armoured Division had managed to get some elements out of the minefields in positions beyond, but 10th Armoured Division was not so fortunate, and was having a very difficult time. An attack they made at 2200 hours that night, supported by the corps artillery, made little progress.

Altogether I gained the impression that a feeling was developing in some quarters which favoured suspending the forward move, and pulling back under cover of the ridge. I decided, therefore, that this was an occasion when the Army Commander must intervene, and so I called a conference for 0330 hours at our Tactical Headquarters, asking Leese (30th Corps) and Lumsden (10th Corps) to attend. Then I went along to his caravan and woke him up. He appeared to be sleeping peacefully – in spite of a lot of attention from the enemy air force. He agreed with the action I had taken, and told me to bring the two corps commanders along to his map lorry when they arrived.

In due course I led the generals along the little path to the lorry. Montgomery was seated on a stool carefully examining a map fixed to the wall. He greeted us all most cheerfully, motioned us to sit down, and then asked each corps commander to tell his story. He listened very quietly, only occasionally interrupting with a question. There was a certain 'atmosphere' noticeable, careful handling was required, and Lumsden was obviously still not very happy about the role his armour had been given. After a while Montgomery spoke to the commander of the 10th Armoured Division on the telephone, and heard his version of the situation. He then made it quite clear that there would be no alteration to his orders. He also ordered the headquarters of this division to be moved farther forward.

The decision to make no change in the plan at that moment was a brave one, for it meant accepting considerable risks and casualties. But if it had not been made, I am firmly convinced that the attack might

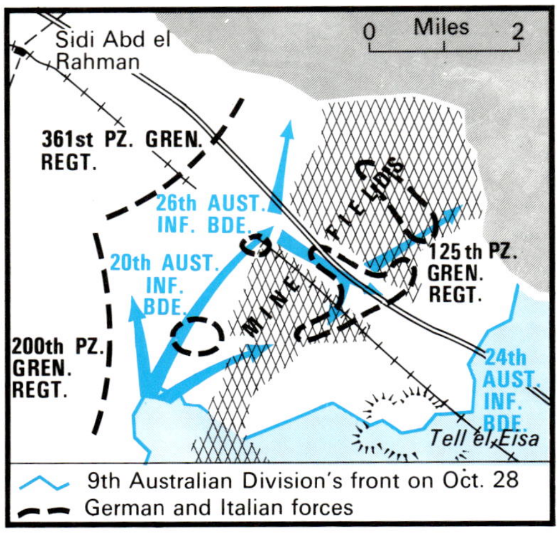

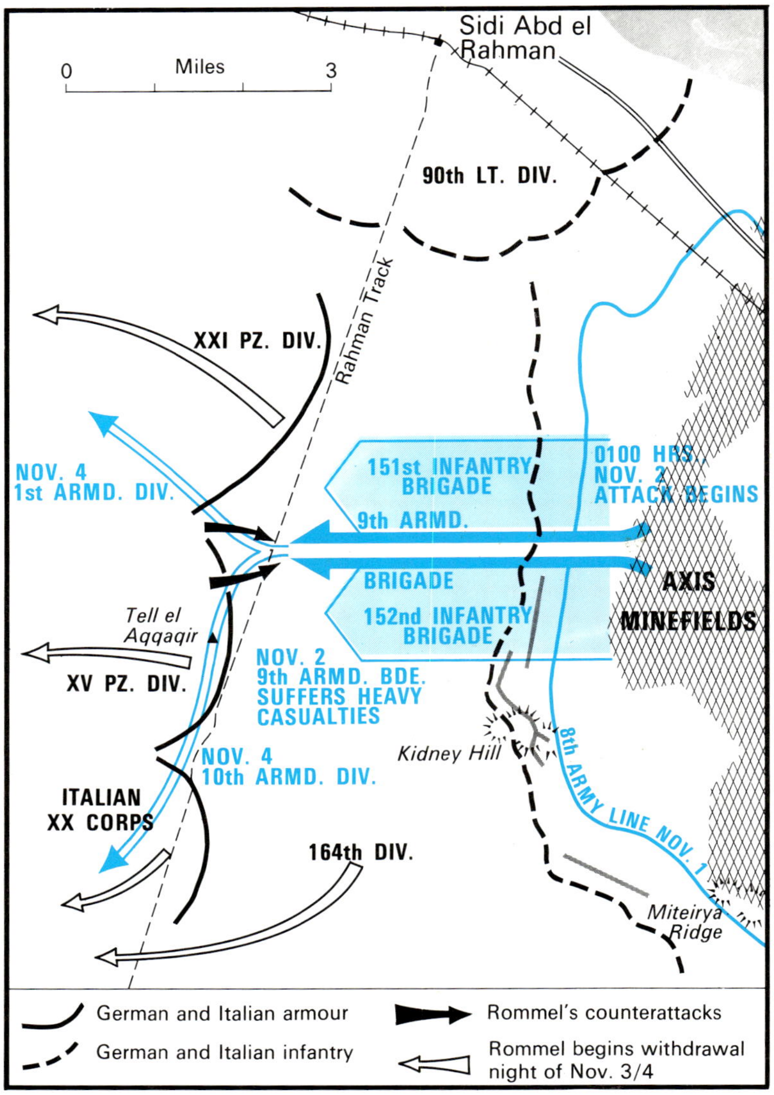

Far left: The Australian thrust which cut off units of two German regiments and persuaded Rommel to concentrate his reserves in the far north. On the morning of November 2, after a heavy barrage, two infantry brigades began 'Supercharge' **(left),** Montgomery's final thrust: the first armoured unit, 9th Armoured Brigade, was severely mauled, but when the 1st Armoured Division followed it and met XXI Panzer coming from the north, there was a confused tank battle in which the Germans lost much vital equipment. By the morning of the 3rd, Rommel had decided to retreat, only to receive a message from Hitler ordering him to hold the Alamein position at all costs. This order he prepared to obey until the news arrived that his defences in the south had been shattered by 14th Indian and 51st Highland Divisions (not shown on map), and General von Thoma had been captured. He was thus forced to fall back precipitately as the British armour threatened to surround his most precious forces

well have fizzled out, and the full measure of success we achieved might never have been possible.

By 0800 hours on October 25 the leading armoured brigade of the 10th Armoured Division was reported to be 2,000 yards west of the minefield area, and in touch with the 1st Armoured Division to the north. In addition, we heard that the New Zealand Division and the 8th Armoured Brigade were clear of the main minefields, and were advancing south-westwards in accordance with the plan, drawing the XV Panzer Division into several counterattacks against us, which were all repulsed with heavy losses.

The attack switches to the north

By about mid-day Montgomery realised that the 'crumbling' operations by the New Zealand Division would prove very expensive and decided to switch the axis northwards, telling the 9th Australian Division to destroy the Germans in the salient. The 1st Armoured Division was ordered to fight its way westwards with the object of threatening the enemy's supply routes in the Rahman track area, where it would also threaten the rear of the enemy holding the coastal salient, but this attack made no appreciable progress until the night of October 26/27.

The Australian attack under General Morshead went well–ground was gained and heavy casualties inflicted on the enemy. Here the enemy's defences were very strong (the garrison was mainly German) and I believe this area saw the most determined and savage fighting during the whole battle and made a major contribution to ultimate victory.

On the 26th the New Zealand and South African Divisions made slow progress, and the Army Commander decided to regroup. The 30th Corps required a pause to reorganise and, although we had forced our way through the main minefields, the enemy still had well organised anti-tank defences opposing us.

This regrouping produced the reserves required for the decisive phase of the battle. The New Zealand Division was pulled out of the line, their place being taken by moving the 1st South African and 4th Indian Divisions northward. The New Zealanders were given first priority for all tank replacements, and spent a day or so resting and bathing. We could see this cheerful body of men spread out along the beach from our headquarters, the horrors of the Miteiriya Ridge behind them, preparing themselves for the ordeal ahead.

During October 27 news came in that two enemy tankers and a merchantman had been sunk near the entrance to Tobruk harbour, and their loss may have had a considerable influence on the battle. At 1400 hours the Army Commander held a conference at which the regrouping plan was explained, and also plans for the continuance of the Australian attack. The 13th Corps was ordered to make final arrangements for moving the 7th Armoured Division and other troops to the northern sector, for during the night of October 26/27 the XXI Panzer Division had moved northwards, and so these forces could be spared. In the morning we had located, by wireless direction-finding, the headquarters of this German armoured division.

For most of the day, the two German Panzer divisions launched attacks against our positions. This suited us well, and the 1st Armoured Division excelled themselves, claiming 50 enemy tanks knocked out, as well as others damaged. In addition, the RAF was doing good work bombing the enemy as they formed up, so altogether it was an exciting and successful day – from our headquarters we could see the tell-tale pillars of black smoke towering up into the sky when tanks and vehicles were destroyed.

Now Montgomery decided that the 1st Armoured Division needed a rest, and withdrew it into reserve, turning their sector to defence, with infantry brigades, moved up from 13th Corps, and available for subsequent operations.

On the night of the 28/29 the Australian Division attacked again, and drove a wedge into the enemy positions which almost reached the road between Sidi Abd el Rahman and Tell el Eisa, and although on the 29th the enemy did all in their power to destroy this wedge, these attacks made with both tanks and infantry completely failed.

October 29 was a very interesting day as plans and preparations went ahead for the launching of the break-out attack – given the code name of 'Supercharge'.

The Army Commander's intention was to launch this attack as far north as possible, but some of us felt that better results would be gained by adopting a more southerly axis; the farther north we went, the more Germans, mines, and prepared defences would be met.

During the morning we were paid a visit by Commander-in-Chief General Alexander, Minister of State Casey, and Alexander's Chief-of-Staff, Lieutenant-General McCreery. The Army Commander described the situation and his plans, and radiated confidence. He stressed that he had always predicted a ten-day 'dog-fight', and he was quite certain that he would win the battle. However, I soon realised that the Cabinet in London, if not some people in Cairo, were beginning to wonder whether Montgomery would after all fulfil his promise of 'Complete Victory'. It was inevitable therefore that interest was focused upon Supercharge and in discussions with McCreery I found that he also felt that it should be launched farther south.

After Alexander, Casey, and McCreery had departed, I felt more than ever worried about the sector chosen for Supercharge. It appeared to me that Rommel would do all

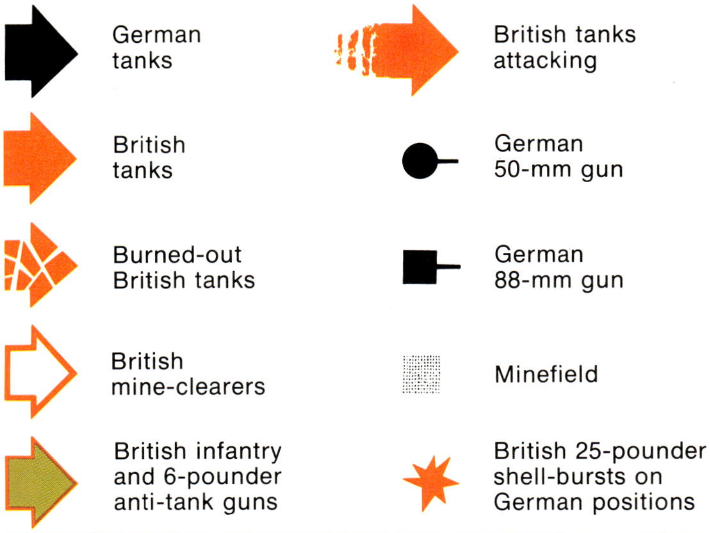

A Set-Piece Desert Battle

Alamein was the first set-piece battle the 8th Army had to fight against an enemy firmly entrenched behind minefields which could not easily be turned. Although on a far larger scale than most subsequent engagements, it set a pattern for a series of later actions in which the 8th Army had to breach the defence lines set up by the retreating Panzerarmee. This diagram shows a typical desert engagement. In the foreground a corridor has been cleared through the Axis minefield, the armour (Crusaders, Grants, and Sherman tanks) has passed through; and one formation is waiting to go in on the near side of a ridge. Meanwhile, infantry are coming up in trucks with their 6-pounder anti-tank guns and the engineers are clearing a second lane. In the centre another tank unit is launching an attack; well spaced out—at least 100 yards between vehicles—they move against the Axis troops who have their 50-mm PAK anti-tank guns in front, and their 88-mm guns lying back. Axis armour waits on the flanks of the position which is being shelled by British 25-pounders

Peter Sarson

Rulers of the Desert Battlefield

To achieve a decisive breakthrough, 8th Army had to breach and clear strong Axis defence lines and minefields. Thus in the early stages new mineclearing vehicles—like the Baron—played an important part, although clearing by hand was still the most reliable and common method. But when the tank-to-tank battles began, in spite of Allied re-equipment and material strength, the Germans still had the outstanding mobile weapon—their Mk IV tank with the devastating long-barrelled 75-mm gun

BARON. A mine-sweeping tank built on the hull of a Matilda, with two additional engines to drive the revolving drum which carried the chains. The tank would be driven at 2 mph with the drum revolving at 72/80 revolutions per minute

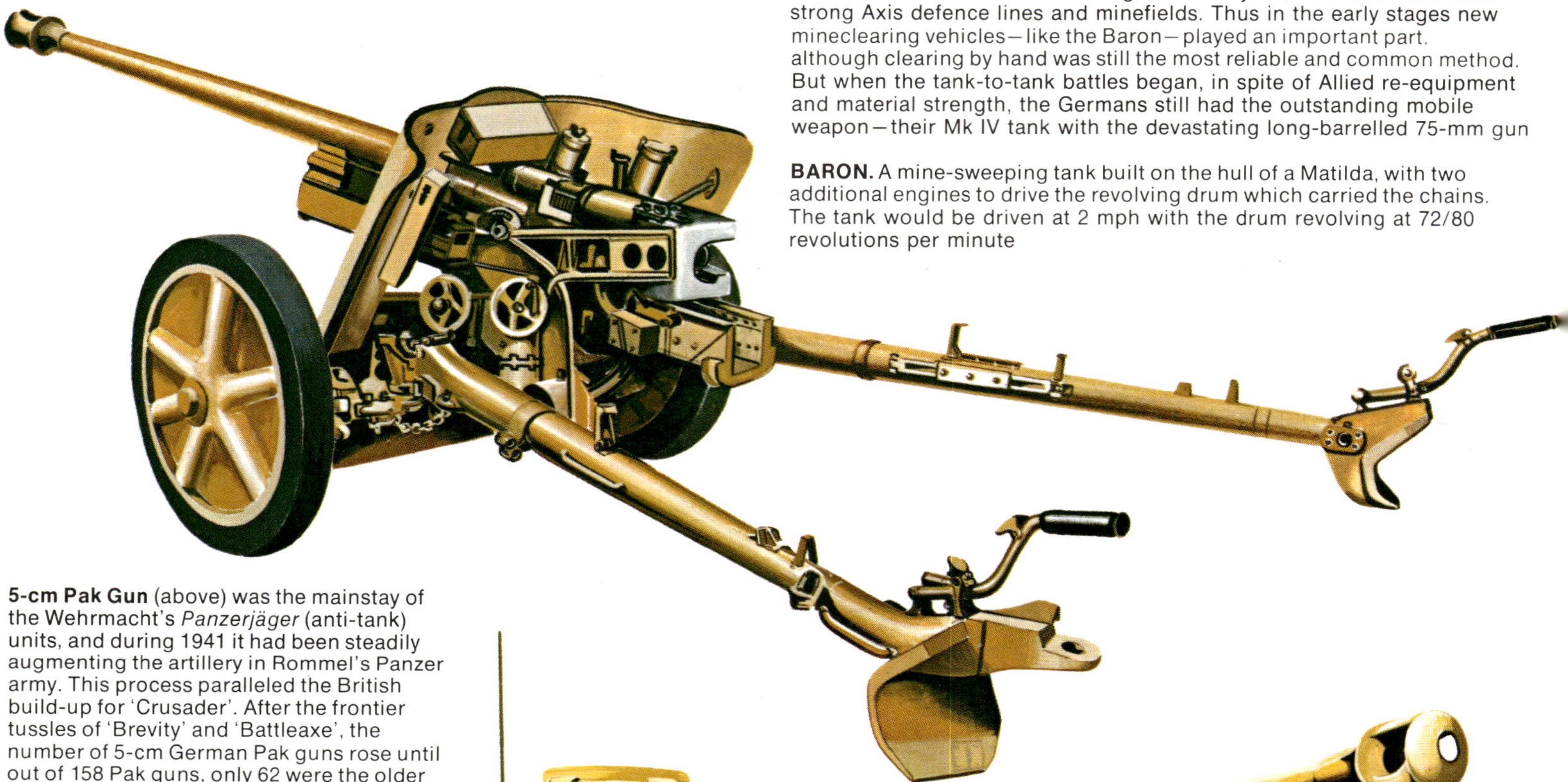

5-cm Pak Gun (above) was the mainstay of the Wehrmacht's *Panzerjäger* (anti-tank) units, and during 1941 it had been steadily augmenting the artillery in Rommel's Panzer army. This process paralleled the British build-up for 'Crusader'. After the frontier tussles of 'Brevity' and 'Battleaxe', the number of 5-cm German Pak guns rose until out of 158 Pak guns, only 62 were the older 37-mm Pak. **Maximum range:** 1,000 yards **Gun crew:** 4

Pzkw MK IVG: *Weight:* 24 tons. *Crew:* 5. *Speed:* 25 mph. *Range:* 130 miles. *Armament:* One long-barrelled 75-mm Kwk 40 (L-43) gun, and two 7.92-mm Type 34 machine-guns

in his power to protect his main supply dumps and his lines of communication which used the coastal road. He could not afford to take any risks on this portion of his front. So I went along to discuss the problem with Bill Williams (G-1 Intelligence) and found that he shared my views. Fortunately the latest intelligence reports showed that 90th Light Division had been moved to the northern sector, no doubt due to successes achieved by the 9th Australian Division. It became obvious therefore that the Axis front farther south had been weakened. I decided to take Williams along to see the Army Commander, and appraise him of the changing situation. Montgomery had previously been much impressed by Williams' explanation of how Rommel had distributed his German troops in order to 'corset' the Italian units, and he was quick to see that the present situation gave an excellent chance of attacking where the enemy was weakest—where most of the defenders were Italian or at least at the junction of the two Axis allies.

Montgomery was never slow in making up his mind—provided, of course, that he had the necessary facts—and in this case he immediately decided to change the axis of the forthcoming attack. I well remember leaving the map lorry in high spirits, and later on that day I rang up McCreery who was quite delighted at hearing the news. This decision was, I'm sure, a decisive contribution to victory.

The Australians continued their attack on the night of 30/31, crossed the coast road, and at one time it looked as if the bulk of the Germans inside the salient would be cut off and destroyed. They managed, however, to get away with the help of tank reinforcements, but this attack to the north had paid a big dividend, for it kept the enemy's attention focused on the coastal area, besides causing great damage among the Germans themselves.

On November 1 we heard that XXI Panzer Division had moved even farther north, and so everything was set for the final phase. After a delay of 24 hours [to rest the troops, and give more time for reorganisation] Supercharge was launched, helped by a creeping barrage at 0100 hours on the morning of November 2. Some 300 25-pounders and the corps medium artillery supported the attack.

The frontage of attack was 4,000 yards, and the depth of the advance 6,000 yards. The infantry (151st and 152nd Infantry Brigades) attacked, and everything went wonderfully well, so on reaching their objective the armour moved through and formed a bridgehead, through which it was proposed to pass the armoured divisions of 10th Corps. The objectives were reached, but the 9th Armoured Brigade suffered heavy casualties from enemy anti-tank weapons. Then the 1st Armoured Division came through to assist, and an armoured battle was fought.

On November 3 we knew that the enemy was beaten, as air reports came in showing that the retreat had started, and we knew that Rommel had insufficient transport or petrol to get back more than a portion of his force.

Yet November 3 still did not see us right out into the open country, for the enemy were still plugging the hole with anti-tank guns, but on the night of the 3/4 a clean break-through was made by the 51st and 4th Indian Divisions, after mounting a sudden attack with the greatest skill.

Bündesarchiv

An Italian machine-gun in action: Italian troops formed the main static element in the Axis line

The battle had been won in 11 days, which was just about the Army Commander's estimate of how long the heavy fighting would last. The enemy was defeated and in full retreat, and our armour and armoured cars were now operating in open country.

When on November 3 all information showed that the enemy was in full retreat, it was hoped that the Desert Air Force would cause havoc among his transport; for reports described a scene of vehicles, head to tail, four and sometimes eight deep, moving westwards either on or just off the road. Indeed we had visions of the retreat being turned into a complete rout, bearing in mind the fact that we enjoyed virtual air superiority. In the event, the results were very disappointing. When setting out along the road between the Alamein battlefield and Daba, I had expected to see a trail of devastation, but the visible signs of destroyed vehicles were few and far between. The fact is that at this period of the war we had not learned the technique of low strafing, for our fighter bombers had been employed in air fighting and bombing. I believe the attacks on the retreating columns were made mostly with bombs, and that the aircraft were not allowed to come down low; no doubt because our pilots had not been trained in low-flying attacks with cannon. I feel, however, that an opportunity was lost, and that it should have been possible to have produced a form of paralysis in the enemy's rearward movement.

It was also a great disappointment that we were unable to cut off completely Rommel's surviving forces and so save the long and arduous series of operations that took us to Tripoli and beyond. Montgomery, however, knew that it was only a matter of time, and in any case he was very unlucky, for the forces which he had ordered to cut off the enemy at the bottlenecks of Fuka and Matrûh were deprived of fulfilling their object through the interference caused by some most unusually heavy rain storms, which 'bogged' them down within a stone's throw of the retreating enemy.

The Hinge of Fate

1942 October 6: General Montgomery issues his final plan for 8th Army's offensive.
October 23: 2125 hours; artillery bombardment begins in the 13th Corps sector. 2140; 30th Corps bombardment begins. 2200 hours; 30th Corps with four divisions and 13th Corps launch two attacks—on Himeimat and Gebel Kalakh.
October 24: 0200 hours; leading elements of 1st and 10th Armoured Divisions begin to move through the corridors. By dawn most units of 30th Corps have reached their 'Oxalic' line objectives, but 10th Corps has been unable to clear the bridgehead and reach 'Pierson'. After a successful start, 13th Corps is held up between the minefields, but is successful in keeping XXI Panzer Division in its sector. By the evening, 1st Armoured Division has got some units out of the minefields, but 10th Armoured Division's attack at 2200 hours makes little progress.
October 25: 0200 hours; congestion in the southern corridor reaches a dangerous level, but after a conference at 0330 hours, Montgomery confirms that the attempt to break out must continue. 0800; the leading brigade moves clear. The New Zealand Division and 8th Armoured Brigade also clear the main minefield and turn to advance south-westward, fighting off counterattacks by XV Panzer. 1200 hours; Montgomery decides to switch the axis of the attack to the north—9th Australian Division is to strike northward and 1st Armoured Division westward behind the coastal salient.
October 26: The 9th Australian Division gains ground, but all other attacks are held; Montgomery decides to regroup—the New Zealand Division moves back into reserve, and is replaced by the 1st South African and 4th Indian Divisions. Two German tankers—the *Proserpina* and the *Tergesta*—are sunk; Panzerarmee's fuel problem becomes acute.
October 27: XXI Panzer moves northward; the British redeployment continues with 7th Armoured Division being withdrawn from 13th Corps and brought north. A series of German attacks on 1st Armoured Division are thrown back with a loss of 50 tanks.
October 28/29: Further attacks by 9th Australian Division in the northern sector drive a wedge into the enemy position.
October 29: Montgomery decides to launch the break-out (Supercharge) as far north as possible, but revises his decision (on hearing that the German 90th Light Division has also moved north) in order to strike Italian not German troops.
October 30/31: The Australian attack continues in an attempt to cut off the enemy forces in the coastal salient.
November 2: 151st and 152nd Brigades launch Operation Supercharge, they reach their objectives successfully, and at 0615 9th Armoured Brigade advances, but is held up by heavy anti-tank fire. The 1st Armoured Division moves through to eliminate the opposition. At 2015 hours, after a conference with General von Thoma, Rommel decides to begin the retreat to the Fuka position.
November 3: Confused fighting, but during the night the break-through is achieved by the 51st and 4th Indian Divisions in the south.
November 4: After further fighting, Axis troops begin to retreat, followed by 1st, 7th and 10th Armoured Divisions.

Operation Torch was notable for the long approach voyages – troops came straight from the US and the UK to the beaches

TORCH AND THE TUNISIAN BRIDGEHEAD

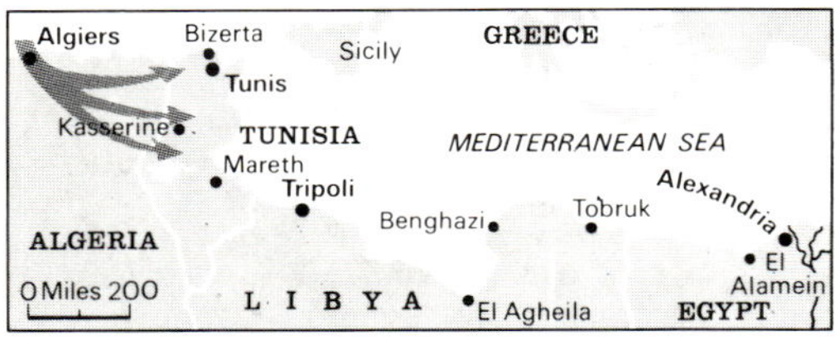

On the morning of November 8, 1942, a force of over 100,000 American and British soldiers went ashore on the coast of Vichy French North-West Africa, and a period of close Anglo-American co-operation began. Altogether over 500 ships had carried and guarded the assault force: 102 of them crossing the Atlantic from America; the remainder sailing in two convoys – one fast and one slow – from Britain. They all arrived at their destinations within a few hours of each other and a pattern of smooth timing and organisation had been set.

Once on North African soil, however, the reactions and responses of a third nationality were soon to complicate events, adding to them at the same time a purely Latin flavour of tragicomedy. The American belief that they were so beloved by the French while the British were so hated as to make the essential difference between welcome and resistance in North Africa had already caused unnecessary complications in the tactical planning (in that the landings had to appear to be all-American). But the French desire, on the one hand to avoid retribution at the hands of the Germans if the landings proved a failure, and on the other

Imperial War Museum

Imperial War Museum

US Army

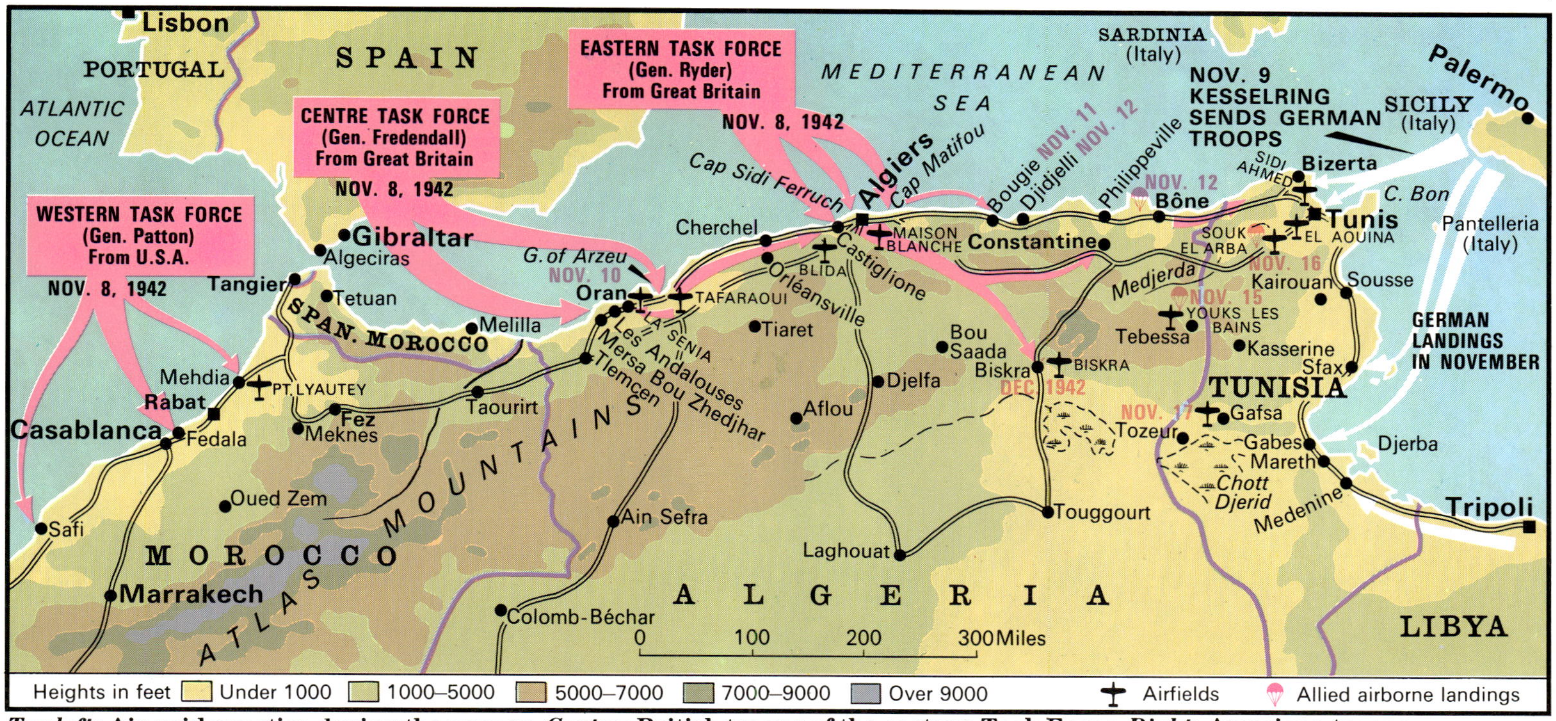

Top left: **Air-raid practice during the voyage. *Centre:* British troops of the eastern Task Force. *Right:* American troops**

An American soldier carrying his rifle – the famous Garand ·30 M1, described as 'the best battle implement ever devised'

to play an important part in their own liberation should they succeed, complicated the situation immeasurably more. However, by one of history's oddest twists, the Gordian Knot was cut by the very man who had most reason to hate the British, and good reason to suspect the Americans. Admiral Darlan, the Vichy C-in-C who was visiting the area at that time for purely personal reasons, was one of the few French leaders with the authority to order the French forces to stop their desultory resistance and join the Allies. After some hesitation he ordered a ceasefire and the Allies could at last turn their energies to the more important military objectives – the ports of Tunis and Bizerta.

The Oran landings were followed by smooth disembarkation

US Army

A Sherman tank of the 1st Army: neatness was their hallmark

Shortly after the main landings in Algeria and Morocco, the British 1st Army drove into Tunisia to clear the coastline and link up with the 8th Army, now advancing from El Alamein. But the swift liberation of Algeria and Morocco had been untypical; in Tunisia the Germans reacted with speed and efficiency, and rapidly built up their forces. Within three days of the Allied landings, German airlifts were bringing troops and equipment into Tunis, and by the end of the month 15,000 well-armed and experienced German soldiers and 9,000 Italians were expertly deployed to block Allied plans. By pouring troops into this 'Tunisian Bridgehead' Hitler was hoping to prevent or at least delay an Allied attack on southern Europe. By the end of January the Axis had over 100,000 troops in Tunisia and had brought the Allied advance to a halt.

Meanwhile at the other end of the Mediterranean Rommel was also heading for Tunisia. Four days before the Torch landings took place, the Axis defences at El Alamein had finally given way and the 8th Army began the last pursuit of the Afrika Korps – who with typical efficiency succeeded in fighting repeated and stubborn rearguard actions despite their exhaustion and lack of supplies.

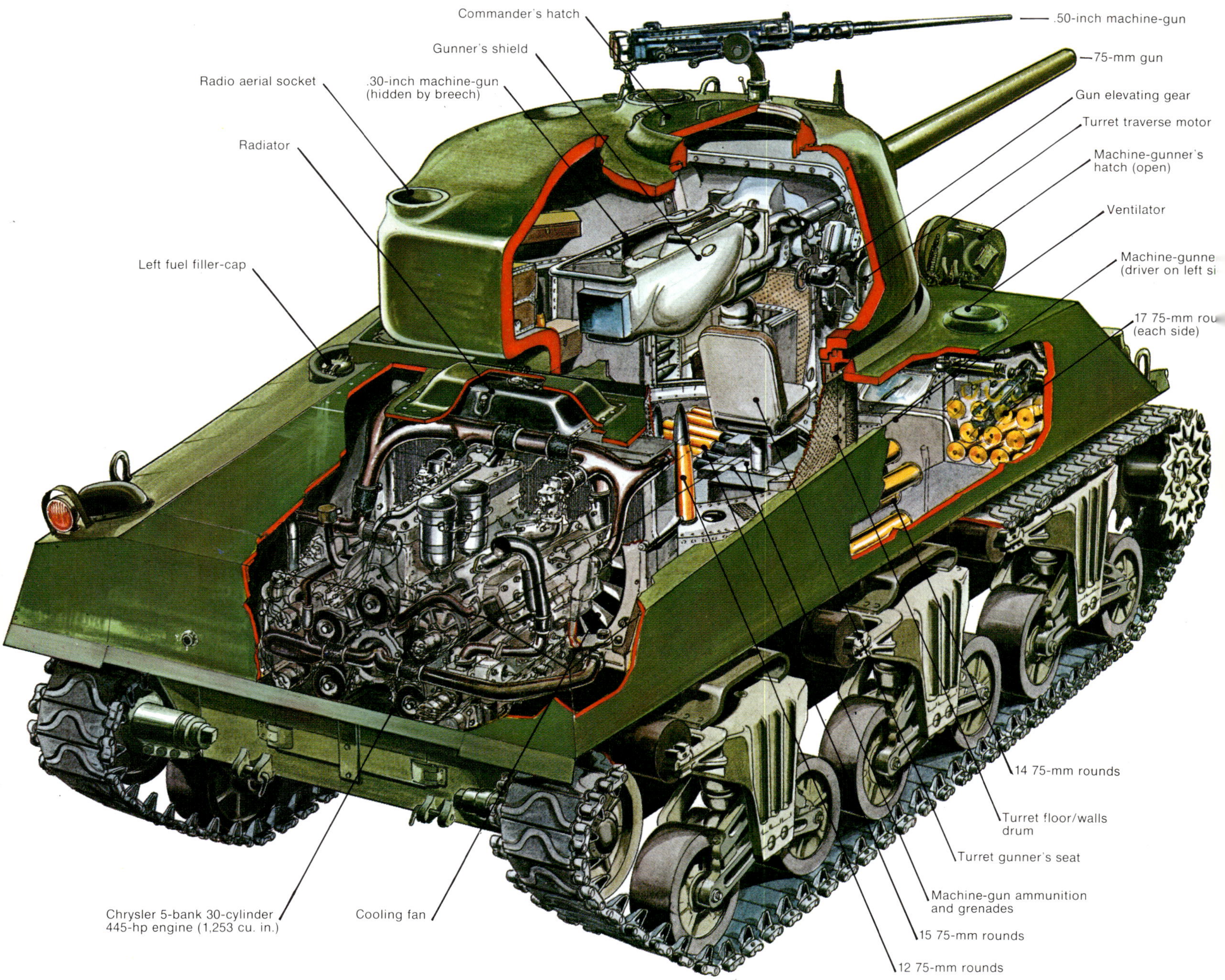

The Allied Juggernaut

After the earlier designs of the Grant and Lee tanks – which had themselves performed invaluable services with 8th Army in early 1942 – the main American and Allied battle tank came to be the Sherman. Its mass delivery to the Allied armies in North Africa and southern Europe was the result of an unprecedented feat of production. In 1941, American factories turned out 14,000 Shermans; in 1943, this rose to 21,000. And these numbers alone, matched by the virtues of mechanical reliability, gave the Sherman a very significant counter to the German gun and armour superiority. Solidly armoured, formidably armed, this model's most extraordinary feature was its Chrysler engine, built up from five 25-hp truck engines. *Max speed:* 23 mph. *Range:* 80 miles in average conditions. *Crew:* five. *Weight:* 71,900 lb. *Engine:* Chrysler model A57 (30-cylinder, 460-BHP). *Armament:* one 75-mm M3 gun, one ·50-inch machine-gun in hull, one ·30-inch machine-gun on flexible mounting

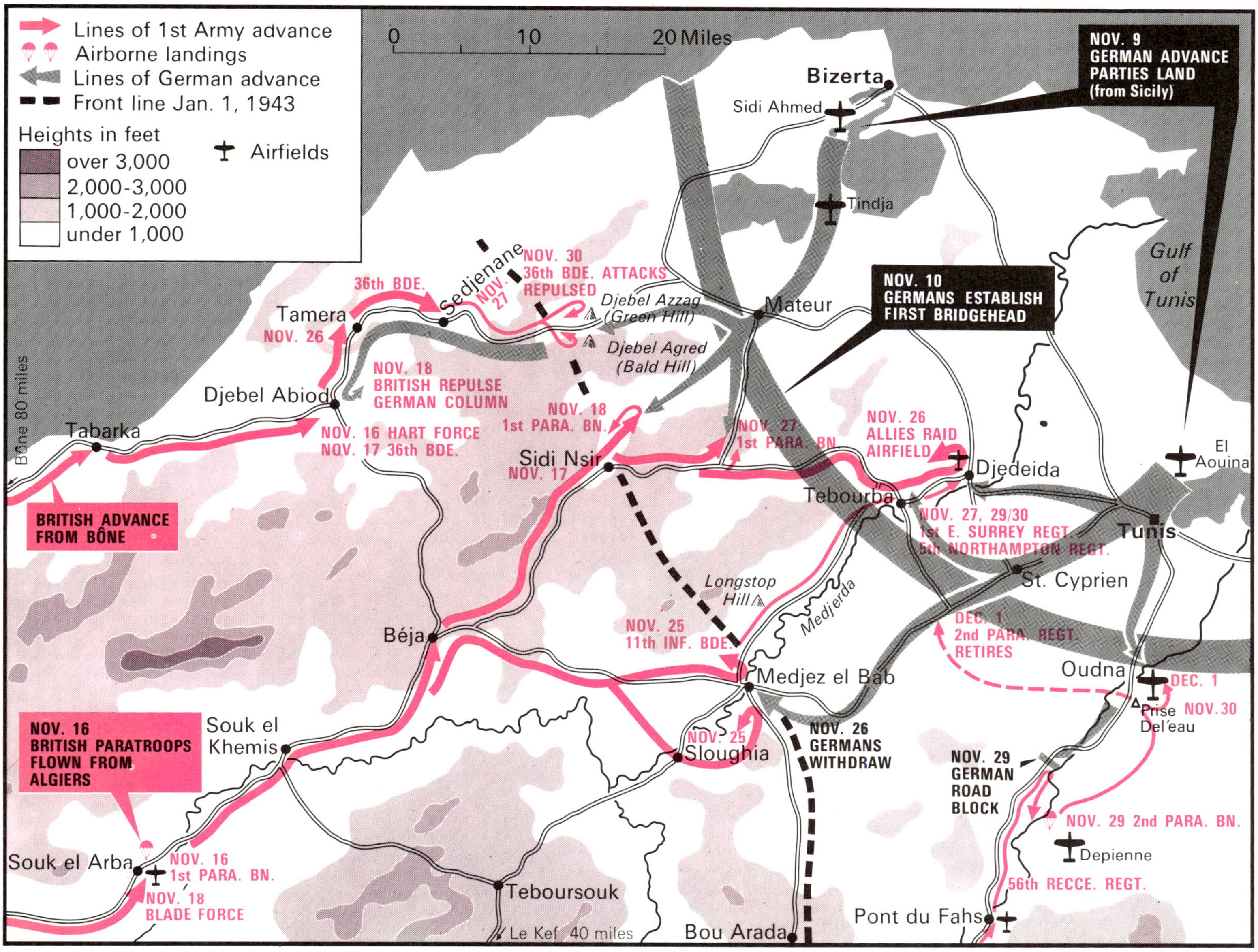

One of the weaknesses of the Torch planning was that no provision had been made to neutralize Tunisia during the initial stages. German reaction was faster than Allied planners had thought possible, and a race developed between the 1st Army and the German advance parties—first to seize certain vital airfields with airborne troops, and then to occupy the passes leading into the Tunisian plain with orthodox forces. The Allies won the first, lap, but their advance towards Tunis and Bizerta was stopped by the Germans on a line running from Oudna through Tebourba towards Mateur. By this time, the 1st Army had outrun its supply lines and lacked the impetus to break through the German defences. Meanwhile, the Germans and Italians continued their build-up, pouring in troops and aircraft. The prime German deficiency was in artillery: guns of all types numbered less than 40, but operations were in fact hardly hampered—the Stukas provided intense fire-support by day and the mortars were a deadly supplement. It was the mountainous terrain, however, which most aided the Axis defence.

Once Admiral Darlan had agreed to support the Allies, French resistance in Algeria and Morocco came to an end and the Allied forces were able to move out from the main cities and complete the occupation of the country swiftly and easily

United Press

New Tide from the Atlantic

1942 July 24/25: The combined British and American Chiefs-of-Staff decide to adopt the 'Super-Gymnast' plan—a major Anglo-American invasion of north-west Africa. Churchill renames the operation Torch; General Eisenhower is given overall command.
October 22/23: American General Mark Clark makes a secret landing on the Algerian coast for talks with key French officials. The first assault forces for Oran and Algiers sail from Britain.
November 2: Rommel gives Afrika Korps orders to withdraw from El Alamein.
November 3: On receiving Hitler's refusal of permission to withdraw, Rommel orders his units to take up new defensive positions.
November 3/4: 8th Army breaches the German defence line, Afrika Korps loses about 200 tanks and armoured vehicles.
November 5: Rommel establishes a new halt-line at Fuka, where his units can reorganise, but it is penetrated by the 8th Army.
November 6: Heavy rain slows up the 8th Army's pursuit.
November 7: French General Giraud, principal candidate to lead the French in Africa, is picked up on the south coast of France by a British submarine, and taken to Gibraltar to await the results of the landing.
November 8: The Allied assault forces land near Casablanca, Oran, and Algiers. At Casablanca, landing troubles delay the invaders, but the other forces are not opposed until they begin to move toward their objectives.
November 9: Following discussions with General Clark in Algiers, Admiral Darlan issues an order to cease fire. After pressure from the Germans this is countermanded by the Vichy government, but the French forces in North Africa obey. On hearing of Torch, Rommel decides to retreat in one bound to El Agheila. Sidi Barrani is evacuated.
November 11: German forces overrun the unoccupied part of France, and begin to pour into Tunisia, as the British 1st Army begins to advance towards Tunis and Bizerta. Afrika Korps evacuates Halfaya Pass. 36th Brigade lands at Bougie.
November 12: Paratroops of British 1st Parachute Brigade occupy Bône Airfield.
November 13: Advance guard of the 8th Army enters Tobruk.
November 16: Souk el Arba airfield is captured by the 1st Parachute Battalion; it begins to advance towards Tunis. The headquarters of 78th Division is established at Bône.
November 20: 8th Army reaches Benghazi.
November 23: Afrika Korps falls back from Agedabia; Montgomery slows up the pursuit in order to reorganise his fighting forces and supply lines.
November 26/30: Medjez is evacuated by the Germans and occupied by 11th Brigade. 36th Brigade reaches Tamera, and continues to probe towards Mateur. It meets strong resistance, and 1st Army's advance is held up on a line Mateur/Medjez. Djedeida is occupied for a short time, but the Germans recapture it.
November 29: The 2nd Parachute Battalion lands at Depienne airfield, and marches to Oudna, but it has to withdraw when 1st Army fails to break through at Djedeida and link up with it.
December 12/13: 8th Army attacks the German line at Mersa Brega, the Afrika Korps withdraws to avoid a major struggle.
December 14/18: Rommel evades an attempt to surround his forces at El Agheila.
December 24: Admiral Darlan is assassinated.

Debut of the Parachute Regiment. By the time of the Torch landings, the British had recruited a small force of airborne troops which was to prove vital during the opening stages of the race into Tunisia. The operations to capture the airfields at Bône and Souk el Arba were among the first occasions in which the new parachute battalions were used in action, and since at this stage they had not acquired a new badge, the men wore the distinctive red beret with the badges of their old regiments. A parachute battalion at this time consisted of about 538 men of all ranks—a headquarters company and three rifle companies—and would be accompanied into action by a variety of specialists: troops from the Royal Engineers, Royal Signals, and Royal Army Medical Corps. The operations in Tunisia were also the first time that the airborne troops used the aircraft which was to become their standard mount for the rest of the war—and the workhorse of almost all the Allied forces in every theatre.

Douglas C-47 Dakota. A military version of the DC-3 airliner, the Dakota had a strengthened floor and larger cargo-handling door on the port side. Rugged and extremely reliable, over 10,000 Dakotas had been produced by the end of the war—1,200 of them being supplied to the RAF—and many were still in use 20 years after the war ended. **Speed:** 230 mph (maximum), 167 mph (cruising). **Range:** 1,300 miles. **Crew:** Three. **Load:** 9,028 lb of cargo, or 18/24 paratroops

(Below) Dakotas in flight during the advance into Tunisia
(Below right) British paratroops inside a Dakota en route to Bône airfield

Dakota: Workhorse for the Allies

Imperial War Museum

Weapons for the Final Desert Drive

The first British attempts to produce efficient self-propelled guns were not encouraging. The Bishop *(below)* was weak in design and construction, slow, uncomfortable, and usually more trouble than it was worth; the Sexton *(right)* was better, being constructed from more reliable components. But in the 5·5-inch and 3·7-inch guns the British artillery had two splendid weapons, which were equal to any of their Axis counterparts; and although the 3·7 was never allowed to give of its best in the anti-tank role, the 5·5 served with distinction, proving invaluable in the interminable bombardments among the Tunisian hills

Bishop Self-Propelled Gun
No two variants were ever exactly alike, but the type basically consisted of a 25-pounder mounted in a Valentine hull. It was not a happy combination, as the two components were usually battle-weary from past campaigns. *Weight:* 18 tons. *Crew:* four. *Max armour thickness:* 51-mm

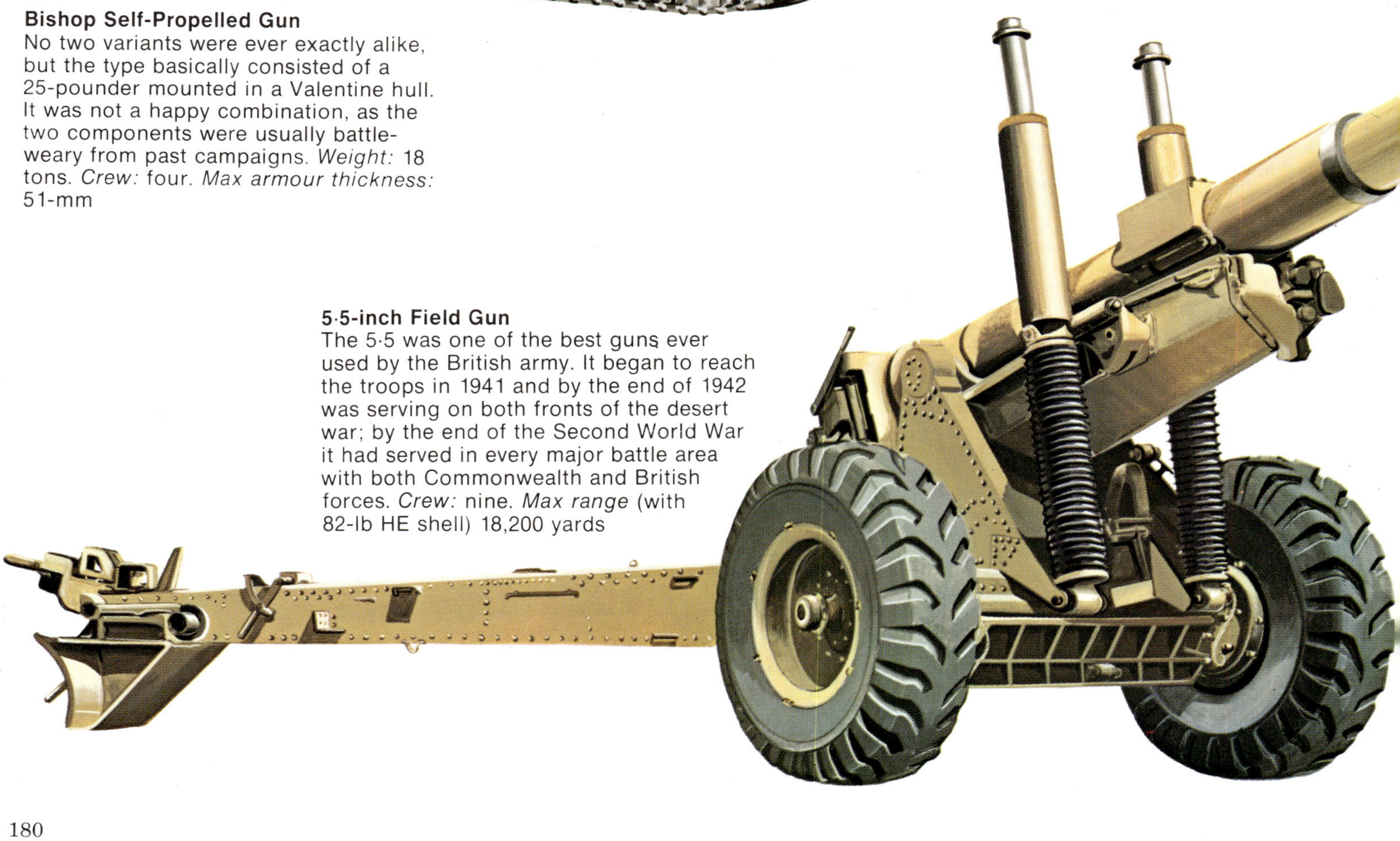

5·5-inch Field Gun
The 5·5 was one of the best guns ever used by the British army. It began to reach the troops in 1941 and by the end of 1942 was serving on both fronts of the desert war; by the end of the Second World War it had served in every major battle area with both Commonwealth and British forces. *Crew:* nine. *Max range* (with 82-lb HE shell) 18,200 yards

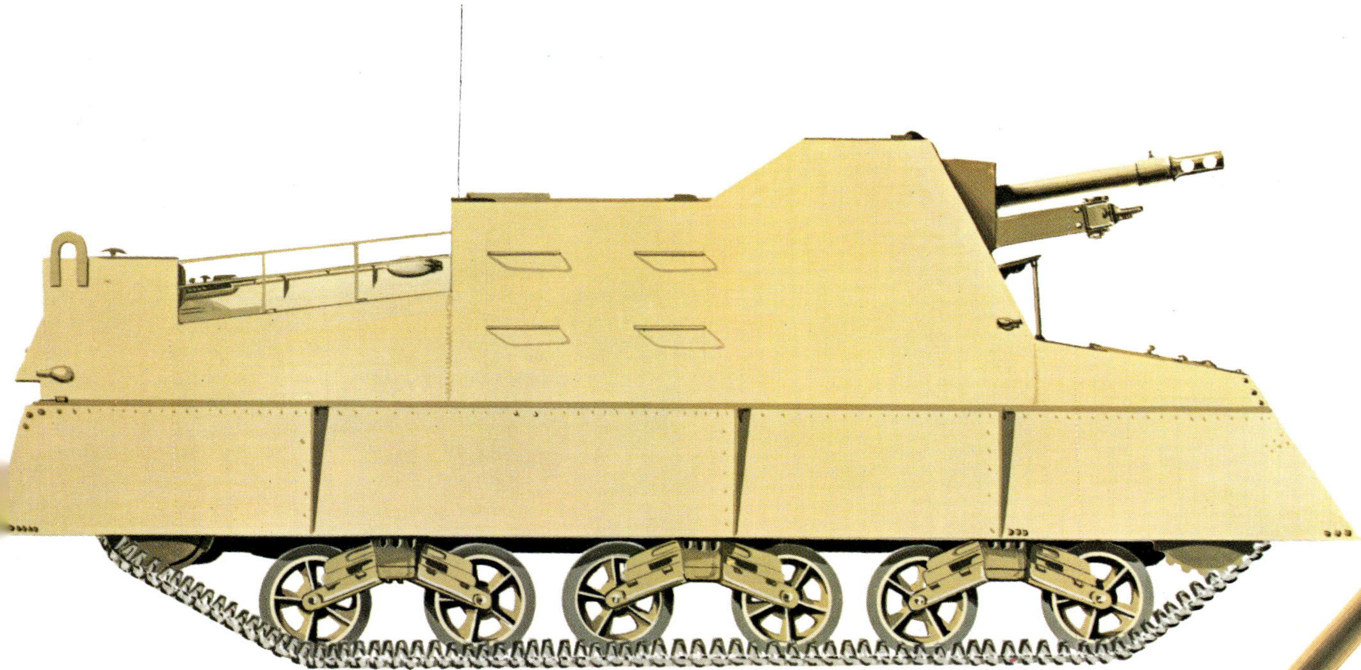

Sexton Self-Propelled Gun
The Sexton began to appear when the flood of American equipment had reached the desert theatre; it was constructed along the same lines as the Bishop, with a 25-pounder or 75-mm gun mounted in a Grant or Sherman hull. *Weight:* 25 tons. *Crew:* four. *Max armour thickness:* 65-mm

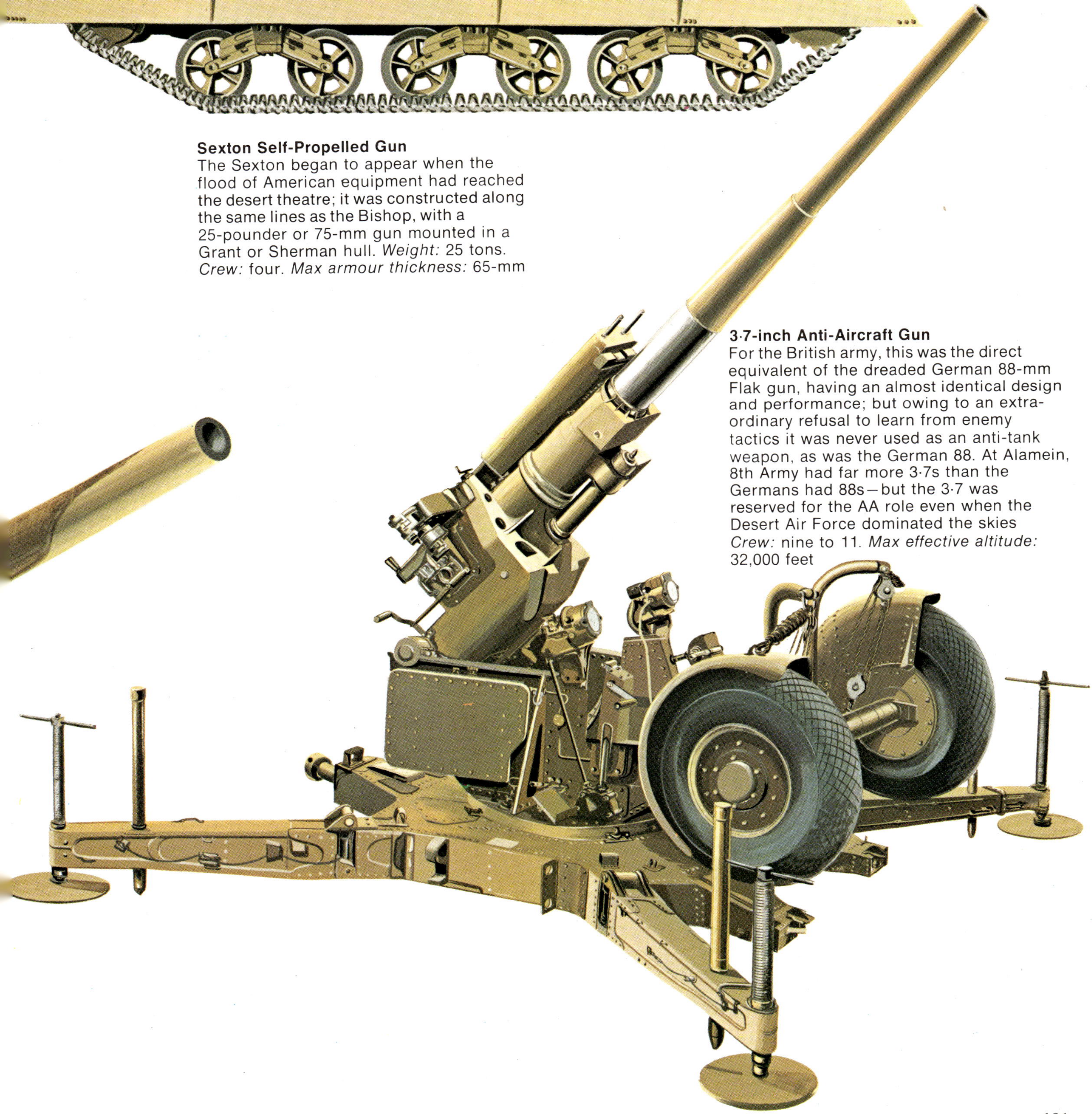

3·7-inch Anti-Aircraft Gun
For the British army, this was the direct equivalent of the dreaded German 88-mm Flak gun, having an almost identical design and performance; but owing to an extraordinary refusal to learn from enemy tactics it was never used as an anti-tank weapon, as was the German 88. At Alamein, 8th Army had far more 3·7s than the Germans had 88s—but the 3·7 was reserved for the AA role even when the Desert Air Force dominated the skies *Crew:* nine to 11. *Max effective altitude:* 32,000 feet

THE CHASE TO MARETH

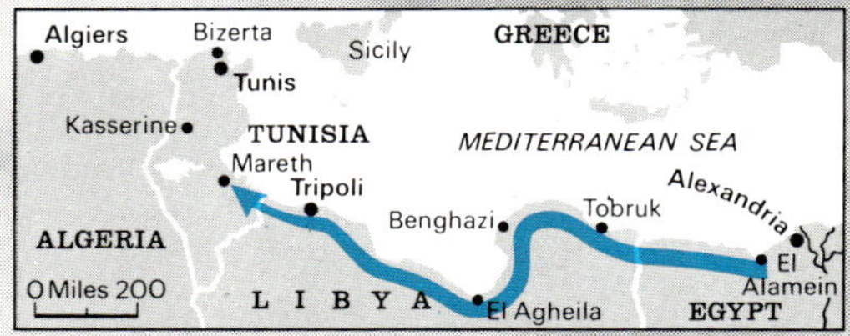

If after El Alamein Rommel had any hopes of once again turning the tables on the 8th Army they were quickly dashed by the Allied landings in Morocco and Algeria. His only chance of survival from then on lay in a successful, defensive withdrawal to the 'Tunisian Bridgehead'.

At the opening of the battle, Rommel had been away sick in Austria, but flew back at once. Weighing up the situation, he planned to withdraw his army to the Fuka position, 60 miles west of El Alamein. That step would have thrown Montgomery's battle-machine out of gear. But Rommel's intention was overruled by Hitler's insistence that no ground must be yielded. So retreat was deferred until after defeat. Then Rommel executed it with his usual celerity and ruthless calculation – abandoning his less mobile and less expert troops, including the bulk of the Italians, in order to bring away his picked troops in the motor transport available.

The chance of cutting him off was lost because the pursuit was not sufficiently indirect or extensive in its circling sweep. In the first place, it turned in too soon to catch the bulk of the forces retreating along the coastal road. Then a longer-range turn-in at 'Charing Cross', near Marsa Matrûh (120 miles west of El Alamein), failed to cut them off through running short of petrol after being impeded by heavy rain. A wider move through the desert, farther inland, would have avoided the rainy belt.

Once Rommel had slipped through the jaws of his armoured pursuers, he did not pause until he had reached his favourite backstop position near El Agheila at the far end of Cyrenaica – 700 miles back from El Alamein. In a fortnight's swift retreat he had outstripped the pursuit, and left few prisoners or supplies behind.

Imperial War Museum

The crew of one of Rommel's Panzers surrenders at Alamein

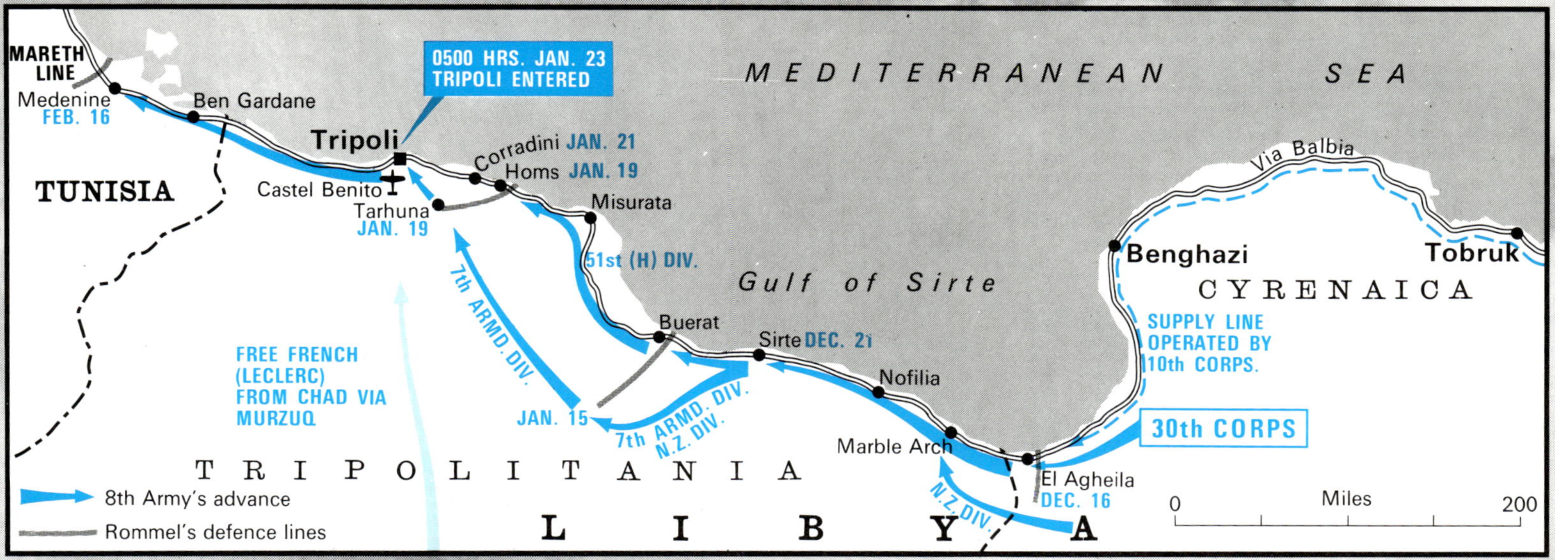

Rommel's forces were so weak that he could not even hope to hold a defensive line for long, let alone mount a counterattack. Instead he fought a masterly withdrawal, causing the 8th Army the maximum of trouble while keeping Panzerarmee in being and its morale high.

Imperial War Museum

The 8th Army in pursuit of the Afrika Korps at Alamein

Imperial War Museum

But this time the odds against him were too heavy to permit any riposte, or even a long-sustained stand at El Agheila. A pause of three weeks occurred before the 8th Army could bring up its strength and mount an offensive against the El Agheila position. Just as the offensive developed, Rommel began to slip off. Rommel halted again on the Buerat position, a further 200 miles back. He stayed there three weeks, but when the 8th Army closed up and launched its next offensive, in the middle of January 1943, he fell back again.

This time he made an almost continuous withdrawal for 350 miles, past Tripoli, to the Mareth Line inside the frontier of Tunisia. His decision was the consequence not merely of his weakness of force and the sinking of the majority of his supply-ships, but of the new situation produced by the Anglo-American invasion of Morocco and Algeria – Operation Torch – in November 1942. That move had closely followed the El Alamein offensive, some 2,500 miles away at the other end of North Africa.

As originally conceived, the Allied landings were to have taken place only on the Atlantic coast of Morocco. This would have meant a purely frontal advance, giving the French forces the fullest chance of effective resistance. The advance would have started 1,200 miles away from Bizerta, the key to the whole North African theatre of war, so that the Germans would have had time and opportunity to stiffen the French resistance to the Allied invasion. Fortunately for the Allied prospects, landings on the Mediterranean coast, near Oran and Algiers, were added to the plan. American diplomacy smoothed the path of these landings by securing the acquiescence or quiescence of numerous Frenchmen in authority. Once lodgements were achieved at these points they created a decisive leverage on the backs of the French forces on the west coast, where the initial resistance threatened to be more stubborn.

The landings near Algiers reduced the distance from Bizerta to barely 400 miles. At that moment, a mere handful of motorised troops could have run through to Bizerta and Tunis without hindrance except from the mountain roads. Alternatively, either seaborne or airborne landings nearby would have met scarcely any opposition. But the naval authorities were chary of attempting even small-scale landings so far ahead of air cover, and the overland advance was too cautious.

Meantime, the Germans' reaction was swift, though the landings had taken them by surprise. From the third day onwards they began to rush troops to Tunis in all available troop-carrying aircraft

A field gun of Rommel's Army Group Africa in action as the Germans and Italians make their final retreat into Tunisia after the defeat at El Alamein

Sado (Wolff und Tritschler)

as well as in small coasting vessels. Although the total was still small, it was just sufficient to check the leading troops of the Allied 1st Army when these reached the immediate approaches to Tunis two-and-a-half weeks after the initial landings. The result of this check was a five-month deadlock in the mountainous arc covering Bizerta and Tunis.

Nevertheless, this failure worked out to the Allies' advantage in the long run. For it encouraged the enemy to continue pouring reinforcements across the sea to Tunisia, where the Allies could cut off their supplies through developing the stranglehold of superior sea-power, and then cut off their retreat. Ironically, Hitler was led to stake larger forces on the retention of Tunisia than he had ever devoted to the capture of Egypt. By drawing so many of the German and Italian reserves across the Mediterranean and putting them 'in the bag' there, the way was eased for the Allies' subsequent invasion of Europe. North Africa thus became as fatal a strategic bait to Hitler as Spain had been to Napoleon, in conjunction with their respective invasions of Russia.

Sado-Opera Mundi

German transports head for the front past a burning US truck

BATTLE OF KASSERINE

The 1943 campaign in Tunisia opened, however, with a German counterstroke that gave the Allies a bad shock. It came just when their two armies – the 1st from the west, and the 8th from the east – seemed about to crush the Axis forces between their jaws. The Axis command aimed to forestall that danger by dislocating both jaws, and for such an aim the conditions had become more favourable than was apparent on the surface of the situation. By now the reinforcements sent to Tunis had been built up into an army, under General von Arnim, while at the same time the remnant of Rommel's army was acquiring fresh strength, and equipment, as it came nearer to the supply ports in its westward retreat. Profiting by this temporarily favourable turn in the situation, Rommel's design was to exploit his central position between the two converging Allied armies to strike, and cripple, them separately and successively. The design had brilliant promise, but its execution suffered a heavy handicap in being largely dependent on forces which were not under Rommel's control. For when the operation was launched Arnim's army was independent, and even the veteran XXI Panzer Division, which was to deliver the main thrust, had passed to Arnim's command when it had been sent back to help in holding open Rommel's line of retreat and supply.

The American 2nd Corps (which included a French division) was the immediate target of the counterstroke. Its front covered 90 miles, but was focused on the three routes through the mountains to the sea, with spearheads at the passes near Gafsa, Faid, and Fondouk. These passage-ways were so narrow that the occupiers felt secure. But at the end of January, the XXI Panzer Division made a sudden spring at the Faid Pass, overwhelmed the French garrison

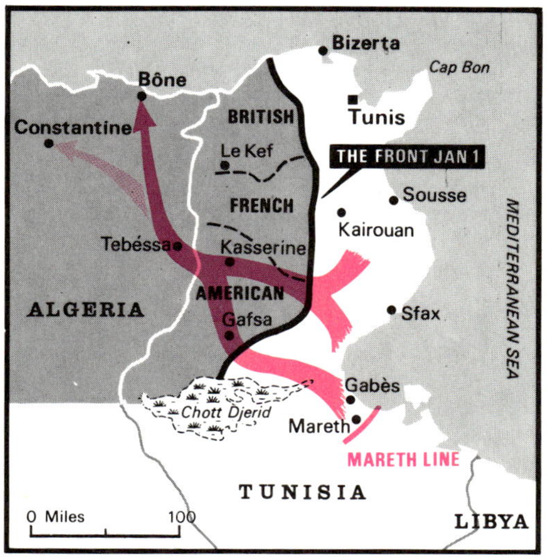

The small map shows the ultimate targets of *Frühlingswind* – the German offensive in southern Tunisia. To break through the mass of Allied men and material between the Tunisian front and the Allied bases of Bône and Constantine was a formidable task – but the confusion which was caused by the first attacks **(below)** seemed to promise fulfilment of all Rommel's hopes. The Axis troops in the Mareth Line were saved from the threat of an American attack from the west – but Commando Supremo failed to appoint a unified command and thus concentrate the Axis strike forces for a further advance. By the afternoon of February 22, Rommel had lost faith in the attack and had begun to withdraw; and the badly-shaken Allied armies recovered themselves

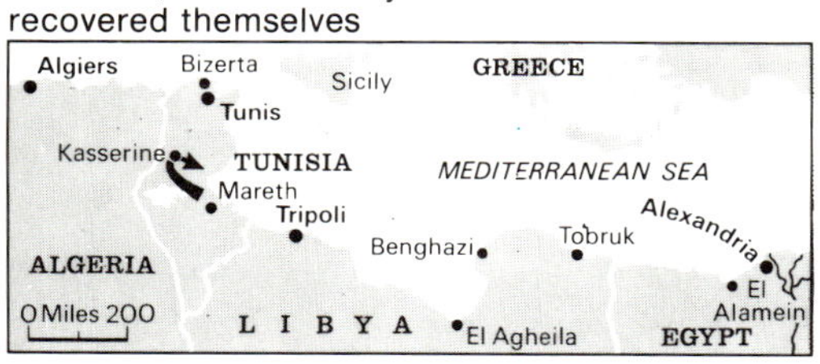

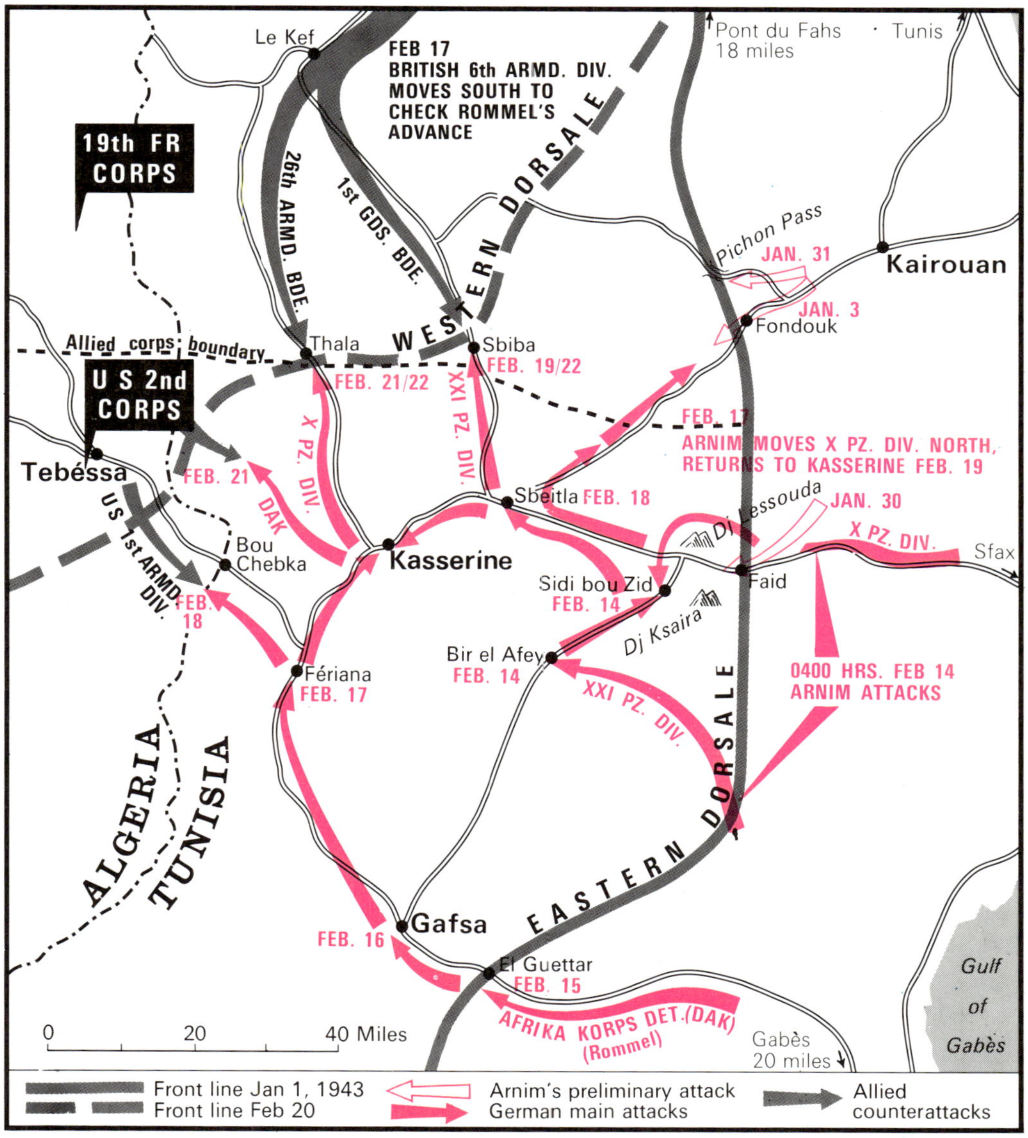

'NEBELWERFER' 150-MM ROCKET-LAUNCHER: The most widely used of the family of launchers developed by the Germans, the six-barrelled Nebelwerfer ('fog-thrower') was used to lay down extremely heavy short-range bombardments or smoke screens. As compared with conventional artillery, the Nebelwerfer fired a heavy projectile (below) from a light carriage, and was thus very manoeuvrable, but it was far less accurate. The six barrels had to be fired separately (this took 10 seconds) to prevent the carriage overturning; the tubes could be reloaded in 90 seconds. *Weight of launcher:* 1,195 lb. *Range:* 7,330 yards with high explosive, 7,750 yards with smoke shells. *Weight of rocket:* 75·3 lb (high explosive), 78 lb (smoke)

before American support arrived, and thus gained a sally-port.

On February 14 the real blow came, starting with a fresh spring forward from the Faid Pass. Arnim's deputy, Ziegler, was in charge here. Rommel urged Ziegler to drive on during the night and exploit the success to the full, but Ziegler waited for 48 hours until he received Arnim's authorisation before pushing on 25 miles to Sbeitla, where the Americans had rallied. Even then he was able to throw them back again, although the fight was harder and they rallied again at the Kasserine Pass.

Alexander, who had just been placed in charge of both the Allied armies, and now arrived on the scene, said in his dispatch: 'I found the position even more critical than I had expected, and a visit to the Kasserine area showed that in the confusion of the retreat American, French and British troops had been inextricably mingled, there was no co-ordinated plan of defence and definite uncertainty as to command.'

Rommel wanted to exploit the confusion and panic by a combined drive with all available mechanised forces through Tebéssa towards the Allies' main communications with their Algerian bases. But it was not until early on the 19th that a signal came from Rome authorising a continuation of the thrust, and Rommel to conduct it—but ordering that it should be made due *northward* to Thala, instead of *north-westward* to Tebéssa as Rommel had proposed.

Thus the thrust came along the line which Alexander had expected, and where he was best prepared to meet it. He had ordered the army commander to 'concentrate his armour for the defence of Thala', and British reserves from the north were being rushed down to that sector. The Americans, too, had collected in strength on the line of approach to Thala, and held on so stubbornly to the Kasserine Pass that the Germans did not break through it until the evening of the 20th. Next day they drove into Thala, exhausted, and were pushed out by the British reserves that had now arrived there.

This too-direct approach not only proved an expensive failure itself but caused delay in releasing the divisions needed for Rommel's intended second stroke—against Montgomery. By March 6, when Rommel struck, Montgomery had quadrupled his strength—besides 400 tanks he had now over 500 anti-tank guns in position. Thus in the interval Rommel's chance of striking with superior force had vanished. The attack was brought to a standstill by the afternoon and the Germans' loss of 50 tanks was a serious handicap in the next phase of the campaign. By then they had also lost Rommel, who had gone back to Europe sick, and frustrated.

For their ultimate victory, the Allies owed more to the enemy's misjudged offensive efforts than to the effect of their own assaults. The Allies' chance to turn the tables only came after the Germans had overstretched themselves in the offensive.

MARETH LINE

The 8th Army's attack on the Mareth Line was launched on the night of March 20. The main blow was a frontal one, intended to break through the defence near the sea and make a gap through which the armoured divisions could sweep. At the same time, the New Zealand Corps made a wide outflanking march towards El Hamma in the enemy's rear, with the aim of pinning down the enemy's reserves that were placed there. The frontal attack failed to make an adequate breach. So, after three days' effort, Montgomery changed his plan, side-stepping inland and sending the 1st Armoured Division to the enemy's rear.

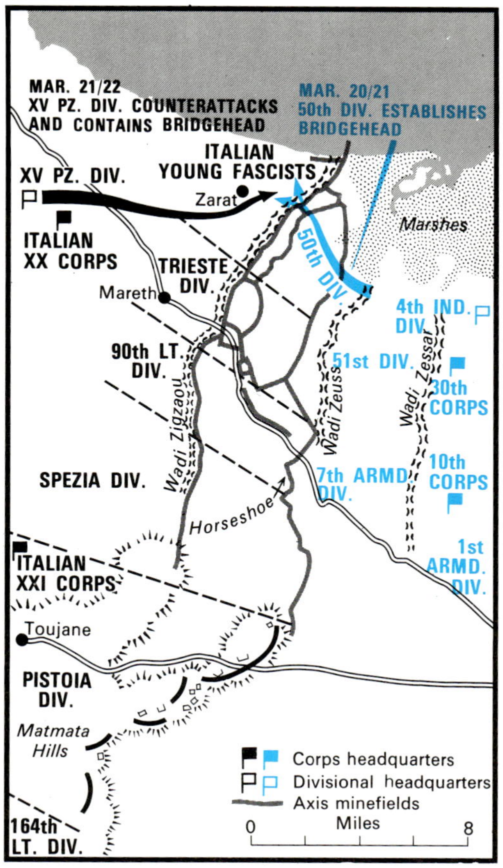

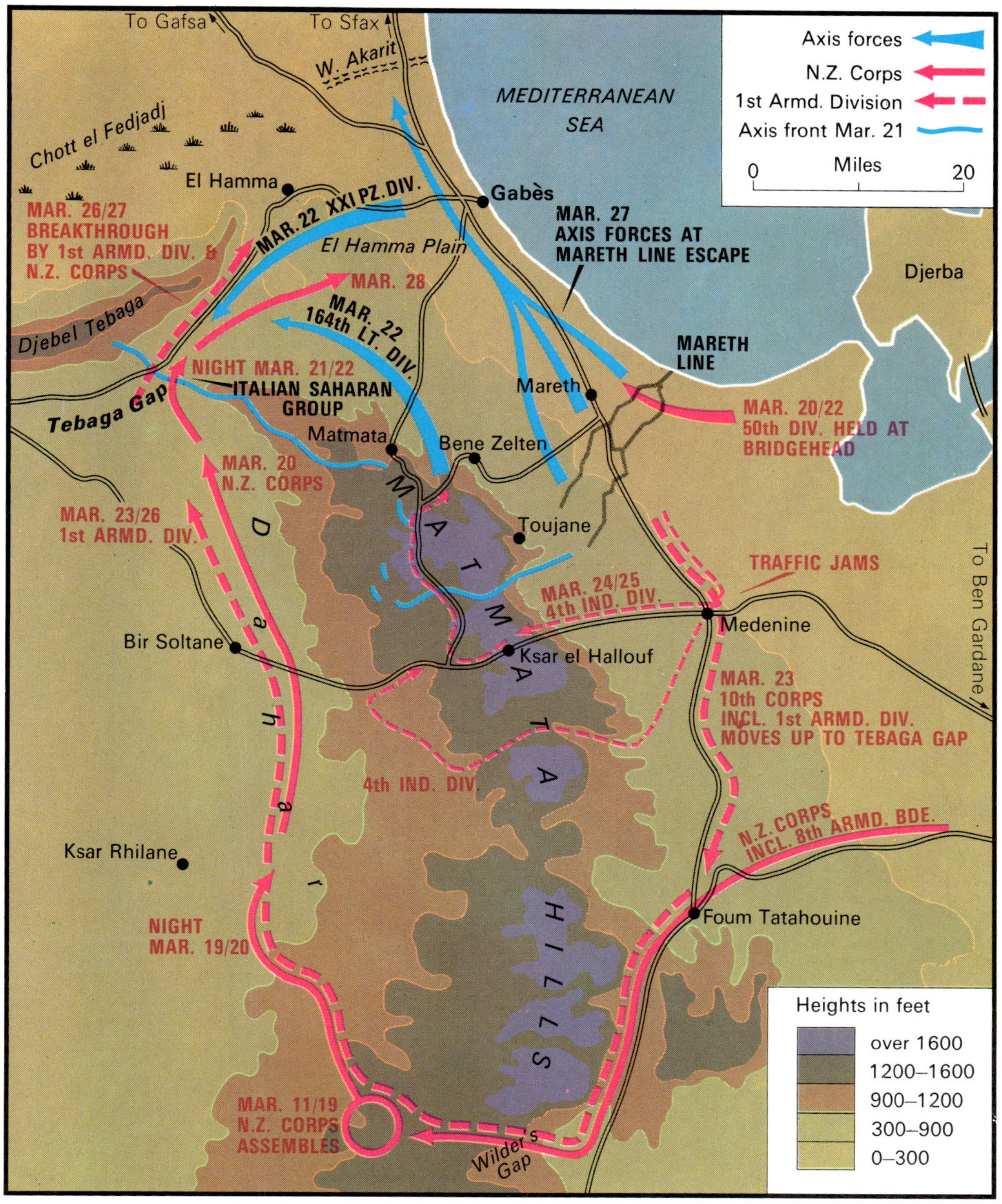

The main defences of the Mareth Line ran along the formidable natural barrier of the Wadi Zigzaou. The 50th Division succeeded in forcing a bridgehead across the Wadi after bitter fighting, but it was contained and almost destroyed in a well-timed counterattack by XV Panzer Division. To outflank the Mareth Line, stretching from the sea to the foothills of the Matmata Hills, troops of the 8th Army were sent through Wilder's Gap and across the waterless Dahar to Tebaga Gap to eventually emerge on the El Hamma Plain. Montgomery saw this outflanking move purely as a diversion, while the main thrust would be through the Mareth Line. When the first attack was pinned down, however, he rapidly transformed the 'left hook' into the main offensive

British troops using ladders to climb the sides of Wadi Zigzaou, the most formidable obstacle along the Mareth Line

Imperial War Museum

Even then, the British attacks were checked by the German backstop defences at El Hamma. Thus, although the threatened cut-off led the enemy to abandon the Mareth Line, he was able to hold the gate open and draw off his forces without much loss.

He stopped again barely 10 miles behind El Hamma, along the Wadi Akarit which spanned the Gabes Gap—a very narrow-fronted position between the sea and the hills. The Americans had already tried to forestall the enemy on this position and to pounce on his back while he was gripped by the 8th Army, but they had again been checked before they could debouch from the hills. Then, in the early hours of April 6, the 8th Army attacked the Wadi Akarit under cover of pitch darkness. That tactical innovation resulted in a penetration, though the exploitation was checked by the Germans when daylight came. On the next night they broke away and retired rapidly up the coast towards Tunis.

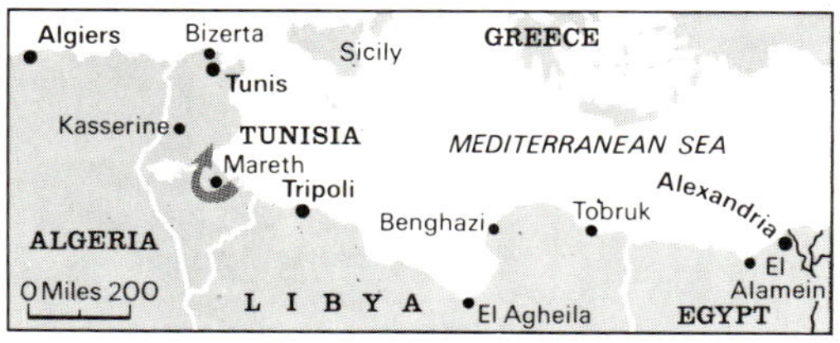

Within a few days the enemy's two armies had joined hands, to offer a united defence along the mountain arc covering Tunis, and it looked as though they might there maintain a prolonged resistance. Alternatively, they might utilise the breathing space gained, by the swift withdrawal, to evacuate their forces to Sicily.

The German Supreme Command, however, was led to attempt a prolongation of the campaign in Africa, rather than draw in its horns and base its defence of Europe upon the southern shores of Europe. Even in Tunisia it tried to hold too extensive a front for its resources —a 100-mile perimeter—in the endeavour to preserve both Tunis and Bizerta.

On April 20 the offensive was opened by the 8th Army with an attack on the enemy's left flank. But the coastal corridor became very narrow beyond Enfidaville, and the advance soon slowed down, coming to a halt on the 23rd. On April 21 the 5th Corps attacked from the left centre, through the hills leading to Tunis. Next day the 9th Corps struck from the right centre near Goubellat, with the aim of achieving an armoured break-through. But the effort failed to pierce the enemy's defences, though it strained them severely and further weakened the enemy's remaining tank strength. A pause of nearly a fortnight followed on most of the front, but in the north the Americans brought up from the south and a corps of French African troops continued to make a gradual penetration, which brought them within 20 miles of Bizerta.

Infantry advance through smoke in an attack on Longstop Hill

MEDJERDA: THE END IN AFRICA

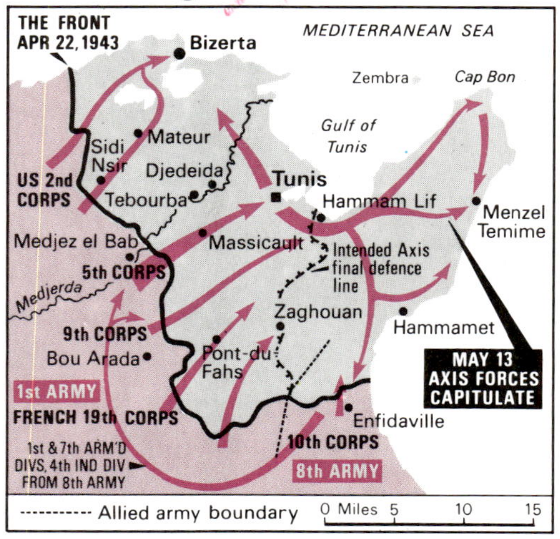

After the abortive attempts by 8th Army to break through the Axis defences in the south and thus earn the glory of ending the Tunisian campaign, the rest of the battle to liquidate the bridgehead fell into two distinct parts. In a series of attacks on April 26/30, 1st Army attempted to seize the last Axis strongpoints barring the way to the plain; but it met such stubborn resistance that the offensive halted, having threatened to lose all momentum. It was then that Alexander stepped in and, taking advantage of Montgomery's offer of help, shifted several of 8th Army's units north to prepare for the final breakthrough

Meantime Alexander again reshuffled his hand. Leaving only a screening force in the right centre near Goubellat, he moved the bulk of the 9th Corps over to the left centre, concentrated it behind the 5th Corps, and reinforced it with two picked divisions from the 8th Army—the 7th Armoured and 4th Indian. The effect of the deception-plan was reinforced by the reputation of the 8th Army, and of Montgomery, so that General von Arnim kept a disproportionate part of his strength in the south. But Arnim had little chance of perceiving the deception, or of re-adjusting his dispositions after the blow fell, because of the Allies' command of the air.

Auster AOP-1. AOPs (airborne observation posts) played an important role in the desert, spotting for the fire of artillery and ferrying commanders to important sectors of the battlefield.
Operating speed: 102 mph
Operating range: 375 miles. No armament; two seats

The assault of the 9th Corps, now under General Horrocks, was launched in the starlit but moonless early hours of May 6. It was preceded and covered by an intensive artillery bombardment from over 600 guns, upon a sector less than 2 miles wide, in the Medjerda valley leading to Tunis. After daylight, the air force extended the blast with a terrific storm of bombs. The stunned defenders of the gateway were soon overrun by the infantry of the 4th Indian and 4th British Divisions. Then the concentrated tanks of the 6th and 7th Armoured Divisions drove through the breach. But they lost time in dealing with various small pockets of German resistance. By nightfall they were still some 15 miles from Tunis.

In the morning, however, it became clear that the opposing army as a whole was still paralysed by the combined air shock and strategic shock to such an extent that it could not develop any tactical countermeasures. By the afternoon the leading troops of the British armoured divisions had swept into Tunis. Almost simultaneously, the Americans and French poured into Bizerta.

The enemy command had been caught off its balance, and then its machine was thrown out of gear by the combination of air pressure overhead and tank impact on its back. Dislocation of control was the primary cause of collapse, while the breakdown of communications accentuated the demoralising effect of lack of reserves and disruption of supplies. Another factor was the closeness of the enemy's bases to the broken front. The rapid penetration into the bases was as dislocating to morale as it was to the administrative system. The loss of their bases deepened the depressing sensation of fighting with their backs to the sea—a sea now dominated by the Allies' sea power and air power.

Although disappointing as an interceptor, the Curtiss Kittyhawk – which had been widely supplied to the RAF under lend-lease – came into its own during the North African campaign. Its ruggedness made it one of the most widely used aircraft for the new close-support techniques the RAF was developing there.
Maximum speed: 362 mph at 15,000 feet **Range:** 700 miles
Armament: Six .50-inch machine-guns and two 250-lb bombs

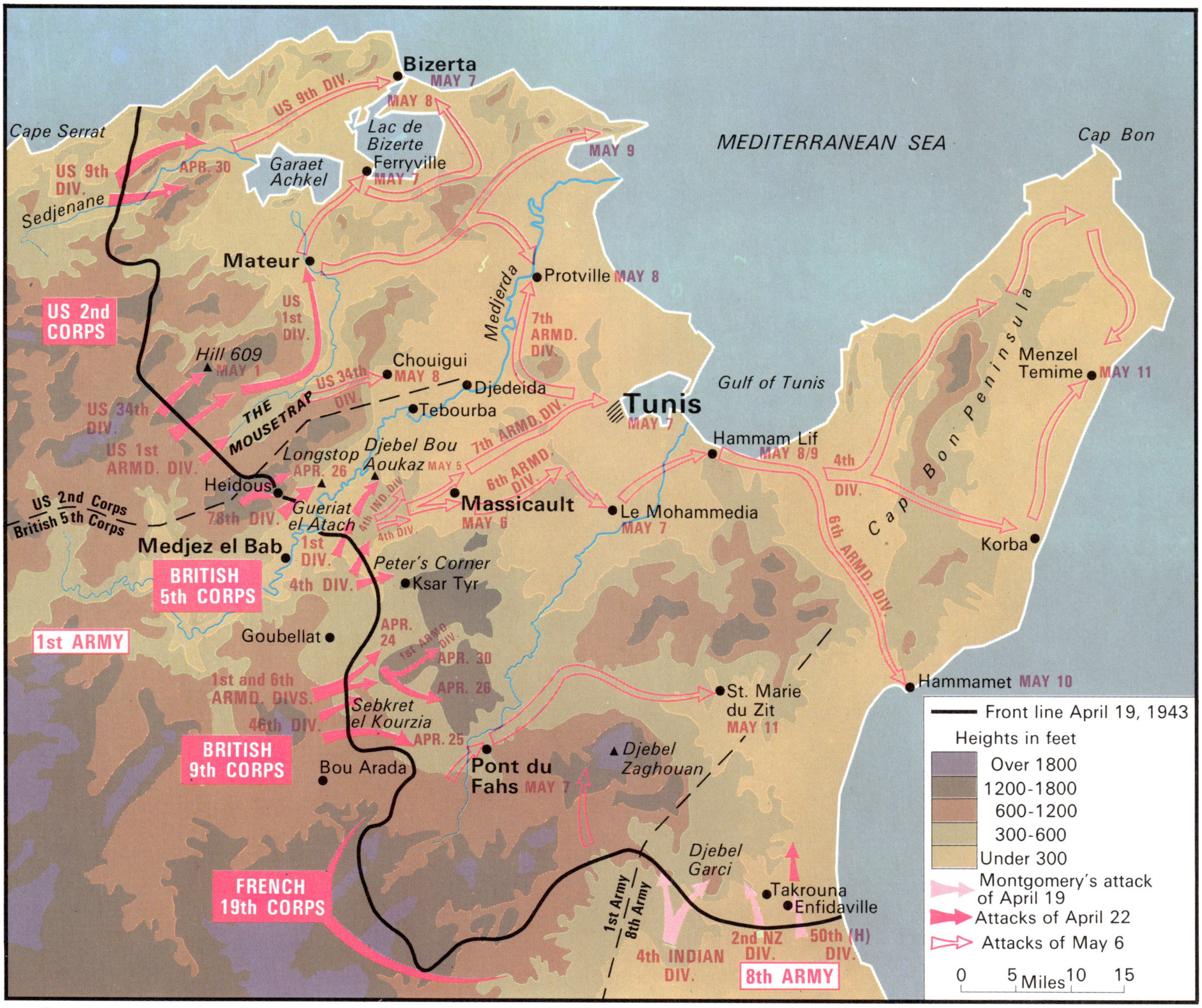

Popperfoto

D-DAY
INVASION OF HITLER'S EUROPE

British and Canadian troops wade up 'Juno' beach to Bernières against only sporadic German resistance, as high tide comes in

United Press

Operation Overlord

THE PLANS TAKE SHAPE

With the coming of summer 1944 the Allies prepared for their greatest trial – 'Overlord', the invasion of Occupied Europe. Previous attacks on German-held coasts – Dieppe, Salerno, and Anzio were the most notorious – had taught some bloody lessons: if Overlord were to succeed, the Allies would have to amass huge air and sea armadas which could land the armies and supply them in an unbroken chain of operations. In this article, Major-General R. H. Barry explains how it all began

Churchill had been the first to foresee the necessity for an Allied re-entry of the continent of Europe. Only shortly after Dunkirk, when British fortunes were apparently at their lowest ebb, he had directed that planning should be initiated with this ultimate end in view.

The Russians had been pressing for the opening of the Second Front ever since the end of 1941, and as the Americans began to gather strength in the European theatre, their eyes turned naturally to the direct assault on 'Fortress Europe' as the major and decisive operation of the war. Owing to the vicissitudes of the war, however, and the calls of other theatres, particularly the Far East, no major concrete steps were taken to start planning for what subsequently became known as 'Overlord', until the Casablanca Conference of 1943. There it was decided to set up an Allied Staff to plan the operation under a 'Chief-of-Staff to the Supreme Allied Commander (Designate)' – COSSAC – and a British officer, Lieutenant-General F. E. Morgan, was appointed to the post in March. At the Washington Conference in May 1943 absolute priority was allotted to Overlord and the target date for the operation was laid down as May 1944.

Left to right: **General Eisenhower, Supreme Commander of Overlord; Air Chief-Marshal Leigh-Mallory, commanding Allied Expeditionary Air Force; Air Chief-Marshal Tedder, Deputy Supreme Commander; General Montgomery, commanding 21st Army Group**

By the time the Quebec Conference assembled in August 1943, COSSAC had produced an outline plan. His first problem naturally had been to select the area of the assault. The choice was rapidly narrowed down to two alternatives – the Pas de Calais and the Normandy coast east of the Cherbourg peninsula and its port. The advantages of the Pas de Calais were obvious: it offered the shortest sea crossing and the most direct route to Germany, the ultimate objective; it would allow the Allied air forces to produce the maximum weight of support. Unfortunately these advantages were equally obvious to the Germans, and it was here that the bulk of the German forces were concentrated and the coastal defences at their most effective.

There was a further and decisive disadvantage – lack of mounting ports. The entire operation would have to be mounted from the comparatively restricted areas of Dover and Newhaven with Portsmouth and Southampton as somewhat distant adjuncts; an assault further west would allow the main body of the operation to be mounted from the great port complex, Portsmouth, Southampton, Poole, Portland. The choice, therefore, fell on Normandy, where the Cherbourg peninsula would protect the landing beaches from the Atlantic weather and where the German defences were thinner; the price, a longer sea crossing and increased dead flying time for the air forces (particularly the fighters), had to be accepted.

Eisenhower selects his team

In November 1943 Roosevelt and Churchill met again in Cairo. Here the main outlines of the plan were settled and – more important still at this stage – the command structure was agreed and the key appointments made. General Eisenhower was nominated Supreme Allied Commander with Air Chief-Marshal Tedder as his Deputy. Eisenhower chose as his Chief-of-Staff, responsible for forming his headquarters, General Walter Bedell Smith, who had served him so well in North Africa. Subordinate to this headquarters were to be two army groups, a US army group under General Omar Bradley and a British army group under General Montgomery; the latter was to be in command of all the land forces during the assault phase and until the area captured was sufficient to permit the deployment of the two army groups. A British officer, Admiral Ramsay, was appointed to command the naval forces; under him the US naval forces were commanded by Admiral Kirk and the British by Admiral Vian. Another British officer, Air Chief-Marshal Leigh-Mallory, commanded the Allied air forces, of which the British and Canadian component was under Air Marshal Coningham, and the American under General Brereton.

Choosing the target

The final presentation of the combined D-Day plans took place under the supervision of SHAEF (Supreme HQ, Allied Expeditionary Force) at a conference held at St Paul's School on May 15, 1944, before a distinguished gathering, which included the British Monarch, the Prime Minister, the Chiefs-of-Staff, the Supreme Commander, and his senior commanders.

The plan in its final shape belonged to General Sir Bernard Montgomery, the Ground Force Commander; Admiral Sir Bertram Ramsay, Commander-in-Chief Allied Naval Expeditionary Force; and Air Chief-Marshal Sir Trafford Leigh-Mallory, Commander-in-Chief Allied Expeditionary Air Force. For five months the headquarters of these three had built upon the solid foundations laid by COSSAC and his Allied staff. The final work bore many 'signatures', owing its existence to the constant planning of Naval and Combined Operations Headquarters, and the original 'Combined Commanders'.

By May 15, the plan had expanded west of the Vire estuary to the beaches of the Cotentin peninsula, and eastward to the Orne (see map). Its three divisions in the assault lift had become five, supplemented by 14 tank regiments, Commandos, and special service troops. The airborne lift had grown from two-thirds of a division for which COSSAC had not been granted sufficient air transport, to three airborne divisions. The naval tasks had expanded steadily in proportion. Nevertheless, the plan remained fundamentally the creation of COSSAC. He had been forced to build with shadows, spinning invisible webs, and sustained by drive and faith.

The target date – Y-Day – was June 1. The day – D-Day – would follow at the earliest possible moment thereafter. The earliest possible moment was Y+4. The conditions essential for the assault had been agreed between the Supreme Commander and Admiral Sir Bertram Ramsay on May 1. The extensive mine-laying operations of the enemy, coupled with the great mass of mined obstacles sprouting from the beaches and planted far out beyond the low water mark, called for a landing on a rising tide as soon after low tide as possible, and in daylight as near to dawn as possible. A moon was desirable by night. These considerations fixed the possible dates as June 5, 6, and 7. The 5th and 6th were both good, the 7th not so good. After that, no further opportunity would occur until June 19, and without the moon.

The possibility of a forced delay of two weeks, dire in its inferences, had been planned for in all its stark detail. It involved the halting of an avalanche of men and supplies, and all that must go with them, already on shipboard, and half of them at sea. About 1,000,000 more men, armour, artillery, transport, and 1,000,000 tons of supplies were in the pipe lines, converging on the embarkation points; 1,000,000 more behind them, reaching back across the Atlantic.

The thought made men shudder. 'The problems arising out of a postponement of 12-14 days to the next suitable period are too appalling even to contemplate,' wrote Admiral Ramsay. Nevertheless, the problems were fully contemplated, and the implications faced.

On May 8, the Supreme Commander tentatively agreed D-Day with his commanders on land, sea, and air, as June 5. The navy and air forces had been laying mines for three weeks to protect the convoys; the far more complex task of mine-sweeping lay ahead. Ten channels to Normandy must be swept from the assembly point known to the Royal Navy as 'Piccadilly Circus', and officially as 'Area Z' just south of the Isle of Wight. The state of the tide for the landing meant that the mine-sweeping would have to be done across the tide setting strongly to the east in the opening stages, and setting westward at about the half-way mark. Mine-sweeping had never before been carried out in such conditions, and great difficulties in timing were involved; 12 mine-sweeping flotillas were assembled for the job.

By the end of the first week of April, Montgomery, with the commanders of the naval and air forces, was able to announce his full plans to his general officers, and hammer out the possibilities with his senior field officers. His intention, as he expressed it, was:

'To assault, simultaneously, beaches on the Normandy coast immediately north of the Carentan Estuary and between the Carentan Estuary and the Orne river, with the object of securing as a base for further operations a lodgement area.'

The lodgement area must include, at the earliest possible moment, airfield sites south-east of the important road centre of Caen, and the port of Cherbourg. He expounded his plan to develop a major threat to break out on the eastern flank, thus to draw the main weight of the enemy reserves and strength against the British and Canadians. Having established a firm hinge pivoting upon Caen, and drawn the enemy to full commitment in the east he would break out with Bradley's US armies to cut a wide swathe 'to cut off all the enemy forces south of the Seine, over which river the bridges were to be destroyed by air action.'

The US 1st Army, with three regimental combat teams, would assault astride the Carentan Estuary, to capture Cherbourg and develop their attack southward upon St Lô to conform to the British 2nd Army.

The British 2nd Army, with five brigades, would assault between Asnelles and Ouistreham, with the Canadians in the centre, to develop a bridgehead south of a line St Lô, Caen, and south-east of Caen to secure airfield sites and to protect the eastern flank of the US 1st Army.

Both armies would be supported by specialised engineer troops, armour, Commandos and US Rangers.

The US 82nd and 101st Airborne Divisions would land south-east and west of St Mère Eglise, astride the flooded Merderet river, to capture crossings and to secure the line of the Douve river, thereby to assist the seaborne assault on Utah beach and prevent the movement of enemy reserves into the Cotentin.

The British 6th Airborne Division would land east of Caen to seize crossings over the Orne river at Bénouville and Ranville.

It was hoped to land 1,500 tanks, 5,000 tracked fighting vehicles, 3,000 guns, and 10,500 vehicles ranging from jeeps to bulldozers on D-Day. Such in broad outline was the land force task, and it gave the senior officers present plenty to talk about all through the day following the opening of the conference. There would be little room for manoeuvre, no opportunity 'to feel a way in'. Supported from the sea and sky by a colossal weight of fire most skilfully devised, the assault troops had to gain their footholds by direct, uncompromising assault, and force their ways in. There would be no way back, only forward.

The US forces were on the right, the western flank, for reasons of supply. As soon as Cherbourg and the Brittany ports could be opened they would be supplied direct from the United States. The British would finally rely upon the Channel ports and Antwerp.

The enemy were expected to hold some 60 divisions in the west under Field-Marshal von Rundstedt. Montgomery's immediate opponent would be Field-Marshal Rommel, commanding Army Group B, consisting of the German VII Army in Normandy and Brittany, the XV Army in the Pas de Calais and Flanders, and the 88th Corps in Holland. The greatest concentration of enemy strength behind the most powerful fortifications lay in the Pas de Calais. It had been the business of the Allies throughout many months, by feints, rumours, diversions, to keep them there, and to bolster the natural enemy fears based on the simple proposition that a straight line is the shortest distance between two points.

Air Chief-Marshal Sir Trafford Leigh-Mallory explained the main tasks of the British 2nd and the US 9th Tactical Air Forces in close support. He feared greatly the results of the airborne attack on the right flank, and expressed his fears up to the final hour. The attacks sustained against railways, roads, and bridges were well known. The extent of the success was not remotely realised. On 'The Day' the air forces would maintain a sustained density of ten fighter squadrons over the beaches, five British and five American. Six squadrons would be alerted to support the beach cover. Five squadrons would cover the main naval approaches, and a striking force of 33 fighter squadrons would be in reserve.

Following the fulfilment of escort duties for the airborne troops a total of 171 squadrons would be apportioned, 54 squadrons to beach cover, 15 squadrons to shipping cover, 36 squadrons to direct support, 33 squadrons to offensive operations and bomber escort, and 33 squadrons as a striking force.

On paper, the Luftwaffe still maintained impressive figures. In the air it could do nothing to counter the immense weight of Allied air power, and little even to harry it.

In round figures, some 5,000 ships and 4,000 ship-to-shore craft would be at the service of the assault. Their fire power, from the heavy armament of the battleships and cruisers down to the destroyers, the rocket ships, the armour and artillery firing from their craft on the run-in, was truly colossal.

Operation 'Neptune' would launch Operation 'Overlord'.

1. Normandy or Calais?

The Allied planners knew that the Germans expected an invasion across the Narrows of the Channel, where the distance was short both for shipping and air cover. But this would mean long distances along the south coast for all ships based on the western ports. If Normandy was the target, however, all convoys would converge on an assembly area equidistant from all the major ports

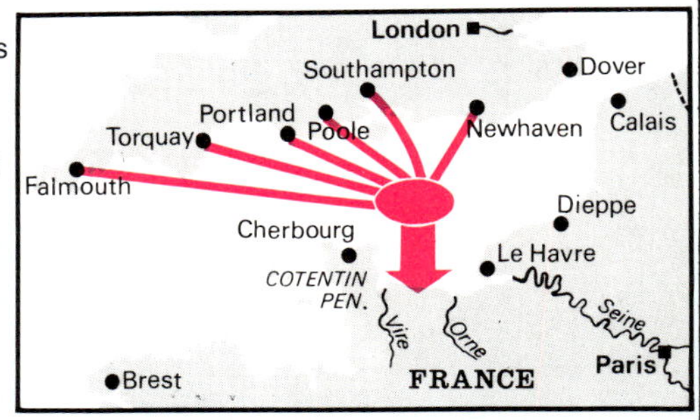

2. The COSSAC plan

In drawing up the preliminary plans for the invasion of Europe, COSSAC had to cut his coat according to his cloth. He was only able to lift two airborne brigades to cover the flanks—and only envisaged landing three assault divisions on the sector between the Vire and the Orne

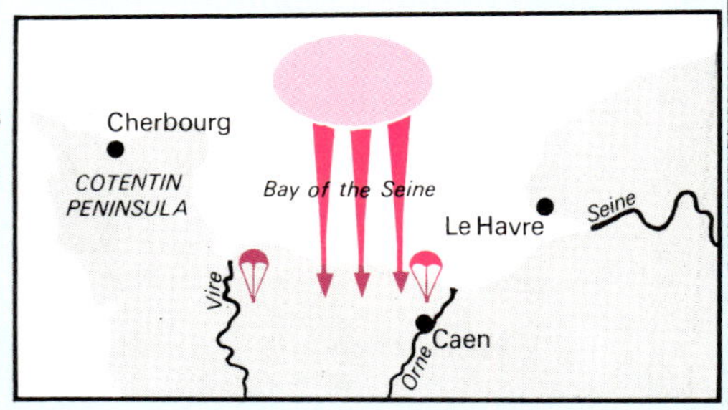

3. Montgomery's amendment

Montgomery's first reactions to the Overlord plan were highly unfavourable. He wanted five divisions, not three; separate sectors for US and British forces, each corps to have its own landing-beach—and at least two full-strength airborne divisions

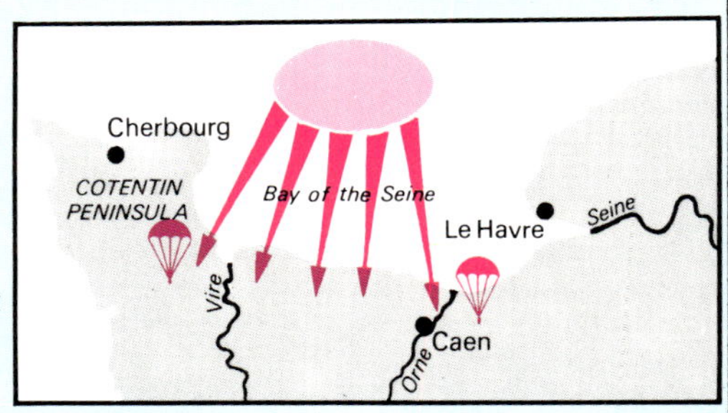

4. The final plan

Eisenhower's staff backed Montgomery's broadening of the assault plans and added a third airborne division. Build-up preparations, too, were intensified: it was now intended to get 18 divisions ashore by D+10

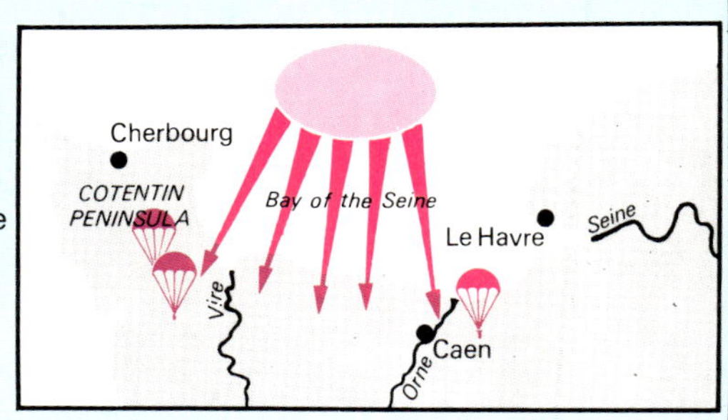

NEPTUNE'S INVASION FLEET

To carry the overall total of 40-50,000 men with their vehicles and equipment, an armada of over 4,000 landing ships, landing-craft, and barges of varying types was required; only about half of these were capable of crossing the Channel under their own power, the remainder having either to be towed or carried aboard the larger ships. When it is remembered that every man and every vehicle had to be allotted to a specific ship or landing-craft, that every vehicle before embarkation had to be waterproofed, that men and vehicles had to arrive at the right time at the 'hards' (improvised landing places) at which their particular landing-craft was beached —the complications of planning and organisation can easily be imagined. Only when all this had been done, did the huge task of the Royal Navy in assembling, marshalling, and shepherding this heterogeneous collection of vessels across the Channel into paths swept through the enemy minefields, in landing them on the correct beaches, and providing the necessary fire support begin.

Apart from the non-combatant ships and landing-craft carrying men, vehicles, and stores, the US Navy and Royal Navy assembled for the escort and support of the operation a fleet of over 1,500 vessels, ranging from battleships to armed landing-craft. They were divided into two 'task forces', the Western Task Force from the US Navy supporting the US landing, and the Eastern Task Force, provided primarily by the Royal Navy, supporting the British/Canadian landing. Each task force was further sub-divided into 'forces', one to each beach, responsible for escorting the assaulting force concerned, positioning it correctly, and providing fire support for the landing. The assault looked primarily to naval gunfire to silence the German coastal batteries and strongpoints.

The magnitude of the naval effort can be judged by the fact that the forces included seven battleships, 23 cruisers, 148 destroyers, as well as a swarm of smaller vessels—sloops, frigates, trawlers, corvettes, patrol craft and minesweepers. In addition, a fleet of 350 specially designed landing-craft carrying guns, rockets, anti-aircraft guns, and machine-guns was assembled for the close support of the actual assault.

The air effort in direct support of the assault was on a similar immense scale. It comprised the most modern types of aircraft available at the period, primarily the Spitfire, Mustang, Typhoon, Lightning, and Thunderbolt.

The exact timing of the assault proved a most complex problem which had its repercussions upon the dates on which the operation could be launched.

Although from the point of view of the assaulting troops there was much to be said for an assault in darkness, both the navies and air forces had to have daylight to carry out their bombardment tasks, and darkness would dangerously increase the likelihood of troops being landed in the wrong place. To assist navigation and for the airborne landings, moonlight was essential. Finally, the German underwater beach obstacles meant that landing must begin three to four hours before high tide. The only suitable periods for the operation therefore were those when there was four to five hours' daylight between dawn and high tide and at the same time good moonlight was available. All these conditions could only be satisfied on approximately three days in each lunar month.

However powerful and successful the assault, it would clearly be valueless unless the forces ashore could be built up more rapidly than those of the enemy and properly maintained when there. This involved three problems: the planning, escorting, and routing of the follow-up convoys; ensuring that those convoys contained the right personnel, vehicles, and equipment arriving in the right order; and finally ensuring that they could be rapidly unloaded on arrival.

Fifteen personnel ships, 74 ocean-going merchant ships, and more than 200 coasters were loaded before D-Day and these were to form the first wave of the build-up; the requirement thereafter was for eight convoys a day. Once having got the assault force across, however, movement of these convoys was not likely to present any particular problem for the Allied navies.

The question of what they should contain after the initial preplanned flight was more difficult, and a special organisation known as 'Build-Up Control' (BUCO) was set up in Southampton to ensure that what was shipped across the Channel was geared to the requirements of the battle.

The question of rapid unloading initially appeared the most difficult of all; it could clearly not be done across the beaches as a long-term measure and the likelihood of capturing port facilities intact appeared small, at any rate in the early stages. The problem was solved by perhaps the most famous devices of the entire operation —the artificial harbours known as 'Mulberries'. They owed their existence primarily to the foresight of Churchill himself, who had directed their development as early as 1942, with his oft-quoted minute: 'They *must* float up and down with the tide. . . . Don't argue the matter. The difficulties will argue for themselves.' They consisted of an outer breakwater formed partly of sunken blockships and partly of concrete 'caissons', 200 feet long, which had to be towed across the Channel; in the area of sheltered water so created were floating piers adapted to take coasters, landing ships or barges; unloading was further assisted by a fleet of amphibious lorries known as DUKWs. The success of the system may be judged by the fact that shortly after the assault, an average of 6,500 vehicles and nearly 40,000 tons of stores was being landed weekly.

The supply of motor and aircraft fuel presented a particular problem. Initially tankers were moored offshore and the fuel fed by buoyed pipeline into depots on land. Preparations were made, however, for an underwater pipeline direct from England to the

***Bangor*-Class Minesweeper** (reciprocating engine)
A wide minesweeper class—it formed a large part of the Neptune minesweeper strength of 287. *Bangor*-class 'sweepers were built in three versions—diesel, turbine, and reciprocating engines. Displacement: 672 tons. Crew: 60. Speed: 16 knots. Armament: 1 × 3-in, 1 × 40-mm, 4 × .303-in mg

French coast – PLUTO, or 'Pipe-Line-Under-the-Ocean' – and eventually, though not in the early stages, fuel supply was in effect drawn direct from England.

The impression so far given may well be that this was an exclusively British/American/Canadian operation, but the contributions of the other Allies must not be forgotten. The French, for instance, provided two cruisers, one destroyer, one armoured division, and four squadrons of aircraft; the Belgians one brigade and two squadrons; the Dutch two gunboats, one brigade, and two squadrons; the Poles one cruiser, two destroyers, one armoured division, and nine squadrons; the Norwegians three destroyers and four squadrons; the Czechs three squadrons; the Australians five squadrons; and the New Zealanders five squadrons. Practically every occupied country of Europe was represented in one way or another.

Finally, it must not be forgotten that the invading forces could expect assistance from an ally inside France. In this context the French resisters deserve to be included in the catalogue of forces available to the Allies. SOE had been doing its best to organise and arm them and from early 1943 German demands for labour had assisted recruiting; by 1944 some 100,000 young men had taken to the 'Maquis'. The vast majority of the resisters' plans were, of course, geared to the great day when the Allies would land in France once more; in 1943 they had put forward a series of seven ambitious plans to deal with railways, road movement, telecommunications, ammunition dumps, oil fuel installations, headquarters, and railway turntables. By the beginning of 1944, however, many resistance networks had been broken up by the Gestapo and only the railway demolition plan appeared to be capable of any certain implementation. Nevertheless both numbers available and arms supplied were considerable: by May 1944 80,000 Sten-guns, 30,000 pistols, 17,000 rifles, and nearly 3,500 Bren-guns had been parachuted into France; overall there were probably some 100,000 men plus another 35-40,000 in the Maquis who had a weapon of some sort.

To assist the Resistance and ensure that as far as possible its operations were co-ordinated with those of the Allies, SOE prepared a number of three-man teams (American/British/French) to be parachuted – in uniform – into areas where resistance was expected to flourish, so as to act as liaison between the resisters and the regular forces. In addition the British Special Air Service and the American Operational Groups were entrusted with various raiding and harassing operations for which it was hoped that they could obtain the assistance and support of the Resistance.

Finally, preparations had to be made to take over and run civil affairs in the liberated areas of France pending recognition of a French government. Here also assistance from the Resistance organisation was hoped for.

RAF Air/Sea Rescue Launch
These boats saved about 13,000 airmen during the war, and were the natural seaborne counterpart to the huge Allied air umbrella which would cover the Neptune operations. Length: 68 feet. Speed: 38 knots. Armament: 3 × .303 Lewis mg

Armed Salvage Tug
Quite apart from the job of moving the huge Mulberry units to the Normandy coast, the fleets of tug-boats had to cope with about half the landing-craft – those unable to cross the Channel under their own power, and which could not be carried on the decks of transports. Displacement: 700 tons. Speed: 13 knots. Crew: 30. Armament: 1 × 3-in, 2 × 20-mm, 2 × .303-in mg

So the balance sheet of this immense operation shows the following staggering figures:

- 50,000 men in the assault drawn from five divisions;
- Over 2,000,000 men to be shipped to France overall, comprising a total of 39 divisions;
- 138 major warships used in the assault, together with 221 smaller combat vessels (destroyer category and below);
- Over 1,000 minesweepers and auxiliary vessels;
- 4,000 landing ships or craft;
- 805 merchant ships;
- 59 blockships;
- 300 miscellaneous small craft;
- 11,000 aircraft, including fighters, bombers, transports, and gliders;
- Over 100,000 partially armed men of the Resistance ready to lend such support as they could.

With such a weight of numbers and material it might well be thought that the assault would be practically irresistible, but two factors must be remembered: first, the hazards and extreme complexity of an amphibious operation of this magnitude, for which there was no precedent; all the most meticulous arrangements could be upset and the utmost confusion caused by some chance occurrence or unpredicted change in the weather: second, the great inherent superiority of the defence over the attack in an amphibious operation, especially against prepared coastal defences; however great the Allied superiority, there could be no certainty that the force would succeed even in securing a foothold. Surprise and deception were the essence of the operation—and complete surprise there could not be, for the Germans knew that the invasion was coming; all they did not know was when and where.

Finally, it was clear to both sides that this was the decisive operation of the war. If the landing succeeded, Germany must eventually be crushed sooner or later between the advancing forces of the Russians and the Allies. Should the landing fail, the Allies might well take years to recover from their losses in men, material, and morale; the peoples of Occupied Europe would give up hope and Germany would be left free to turn and square the account with the Russians.

The broad shoulders of General Eisenhower carried an immense burden.

Armed Trawler
Trawlers—with the minesweepers and other light flotilla craft—were to perform invaluable services as convoy escorts shepherding and marshalling the transports. Hundreds of them were pressed into service for this role. Typical specifications were: Displacement: 378 tons. Speed: 11½ knots. Crew: 30. Armament: 1 × 4-in, 3 × 20-mm, 2 × .303 mg; about 20 depth-charges

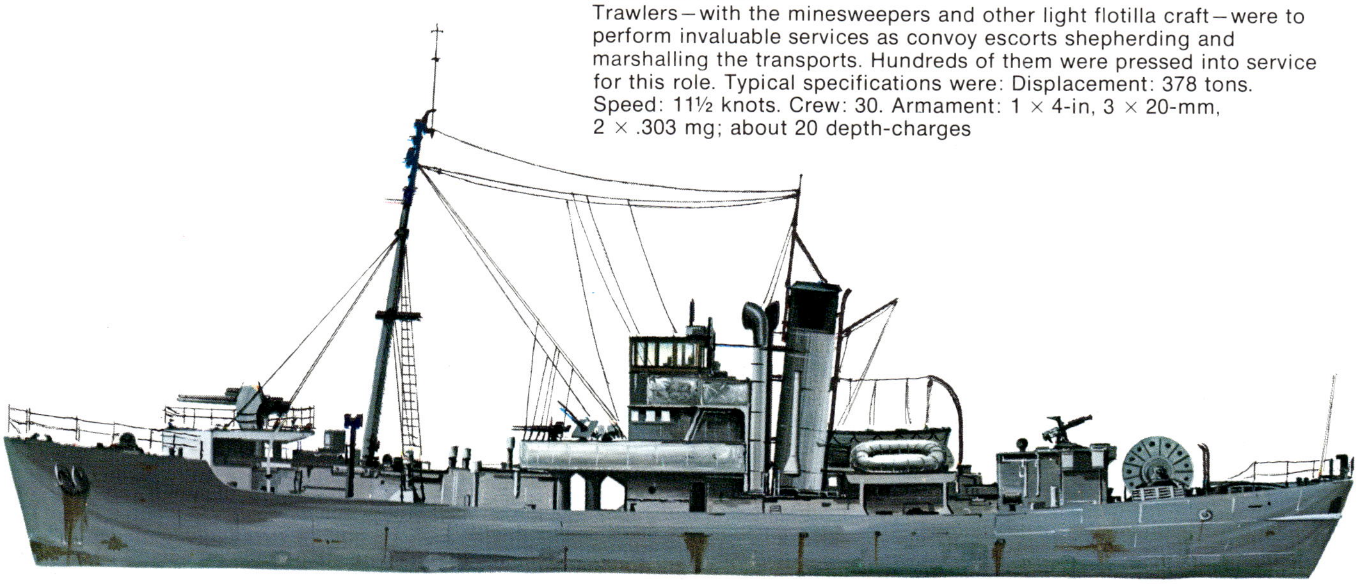

From the Liverpool docks a tug hauls a Mulberry Harbour section on the first stage of its journey to the Normandy beachhead

Imperial War Museum

NEPTUNE'S WHALES

Imperial War Museum

LST (Landing Ship Tank)
The 'Landing Ship Tank' was an upscaled shallow-draught landing craft. Unable to get as close inshore as its smaller sister craft, it could launch DD 'swimming' tanks in large numbers. Crew: 98. Capacity: 2 LCMs and 22 25-ton tanks or 18 30-ton tanks or 33 3-ton trucks and 217 troops. Speed: 12 knots. Armament: 4 × 2-pdr AA, 6 × 20-mm AA

Royal Marine Commandos pour ashore from Landing Craft Assault on a pre-D-Day training exercise

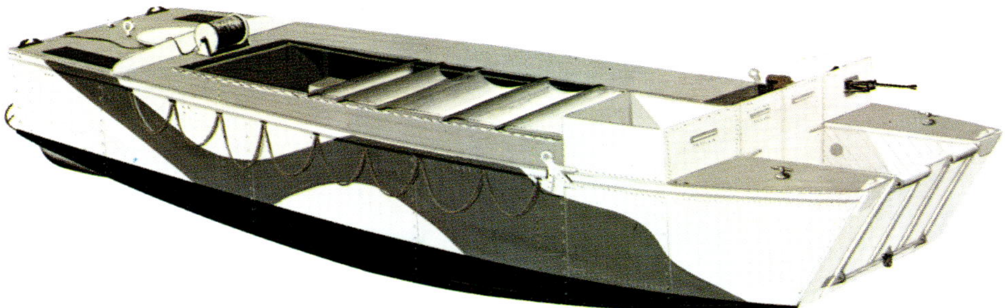

LCA (Landing Craft Assault)
'Landing Craft Assault' were designed as the infantry carrying workhorse, with some light armour and a shallow draught. Crew: 4. Capacity: 35 troops or 800-lb equipment. Speed (loaded): 6 knots. Armament: 1 × Bren-gun in port cockpit

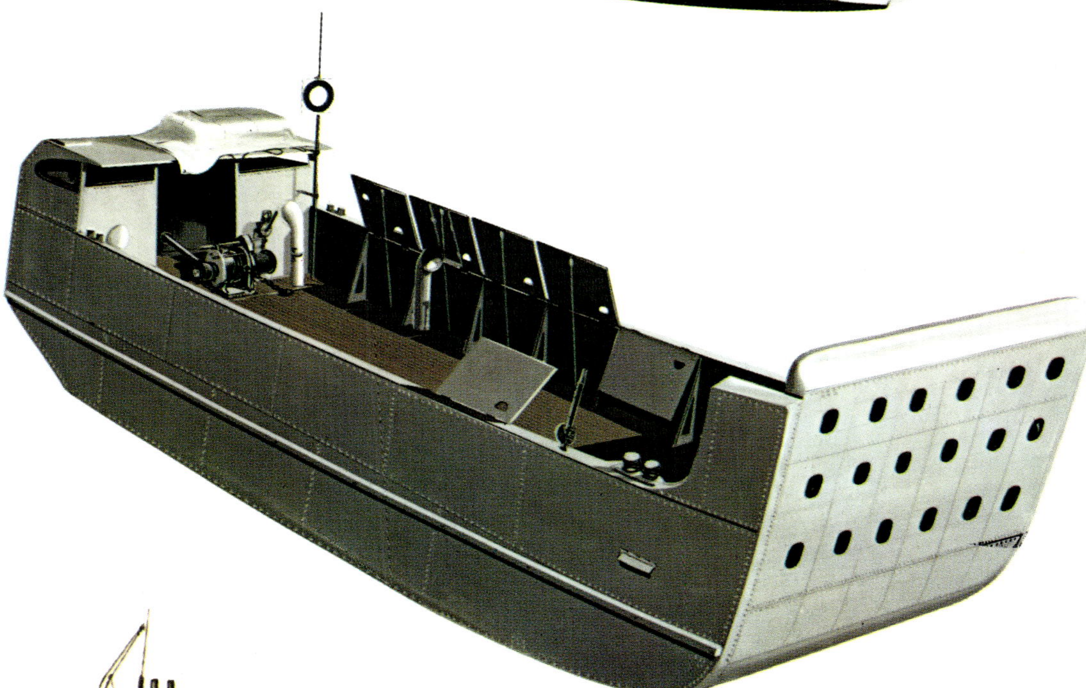

LCM (Landing Craft Mechanised)
The 'Landing Craft Mechanised' could carry a single vehicle or a light tank or put a large amount of men ashore. Crew: 6. Capacity 100 men or 1 tank or vehicle under 16 tons. Speed: $7\frac{1}{2}$ knots. Armament: 2 × .303 Lewis mg

LCT (Landing Craft Tank)
The 'Landing Craft Tank' were developed as larger versions of the LCM, able to bring a larger load as close inshore. Crew: 12. Capacity: 5 × 40-ton tanks or 10 × 3-ton trucks. Speed: $10\frac{1}{2}$ knots. Armament: 2 × 2-pdrs or 2 × 20-mm Oerlikons

THE BALANCE OF ARMOUR

If in no other respect, the British and Americans possessed quantitative superiority in armour, and that, in itself, was no mean industrial achievement when it is recalled that, after Dunkirk, Britain had only 200 tanks fit for battle, while the Americans owned hardly a single operational tank worthy of the name.

Whatever British industry could make in 1940 had to be churned out at once, regardless of quality, to rearm the rescued BEF: indeed, Churchill insisted that, for the time being, all research and development should stop in order to concentrate every ounce of energy on production. So, those tanks already in, or about to enter, production—Matilda, Valentine, Cruisers IV, V, VI, and the new heavy Churchill, all armed with the obsolescent 2-pounder gun—rolled forth in growing numbers while the next generation of vehicles waited in abeyance.

To add further to confusion, the British tank supply organisation tottered on rotten foundations. A month before the outbreak of war, what few tank technologists the War Office boasted had been grabbed by the new Ministry of Supply, isolating the War Office from informed tank advice. A purely politically inspired Tank Board had been set up, to head tank affairs in the right direction, but suffered from a surfeit of responsibility, a lack of power—and a flood of resignations and reappointments. It failed in its task. The last in the line of Britain's great tank enthusiasts, Major-General Hobart, had been dismissed from command of 7th Armoured Division in the desert by Generals Wilson and Wavell, because the former had 'no confidence' in Hobart's way of command. When Guderian proved Hobart right in May 1940, the latter was being promoted to Lance-Corporal in the Home Guard; but by autumn of that year he was on his way back to power, having devised a plan in conjunction with General Pile (another tank expert then in command of the anti-aircraft command) for a new armoured army, governed by a charter strikingly similar to that to be written by Guderian over two years later.

On the insistence of Churchill, Hobart was recalled, ostensibly to raise a new armoured division, but primarily to train all the tank forces. Neither the CIGS, General Dill, nor Commander Home Forces, General Brooke, felt able to accept Hobart's complete plan, so Hobart got his armoured division and General Martel, another of the early tank pioneers, took the watered-down training job, without a charter. For the next two years the tale of British defeat could be linked with mediocre handling of inferior vehicles by officers and men whose courage alone made up for the other deficiencies.

Tank production mounted apace with the aim of filling the establishments of ten armoured divisions each of about 400 tanks. However, the insistence of the pre-war General Staff that a large number of slow, heavily armoured infantry support vehicles would be needed to lead a basically infantry army now led to a short-fall in the number of fast cruisers being built for the armoured divisions: not until later, when US production was tapped, could this deficiency be rectified, so, in the meantime, infantry tanks had to fill spaces in the armoured divisions. In any case, the next generation of cruiser—Mark VII called 'Centaur'—ran into technical troubles, never met its specification or delivery date, and was superseded by a revised Mark VIII 'Cromwell', before the former could be brought into action. And Cromwell, when at last it appeared in 1944, went to battle outgunned and incapable of accepting a larger weapon than the comparatively low-powered 57-mm (6-pounder) or 75-mm gun with which it was provided.

This semi-permanent state of under-gunning stemmed from the earlier, but untested, belief that tank armament could take lower priority after speed and armour, on the assumption that field artillery would supplement the high-explosive dispensing capability the tanks did not possess—a theory which died an instant death in the first major armoured battles when it was discovered that, in a fast-moving encounter, tanks had to be able to provide all sorts of self-support at short notice and that the slower artillery methods often could not compete. Thereafter the delay in making and mounting 57-mm and 75-mm (and later the 17-pounder) guns occurred mainly because of weakness in communication between the War Office and Ministry of Supply—the former not stating their require-

Associated Press

US-built Shermans of a British armoured regiment halted 'somewhere in England' on their journey to the South Coast

ments with sufficient clarity, leading to the army being given whatever the latter thought good for the soldiers. Acrimony ran rife, for instance, when the Ministry of Supply said, in 1942, that it would be impossible to mount the 17-pounder in the Sherman, leaving the War Office to prove it feasible in 1943 and thrust the modification through against protocol barely in time for June 6.

Reorganisation of British armoured forces took place about once a year under the impetus of fresh thought and the demands of front-line soldiers. In 1941 a cry for more armoured divisions to replace infantry ones led to several infantry (including Guards) battalions being converted to armour – an admission that pre-war policy had been wrong, tied to a staunch attempt at retaining old regimental traditions in a changing world. But the disruption in the minds of infantrymen transposed to an entirely new way of thinking and fighting could take at least a year to appease. So when, at last in 1942, the transposition was beginning to make headway, a fresh decision was taken to cut the armoured content of the armoured division by half (and to substitute more lorry-borne infantry) while transferring the redundant armour to independent brigades charged with the task of supporting infantry formations – and this made confusion doubly compounded. Thus British armour multiplied in a state of annual transplantation, the victim of vacillation at the whim of a hierarchy which had never consolidated its concept of future operational procedures.

For the invasion, therefore, the British army, with its large Canadian contingent and the 1st Polish Armoured Division, came to consist of five armoured divisions and eight independent armoured brigades, plus certain specialised armoured formations – of which more later – in all some 3,300 Shermans (barely 1 in 20 with 17-pounders), Churchills (including 100 of the new more heavily armoured Mark VII), and Cromwells – the whole backed by sumptuous material reserves.

America: a New World impulse

The American armour force had not endured the same vicissitudes as the other nations after 1940 because then it hardly existed at all and owned but a few hundred obsolete models, and a small cadre of crews trained in cavalry methods. Its modern battle organisation was of its own devising, but based on a close study of the ideas of the warring nations since, until 1940, American armour had been smothered first by its subservience to the infantry and then the cavalry. The main American battle tank came to be the Sherman armed with either the 75-mm or the slightly superior 76-mm gun. In early 1941 American tank production turned in gestation: in 1942 it gave birth to 14,000 Shermans, followed in 1943 by another 21,000 – the rate still rising at the demand of the sort of mass-production urge so characteristic of New World impulse. Numbers alone, matched by the virtue of mechanical reliability, gave the Sherman (and thereby the Allies) their one significant counter to the German gun and armour superiority; while the seething American training organisation churned out a concourse of mass-trained crewmen, full of confidence but still with much to learn, inspired by the drive of that most colourful of armoured generals – the American counterpart of Guderian and Hobart – George S. Patton.

M-4 Sherman
Shermans equipped the bulk of the Allied tank forces that fought for Normandy. Available in massive quantity, they were outclassed by the German opposition. Weight: 33 tons. Engine: 425 hp. Crew: 5. Armour: 81 mm. Speed: 25 mph. Armament: 1 × 75-mm. 2 × mg

In 1943, however, the USA could have had – and should have had – a powerful successor to Sherman: the T-20, mounting a 76-mm gun, which could have seen action in 1944. But a belief that Shermans in large numbers would be good enough to saturate the German defences as well as act with reliability and speed in pursuit, prompted a decision to stop production of the T-20 in order not to disrupt the flood of Shermans coming from the factories. It is the privilege of vast nations to employ big battalions regardless of finesse, and to a considerable extent this was American policy in 1944.

Updating the tank tactics

Every combat army had learned the need to combine infantry and artillery with tank action, although the levels at which co-operation took root differed as did the detailed methods of command. The Germans plumped for mixed battle groups of flexible composition within the division; the British tended to draw a line between armoured and infantry formations, regrouping no lower than brigade level if they could help it; while the Americans followed the German example in the main, but enhanced flexibility by refining control through special Combat Commands (two per armoured division) upon mixed battle groups drawn from a divisional tank strength of 270 (including 83 light Stuarts). This was the latest of several variations on the American theme and was in use by the six US and the French 2nd Armoured Division in mid-1944.

However, unlike the Germans who employed their assault gun units purely in the infantry support role, the American philosophy reached towards the British by setting aside specific GHQ tank battalions to work closely with infantry divisions. This reflected the fundamental difference between Allied and German armour doctrine, for the latter insisted on the merits of armoured divisions being grouped exclusively in armoured corps. Each system had its advantages, depending not a little upon the insight of commanders into the potentialities of armour, but not least upon the restrictive nature of ground and room available for manoeuvre. In Russia the rolling steppes favoured the German armoured corps: in Normandy the intensely close bocage threatened to impose an anti-tank barrier infested by well-supported infantry – a situation which favoured the British system.

The greatest changes in the armoured balance since 1940 had been wrought by advances in the nature of field defences, by improvements in the power of anti-tank weapons, and by the proliferation of mines. Whereas the standard towed German anti-tank gun of 1940 had been the 37-mm, by 1944 it was the long 75-mm Pak 40, supplemented by the big, clumsy 88-mm Kwk 43 – the latter capable of penetrating 168-mm of sloped armour at 1,000 yards. A German infantry division deployed 31 anti-tank guns augmented by towed 88-mm guns from army resources, this formidable array knitting together the main fabric of an anti-tank curtain behind which hid the mobile reserves of armour. And from the close range of 100 yards, an infantryman had the new-found ability to penetrate the thickest armour using a recoilless *Panzerfaust* or *Panzerschreck* hollow-charge missile – equivalent of the British PIAT and the US Bazooka.

Of course, the Allies assembled almost as tough a collection of anti-armour weapons in addition to their own assault guns – a US infantry division having both 37-mm and 57-mm anti-tank guns as well as 558 Bazookas; and a British division was no less well equipped and had the well-tried 17-pounder gun. Towed anti-tank guns are strictly a defensive weapon and require time to arrange mutually supporting arcs of fire, to settle in their positions and conceal such protective digging as may be necessary. Hence, anti-tank guns were of more use to the Germans, since they nearly always fought on the defensive from previously established positions. For the same reason, the Germans could make extensive use of minefields to shield their positions and to delay penetrations by Allied armour: thereby they gave their mobile reserves more time to shape counteraction at the critical points of rupture. And on the beaches, the mines lay thickest among a cunning arrangement of artificial

obstacles linked with the natural sea defences and deep inundations.

Every defensive feature favoured the Germans and pulled the balance of armour towards their side of the scales. However, the more powerful weapons are almost inevitably bigger, clumsier, and demanding of increased man- and machine-power resources to move them about the battlefield, culminating in a multiplication of difficulties when seeking satisfactory emplacements. Moreover, the faster a high-velocity shot flies, the greater the difficulty of seeing by what distance it has missed its target (since it gets there before the smoke and dust of discharge have subsided), and so correction of fire is repeatedly made haphazard by this sort of obscuration with a consequent degradation in hit probability. These difficulties all tell against big fieldpieces, the positions of which are compromised once the flash and smoke of discharge appear: ironically they helped restore some of the advantage in favour of armour in 1944.

The German static defences erected along the coastline, set in belts inland and drawn close around vital points – such as the radar station at Douvres in Normandy – raised far more serious hazards to the assault than anything of the sort met so far in the Second World War: they were the products of four years' thought and labour, galvanised by a few months of Rommel's dynamic enthusiasm and his belief in the importance of holding the beaches as a hard crust. Indeed, the Americans seem to have come apathetically to accept these obstacles as a deterrent to the use of massed armour in the lead of the assault: but to the British, recalling their bitter experience at Dieppe, the obstacles acted as a spur to finding ways of destroying them by unconventional methods.

Wholesale slaughter at the water's edge was unthinkable to the British – and the emotions of Churchill ran riot at the nightmare that, once again as at Gallipoli, British infantry might be mown down in heaps at his behest. At Dieppe the Canadians had already suffered something like this fate as, when the tanks came ashore, they were prevented from breaking through the shore obstacles and left the infantry unsupported beyond: while, as the engineers tried to clear pathways for the tanks, the vicious circle drew tight and they were shot down because the unsupported infantry could not subdue the German machine-gun nests.

Special devices

In March 1943 the CIGS, General Brooke, decided to create special armoured units whose purpose would be to land in the van of the assault, open gaps on their own even before the first waves of infantry got ashore, and then dominate the defences without exposing more than a few unarmoured men to direct fire. Teams of specialised armour were visualised as progressively smothering the German defences with aimed fire, detonating the beach minefields, breaking down the artificial barriers, demolishing or bridging the next row of sea walls, concrete blocks, or deep ditches, then disposing of more minefields, while subjugating the remaining pill-boxes, before accompanying the next wave of assault infantry and armour deep inland. Speed came first in these complex operations, particularly in the British sectors, where the nature of the ground aided German armoured counterattack, since the need quickly to gain depth and space inland, to fight a mobile battle, took precedence over almost every other requirement once a lodgement had been made.

Before 1943, most of the essential kinds of special device needed had reached some form or another of experiment or development – indeed, the ideas for most of them originated from the First World War. Primitive flails had been employed in Africa to detonate mines; an Armoured Vehicle Royal Engineer (AVRE), carrying demolition teams and a variegated selection of bridges or fascines for crossing walls and ditches, had been invented (appropriately by a Canadian, named Donovan) after Dieppe and mounted on the Churchill tank; early efforts to help tanks swim had hardened into a simple arrangement whereby a canvas screen, temporarily erected round the vehicles, displaced the tank's weight while its engine drove two propellers – this was Nicholas Strausler's invention, the Duplex Drive tank (DD); another type of Churchill tank had been fitted with flame-throwing equipment, with pressurised fuel carried in an armoured trailer, the whole device called Crocodile; there were also tanks mounting a powerful searchlight called a Canal Defence Light (CDL). Later a host of other inventions came up for trial, to be rejected or accepted, improved, put into production in quantity, the crews trained and methods found to combine them in teams taught to act in the elimination of every possible obstacle combination.

Cromwell IV
Reliable, fast, the Cromwell was in the forefront of British tank design, but already hopelessly outclassed by the new generation of German tanks and barely a match for the old. Weight: 28 tons. Engine: 600 hp. Crew: 5. Armour: 76 mm max. Speed: 38 mph. Armament: 1 × 75-mm, 2 × mg

Churchill AVRE with fascine
Where the British fell down in battle tank design, they made up in specialised armour. The 'Armoured Vehicle Royal Engineers' doubled as a mobile demolition and construction team, able to bridge a trench or blast a hole in a concrete sea-wall. Weight: 39 tons. Engine: 350 hp. Crew: 5. Armour: 88 mm. Speed: 15 mph. Armament: Petard mortar, 1 × mg

General Percy Hobart, the armoured innovator of the 'thirties, with his brother-in-law Montgomery, who grasped the vitally important role of the 79th Armoured Division's weapons

Lady Hobart

Sherman Duplex-Drive DD
In the very spearhead of the attack came Sherman battle tanks able to wade out of the sea by the combination of propellers and a collapsible canvas flotation screen displacing the tank's weight. Many foundered, but many more got through to the beaches

Churchill AVRE with SBG Bridge
The AVRE's Petard mortar could throw a 25-lb charge called a 'flying dustbin', specially designed to demolish beach obstacles, a distance of 120 yards. For the crossing of trenches the 'Small Box Girder' Bridge could be quickly manoeuvred into position

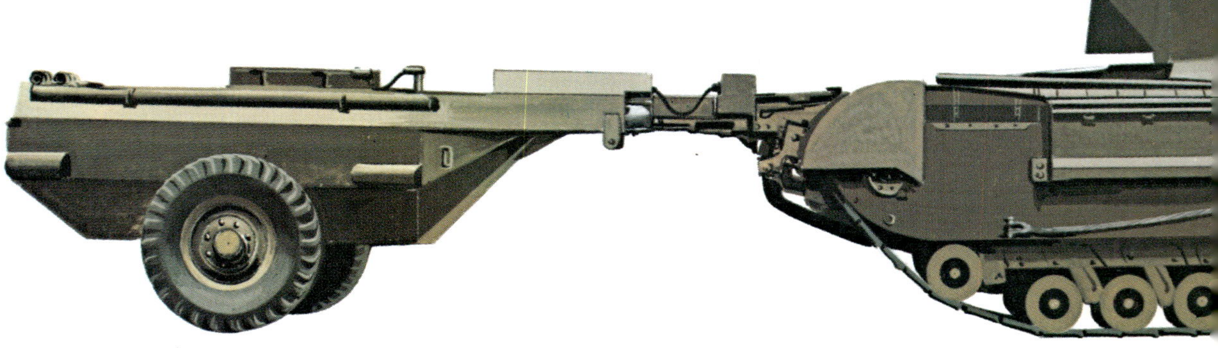

Sherman Crab
Designed to flail a path through beach minefields, the Crab mounted a flail drum driven from the main engine. A thick cloud of dust was thrown up and a maximum speed of only $1\frac{1}{2}$ mph could be reached, nor could the main armament be used, hence other gun tanks escorted them on the beaches

This was to be the Twentieth-Century equivalent of a medieval siege train, constructed to substitute machines for manpower and restore mobile, armoured dominance at every stage in an assault, even where the defences were strongest. With only 14 months to spare, Brooke searched for a man to spring a miracle – pitching his choice on Hobart who, at 58 years of age, still looked the only one with deep enough experience of armour in all its aspects, joined with ruthless energy capable of accomplishing so enormous a task in such a short time. But cutting a hole through the Atlantic Wall was but the last stage of Hobart's task: first he had to persuade and bulldoze the military and industrial machines to improve and construct the necessary equipment to his specifications at his speed: above all he demanded that each special vehicle should retain the ability to fight on its own should it be necessary, and then he had to drill ordinary tank crews in the spirit of dauntless improvisation which recognised no insuperable defence. Against all sorts of frustration Hobart succeeded in his task and was ready, early in 1944, to show a wide range of armoured hardware to General Eisenhower, and to his own brother-in-law, General Montgomery, when they came home to take charge of the invasion forces.

There was a brigade each of DD Shermans and Crab Flail Shermans, and another of Churchill AVREs armed with the Petard demolition projectile, a regiment of Crocodiles and a brigade of Grant CDLs, the latter never, in the event, put to use in their intended role of illuminating the battlefield in order to continue an advance in the dark. Other devices with animal names – 'Hobo's Menagerie' or 'The Funnies' as they came to be known – followed in the months to come, but the combination of DD, Flail, and AVRE were the basic elements of the beach assault team which worked ahead of the infantry on June 6.

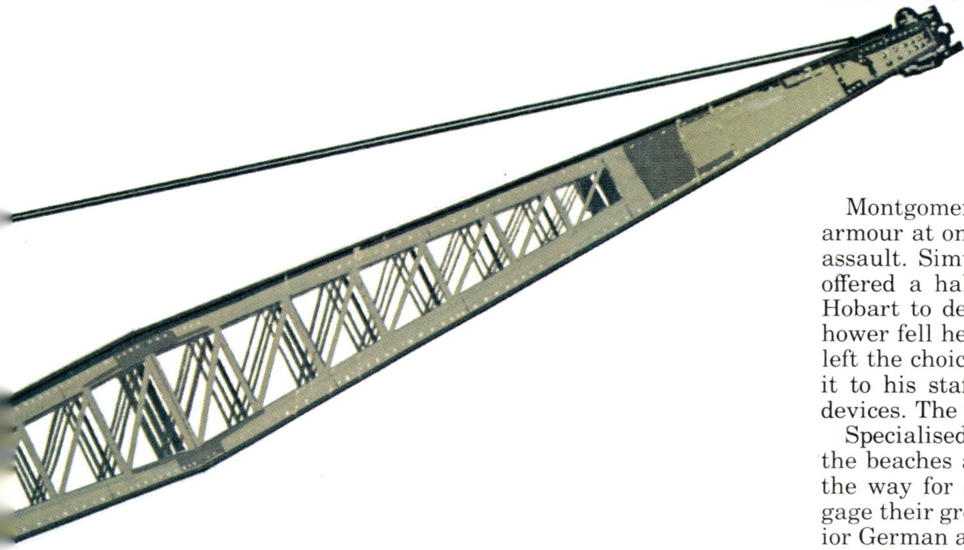

Montgomery grasped the purpose and significance of specialised armour at once, calling for the necessity of armour to spearhead the assault. Simultaneously, he insisted that the Americans should be offered a half share of everything the British had made, getting Hobart to demonstrate each device to his allies. But, while Eisenhower fell heavily for the DDs, and demanded a brigade's worth, he left the choice of the other items to General Bradley, and he passed it to his staff who, for various reasons, mostly thin, rejected the devices. The terrible outcome of this omission will appear later.

Specialised armour promised to restore balance to Allied armour on the beaches against mines and obstacles. In so doing it might open the way for conventional vehicles to press quickly inland and engage their greater numbers in open battle with the technically superior German armour and anti-tank guns. There was nothing to choose between the determination and gallantry of the men of either side – there never had been – so it remained to be seen if the heavier losses inflicted by a qualitatively superior foe on a numerically superior one might eventually undermine the élan of the latter. Here dwelt a deadly but imponderable threat, hidden behind the soaring morale of the confident British and Americans. In the end a single Tiger which had destroyed a squadron of Allied tanks might be overwhelmed, but would the survivors of that sort of Pyrrhic victory be so ready to stalk the next Tiger when it appeared? And could they go on doing so until the last Tiger had been shot – that is, when no more could reach the battle-front down ramshackle roads and railways from the German interior?

Indeed, the likelihood of the Germans being able to sustain the routes carrying reinforcements and, above all, the fuel and ammunition to nurture a mobile battle, hung in doubt. Here was the crux of the battle – since half replenished fuel stocks in mechanical war can be almost as crippling as no stocks at all, for planning gets clogged by imponderables. In the ability of the Allied air forces to disrupt fuel supplies resided an indirect threat infinitely more potent than their erratic claims to be able to knock out armour with unstable rockets and bombs.

In 1940 the balance of armour could be reduced to comparatively simple terms and almost in splendid isolation, with the other combat elements playing walking-on parts after the tank heroes had trodden the centre of the stage. Now, in 1944, armour still filled a vital role but merged tightly with every other fighting asset of each army. Yet both sides came to grips again acutely aware that aerial supremacy tipped the scales most profoundly, but not irrevocably, while destruction or neutralisation of armour most certainly would be decisive in the final analysis.

Churchill Crocodile Flame-Thrower
The Crocodile kept the Churchill's main gun armament, but substituted a flame-thrower for the hull machine-gun. Towing 400 gallons of fuel in an armoured trailer, the Crocodile assaulted pillboxes and bunkers, squirting a jet of flame through loop-holes to exhaust the oxygen

THE PANZERS: FRONT LINE OR MOBILE RESERVE?

Sturmpanzer IV
An infantry assault gun built on the Pzkpfw IV chassis, the Sturmpanzer proved its worth in the close fighting behind the beachhead, 'shooting in' counterattacks. Weight: 25 tons. Speed: 23 mph. Crew: 5. Armour: 80 mm. Armament: 75-mm gun, 2 × mg

Jagd Panther
A marriage of the Panther suspension and the 88-mm gun in a low silhouette hull produced this potent 'hunting' anti-tank vehicle. Weight: 46 tons. Speed: 35 mph. Crew: 5. Armour: 80 mm max. Armament: 88-mm gun, 2 × 7.92-mm mg

Field-Marshal Gerd von Rundstedt, C-in-C West, held a poor opinion of Rommel as a strategist, though he shared his distrust of the Atlantic Wall's capabilities. He believed that the attack would come in the Pas de Calais and that the Panzers should deliver a counterstroke *after* the Allies broke through the outer crust

Keystone

Panzerkampfwagen V Panther Ausf D
Based on experience gained in Russia, the Panther design was a fine balance of speed, armour and firepower and completely dominated Allied opposition. Weight: 43 tons. Armour: 120 mm max. Speed: 30 mph. Crew: 5. Armament: 75-mm gun, 2 × 7.92-mm mg

Panzerkampfwagen VI Tiger
Massively armoured and heavily armed, one Tiger could hold up a squadron of Shermans. But its size and immobility stranded the mighty Tigers far from the battlefront under the hammer of Allied air attack pounding at all road and rail communications. Weight: 55 tons. Armour 110 mm max. Speed: 25 mph. Crew: 5. Armament: 88-mm gun, 2 × 7.92-mm mg

Ullstein

Rommel looks out over the Channel and its defences

The German tank forces had shown in 1940 that a continuous line of defence is as strong as its weakest point. In the spaces of Russia the panzer crews had learnt offensive and defensive mobile warfare on a massive scale. Now the tank commanders in the West were ordered to buttress a static defensive crust 2,000 miles long—the Atlantic Wall. Both Field-Marshals von Rundstedt, C-in-C West, and Rommel, Commander of Army Group B covering the Channel, agreed that the final outcome of the battle would be decided in mobile battle by tanks, however ingenious the static defence or intense the intervention by aircraft. Where they disagreed was how and where the Panzers should be used.

Rommel, touring the miles of ferro-concrete and barbed wire, could see the cracks in the vaunted Atlantic Wall. In using tanks as a bludgeon behind the sagging rampart, he was aware of a dual problem. The Allies were lavishly provided in equipment, backed by a colossal war-machine—their attack must be smashed on the beaches themselves. Experience in North Africa left him the haunting memory of how air power could cripple the movement of a central armoured reserve. From his command bunker at St Germain-en-Laye, Rundstedt saw the air argument differently. Air power could trap armour grouped close to the beaches, far from the scene of the main assault. The old Field-Marshal, like Geyr von Schweppenburg, commander of the Armoured Reserve, was used to the tactics of the Russian steppe, when intervention from the air was minimal. The 'Russian School' believed in grouping the Panzers in a central region prior to moving it for a blow against the main Allied effort—when it had been identified.

Front line defence or mobile reserve? This was the agonising strategic dilemma which compromise could only further aggravate. By June 1944 the German armoured force in the West could muster 10 Panzer Divisions, a Panzer Grenadier Division, and several Assault Gun Battalions. These units were of varying complements and strength, but they were equipped with fighting vehicles superior to anything that would wade out of the Channel.

German tank design and organisation had profited from the bloody school of the Russian Front, where the lightning thrusts of the *blitzkrieg* era had turned into a titanic armoured slugging match. The formidable combination of General Heinz Guderian, Inspector General of Armoured Troops, and Armament Minister Albert Speer had begun the rationalisation of fighting vehicle production and training with a dual aim—to produce quantity by building up-gunned and up-armoured versions of the old Pzkpfw IV in large numbers, and quality in the formidable new breed of Tigers and Panthers. The *Panzerkampfwagen* V Panther, with its sloped armour, excellent ballistic qualities and 'long' 75-mm gun, was a fine balance of speed, armour, and hitting power. Pzkpfw VI Tiger, with its lavish armour and formidable 88-mm gun, had shown its ability to decimate Allied armour. Both Tiger and Panther suffered from reliability problems and Tiger particularly from lack of mobility, but in battle only numbers could overwhelm them. Backing them up were a wide range of assault guns *(Sturmgeschütz)* and tank-destroyers *(Jagdpanzer)*, an armoured anti-tank force to provide defensive hard shoulders round which the battle tanks could manoeuvre.

Rommel's problem was not only how and where to deploy this force, but in securing new equipment from other theatres. On this depended the erratic but absolute dictates of Adolf Hitler.

Hitler's Atlantic Wall

THE GREATEST FORT OF ALL TIME?

'I am the greatest fortress builder of all time' boasted Hitler; 'I built the West Wall; I built the Atlantic Wall . . .' But the much-vaunted Atlantic Wall, against which the invading Allies were intended to dash themselves into ruin, was only a figment of Hitler's imagination. He had never visited the invasion coast; and despite Rommel's frantic efforts to create a strong defence system, it was only in the Pas de Calais that the 'Wall' existed in anything like its intended form. And the Pas de Calais was not the Allied target area . . .

From the moment of Germany's offensive against Russia her forces had been totally inadequate for the defence of the 3,000 miles of western coastline she controlled. Field-Marshal von Rundstedt, transferred from his command in the West in April 1941, to command Army Group South in the attack against Russia, confessed that the bareness at his back gave him a feeling of chill. He expected Britain to walk in. This is not only illustrative of the Nazi weakness in the West, but of German ignorance of the true condition of the almost unarmed remnants of the British army that had survived Dunkirk. Such thinking helped to save Britain from invasion.

Returning to command in the West in 1942, Rundstedt found the situation little more to his liking. Throughout that year France had been used as a rest area for divisions badly mauled on the Eastern Front. The 50 or 60 divisions available at all material times on paper seldom mustered 25 field divisions of reasonable quality, and seldom at full strength. A Nazi decision that it would be more profitable to use prisoners of war as soldiers rather than to exterminate them, or induce them to rot in their 'Belsens' led to a complex situation, but it relieved the growing strain on German manpower. In 1942, foreign battalions were being drafted into German divisions, and in one German regiment no fewer than eight different kinds of 'Pay Book' were in use, covering at least a score of Eastern 'tribes'. A hotch-potch of races under German officers made up at least 10% of the strength of many divisions, and up to 25% of the strength of a few.

It can be seen at a glance – and it was seen at a glance by Rundstedt – that 50 or 60 divisions, even of the highest quality, will 'go' at least ten times too many into 3,000 miles of coastline. One division to 3 miles was not excessive in defence; one division in 50 or 60 miles was hopeless. One of the main enemy problems, therefore, was to decide where as well as when a major assault from the West might be expected. Whatever decision is made, wide areas must be left bare. The problem of reserves becomes insoluble.

The appreciation of Field-Marshal von Rundstedt, which remained constant, was that the Western Allies would assault against the Pas de Calais area, probably astride the Somme, not only because it was the shortest route from shore to shore, simplifying sea and air cover and a quick turn-round, but because it offered the shortest route to the Rhine, and on into the heart of the Reich. The fact that it was obvious could not exclude it, and the view from France was very different from the view from Britain. While the Allies saw the strength of the enemy positions, Rundstedt was acutely aware of the weaknesses. If the 'Atlantic Wall' was more than the 'propaganda structure' Rundstedt considered it, it was also much less than Hitler had led himself or the Allies to imagine. The materials and labour were never available to carry out his dreams, and even had the dreams been practical the fate of the immensely powerful Maginot Line had proved that defences were no stronger than their weakest links, or their defenders. The 'Atlantic Wall' existed in something like its 'propaganda strength' in the Pas de Calais, and nowhere else.

Throughout 1943, as the Nazi armies were bled white in the East, and the Allied strategic bombing offensive moved steadily towards its terrible crescendo, Rundstedt strove to reorganise the meagre and poor quality troops at his disposal. Static coastal divisions were formed, carrying a high proportion of second grade troops, but with the virtue of gaining familiarity with their allotted areas.

The Allied landings in North Africa in the late autumn of 1942 put Hitler 'constantly on the jump', in the words of General Blumentritt. He expected landings anywhere and everywhere. His anxieties included Holland, Portugal, Spain, and the Adriatic. The fall of Tunis led him to believe that the south of France was immediately threatened. At the same time his fears for the vulnerability of Norway matched Churchill's recurrent desire to make these fears come true. It was an impossible situation for his generals, almost all of whom were kept in ignorance of the progress of war outside their immediate command areas. In April 1943, Geyr von Schweppenburg, then commanding the 86th Corps, was ordered to prepare Operation 'Gisela' in which five mechanised divisions would fan-out through Spain, four divisions making a 'dash' for Madrid while the fifth anchored on Bilbao. It is not to be wondered at that Geyr described the project as 'This folly'.

But although the generals did not share the wide range of their Führer's haunting apprehensions they were compelled to act upon his hunches, especially when they pointed to the region of the Somme and Normandy.

In September 1943, the elaborate exercise carried out in Britain, partly as a rehearsal of the massive and complex troop movements and loadings problems for Overlord, and partly to mislead the enemy, failed in its second purpose. The bluff, Rundstedt thought, was 'too obvious', and it seems that the Germans were misled and alarmed more by the natural rumours abounding in the occupied countries than by the stories planted by the Allies.

The autumn of 1943, bringing with it the first heavy seas and the promise of winter, limited the areas of possible Allied attack, and a respite to the enemy. All was probably secure until the spring of 1944. All that could be done was to strengthen the 'Atlantic Wall', increase the minefields guarding the approaches, and improve the training and rather miscellaneous weapon strength of the available troops. The placing and use of the armoured reserve was already looming as a difficult matter, and one which the suspicions of Hitler and the air power of the Allies, would make impossible.

Through the year the quality of the French Resistance had greatly improved, the quarrels of the various groups had abated, and the whole movement had responded well to British aid and organisation. By the winter of 1943/44 the Resistance had become a serious problem for the Germans, sabotaging railways and transport, and undermining morale with the fears that there might always be a bomb under the bed or in the wardrobe, that trains might leave the rails, or mysteriously blow up. And these things happened with growing frequency. The signs that the moment of crisis in the West was approaching could not be misread. 1944 would be the year, Western Europe the place, the spring or summer would bring the hour.

The snout of a German coastal gun emerges from its bunker

Information reaching the Axis through a German Foreign Office report dated January 8, 1944, by way of Ankara, gave the code name of 'Overlock' to the Allied plans, and provided 'conclusive evidence that the Anglo-Saxons are determined to force a show-down by opening a "Second Front" in 1944. However, this Second Front will not be in the Balkans.'

An Intelligence analysis by the Chief of Western Military Intelligence followed a month later:

For 1944 an operation is planned outside the Mediterranean *that will seek to force a decision and, therefore, will be carried out with all available forces. This operation is probably being prepared under the code name of OVERLORD. The intention of committing large forces becomes clear from the fact that the operation is expected to produce the final military decision within a comparatively short period of time.*

The exact area to be attacked eluded the enemy, but an Intelligence report dated February 21 re-affirmed that:

The frequently expressed determination to bring the war to an end in 1944 *is to be considered* the keynote of the enemy's operational planning. *It is also repeatedly mentioned as a definite fact that the decision will be sought by a* large-scale attack in Western Europe.

The Germans expected the attack either in the first or the third quarter of the year. Their Balkan fears were at an end. Time had narrowed down to May-August, 1944; place could be narrowed perhaps to the Pas de Calais . . . or Normandy.

Rommel faces the facts

The appointment of Field-Marshal Rommel in November 1943, to inspect and improve the defences of the Western coastline from Denmark to the Spanish border complicated an already difficult command situation. Possibly General Blumentritt exaggerated when he said that 'soon the armies did not know whether they were under command of Rundstedt or Rommel'. Rommel's direct line through to Hitler certainly invested him with great influence, but equally there is no doubt that he respected Rundstedt, C-in-C West, and observed the proper etiquette. Rundstedt, while holding a poor opinion of Rommel as a strategist, has paid tributes to his courage and loyalty. In the hands of one of the Nazi upstarts the appointment would have rendered the position of the C-in-C intolerable.

It was, inevitably, an uneasy situation, eased over the months by Rommel's appointment to command Army Group B, with responsibility under Rundstedt for the vital sectors of the Channel coast from the Dutch-German border to the Loire. Later, the appointment of Colonel-General Blaskowitz to command Army Group G covering the Biscay and Mediterranean coasts of France, clearly, if unsatisfactorily, clarified the 'Ground Force Command'.

But the Ground Force Command, even in isolation, and it was virtually in isolation, remained subject to powerful influences, arising not only out of the divergencies of opinion between the C-in-C West and the Commander of Army Group B, but also from General Guderian, Inspector General of Armour since March 1943, and from General Geyr von Schweppenburg, commanding Panzer Group West, and controlling the armoured reserve.

Rommel, sharing Hitler's view that Normandy would be the main Allied target, and believing that the enemy must be annihilated, if possible on and in the sea, and certainly on the beaches, wanted the armour close up under his hand ready to deliver an immediate and massive counterstroke. He had had painful experience of Allied air supremacy in the Western Desert, and knew well the fate of armoured columns attempting to move by daylight under 'open bomb sights'. If the armour was not 'there' he doubted its ability to get there, and certainly not in time. It was, in any case, virtually impossible to move armour on the stricken roads by day.

None doubted the magnitude of the Allied air threat, of which they were having daily and nightly experience, but at the same time neither Rundstedt nor the Panzer generals agreed with Rommel's tactics, or shared his beliefs about the site of operations. First, Rundstedt visualised delivering massive counterstrokes after the Allies had broken through the outer crust of the sea defences; second, he did not share Rommel's views on Normandy; third, he could not agree to the commitment of the armoured reserve close up before the event. The air argument which rendered the armour difficult to move might easily trap it and destroy it if Rommel had his way, and the main assault should come in against the Pas de Calais, or elsewhere.

Guderian, greatly worried about the situation in both the East and West, breakfasted alone with Hitler in early January 1944, and urged upon him the necessity to strengthen the Eastern defences

Hitler boasted of his Atlantic Wall as the greatest rampart in history. But Rommel saw its weaknesses, which only effort and time could amend – but time was running out

Alfredo Zennaro

Ullstein

Whole forests were cut down to make beach obstacles, designed to rip open a landing craft – but there were 3,000 miles of coast

and release much needed reserves to the West. This touched off a typical Hitler outburst:

'Believe me! I am the greatest builder of fortifications of all time,' Hitler ranted. 'I built the West Wall; I built the Atlantic Wall . . .' He then began to deluge Guderian's ears with 'tons of concrete' and a mass of statistics. In fact, Hitler had never visited the 'Atlantic Wall', and it existed, like the Emperor's clothes, largely in his imagination.

Guderian then toured the West, and was at once alarmed by Rommel's intended dispositions, and his intention to commit the Panzer divisions close up before the 'Day'. 'Disposed thus,' he wrote, 'they could not be withdrawn and committed elsewhere with sufficient rapidity.'

Back at Supreme Headquarters, Guderian took the opportunity to point out 'this error' in conference. Hitler refused to countermand the orders of the 'man on the spot', and advised Guderian to 'go to France and discuss the matter once more with Rommel'.

Guderian and Schweppenburg then visited Rommel at his Headquarters at La Roche Guyon. The Field-Marshal explained his views fully, but was not disposed to argue. Apart from his belief that Normandy would be the sector of assault, he was convinced that the enemy must be destroyed without gaining a foothold. Given his own way he might deliver such a blow to the enemy in the shallows and on the beaches that it would be impossible to mount a further assault, at least in that year. And if he were right in these beliefs, which he shared with Hitler, then he must be right about the disposition of the armour close up. The risk, admittedly was great, but there was no escape from that. Clearly Rommel did not share Rundstedt's view that a battle of mobility might be won.

Disastrous compromise

Hitler, meanwhile, clung to his intuitions, reinforced by his reasonable deductions from Allied troop placings, especially in the south-west of England, that Normandy would be the main target, and that Cherbourg would be the natural port for the Allies to aim at. But the nagging possibility of a second assault – even a major effort – elsewhere, began to divide his mind, disposing him far more than the commanders on the spot to the ultimate disasters of compromise.

Guderian had made a third attempt to convince Hitler of the dangers of Rommel's armoured dispositions, but early in May, Schweppenburg, fearing that Rundstedt was moving closer to Rommel's views, appealed to Hitler on his own account. He wanted to hold the bulk of his armour north and south of Paris, and at last Hitler dithered. The result was a disastrous compromise whereby four Panzer divisions were held as an assault reserve under the command of OKW, Supreme Headquarters. This weakened Rundstedt's command, for the old Field-Marshal, already thwarted in his attempts to organise an infantry reserve in Normandy by withdrawing strength from south of the Loire, now found himself deprived of the means to deliver an effective counterstroke against the beaches, or later, without seeking permission from OKW.

Thus Schweppenburg had unwittingly brought about a situation which was to prove fatal.

These were worries enough, but they were but one expression of a general weakness based on suspicion and decay at the top.

Whereas Rommel, in his natural desire to have full control of the battle his armies must fight, was in a position comparable with Montgomery's, Rundstedt's position was not in any way comparable with Eisenhower's. Not only was Rundstedt deprived of full control of his ground forces, but he was also forced to 'request' air and naval support when he might need them. There was no machinery for combined planning between the services. Worse, the German navy controlled the coastal batteries which must play a major part in repelling an assault. The fact that naval and air strength had been reduced to very small, almost negligible proportions, strengthened rather than weakened the need to co-operate and co-ordinate all available defences.

Admiral Theodor Krancke, C-in-C, German Naval Group West, had his small fleet of some 60 miscellaneous craft, hemmed into port under incessant Allied air attack. Clashes in the Channel reduced his destroyer flotilla to two operational vessels. For the rest he could muster two torpedo boats, 31 motor torpedo-boats, and a handful of patrol vessels and mine-sweepers. In addition 15 of the smaller U-boats in Atlantic ports were to be made available, but were not under his command.

In the event, even this small 'fleet' was virtually unable to put to sea.

The German Luftflotte III, commanded by General Hugo Sperrle, was equally a broken reed. Compelled to use half-trained pilots its effectiveness, even with its dwindling numbers, was poor, and it was harried constantly on the ground as well as in the air. At the beginning of June 1944, Luftflotte III mustered some 400 aircraft operational 'on paper'. Again on paper these were divided between Jagdgeschwader IV and V under II Fliegerkorps. Those of Jagdgeschwader IV had the priority task of intercepting Allied bombers bound for the Reich, but could be diverted in the event of Allied assault landings. In the event none of the units of II Fliegerkorps had aircraft available to make their presence felt on the 'Day'. The promised fighter 'wings' on the way from Germany mostly failed to arrive. Few pilots knew France; few could read maps. The Chief-of-Staff of II Fliegerkorps estimated that he had no more than 50 aircraft under command.

Thus, the Western Allies could not be challenged at sea or in the air, and Rommel had few illusions about his task. It was, in a sense, simple: the German armies in the West, battered incessantly from the air, short of training, short of essential transport, and of poor quality, deprived by the disruption of their radar installations of

Ullstein

Beneath millions of tons of concrete the Germans set their long-range guns – but they were prime targets for Allied gunners

the full use of their 'eyes' and 'ears', stood alone, waiting.

For nearly six months Field-Marshal Rommel devoted his tremendous energies to the task of making the coastal defences impregnable from Cherbourg to the Somme, giving as much attention as was permitted to the problems of Normandy. Moved by a profound pessimism, untrammelled by the limitations of the orthodox military thinking which patterned the minds of Rundstedt and the older school, perhaps even sub-consciously aware that there could be no compromise for Germany while Germany was Hitler, he knew that the enemy must be beaten on the beaches. Perhaps he knew also that it was a forlorn hope: there was no other.

There is no evidence to suggest that Rommel would have disliked a battle of manoeuvre. It was simply that he knew it would be too late, and lost. There was no room, therefore, for Rundstedt's belief that the Allies were bound to gain a foothold, and that the battle for Normandy would then be fought.

To Rommel such optimism was another name for despair, and Hitler, with the shadow of disaster already darkening his door, knew it also. Blumentritt remarked that messages from OKW at this time invariably began: 'The Führer fears . . .' He was full of fears, centring on Normandy where the Valkyrie rode the skies. But whereas Rommel was a realist concerned with men and materials, concrete and mines, guns and ammunition, Hitler was a visionary, seeing figures in a glass darkly. His support for Rommel was split too many ways, and never effective. He stated clearly, to Warlimont and others: 'If we do not stop the invasion and do not drive the enemy back into the sea, the war will be lost.' He had the greatest faith in Rommel, yet apart from ordering a few anti-tank and anti-aircraft units to reinforce Western Normandy, he did almost nothing about it. US troop concentrations and assault landing exercises in south-west England pointed ever more clearly to Normandy, and to Cherbourg, but Hitler vacillated. Neither he, nor anyone else, had conceived the possibility of the harbours the Allies planned to tow in their wake.

A powerful factor in the indecision in regard to the armoured reserve was the haunting fear that Normandy might not be the place, or only one place. The extreme lack of mobility of the German armies in the West haunted the minds of the Commanders.

155-mm Coastal Gun
Along the invasion coast these guns were dug in in batteries of three or four. Set back from the cliff edge, and protected by a carapace of ferro-concrete, their main purpose was to break up an Allied invasion fleet before it reached the inshore approaches. But they were large and the natural first target for Allied bombardment. Crew: 12. Max range: 12 miles. Ammunition: 200 rounds

1 155-mm gun
2 Reinforced concrete carapace, capable of withstanding a 500-lb bomb without shattering
3 Entrance, protected against rear fire
4 Magazine (shell room other side)

The Allied air forces would not only be able, in Rommel's considered opinion, to prevent troop movement in battle, but they had already knocked the wheels from under the ground troops, condemning them to static rôles.

It was impossible to make the best of it. In spite of repeated demands Rommel did not receive the command control essential to the carrying out of his basic plans even on a minimum basis. His demands for labour and materials could not be 'orders', but merely 'requests' through the normal channels. Denied the help of the Todt Organisation, fully extended on fortress work mainly in the Pas de Calais, and unable to cope with the sustained Allied air attacks which were wrecking the transport services, Rommel used his troops as labourers to the detriment of their essential training. Some units were employed for three full days a week on labouring tasks, and much of the remainder of their time was taken up with special guard duties.

In February, Rommel issued a directive to his army commanders, and repeated it again towards the end of April:

In the short time left before the great offensive starts, we must succeed in bringing all defences to such a standard that they will hold up against the strongest attacks. Never in history was there a defence of such an extent with such an obstacle as the sea. The enemy must be annihilated before he reaches our main battlefield. We must stop him in the water, not only delaying him but destroying all his equipment while it is still afloat.

Repeatedly he emphasised to his commanders and staff that the first 24 hours would be decisive. He conceived an elaborate system of obstacles between high and low water marks covering the beaches, which would make the passage even of flat-bottomed boats perilous in the extreme, if not impossible. Rommel planned to lay over 50 million mines as the first line of sea defence, and sow minefields over the beaches. The mines were never available, and when at last inadequate deliveries were made, the minelayers were immobilised by Allied air attack and unable to put to sea. In the event not more than 6 million mines were laid, little more than one-tenth of the minimum programme.

Regarding Rundstedt's 'Zweite Stellung', or second line of defence as 'a waste of time', Rommel ordered all work upon it to cease, and the entire effort concentrated upon strengthening the forward positions. Innumerable 'hedgehogs' and anti-tank obstacles were moved forward to reinforce the massive concoctions of angle iron, the 'Tetrahydra' and 'Belgian Gates', which with thousands of mined stakes slanted seaward, mazed the approaches to the beaches. So grave was the shortage of labour that the 352nd Division, covering the vital stretch of beach from Grandcamp to Arromanches, had to cut and haul its own stakes from the Cerisy forest, 11 miles inland, and drive each stake by hand into position.

In the areas behind the Cotentin, Rommel had planned an extensive network of poles linked by wires and mined as a defence in depth against airborne landings. When the work should have been completed in the middle of May he visited the site and found that the task was only in its opening stages. The 13,000 shells necessary to set off explosions were not available.

Luftwaffe jealousy

The acute shortage of labour, mines and materials of all kinds, and the reduction of transport to the horse and cart and the bicycle, made the carrying out of a massive defensive plan impossible. Of 10 million mines needed for the 30-mile front of the 352nd Division only 10,000 were forthcoming, and these did not include any Teller mines. The situation of the 716th and 711th Divisions covering the vital frontage behind the Normandy beaches was no better. Not more than two-thirds of the coastal guns covering the army group front had been casemated by the end of May. A system of strongpoints spaced from 800 to 1,300 yards apart were in the main unprotected. 'Of the installations in the sector of the 352nd Division only 15 were bombproof; the remainder were virtually unprotected from air attack.' The 716th Division regarded its situation as even worse.

The minimum daily need of the VII Army in Normandy to fulfil its construction tasks was for 240 carloads of cement alone. In one typical three-day period the records show that it received 47 carloads. The forced closure of the Cherbourg cement works for lack of coal aggravated the extreme shortage. This was, above all, due to the Allied attacks on road and rail transport.

These desperate shortages sharpened the edge of Rommel's bitter criticism of the Luftwaffe. He pointed out that the Luftwaffe employed 50,000 men to maintain its communications, and engaged a further 300,000 on ground services. This worked out at 100 men on the ground to every man in the air. That Hugo Sperrle, commanding Luftflotte III, largely shared his views availed nothing. The situation existed to feed the grandiose dreams of Göring.

Rommel's repeated attempts to gain the services of the III Flak Corps in Normandy were thwarted, and it remained under the Luftflotte III, subject to the whims of Göring, and useless in defence. It might have done much to counter the overwhelming air strength of the Allies, and would have given some comfort and a sense of 'hitting back' to the battered troops in their dug-outs. Even the II Parachute Corps, tactically under VII Army, remained administratively and for training under the Luftwaffe. Göring refused to permit these troops to be used to help in defence works.

Thus, as June opened, the gaps in the defences were frightful, and each new device had been observed by the Allies, and often tested through the courage of the small teams of men who explored the shallows by night. By abandoning the 'Zweite Stellung' the defences had been deprived of depth, and reduced to an outer crust too fragile to withstand the immense weight of assault in store for it. Nevertheless, the fault was not Rommel's. He had attempted the impossible, and had achieved much. He had inherited a myth, and had given it 'teeth' to inflict a dangerous, if not deadly, bite. He had also greatly improved the dispositions of his troops.

On the eve of 'D-Day', Field-Marshal von Rundstedt's command in the West numbered 60 divisions, one of them, the XIX Panzer Division, refitting after a severe hammering on the Eastern Front, another in the Channel Islands, reducing the effective total to 58 divisions (see map).

Of these, 31 divisions were in static rôles, and 27, including 10 armoured divisions, were as mobile as the suspicions of the Führer and the available resources allowed. They were disposed from Holland to the Atlantic and Mediterranean coasts, five divisions in Holland in the 88th Corps, including the 'lame' XIX Panzer, 19 in the Pas de Calais between the Scheldt and the Seine, 18 between the Seine and the Loire. The remainder were south of the Loire.

Some 43 divisions out of the grand total of 60 were grouped under Field-Marshal Rommel's Army Group B, the 88th Corps in Holland, the powerful XV Army in the Pas de Calais, the VII Army in Normandy. The XV Army, commanded by Salmuth, was virtually anchored in its positions mainly by the incapability of the German military mind to disengage itself from a pre-conceived idea. The Western Allies did their best to nurture the illusion.

By the eve of D-Day, Field-Marshal Rommel had succeeded in improving and strengthening the dispositions of the VII Army under Dollmann which, he believed, must fight the decisive battle on the beaches. The 352nd and 716th Infantry Divisions lay in their dug-outs and resistance 'nests' along the coast of Calvados from the Vire river to the Orne. On the German left flank the 91st Division, with the VI Parachute Regiment under command, covered the left flank of the 352nd in the area of Carentan. The 709th Division covered the eastern coastline of the Cherbourg Peninsula.

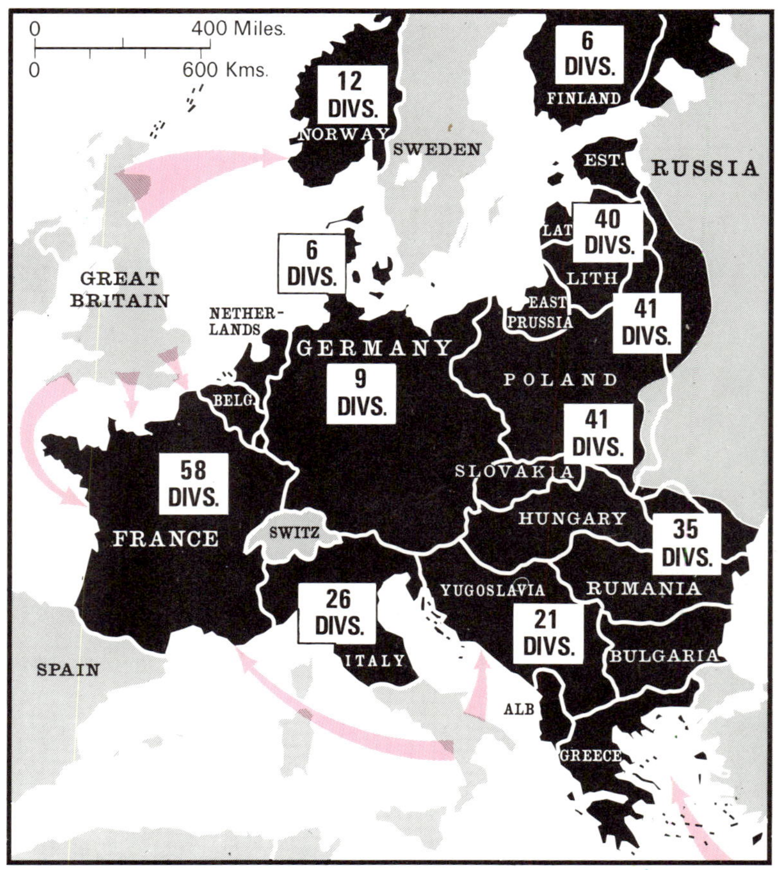

Behind its right flank positions, known to the Allies by the code name 'Utah' beach, the extensive marshes and the flooded areas following the courses of the rivers Dives and Merderet from Carentan to le Port Brehay, were regarded as safeguarding the rear, and blocking the exits from the beaches. The 243rd Division faced west in the Peninsula.

On the German right flank the 711th Division with one regiment of the 346th Division under command covered the coast from the River Orne to the Seine Estuary opposite Le Havre.

The 709th, the 352nd, and the 716th Infantry Divisions would, therefore, meet the Allied assaults on the beaches codes named 'Utah', 'Omaha', 'Gold', 'Juno', 'Sword'. Against the will of Rundstedt, Rommel had succeeded in bringing up the XXI Panzer Division to the Caen area, poised to strike against the Allied left flank. The three armoured divisions, the XII and 116th Panzer, and the Panzer Lehr, the Army Group B reserve, capable of delivering a massive punch, lay in the rectangle Mantes-Gassicourt, Chartres, Bernay, Gacé, the 116th forward. But the fears of Rundstedt, Guderian, and Schweppenburg had placed the force under OKW, subject to the will of Hitler. Thus, the outcome of the day of decision lay with the coastal batteries and with the three divisions entrenched along the Normandy coast, the 91st Division and its parachute regiment on the left, and the XXI Panzer Division on the right.

The Allied assault had been expected in the middle of May, and in spite of warnings from the German Naval Command in the West, the military view was that the assault would be at high tide. When the middle of May had safely passed there was a tendency to relax, in the belief that the attempt would be delayed until August. Enemy appreciations continued to be governed by the belief that the Allies must gain the use of a port or ports, and naval opinion moved away from the Pas de Calais, hardening in the belief that Le Havre and Cherbourg would be the main objectives. Allied troops and shipping concentrations in the south and south-west of England strongly supported this view, as also did the comparative freedom of the two ports from air attack, and the general pattern of Allied bombing at the end of May. The navy also believed that the rocky shallows covering the eastern sector of the Normandy coast would rule out landings, and expected that a major effort would come in against the Cotentin, together with airborne landings.

By the end of May, Admiral Krancke, Navy Group West, had lulled himself into an optimism, the more remarkable in view of the almost total immobilisation of his naval force. He believed that his coastal batteries could blow the Allied armada out of the water, and noted that Allied air attacks on the batteries had accounted for only eight guns, five of them between Le Havre and Le Treport, and three in Normandy. The Admiral began to believe that the massed shipping in British ports, the immense activities, the assault exercises, of which the enemy had some knowledge from isolated air reconnaissance and the reports of agents, were all part of a bluff.

The rapid deterioration of the weather in the first days of June ruled out the possibility of invasion in the mind of the enemy. The interceptions of warning messages broadcast to the Resistance and handed to Admiral Dönitz, failed to weigh against the high winds and rising seas in the Channel. On June 4, while General Eisenhower met with his admirals, air marshals, generals, and weather forecasters at Portsmouth, and the approaches to the Channel already seethed with the ships of the spearhead troops, Admiral Krancke in Normandy reached the view that no attack was or could be imminent. General Blumentritt, Chief of Staff, OB West agreed with him.

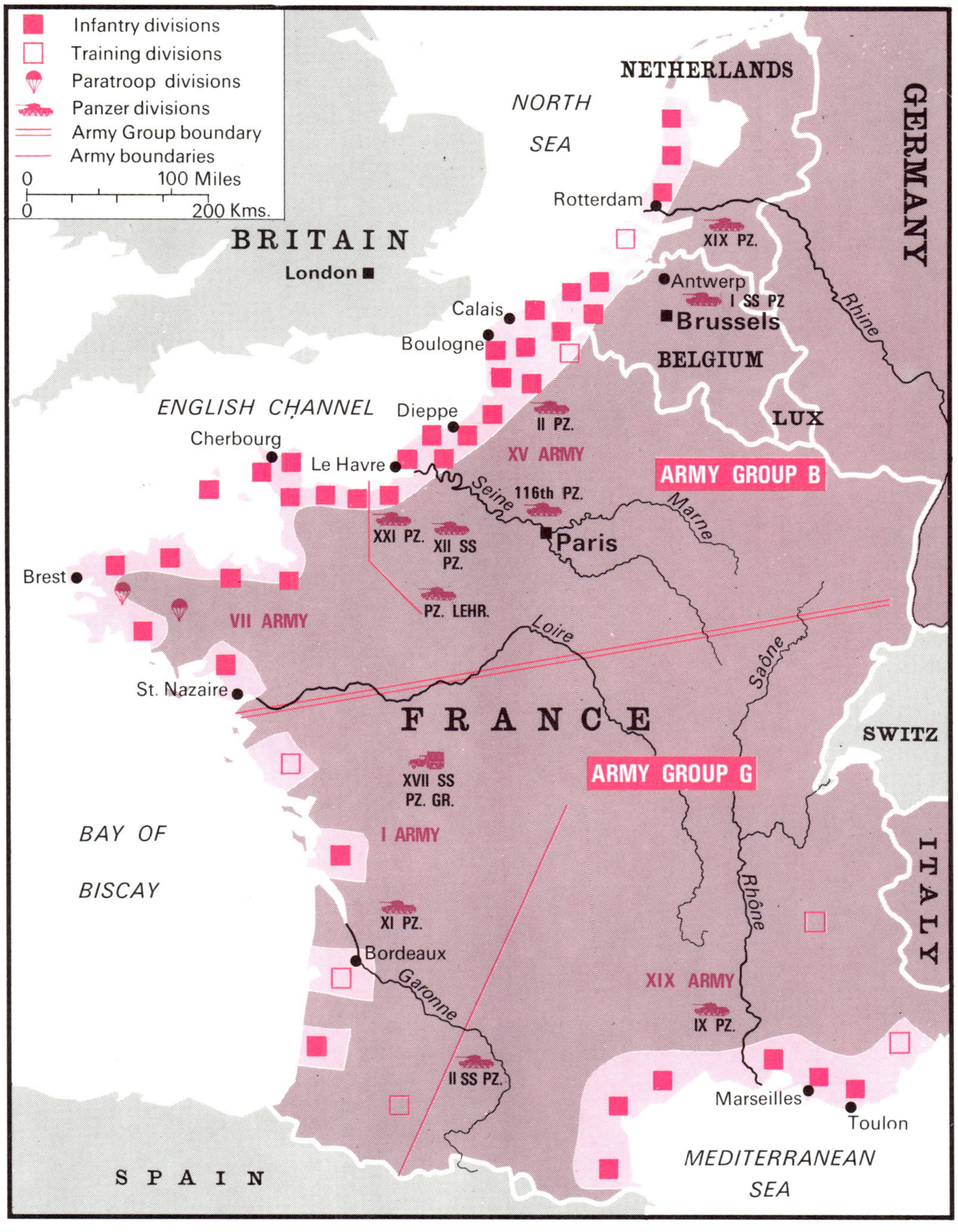

Right: Rommel could not believe that the Allies would ignore the Pas de Calais, and therefore he did not try to diminish the German forces already massed there. But he knew that if the Allied beachheads were to be smashed before they could be built up into secure jumping-off points, the Panzer divisions would have to be stationed near the beaches; for Allied air superiority would prevent all large-scale reinforcement from moving up to the front. And he had lost his battle to put the Panzers where he wanted them: OKW insisted on retaining the armour inland, as an inner ring of strategic defence – the classic pattern of mobile reserve. Rommel lamented: At one time they (OKW) looked on mobile warfare as something to keep clear of at all costs, but now that our freedom of movement in the West has gone, they're all crazy after it . . . thanks to the Allied air forces we will have nothing there in time. The day of the dashing cut-and-thrust tank attack of the early war years is past and gone . . .

Left: By June 1944 the Germans knew that the launching of the Allied Second Front could not be long delayed, and that the main blow would be a cross-Channel invasion. But Hitler expected supplementary invasions everywhere – and even Rommel came to believe that the Allies would follow up their first landings with other operations in France. And so the West was allocated some 58 divisions – but they had to be spread from the Netherlands to the Italian frontier, and divided between two separate army groups

Air Power

WHERE TO DROP THE BOMBS?

The importance of air power in particular relation to the success or failure of Overlord was fully realised in the summer of 1943. The combined bomber offensive, authorised at Casablanca in January, designed to destroy the enemy economy and to undermine the morale of the German people, had not, at first sight, brought satisfactory results. In July, General Morgan – now known as COSSAC – revealed his disquiet:

The most significant feature of the German Air Force in Western Europe is the steady increase in its fighter strength which, unless checked and reduced, may reach such formidable proportions as to render an amphibious assault out of the question. Above all, therefore, an overall reduction in the strength of the German fighter force between now and the time for surface assault is essential. . . . This condition, above all others, will dictate whether amphibious assault can or cannot be successfully launched on any given date.

A month earlier it had been noted on a higher level that unless the fighter strength of the enemy could be broken 'it may become literally impossible to carry out the destruction planned'. A new plan was drafted, Operation 'Pointblank', raising the reduction of the German fighter strength to the first priority while retaining the ultimate object of the bomber offensive.

These conclusions, with their notes of pessimism, were not shared by the bomber commanders, and were echoes of a new problem of immense significance. Air power, and particularly the bomber, had introduced a new dimension into warfare. Despite results, which were at best inconclusive, and the continued growth of enemy fighter strength, the commanders of the Allied strategic air forces had reached the conclusion that they controlled the decisive instrument; that they could achieve victory alone. General Spaatz, commanding the US Strategic Air Force Europe (USSAFE), believed simply that Overlord was unnecessary. Air Chief-Marshal Harris, his British opposite number, agreed with him. General Arnold, the representative of the US air arm on the Joint Chiefs-of-Staff, had reached a similar conclusion. None of these commanders 'objected' to Overlord, or resented its demands upon their forces. They believed simply that if they continued with their bombing strategy the demands would be met.

Keystone

General Spaatz, who was certain that a well-conducted strategic bomber offensive would cripple the German economy and make Overlord unnecessary

In the early days of 1943, the Americans had refused to profit by British experience and had sustained heavy losses in daylight raids, particularly over Stuttgart and Schweinfurt. By the end of the year these growing pains had been overcome, and the strategic air forces of the two nations were well integrated in an almost continuous all-round-the-clock bombing programme. The continued growth of the German fighter force, despite the priorities of Pointblank, was not necessarily a guide to its real strength, and the confidence of the bomber commanders remained unshaken. They 'knew' – they 'felt' – that they were winning, even if the statistics failed to prove it.

All this was highly unsatisfactory to the military commanders

Keystone

Air Chief-Marshal Harris, who agreed that Overlord was unnecessary. He believed that the quickest way to cripple Germany would be to shatter civilian morale by bombing the cities

and planners, and Air Marshal Tedder wrote later: 'I could not help feeling a certain sympathy for my soldier and sailor colleagues in the earlier days who could not understand why, before their operations began, I could only say that I "thought" and "felt" the air situation would be all right . . .'

Even if the claims of the Air Marshals were not yet wholly true – and they would never be true while war held its historic meaning – the signs were sufficiently ominous. Nazi Germany was being dissected, and destroyed behind its armies. The vast concentrations of heavy industry in the Ruhr and Saar valleys, coal, oil, synthetic fuels, ball bearings, roads, railways, cities, and hamlets were all being steadily reduced to rubble at the whim of this man or that. The bomber chiefs were agreed on their mission, but not on their choices of targets. Oil, General Spaatz believed, was the essential upon which a modern nation at war must depend. Ball bearings, said another. Communications and morale, yet others.

These beliefs made the commanders of the strategic bomber forces careless of the tactical demands of armies. Strategically, they declared, the bomber is winning the war. To divert the bomber from its strategic mission was old fashioned and short-sighted. The German armies in the field, immensely powerful as they were, were nevertheless powerless to prevent the utter destruction of the homeland and people it was their rôle and purpose to defend.

The rocket threat

Military thinkers, prominent among them Captain B. H. Liddell Hart, discerned the new pattern and portent of 'war' with which we now uneasily co-exist. Liddell Hart's warning that 'You cannot surrender to a bomber in the sky' went unheeded. Meanwhile, on the very highest levels there were forebodings of a very grave nature. Early in 1943, air photography and espionage, aided by the daring of Polish allies, had produced physical evidence of the enemy progress in the development and manufacture of rockets and pilotless aircraft capable of carrying warheads of high explosive dis-

United Press

Air Chief-Marshal Tedder, who led the fight to control the bomber chiefs and ensure that all Allied air power would be available to support the build-up for Overlord

tances of 150 miles plus. Such weapons might prove devastating in a high degree, and posed new problems of defence. In addition, the terrible secret of atomic progress engendered fears of enemy achievement in that field. The world had begun to fill with dark shadows, altering all accepted values, forewarning that the days of courage, ethics, morality, 'right or wrong', and those attributes of humanity known as 'virtues', were drawing to a close. The implications must undermine the faith in a just cause, in the virtues of steadfastness which, hitherto, had stimulated and sustained peoples to defend themselves successfully against odds.

Politics, and its age-old weapon of war, was giving way fast to blackmail, and its weapon of the 'push button'. The odds were new

Imperial War Museum

Air Chief-Marshal Portal, who reconciled the opposing views, and ensured that the strategic and tactical bomber forces would co-operate for the pre-D-Day attacks

and had to be considered urgently in the context of survival in a fight to the finish against an enemy who, it could be predicted, would stop at nothing. Never was the calm light of reason more necessary to mankind; seldom has it been less in evidence.

The bomber commanders, confident in their power, accepted an urgent mission to add the destruction of rocket and 'flying bomb' sites and bases to their commitments, and on August 17 Air Chief-Marshal Harris opened the attack with 571 heavy bombers on the enemy rocket base at Peenemünde. Finally, bombed out of Peenemünde, the German rocket experts under General Dornberger moved into 'factories' deep in the Harz mountains, and continued their production on a reduced scale; while the 'ski-sites' for launching their pilotless aircraft grew in numbers, demanding constant vigilance and hammering from the air.

The main burden of the attacks against rocket bases and ski-sites was borne by the tactical air forces. By the end of 1943, 93 sites for launching the pilotless aircraft known as the V-1, and to Air Intelligence as FZG-76, were pin-pointed within a 150-mile radius of

Opposite: RAF Mitchells attack a tactical target behind the beachhead. Road and rail targets were highest priority

London, and most of them in the Pas de Calais region. Nine thousand sorties were flown against these sites in the ensuing three months, and the enemy was forced to find alternative means of launching. Meanwhile the attacks by heavy bombers had severely hindered German development of the A-4, presently to be known as the V-2, and the major fear of the Overlord command was confined to the lesser, more recognisable – and defensible – danger of the V-1.

Despite successes it seemed that the Allies were faced with a grim race against time, even up to the end of March 1944. It was by then known that the enemy had improvised some form of modified launching site, very easily hidden from view. Many of these were suspected to exist in the Pas de Calais and the Cherbourg Peninsula, but the heavy and varied demands on the entire Allied air strength as Overlord approached its hour, made it difficult to press consistent attacks.

Popperfoto

Reconnaissance analysis of an attack on a V-1 launching site

The army commanders were at no time inclined to underestimate the gravity of the threat, and in early December COSSAC had made an assessment. The immediate decision was to 'leave things as they were', but it was not until March 28 that Eisenhower, emerging from 'a sea of troubles', reported that the 'secret weapon' attack 'would not preclude the launching of the assault from the south coast ports as now planned, and that the probable incidence of casualties does not make it necessary to attempt to move the assault forces west of Southampton'.

The task would have been monumental. From the Wash southward and westward to the Severn Estuary, Britain was girdled with a belt 10 miles deep, a maze of assembly points, dumps, vehicle parks, camps, training grounds, embarkation 'hards', barbed wire, airfields, anti-aircraft and searchlight sites, and everywhere the massing paraphernalia of war, while every port, large or small, on the island's coasts bristled with shipping. Wherever Britain, from the extremities of Scotland and Wales to Cornwall and the Kent coast, was less than a camp, a dump, a training ground, or any other of the multitude of activities relevant to the cross-Channel assault, it was a munitions works.

The problem of attempting to move all this was a greater hazard than the threat of the V-1s and V-2s on London and the south coast ports. The chance of massive enemy interference had to be taken.

The attitude of the 'Bomber Barons', who, in General Morgan's words 'remained obstinately aloof', manifesting many of the characteristics of a 'new élite', made it inevitable that a serious command crisis would follow upon the appointment of a supreme commander for Overlord. General Eisenhower was not slow to point out that: 'The strategic air arm is almost the only weapon at the disposal of the supreme commander for influencing the general course of action, particularly during the assault phase.'

This is a simple statement of fact, and no supreme commander worth his salt could have accepted the attitude of the strategic air force commanders, and abrogated his right to command. The command of the ground forces was in the hands of General Montgomery, and with General Bradley commanding the US 1st Army, Commander Designate of the US 12th Army Group. The great invasion fleet was under Admiral Ramsay, and it was not until April that the obstructive and obstinate Admiral King authorised the full complement of US naval resources. Without the command of the air forces in his hands the Supreme Commander would be reduced to a cipher, a mere pusher of the button, afterwards to sit back, certainly for days, possibly for weeks, with no real prospect of influencing the battle. In this context Eisenhower's statement to Churchill on March 3 that he would 'simply have to go home', and his subsequent memo to Washington, dated March 22, 'unless the matter is settled at once I will request relief from this command', lose all trace of petulance.

The fact was (and is) that the Supreme Commander in his fight with the strategic air force commanders in 1944, and to a great extent with the British Prime Minister and the Chiefs-of-Staff, emphasised the obvious truth that air, sea, and land forces had become the three prongs of a single weapon. The proud and jealous distinctions, worse than 'nationalism', between the services, were already becoming blurred. A supreme commander must command them all, and in submitting each service must lose some part of its separate identity.

Welding the air/sea/land forces

In a small way Combined Operations Headquarters had functioned as an embryo of this trend. It had welded land and sea forces into a potent combined weapon, and had often 'used' the air weapon effectively in close support, at first under Lord Louis Mountbatten, and then equally well under General Laycock.

But the stand of the strategic air force commanders, and their supporters, was not aimed solely at the Supreme Commander. Apart from the fact that they believed they knew best how to use the strategic air arm, they objected also to relinquishing some of their command power into the hands of Air Chief-Marshal Sir Trafford Leigh-Mallory, Air Commander-in-Chief, Allied Expeditionary Air Force, on the grounds that his experience in Fighter Command, which had been mainly exercised in the defence of Britain, had not fitted him for an aggressive rôle with the strategic air weapon. But primarily they feared that he – and the Supreme Commander – would use strategic air power tactically.

In fact the demands of Overlord and Pointblank, the combined bomber offensive, were certainly not mutually exclusive or incompatible. The Supreme Commander had made it clear that in seeking command of the air forces he had not the smallest intention of interfering with, for example, Coastal Command. He had no quarrel with the strategic aims pursued by the bomber commanders, as far as they went, but he and his staff must have the right to state and to press their views on the use of air power in direct relation to Overlord, and to control it, at least, in the assault stages, and now, urgently, in the last 90 days.

Coincidentally, therefore, with the rather confused command arguments, an argument raged on the best way to serve Overlord from the air. The Deputy Supreme Commander, Air Chief-Marshal Sir Arthur Tedder, became the champion and chief exponent of what was known as 'The Transportation Plan' against General Spaatz, the champion and chief spokesman of 'The Oil Plan'. The argument, at times bitter, carried also grave political implications, and was pursued in an atmosphere of 'tense anxiety' until April.

All these difficulties were resolved by the middle of April largely

Allied Expeditionary Air Force attack on a V-1 site

Popperfoto

US B-25 Mitchell
Some versions of this widely used medium bomber were specially equipped for ground attack with a 75-mm cannon in the nose.
Span: 67 ft 6 in. Length: 52 ft 10 in Max speed: 284 mph at 15,000 ft.
Range: 1,525 miles at 233 ft. Armament: 14 × 5-in mg, 4,000-lb bombs.
Crew: 6

by the efforts of two of the most experienced airmen in the world, both of whom happened to be men of outstanding character and ability, Air Chief-Marshal Sir Charles Portal, a member of the Chiefs-of-Staff, and Tedder, Eisenhower's Deputy Commander.

Briefly, the Transportation Plan aimed at the disruption of the enemy communications, the destruction of railways, locomotives, marshalling yards, repair and maintenance facilities, roads and bridges, and the prevention of enemy reserves reaching the battlefield. This, in General Eisenhower's view, was 'the greatest contribution he could imagine' to the success of Overlord, and Tedder was his worthy champion.

Some idea of the feeling generated by this argument may be gathered from a remark made by General Spaatz to General Arnold, that he hoped 'the AEAF plan (the Transportation Plan) will be repudiated by Tedder of his own accord, thus avoiding hard feelings'.

But Tedder stuck to his guns, which were also the Supreme Commander's guns. Early in March he set about the dual tasks of reconciling the bomber commanders to the minimum command needs of the Supreme Commander, while at the same time fighting for the Transportation Plan, not only against Spaatz and Harris, but against 'the facts' produced by Air Intelligence, the doubts of 21st Army Group, and the grave misgivings of the British Prime Minister and the War Cabinet. It was one of the very few matters in regard to strategy upon which the British War Cabinet was consulted. This does not indicate that the War Cabinet was a rubber stamp, but that it had plenty of work to do without commenting on command problems, unless called upon to do so.

Eisenhower wins use of air power

In the final resolution of these two important matters, the command problem, and the air targets to be adopted in support of Overlord, Sir Charles Portal acted in the rôle of 'umpire', 'chairman', 'interpreter' to the Prime Minister and the Chiefs-of-Staff, holding the balance of the arguments with great skill while retaining a powerful personal judgement and opinion. On March 9 Tedder drafted a scheme of command acceptable to Eisenhower, and on March 27, with Portal's aid, he 'supervised' the Strategic Air Command for Overlord, co-ordinating the combined air effort with Leigh-Mallory's tactical air forces. On that day, also, having won agreement for the Transportation Plan, he relieved Leigh-Mallory of responsibility in the running of it. Thus the Deputy Supreme Commander became Eisenhower's direct channel of air command for Overlord, while the Combined Chiefs-of-Staff retained the last word in strategic matters.

This arrangement did not suit everyone, but it was the best possible in the difficult circumstances. The US Joint Chiefs-of-Staff objected to the word 'supervised', and wanted the stronger word 'directed'. The vital point was that the Supreme Commander had won the use of the air power he needed for Overlord and would retain essential control over it in the relevant period.

The target argument, waged by the main protagonists, Tedder and Spaatz, was less confused. In early March, General Spaatz produced a reasoned and carefully worked out Oil Plan, while Tedder produced his plan for the disruption of communications. This was not an attack on combined bomber offensive strategy embodied in Operation Pointblank. Eisenhower and Tedder were agreed that the destruction of the Luftwaffe bomber and fighter strength – which had continued to grow in numbers – must remain the first priority. They had no quarrel with Pointblank, as far as it went, but they were resolved to prevent the movement of enemy reserves into the battle area. Spaatz, they felt, might be right in his belief that by depriving the enemy of oil both the Luftwaffe, and almost all ground movement, would cease. They did not object to the Oil Plan, except as an alternative to their own. It was all

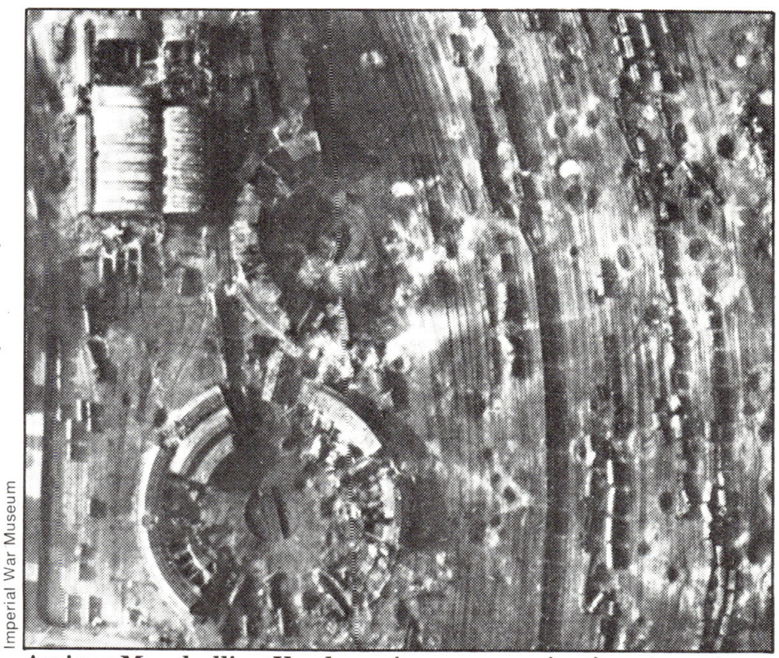

Imperial War Museum

Amiens Marshalling Yard, a prime communications target

very well for the commanders of the strategic air forces to state with conviction that the power of the enemy was being sapped at source, that at a given moment the whole 'house' would collapse, but the evidence for such an optimistic view was not conclusive. At best, it would be a nerve-racking wait as zero hour approached.

The real crux of the argument lay probably in the use of air power as an independent air weapon, and its use, as Ehrman put it, 'within the context of other operations'.

While the arguments and counter-arguments were pursued hotly throughout March both plans were virtually in operation. Pointblank, designed as an operation in support of Overlord, had been in action for a full nine months. Tedder's 'Transportation Plan' had been partially in operation since the beginning of the year. Neither

Martin B-26 Marauder
At first dubbed the 'widow-maker' due to a large number of early accidents, the B-26 proved a useful weapon in the tactical air forces armoury. Span: 71 ft. Length: 58 ft 3 in. Max speed: 282 mph at 15,000 ft. Range: 1,150 miles at 214 mph. Armament: 12 × .5-in mg, 4,000-lb bombs

plan was, therefore, wholly speculative.

The original Transportation Plan put forward in January by Allied Expeditionary Air Force Headquarters was based on an analysis by Professor Zuckerman. It called for a sustained 90-day attack directed against 72 carefully chosen targets, 39 of them in Germany and 33 in France and Belgium. The plan, constantly shorn of its targets, which were subject to constant pressures and permutations from air, civil, and military authorities, operated on a limited basis while the arguments were being hotly debated. The strategic views expressed by General Spaatz, Air Chief-Marshal Harris and their supporters, were that it would be quixotic and totally wrong to divert strength from the main bomber offensive at a time when it was beginning to take powerful effect; and, secondly, that railways and marshalling yards were notoriously difficult targets, and that no effective slow-down of enemy transport would be achieved in time for D-Day.

The British Chiefs-of-Staff, largely sympathetic to this view, and beset by grave fears of the consequences of heavy bombing in France and Belgium, were reluctant to clear the 'Zuckerman' targets, changed their minds constantly, and forced the AEAF to operate under grave handicaps against limited objectives.

Assessments of early results by Air Intelligence, by SHAEF G-2, and by 21st Army Group HQ, pointed to almost total failure of the effort. As late as May 9, 21st Army Group, more directly concerned in the end results than any other body, referred to the Transportation Plan, as 'pin-pricking on rail communications'. They were frankly scornful.

Never have assessments been more wide of the mark. The German communications were at the point of almost total collapse, for it was misleading simply to count trains and engines destroyed. Hundreds of engines, physically still 'in existence', were on the verge of breakdown, and the maintenance and repair facilities had sustained such a hammering, that it would prove impossible to get most of the battered trains on the move.

Nevertheless, at the height of his argument for the Transportation Plan most of the facts seemed to argue against Tedder. He stood as firm as a rock, convinced of the correctness of his view, and that nothing else would be of direct physical aid to Overlord. But it would have taken arguments of greater potency than those put forward by Harris, Spaatz, and their Intelligence supporters to prevail against the direct and urgent desire of the Supreme Commander. The arguments of greater force concerned the fear that the French and Belgians would suffer heavy civilian casualties, which, it was believed, must inevitably follow upon intensive bombing of marshalling yards. Some authorities put the expectation of civilian casualties as high as between 80-160,000. The possibility gave Churchill, among others, grave misgivings, and Portal was forced to draw the attention of the air planners to the fact that attacks on occupied countries, which might cause heavy civilian casualties and damage, were prohibited under a ruling dated June 3, 1940.

None of the difficulties had escaped Tedder. Even, he believed, if the enemy rail traffic could be reduced by 10% by D-Day it would be worth while. He and the Supreme Commander were convinced beyond a doubt that only in this way could air power make a direct contribution to Overlord.

The arguments, heart searchings, accompanied by constant

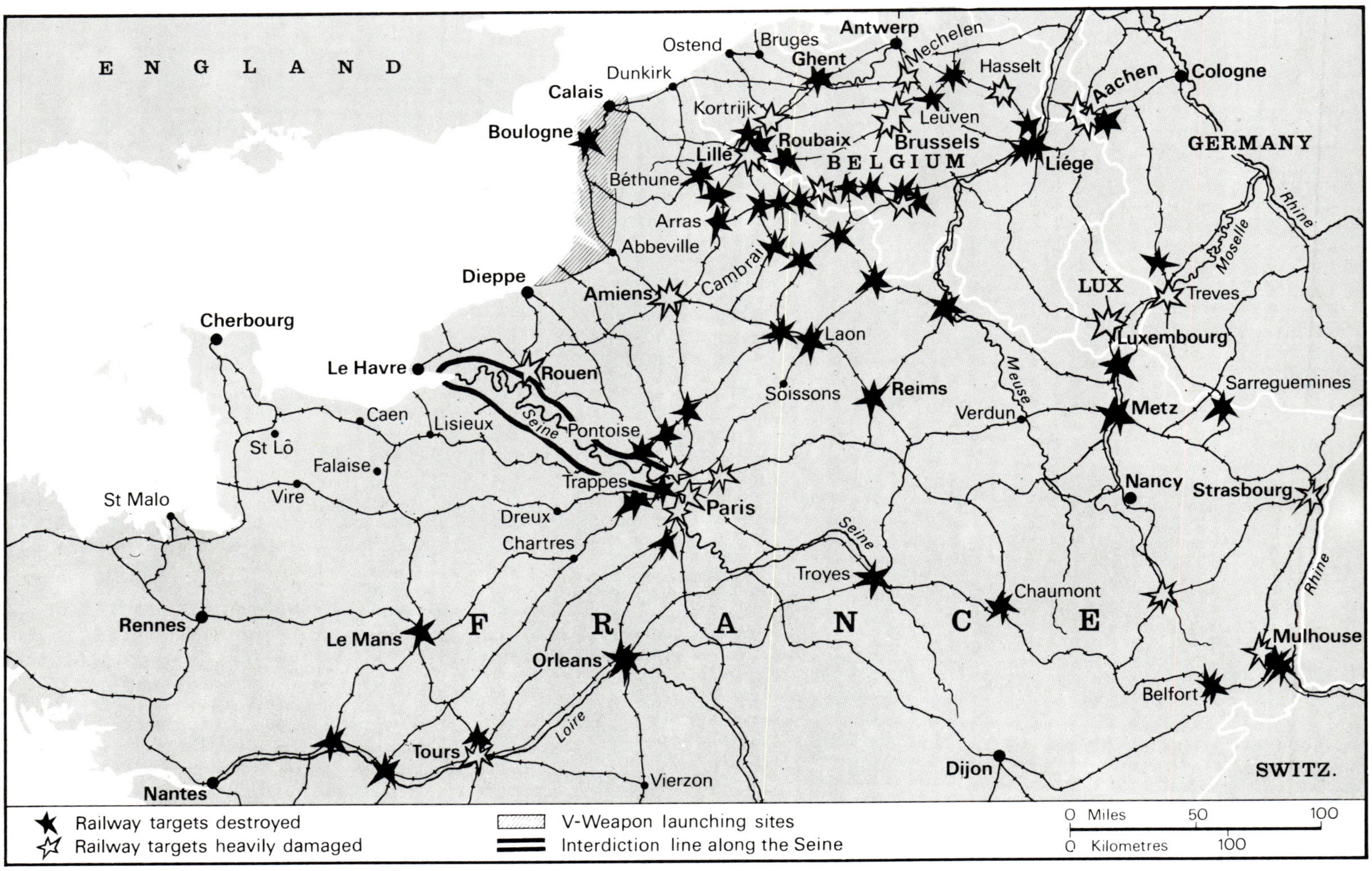

changes of targets, and the inclusion of roads and bridges, continued almost up to the eve of D-Day, as also did the derogatory and derisory intelligence estimates of the effects on traffic, and of the 'load of hatred being generated in the hearts of the French people'. They were hopelessly wrong on both counts. The civilian casualties were less than 10% of the worst fears, and were suffered without rancour.

Meanwhile, on March 25, Portal called a meeting with the object of reaching a decision. There was no longer room for delay. The Air Ministry, the War Office, the Ministry of Economic Warfare, the Joint Intelligence Committee, were all represented. The Supreme Commander, his deputy Tedder, together with Leigh-Mallory, Harris, and Spaatz, attended with their staffs. The debate favoured Overlord, and with that, on March 27, the Deputy Supreme Commander co-ordinated air operations in support of Overlord, and assumed responsibility for carrying out the 'Transportation Plan'.

The British Prime Minister, however, continued to urge upon Eisenhower the need to avoid civilian casualties, and remained uneasy until the middle of May, far from sure that military implications should outweigh the possible political implications. In the end he was fully reconciled. The results were significant.

Throughout all the arguments and disagreements, covering command, strategy, and tactics, the Allied air forces met all the great variety of demands upon them, and pursued their offensive with unabated vigour, while planning and training to lift three airborne divisions simultaneously into Normandy. Even General Spaatz continued to hammer away at his oil targets, and one is inclined at times to wonder what all the fuss was about.

In March, a minor command crisis followed Leigh-Mallory's establishment of an advanced headquarters of AEAF under Air Marshal Sir Arthur Coningham to operate in direct support of the ground forces. The objections of the bomber commanders to this appointment may not have been more than a last sop to their prejudices. In spite of everything Operation Pointblank had operated for a full ten months by the eve of D-Day. Up to the end of March, with the combined bomber offensive the aims were:

- The reduction of the Luftwaffe;
- The general reduction of the German war potential;
- The weakening of the will of the German people.

In the last phases the direct demands of Overlord, and of the assault landing, Neptune, took priority with five primary tasks:

- To attain and to maintain an air situation whereby the Luftwaffe was rendered incapable of effective interference with Allied operation;
- To provide continuous reconnaissance of enemy dispositions and movements;
- To disrupt enemy communications and supply channels for reinforcement;
- To deliver offensive strikes against enemy naval forces;
- To provide airlift for airborne forces;

In the assault phase the plan was designed:

- To protect the cross-Channel movement of assault forces against enemy air attack, and to assist the naval forces to protect the assault against enemy naval attacks;
- To prepare the way for assault by neutralising the beaches;
- To protect the landing beaches and shippings concentrations;
- To dislocate enemy communications and movement during assault.

Left: The air-planner's problem. A multitude of targets and of doctrines – but now with one aim: success on D-Day

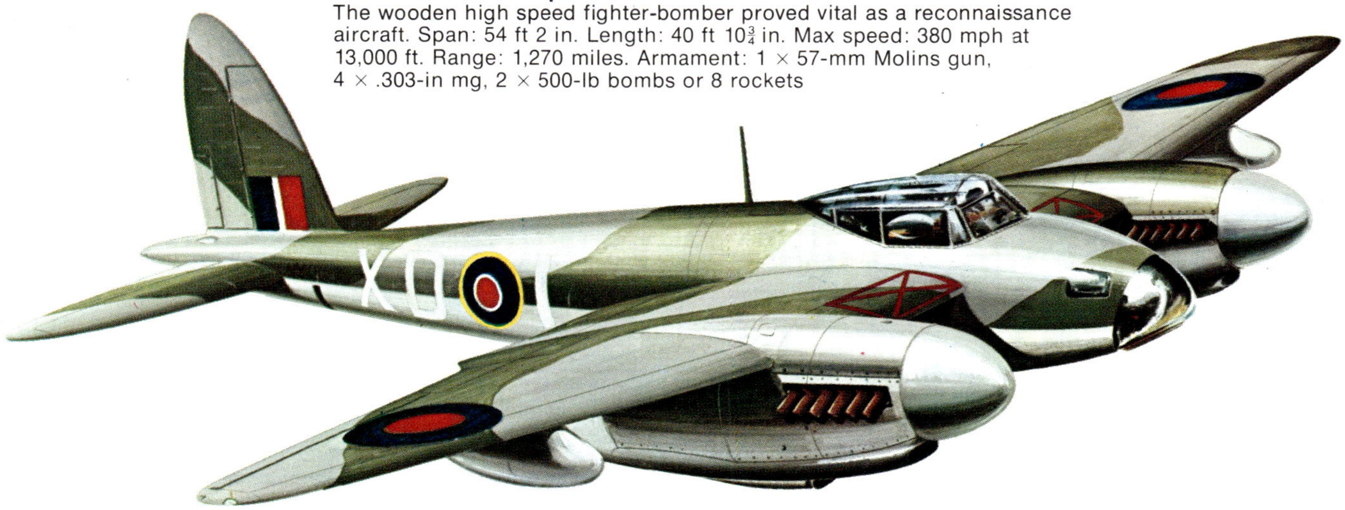

De Havilland Mosquito Mk XVIII
The wooden high speed fighter-bomber proved vital as a reconnaissance aircraft. Span: 54 ft 2 in. Length: 40 ft 10¾ in. Max speed: 380 mph at 13,000 ft. Range: 1,270 miles. Armament: 1 × 57-mm Molins gun, 4 × .303-in mg, 2 × 500-lb bombs or 8 rockets

In addition to all these tasks a sustained attack was pressed against the flying bomb sites and rocket bases, thus to stave off the threat to the assembly areas, the massed shipping, and all the intricate preparations within range of the new weapons.

To meet these commitments Air Chief-Marshal Leigh-Mallory disposed some 5,677 aircraft of the US 9th Air Force and the 2nd Tactical Air Force of the Royal Air Force. Of these, 3,011 were medium, light, fighter, and fighter-bombers, and the remainder transport aircraft, gliders, reconnaissance, and artillery observation aircraft.

Between February 9 and D-Day these forces, aided by the heavy bombers of combined bomber offensive, attacked 80 rail and road targets with 21,949 aircraft dropping 76,200 tons of bombs. Some 51 targets were destroyed, 25 severely damaged, and slight damage was caused to the remaining four. On March 6 Bomber Command made the first heavy attack on Trappes, some 20 miles to the north of Paris, claiming 190 direct hits. The final effect revealed the inadequacy of the existing Intelligence estimates, and went some way towards justifying the claims of the air marshals that they 'felt' and 'thought' they were achieving their various objects. By D-Day railway traffic within 150 miles of the battlefield was at least 75% unusable, and the whole railway system of north-west Europe had been dislocated. Air photography, or even visual observation on the ground, failed to reveal the condition of locomotives and rolling stock still 'in existence', but often held together 'by the last cotter pin' and in no operational state.

Early in May, the tactical air forces opened an all-out assault on trains, railway bridges, and road bridges over the Seine below Paris. Heavy attacks were pressed on Mantes-Gassicourt, Liége, Ghent, Courtrai, Lille, Hasselt, Louvain, Boulogne, Orleans, Metz, Mulhouse, Rheims, Troyes and Charleroi. The pattern of the bombing might as easily have been designed to isolate the Pas de Calais as Normandy, and did not reveal the planned area of the Allied assault. Substantial attacks against road and railway bridges over the Loire waited upon the day. In the event, every bridge serving the battlefield was down.

Attacks on radar installations, wireless telegraphy, and navigational stations paralysed enemy signals, and made air and sea reconnaissance virtually impossible. A total of 49 coastal batteries covering the sea approaches were also attacked with some success, while the long sustained assaults on the German aircraft industry had reduced production by some 60%. It was known that more than 5,000 enemy aircraft had been destroyed in combat between the middle of November and D-Day. These facts, combined with the constant harassing of airfields, and the German losses in trained pilots, effectively banished Luftwaffe interference from the battlefield.

Meanwhile the combined bomber offensive pursued by Harris and Spaatz steadily sapped the industrial strength of the German nation, reducing it to a meagre skeleton, yet with astonishing powers of endurance.

An important side-issue of the offensive against the railways was that 18,000 men of the Todt Organisation (the German forced labour organisation) were forced off urgent work on the strengthening of the 'Atlantic Wall' to undertake the even more urgent tasks of railway repair.

In the last weeks before D-Day German troops, many of them of low calibre, lay almost helpless under the Allied bombs by night and day.

Such is a brief glimpse of the overwhelming contribution of air power in direct support of the Normandy landings. It was enough.

Britain prior to D-Day

AN ISLAND AT WAR

For four years, ever since the withdrawal from Dunkirk, the ultimate inspiration of all British and Allied policy had been the need to strike across the Channel and break Germany's power by occupying her homeland. For the inhabitants of Britain, this had meant a dramatic impact on every facet of civilian life and a subordination of everything to the needs of the most complex and vital military operation in history – an operation which could not afford to fail

Imperial War Museum

GIs fraternise with the natives – English housewives

Imperial War Museum

No visitor to Britain in the early spring of 1944 – and there were some 2,000,000 visitors – could have failed to observe the sources of the island's strength. The evidences of her maritime power, which had enabled her through the centuries, not only to repel the threats of Philip of Spain, Napoleon of France, and Hitler of Germany, but also to found an empire covering one-fourth of the surface of the earth, lay not only in the seas around her, patrolled constantly by big and little ships of war, in the hundreds of ports seething with shipping in astonishing variety, in the numerous 'hards', or ramps, enabling her to launch and land craft of many kinds from beaches and estuaries, in the shipyards bristling with the naked struts and ribs and stays of a great multitude of vessels under construction, and all the immense activities of her coasts, but also deep inland, in her resources in coal, iron, and steel, in heavy and light industry, and above all in the preoccupation of the people.

Ships were not confined to shipyards, they grew in narrow streets, in alleyways, prefabricated in scores of workshops. Not only ships and craft, but 'things to float' rose under the hammers of tens of thousands of workmen. Shipbuilding, it almost seemed, had become a 'cottage industry', and children homing from their schools stopped to stare at the welders and the riveters, fascinated by the steel skeletons taking shape outside their doors.

Even many of the principal activities of the army had a snatch of the sea. Naval and military men worked together in numerous 'combined' tasks under Major-General Sir Percy Hobart's orders.

Churchill and Sherman tanks, after much trial and error, were adapted to deal with the scores of obstacles to be faced in the assault on the Normandy beaches. The 79th Armoured Division grew to nearly 1,000 armoured vehicles, destined to lead the assault.

The demand for crews for the many hundreds of specialised vehicles put a great strain on manpower already strained to the limits, for the crews must be men of skill, courage, and resource, and of strong character, and it seemed that the combined demands of the mass of specialised land and sea vehicles, as well as the naval, military, and Marine Commandos, might strip the conventional services of many of their best personnel. While Hobart was training crews for his amphibians, the navy was training crews for its great host of landing-craft, tank landing-craft, assault landing-craft, gun landing-craft, craft mounted with batteries of rockets which could devastate whole villages with a salvo and which seared the decks of their parent vessels with flame, landing-craft adapted for special survey work, even small submarines known as X-craft to lay off the enemy shore in the shallows. All had to be manned with brave and expert crews, and many were involved in constant action against the enemy through their periods of training.

It is important to underline the remarkable integration of the services in combining sea and land power into a single potent weapon which, in fact, was the 'tin-opener' into Normandy.

In the early spring of 1944, most of these activities were reaching their peaks. The extra month, so desperately needed, so grudgingly gained, before 'D-Day', was revealed as indispensable to success. Without that extra month the great artificial harbours upon which success in sustaining the battle for Normandy must depend, could not have been ready, and the assault, however well it might fare, would have been in vain. These great artificial harbours known as 'Mulberries' and protected by breakwaters known as 'Gooseberries' were of singular complexity, comprising roadways known as 'Whale' units, caissons of steel and concrete, known as 'Phoenix' units, 'Beetles', and a whole 'menagerie' of accessories. A total of 146 Phoenix caissons was needed, ranging from 10 of the smallest size, each of 1,672 tons through six sizes to the 60 largest, each of 6,044 tons. 600,000 tons of concrete, 31,000 tons of steel, and 1,500,000 yards of steel shuttering were consumed in their construction. Eight dry docks and two wet docks, made available with great difficulty, had to be supplemented by 12 great holes excavated on Thames

British troops at bayonet practice. The British Isles became a gigantic training school with the Allied armies as its pupils

side below water level, and leaving a barrier of earth between them and the river. The earth barriers would be breached when the caissons were ready to float out into the stream. Some 20,000 men worked overtime for months while the pumps continuously fought the encroaching waters.

But to construct these strange objects, completely baffling to German air reconnaissance, was not enough. They had not only to float, but to sink, and sink fast in varying depths according to their sizes. After much trial and error the sinking time of the largest caissons was reduced from 1½ hours to 22 minutes. Each 'Phoenix' was also a 'kind of ship', provided with quarters for a crew, and mounting two Bofors guns with 20 tons of ammunition. They could not sail under their own steam, however, and when they were completed it was found that the towing fixture gear was inadequate. Teams of riggers in Chatham naval dockyard worked day and night in the last weeks to make them secure for the tugs.

The safe passage of 146 of these 'monsters' was only one of many towing problems, demanding a great fleet of tugs to deliver them safely across the Channel and manoeuvre them into their exact positions based on the gradient of the sea bottom. There were also, as an item, some 70 old ships, many of them old warships with proud names, to be towed out and sunk to form the 'Gooseberries'.

There were in all more than 3,000 small craft, lighters, and barges, manned by 15,000 men, involved in the 'artificial harbour project', which was going into service direct from the drawing boards. As an item the pier heads, each of 1,000 tons of steel, were needed to anchor on the beaches, and the mass of material behind them, the thousands of yards of 'floating bridge' roadway, had to rise and fall 20 feet with the tide, all within the 24,000 feet of breakwater provided by the sunken blockships.

By such means, Admiral Ramsay, commanding the Allied naval forces, hoped to build a stable bridge to France, and to achieve a delivery of up to 12,000 tons of supplies each day to the 33 divisions to be fed with food and ammunition at the peak of the Mulberry service from the shores of Arromanches. Meanwhile 'Pluto' (Pipe-Line-Under-The-Ocean) was designed to carry oil fuel to Cherbourg, and later to more accessible points on the French and Belgian coasts.

To describe these activities as a microcosm of the tasks involved in launching a successful assault across the Channel against a 60-mile-wide stretch of the 'Atlantic Wall' is perhaps an under-statement, but it is not a serious under-statement. Rear-Admiral W. G. Tennant, who had achieved great things as a captain on the beaches of Dunkirk, saw the 'Mulberry' project through with a naval staff of 500 officers and 10,000 men apart from the large labour force involved. The enterprise tied in with a remarkable galaxy of organisations bearing 'mystical' code names which, from those days, wrote themselves temporarily into the language so that each service developed a form of jargon. 'Buco' stood for the build-up control organisation, 'Turco' for the turn-round control, 'Corep' for the control repair, 'Cotug' for the control tug organisation, and these bred many lesser brands of initials like a warren of rabbits.

Patience and ingenuity

But all these major projects and activities, indeed all the activities taking place in the island, covering all the known facets of war, and many previously unknown, all the intricate plans, the miracles of production, transport, assembly, training, and organisation, were dependent in great measure for success upon the activities of a very small and select band of men combining qualities of great daring with extraordinary patience and ingenuity. Upon the accuracy of the information these men provided would depend success or failure. Air photography, valuable as it was, was not enough. It was essential to know, for example, the exact geological composition of the beaches, the rocks, the runs-in, over 60 miles of enemy-held coast subject to constant vigilance and incessant enemy activity.

It was to such men that General Omar Bradley paid tribute in his book, *A Soldier's Story,* when he feared that his trucks might bog down at one of the planned unloading points on 'Omaha' beach. 'How much dope can you get on the subsoil there?' he asked his G-3. He goes on to record that 'Several days later a lean and reticent British naval lieutenant came to our briefing . . . From his pocket he pulled a thick glass tube. He walked over to the map on the wall. "The night before last," he explained drily, "We visited Omaha beach to drill a core in the shingle at this point near the draw. You can see by the core there is no evidence of silt. The shingle is firmly bedded upon rock. There is little danger of your trucks bogging down." '

General Bradley went on to explain how this lieutenant had taken a submarine through the minefields, paddled ashore 'one evening' in a rubber boat under the muzzles of the German guns, and calmly done his work.

Imperial War Museum

Mulberry pre-fab harbour sections under construction. 'They must float up and down with the tide,' said Churchill. 'Don't argue the matter, the difficulties will argue for themselves.'

Inevitably such men were sometimes caught, and many were killed. Alive or dead they never talked.

In addition, it was of great help to the engineers who would go in ahead of the assault troops, often under water, to know exactly the nature of the many lethal obstacles the enemy constantly devised and sowed in swathes in the sea approaches. These included massive 'Tetrahydra', 'Belgian Gates', and 'Element C'. To know them was to disarm them, and to discover these things, and many others, to explore the estuaries of the Orne, the Vire and lesser streams, to neutralise the German mining of locks that would block the entry of Allied barges and lighters, was the rôle of small tight groups of young men of a physical and nervous calibre to withstand extremes of temperature, to be still almost under the feet of the enemy, to endure many lonely vigils, and with no resources other than the human spirit to sustain them.

Many such men there had been since the days of Dunkirk, and their services were incomparable. For these war provided the opportunities men often seek in vain in peace. Night after moonless-night in summer and winter they left the shores of the island, sneaking out from the quiet estuary of the Hamble, from the Solent, and homing back to the green grass domes of the old Forts Brock-

A shipyard crew work to swell the armada of landing craft

Fox Photos

hurst and Gomer with their 'spoils of war'. Towed in their landing craft adapted for survey work behind naval motor launches, they left their parent craft to propel themselves ashore in folboats or to take at once to the water, using the apparatus for underwater swimming. Thus they moved in the shallows through lethal forests, sometimes laying charges, more often removing those of the enemy, making mental notes from which to produce accurate diagrams, noting tidal conditions, changes of the sea bed, and collecting samples from scores of points for the experts to consider. A sudden doubt in an expert mind would send a party at once back to any given point to check, for on such things must depend the movement of armour out of the sea.

These men, volunteers from the navy and army, comprising many junior officers of the Royal Naval Volunteer Reserve, Royal Marines, Commandos, sergeants, corporals, petty officers, and men, were the weakest link by which the strength of the great chain of Allied effort must be measured. But they were not weak. Their exploits defy exaggeration and invite tears. Frenchmen, Dutchmen, Norwegians, Czechs, Poles, and Belgians made up their numbers, and men of a self-same spirit and humility trained in hundreds to provide naval beach units to organise and lead the men ashore. Long before D-Day they had learned to live with danger and sudden death.

Civilian life had ceased to exist

By February 1944, the island was shrinking fast to grip the hard-pressed inhabitants in a strait jacket, and deprive them of the last shreds of their freedom.

'Over the war years,' wrote COSSAC, 'indignity and inconvenience had been heaped upon the devoted backs of [the people] almost to breaking point.'

In the last few months before D-Day security demanded the imposition of the 'last straws'. The coastal belt of the island was frozen 10 miles deep from the Wash southward and westward to Land's End, and from Dunbar to Arbroath in Scotland. Innumerable prohibited areas, including forests such as Sherwood, had become ammunition dumps, and mazes of airfields, camps, and vehicle parks still further confined the civilian population. Millions of men and women lived within the wire against the sea, millions more inhabited the inner cage, no less restricted than the sealed-off troops. In fact civilian life had almost ceased to exist, yet it was essential that many of its functions should be preserved.

On March 10 all movement, communications, and mail became subject to strict control, but even without control the immense weight of military traffic on roads and railways made civilian movement next to impossible. Few had travelled in comfort for at least three years. Few attempted to go anywhere, although to do so was an immense relief. National Registration and rationing of all food and essential commodities had long since reduced the inhabitants to 'statistics'. Apart from doctors, others on essential business, and a few limited privileged groups, no civilian had the means to use the roads other than by bicycle or on foot. The roads, in any case, had become death-traps over which fast convoys had begun to roar at breakneck speeds in endless streams, so that houses bordering the narrow streets of towns and villages shuddered through all the hours of day and night to the thunder of wheels.

On April 6, all military leave was stopped, and the last slack in the censorship of mails and communications of all kinds was drawn tight. The War Cabinet, gravely troubled, but unable to refuse the reasonable wishes of the Supreme Commander, imposed severe restrictions on diplomatic privileges, held up diplomatic bags, and watched embassies. It was difficult, if not impossible, to grade foreign embassies in a security sense, for the most loyal of allies might harbour enemies or fools. It was simpler to watch all equally rather

Imperial War Museum

US soldiers practise landing craft embarking on a training rig

than to attempt to watch this man or that man more than the next.

These impositions led to serious difficulties, especially with the sensitive Free French, and there remained always the 'Achilles Heel' of Eire, in whose capital city German agents walked freely, listened eagerly, and from whose shores ships might still sail without 'let or hindrance' beyond the inevitable lets and hindrances of a world at war.

Every possible step was taken to seal off all conceivable channels of leakage to the Germans, and in the event only one real scare occurred. This was when a postal package burst open in the Chicago Post Office to reveal secret documents concerning 'Overlord'. A sergeant in *Etousa* Headquarters, London, had posted them to his sister in error. His loyalty was not in doubt. In a different degree, a high-ranking US officer, a class-mate of the Supreme Commander's at West Point, boasted the date of D-Day at a reception in Claridges Hotel. His friendship with the Supreme Commander did not save him from his master's wrath, and shipment home reduced to his basic rank. Even General George Patton, a man of immense warmth, of deep and unusual awareness of the plight of the British people, earned severe reprimand for an 'irresponsible' statement at a party he genuinely believed to be 'within its four walls'.

Yet, at their worst the indignities to which the British people submitted, with growing uneasiness, but with a minimum of grumbling, were trivial to those suffered by the peoples of the

A platoon of black GIs demonstrate 'jazz marching'

Imperial War Museum

occupied countries. They were deeply aware, too, that they wore the very shackles—self imposed, it is true—they fought to destroy, and the arrival of tens of thousands of troops from a huge land, untouched by war, accentuated the 'inequalities of experience' which must inevitably add to the difficulties of mutual understanding when the fight was over.

Indeed, in the spring of 1944, the mood of the British people was undergoing a subtle change, compounded of unease and relief in roughly equal proportions. They were glad of the outward and visible signs of the physical aid they so sorely needed; they feared the unspoken implications of the huge 'invasion' which changed the nature of the island, it might be forever. They were closer in a hundred ways to the refugees, the Europeans and the Scandinavians, in their midst, fighting at their side on similar 'shoestrings' for the return to their Continent, than to the men of the New World with their alien habits and customs, their wealth of food, clothing, money, and with their eyes focused on a different vision. Perhaps it was easier for Churchill with his American blood to know them as 'cousins', to accept the inevitable passing of the precious sovereignty of Britain into hands that he did not regard as alien.

If indeed Britain had admitted a Trojan Horse within her gates, it was none the less certain that the hordes of troops pouring in from it were animated by the best possible intentions, including the very natural desire to return to their own land at the earliest possible moment. Each man had been well briefed on some of the outstanding eccentricities of the British people, and was 'armed' with a booklet designed to aid him in avoiding treading too heavily upon the 'long toes' of the islanders.

Overcrowded island

There were 750,000 members of the United States forces in Britain on January 15, 1944, and new arrivals swelled the number to over 1,500,000 in the following five months. They brought with them an immense variety of weapons, ammunition, equipment, food, and transport, and at a build-up rate of 750,000 tons of supplies a month. All these men and materials had to be channelled through 'their own' ports to the areas assigned to them. It had been fully understood by COSSAC, and his American aides, at an early date, and was constantly emphasised by General Montgomery in the later stages, that it would be disastrous to permit the lines of supply and communication of the Allied armies to cross. Methods of organisation and administration, as well as equipment and supplies, were too diverse to blend.

The fact of two very large armies and all their services and stores based upon the same small and overcrowded island, preparing to sail on the same day to take part in the same assault, and yet to be kept severely apart, posed problems of the utmost intricacy. Warehouses swiftly overflowed, and supplies were camouflaged all along the routes to the embarkation areas.

In the main the Americans occupied the west and south-west coastal belt, their huts and tented camps dotting Cornwall, Devon, and Dorset, with their supply and service 'tails' stretching far back into the Midlands. Hundreds of pieces of private property, farmlands, and whole villages had been taken over in the face of fearsome legal difficulties, and even so the areas suitable for intensive assault training were barely adequate. For the US airborne forces marshalling areas had been set aside north-west and north-east of London, glider troops in the west Midlands, the US 101st Division between Newbury and Exeter, the US 82nd Division in the east.

The British and Canadian forces were assembling in the south, basing themselves mainly upon the Hampshire and Sussex coasts, while the 'armies' of men and women to serve the armies grew alarmingly. One authority records that 54,000 men, 'including the temporary housekeeping services of the entire 5th Armoured Division, were required to establish and maintain installations for mounting the seaborne assault forces alone, and to perform services necessary to make them ready for sailing'. More than 4,500 cooks were trained to cook for them in the first three months of the year, and more than 3,800 trucks moved their supplies.

On another level the generals commanding the assault were fighting to keep down the vehicles to a maximum of 2,500 per assault division against the minimum estimates of 3,000. It seemed impossible to halt the growth of this remarkable case of 'Parkinson's Law' by which ten men would be needed to keep one man in the battle. It meant an even greater strain on the already strained resources in craft to carry and supply this immense load across the Channel.

Meanwhile a thousand feats of skill and daring went unsung in those days when 'scratch' crews set sail cheerfully day after day to cross the Atlantic in 'ships' which would give a rough ride in coastal waters. US tank landing craft crossed to Britain under their own power right up to D-Day. It proved impossible to maintain the high standard of training for all the crews, nevertheless the standard was higher than it had ever been before.

Similar problems of supply and training confronted the airmen to meet the demands in transport planes and crews to carry the three airborne divisions assigned to the Day.

The most meticulous planning of detail was necessary to ensure that all this mass of men, vehicles, and shipping should come together at the right places at the right times, and with all that they would need, organised in the right order behind them. The last things in would be the first things out, and the supply lines had to be organised accordingly. At the same time the concentrations of men and shipping had to be camouflaged as much as possible from the enemy, and the innumerable activities of warfare slanted always to give a false impression of the target. The smoke of many fires rose from scores of dummy camps, while diversionary sorties in the Channel and far to the north were the constant pre-occupations of

US Air Force

Stockpile of bombs on a US air base. Montgomery forecast that air power would 'hold the ring' over the beaches

naval and air forces. Some sections of a Mulberry were sunk off Dungeness to mislead the enemy. Extensive mine-laying operations bore a curious pattern from the southern Baltic, between Sweden and Denmark, and down to the Pas de Calais, and air attacks against U-boats off the Norwegian coasts were designed to feed the fears of the enemy that an assault might be expected in that quarter. From Milford Haven to Harwich the southern ports of Britain were crammed with invasion shipping, and this led to an enormous concentration of ships of every conceivable kind in the northern and north-eastern ports. The 'look' of the island, and the patterns of its actions could be read to mean an assault against almost anywhere. Carefully planted stories among elements of the resistance forces from Norway through Holland and France still further misled the enemy.

Intensive training for the Day took place on land, sea, and sky side by side with the live operations of war. Brigades were landed with live ammunition under covering fire on the shores of Suffolk, north and south Devon, and Dorset, as tens of thousands of Americans, Canadians, and British rehearsed the ordeals they must face, and the crews of the landing craft learned to beach and unbeach their craft. In the more rugged parts of Scotland, Commandos brought themselves to the peak of training, nearly all of them blooded in a score of assaults.

In September 1943, the US Lieutenant-Colonel Paul Thompson had established a training area on the perfect sweep of sandy beach between the headlands of Morte and Baggy on the north Devon coast, and many hundreds of Americans owe their lives to his ingenuity, his ability to learn as well as to teach, and to imagine almost every possibility. From January to May 1944, Colonel Thompson put all the regiments of the US 29th Division and 4th Division, the 16th Infantry Regiment of the 1st Division, and elements of the 101st Airborne, through courses simulating war.

Coils of barbed wire snaked out of the sandy draws of the combe, mines and bombs erupted in spouts of black smoke, flame, and sand, and thousands of men leapt from their assault craft, up and over the beaches to the violent music of war. The authentic din of battle was there, but the leading actor did not attend rehearsals. Men did

On an RAF base US C-47 transport aircraft taxi to dispersal. Not only bombs but men would rain from the skies on D-Day

US Air Force

not choke and drown in their own blood, gaps did not open to leave men 'naked and alone', spattered with the entrails, blood, and brains of their friends, nor did flying limbs and fragments torn from the bowels of men smite survivors haphazard, as though the world had become suddenly the playground of some hideous poltergeists. Nor were the coils of wire littered with the obscene offal of war.

It was exciting; it was the best that could be devised, but the indescribable tension when the ramps go down was lacking. Only the Day would produce the reality.

Through all March, April, and May, enemy naval and air activity increased in the Channel. Motor launches and E-boats clashed as the enemy moved his slender naval resources in small craft from Brest to Le Havre and Cherbourg. Twice destroyers fought with equal loss to both sides. On every dark night enemy aircraft sowed mines in the southern coastal waters of the island, and a few bombs did negligible damage. In the middle of May the first U-boat was sighted in the Channel, but the major worry of Admiral Ramsay came from the enemy concentrations of mines, the greatest threat to the success of 'Neptune'. Swiftly the mine-sweeping flotillas were alerted, and detailed plans made for the greatest mine-sweeping operation ever to be contemplated. For the Day, the broad clear channel must be swept to France, and the buoys placed to mark the way. There would be no time, or opportunity, for rehearsal, but for the men manning the flotillas their daily and nightly tasks were the 'real thing'.

On April 26, the invasion forces for the assault were finally sealed in their embarkation areas. The 'mighty gun' was primed. Two thousand security men watched and waited over the Americans in the south-west and south, hundreds of security troops likewise watched the British and Canadian perimeters. The ships in the ports, the estuaries, the anchorages, were sealed. The Wrens serving the little ships, ciphering, secretarying, driving, were as steadfast as men, and knew or guessed the secret things. But there was no place in all the island, within or without the wire, where the great silence was not felt, and understood. It was like a gigantic boil coming to a head.

E-boat sweep

Two days after the sealing the worst tragedy of training overtook the infantry landing ships and men of part of the American Force U, exercising in the Channel in one of the two final assault rehearsals, code named 'Tiger' and 'Fabius'. Two German E-boat flotillas swooped in to sink two tank landing ships and damage a third. It is known that 749 men, predominantly engineer troops, lost their lives.

Perhaps no other incident reflected so grimly the shortage of assault shipping, for the Supreme Commander at once reported to the Combined Chiefs-of-Staff that the loss of the LSTs had reduced the reserve 'to nothing'

The D-Day problem involved the pre-loading of 185,000 men and 20,000 vehicles in the initial assault lift, and thereafter the maintenance of a steady flow of men, equipment, and stores to the beaches. These would be carried in 4,200 landing ships and craft, supported by 1,200 merchant ships and ancillary vessels, and with 1,200 warships, including seven battleships and 23 cruisers. In the wake of this vast armada all the strange floating shapes of concrete and steel of the Mulberries would lollop through the waters towed by a fleet of 100 tugs and ferries. Beach organisations would be set up ready to meet them, and trained crews would begin the complex task of erection. Frogmen and engineers working in the shallows would clear the forests of obstacles, and dismantle heavily mined contraptions of angle iron and steel.

Through the hours of darkness before the dawn the airborne vanguard, nearly 20,000 strong, would be carried in 1,087 transport aircraft and gliders to their dropping zones behind the beaches. Some 10,000 aircraft would add to the immense weight of naval fire power, which itself would be the heavy orchestra behind the rocket batteries and Bofors of the support landing craft, and the guns of tanks and artillery firing from their landing craft on the run in.

The Neptune plan, covering every phase of the assault, except the air, made a printed book foolscap size 3 inches thick. The first 47 convoys were fully mapped, together with minesweeper flotilla positions hour by hour, and the courses of innumerable tank landing craft and other vessels were plotted in a shuttle service to and from their 'home' beaches to their 'home' ports, to cut navigational sailing hazards to a minimum. Each ship and its destination was at once recognisable by code lettering and numbering prominently displayed. The loads of ammunition, armour, equipment, and men awaited them at every turn-round, and their own guns would be cleaned and replenished by dedicated teams of men and women who had lived by and served their little ships in the estuaries and ports through the long days and nights of waiting. An elaborate organisation for salvage and repair had been worked out to the last detail.

On April 26, Admiral Sir Bertram Ramsay, Commander-in-Chief, Naval Forces, moved into his advanced HQ at Southwick House, Portsmouth, and the five divisions chosen to assault the five main Normandy beaches in the Bay of Seine, moved into their embarkation areas with all their specialised assault troops, armour, and ancillaries.

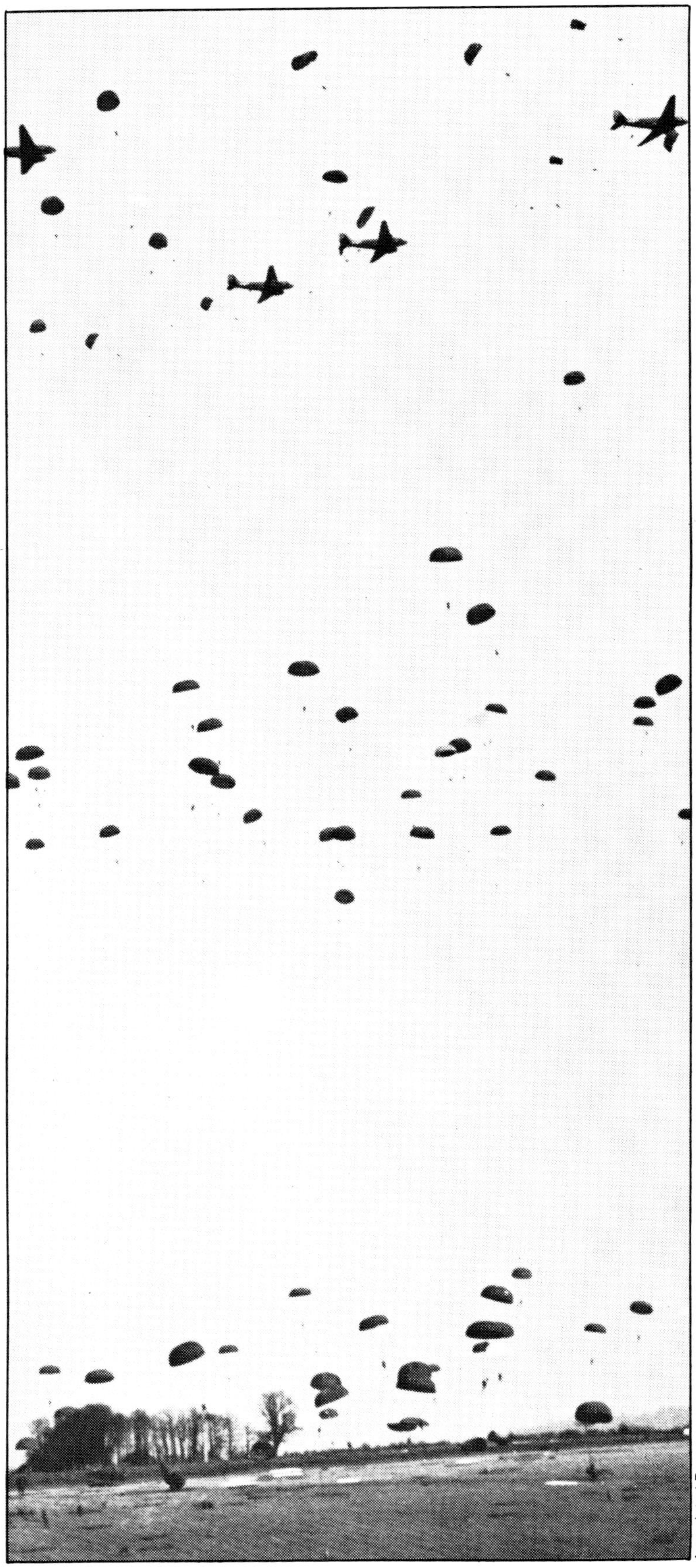

Associated Press

Left: Beneath low flying Dakotas the parachutes of US paratroops billow during a training drop over southern England

Right: With toy soldier precision and with neatly marked mine-free lanes, British soldiers practise beach landing

Imperial War Museum

The moment of transfer from mother ship to landing craft called for a high degree of seamanship and rehearsal

Each assaulting force bore the initial letter of the code-name given to the beach it would assault.

- The western force, U for 'Utah', the US 4th Infantry Division of 7th Corps of the US 1st Army, spearheaded by 8th RCT concentrated upon Torbay, Brixham, Dartmouth, and Salcombe, would assault the Cherbourg Peninsula north-west of the Vire river on the extreme right flank.
- Force O for 'Omaha', the US 1st Infantry Division of 5th Corps of the US 1st Army, spearheaded by 16th RCT, would assault east of the Vire, concentrated upon Weymouth, Portland, and Poole.
- The follow-up Force B, the US 29th Infantry Division, spearheaded by 116th RCT and with two battalions of US Rangers on its right, would assault on the right of the 1st Division, concentrated upon Plymouth, Falmouth, Helford river, and Fowey. Behind them the build-up divisions concentrated upon Bristol Channel ports.
- The eastern force, G for 'Gold', spearheaded by the British 50th Division of the 30th Corps of the British 2nd Army, with No. 47 Commando strengthening its right, would assault Arromanches, east of Port en Bessin, concentrated upon Southampton facing the Channel.
- Force J for 'Juno', concentrated upon Southampton, the Solent, and Spithead, was spearheaded by the Canadian 3rd Division of the 1st Corps of the British 2nd Army, and would assault astride the Seulles river between la Rivière and Courseulles sur Mer.
- Force S for 'Sword', concentrated upon Portsmouth, Newhaven, and Shoreham, was spearheaded by the British 3rd Infantry Division of the 1st Corps of the British 2nd Army, and with the 1st and 4th Special Services Brigades on the right, and the No. 4 Commando on the left, would assault the beaches covering Douvres and Ouistreham.
- The follow-up Force L, the 7th Armoured Division of the 30th Corps, concentrated upon Harwich and the Nore, and would assault behind the 50th Division. The build-up divisions concentrated upon Thames ports.

The flails and specialised armour of Hobart's 79th Armoured Division would be at the service of the British and Canadians, but were refused by General Bradley. DD 'swimming' tanks would be supporting the entire assault.

In the assault the US 1st Army would be commanded by General Omar Bradley, until the arrival of the US 3rd Army commanded by Lieutenant-General George S. Patton, when Bradley would assume command of the US 12th Army Group.

The British 2nd Army was commanded by Lieutenant-General Miles Dempsey. The Canadian 1st Army, commanded by Lieutenant-General Crerar, would follow. The 21st Army Group was commanded by General Sir Bernard Montgomery, Ground Force Commander for the assault and the Battle for Normandy.

State of suspense

Thus on April 26, the first rumblings of the great avalanche in its initial heave could be felt in every corner of the British Isles. At that time neither D-Day nor H-Hour had been fixed. The last arguments on time and tide, phases of the moon, even daylight or dark, had not been thrashed out to a final conclusion. Nevertheless, none doubted, however little 'in the know', that the hour was drawing near, that it could not be long delayed, that it seemed, in an eerie way, almost 'out of the hands of men', gathering its own momentum. A state of suspense gripped the inhabitants of the island; soldiers, sailors, airmen, the millions in shipyards, the foundries, the factories, the fields, the homes, the railwaymen, the dockers, the police and firemen, and public servants, all were at war. The distinction between 'soldier' and 'civilian' had become blurred to the point when it had become almost meaningless, save for the élite, that dwindling band of men who would confront the enemy in the vanguard of battle.

'Sooner or later,' General Wavell had said, 'the time will come when Private Snodgrass must advance straight to his front.'

The hour was at hand.

Imperial War Museum

The Waiting is Over

THE GREAT GAMBLE BEGINS

They had trained on remote beaches. They had been shuttled and shunted in darkened trains. The Allied armies were like a gigantic coil spring winding and waiting in grey limbo—aware that a moment would come when they would be disgorged upon an enemy shore, bristling with devices of death, swept by withering fire. All they were waiting for was the weather.

By June 4 the weather was so bad that the invasion had to be delayed for one day. On the 5th, though conditions were still terrible, there was some slight chance of improvement. Appalled by the chaos which must ensue if there was any more delay, Eisenhower decided that the great gamble must be taken: D-Day, the assault on Hitler's Europe, would be June 6

US Army

US Navy

287,000 men and a host of armoured fighting vehicles were pre-loaded into ships, as early as the first of the month

Imperial War Museum

△ Grim-faced American troops file aboard a landing ship.
▽ British soldiers pass the time learning about their target.

Imperial War Museum

Imperial War Museum

The Airborne Assault

COUNT DOWN TO H-HOUR

The day had dawned: the first Allied troops drifted down from the sky and struggled from the sea to begin the battle for Europe. For some it was to be an anti-climax to the months of waiting, training, thinking, wondering. For others it was to be chaos, confusion, and death. On one beach men walked ashore with next to no opposition, on its neighbour they were pinned down and massacred. There were moments of near disaster when a resolute German attack might have shattered the Allied beachheads, but the Germans too were confused and bewildered by the weight of the massive attack. By evening the Allied foothold was secure: the great gamble had paid off

Airborne Pathfinders, leaders of the paratroop drops which heralded the invasion, check their watches before take-off

Lieutenant-Colonel Hoffmann had just glanced at his watch. The time was forty minutes past midnight. June 6 was less than three-quarters of an hour old. For the past hour there had been a continuous drone of aircraft above the battle headquarters of III Battalion, 919th Grenadier Regiment, east of Montebourg.

Another wave was approaching. The roar grew louder.

Hoffmann stepped outside the bunker. He gave a start. Six giant birds were making straight for his battle headquarters. They were clearly visible, for the moon had just broken through the clouds. 'They're bailing out.' For an instant Hoffmann thought the aircraft had been damaged and its crew was going to jump. But then he understood. This was an airborne landing by paratroops. The white mushrooms were floating down – straight at his bunker.

'Alarm! Enemy paratroops!' The men at III Battalion headquarters had never pulled on their trousers so fast before.

'Alarm! Alarm!'

The sentries' carbines were barking. They were firing at the parachutes floating down from the sky. Then the moon hid itself. Darkness enveloped the descending enemy. Hoffmann grabbed a rifle. Then the darkness was rent by the first burst of fire from an American submachine-gun.

The battle for Normandy was on.

Fifty miles south-east of the battle headquarters of III Battalion, 919th Grenadier Regiment, on the far side of the Orne, things were also fairly noisy. The German sentry on the eastern end of the bridge over the Caen canal at Bénouville jumped as some 50 yards in front of his concrete sentry-box a spectral aircraft swooped towards the ground without any engine noise. A moment later there was a crash and a splintering sound, then quiet.

The sentry snatched his carbine from his shoulder and loaded. He held his breath, listening. 'A crashed bomber,' was his first thought. After all, enemy bomber formations had been roaring overhead in from the coast for well over an hour. From the Caen direction came the noise of explosions. Anti-aircraft guns were barking from the neighbourhood of Troarn.

'They've had it,' thought Private Wilhelm Furtner. Then a searing flash blinded his eyes. He no longer heard the burst of the phosphorus grenade.

His comrades in the dugout by the approach to the bridge leapt up. They raced to their machine-gun. They fired a burst at random. They saw nothing. Suddenly they heard voices calling: 'Able-Able.' They did not know that this was the recognition signal of A Detail of a combat team of the British 6th Airborne Division, one of whose gliders had just crash-landed there in front of them. The lance-corporal of the guard was about to lift up the telephone to give the alarm to his platoon commander on the far side of the bridge. But there was no time. Two hand-grenades came sailing in through the aperture of the pill-box. Finished.

There was no point now in keeping quiet. The hand-grenades were bound to have roused the guard on the far side. With shouts of 'Able-Able' the Tommies galloped across the bridge.

They heard other gliders crashing. They also heard the rallying cries of B Detail: 'Baker-Baker.' And a moment later they could hear C Detail as well: 'Charlie-Charlie.'

The German machine-gun was blazing away over the bridge. The first Tommies were falling. But the bulk of them got through. A short skirmish. The guard on the bridge was overwhelmed. The crossing of the Caen canal at Bénouville was in British hands. Only Lance-Corporal Weber got away. He tore through the village to the commandant. 'British paratroops have seized the canal bridge.' What he did not know was that the nearby bridge over the Orne at Ranville had also been seized by men of the British 5th Parachute Brigade in a surprise attack. At 2nd Battalion, 192nd Panzer

Associated Press

Grenadier Regiment, at Cairon the field telephone rang: 'Launching immediate counterattack against enemy paratroops in Bénouville bridgehead.'

At the Dives bridge, on the Varaville-Grangues road, another sentry was peering into the night. The watch at the bridge was mounted by II Battalion, 744th Infantry Regiment, which was barely a platoon in strength. The men had every reason to curse the bridge. Four weeks previously III Battalion had organised a night exercise without warning neighbouring units, and staged a dummy attack on the bridge. The sentry, of course, could not have known that the shots that suddenly came from the approach to the bridge were blanks. He had thought the balloon had gone up in earnest and opened up with his machine-gun. There had been several wounded and two men killed. There was a terrible rumpus and some very unpleasant investigations. All that flashed through the mind of the sentry on the bridge when, shortly after midnight, he saw three men with blackened faces charge up the embankment. 'Silly fools,' he called out to them contemptuously. But then he jumped. Too late. He was given no time to call out or to scream. Without a sound he collapsed, stabbed by a long paratroop knife. From then onward it was an easy matter for the Tommies. Five minutes later the bridge was blown sky high.

'Let's wait and see'

It was exactly 0111 hours when the field telephone rang on General Marcks's desk at 84th Corps headquarters in St Lô. Marcks and his staff officers were still sitting over their maps. The general himself picked up the receiver. He listened. He raised his head and motioned his chief-of-staff to listen in with him. The call was from chief of operations, 716th Division. Hurriedly the words tumbled out of the earpiece: 'Enemy paratroops have landed east of the Orne estuary. Main area is Bréville-Ranville and the northern edge of the forest of Bavent. Main objective apparently the Dives bridges and the crossings over the Orne. Countermeasures are in progress.' The news had the effect of a thunderbolt. Was it the invasion? Or were they merely strong liaison groups dropped to link up with the French Resistance? These were the questions to be answered. After a little hesitation Major Hayn shook his head. 'Too close to our front line. The Resistance people would never risk that.' His conclusion was: 'This is the invasion.' General Marcks nodded. 'Let's wait and see.'

They were still arguing the pros and cons when Colonel Hamann, acting commander, 709th Division, came through on the telephone: 'Enemy paratroops south of St Germain-de-Varreville and at Ste Marie-du-Mont. A second group west of the Merderet river and on the road at Ste Mère-Église. Headquarters of III Battalion, 919th Grenadier Regiment, holding prisoners from the US 101st Airborne Division.'

The time was 0145 hours. Five minutes later, at exactly 0150, the telephones were also ringing in Paris, in a big block of flats on the Bois de Boulogne. The chief of operations of Naval Group West, Captain Wegener, summoned his officers to the situation room. 'I think the invasion is here,' he said calmly.

Admiral Hoffmann, the chief-of-staff, did not even wait to dress. He grabbed a dressing-gown and rushed into the situation room. The reports from the radar stations under Lieutenant von Willisen were unanimous: 'Large number of blips on the screens.'

At first the technicians thought the huge number of blips must be caused by some interference. There just could not be so many ships. But presently no doubt was left. A vast armada must be approaching the Normandy coast.

'This can only be the invasion fleet,' Hoffmann concluded. He ordered: 'Signal to C-in-C West. Signal to the Führer's headquarters. The invasion is on.'

But both in Paris and in Rastenburg the news was received sceptically. 'What, in this weather? Surely your technicians must be mistaken?' Even the chief-of-staff of C-in-C West scoffed: 'Maybe a flock of seagulls?' They still would not believe it. But the navy was certain. Naval headquarters alerted all coastal stations and all naval forces in port: 'The invasion fleet is coming!'

[*From* Invasion – they're coming! *by Paul Carell (George Harrap & Co. Ltd.)*]

Through the hours of darkness the immense convoys moved steadily, unmolested, on their courses in the buoyed channels cleared by the mine-sweeping flotillas, a wedge more than 50 miles wide, and with scores of small fighting ships ranging far out on the flanks probing for the enemy. There was nothing. The long lines of ships seemed to unwind on fabulous spools, drawing their component threads from a hundred havens of the English coast, to weave them into thick skeins to the Bay of Seine. The fierce turbulence of wind and sea failed to mask the strange 'unnatural' silence of the night. The sustained thunder of the fleets of bombers overhead, quenched for those below by the drenching sounds of sea, and the shuddering stresses of steel plates, seemed to accentuate the absence of the enemy. It seemed impossible that such an avalanche of ships and men could muster through the months, at last to fill the English Channel from shore to shore, and remain undetected. Surely no instrument more 'scientific' than the human ear would be needed to hear so vast a throb of power!

No signs of detection

Before the sun had set on the evening of the 5th, two flotillas of mine-sweepers stood off the coast of Normandy, well within sight, and easily able to distinguish houses on shore with the naked eye. The midget submarines of Lieutenant Honour's command were at their stations, close inshore marking the eastern flank and the dangerous rocks. There were no signs of detection. From 0200 hours on the 6th, the HQ ships of the assault moved into their transport areas, and prepared to put their assault craft into the water. The only interference came from the unfriendly sea, and the weather was not alone to thank, or blame, for this.

The sustained attacks from the air on the elaborate Early Warning System of the enemy had succeeded almost too well. In the entire Neptune Area from Cap d'Antifer to Barfleur, 74 radar stations were out of action, and the 18 still capable of working were silent. But it was not enough simply to blind the enemy, it was important also to mislead. For this purpose ten stations were deliberately left in working order north of the Seine, and on to these screens the Royal Navy contrived to produce a misleading web of shapes and echoes. It seems extravagant that such a claim is made, for it reveals a predominance over the enemy that reduces his forces to a stricken body, lacerated on all sides, unable to fly or float, but capable of inflicting grievous, even crippling, wounds upon those seeking to deliver the *coup de grâce*.

But there was no inclination on the part of the Allies to underestimate the powers of the German army in the west. Thus all through June 5 and the night, 105 aircraft of the RAF and 34 little ships of the Royal Navy contrived by means of weaving patterns over the sky and sea, and flying barrage balloons, to produce the 'echoes' in the enemy radar ears of a substantial fleet approaching the Pas de Calais. At the same time jamming operations and diversions were carried on against Cap d'Antifer and Barfleur. The silent approach of the great armada to spread out in a fan from 8 to 12 miles offshore enclosing the Bay of Seine is the measure of success.

Soon after 9 o'clock, the unusual length and content of the BBC broadcast warning to the French Resistance alarmed the Germans, and the XV Army in the Pas de Calais was alerted, while the VII Army in Normandy remained undisturbed. Nothing, it seemed, could prise von Rundstedt's mind away from its preconceived fixations, even the deadly facts of the elements of three airborne divisions dropping in the midst of his forces. Well before the first assault craft of the seaborne forces were in the water, the battle on land was joined.

AIR DROP IN THE WEST: 'CHAOS WILL REIGN'

Within half-an-hour of sunset on the night of June 5, while the leading ships of the seaborne assault moved into the buoyed channels to steer for France, the Pathfinders of the United States and British air forces took off from their English fields to light their beacons in the fields of Normandy. Soon after midnight these small vanguards of élite troops were moving silently in the midst of the enemy, the British to mark the dropping zones for the 6th Airborne Division to the north-east of Caen on the eastern flank, the Americans astride the Merderet river, and the road Carentan-Montebourg-Cherbourg in the area of Ste Mère-Église. Behind them more than 1,200 aircraft bore nearly 20,000 men into battle; then the gliders for which the paratroops must clear the way.

The last warning of the brigadier commanding the British 3rd Parachute Brigade may well serve for all: 'Do not be daunted if chaos reigns: it undoubtedly will.'

The drop of the US 101st Airborne Division, as fully plotted as all subsequent information has made possible, spatters the map over an area 25 miles long by 15 miles broad, and with small isolated elements even further afield. Very few of these had even an outside chance of becoming part of the division. The men had been loosed, as it seems, recklessly upon the winds, and thence to the flooded hinterlands, and maze of closed country, behind Utah Beach.

The US 82nd Airborne Division, largely due to the arrival of one regiment reasonably on its objectives, fared a little better, but of the remainder of the division only 4% were dropped in their zones west of the Merderet river. Thus the tasks of the division west of the Merderet, and the crossings of the Merderet and Douve rivers, could not be fulfilled. The division had become a regiment.

At dawn, when the seaborne landings were coming in on Utah Beach, the 101st Airborne Division mustered 1,100 men out of 6,600. By evening its strength had grown to 2,500 men. The 82nd Airborne Division, at least 4,000 men short on the day, was still only at one-third of its strength three days later. Both divisions had lost great quantities of equipment, and almost their entire glider-borne

Associated Press

AS DAWN BREAKS

artillery, much of it in the floods of the Merderet and Douve rivers. Neither division was able to prepare adequately for the arrival of its glider-borne follow-up, the losses were severe and tragic.

Yet the remarkable fact is that so great a confusion was created in the enemy by this incoherent scattering of men in their midst that there was no possibility of reserves supporting the beach defenders.

No coherent pattern has ever emerged from the struggles of the isolated remnants of the airborne divisions on that day; nor will such a pattern ever emerge. The individual contributions of many men who fought bravely alone or in twos and threes will never be assessed. Even those who gave up without a fight added to rather than subtracted from enemy bewilderment. The Pathfinders of the airborne divisions did not do well. Many failed to find and to mark the dropping zones; some beacons were missing entirely, especially west of the Merderet in country infested by enemy; others were wrongly placed.

Major-General Maxwell Taylor, commanding the 101st, dropped with a nucleus of his divisional HQ, and struggled all through the day to make contact and to bring some sort of order out of chaos. He felt 'alone on the Cotentin'. In the upshot the pattern may be seen dimly in the struggles of half-a-dozen colonels, each managing to group between 75 and 200 men round him, aided by the tell-tale click-clack of the toy 'crickets' with which every man was provided.

By a stroke of remarkable fortune a small band of men ambushed and killed the commander of the German 91st Division, returning from an 'exercise' conference to his headquarters. Thus the 91st Division, trained in the role of defence against airborne attack, and forming almost the sole available reserve behind the defenders of the Cotentin coast, was deprived of its commander and severely handicapped.

While many German officers were sure that this must be the beginning of the main Allied assault – so long awaited and expected – and that the battlefield was Normandy, others, including Lieutenant-General Speidel, Rommel's Chief-of-Staff, and Lieutenant-General Blumentritt, Chief-of-Staff to Rundstedt, were doubtful. Thus the German military machine remained hesitant and palsied, its slender reserves uncommitted, its armour waiting, Rommel out of touch, Hitler sleeping. These things gave the airborne troops on the western flank an initial advantage of which, perforce, they were unaware, and saved them from the possibility of annihilation.

Throughout the whole day and night the 101st Airborne Division, reduced to much less than the effective strength of a single regiment, was not only isolated from its own widely scattered units, but also in complete ignorance of the fate of the 82nd Airborne Division. Ironically, it may have achieved at least as much in its confusion as it could have hoped for in coherence, for chaos bred chaos.

The story of the 82nd Airborne Division is simple. Two of its regiments with the tasks of clearing the area west of the Merderet river and in the angle of the Douve, were not in the fight. It fell to one regiment to save the day, and to fight the one clear-cut battle fought by the US airborne forces on D-Day. While scores of men struggled in the swamps of the Merderet, dragging themselves towards the dry land of the railway embankment, concerned in the main with the problem of survival, the third regiment had dropped in a fairly tight group to the north-west of Ste Mère-Église. This was not due to chance, but to the determination of the pilots to find their targets. Long before the dawn, Lieutenant-Colonel Krause, finding himself on the outskirts of Ste Mère-Église with roughly a quarter of his battalion, bounced the town without waiting for more, and taking the enemy completely by surprise began to establish a solid base and by the afternoon the town was securely held.

The 82nd Airborne had dropped on the fringe of the assembly area of the German 91st Division, and its position from the outset was much more precarious than that of the 101st. All troops, however fragmentary, were at once in the midst of the enemy, and fighting for their lives within minutes of finding their feet. Some small groups up to 50 or 60 strong fought all day in the ditches and hedgerows within 1,000 yards of others with whom it was impossible to make contact. Often they were unaware of their nearness.

The performance of the 101st and 82nd Airborne Divisions on D-Day may only be seen in fragmentary terms. At the end of the day the divisions had not made contact. Each believed it had lost some two-thirds of its troops. Neither one had cause for satisfaction, or the haziest idea of what was happening. All that they could do was to wait for the morning.

Fortunately, the enemy's confusion was equivalent to almost total breakdown. Hammered savagely and incessantly from the air, handicapped by the chance of a conference at Rennes of their senior commanders coinciding with the assault, their communications disrupted, and with, as it seems, a premonition of inevitable doom, their resistance was as fragmentary as that of the airborne troops infesting their imaginations as well as their fields. Many surrendered almost without a fight. Major von der Heydte, commanding the German VI Parachute Regiment, probably the finest enemy troops available in the Carentan area, has told of his difficulties in getting orders from his senior commanders. From the church steeple of St Come-du-Mont he had a personal view of the seaborne armada on the western flank. It seemed to him curiously detached from reality, almost peaceful. At noon the sun was shining, and the whole scene reminded him 'of a summer's day on the Wannsee'. The immense bustle of landing craft, and the warships fading into the horizon, lacked to his ears the orchestration of battle.

Von der Heydte sent his three battalions into battle, one to the north to attack Ste Mère-Église, another to the north-east to protect the seaward flank in the area Ste Marie-du-Mont, the third back on Carentan. Von der Heydte almost at once lost contact. Organised defence on the western flank had crumbled.

H-HOUR DRAWS NEAR

H-HOUR AND THE RAMPS ARE DOWN

At 0200 hours on June 6, the leading ships of Force U, organised in 12 convoys comprising 865 vessels commanded by Rear-Admiral Moon, USN, moved into their assembly area 12 miles off the western coast of the Cotentin Peninsula, opposite the dunes of Varreville—Utah Beach. The assault upon Utah Beach on the extreme western flank was virtually an isolated operation. If all else failed it might have been reinforced to establish a bridgehead, to cut off the Cotentin Peninsula, gaining Cherbourg as a major port from which to mount some subsequent effort. In that event Overlord would be no more.

Field Order 1 states: '7th Corps assaults Utah Beach on D-Day at H-Hour and captures Cherbourg with minimum delay.'

Steadily in the hours before dawn the orders to 7th Corps reduced down to those few who would debouch into the shallows of the unfriendly sea. The 4th Infantry Division would establish the bridgehead; the 8th Infantry Regiment leading—the 1st Battalion on the right, 'Green beach'; the 2nd Battalion on the left, 'Red beach'; two companies of each battalion forward; 30 men to each landing craft; five landing craft to each company, 20 landing craft carrying 600 men in the van, with two companies of the 70th Tank Battalion in the first wave (see map on pages 1806/07). Behind them, wave upon wave of their fellows and the waves of the sea, H+5, H+15, H+17, H+30, on and on through all the day and night, and beyond; infantry, armour, engineers, into the shallows, through the obstacles, the mine-fields, over the beaches, the sea wall, the causeways, the floods, inland to the villages and fields; 27 miles across the neck of the peninsula, Carentan to Lessay; north to Cherbourg.

H-Hour on the western flank was 0630 hours, but along the invasion beaches tidal-variations decreed four different H-Hours from right to left, from Utah Beach to Sword Beach, a span of one hour and 25 minutes. But the men on the right were in their own cocoons of loneliness. Now, in the bitter morning, they were being buffeted in the shallow draft vessels, the dark sky above them wild with the roar of aircraft, the crescendo rising, the blasting roar of the main armament, the scream of shells, and all around a turbulence of men and craft.

To the left, for nearly 50 miles, variations on the theme were unfolding over the waters, Omaha, Gold, Juno, Sword, and over the dark shore-line from end to end the dust was rising, blasted in towering columns by shells and bombs to hang, an opaque and ominous curtain, above the stage.

Enemy shells air-bursting over the water, the spasmodic explosions of mines, the shouts of men floundering, arms flung out, weighed down by equipment, created an uproar in the mind and senses in which the last cries of the lost, the total personal tragedies, were no more than the plaintive squeakings of mice in a cage of lions. The 60 men of Battery B, 29th Field Artillery Battalion, became a statistic on the debit side, dark shadows threshing in the water, under the water, part of the pattern at the bottom of the sea.

But the pattern advanced, untroubled by calamity, the second wave, the bulldozers on their craft, the special engineer units, all in position, the heavy armament of the bombarding squadron blasting the grey dawn to crimson shreds, 40 minutes to go. Some 276 aircraft of the US 9th Air Force roaring in over the beach defences, delivering their bombs, 4,404 bombs each of 250 pounds upon seven targets, 'according to the book'.

Seventeen of the 33 supporting craft seemed to tear the crackling scalp off the universe in an unbearable rasping agony as their mattresses of rockets shuddered inshore. Other craft were machine-gunning, perhaps in the hope of detonating mines, perhaps simply to boost morale, but all 'drenching the beaches with fire'.

About 700 yards to go, and on time, ten assault craft, 300 men on the left, ten assault craft, 300 men on the right; in their wakes 28 DD tanks, swimming, slopping the choppy water across their grey backs, the long muzzles of their guns like snouts, a seeming miracle thanks to the bold initiative and swift decision of their commander to launch close in at 3,000 yards, 'not according to the book'.

From their flimsy assault craft, pitching in the surf, US troops hit the beaches and a frantic rush against an unseen enemy

US Coast Guard

US Navy

The beach was almost invisible behind the sand pall, blasted by gunfire and bombs, joining it to the sky, and in it, under it, the enemy – if there could be an enemy!

Some 67 of the bombers had failed to release their bombs, one-third of the remainder had fallen between high and low water mark, the bulk of the rest on the fortifications of La Madeleine.

A swift, painless landing

Out of the leading wave of the assault craft smoke projectiles hurtled to the sky, demanding silence from the gunners of the bombarding force. About 300 yards to go, and the ramps down, 300 men of the 2nd Battalion, waist deep in water, floundering, finding their feet, wading in, rifles held high, to the dry sand, and the sudden upsurge of spirit. Normandy, the first men ashore, and not a shot out of the haze of battle, the grey shapes of the tanks crawling up out of the sea in their 'skirts', striking terror to the few who still lifted up their heads in the defences and dared to fire, a few wavering shots, 'desultory fire'.

These few men, and their comrades in the van, landing within minutes on their right, did not know that the south-easterly set of the tide had carried them more than a mile south of their target. It was a fortunate chance. Two hours later the leading troops were off the beach. The enemy strongpoints yielded to mopping-up operations in company strength, and the sea wall did not demand assault. Six battalions of infantry had begun to move off the beach by 1000 hours, and little more than an occasional air burst hampered the engineers at their toil, or reminded them of their extreme vulnerability as they placed their charges by hand. By noon the beach had been cleared at a cost of six men killed and 39 wounded out of the 400 involved in static roles, all of them sitting ducks without cover, and without armour.

Shortly after midday three battalions of the 22nd Infantry Regiment were moving north to open the northerly exit, the 3rd Battalion along the coast road to anchor a flank on Hamel-de-Cruttes, the 1st and 2nd Battalions wading diagonally, and miserably, waist deep, and often armpit and neck deep, across the floods all the way to St Germain-de-Varreville.

The 12th Infantry Regiment found the going worse, wading from the Grand Dune position immediately backing the beach, and crossing the line of march as they reached dry land, many of them soaked to the ears.

In all that day, the 8th and 22nd Infantry Regiments lost 12 men killed. Twenty times the number would have been counted fortunate; 100 times the number a misfortune to be looked for. A single resolute man armed with a flint lock could have accounted for more than 12 men on the beach in the first half-an-hour, including a brigadier-general and a colonel. The struggle of the 4th Infantry Division was mainly against the forces of nature, which were considerable. Eastwards it was different.

OMAHA BEACH: THE BLOODBATH

The beach of Omaha lies between the outcropping rocks of Pointe de la Percée in the west, and Port-en-Bessin in the east, a shallow arc of sand enclosed inland by bluffs rising in a gentle slope 150 feet to a plateau of tiny hedge-enclosed fields, deep lanes, and scattered hamlets built solidly of stone. It is a thinly populated region, the largest village, Trévières, 3 or 4 miles inland on the south side of the Aure river, counting not more than 800 inhabitants.

Three coastal villages, Vierville, St Laurent, and Colleville lie behind the beach at regular intervals a mile and a half apart, and linked by a narrow lane from 500 to 1,000 yards in from the shore line. A stretch of paved promenade along the 'front', and with a score or more of good houses between Vierville and St Laurent, backs a low sea wall of masonry and wood. Gullies opening from the beach give access up narrow lanes to the villages.

At low tide the sands slope gradually to the sea wall, and in places to a heavy shingle bank of stones 3 inches in diameter, a barrier 8 to 10 feet high between the beach and the reedy grasses of the bluffs. Seaward the stresses of the sea and the strong currents carve runnels in the wet ribbed sands.

The rocky shoulders of the bluffs of Omaha, flanking the crescent of the beach, provided concealed gun positions to enfilade the fore shore and the sea approaches, and behind the obstacle of the heavy shingle bank and the wall, the enemy defended entrenchments linking strongpoints, pillboxes, and concrete gun emplacements

US Army

Imperial War Museum

French Canadians land on Juno Beach. Waiting until the tide had risen meant that theirs was the last assault to go in sited to bring devastating cross-fire to bear upon the beach. Theoretically, at least, light and heavy machine-guns, 75- and 88-mm artillery pieces, would make a beaten zone of the entire beach area from end to end. And behind the forward defensive positions the terraced slopes of the bluffs gave cover to further trench systems, machine-gun nests, and minefields.

The beach itself was moderately mined, especially in the areas between the gullies, and from low to high water mark an elaborate system of staggered lethal obstacles seemed to defy the passage of any craft larger than a matchbox. But all these things had been studied in some detail by small parties visiting the beaches by night, and from countless air photographs.

Omaha Beach held no mystery and no surprises. Even the bringing in of a new and vastly superior division – 352nd – had been observed by British Intelligence, and passed on to US 1st Army. Unhappily, this piece of information had seemed suspect to the 1st Army Command, and the assault troops were not informed. Yet it is inconceivable that they had been briefed to expect less than the worst the enemy could be expected to perform. To attack this superb defensive position General Bradley had rejected Hobart's magnificent array of assault armour, and had accepted DD tanks only with reluctance.

A terrible confusion

At 0300 hours on June 6, Force O, commanded by Rear-Admiral Hall, USN, and carrying 34,000 men and 3,300 vehicles and with a follow-up force, almost its equal, a few hours astern, began to put its assault craft into the water 12 miles off shore. There followed four hours of a macabre Dantesque confusion, through which men struggled blindly with the sea, a prey to despair, knowing the dregs of misery. While the larger vessels moved forward, finding difficulty in maintaining their stations in the heavy sea, the smaller craft were exposed to the full force of the north westerly, fighting seas up to 6 feet high, unstable and making water too fast for the pumps.

Some of the larger ships had put their assault craft into the water fully loaded, but others had put their men over the side into craft pitching and rolling wildly, an ordeal for men wracked with sea sickness. The sea, unfriendly through all the hours of the long passage, became in minutes a dark heaving formless jungle upon which men and boats wrestled like the damned in a labyrinthine maze of driven spume.

Almost at once ten small craft foundered, and upwards of 300 men struggled for their lives in a darkness which seemed to contain a kind of uproar in its relentless impersonal violence. Rudderless, foundering small craft and the sodden wreckage of equipment added to the menace, buffeting the men in their life jackets.

In nearly 200 assault craft, the crews and troops who must presently assault the enemy across open beaches in the face of withering fire, baled with their tin hats for their lives, in some boats 100% sea-sick, in all boats sodden, cramped, and cold. At last on the verge of nervous and physical exhaustion the assault troops neared the shore, and their craft strove to manoeuvre for the final run-in.

These men in the vanguard were more naked than they knew or greatly cared. Behind them the seas had stripped them steadily of guns and armour, and the teams of combat engineers had suffered no less than they. With a reckless irresponsibility the commander of the tank landing-craft carrying 32 DD tanks due to land at H – 5 launched his massive vehicles into the steep seas 6,000 yards off shore. Even with well-trained crews there would have been small hopes for the tanks; as it was 27 were swamped within minutes and sank. Two, by brilliant seamanship and chance, managed to reach the shore. Three others were saved the ordeal by the jamming of the ramp of the landing craft, and were carried in. Thus the 96 tanks planned to provide vital close support for the 1,450 men of eight companies, and the first wave of the engineer teams, in the moment of assault had dwindled by almost a third of their number.

Disaster had also met the attempts to ferry the supporting artillery ashore in DUKWs. The small overloaded craft, almost unmanageable, quickly foundered. The 111th Field Artillery Battalion lost all its 105-mm howitzers save one. The 16th Infantry Cannon Company shared the same fate, and the 7th Field Artillery was very little better. The engineer teams, off-loading their heavy equipment from LCTs to LCMs, also had their troubles and losses.

It was a battle of material, of landing craft and armour, but it was men who had to walk up the beaches – and pay a price

Commandos go ashore in the British sector, their specialised armour already at work flailing a path across the beaches

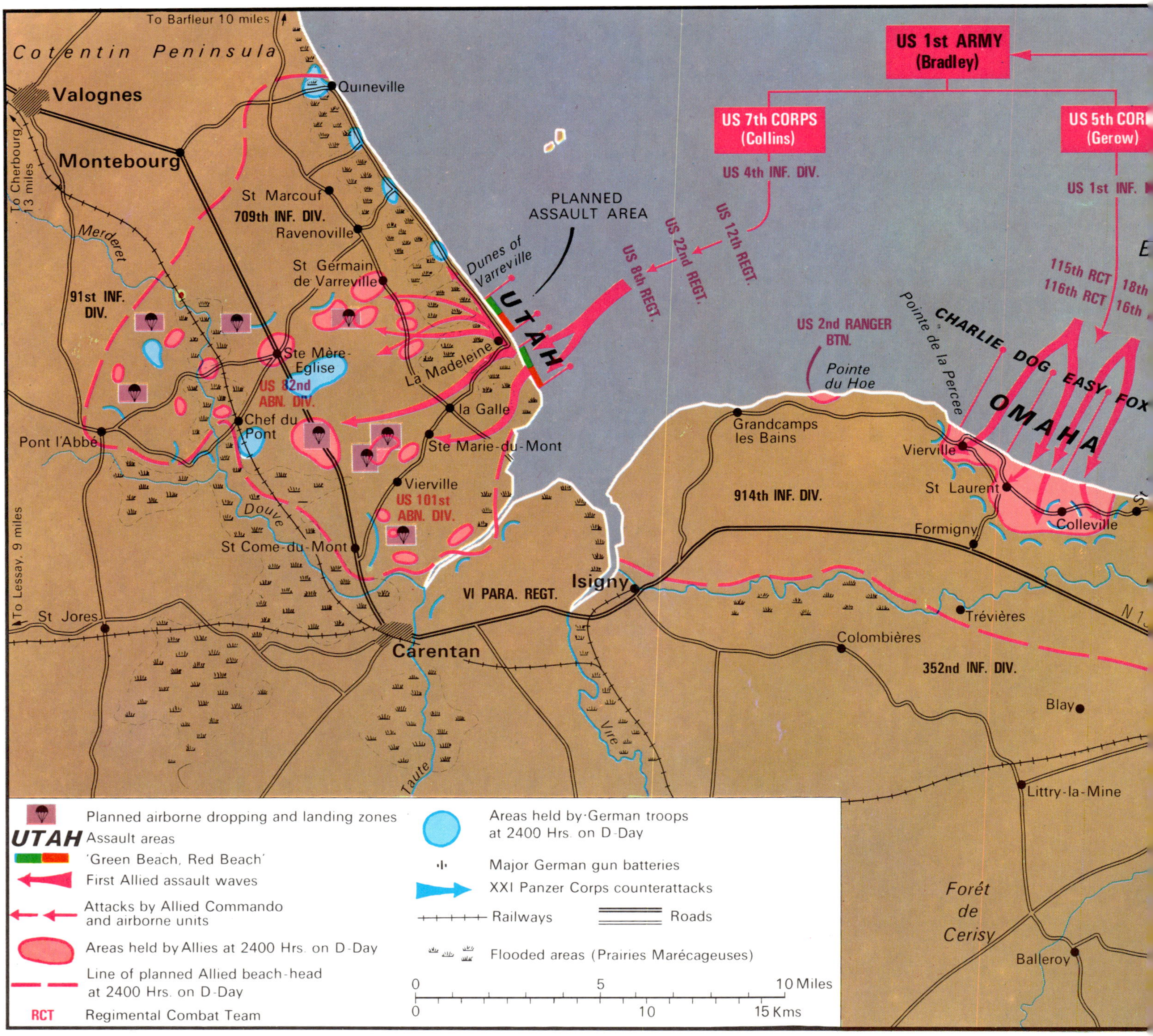

Nevertheless, in the last hour a great concourse of men, guns, and armour approached the lethal regions of the shallows, their initial losses far less than must have been inflicted by an enemy capable of even a moderate challenge on the sea and in the air. But the sea and air belonged to the Allies. With 40 minutes still to go the powerful bombarding squadron opened fire on the coastal defences with a great armament from the 16-inch guns of the battleships to the 5-inch guns of the destroyers, deluging the line of the bluffs with fire and smoke. At the same time 329 out of the 446 Liberators sent to do the job attacked 13 targets on and about the beaches with more than 1,000 tons of bombs.

The leading assault craft were some 800 yards out when the barrage behind them lifted and the vast uproar muted to the violent staccato sounds of the guns in the close support craft in their wakes. The crash of bursting mortar bombs, of shells, and the smash of machine-gun bullets against the ramps warned the assault troops that the enemy held them in his sights. The cries of men in the water, the sudden searing sheets of flame, the thunderous explosions as craft were hit by enemy shell and mortar fire, caught them up and splintered their isolation to fragments, and the ramps went down.

There is a devastating simplicity about disaster. There were no dry landings. The assault craft, and the larger LCVPs and LCMs grounded on the sandbanks, slewed in the sand runnels, and cast scores of men knee, waist, and neck deep into seas lashed not only by the wind, but by mortar bombs, shells, and machine-gun bullets. While isolated groups waded to the shore, dazed and bewildered by their loneliness on that 5-mile-long wilderness of sand, blinded by the smoke of many fires raging on the bluffs, uncertain what to do, others, the great majority, were in the midst of infernos of exploding ammunition and engineer charges set off by direct hits. Here and there craft blew up in ferocious ovens of flame.

The LCTs of the 743rd Tank Battalion leading in the van on the right flank surged on with men diving from stricken craft on either side, seeking the shelter of the waves, while others fought for footholds, clawing their ways to the beach, weighed down with equipment, some on hands and knees, others dragging forward on their bellies, with their wounded and their wounds. But it was safer in the sea.

A direct hit on the leading LCT killed all the company officers, save one, but eight of the DD tanks landed on the rim of the sea to open fire on the Vierville strongpoint: range 200 yards. The tanks of the 743rd were getting in further east, but the men without armour had little chance. When the ramps of the leading assault craft went down the enemy machine-guns tore through living flesh so that the front cavities of the vessels became in seconds raw wounds, thick with blood. Dozens leaped this way and that for their lives.

Within half-an-hour of H-Hour there were at least 1,000 assault infantry and engineers alive on the beach and in the shallows, but they were not fighting the enemy; they were fighting quite simply for

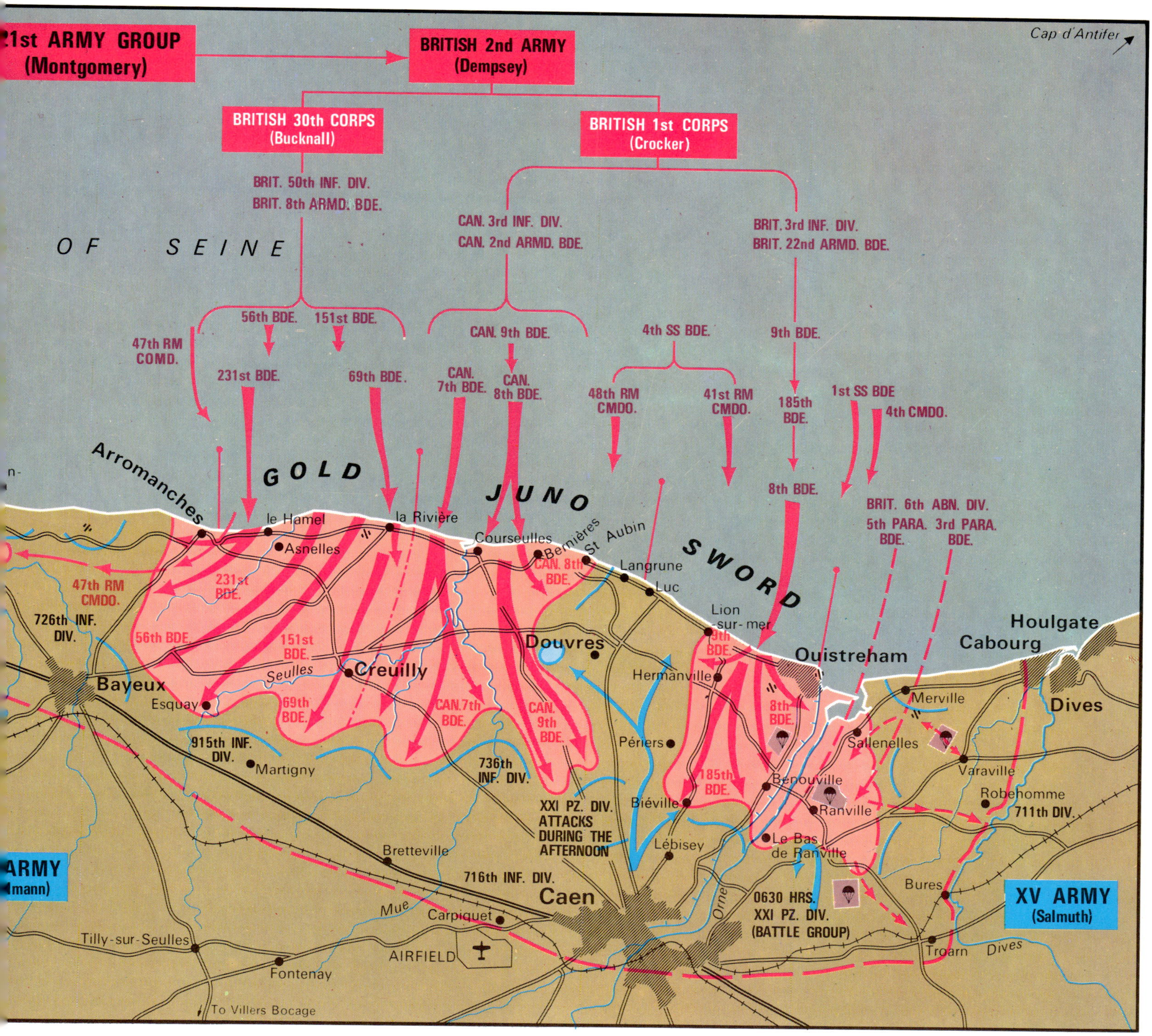

Overlord began with the airdrops: in the west to isolate the Cotentin Peninsula, in the east to hold the left flank on the Orne. Despite widely scattered landings, both objectives were achieved. Opposition to the seaborne landings varied. On Utah Beach US troops were off the beaches by 1200 hours. On Omaha lack of special armour pinned the infantry down in a deadly firefight. On Gold and Juno the 'Funnies' carried the British and Canadians towards Caen, and on Sword Commandos were linking with the paratroops by 1400 hours, turning the counterattack of XXI Pz Div from behind

survival, many exhausted, all too weary to drag their equipment across the beach, very few among them able to run, to assault, head-on, the enemy strongpoints.

Some went back to the water, and came in with the tide until at last it brought them, like flotsam, to the meagre shelter of the sea wall or the shingle bank. Very few of those scattered, almost at random, along the length of that beach, and all trained for the specific tasks with which, it was planned, they would be faced, knew where they were. Very few had come in on those 'stages' for which they had rehearsed. Boat teams, organised as fighting units, were miserably scrambled, and often alone, a detachment here, another 200, 300, even 1,000 yards away. For all many of them knew they were alone on the beach known as Omaha. The sea was behind them, and the blinding smoke, saving them from enemy fire in the lucky places, dazed them. The few officers were often slow to get their bearings, or to make up their minds what to do. Few found the leadership in that first hour which alone could have got them off the beach. Above all they were exhausted, and there was no refuge.

The engineer combat teams, coming in on the heels of the assault infantry, had suffered severely on the run-in, losing much of their vital equipment. Direct hits had blown some of their craft to pieces. Of 16 teams, each trained for its special role in its sector, only five came near to their assignments, and of these, three were utterly alone, unprotected by man or gun, naked to the enemy. Within minutes only three bulldozers out of 16 survived for the work of heaving aside the heavy barriers of angle iron and obstacles, and these lost their ability to manoeuvre as men took cover behind them.

Yet despite their crippling losses, and their exposure to the full force of enemy fire, the engineers salvaged what gear they could and strove to clear lanes through which the follow-up forces hoped to pass. Heavy mortar and shell fire detonated chains of fuses painfully laid by hand, and blew up whole detachments of engineers before they could get clear. The swiftly rising tide foamed round their feet, their waists, submerging the outer obstacles, and forcing the survivors to the sea wall and the shingle before their tasks were a tenth-part done. On the whole sector of the 116th RCT they had cleared two gaps. Far to the east, where scarcely a man had landed, they had cleared four gaps, but of them only one was marked. The effort had cost more than 40% of the engineer strength.

Burning tanks of the first wave lie stranded amongst the beach obstacles the DDs and the 'Funnies' had overcome

But always behind the engineers, not only the rising tide, but the tremendous tide of men and vehicles pressed on, steadily wave upon wave, building up on the beaches, in the shallows, demanding an outlet. After three terrible hours the foreshore was a wilderness of wreckage, of burning vehicles, of shattered craft, and shattered men. Not one of the exits from the beach was open, not one of the defensive positions had been stormed, and a message went back to the sea to land no more vehicles, but only men.

Nevertheless, long before the destroyers of the naval force came close inshore to blaze away at the enemy strongpoints at little more than 1,000 yards, a desperate beginning of order was growing out of chaos, and men, tried to the limits of endurance, regained their feet, lifted up their heads, and began to fight for more than their lives. They had paid a terrible price for General Bradley's rejection of the specialised armoured fighting vehicles Montgomery had offered him, for these were the 'tin openers' to Normandy.

AIR DROP IN THE EAST: ALMOST OVERWHELMED

The task of the British 6th Airborne Division was to establish a bridgehead across the Orne river and the Caen Canal, midway between the city of Caen and the Normandy coast, and to protect the eastern flank of the seaborne landings. In its initial stages the task was both complex and of a desperate simplicity; complex because the pieces in the pattern were many, simple because there was no room for finesse, no time. A number of *coups de main* must succeed, and become one simple *tour de force*.

Two parachute brigades would land in the very midst of the enemy, on the boundary of the German VII and XV Armies, seize the vital objectives, and at all costs prevent reinforcements from reaching the main battlefields.

Powerful elements of the German 711th and 716th Divisions defended every village, strongpoint, and bridge; the XXI Panzer Division poised and ready to strike was on their right flank, and behind them the whole weight of the German armoured reserve lay within striking distance. Unless, therefore, the two leading brigades of paratroops could strike their blows like lightning out of the sky, and consolidate, unless they could clear landing places for the glider-borne brigade, and could have with them anti-tank guns, mortars, and the bulk of their heavy equipment, their task would be beyond hope. Whatever might be won by lightning strokes must inevitably be lost, even before the sun was up, and assuredly before the sun was down.

The 5th Parachute Brigade would seize the bridges across the Orne and the Caen Canal north of Ranville, clear and protect landing zones for their gliders, and establish a firm bridgehead.

The 3rd Parachute Brigade would demolish the bridges across the flooded Dives river at Troarn, Bures, Robehomme, and Varaville. They would block and hold all routes leading in from the south-east. They would destroy the powerful Merville battery of 155-mm guns and its garrison before it could enfilade the left flank of the seaborne attack with devastating fire. For this latter task there would be a maximum time of one hour.

It was 2330 hours on the night of the 5th when the first of six Albemarle aircraft of the Pathfinder force took off from their English field with 60 men who must light the beacons to lead the way. At the same hour, six gliders bore a small force of the 2nd Battalion, the Oxford and Bucks Light Infantry, and Royal Engineers to seize crossings of the Caen Canal and the Orne. It was a night of drizzling rain and gusty winds, and lit by tattered patches of moonlight; a night filled with the roar of aircraft, the bombers, the transports, the tugs and their gliders in their thousands teeming through the Channel sky from Le Havre to Cherbourg. Below them the wakes of 5,000 ships cleaving the gun-metal sea into greenish-white trails of foam.

At 0030 hours, the first of the Pathfinders touched down on the soil of France, two-thirds blown awry by the winds, beacons lost, equipment damaged, but enough on their targets to do the vital minimum as best they might. Within minutes the leading glider of the first of the *coup de main* parties crash-landed 47 yards from its objective, overwhelmed the enemy with the sleep still in their eyes, and seized intact the bridges over the Caen Canal and the Orne. Already the enemy tracer looped the sky, and the flak streaming up into the cloud-banks exacted a price in gliders and transports over the coast. A hot reception met the men of the 7th, 12th, and 13th Battalions of the 5th Brigade tumbling out of the cloud-banks. While many landed fighting, at once at grips with the enemy, others hung suspended in the trees, sitting ducks, few to survive.

A flare lighting up the medieval tower of Ranville Church pinpointed the position, and nearly half of the 7th Battalion was able to move swiftly to reinforce the bridgeheads. Civilians, possessed of an awful optimism, both hindered and inspired the British. By 0230 hours, the 7th Battalion was engaged desperately on both banks of the Orne against units of the German 716th Division and two battalions of Feuchtinger's XXI Panzer Division, which had been committed soon after 0100 hours. One company of the 7th, hard pressed at Bénouville, held on, fighting against time, knowing that relief could not reach them until early afternoon, but the colossal detonations of the naval bombardment preceding the seaborne landings brought inspiration.

The 12th Battalion, having seized Le Bas de Ranville, found itself in need of luck as well as inspiration. Its forward platoons, outnumbered twenty to one, faced 88-mm guns firing point blank at 70 yards, and with the breech block of their solitary 6-pounder smashed on landing, their only hope lay in the uncertainty of the enemy, and fortunately this was great. While Blumentritt strove to arouse an adequate sense of urgency in the German High Command, and obtain the release of the armoured reserve, Speidel was advising Rommel of the situation with equal urgency, and receiving orders for the employment of the XXI Panzer Division.

Imperial War Museum

Horsa gliders and parachutes litter the fields of Normandy. It took the airborne troops hours to link up as a coherent force

But Feuchtinger had committed a battle group of the XXI Panzer Division on his own initiative soon after 0600 hours. Had this battle group pressed its attack it must have overwhelmed the defenders of Le Bas de Ranville, and greatly restricted the bridgehead. As it was, the confusion in the enemy command, the widespread threats developing over the entire Normandy coast, was the luck the paratroops needed. At about mid-morning the German armour turned its back upon Le Bas de Ranville leaving the battered defenders in possession.

The effects of the struggle in the early hours on the extreme left flank were to have a vital significance in the crises developing on Omaha Beach, for when Feuchtinger was ordered to move his infantry battalions to counterattack the Americans, he was unable to extricate them from their fight with the 5th Parachute Brigade. His anti-tank battalion was also deeply committed in an attempt to save the 716th Infantry Division from the seaborne infantry and armour. Thus no reserves were available to move against 'Omaha' at the vital hour.

When the first of the Commandos fought through from the beach at Ouistreham, reaching the Orne bridgehead only two-and-a-half minutes behind schedule, the small force of the Oxford and Bucks

Light Infantry, with the help of the 7th Battalion, had held for 12 hours against powerful counterattacks supported by artillery and mortars. One company, with all its officers killed or wounded, held on without relief for 17 hours. It was 1400 hours when No. 6 Commando crossed the Orne bridge on its way to reinforce the 9th Battalion of the 3rd Parachute Brigade. The Commando had then fought its way through enemy strongpoints, destroyed a battery in full blast against the beaches, and marched 9 miles.

Daring of a high order

It seemed impossible that a coherent pattern could emerge from the complex missions of the 3rd Parachute Brigade, or that seven major tasks, covering a 7-mile front from the town of Troarn, due east of Caen, to the coast at Merville, could be successfully fulfilled. Each demanded daring of a high order, meticulous planning, impeccable timing, and above all the ability to improvise if, as was almost certain, things went wrong.

The Albemarles carrying advance parties with the urgent role of clearing a way for a small glider-borne force with anti-tank guns, dropped their cargoes reasonably near their objective, but the brigadier, wounded and wallowing in the flooded Dives with his HQ, and elements of the 1st and 9th Battalions, did not regain the main body of the brigade before dusk. The 3rd Brigade had a bad drop. The smoke and dust from the heavy bombing of the Merville battery position obscured dropping zones on which many beacons were damaged, and failed to show up. Flak and the strong wind gusts played their parts; gliders parted from their tugs, many were hit, but above all, perhaps, 46 Group in particular had lacked the time for training. Now, on the day, on sea and land, the miserable and bitter battles waged by the Overlord planners for air and sea landing-craft, always denied until the last moment, were reaping a harvest in lives from end to end of the Peninsula.

On the left the Canadians of the 1st Battalion found sufficient strength to press home immediate attacks on their objectives at Varaville and Robehomme. While all kinds and conditions of civilian men, women, and children, including a boy of eleven and a Cockney woman of 55, a native of Camberwell, helped stragglers to rejoin their battalion, the solid nucleus of one company attacked Varaville, destroyed the bridge, and at once became too heavily engaged to extricate itself until late in the morning. Meanwhile a captain of Royal Engineers, with elements of the battalion, blew the Robehomme bridge.

These exploits, performed with satisfactory speed in spite of the chaos predicted by the brigadier, were outshone by a deed of a different order. This was the assault on the Merville Battery position.

The 150-mm guns of Merville were housed in concrete emplacements 6 feet 6 inches thick, reinforced by 12 feet of earthworks, and protected by steel doors. The perimeter fence, lined with a concertina barbed wire barrier 15 feet wide and 5 feet high, enclosed an area of some 400 square yards defended by a garrison of 130 men. At least 20 weapon pits and machine-gun positions were sited to protect every possible avenue of approach through surrounding minefields, and with no cover from fire for attackers over the open fields and orchards. At least one 20-mm dual-purpose gun completed the known armament of a battery which threatened the left flank of the seaborne assault at close range. It was imperative that the Merville guns should be destroyed. Direct hits by heavy bombs had failed to penetrate the casemates, and the naval gunfire, to be directed against the battery if all else failed, could only hope to put the guns out of action by direct hits through the embrasures or up the 'spouts'. Such hits occur by mere chance, and are not to be looked for.

A force of 1,000 Lancasters unloading a deluge of 4,000-pound bombs shortly after midnight failed to hit the target, but killed a number of cattle and provided some deep craters which might be useful cover for the attackers.

In the last four or five minutes of the flight from England, enemy flak forced pilots to take evasive action, and tumbled the battalion commander of the assault force into the garden of a German headquarters. The rest of the force lay scattered over an area ten times as large as it should have been. Yet at 0250 hours the battalion commander had assembled 150 men, one Vickers heavy machine-gun, a bare minimum of signals equipment, and 20 lengths of bangalore torpedo. Jeeps, 6-pounders, mortars, sappers, mine detectors, had all gone astray. With this force, organised in groups 30 strong, each with a special mission, the commander attacked. Within a minute or two of 0430 hours the assault went in. Half an hour later, after a hand to hand mêlée of a desperate and deadly intensity, the success signal blazed out. It had been a fight of gaunt shadow shapes against a spasmodic background of smoke, flame, and violent explosion. One of the battery guns had been destroyed by firing two shells simultaneously, and the other three by gammon bombs. A lieutenant, dying of his wounds, checked the destruction and was added to 66 British dead. Some 30 men were wounded, 20 of them seriously. Not a man of the party was over twenty-one years of age, and few had fought before.

By early evening, the two brigades of the British 6th Airborne Division, anxiously awaiting their glider and seaborne reinforcements, had carried out their tasks, and established bridgeheads across the Caen Canal and the Orne. They had been strengthened by the arrival of the 1st Commando Brigade, and had blocked all roads from the east. Their future – if they were to have a future – must depend on the success or failure of the British 3rd Infantry Division, spearheading the left flank assault on the beaches.

By evening it had become clear that the advance out of the beachhead was too slow. Infantry had dug in too soon, when they should have pressed on. Traffic jams building up on the beach prevented the British from shaking loose until early afternoon, and Feuchtinger's armour, at last with its orders, was driving down, nearly 90 tanks strong, to the sea at Lion-sur-Mer. Nevertheless, the diversion of the German armour to meet the major threat of the British landing had saved the airborne from being overwhelmed.

SWORD BEACH: HITLER WAKES UP

The battle for the Orne bridgehead was already six hours old when Hobart's armour led the British and Canadian seaborne assaults to the rock-enclosed strips of beach fronting Ouistreham and Lion-sur-Mer, Langrune and Courseulles, la Rivière and le Hamel. Far away on the right, beyond the outcropping rocks of Port-en-Bessin, the Americans had suffered for a full hour under the guns of the enemy strongpoints on the long bare stretch of Omaha. The hopes of surprise in the east had seeped away, but it appeared to make no difference to an enemy hammered from the sea and sky.

A smoke screen veiled the whole British left flank from the powerful guns of the Le Havre batteries, which had withstood a hundred batterings from the air, and were a graver menace than

Imperial War Museum

the rough sea to the convoys assembling 7½ miles offshore, and putting their hordes of small craft into the water. Enemy E-boats, choosing their moment to venture out of Le Havre, emerged momentarily from the smoke to discharge four torpedoes, one to sink a Norwegian destroyer, another to force the command ship, HMS *Largs*, full astern in evasive action, the remaining two to pass harmlessly between the warships.

Torrents of bombardment from the air soon after dawn were followed by greater bombardments from the sea, concentrating an enormous weight of metal and explosive upon the narrow coastal strips, the grey lines of buildings protruding like desolate crusts out of the mists of smoke and flame which tore the amphitheatres to shreds. The helmsman of an assault craft was seen to be hanging out over the stern acting as a human rudder. Men floundered to death by drowning; the assault and landing craft surged on, as if borne on the screaming, crashing ferocity of their own gun craft, which blazed away with 4·7s, rockets, Oerlikons, and machine-guns, while the armour and field artillery went into action from their carrying craft. Mines, mortar bombs, and shells erupted small craft out of the water to fill air and sea with falling wreckage; explosions tore the entrails out of larger vessels, and leapt into furnaces in which, miraculously, men survived.

The high wind was piling the rising tide above the outer belts of obstacles, and there was nothing for it but to ride in, attempting to navigate the lethal forest of angle iron, stakes, and steel, and crash down in the foam of waves breaking on the shore.

H-Hour was 0730 hours, with the armour leading in at H – 5. Force S for Sword had put its DD tanks into the water 3 miles out, and it was clear that only fine seamanship on the part of their crews, the 13/18th Hussars, would bring them in on time, or at all. Low in the water, beaten by waves 4 feet high, the grey upper works were almost invisible, and a line of tank landing craft cutting across their bows sank two, and might have swamped a score but for a mattress of rockets falling short, and forcing the tank landing craft to alter course away from the fragile DDs swimming in the water.

When the bombardment of the warships began to lift, the shore approaches were a turmoil of weaving craft and wreckage, and almost to the minute the flail tanks crawled on shore in the lead, eight assault teams, beating up towards the beach exits, engaging enemy guns point blank, followed by the whole strange 'menagerie' of armoured monsters, the bridging tanks, the bobbins, the petards, and 33 out of 40 DD tanks crawling up out of the water in time to shoot the infantry over the hazardous stretch of beach.

Within minutes, the wreckage of armour added a grotesque dimension to the inferno. A flail, losing its tracks, continued to engage an enemy 88, another brewed, a bridging tank lost its bridge, and somewhere a DD tank foundered in a bewildering mass of steel. Sappers leaving their armoured vehicles pressed on, clearing by hand. Men leapt from blazing craft in the shallows, and struggled towards the beach through the crumpled ruins of men and equipment.

On the right, the 1st Battalion of the South Lancashire Regiment, spearheading the 8th Infantry Brigade, quickly cleared the beach in the wake of the armour, and began to assault the strongpoints. The 2nd Battalion, the East Yorkshire Regiment, their brothers-in-arms on the left, fought their way more slowly to a foothold. Over all the beach, left and right, enemy mortar and small-arms fire was intense, thickened by the anti-tank guns sited on Périers Ridge, and the divisional artillery ranging on the barrage balloons.

Order out of chaos

Out of the seeming chaos and confusion, and the increasing wreckage on the beach, the threads of order began to emerge. By 0930 hours, Hobart's armour – manned by the 22nd Dragoons, the Westminster Dragoons, and two squadrons of the 5th Assault Regiment, Royal

British assault troops run for cover, the beach behind them crowded with an ever-growing arsenal of heavy equipment. Inset: A bespectacled RM Commando lands on Juno Beach

Engineers—had cleared seven out of the eight lanes through the exits. At La Riva Farm, the squadrons were rallying, some to aid Commando troops fighting for possession of the Ouistreham Locks, and for Lion-sur-Mer, others making ready to spearhead the infantry on the road to Caen.

The South Lancashires reached Hermanville in good time, one-and-a-half miles inland, confronting the vital Périers Ridge, bristling with Feuchtinger's anti-tank guns and defended by infantry of the 716th Division. But the 8th Infantry Brigade had lost its vital momentum. Enemy guns broke up armoured sorties, and the infantry dug in at Hermanville.

Meanwhile, by 1100, the 185th Brigade was assembling its three battalions in the orchards beyond Hermanville, and an immediate attack should have been pressed home against the Périers Ridge, not only to open the road to Caen, but for the urgent relief of the Orne bridgehead. Where Commando troops had marched boldly through, the infantry, dourly led, performed its slow set-piece gyrations.

A contributory cause of the slowness in front was, however, the growing mass of men and armour, striving to break loose from the beaches, and the impossible tangles of traffic in the narrow streets, the laterals, and leads out of the exits. The tanks of the Staffordshire Yeomanry, with the role of carrying the men of the King's Shropshire Light Infantry on the road to Caen, could not be prised loose from the mêlée. It was late when the guns of the Périers Ridge were silenced, and the Shropshires took the road alone.

The infantry of the line did all that its leaders demanded of it, but it was not enough. The East Yorkshires had taken a severe hammering, losing five officers and 60 men killed, and more than 140 wounded, in gaining their objectives. The Shropshires on the lonely road out of Hermanville were marching boldly into the midst of the enemy, their flanks bare. At 1600 hours, the battalion, joined by the self-propelled guns and armour of the Staffordshire Yeomanry, reached Biéville, barely 3½ miles short of Caen.

It was, in fact, a position of extreme difficulty, for at last Feuchtinger had his clear orders, Rommel was speeding on his way to his command, Hitler had awakened from the effects of his sleeping pills, and the German armour was on the move. At Biéville 24 tanks leading a powerful battle group of the XXI Panzer Division, probing for a crevice in the British assault, clashed head-on with the Shropshires and their armour. Self-propelled guns accounted for five enemy tanks, and the enemy withdrew. In spite of the armoured threats the Shropshires strove to press on, only to be halted by intense fire from the thickly wooded Lébisey Ridge. Casualties were growing steadily; a renewed armoured attack might develop at any moment, and the flanking battalions of the 185th Brigade were making very slow progress. Caen was a fading dream.

But Feuchtinger's armour was not coming that way again. The British, now in command of the Périers Ridge, had pushed the battle group further west, and the spearhead, bouncing off the Shropshires, and again off the British guns, was pounding northward down the wide gap between the British and Canadian landings, 90 tanks strong. There was nothing to stop them.

Imperial War Museum

A Churchill AVRE bridgelayer goes into action. Against the defenders' ingenuity the British set their specialised tanks

GOLD BEACH

HOBART'S TIN-OPENERS WORK

The main weight of the British seaborne assault fell on the right, on the beach code-named Gold, a shallow arc streaked with treacherous strands of soft clay, and behind that to the west the powerful strongpoints and fortified villages of Arromanches and le Hamel, and to the east, la Rivière.

It was 0725 hours when the leading flotillas carrying the flail tanks and armoured fighting vehicles of the Westminster Dragoons and the 81st and 82nd Assault Squadrons, Royal Engineers, closed the beaches of le Hamel and la Rivière. It was at once clear that the heavy air and naval bombardment had failed to silence the enemy guns, especially on the right. Only one of the flails serving the 231st Brigade's right flank succeeded in beating a lane up and off the beach, while in its wake others foundered, losing their tracks to mines and heavy machine-gun fire. On-coming craft, driven like surf boats by the strong wind and heavy seas, fouled obstacles and armour, creating a sense of chaos on the edge of the sea.

The squadron commander of the right flanking teams was killed at the outset in the turret of his AVRE, but many armoured vehicles, temporarily unable to crawl, engaged the enemy with their main armament, and were a valuable cover. But further to the east, beyond the immediate beaten zone of fire from the le Hamel strongpoints, the three assault teams serving the left flank of the brigade made good progress. While flails lashed the beach, lumbering on in the midst of eruptions of mines, mud, and sand, to gain the coast road, the bobbins laid mattresses over patches of soft blue clay; and fascine bridging tanks crawled over the beach with their huge unwieldy burdens, finally to fill craters, to make anti-tank barriers crossable, to pave the way for infantry, armour, and the great mass of vehicles bearing down, with a pressure impossible to deny, upon the beaches.

The DD tanks, finding the sea passage to the beach hopeless under their own power in the rough conditions, had been held back, later to beach dry shod, and add greatly to the early armoured firepower. Meanwhile, the spearhead role belonged to the flails and their supporting AVREs.

Well within the hour Hobart's armour had emerged from the turmoil of the water's edge and cleared four safe lanes out of six over the le Hamel beaches, and spearheaded the leading battalions of the 231st Brigade on to their objectives. Petard tanks all along the line were dealing out murderous treatment to fortified houses and strongpoints which would have tied up infantry platoons and companies, perhaps for hours, and taken a steady toll in dead.

On the 69th Brigade front facing la Rivière the flails and AVREs of the assault teams fought their way with infantry across the beaches in the face of intense mortar, anti-tank, and machine-gun fire directed from well-sited pillboxes, and houses linked together in systems of strongpoints. Three clear lanes were opened out of six from the edge of the sea to the edge of the marshland beyond the coast road. While petard tanks supporting the infantry blasted the coastal crust of strongpoints with their giant mortars, like ancient cannon, AVREs filled craters and anti-tank ditches with fascines, provided soft landings for armour behind walls, bridged culverts, and bulldozed tracks for the host of vehicles and men coming in fast on the rising tide. Within the hour armour and infantry were more than a mile inland, and the hard outer crust of the defence was broken.

Saved by the 'specials'

On the right flank of le Hamel there might have been a 'little Omaha' but for Hobart's armour. The 1st Battalion of the Hampshire Regiment, leading on the right flank, had had an uneasy passage. For them the sea-sick pills had not worked. They debouched from their assault craft 30 yards out into waves beating about their thighs and dragging at their feet as they struggled to dry sand. If they were grateful for anything it was simply that the movement of the sea had stilled, no longer to rack their guts with sickness. They had come in supported by self-propelled guns and field artillery firing from their carrying craft, aware of mortar and machine-gun fire from the enemy over the last half-mile. It had been uncomfortable rather than deadly. Smoke and flame obscured the beaches, but it seemed that the terrific bombing, followed by the naval bombardment, had failed to silence the enemy.

On the beach, in their first moments of comparative immunity before they came within the traverse of the le Hamel guns, they saw only the confusion of disabled armour, and swiftly discovered that for two-thirds of their numbers there were no safe lanes across the shambles of the beach. An immense weight of fire stopped them in their tracks as they strove to move up the beach, and no gunfire from the sea could bring them aid. With their battalion commander twice wounded and forced out of action, their second-in-command soon killed, there was nothing for it but to abandon the direct approach. Moving east the left flanking companies of the battalion gained les Roquettes, an objective of the 1st Dorsets on their left, and then swung right handed, seized Asnelles-sur-mer, and prepared to assault the le Hamel sanatorium. But it was afternoon before the sanatorium, resisting all infantry attacks, finally caved in to the devastating 'dustbins' of a petard, not the least of Hobart's 'specials'.

Meanwhile the 1st Dorsets, out of reach of the le Hamel guns, had stormed over the beach, covered by the guns of the 'specials', and swung right handed to gain the slight rise of Arromanches.

On the beach of la Rivière the 5th Battalion of the East Yorkshire Regiment and the 6th Battalion the Green Howards, leading the assault of the 69th Brigade, were in no doubt about the value of the armour. From the first, infantry and armour, greatly aided by close-support fire from gun craft, stormed the beach defences in complete co-ordination, and fought a tight battle through the streets, eliminating 88s and pillboxes, cutting out the enemy like a canker, and moving inland. Things had been bad, but not bad enough to curb their momentum on landing, and if men could hurl themselves over the first obstacle of the beach they must win. There was no other place to stop them but in the shallows and on the beaches.

By 1100 hours, seven lanes had been cleared on Gold Beach, the DD tanks were moving fast inland, and with them the 56th and 151st Brigades, carving out the centre, keeping the enemy off balance at all costs. Long before the le Hamel sanatorium had fallen the bridgehead was 3 miles in depth, the 56th Brigade was going well astride the la Rivière-Bayeux road, the 151st, on its left, racing for the high ground, and beyond into the Seulles valley, while left again the 69th pressed on for Creully. Even the right flank, delayed at le Hamel, had cut the Arromanches-Bayeux road, while the 47th Royal Marine Commando was working round to assault Port-en-Bessin.

The Commando had outstripped them all. Coming in to land west of le Hamel they had come under fire from the cliffs and lost four out of their 14 assault craft. Finally, forced eastward, they had run in east of the le Hamel position, hoping to find the way cleared ahead. It wasn't. They had had to fight their way through the coastal villages, each man humping 88 pounds of equipment, and covering 10 miles by early afternoon. By the time the 231st Brigade began to ease their sense of isolation they were occupying the high ground south of Port-en-Bessin. No men on their feet had done more.

JUNO BEACH: SOLID FOOTHOLD

By the time the Canadians stormed ashore with two brigades up astride the Seulles estuary, and raced for the sea walls, the rising tide had reduced the gauntlet of the beaches to as little as 100 yards at the narrowest point, and the battles of the beaches on the flanks were already from one to two hours old. The Canadians had no intention of being left behind.

The Canadian 7th Brigade, the Royal Winnipeg Regiment and the Regina Rifles leading, came in on the right, west of the Seulles river,

The assault on the invasion coast was spearheaded by the specialised armour of the British 79th Armoured Division. On the day they were highly successful, and where they were not used on Omaha Beach the price was a high toll in casualties. 1: DD Sherman tanks were the first ashore, engaging enemy positions from the water's edge. 2: They are followed by the flail tanks beating overlapping mine-free lanes. 3: To breach the sea wall and any anti-tank ditch, an AVRE would place its SBG bridge, allowing DD gun tanks to close the range. AVRE-dropped fascines would then fill the ditch. By now infantry (red arrows) would be crossing the beach. 4: The flails continued to clear the minefields, widening the beachhead. Petard and flamethrower tanks would mop up any remaining pillboxes.

US Coast Guard

An American soldier lies dead, still wearing his lifebelt

beating the Canadian 8th Brigade to the beach by a minute or two. With them were eight, possibly ten, DD tanks manned by the Canadian 1st Hussars. The tanks had taken to the water 800 yards out, threatened by the turbulent sea, in constant danger of swamping, threading their ways through a maze of scantlings jutting out of the water like the stumps of some petrified forest.

On the left, the Queen's Own Regiment of Canada and the North Shore Regiment led the Canadian 8th Brigade without armour, and raced for the sea wall, the heavy machine-guns of the enemy cutting swathes out of the Queen's Own in the 30 seconds or so it took them to reach the shelter of the wall. The landing craft carrying the assault armour of the engineers were still battling with the heavy seas and obstacles, and the DD tanks were coming in to land dry-shod when the spearhead infantry were well away, blasting the enemy out of Courselles and Bernières, and pressing on. When the Régiment de la Chaudière came in 15 minutes later there was scarcely a shot.

The Canadian battalions were borne in on a rough sea driven by the wind which flung them onto the beaches, and in one bound across them. The dangerous reefs and rocks of that narrow coast forced the assault craft to wait for the tide, and when at last they were clear of the reefs the larger craft had to charge the obstacles, hoping for the best, while the small craft strove to swerve and weave through tangles of angle iron and stakes. At one point 20 out of 24 assault craft blew up, and men struggled for the shore with the splinters of their landing craft falling from the skies about their ears. According to the record, 'chunks of débris rose a hundred feet in the air and troops, now hugging the shelter of a breakwater, were peppered with pieces of wood'.

Driven by the wind, the rapidly rising tide piling up the heavy surf, the helmsmen of the assault craft could only hang on and pray. The first three craft coming in on the Canadian left blew up, but their entire complement, save two killed, struggled out of the débris and water to make the beach and fight.

There were many brave men manning the landing craft all along the line from Sword to Utah, men fighting lone battles against outbreaks of fire and exploding ammunition, one man at least, a man named Jones, saving wounded from drowning in a flooded hold and amputating two horribly mangled legs. He was no doctor, merely a sick-berth attendant, but he did the job. And there were scores of 'Joneses' at sea that day off the beaches, but none had a struggle as grim as that of the men who carried the Canadians ashore on Juno.

The LCOCU (landing craft obstacle clearance units) of the naval demolition teams, and the beach units, striving to sort out the horrible muddle of mined obstacles, machines, and men, were under shell fire from enemy corps and divisional artillery long after the last mortar, machine-gun, and 88 of the beach defences, even the last sniper, had been silenced. Bulldozers not only bulldozed débris out of the way, but bulldozed beached craft back into the sea, giving them a start on the way back.

When the engineer assault armour of the 22nd Dragoons and the 26th Assault Squadron, Royal Engineers, reached the beach on the Canadian 7th Brigade front, the DD tanks which had landed with the infantry had settled the score with the worst of the enemy strongpoints mounting the 75-mm guns and the heavy mortars and machine-guns, but there was plenty of mortar and automatic fire coming in from a bit further back. The flails were urgently needed to carve clear lanes through to the exits for the mass of armour and vehicles building up, and the petards and bridging tanks lumbered up behind them, to keep the infantry going at high pressure.

East of the Seulles the going was good, and on both sides of the river the flails had opened the exits before 0930 hours, the fascines and bridging tanks had bridged the worst of the craters and culverts, and opened the sluices of the Seulles to drain a crater as large as a village pond, and twice as deep.

On the left at Bernières, flails and petards had smashed exits through the 12-foot-high sea wall, and cleared lanes and laterals well in time to work in with the infantry against the pillboxes and strongpoints. Before noon on the right flank the flails were advancing inland under command of the Canadian 2nd Armoured Brigade.

Twelve lanes were cleared that day on the Juno beaches by Hobart's armour, and the exits linked right through to join the brigade fronts. The DD tanks, beaching dry shod an hour behind the infantry, were swiftly off the beach, adding their firepower to the men storming on inland to keep the enemy off balance and not giving him a chance to form a second line. By late afternoon the Canadian 7th Brigade was challenging the 69th Brigade of '50 Div' for the lead, its armoured patrols probing for the main Bayeux-Caen road at Bretteville, while on the left, the Canadian 9th Brigade, breaking loose from the chaos and confusion on the beach, was through the 8th Brigade, and going well astride the Courselles road to Caen.

The centre bridgehead from Langrune to Arromanches was solid, 12 miles wide and growing deeper every hour. The bottleneck was behind, in the congestion of the narrow beach, the struggle of armour, vehicles, and men, to break loose from the appalling traffic jams. And on the right, there was the growing awareness of an ominous gap, the dangerous toe-hold of Omaha, the Americans inching slowly off the beach, their progress measured in yards.

Whatever happened the enemy reserves must be prevented from reaching Omaha, and it was this above all which made Dempsey pause, ready to reach out a helping hand, holding back his armour.

Left: British Commandos have broken out of the beaches and into a coastal town, hugging the walls as cover against snipers

AT THE END OF THE DAY

A FOOTHOLD ON THE CONTINENT OF EUROPE

It was late afternoon before the German High Command began to emerge from confusion. The lack of air reconnaissance, the blocking of radar, the dislocation of communications of every kind, had reduced observation almost to the eyes and ears of men. Reports could not be quickly confirmed, or information co-ordinated. Uncertainty inhibited the violent counterblows which alone could have driven the British and Americans back into the sea. And the instrument was lacking. The I Panzer Corps lay west of the Seine, immobilised, awaiting the decision of the Führer.

Field-Marshal Rommel had been right about the first 24 hours: they would be decisive. He had made repeated efforts to move the XII SS Panzer and the Panzer Lehr Divisions on a line St Lô-Carentan. Had these divisions been there, the Omaha beach-head must have been smashed; even had Rommel himself been there on the day, able perhaps to rouse Hitler out of his early morning dreams, it might not have been too late. It was too late when Hitler held his afternoon conference, and released the XII SS Panzer Division.

All that could be done against the Allied air and seaborne assaults had been done by the forces immediately available. Feuchtinger,

From behind the shallow cover of the sea wall US troops begin to move off Utah Beach. By nightfall 20,000 men were ashore

Keystone

United Press

British men and vehicles advance through a coastal village. Such bottlenecks delayed the advance from Gold Beach

Imperial War Museum

American combat engineers strive to bring order out of chaos on the beaches – working to keep the advance going

commanding the XXI Panzer Division, the only counterattacking force within reach, had reacted swiftly against the British airborne landings on the Orne, according to his standing orders. But at once there followed a long period of uncertainty, due partly to a breakdown in communications. When at last the division was put under command of the 84th Corps, General Marcks, the corps commander, was right in his appreciation that the British 3rd Division was the more potent threat, and that Caen must be at once powerfully screened. Nevertheless, too much time had been wasted, and he might have done better to commit the division against the airborne bridgehead. Had that been done the great glider-borne force might have arrived to a terrible reception.

As it was, Feuchtinger could not disengage his infantry battalions from the British, nor his anti-tank guns from the German 716th Division. He had been shot away from the Périers Ridge by British guns when he might have shot the British armour out of the way with his own guns – if he had had any.

But XXI Panzer Division did very well in view of its difficulties. Had they not taken fright at the impressive spectacle of 250 air-tugs towing their gliders full of reinforcements for the airborne divisions on their flank, and at the evening sky black with the fighter escorts, the battle group, powerfully and swiftly reinforced, might have disrupted the British right flank on Sword Beach, and driven a dangerous wedge between the British and Canadians, down to the sea. Instead it withdrew to take up a position to the north of Caen. There was no second chance.

But it is unlikely that the XXI Panzer could have prevailed, even the first time. Air power had done its work for the Allies, sealing off the battlefield, holding the ring, denying mobility to the reserves, making of each day a hideous nightmare, and of each night a tortured crawling progress. Of the more than 11,000 sorties flown by the Allied air forces on June 6, not one single aircraft was lost to the Luftwaffe. Air superiority, it has been estimated by some staff authorities, multiplies superiority on the ground by three. On D-Day, Allied air power was overwhelming, and decisive.

The pattern of the Battle for Normandy was beginning to set by the end of the first day, with the British and Canadians thickening a stout shoulder on the left, holding off the entire enemy armoured reserve, while the Americans made ready to exploit the open right flank. If – if that right flank could have been smashed at the outset, vulnerable, almost defenceless, on the long beach of Omaha, then a terrible, nagging battle of attrition might have gone on and on, the British bridgehead virtually sealed off. But the 6th Airborne, and then the British 3rd Division, and then the Canadian 3rd Division, had made that 'if' impossible. General Bradley may have feared a German counterattack, but General Kraiss, commanding the German 352nd Division, knew that counterattack was impossible.

And the maintenance of an 'open right flank' was essential to Allied victory. That was the point and purpose of General Montgomery's strategy, and by the end of the day he knew that he would win; that he would impose his will on the shape of the Battle for Normandy. He didn't care much for 'phase lines' and estimates of progress. He was concerned with the end result.

Meanwhile, by taking a chance, Rundstedt had dared to move a powerful force of the XII SS Panzer Division to Lisieux, and as soon as the release order came through from the High Command, this group, under Kurt Meyer, was ordered at once to the battlefield. By midnight, constantly harassed and desperately short of fuel, it reached Evrecy, 9 miles south-west of Caen, to find its petrol dumps a burned-out ruin. When it was able to move it had to counter a powerful Canadian threat, for it was opposite the line of advance from Juno Beach. Thereafter, the British and Canadian 3rd Divisions absorbed its offensive power, and sapped its defensive strength.

The Panzer Lehr Division was nowhere near the battlefield on D-Day; or the day after.

'As a result of the D-Day operations a foothold has been gained on the continent of Europe,' General Montgomery was able to report.

For General Bradley, commanding the US 1st Army, it must have been a night of grave anxieties, even – but there is no evidence – of some self-questioning. For General Dempsey, commanding the British 2nd Army, there was cause for some satisfaction, but not for jubilation. Dempsey, of whom very little has ever been written, is a quiet, gentle man, a good strategist and a sound tactician. He confined himself absolutely, and with a remarkable devotion, to his work of soldiering. On that night of June 6, Dempsey knew that his army had done enough. It was a good army, perhaps the last real 'army' Britain would ever produce. The dreams had faded; as they had been almost sure to fade. The vital momentum which might – might – have carried the Canadians and the British into the open country beyond Caen was never there. Beyond the Caen-Bayeux road there was no open country, only the bocage, the close-hedged, deep-ditched fields, the narrow lanes, the steep wooded valleys. The real open country had never been truly 'in the sights'. Perhaps it did not matter. The pattern of the struggle would have been different, but not necessarily more favourable to the Allies.

The first of the landing craft, turning about, had reached the hards of England, the small ports, the estuaries, in the afternoon, swiftly replenishing ammunition, stores, men, cleaning and greasing the guns, setting forth a second time through the great maze of shipping. Through all the day and night the Mulberry tows were breaking loose, the tugs fighting scores of desperate battles with hawsers, winches, and chains, clawing at the huge unwieldy objects they sought to drag through the seas. Some 40% of the 'Whale' units broke away and were lost. But it would go on, and on.

It was a strange day and night on and off the beaches. Men clung marooned to obstacles and debris, on rocks, on the tops of drowned vehicles, while naval and small craft, DUKWS and outboard motors, buzzed and weaved about their business, impervious to croaking cries for help, and to the full-blooded curses of frustrated, angry, frightened men. Many of those picked up by craft on the 'turn-about' were carried straight back to England whether they liked it or not. There were a good many men wandering about for days.

There was not much chance to rest in the bridgehead. The smoke rose from the burned-out houses lining the battered sea fronts from Ouistreham to Arromanches, and beyond to the desolation of Omaha and the isolation of Utah, the dunes of Varreville. In the midst of the monstrous chaos of the beaches, in the jungles of shattered craft, tank tracks, wheels, and twisted masses of iron and steel, the bodies of men lay under gas capes, awaiting burial.

At Sallenelles on the left, in the 3-mile gap between Sword and Juno, and in the chasm between Gold and Omaha, there was no rest. The airborne and the Commandos were having a rugged time. Yet some lay in the meadows, and wrote home about 'butterflies' and 'bird song', which seemed the oddest things of all in the day.

Morale was high. To most of those not 'in contact', and not 'fighting' – and a minority is 'in contact' doing any 'fighting' – it seemed an anti-climax. One man called it 'a crashing anti-climax'. In a sense it was an anti-climax not to be dead, after so much waiting, training, thinking, and expecting 'God knew what'.

Some thought that the French were warm and friendly, others that they were suspicious and unfriendly, still others that they were indifferent. Many were startled by the extreme youth, or age, of the captured enemy and inclined to believe that it was going to be, what they called in those days, 'a piece of cake'. But the men who had charged the strongpoints, and gone into the cellars behind grenades, knew better. The German 716th Division had been cut to pieces, but its isolated 'bits' fought on.

The men, above all, who felt themselves to be 'out on a limb' that night were the US 82nd Airborne, holding on in Ste Mère-Église and with the 101st in scores of tiny 'pockets', wondering when their small seaborne 'attachment' was going to catch up. They didn't realise that many of their small bits and pieces would presently come together and give a much greater length and depth to the Utah bridgehead than it looked.

But the Utah bridgehead was sound. The entire 4th Division was

US Army

American wounded. The day claimed 2,500 killed, 1,000 of them on Omaha Beach where the special armour was not used

The US flag laid out for Allied aircraft recognition on a shattered German bunker as GIs winkle out the defenders

US Army

US Navy

Imperial War Museum

on shore well before midnight, and much more besides, 20,000 men and 1,700 vehicles in round figures. The two leading regiments had lost twelve men killed between them. General Collins, the corps commander, was far more worried about the possible actions – or lack of actions – of Admiral Moon, than about the bridgehead. The General wanted to go on shore, but he dared not leave the *Bayfield*. The Admiral, worrying about his losses, wanted to suspend landing operations through the night, and General Collins had 'to hold down Admiral Moon', as Bradley put it.

General Gerow, commanding the US 5th Corps, with no such sea cares, but with plenty on shore, had set up his command post on the bluffs of that desolate stretch of coast. There were 'no rear areas on Omaha' that night, according to the record, no comfort, no feeling of security. Enemy were still firing from beach positions, sniping all night, and all through the next day. Barely 100 tons of supplies had come on shore, and the men were hungry, weary, hanging on grimly, short of ammunition, sleep, short of most things. At the deepest point the penetration on Omaha was not much more than 1,500 yards, and there wasn't a line, not even the planned 'Beach Maintenance Line'. It was a miracle that they had gained a foothold, but they had. Men without armour.

No one may ever know what General Bradley thought about it. Why had he refused the flails, the petards, and all the rest of Hobart's armour? Chester Wilmot believed that it was Bradley's contempt for British 'under confidence and over-insurance'. Captain Sir Basil Liddell Hart summed up: 'Analysis makes it clear that the American troops paid dearly for their higher commander's hesitation to accept Montgomery's earlier offer to give them a share of Hobart's specialised armour.'

And the Supreme Commander's report states:

Apart from the factor of tactical surprise, the comparatively light casualties which we sustained on all beaches, except 'Omaha', were in large measure due to the success of the novel mechanical contrivances which we employed and to the staggering moral and material effect of the mass of armour landed in the leading waves of the assault. It is doubtful if the assault forces could have firmly established themselves without the assistance of these weapons.

The cost of the day in killed was not more than 2,500 men, 1,000 of them on Omaha Beach. At Towton Field, on 29th March, 1461, 33,000 men perished by the sword and were buried there. Nearly 20,000 British troops were killed on the first day of the Battle of the Somme in 1916. War had become a battle of machines against machines. Tens of thousands of tons of explosive, of copper, tungsten, bronze, iron, steel, bombs, bricks, mortar, concrete, guns, tanks, vehicles, ships, all 'blown to smithereens'. Bridges, railways, dumps, factories, whole towns, flattened to rubble, a war for bulldozers.

And presently the men controlling the bombers sensed their power, making it almost impossible for men on their feet to get through. It will be an unhappy day for the world when men on their feet cannot get through.

After the battle came the liberation. Here, French men and women march across the city square in Rennes, North France waving the 'Stars and Stripes'

US Navy

US rocket bombardment before the Leyte landings

BATTLE OF THE PACIFIC

Imperial War Museum

PEARL HARBOR: A BLOW FOR EMPIRE

For years before Pearl Harbor, Japan's military and political leaders had been flexing their Imperial muscles on the mainland of China in an attempt to win territory both along the coast and inland in the productive wastes of Manchuria.

In contemplating an extension of this Imperial war in Asia, those same Japanese leaders had one idea fixed firmly in their minds: that a war involving the United States was quite feasible in the short run, but should that war last more than a year then America's enormous industrial capacity would inevitably become the decisive factor.

Japan's initial war strategy was, as a result, quite simply to direct all her military and naval might southwards against the productive, oil-rich states of South-East Asia – Thailand, Malaya, the Philippines and the Dutch East Indies. Subsequently put into practice and known to historians as the 'Oriental Blitzkrieg', this strategy was intended to rapidly establish a Japanese Empire and a sound industrial base in South-East Asia – an Empire so costly of American lives to eliminate that any negotiated peace settlement would leave it essentially intact.

This strategy was, however, to be dramatically modified before it was ever put into action. Aware that the 'Oriental Blitzkrieg' would, anyhow, bring the United States into the war, Admiral Yamamoto – C-in-C of the Japanese Fleet – reasoned that if war with the USA was inevitable, then it should be provoked to Japan's best advantage.

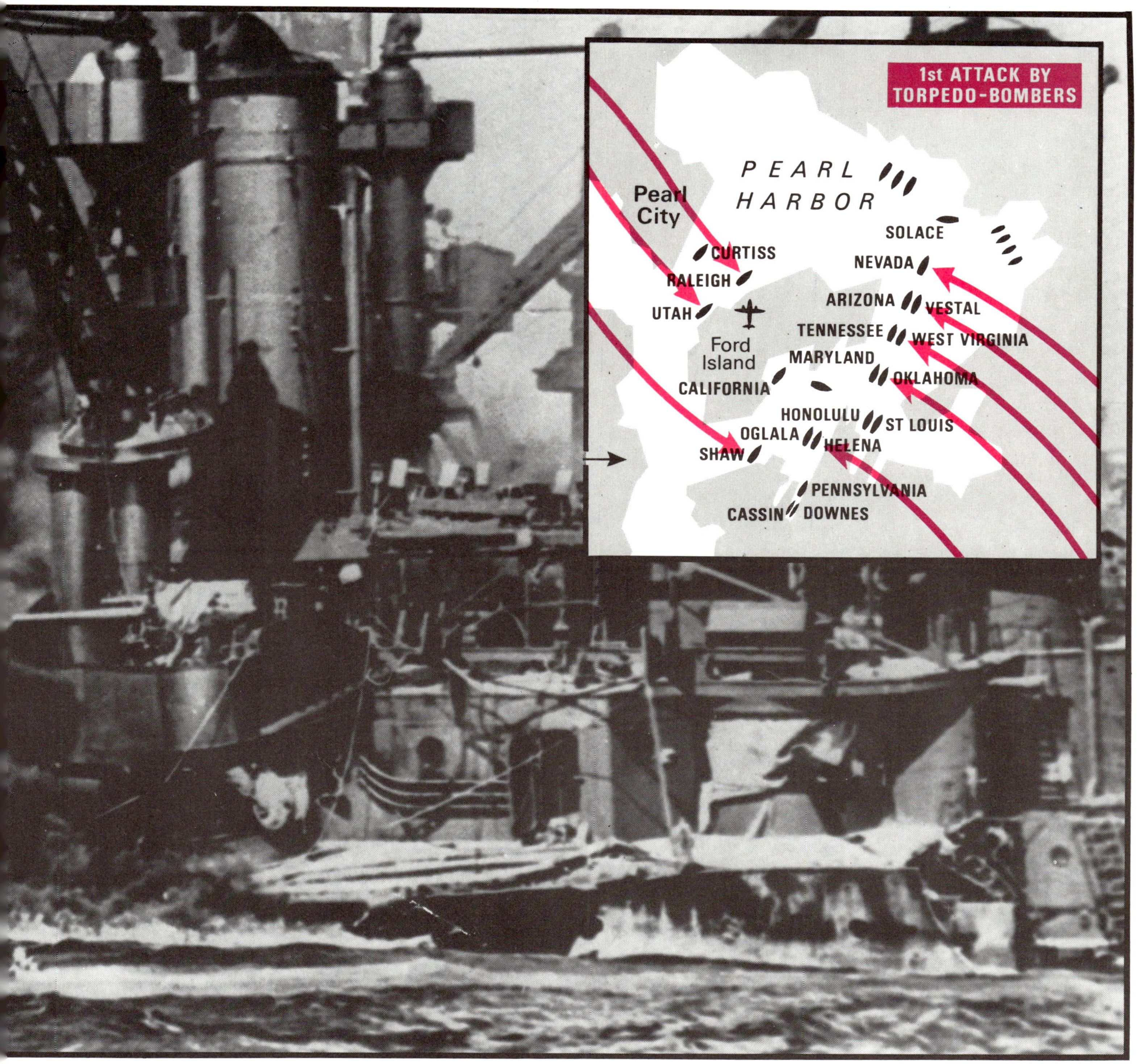

The way to do this, he insisted, was to strike a direct blow against America's greatest military asset in the Pacific – her Fleet, whose home base was Pearl Harbor.

As a result – and after Yamamoto's ideas had only weeks before overcome the opposition of the Japanese army and navy Establishment – the morning of November 26th, 1941, saw six Fleet carriers, two battleships, three cruisers and numerous other warships and supply ships of Admiral Nagumo's Fast Carrier Strike Force slip anchor from their staging-post off the Kurile Islands to the north of Japan and, observing strict radio silence, head off 3,000 miles east across the Pacific. Their destination was to be the launch-point for a massive air-strike planned to deal 'a devastating blow against the sea power of the nation standing between Japan and the glorious destiny mapped out by her leaders.'

L to R: *West Virginia, Tennessee* and *Arizona* after the attack

Meanwhile, despite their knowledge of Japanese diplomatic codes, their monitoring of naval radio communications and the certainty that Japan was, indeed, about to open hostilities against the USA, no one on the American side had any idea of the movement of the Fast Carrier Strike Force . . . nor, on that sunny, early morning of December 7th, 1941, had any particular alert been ordered to protect the warships riding placidly at their Hawaiian moorings around Ford Island, Pearl Harbor.

The great blow was at hand. America was about to be plunged into a World War that would only end some four years later in the holocausts of Hiroshima and Nagasaki . . .

. . . Pearl Harbor was under air attack.

Since 0615 hours the first wave of Japanese aircraft had been winging their way southwards led by Commander Mitsuo Fuchida, the air group commander, in the leading high-level bomber. A pair of trainee radar operators at the mobile station at Opana, practising with the equipment beyond the normal closing-down hour of 0700 hours, saw them appear on the screen at a range of 137 miles and plotted their approach just as a matter of interest: they were told by the information centre, to which they reported, that the contact could be disregarded as it was probably a flight of Fortresses due to arrive that morning from the mainland.

Fuchida led his swarm of aircraft down the western coast of Oahu, watched with idle curiosity by the many service and civilian families living along the shore, who took them for the air groups returning from the *Lexington* and *Enterprise*. By 0750 hours Fuchida could see across the central plain of the island to Pearl Harbor, its waters glinting in the early sunshine of a peaceful Sunday morning, and through binoculars he was able to count the seven capital ships moored two by two in 'Battleship Row' on the eastern side of Ford Island.

Surprise was complete: he gave the order to attack.

From endlessly repeated practice and meticulous study of maps and models of Oahu and Pearl Harbor, every Japanese pilot knew exactly what he had to do. While the squadrons of dive-bombers split up into sections which were to swoop simultaneously on the several army, navy, and marine airfields, the high-level bombers settled on to their pre-arranged approach course, bomb aimers adjusting their sights, and the torpedo-bombers began the long downward slant to their torpedo launching positions abreast the battleships. A few minutes before 0800 hours, to the scream of vertically plummeting planes, bombs began to burst among the aircraft drawn up, wing-tip to wing-tip in parade-ground perfection on the various airfields. Simultaneously the duty watch aboard the ships in 'Battleship Row', preparing for the eight o'clock ceremony of hoisting the colours, saw the torpedo-bombers dip low to launch their tor-

Sunk at Pearl Harbor, the USS **California. Length:** 624 feet. *Beam:* 97·5 feet. **Draught:** 32 feet. **Displacement:** 32,600 tons. **Speed:** 21·5 knots. **Armour:** *Belt:* 14 inches; *Conning tower:* 16 inches; **Armament:** 1 x 14-inch and 12 x 5-inch guns. **Launched:** 1921

Ford Island and 'Battleship Row' under Japanese attack. Note Japanese aircraft and explosions on far side of Ford Island

US Navy

pedoes and watched, horror-stricken, the thin pencil line of the tracks heading for their helpless, immobile hulls. Not an American gun had yet opened fire. Not an American fighter plane had taken off.

Moored together in the harbour, five of the battleships – *West Virginia, Arizona, Nevada, Oklahoma,* and *California* – were rent open by torpedo hits in the first few minutes; only the *Maryland* and *Tennessee,* occupying inside berths, and the flagship *Pennsylvania* which was in dry dock, escaped torpedo damage. Other ships torpedoed were the old target battleship *Utah,* and the light cruisers *Raleigh* and *Helena.*

Nevertheless, although to the shudder and shock of underwater explosions was soon added the rising whine of dive-bombers and the shriek and shattering detonation of bombs from them and from the high-flying bombers, the American crews, for the most

part, went into action with speed and efficiency, shooting down several of their attackers. Damage-control parties worked manfully to minimise the consequences of flooded compartments, counter-flooding to keep the foundering ships on an even keel, restoring electric and water power and communications, fighting the fires.

Meanwhile, however, high up above the smoke and confusion, hardly able at first to credit the total absence of any fighter opposition, and little inconvenienced by the sparse gunfire directed at them, Fuchida's high-level bombers were calmly selecting their targets and aiming with cool precision. An armour-piercing bomb sliced through the five inches of armour of a turret in the *Tennessee* to burst inside it; another plunged down through the several decks to explode in the forward magazine of the *Arizona,* which blew up. Both the *Maryland* and the *California* were hit with devastating effect.

When a lull occurred at 0825 hours, as the first wave of Japanese aircraft retired, almost every US aircraft at the air bases was damaged or destroyed, the *West Virginia* was sinking and on fire, the *Arizona* had settled on the bottom with more than a thousand of her crew fatally trapped below. The *Oklahoma* had capsized and settled on the bottom with her keel above water; the *Tennessee,* with a turret destroyed by an armour-piercing bomb, was badly on fire; and the *California* had received damage that was eventually to sink her, in spite of all efforts of her crew. Elsewhere, all that was visible of the *Utah* was her upturned keel. The *Raleigh,* deep in the water from flooding and counter-flooding, was being kept upright only by her mooring wires.

While all this had been taking place, at least one Japanese midget submarine succeeded in penetrating the harbour, passing through the gate in the boom defences which had been carelessly left open after the entry of two minesweepers at 0458 hours. During a lull in the air attacks this submarine was sighted just as it was firing a torpedo at the seaplane tender *Curtiss.* The torpedo missed and exploded harmlessly against the shore, as did a second one. The submarine was attacked by the destroyer *Monaghan* and sunk by depth charges. Of the other three midgets launched from their parent submarines, two were lost without trace; the third, after running on a reef and being fired at by the destroyer *Helm,* was finally beached and her crew taken prisoner. The parent submarines and the 11 other large boats of the Advanced Expeditionary Force achieved nothing.

The second wave of Japanese aircraft – 54 bombers, 80 dive-bombers, and 36 fighters, led by Lieutenant Commander Shimazaki of the aircraft-carrier *Zuikaku* – had taken off an hour after the first wave. They were met by a more effective defence and thus achieved much less. In the breathing space between the two attacks, ammunition supply for the US anti-aircraft guns had been replenished, gun crews reorganised, and reinforced; and a number of the Japanese dive-bombers were shot down. Nevertheless, they succeeded in damaging the *Pennsylvania,* wrecking two destroyers which were sharing the dry-dock with her, blowing up another destroyer in the floating dock, and forcing the *Nevada* – feeling her way towards the harbour entrance through the billowing clouds of black smoke from burning ships – to beach herself. Meanwhile the high-level bombers were able to make undisturbed practice and wreak further damage on the already shattered and burning US ships.

At 1000 hours it was suddenly all over. The rumble of retreating aircraft engines died away leaving a strange silence except for the crackle of burning ships, the hissing of water hoses and the desperate shouts of men fighting the fires. For the loss of only nine fighters, 15 dive-bombers, and five torpedo-bombers out of the 384 planes engaged, the Japanese navy had succeeded in putting out of action the entire battleship force of the US Pacific Fleet.

To the anxious Nagumo the success seemed so miraculously complete, and the price paid so small, that when Fuchida and other air squadron commanders urged him to mount a second attack, he felt it would be tempting fate to comply. Against their advice, he gave orders for his force to steer away to the north-west to rendezvous with his replenishment aircraft-carriers, and thence set a course for Japan.

This was a bad mistake – but Nagumo, who was no airman, was not alone at that time in a lack of appreciation of the fact that the massive gun armaments of majestic battleships were no longer the most effective means of exercising sea power. In the vast spaces of the Pacific, only the aircraft-carrier had the long arms with which to feel for and strike at an enemy fleet – and a rich reward would have awaited a second sortie by his exultant airmen. Not only was the *Enterprise* approaching Pearl Harbor from her mission to Wake, and could hardly have survived a massed aerial attack, but the repair facilities of Pearl Harbor and the huge oil-tank farm, its tanks brimming with fuel, still lay intact and now virtually defenceless. Without them the naval base would have been useless for many months to come, forcing what remained of the US Pacific Fleet to retire to its nearest base on the American west coast, out of range of the coming area of operations in the Pacific.

Thus Yamamoto's daring and well-planned attack failed to reap the fullest possible harvest – though undoubtedly the blow it delivered to the United States navy was heavy indeed. But it had one effect even more decisive than that on sea power, for it brought the American people, united, into the war.

Perhaps only such a shock as that delivered at Pearl Harbor could have achieved such a result.

Associated Press

...WITHIN HOURS OF PEARL HARBOR
THE FIGHT FOR WAKE

Colonel Robert D. Heinl, Jr

Grumman F4F Wildcat was Grumman's first monoplane fighter for the US Navy. Tubby and highly manoeuvrable, it put up heroic resistance to the Japanese onslaught of 1941 and early 1942. The same plane was rushed into British service as the 'Martlet 1'

Max Speed: 330 mph at 21,000 feet. **Range:** 845 miles at cruising speed. **Armament:** 4×·5-inch machine-guns

Seven of Wake's 12 Wildcats lie destroyed after a bombing raid on December 8

Admiral Kimmel, the ill-fated commander of the Pacific Fleet at Pearl Harbor, had predicted that one of the first Japanese operations on the outbreak of war would be against Wake; and the first troops had arrived in August 1941. By November, while all weapons had been emplaced, there were still less than 400 Marines to man them. Besides having only one-third of its garrison, Wake suffered from other shortages. Much fire-control equipment had not arrived. Radars intended for Wake were awaiting shipment at Pearl Harbor. There were no mines, no barbed wire, no revetments for aircraft.

On December 4, however, the fighters arrived. Twelve new Grumman Wildcats of Marine Fighting Squadron 211 (VMF-211), flew ashore from USS *Enterprise*. This brought the total of Marines —ground and air—to 449. Commanding the ground defences on Wake was Major James P. S. Devereux; the commander of VMF-211 was Major Paul. A. Putnam. The atoll commander, who had relieved Devereux on November 28, was Commander W. S. Cunningham.

At 0650 hours on December 8, 1941, a signal blurted through from Hawaii: Pearl Harbor and Hickham Field were under Japanese attack. Moments later, 'Call to Arms' was blaring for the Marines. Troops piled out with rifles and steel helmets, and trucks jolted over the coral towards the gun-positions.

About noon, rain-squalls masked Wake. While

the Wildcats patrolled north, 36 grey Japanese bombers came in low from the south. The CO of an AA Battery saw them first. Barking the report into a field telephone, he signalled his gunners to commence firing.

Wake's airstrip took the brunt. Seven American fighters were burnt out or blasted. Fires engulfed the squadron's scanty stocks of tools, spares, and manuals. The air-to-ground radio was riddled. Out of 55 officers and men on the ground when the Japanese struck, VMF-211 had 23 killed (including three pilots) and 11 wounded.

Methodical to a fault, the bombers returned next day at 1145 hours. Before they could release their bombs, Putnam's four air-worthy fighters slashed in. One bomber faltered and spun down; then the batteries opened fire. Another bomber disintegrated, and others trailed smoke. Battered by flak, the Japanese pounded Wake again, leaving ruin and flame behind them—but this time only 14 bombers limped home.

Even though the flak and the fighters still fought back—three more bombers were shot down on the third day—Admiral Kajioka felt satisfied with the damage inflicted on the Wake defences to date. Structures razed, heavy explosions, large fires, and extensive cratering reported—all presented a picture of destruction. And on December 9 the Japanese fleet set sail

to capture Wake. Arriving off Wake before dawn on December 11, the Japanese landing force began to transfer to the boats. As day broke, Kajioka's flagship, two other cruisers, and six destroyers commenced bombardment. Gradually closing in, the Japanese shelled Wake heavily—and received no reply.

At 0615 hours, after a bombardment of 45 minutes' shelling, Major Devereux knew that the moment had come: the Japanese were well inside the range of Wake's guns. He gave the order to open fire. The battery on Peacock Point drew first blood. On the waterline of Kajioka's flagship, two 5-inch projectiles punched through and burst. Steam and smoke belched from the holes, and another salvo hit just aft of the first. Slowing down, *Yubari* turned away while a destroyer made smoke to screen the wounded cruiser.

At the other end of Wake, the Wilkes Island 5-inch battery had been tracking three destroyers. When *Yubari* was hit, these ships closed the beach, firing as they came. Nearing the reef, *Hayate,* leading, turned parallel to the shore. At 4,000 yards, broadside on, she was a tempting target for a battery whose range-finder had been destroyed during the bombing. Estimating range, the battery commander opened fire; and on the third salvo, the *Hayate* was obliterated by a violent explosion. As smoke, spray, and debris cleared away, the American gunners saw that she had been disabled and was sinking rapidly but her crew managed to beach her. She was the first Japanese warship destroyed in the war.

The battery resumed fire on the next ship in column. She too was hit and, like *Yubari,* turned into the smoke. Then the gunners scored hits on another cruiser, on a transport hastily hoisting in boats, and on two more destroyers. Soon after 0700 hours, Kajioka was in retreat.

Now came VMF-211's turn. Putnam had taken off with his four fighters at dawn to intercept any aircraft accompanying the attack—but also armed with bombs in case the Japanese fighters did not intervene. Seeing Kajioka retire, Putnam led his Wildcats in a steep dive through heavy flak and bombed two cruisers. As each pilot dropped his bombs, he swooped back to Wake to re-arm. The second sorties brought even better hunting. Incredibly carrying a deck-load of depth-charges, the destroyer *Kisaragi* was bombed by Captain Henry T. Elrod. The depth-charges exploded with a crash—and *Kisaragi* vanished.

Wake's guns and handful of aircraft had stopped an amphibious attack, sunk two warships, damaged seven more, and inflicted about 700 casualties on the Japanese (mostly dead).

For the defenders of Wake, the days following the attack fused into each other. Each day there was at least one heavy air raid, but fighters opposed every attack and the guns shot back even though there was only one serviceable director and one height-finder left.

Wake's resources were wearing thin. On December 17, the atoll commander told Pearl Harbor that over half the vehicles and engineering equipment were destroyed, the petrol mostly consumed, all workshops and warehouses obliterated, and civilian morale poor.

On December 21, Kajioka sailed again from Roi. This time he had additional cruisers and destroyers, and a landing force battalion hastily transferred from Saipan. He also had two fleet aircraft-carriers, *Soryu* and *Hiryu*. Companies of the landing force were aboard two ancient destroyers which, at any cost, were to be rammed ashore on Wake. And, most important, Kajioka knew that Wake's last aircraft had gone: it was lost in desperate combat with Zeros and dive-bombers from the carriers, on December 22.

Soon after midnight on the 23rd, amid squalls and foul weather, the Japanese formed up off Wake's south shore. Landing-craft were to flank the destroyers' lunge on to the beaches; infiltrators in rubber boats were to enter the lagoon. On the signal, they headed for the shore; and the destroyers grounded.

A searchlight flashed on and machine-guns opened up. The only gun bearing on the grounded destroyers was near the airstrip; its scratch crew of Marines and civilians put 15 shells into the nearer destroyer. As Japanese troops tumbled clear, the ship exploded and broke her back. In the lurid light, the thin groups of defenders could see the Japanese swarming ashore from the other ship and from barges along the beach.

By dawn at least 1,000 Japanese were ashore, fighting amid brush and boulders along the southern leg of Wake Island, overrunning the airfield, but stopping at the perimeter manned by the surviving officers and men of VMF-211 who, in the tradition of their corps, had formed as infantry when the last aircraft was gone. North of the airstrip, Major Devereux had a precarious line across the other leg of the island, but there was no knowing how long this could hold—40 riflemen against hundreds. Now the sun was up, dive-bombers and cruisers hammered the island.

Devereux went to Cunningham. When the answer was negative, Devereux explained the hopelessness of the situation, and Cunningham went to find a dress uniform for the surrender. With a white flag, Devereux marched sadly towards the Japanese.

Lacking radar, with less than half the crews for its guns, with no infantry reserve, Wake was foredoomed when its fighters could no longer contest the sky. That this handful of Marines could hold out more than two weeks, sinking Japanese ships, downing 21 Japanese aircraft, and fighting to the last with rifle and bayonet, gave encouragement and resolution to their countrymen.

At a press conference in 1942, a reporter, contrasting less brilliant performances elsewhere, asked the Major-General Commandant of the Marine Corps how he explained Wake's stout resistance. The reply spoke like a howitzer: 'Just what did you expect of the Marines, anyway?'

US Navy Dept.

AMERICA'S AIR ARM

When the war in the Pacific opened, the American and Allied air forces were tactically and numerically inferior. Their standard fighter aircraft (F-2A Buffalo and the P-40) were totally outclassed by the Japanese Zero. The B-17 Flying Fortress bomber proved a formidable weapon, but for all its toughness and hitting power its value was jeopardised by the lack of Allied fighter protection—and this only time could remedy

Boeing B-17 Flying Fortress served with the US Army Air Force throughout the war, also serving with the RAF. Japanese pilots respected its bristling armament. **Max speed:** 300 mph. **Range:** 1,850 miles. **Armament:** up to 13 ·50 machine-guns; up to 8,000 lbs of bombs

FROM THE JAPANESE ARSENAL

The Japanese army was primarily an infantry force, and consequently its field units were relatively well supplied with artillery. The equipment compared well with that in other armies, being soundly constructed, reliable in action, and with good range and hitting power. All these howitzers had their gun counterparts, but these were less widely used because the terrain made the plunging fire of howitzers and mortars of higher value in the Pacific War

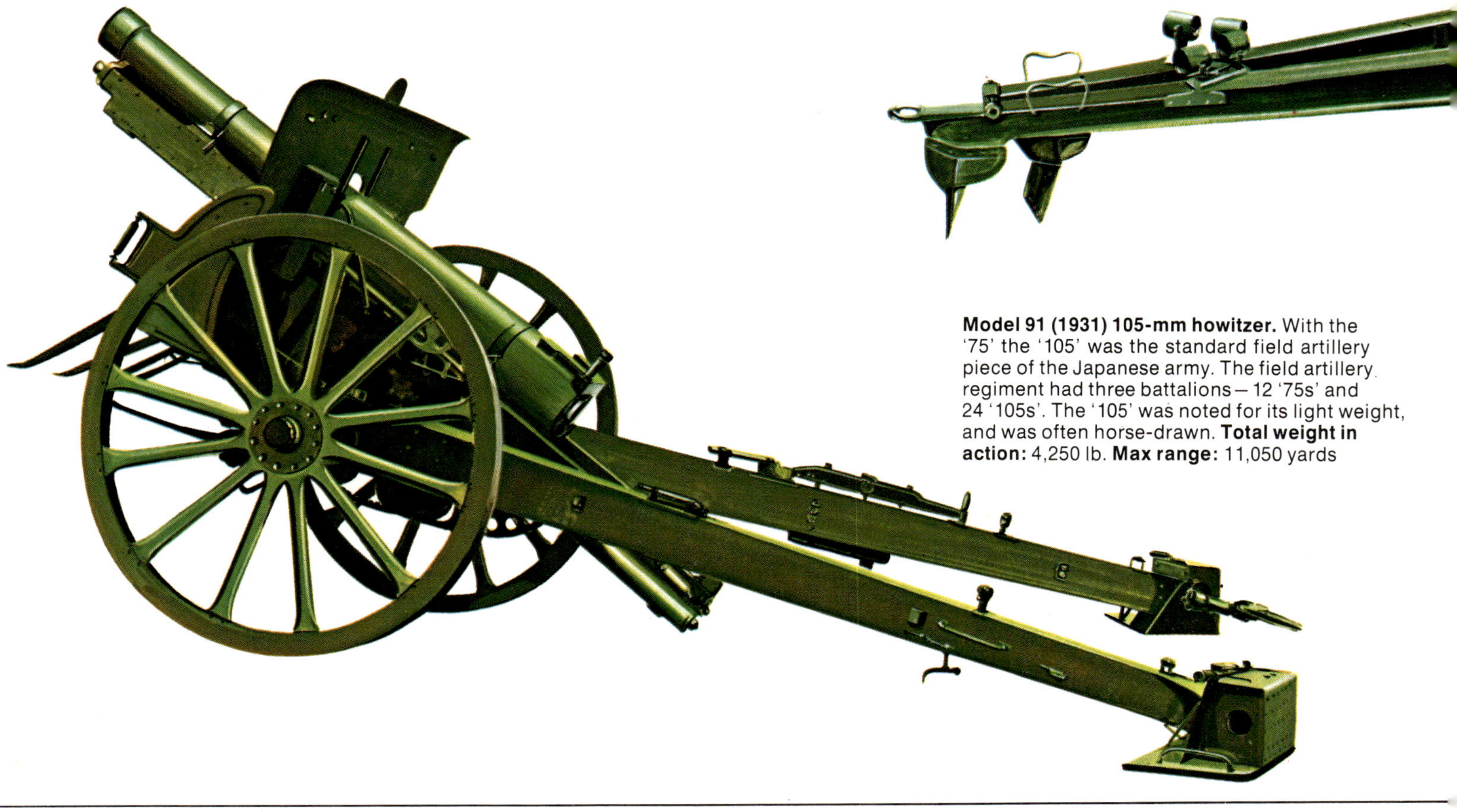

Model 91 (1931) 105-mm howitzer. With the '75' the '105' was the standard field artillery piece of the Japanese army. The field artillery regiment had three battalions—12 '75s' and 24 '105s'. The '105' was noted for its light weight, and was often horse-drawn. **Total weight in action:** 4,250 lb. **Max range:** 11,050 yards

Curtiss P-40 was the first mass-produced US monoplane fighter, and constituted more than half the US fighter strength at the beginning of the war. It was supplied to the RAF, where it was known as the Tomahawk. **Max speed:** 357 mph. **Max range:** 1,400 miles. **Armament:** two ·30, two ·50 machine-guns

Brewster F2A Buffalo was the US Navy's first monoplane fighter. Official vacillation resulted in its near obsolescence by the beginning of the Pacific War. **Max speed**: 313 mph. **Max range:** 650 miles. **Armament:** two ·50 machine-guns

Model 92 (1932) 70-mm howitzer. Every Japanese infantry battalion had a two-gun, two-platoon company equipped with this infantry support weapon. It was light in weight and manoeuvrable, and fired a projectile of relatively large weight. **Total weight in action:** 468 lb. **Max range:** 3,075 yards

Model 4 (1915) 150-mm howitzer. One of the standard medium artillery weapons; each battalion had three companies with four '150s' apiece. The newer model 96 (1936) could be fired at the unusually high elevation of 75° if a deep loading-pit were dug beneath the breech. **Total weight in action:** 6,100 lb. **Max range:** 10,500 yards

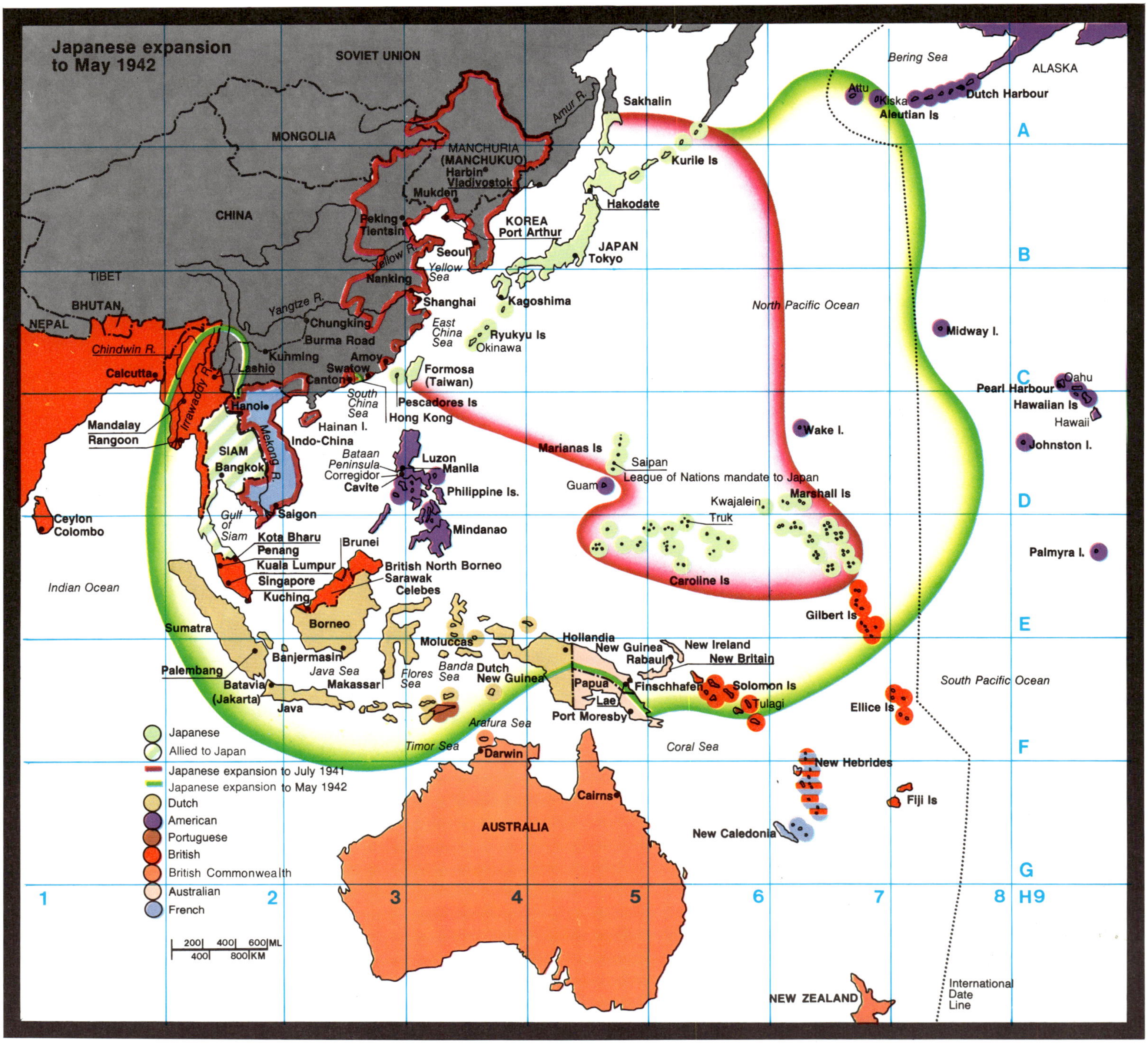

BLITZKRIEG OF THE RISING SUN

On December 8, 1941, while fires around Ford Island, Pearl Harbor, were still burning, Japanese bombers destroyed 42 US planes on the ground in the Philippines. Far to the west, General Yamashita's 60,000-strong XXV Army, together with 459 Army and 159 Navy aircraft of the 111 Air Group and airborne troops drawn from the battlefields of Manchuria arrived in an armada of transports to establish beach-heads in Thailand and the north of Malaya. Way out in the Pacific, to the north of the Marshall Islands group, Japanese forces opened an attack on Wake Island – an attack that was to cost them two destroyers and 1,150 men and take until December 23 to complete. The same day, from their bases on the Chinese mainland, Japanese forces began an assault on the British base of Hong Kong lying one mile offshore.

The first round of the 'Oriental Blitzkrieg' had begun, and everywhere the Allies – though fully expecting an enemy offensive – had been caught unprepared.

In the next few days, though, the situation worsened considerably. Guam, an important American base far out on the Pacific rim, was overrun in only 30 minutes on the 10th. The same day, in the Gulf of Siam, a British battleship force

The sinking of Force Z. Below: *Repulse* narrowly dodges bombs

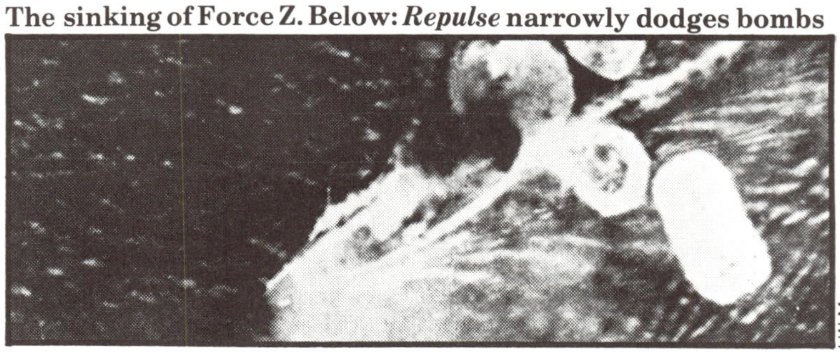

I.W.M.

Left: Japan strikes south. Map showing the expansion of Japan to May 1942—the fruits of the 'Oriental Blitzkrieg'

Above: In Burma, as Japanese infantry charge, a machine-gun covers the advance

Japan's Aerial Élite—Her Long-Range Strike Force

The Japanese Navy and Army Air Forces had a numerous fleet of medium bombers with remarkable ranges, needed to deal with the vast distances of the Pacific theatre. Japanese bombers all suffered to some extent from weak defensive armament—none of them had as many machine-guns as the US B-25 Mitchell, for example. But in the first Japanese sweep through the Pacific—when the Zeros ruled the skies—Japanese bombing-strikes were never effectively challenged; and their weaker army fighters were able to hold their own

Mitsubishi G4M *(Betty)* was the Japanese navy's principal wartime bomber; but the needs of its strike and support role demanded range, which had to be purchased at the expense of defensive armament. This inevitably meant high losses for the *Betty* crews. It served as transport, level- and torpedo-bomber, and reconnaissance aircraft. **Max speed:** 276 mph. **Range:** 2,620 miles. **Armament:** up to five 7·7-mm machine-guns. **Bomb load:** 1,765 lbs

Mitsubishi Ki-21 *(Sally)* was the standard bomber type at the time of Pearl Harbor, and played an important role throughout the war, although it had become obsolescent long before 1945. **Max speed:** 248 mph. **Range:** 1,180 miles. **Armament:** up to five 7·7-mm machine-guns. **Bomb load:** 2,100 lbs

Nakajima Ki-43 *(Oscar)* had the highest production of any of the Japanese army's fighters. It served in all theatres of the Pacific War, although it was far outclassed by later Japanese fighter designs; and it had the typical manoeuvrability of Japanese fighters. **Max speed:** 308 mph. **Range:** 745 miles. **Armament:** two 7·7-mm machine-guns

America's Challenge – Her Carrier-Borne Aircraft

In the first year of the Pacific War, the US carrier-borne force had no fighter which could match the Japanese Zero in manoeuvrability and hitting-power. But both the Dauntless and Devastator strike aircraft–although obsolescent at the time of Pearl Harbor–served with great distinction, and inflicted heavy damage on the ships of the Japanese navy

Douglas SBD-III Dauntless became the backbone of the US carrier light-bomber force. Not only could it absorb considerable punishment, but it also had the lowest loss figures of any US carrier aircraft. **Max speed:** 275 mph. **Max range:** 875 miles. **Crew:** 2. **Armament:** twin ·50 machine-guns; one 500-lb bomb

Douglas TBD-1 Devastator suffered heavy losses because of its inadequate defensive armament, but it formed the mainstay of the US navy's carrier torpedo-bomber force in the early stages of the Pacific War. **Max speed:** 225 mph. **Max range:** 985 miles. **Crew:** 3. **Armament:** one ·30, one ·50 machine-gun; one 1,000-lb torpedo

Grumman F4F Wildcat was the standard US navy fighter in 1941 and the first five months of 1942. It earned undying battle-honours in its defence of Wake Atoll, and also served with the RAF as the 'Martlet'. **Max speed:** 330 mph. **Max range:** 845 miles. **Armament:** four ·50 machine-guns

Above: Japanese troops cheer the news of the surrender of the Hong Kong garrison

sent north from Singapore to intercept enemy transports supplying the landings in Malaya and Thailand (Force Z), was caught without air cover by a flight of Japanese bombers from Saigon. The capital ships *Prince of Wales* and *Repulse* were both sunk within the hour, and with them the fate of Malaya was sealed and Japanese control of the Pacific and Indian Oceans was confirmed.

This control was to be illustrated later in two actions that virtually eliminated any Allied naval presence east of the Persian Gulf. The first, the Battle of the Java Sea, on February 27, 1942, resulted in the loss of 11 out of 14 Dutch, American, Australian and British ships without loss to the Imperial Navy. The second, off Ceylon on April 1, 1942, set the British Eastern Fleet against the victors of Pearl Harbor – Admiral Nagumo's well-trained and practised naval aviators of the Fast Carrier Striking Force. The outcome was yet another disaster for the Allies, with the loss to bombs and torpedoes of the heavy cruisers *Cornwall* and *Dorsetshire*. But still the essential lessons of air cover for naval forces had not been learned, and on April 9 the same Japanese aviators were able to sink the old British carrier *Hermes,* the destroyer *Vampire,* a corvette, a tanker and a fleet auxiliary in a

US Army

Above: Japanese flame-thrower attack on an American blockhouse in the main defence line on the Bataan Peninsula of Luzon
Below: Japanese infantry advance stealthily through a Malayan rail-yard

Imperial War Museum

1941 December 7: The Japanese bomb US naval and air units at Pearl Harbor.
December 8: News of the Japanese attack on Pearl Harbor is received at 0230 hours, but the Japanese still catch the majority of American aircraft in the Philippines on the ground when they attack at 1215 hours. Some 17 B-17s, 56 fighters, and 30 other aircraft are destroyed. First Japanese landing on the island of Batan. Four hours after the Pearl Harbor air-strike, Japanese forces in China begin the attack on the British colony of Hong Kong. From Singapore, Admiral Phillips heads north with *Repulse* and *Prince of Wales* (Force Z) to strike at the Japanese supplies for the beach-heads at Kota Bharu and Singora, which have started the invasion of Malaya and Thailand.
December 8/9: The Japanese seize and retain the initiative in Malaya: the British fall back from Jitra to Alor Star. Force Z abandons its northward sweep, but is sighted and its position reported by a Japanese submarine.
December 10: *Repulse* and *Prince of Wales* are sunk by Japanese air attacks due to the lack of British air cover.
December 10/22: Japanese advance forces land in north and south Luzon, Mindanao, and Jolo, capturing airfields and liquidating local opposition.
December 12: The British begin evacuation from Hong Kong's mainland defences.
December 17: In Malaya, the British withdraw to the Perak river.

JAPAN'S LIGHT TANKS – OUT-DATED BUT UNCHALLENGED

Japanese tanks in 1941 were light – none of their designs were over 22 tons – but in the Pacific theatre this made them easily transportable for attacks on the 'Southern Area', and for later amphibious warfare in the Pacific islands. British troops in the Far East were equipped with obsolete weapons, however, and Japan's armoured attacks in Burma and Malaya faced little positive opposition.

Light Type 95. This Japanese tank saw action both in Malaya and later Pacific campaigns, remaining operational until 1943. **Weight:** 10 tons. **Crew:** 3. **Armour:** 14-mm (max). **Armament:** 1×37-mm gun, 2×7·7-mm machine-guns. **Speed:** 28 mph. **Range:** 100 miles

Below: Surrender at Singapore. Some of the 130,000 Allies lost with the city

Paul Popper

December 18/19: Japanese land large forces on Hong Kong island and establish beach-heads.
December 22: Main Japanese landings at Lingayen Bay and Lamon Bay in the Philippines meet with light resistance. The Japanese now begin to advance on Manila from north and south.
December 23: MacArthur announces a plan for withdrawal to Bataan, leaving Manila as an 'open city'. Japanese receive the surrender of Wake.
December 25: The British garrison of Hong Kong surrenders.
December 26: In Malaya, Japanese forces break the Perak river defences and advance south to Ipoh. Carmen falls, and Japanese gain control of the main road to Manila.
December 29: Japanese aircraft make their first heavy raid on Corregidor.
December 31: Japanese have advanced to within 30 miles of Manila, but their failure to destroy the bridges at Calumpit allows the American and Philippine troops to withdraw and form a defence line between Porac and Guagua.
1942 **January 1:** The US troops on Corregidor are put on half rations.
January 2: Japanese begin air attacks on Rabaul and Balikpapan – the prelude to invasion of New Britain and Borneo.
January 2/9: American and Philippine troops dig in on Bataan peninsula.
January 7: Japanese break the Slim river defences: central Malaya is open to them.
January 9/February 28: Savage fighting in the Philippines, the Japanese suffer heavy casualties while forcing back the defenders.
January 10: The Allies in the south-west Pacific set up a combined command – ABDA (American, British, Dutch, and Australian). General Sir Archibald Wavell is appointed Supreme Commander.
January 11: The Japanese begin their campaign in the Dutch East Indies by attacking Tarakan and Manado. Both targets fall within a few days.
January 11: Japanese enter Kuala Lumpur. The Japanese drive down the west coast of Malaya begins.
January 23/February 9: Japanese forces continue their sweep of the Dutch East Indies by taking Balikpapan, Kendari, Ambon, Ulin, and the port of Makassar.
January 30/31: British and Empire forces withdraw to Singapore Island.
February 3: Port Moresby – a major Japanese target – is subjected to its first air raid.
February 7/9: Japanese land large forces on Singapore Island and establish beach-heads.
February 8: A proposal that the Philippines be granted their independence and declared a neutral area is rejected by President Roosevelt.
February 15: Singapore surrenders to the Japanese on 'Black Sunday'.
February 19: Some 135 Japanese aircraft

Sado-Opera Mundi

Above: Japanese troops go ashore in the attack against North Borneo, part of a massive sweep into the 'Southern Area'

further continuation of the same action.

By this time, though, the situation on land had gone from bad to desperate. On Christmas Day, 1941, the British bastion of Hong Kong fell, leaving the uselessly exposed garrison of 12,000 to their fate as Japanese prisoners of war. In Malaya, 80,000 British and Commonwealth troops – inadequately trained and unprepared to meet an attack from the north – fell back disorganised and demoralised in the face of General Yamashita's specially trained and equipped jungle fighters. On January 31 they reeled into Singapore, where – virtually without air cover and defenceless from the landward side – they could offer little resistance to Japanese landings. As a result, on February 15, the island surrendered – 138,708 prisoners and casualties falling to the Japanese who, at a cost of a mere 9,284 casualties, had inflicted one of the most disastrous defeats in British military history.

But there was still more to come. To the north, in the longest retreat in British

Below: A blazing B-17 bomber after a Japanese air-raid on Bandung airfield, Java

Rijksinstituut voor Oorlogsdocumentatie

Below: Faces of the 'Bataan Death March'

military history, Japanese forces harried the Allies through Malaya, Thailand and Burma. At a cost of 4,597 casualties against the Allies' 13,463, the Japanese eventually pushed the British and Commonwealth troops across the Indian frontier on May 20, 1942.

Meanwhile, on January 11, 1942, the Japanese began their campaign against the strategically vital, oil and mineral-rich Dutch East Indies. Within days Tarakan in Borneo and Manado in the Celebes had fallen. By February 9, Makassar in the Celebes, the island of Ambon, and Balikpapan in Borneo had fallen. Resistance in the ill-defended jungle terrain was virtually impossible, and on March 8 – after the Battle of the Java Sea had destroyed any hope of Allied counter-measures – the Dutch East Indies surrendered unconditionally.

In the Philippines, Japanese landings since December 10 had driven the diseased, demoralised American and Filipino troops – since March 12 without their commander, General Douglas MacArthur, who had repaired on Presidential orders to Australia – onto the Bataan Peninsula and the fortress of Corregidor Island guarding Manila Bay. But there was no escape, and on April 9, 78,000 unfortunate Allied troops surrendered to Japan's General Homma. *En route* to prison camps 65 miles distant, so many of these prisoners were to die that the journey became known as the 'Bataan Death March'.

With the fall of the Dutch East Indies, though, the 'Oriental Blitzkrieg' had achieved its objective, and the first phase of the Pacific War was over. Japan had established an island ring in the Pacific behind which she would consolidate her gains and prepare for the inevitable Allied counter-offensive.

Amid all the optimism born of success, though, the Japanese planners had somewhere lost sight of the reality of the war to which they were now committed. In not destroying those two American carriers at Pearl Harbor or in fleet actions soon after, and in extending their conquests far beyond their ability to resist concentrated attack, they had in fact planted the seeds of their own eventual destruction.

In naval aviation alone, America still had a counter-offensive capability equal to that of Japan, and in the fleet actions that were soon to follow this over-confidence would be dramatically and fatally illustrated.

The 'Oriental Blitzkrieg' was indeed an astonishing military victory, but with its completion the Japanese Empire in the Pacific and South-East Asia had reached its limit.

Nakajima B5N2 'Kate'. This plane was in the forefront of the Pearl Harbor attack, and was later to deliver fatal blows to the carriers *Lexington*, *Yorktown* and *Hornet*. **Max speed:** 235 mph at 11,810 feet. **Max range:** 1237 miles. **Armament:** 1×7·7-mm machine-gun plus 1764 lbs of bombs or torpedoes

Below: May 6, 1942. The final surrender of 15,000 Allied troops on Corregidor

bomb and strafe the port of Darwin in northern Australia. In this one raid alone, 240 people are killed and more than 150 wounded.
February 27: Battle of the Java Sea. Allied ships challenge a superior Japanese naval force in an attempt to stop the invasion of Java. But Allied losses are heavy, and the invasion takes place, delayed for only one day by the action.
March 4: Japanese Zeros attack the harbour and airfield at Broome, Australia: 16 flying boats and seven aircraft are destroyed in the 15-minute raid.
March 8: The Dutch East Indies government, after talks with the Japanese C-in-C, decides to surrender unconditionally.
March 12: MacArthur leaves Corregidor – 'I shall return'.
March 17: The first of three US fighter squadrons arrives at Darwin: from now on, Japanese raids on Darwin begin to lose intensity.
March 24: Japanese begin their attack on Bataan, and begin a regular artillery bombardment of Corregidor.
April 8: Japanese receive the last surrenders of Bataan in the Philippines.
April 18: 16 Mitchell B-25 bombers, launched from US aircraft-carriers, carry out the first air raid on Japan.
May 5: The Japanese forces cross to Corregidor island and establish a beach-head.
May 6: Japanese receive the surrender of Corregidor.

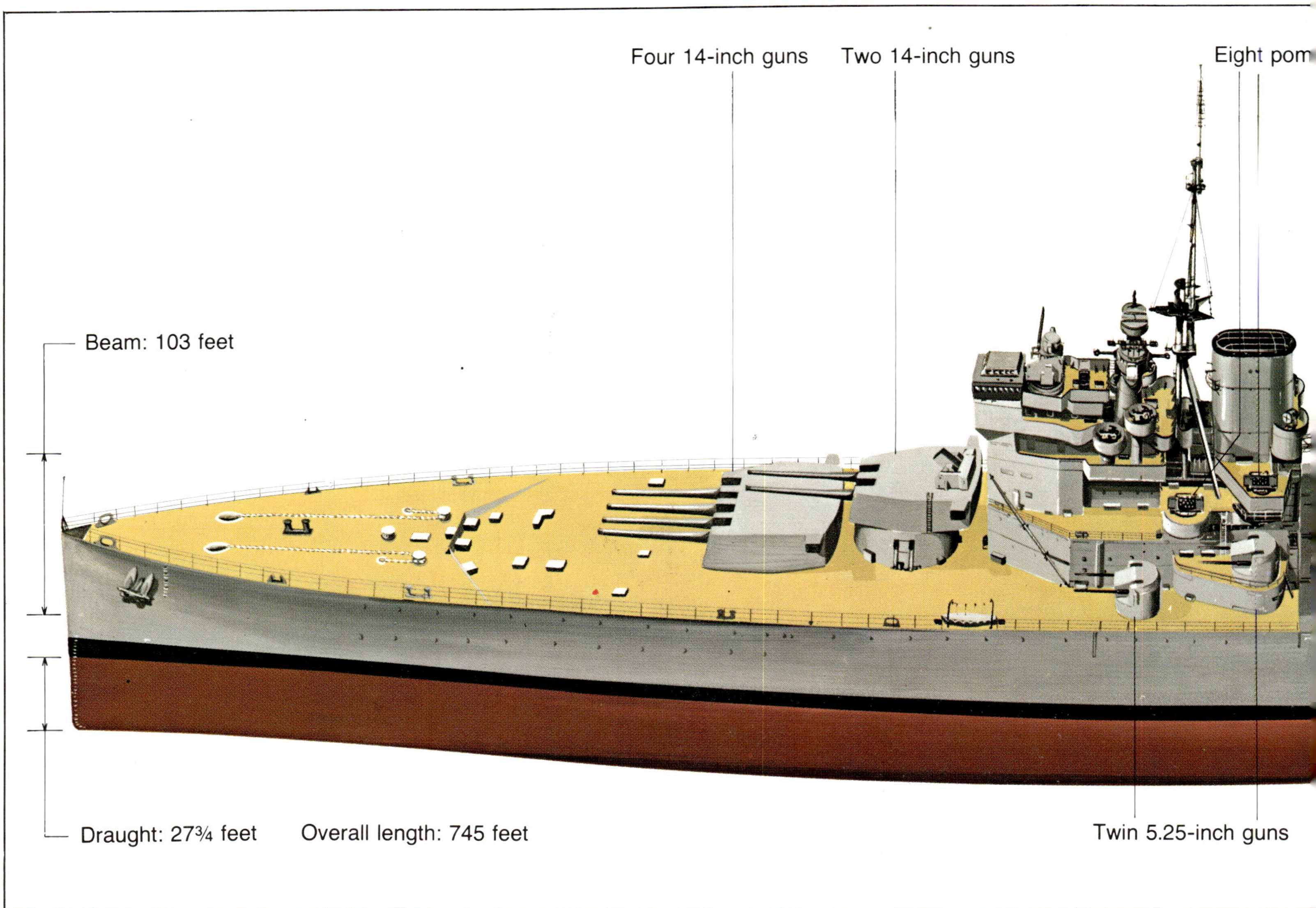
Four 14-inch guns
Two 14-inch guns
Eight pom
Beam: 103 feet
Draught: 27¾ feet
Overall length: 745 feet
Twin 5.25-inch guns

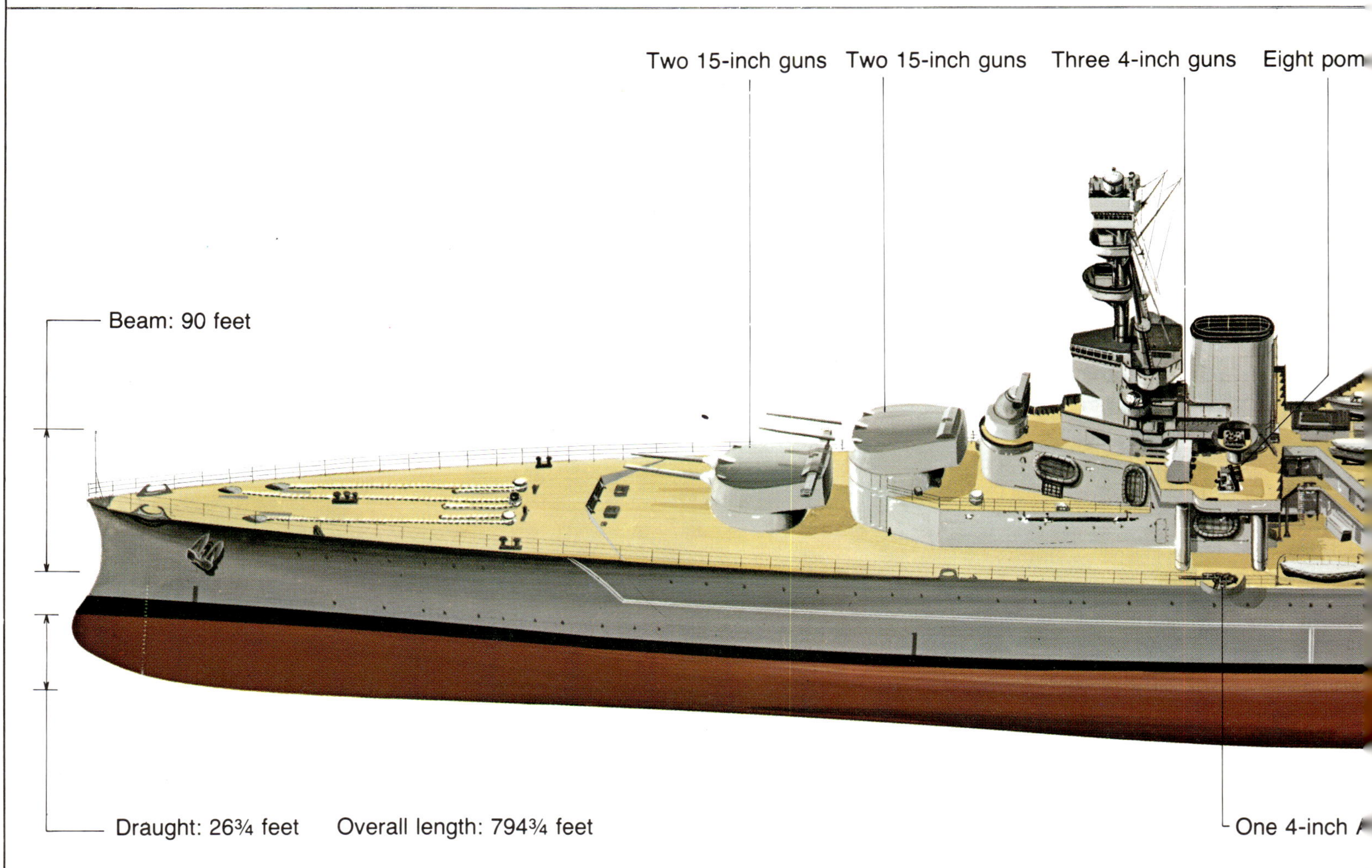
Two 15-inch guns
Two 15-inch guns
Three 4-inch guns
Eight pom
Beam: 90 feet
Draught: 26¾ feet
Overall length: 794¾ feet
One 4-inch

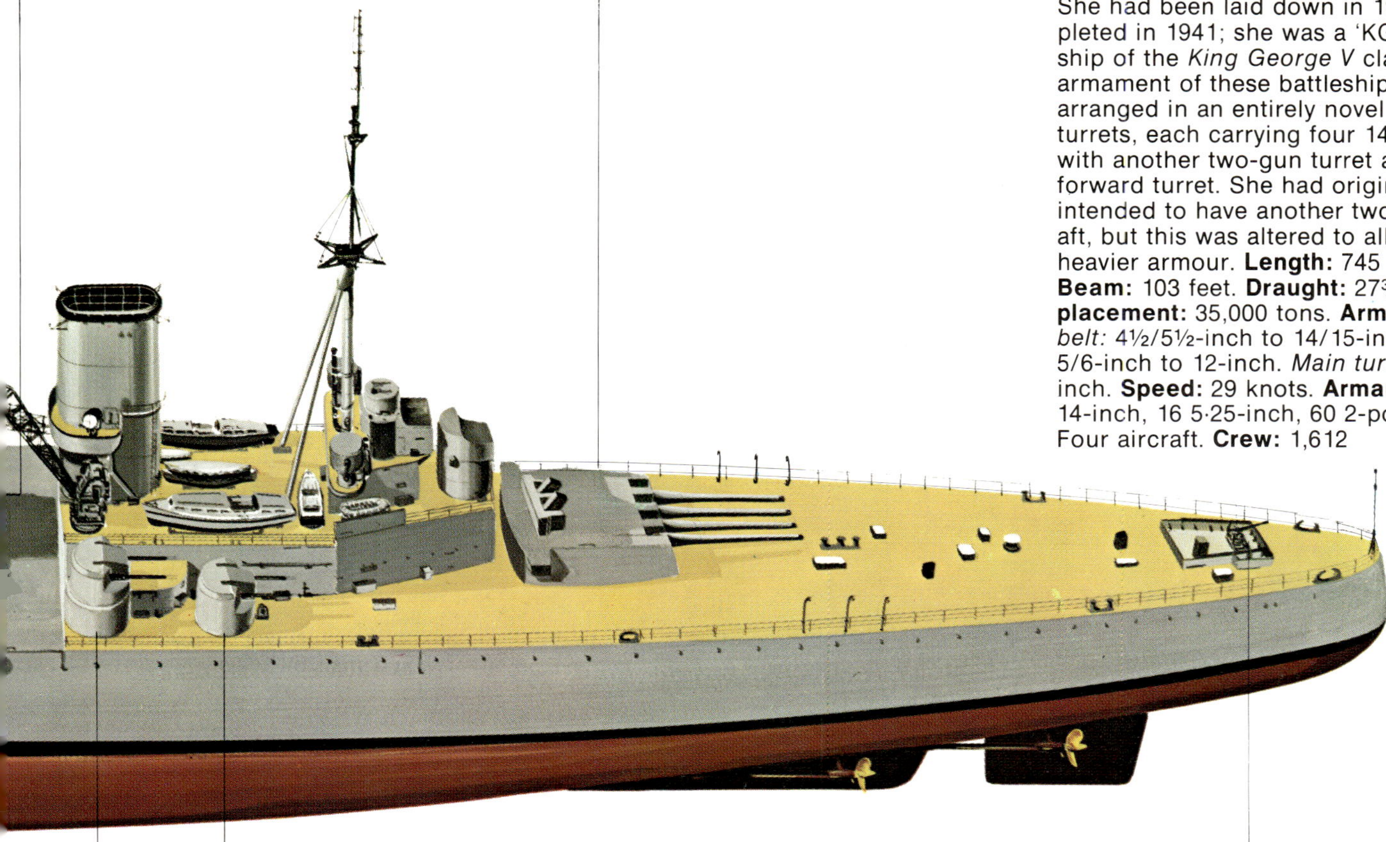

Prince of Wales represented the ultimate in battleship design for the Royal Navy. She had been laid down in 1939 and completed in 1941; she was a 'KG V'—a battleship of the *King George V* class. The main armament of these battleships was arranged in an entirely novel way: two turrets, each carrying four 14-inch guns, with another two-gun turret above the forward turret. She had originally been intended to have another two-gun turret aft, but this was altered to allow for heavier armour. **Length:** 745 feet overall. **Beam:** 103 feet. **Draught:** 27¾ feet. **Displacement:** 35,000 tons. **Armour:** *Main belt:* 4½/5½-inch to 14/15-inch. *Deck:* 5/6-inch to 12-inch. *Main turrets:* 9/16-inch. **Speed:** 29 knots. **Armament:** ten 14-inch, 16 5·25-inch, 60 2-pounder AA. Four aircraft. **Crew:** 1,612

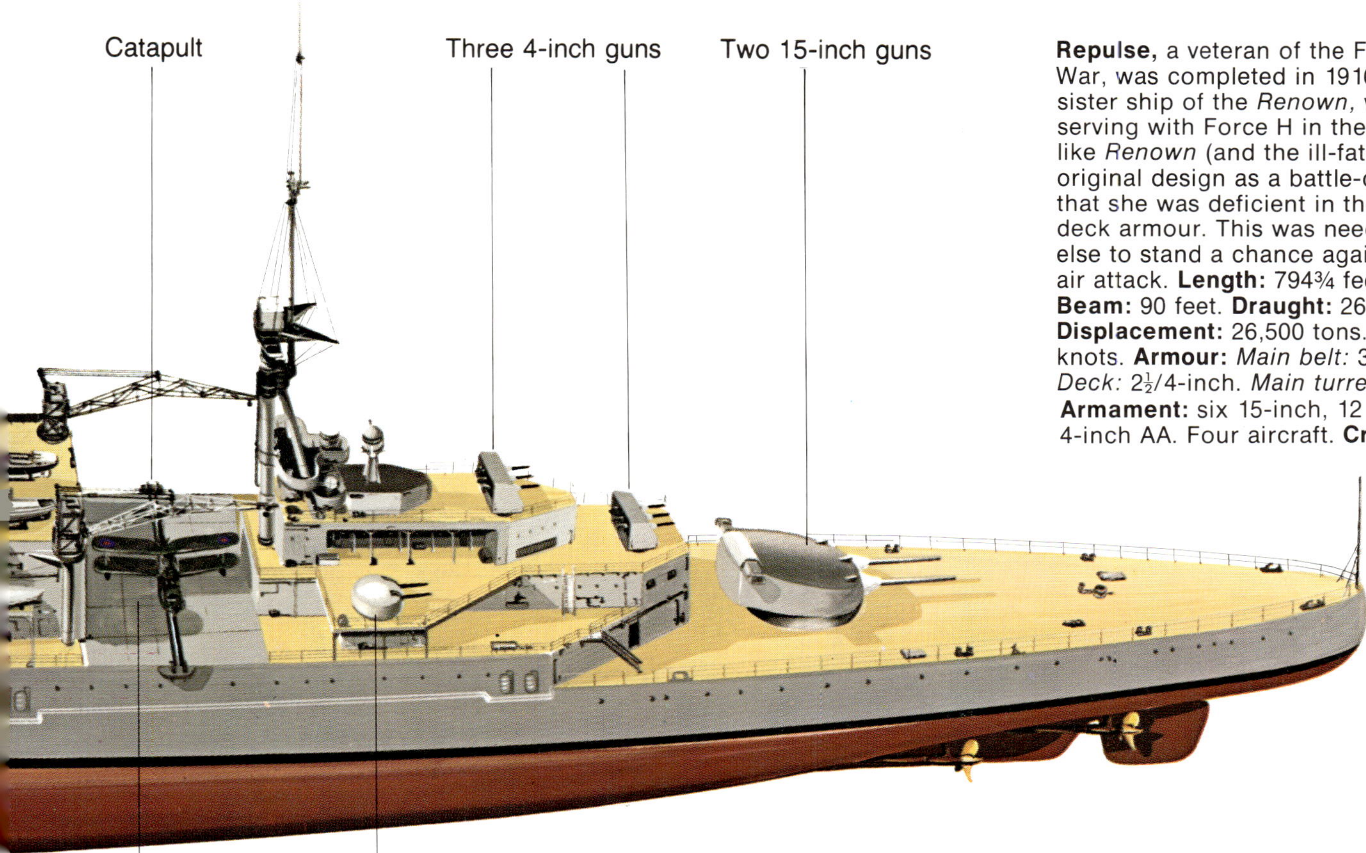

Repulse, a veteran of the First World War, was completed in 1916. She was the sister ship of the *Renown,* which was serving with Force H in the Mediterranean; like *Renown* (and the ill-fated *Hood),* her original design as a battle-cruiser meant that she was deficient in the weight of deck armour. This was needed above all else to stand a chance against determined air attack. **Length:** 794¾ feet overall. **Beam:** 90 feet. **Draught:** 26¾ feet. **Displacement:** 26,500 tons. **Speed:** 29 knots. **Armour:** *Main belt:* 3/9-inch. *Deck:* 2½/4-inch. *Main turrets:* 7/11-inch. **Armament:** six 15-inch, 12 4-inch, eight 4-inch AA. Four aircraft. **Crew:** 1,309

THE BATTLE OF

Brown Bros

US Navy

Above and below: Near misses burst alongside the *Shokaku* as it frantically zig-zags to avoid US bombs. Above, centre and right: The loss of the *Lexington*. Listing and on fire from leaking fuel, the carrier is abandoned by its crew after several violent explosions. Below, centre and right: The *Lexington*'s crew is picked up

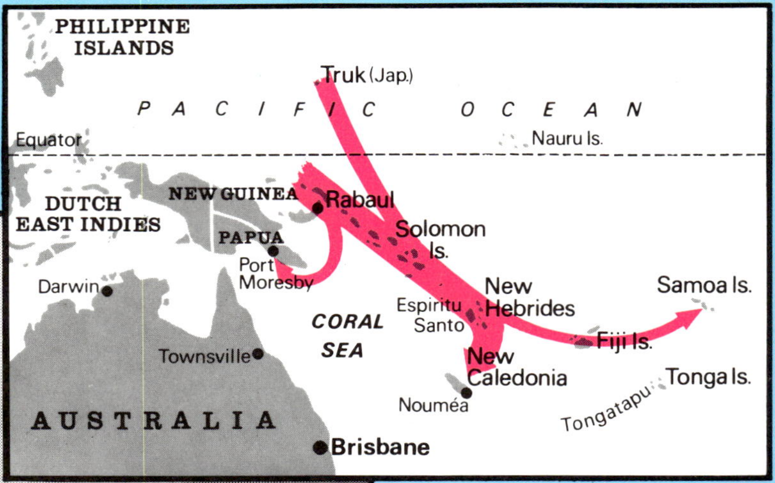

Brown Bros

US Navy

The outstanding success of the 'Oriental Blitzkrieg' in the first months of the Pacific War left Japan in a commanding strategic position. With the conquest of Burma, Malaya, the Dutch East Indies and the Philippines, the defensible perimeter in the Pacific and Southern Asia that her initial war plans called for had been achieved.

By the early spring of 1942, then, Japan's military planners were faced with choosing between the various conflicting possibilities open to them in their conduct of the second phase of the Pacific War.

First, there was the proposal from the Army for an offensive against the powerful Allied base of Port Moresby in Papua, continuing through the Solomons, New Hebrides, New Caledonia, Fiji and Samoa – an offensive that would effectively isolate Australia and put her out of the war.

Second, the Naval General Staff advocated either an advance against India and Ceylon or a direct thrust at Australia.

Third, Admiral Yamamoto – forever aware of the economic might of the United States and the counter-offensive capacity of her carriers still loose within the Pacific defence perimeter – urged a thrust against Midway and the Aleutian Islands to precipitate a decisive battle with what remained of the US Pacific Fleet.

As a result – in a fatal combination of all but the Indian option – the occupation of Port Moresby was scheduled for the beginning of May, to be followed early in June by operations against Midway and the Western Aleutians. The Port Moresby operation – which would not only leave Australia isolated, but also put the Japanese in control of the Coral Sea area – was planned along simple premises, but its detailed operation involved a tactical complexity and separation of forces that was to prove disastrous.

In overall command of the Japanese force heading for the Coral Sea at the end of April, 1942, was Vice-Admiral Inouye. Under him the main elements of the Japanese force of three carriers, 180 aircraft and six cruisers were split into the Port Moresby Invasion Group, a Covering Group commanded by Rear-Admiral Goto and including the light carrier *Shoho*, and a Striking Force under Vice-Admiral Takagi including Rear-Admiral Hara's carriers *Shokaku* and *Zuikahu* of the

THE CORAL SEA

Brown Bros

he small map shows the Japanese strategy behind their outflanking ove against New Guinea. Operations hinged on the vital bastion of Port oresby; and Admiral Nimitz knew that the Japanese were planning yet nother amphibious operation. The Japanese invasion-group, with the arrier *Shoho* and a cruiser force, was to head straight for Moresby round the tail of New Guinea. The carrier striking-force was to cruise to the Coral Sea past the Solomon Islands and ward off any US carrier opposition. The US Navy countermoves *(large map, overleaf)* resulted in the first of the war's great carrier actions – one which lasted three days. In terms of enemy ships destroyed, the Japanese had the higher score; but they were forced to content themselves with occupying Tulagi and Florida islands in the Solomons. Their attempt to seize Port Moresby had been a definite failure – their first major setback of the war, and a major portent of what was to follow at Midway.

US Navy

V Carrier Division charged with the task of repelling any US forces that might attempt to interfere.

But interference was just the thing that Admiral Chester W. Nimitz, C-in-C US Pacific Fleet, and General MacArthur, C-in-C SW Pacific Area, had in mind. Unlike the Japanese, who had divided their ships assigned to the operation into six separate forces, Admiral Nimitz boldly concentrated every ship available to meet the Japanese in the Coral Sea, where – because the Americans had cracked the Japanese naval code – he knew he could expect an attack on Port Moresby on or after May 3.

Nimitz's force of two carriers, 121 aircraft and seven cruisers comprised the *Yorktown* task force under the command of Rear-Admiral Fletcher, the *Lexington* task force commanded by Rear-Admiral Fitch, and a force under Rear-Admiral Grace (RN) comprising the Australian heavy cruisers *Australia* and *Hobart* and the American heavy cruiser *Chicago* and destroyer *Perkins*. Called Task Force 17, the fleet was under overall command of Rear-Admiral Fletcher.

By May 3, 1942, the Allied force had assembled in the Coral Sea area. There, on hearing reports of Japanese landings at Tulagi in the Lower Solomons, Fletcher took the *Yorktown* force north to launch an attack on the 4th. Dauntlesses and Devastators from the carrier took off at 0630 hours and, in a brief action later known as the 'Battle' of Tulagi, despatched an enemy destroyer, three minesweepers and various smaller craft for the loss of three planes.

The following two days, though, were anti-climactic for the Americans who had already tasted blood. Instead of the long-awaited combat, the days were spent refuelling and jockeying for position as reports came in of the movement of the enemy forces into the Coral Sea area, suitably advertised by a bombing attack on Port Moresby on the 5th.

On the evening of the 6th, as news reached the Japanese force of the surrender of the last Allied resistance on Corregidor in the Philippines the Port Moresby Invasion Group was beginning the run up to its objective, covered on its left flank by Rear-Admiral Goto on board the carrier *Shoho*. Further out to sea, Vice-Admiral Takagi's Strike Force was cruising, preparing to move in and support the Invasion Group.

The next day the battle began in earnest. Accepting Hara's recommendation that a thorough search to the south should be made before he moved to provide cover for the Port Moresby Invasion Group, Takagi accordingly launched reconnaissance aircraft at 0600 hours. As Hara later admitted: 'It did not prove to be a fortunate decision.' At 0736 one of the aircraft reported sighting an aircraft-carrier and a cruiser at the eastern edge of the search sector, and Hara, accepting this evaluation, closed distance and ordered an all-out bombing and torpedo attack. In fact, the vessels which had been sighted were the luckless *Neosho* and *Sims*.

After a single Japanese aircraft had attacked at 0900 hours, 15 high-level bombers appeared half an hour later, but failed to hit their targets. At 1038 the *Sims,* by swinging hard to starboard, avoided nine bombs dropped simultaneously by ten aircraft attacking horizontally. However, about noon, a further attack by 36 dive-bombers sealed the fate of the destroyer. Three 500-pound bombs hit the *Sims*, of which two exploded in her engine room. The ship buckled and sank stern first within a few minutes, with the loss of 379 lives.

Meanwhile, 20 dive-bombers had turned their attention to *Neosho*, scoring seven direct hits and causing blazing gasoline to flow along her decks. Although some hands took the order to 'make preparations to abandon ship and stand by' as a signal to jump over the side, the *Neosho* was in fact to drift in a westerly direction until May 11, when 123 men were taken off by the destroyer *Henley* and the oiler was scuttled. But the sacrifice of these two ships was not in vain, for if Hara's planes had not been drawn off in this way, the Japanese might have found and attacked Fletcher on the 7th, while he was busy dealing with the *Shoho*.

Fortune indeed smiled on Fletcher that day. At 0645, when a little over 120 miles south of Rossel Island, he ordered Crace's support group to push ahead on a north-westerly course to attack the Port Moresby Invasion Group, while the rest of Task Force 17 turned north. Apparently Fletcher, who expected an air duel with Takagi's aircraft-carriers, wished to prevent the invasion regardless of his own fate but, by detaching Crace, was in fact weakening his own anti-aircraft screen while depriving part of his force of the protection of carrier air cover.

The consequences of this move might have been fatal but, instead, the Japanese were to make another vital error by concentrating their land-based air groups on Crace rather than Fletcher's aircraft-carriers. A Japanese seaplane spotted the support group at 0810, and at 1358, when the ships of Crace's force were south and a little west of Jomard Passage, 11 single-engined bombers launched an unsuccessful attack. Soon afterwards, 12 Sallys (land-based naval bombers) came in low, dropping eight torpedoes. These were avoided by violent manoeuvres, and five of the bombers were shot down. Then 19 high-flying bombers attacked from 15,000 to 20,000 feet, the ships dodging the bombs as they had the torpedoes.

Before the day was out, Crace had survived another attack, this time from American B-26s which mistook his vessels for Japanese. By midnight he had reached a point 120 miles south of the New Guinea tail, later turning back south on hearing that the Port Moresby Invasion Group had retired.

While Takagi's aircraft were dealing with *Neosho* and *Sims*, the *Shoho*, of Goto's Covering Group, had turned south-east into the wind to launch four reconnaissance aircraft and to send up other aircraft to protect the invasion force 30 miles to the south-west. By 0830 Goto knew exactly where Fletcher was, and ordered *Shoho* to prepare for an attack. Other aircraft had meanwhile spotted Crace's ships to the west. The result of these reports was to make Inouye anxious for the security of the Invasion Group, and at 0900 he ordered it to turn away instead of entering Jomard Passage, thus keeping it out of harm's way until Fletcher and Crace had been dealt with. In fact, this was the nearest the transports got to their goal.

Fletcher had launched a search mission early on the 7th, and at 0815 one of *Yorktown*'s reconnaissance aircraft reported 'two carriers and four heavy cruisers' about 225 miles to the north-west, on the other side of the Louisiades. Assuming that this was Takagi's Striking Force, Fletcher launched a total of 93 aircraft between 0926 and 1030, leaving 47 for combat patrol. By this time Task Force 17 had re-entered the cold front,

Douglas TBD-1 Devastator. The backbone of the US Navy's carrier torpedo forces at the outbreak of the Pacific War, the Devastator was already obsolete. With its light armament and slow approach speed, it was easy prey for Japanese Zeros. **Max speed:** 225 mph. **Max range:** 985 miles. **Armament:** 1×·3-inch and 1×·5-inch machine-guns plus 1×1000-lb bomb or 1×21-inch torpedo

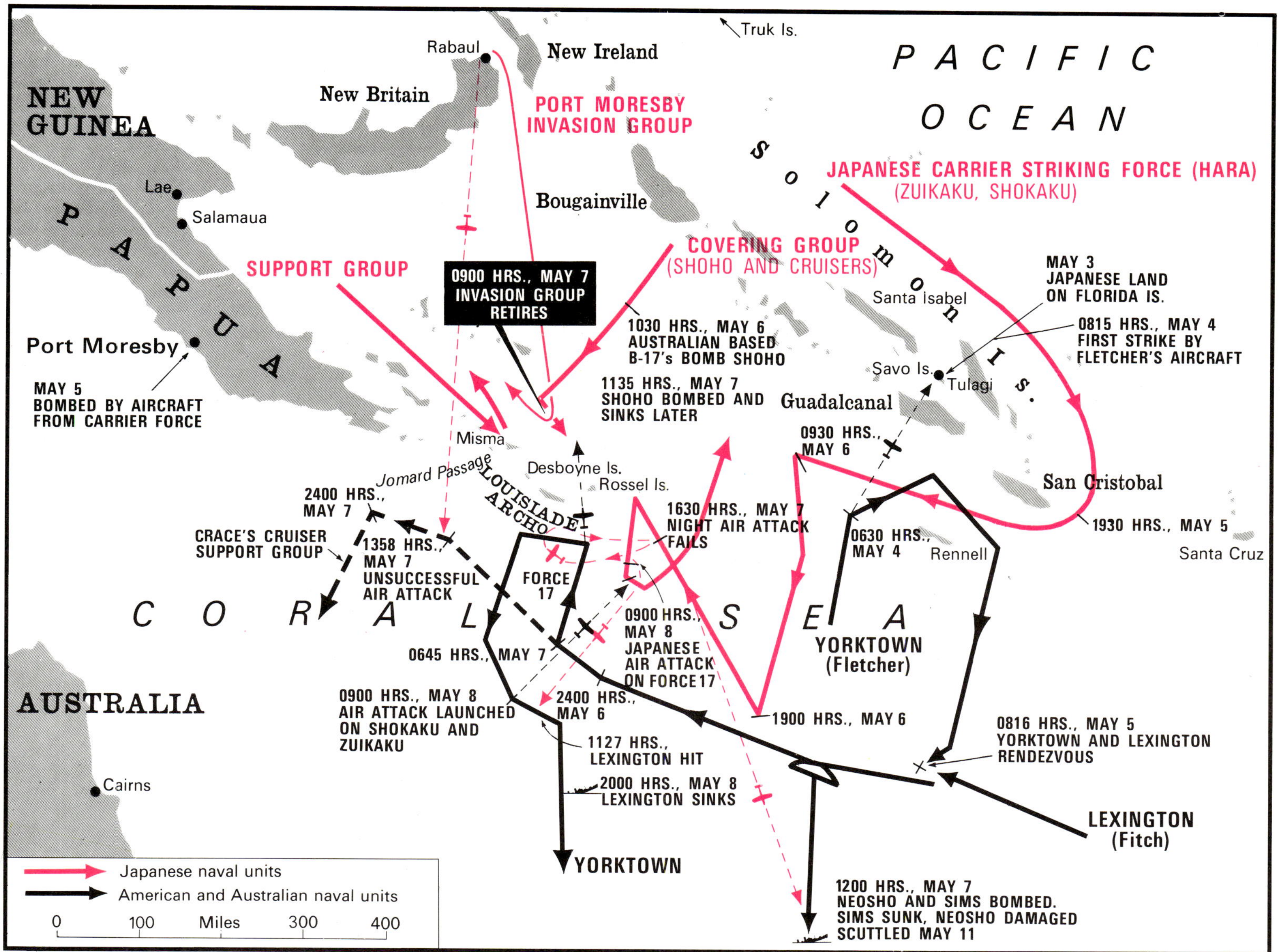

Coral Sea: the progress of the battle

while Goto's force lay in bright sunlight near the reported position of the 'two carriers'. However, no sooner had *Yorktown*'s attack group become airborne than her scouts returned, and it immediately became obvious that the 'two carriers and four heavy cruisers' should have read 'two heavy cruisers and two destroyers' – the error being due to the improper arrangement of the pilot's coding pad. Actually the vessels seen were two light cruisers and two gunboats of Marushige's Support Group. Fletcher, now knowing that he had sent a major strike against a minor target, courageously allowed the strike to proceed, thinking that with the invasion force nearby there must be some profitable targets in the vicinity.

The attack group from *Lexington*, well ahead of the *Yorktown* aircraft, was nearing Misima Island in the Louisiades shortly after 1100, when Lieutenant-Commander Hamilton, leading one of *Lexington*'s Dauntless squadrons, spotted an aircraft-carrier, two or three cruisers, and some destroyers, about 25 miles to the starboard. This was the *Shoho* with the rest of Goto's Covering Group. As the *Shoho* was only 35 miles south-east of the original target location, it was a simple matter to re-direct the attack groups over the carrier. The first attack, led by Commander W. B. Ault, succeeded only in blowing five aircraft over the *Shoho*'s side, but he was closely followed by Hamilton's ten Dauntlesses at 1110, the *Lexington*'s torpedo squadron at 1117, and the *Yorktown*'s attack group at 1125. Under such a concentrated attack, the *Shoho* stood little chance: soon she was on fire and dead in the water – and, smothered by 13 bomb and seven torpedo hits, she sank soon after 1135.

Only six American aircraft were lost in the attack off Misima. Back on the American aircraft-carriers, listeners in the radio rooms heard the jubilant report from Lieutenant-Commander Dixon, leading *Lexington*'s other Dauntless squadron: 'Scratch one flat-top! Dixon to carrier, scratch one flat-top!'

With the air groups safely landed again, Fletcher decided to call off any further strikes against Goto, as he now knew, from intercepted radio messages, that his own position was known to Takagi – although he had not yet located the other Japanese aircraft-carriers himself. The worsening weather dissuaded him from further searches, and he thus set a westerly course during the night of May 7/8, thinking that the Japanese invasion force would come through the Jomard Passage the next morning. He did not yet know of Inouye's timid decision to recall the transports.

May 7 had been a day of serious blunders from the Japanese viewpoint, but Takagi and Hara were determined to try once more to destroy the American aircraft-carriers before the next day. Selecting the 27 pilots best qualified in night operations, Hara launched a strike from the *Shokaku* and *Zuikaku* just before 1630, with orders to attack Fletcher. Although the Japanese aircraft passed close to Task Force 17, they failed to locate owing

Below: A Japanese reconnaissance seaplane casts off from its parent warship

to the foul weather and poor visibility. The American combat air-patrol, vectored out by radar to intercept, shot down nine of Hara's precious aircraft. An hour later, some of the returning Japanese laid a course for home right over the American carriers, which they mistook for their own. At 1900 three Japanese aircraft were spotted on *Yorktown*'s starboard beam, blinking in Morse code on Aldis lamps. Though recognised, they managed to escape. Twenty minutes later, three more attempted to join the *Yorktown*'s landing circle, and one was shot down. Hara was to lose 11 more aircraft which 'splashed' when attempting night landings on his aircraft-carriers. Only six of the original 27 got back safely.

With the day's operations virtually at an end, the commanders on both sides now toyed with the idea of a surface night action. At 1930 the *Lexington*'s radar showed what appeared to be a Japanese landing circle 30 miles to the east, but Fletcher did not receive the report until 2200, by which time he knew it might be impossible to locate Takagi's new position (at that moment the Japanese carriers were actually 95 miles to the east of Task Force 17). Fletcher rejected the idea of detaching a cruiser/destroyer force for a night attack, as the last-quarter moon would not afford much light, and he urgently needed all the anti-aircraft protection he could get for the next day's operations. In his own words: 'The best plan seemed to be to keep our force concentrated and prepare for a battle with enemy carriers next morning.'

Inouye, meanwhile, had ordered Goto's cruisers to rendezvous east of Rossel Island and make an attack on the Allied force, though he did not specify whether the target was to be Fletcher or Crace. By midnight he had reconsidered the plan, ordered the invasion to be postponed for two days, and split Got's cruisers up between the invasion transports and Takagi's force. Takagi, too, on receiving his pilot's reports that the American carriers were 50-60 miles away, considered a night action, but his air crews were tired—and he was in any case forestalled by a call for protection from the transports, which it was his basic mission to protect, and which had now lost the cover of the *Shoho*. Thus the main action was delayed yet again, although both sides expected a decision on the 8th. Everything now depended on locating the enemy as early as possible in the morning.

In the event, reconnaissance aircraft of both sides, launched a little before dawn, located the opposing aircraft-carrier force almost simultaneously, between 0815 and 0838. Fitch, now in tactical command of the American aircraft-carrier operations, had 121 aircraft available, while Hara, his opposite number, had 122. The Japanese had more combat experience and better torpedoes, while the Americans were stronger in bomber aircraft. Thus the two sides began the first ever 'carrier-versus-carrier' battle roughly on equal terms, although by moving south during the night, Fletcher had run out of the bad weather and lay under clear skies, while the Japanese remained under the shelter of clouds and squalls.

The first sighting of the Japanese carriers had been at 0815, by one of *Lexington*'s scouts, the pilot reporting that Takagi was 175 miles to the north-east of Fletcher's position. Later, at 0930, Lieutenant-Commander Dixon sighted the Japanese Striking Force steaming due south in a position 25 miles north-east of the original contact, but about 45 miles north of Takagi's expected position at 0900 as predicted on the strength of that contact.

The discrepancy was to cause trouble for *Lexington*'s attack group, which by this time was airborne. Fitch had begun launching his strike between 0900 and 0925, the *Yorktown* group of 24 bombers with two fighters, and nine torpedo-bombers with four fighters, departing ten minutes before the *Lexington* aircraft. The dive-bombers spotted the Japanese first, at 1030, and took cloud cover to await the arrival of the Devastators. While *Shokaku* was engaged in launching further combat patrols, *Zuikaku* disappeared into a rain squall. The attack, which began at 1057, thus fell only on the *Shokaku*. Although the *Yorktown*'s pilots co-ordinated their attack well, only moderate success was achieved. The slow American torpedoes were either avoided or failed to explode, and only two bomb hits were scored on the *Shokaku*, one damaging the flight-deck well forward on the starboard bow and setting fire to fuel, while the other destroyed a repair compartment aft. The *Shokaku*, now burning, could still recover aircraft, but could no longer launch any.

Of the *Lexington* group, ten minutes behind, the 22 dive-bombers failed to locate the target, leaving only 11 Devastators and four reconnaissance-bombers for the attack. Once again the torpedoes were ineffective, but the bombers scored a third hit on the Japanese aircraft-carrier. Although 108 of the vessel's crew had been killed, she had not been holed below the waterline, and her fires were soon brought under control. Most of her aircraft were transferred to the *Zuikaku* before Takagi detached *Shokaku* at 1300, with orders to proceed to Truk. Although in poor shape, she was not 'settling fast', as the American pilots had reported.

Captain Sherman, in the *Lexington*, had

Aichi D3A2 'Val'. This rugged carrier-borne dive-bomber sank more Allied fighting ships than any other Axis aircraft type. **Max speed:** 267 mph at 9845 feet. **Max range:** 840 miles. **Armament:** 3×7·7-mm machine-guns, 1×550-lb bomb plus 2×132-lb bombs estimated that the Japanese attack on Task Force 17 would begin at about 1100, basing his deduction on Japanese radio traffic. In fact, the *Yorktown* and *Lexington* were to come under attack in the interval between the strikes of their respective air groups on the Japanese aircraft-carriers. The Japanese

had begun launching at about the same time as the Americans, but their attack group of 18 torpedo-bombers, 33 bombers, and 18 fighters was larger, better balanced, and more accurately directed to the target. Although the American radar picked them up 70 miles away, Fitch had far too few fighters to intercept successfully, and was forced to

Below: Coral Sea, an aerial view

Bibliothek für Zeitgeschichte

rely mainly on his AA gunners for protection.

At 1118 hours the battle 'busted out', as one American sailor described it. The *Yorktown*, with a smaller turning circle than the *Lexington*, successfully avoided eight torpedoes launched on her port quarter. Five minutes later she came under dive-bomber attack but, skilfully handled by Captain Buckmaster, escaped unscathed until 1127, when she received her only hit – from an 800-pound bomb which penetrated to the fourth deck, but did not impair flight operations. During this time, the evasive manoeuvres gradually drew the American aircraft-carriers apart and, although the screening vessels divided fairly evenly between them, the breaking of their defensive circle contributed to Japanese success.

The *Lexington*, larger than the *Yorktown*, had a turning circle of 1,500 to 2,000 yards in diameter, compared with the 1,000-yard tactical diameter of her consort. Moreover, she had the misfortune to suffer an 'anvil' attack from the Japanese torpedo-bombers, which came in on both bows at 1118 to launch their missiles at altitudes of about 50 to 200 feet, and about half a mile from the *'Lady Lex'*. Despite valiant manoeuvres by Sherman, she received one torpedo hit on the port side forward at 1120, quickly followed by a second opposite the bridge. At the same time a dive-bombing attack commenced from 17,000 feet, the *Lexington* receiving two hits from small bombs. One exploded in a ready-ammunition box on the port side, while the other hit the smokestack structure. To add to the din of battle, the ship's siren jammed as a result of an explosion and shrieked weirdly throughout most of the attack.

Some 19 minutes later, the aircraft-carrier battle was, to all intents and purposes, at an end. At this point, honours were more or less equal – but for the Americans the real tragedy was still to come. At first it appeared that the doughty *Lexington* had survived to fight another day. A list of 7 degrees caused by the torpedo hits was corrected by shifting oil ballast, while her engines remained unharmed. To her returning pilots she did not appear to be seriously damaged, and the recovery of the air group went ahead. At about 1240 hours, Commander H. R. 'Pop'

Healy, the damage control officer, reported to Captain Sherman: 'We've got the torpedo damage temporarily shored up, the fires out, and soon will have the ship back on an even keel. But I would suggest, sir, that if you have to take any more torpedoes, you take 'em on the starboard side.'

Minutes later, at 1247, a tremendous internal explosion, caused by the ignition of fuel vapours by a motor generator which had been left running, shook the whole ship. Although the *Lexington* continued landing her planes, a series of further violent explosions seriously disrupted internal communications. Yet another major detonation occurred at 1445, and the fires soon passed beyond control. Despite the fact that the destroyer *Morris* came alongside to help fight the blaze, while *Yorktown* recovered all aircraft still airborne, the need for evacuation became increasingly apparent.

At 1630 hours the *Lexington* had come to a dead stop, and all hands prepared to abandon ship. At 1710 Fitch called to Sherman to 'get the men off', the *Minneapolis, Hammann, Morris,* and *Anderson* assisting with the rescue operations. Evacuation was orderly—even the ship's dog being rescued—and Sherman was the last to leave the aircraft-carrier, sliding down a line over the stern. At 1956 the destroyer *Phelps* was ordered to deliver the 'coup de grace' with five torpedoes, and the *Lexington* sank at 2000, a final explosion occurring as she slipped beneath the waves.

The Battle of the Coral Sea was now over. The Japanese pilots had reported sinking both American aircraft-carriers, and Hara's acceptance of this evaluation influenced Takagi's decision to detach the *Shokaku* for repairs, as well as Inouye's order that the Striking Force should be withdrawn. Even though he thought that both American aircraft-carriers had been destroyed, the cautious Inouye still deemed it necessary to postpone the invasion, apparently because he felt unable to protect the landing units against Allied land-based aircraft. Yamamoto did not agree with this decision and, at 2400 hours, countermanded the order, detailing Takagi to locate and annihilate the remaining American ships. But, by the time Takagi made his search to the south and east, Fletcher had gone.

Tactically, the battle had been a victory for the Japanese. Although they had lost 43 aircraft on May 8 (as against 33 lost by the Americans), and Hara had been left with only nine operational aircraft after the *Zuikaku* had proved unable to take on all *Shokaku*'s aircraft, their air strikes had achieved greater results. The sinking of the *Lexington, Neosho,* and *Sims* far outweighed the loss of the *Shoho*.

Strategically, however, Coral Sea was an American victory: the whole object of the Japanese operation—the capture of Port Moresby—had been thwarted. Despite the occupation of Tulagi, later won back by the US Marines at a heavy price, the Japanese had gained very little of their initial objectives. Moreover, the damage to the *Shokaku*, and the need to re-form the battered air groups of the *Zuikaku*, was to keep both these carriers out of the Midway battle, where they might have been decisive.

Though the Coral Sea engagement was full of errors by the commanders on both sides, the Americans did take its lessons to heart. The ratio of fighters to bombers and torpedo-bombers was increased, and improvements were made in the organisation of attacks in the weeks that remained before the next great naval clash. But the really significant feature of the Coral Sea battle was that it opened a new chapter in the annals of naval warfare: it was the first ever 'carrier-against-carrier' action in which all losses were inflicted by air action, and no ship on either side made visual surface contact with the enemy.

The stage for Midway was now set.

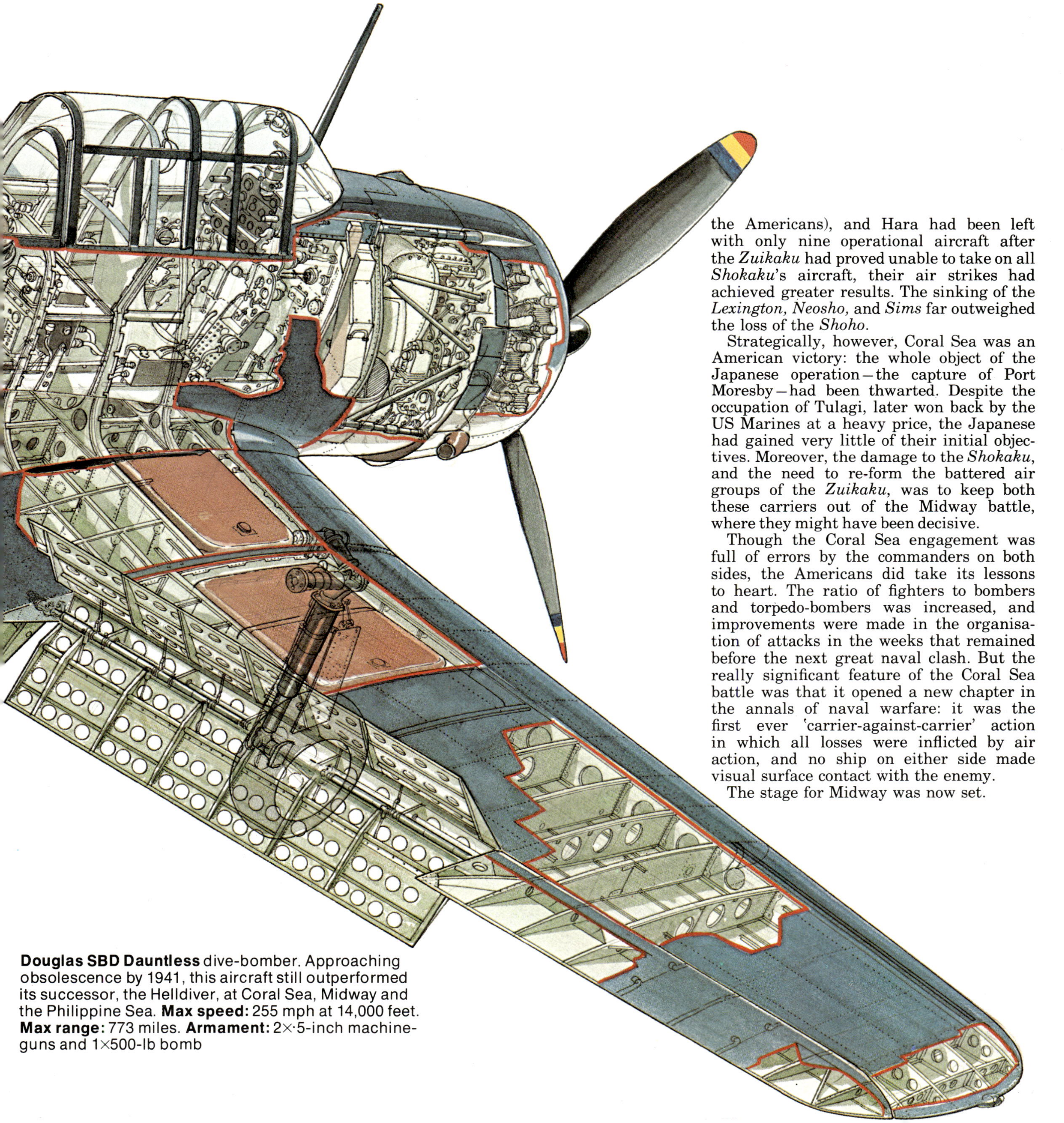

Douglas SBD Dauntless dive-bomber. Approaching obsolescence by 1941, this aircraft still outperformed its successor, the Helldiver, at Coral Sea, Midway and the Philippine Sea. **Max speed:** 255 mph at 14,000 feet. **Max range:** 773 miles. **Armament:** 2×·5-inch machine-guns and 1×500-lb bomb

THE BATTLE OF MIDWAY

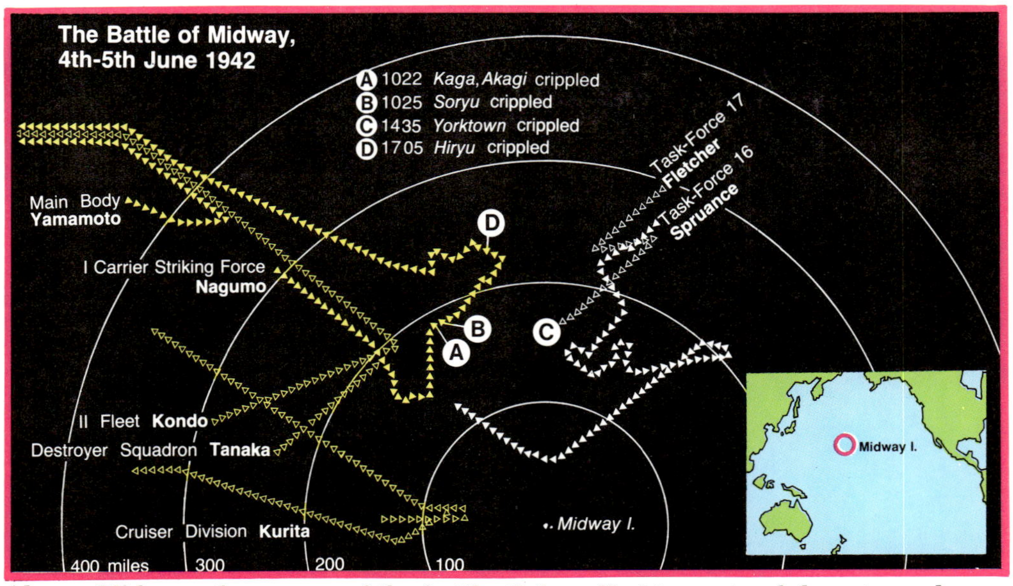

Above: Midway, the course of the battle. Below: *Yorktown* struck by a torpedo

Imperial War Museum

Above: The *Yorktown*, listing and doomed

Imperial War Museum

...TURNING POINT OF WW2

Japan's naval strategists had long prepared for a 'decisive fleet action' with the Americans in the Pacific. At Midway in early June, 1942, they hoped to destroy the surviving vessels of the US Pacific Fleet in just such an encounter.

Admiral Yamamoto, C-in-C of the Japanese Combined Fleet, was rightly convinced that a threat to Midway Island – the westernmost outpost of the Hawaiian island chain – would compel the weaker enemy fleet to challenge overwhelming Japanese forces . . . under whose guns and bombs, he imagined, it could not hope to survive.

At the Battle of the Coral Sea the month before, though, there had been several important indications that should have suggested to Yamamoto that his confidence at the outcome of a fleet action in the Pacific was perhaps misplaced.

Although roughly equal shipping losses had been sustained – the Americans had lost the carrier *Lexington* and 81 aircraft, the Japanese the carrier *Shoho* and 105 aircraft – every advantage had actually fallen with the Americans. Not only had the Japanese attack on Port Moresby been countermanded, but the carriers *Shokaku* and *Zuikaku* had also been withdrawn from service as a result of the action.

Most importantly, though, the US carrier force in the Pacific had lived to fight another day . . . despite all the efforts of a clearly superior enemy force. This had only been made possible because the Japanese tactics of dividing their ships into small, relatively ineffective units operating separately within an overall operational plan had proved indecisive in practice despite their foolproof appearance on paper.

Arrogant and over-confident, unaware of the lessons to be learned from Coral Sea, Japan's naval planners were now about to fall into the same tactical trap once again. The Battle of Midway – when seven Japanese battleships, six carriers, 13 cruisers, 50 destroyers and 325 aircraft lined up against Admiral Nimitz's three carriers, eight cruisers, 14 destroyers and 348 land- and sea-based aircraft – was to prove one of the truly decisive battles of history . . . the turning-point of the Second World War, and the beginning of the end for the ill-starred fortunes of the Rising Sun.

Below: Devastators prepare to leave the *Enterprise*. Only four returned, but the *Yorktown* and *Hornet*'s losses were even heavier

Imperial War Museum

L to R: Spruance, Task Force 17, evaded the trap. Nimitz, who foresaw the enemy moves. Yamamoto, whose plan was too complex. Kondo, of the Support Group. Fletcher, who lost his flagship, *Yorktown*. Nagumo, whose vacillation proved to be fatal

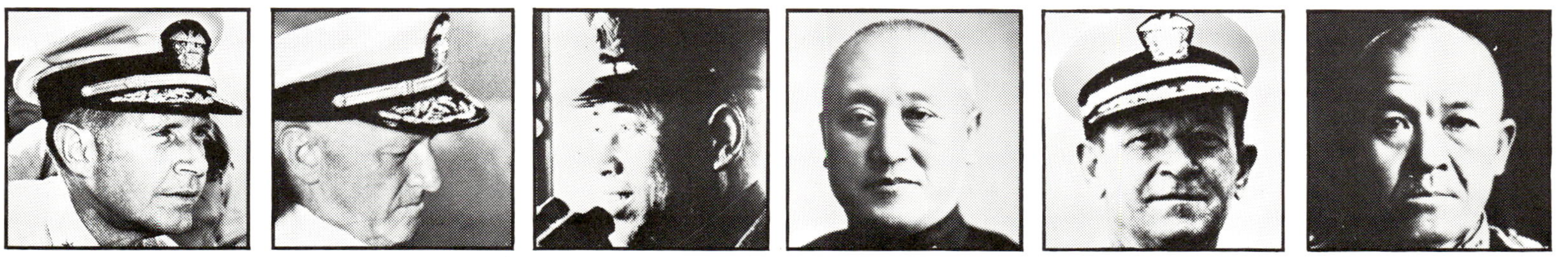

USS *Hornet*
Commissioned in 1941, the *Hornet* had a displacement of 19,800 tons and a crew of 2919. Doolittle's historic raid on Tokyo was launched from her deck, and at the Battle of Midway her Avengers helped shatter two Japanese carriers, the *Akagi* and the *Soryu*. However, she was herself severely damaged, and was finally sunk during the Battle of Santa Cruz after being hit by two torpedoes, six bombs and two Kamikaze planes on October 26, 1942

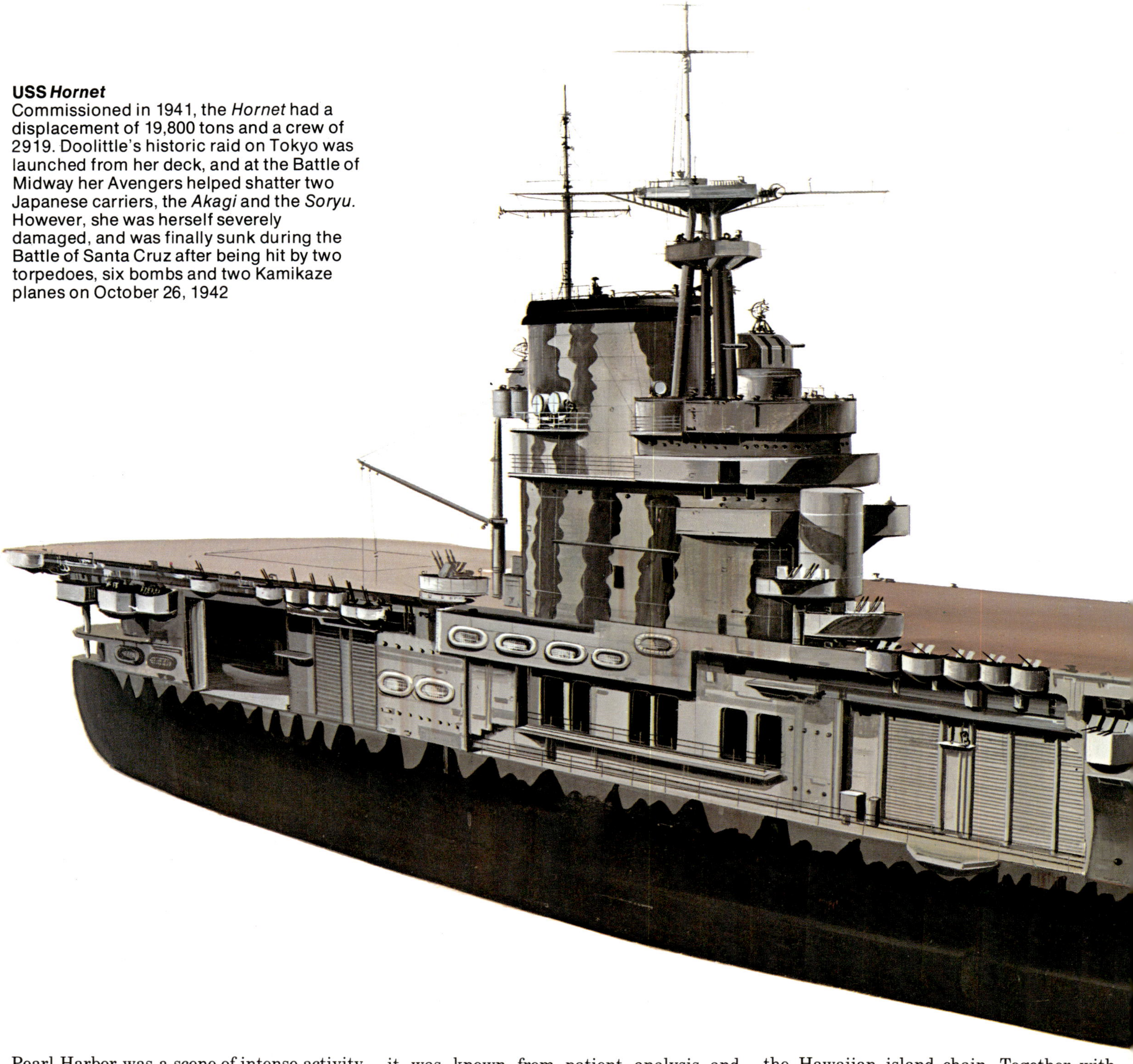

Pearl Harbor was a scene of intense activity during the last week of May 1942: a feeling of great impending events pervaded the atmosphere. On the 26th the aircraft-carriers *Enterprise* and *Hornet* of Task Force (TF) 16 had steamed in and moored, to set about in haste the various operations of refuelling and replenishing after a vain race across the Pacific to try to go to the aid of Rear-Admiral Frank Fletcher's Task Force 17 in the Battle of the Coral Sea. On the next day the surviving carriers of TF 17, the *Yorktown*'s blackened sides and twisted decks providing visible signs of the damage sustained in the battle, berthed in the dry dock of the naval base where an army of workmen swarmed aboard to begin repairs.

Under normal circumstances, weeks of work lay ahead of them, but now word had reached the dockyard that emergency repairs in the utmost haste were required. Work was to go on, night and day, without ceasing, until the ship was at least temporarily battle-worthy. For at the headquarters of the C-in-C Pacific, Admiral Chester Nimitz, it was known from patient analysis and deciphering of enemy signals that the Japanese fleet was moving out to throw down a challenge which, in spite of local American inferiority, had to be accepted.

So on May 28, Task Force 16 sailed again, the *Enterprise* flying the flag of Rear-Admiral Raymond Spruance, and vanished into the wide wastes of the Pacific. Six cruisers and nine destroyers formed its screen; two replenishment tankers accompanied it. The following day the dockyard gave Nimitz the scarcely credible news that the *Yorktown* was once again battle-worthy. Early on the 30th she, too, left harbour and, having gathered in her air groups, headed north-westward to rendezvous with Task Force 16 at 'Point Luck', 350 miles north-east of the island of Midway. Forming the remainder of Task Force 17 were two cruisers and five destroyers.

The main objective of the Japanese was the assault and occupation of the little atoll of Midway, 1,100 miles west-north-west of Oahu, and forming the western extremity of the Hawaiian island chain. Together with the occupation of the Aleutian Islands, the capture of Midway would extend Japan's eastern sea frontier so that sufficient warning might be obtained of any threatened naval air attack on the homeland—Pearl Harbor in reverse. The plan had been given added impetus on April 18 by the raid on Tokyo mounted by Colonel Doolittle's army bombers taking off from the *Hornet*.

Doubts on the wisdom of the Japanese plan had been voiced in various quarters; but Yamamoto, the dynamic C-in-C of the Combined Fleet, had fiercely advocated it for reasons of his own. He had always been certain that only by destroying the American fleet could Japan gain the breathing space required to consolidate her conquests and negotiate satisfactory peace terms—a belief which had inspired the attack on Pearl Harbor. Yamamoto rightly believed that an attack on Midway was a challenge that Nimitz could not ignore. It would bring the US Pacific Fleet out where Yamamoto, in overwhelming strength, would be waiting to bring it at last to a final, decisive action.

The Japanese plan was an intricate one, as their naval strategic plans customarily were, calling for exact timing for a junction at the crucial moment of several disparate forces; and it involved – also typically – the offering of a decoy or diversion to lure the enemy into dividing his force or expending his strength on a minor objective.

Between May 25/27, Northern Force would sail from Ominato, at the northern tip of Honshu, for the attack on the Aleutians. The II Carrier Striking Force, under Rear-Admiral Kakuta – comprising the small aircraft-carriers *Ryujo* and *Junyo*, two cruisers, and three destroyers – would be the first to sail, its task being to deliver a surprise air attack on Dutch Harbor on June 3. This, it was expected, might induce Nimitz to send at least part of his fleet racing north, in which case it would find waiting to intercept it a Guard Force, of four battleships, two cruisers, and 12 destroyers.

Kakuta's force would be followed two days later by the remainder of the Aleutians force – two small transport units with cruiser and destroyer escorts for the invasion of Attu and Kiska on June 5. Meanwhile, from Hashirajima Anchorage in the Inland Sea, the four big aircraft-carriers of Vice-Admiral Nagumo's I Carrier Striking Force – *Akagi, Kaga, Hiryu,* and *Soryu* – would sail for the vicinity of Midway. There, at dawn on the 4th, their bombers and fighters would take off for the softening-up bombardment of the island prior to the assault landing two days later by troops carried in the Transport Group.

The original plan had called for the inclusion of the *Zuikaku* and *Shokaku* in Nagumo's force. But, like the *Yorktown*, the *Shokaku* had suffered damage in the Coral Sea battle and could not be repaired in time to take part in the Midway operation, while both carriers had lost so many experienced aircrews that replacements could not be trained in time.

Yamamoto's battle-squadron

In support of the Transport Group, four heavy cruisers under Vice-Admiral Kurita would also sail from Guam. Finally, three powerful forces would sail in company from the Inland Sea during May 28:

- The Main Body, comprising Yamamoto's splendid new flagship *Yamato*, the biggest battleship in the world, mounting nine 18-inch guns, the 16-inch battleships *Nagato* and *Mutsu*, with attendant destroyers;
- The Main Support Force for the Midway invasion force – two battleships, four heavy cruisers, and attendant destroyers – under Vice-Admiral Kondo;
- The Guard Force (mentioned above).

Parting company with Yamamoto's force after getting to sea, Kondo was to head for a supporting position to the south-west of Midway, while the Guard Force would proceed to station itself near the route from Pearl Harbor to the Aleutians. Yamamoto himself, with the Main Body, was to take up a central position from which he could proceed to annihilate whatever enemy force Nimitz sent out. To ensure that the dispatch of any such American force should not go undetected, Pearl Harbor was to be reconnoitred between May 31 and June 3 by two Japanese flying-boats via French Frigate Shoal (500 miles north-west of Hawaii), where a submarine was to deliver them petrol. As a further precaution, two cordons of submarines were to be stationed to the north-west and west of Hawaii by June 2, with a third cordon farther north towards the Aleutians.

Yamamoto's plan was ingenious, if over-intricate: but it had two fatal defects. For all his enthusiasm for naval aviation, he had not yet appreciated that the day of the monstrous capital ship as the queen of battles had passed in favour of the aircraft-carrier which could deliver its blows at a range 30 times greater than that of the biggest guns. The role of the battleship was now as close escort to the vulnerable aircraft-carriers, supplying the defensive anti-aircraft gunpower the latter lacked. Nagumo's force was supported only by two battleships and three cruisers. Had Yamamoto's Main Body kept company with it, the events that were to follow might have been different.

Far more fatal to Yamamoto's plan, however, was his assumption that it was shrouded from the enemy, and that only when news reached Nimitz that Midway was being assaulted would the Pacific Fleet leave Pearl Harbor. Thus long before the scheduled flying-boat reconnaissance – which in the event failed to take place because French Frigate Shoal was found to be in American hands – and before the scouting submarines had reached their stations, Spruance and Fletcher, all unknown to the Japanese, were beyond the patrol lines and poised waiting for the enemy's approach. Details of this approach as well as the broad lines of Yamamoto's plan were known to Nimitz. Beyond sending a small force of five cruisers and ten destroyers to the Aleutians to harass the invasion force, he concentrated all his available force – TF 16 and 17 – in the area.

He had also a squadron of battleships under his command, to be sure; but he had no illusions that, with their insufficient speed to keep up with the aircraft-carriers, their great guns could play any useful part in the events to follow. They were therefore relegated to defensive duties on the American west coast.

For the next few days the Japanese Combined Fleet advanced eastwards according to schedule in its wide-spread, multi-pronged formation. Everywhere a buoyant feeling of confidence showed itself, generated

by the memories of the unbroken succession of Japanese victories since the beginning of the war. In the I Carrier Striking Force, so recently returned home after its meteoric career of destruction–from Pearl Harbor through the East Indies, and on to Ceylon without the loss of a ship–the 'Victory Disease' as it was subsequently to be called by the Japanese themselves, was particularly prevalent. Only the admiral–or so Nagumo was subsequently to say–felt doubts of the quality of the many replacements who had come to make up the wastage in experienced aircrews inevitable even in victorious operations.

Spruance and Fletcher had meanwhile made rendezvous during June 2, and Fletcher had assumed command of the two task forces, though they continued to manoeuvre as separate units. The sea was calm under a blue sky split up by towering cumulus clouds. The scouting aircraft, flown off during the following day in perfect visibility, sighted nothing, and Fletcher was able to feel confident that the approaching enemy was all unaware of his presence to the north-east of Midway. Indeed, neither Yamamoto nor Nagumo, pressing forward blindly through rain and fog, gave serious thought to such an apparently remote possibility.

Far to the north on June 3, dawn broke grey and misty over Kikuta's two aircraft-carriers from which, soon after 0300 hours, the first of two strike waves took off to wreak destruction among the installations and fuel tanks of Dutch Harbor. A further attack was delivered the following day, and during the next few days American and Japanese forces sought each other vainly among the swirling fogs, while the virtually unprotected Kiska and Attu were occupied by the Japanese. But as Nimitz refused to let any of his forces be drawn into the skirmish, this part of Yamamoto's plan failed to have much impact on the great drama being enacted farther south.

Setting the scene

The opening scenes of this drama were enacted early on June 3 when a scouting Catalina flying boat some 700 miles west of Midway sighted a large body of ships, steaming in two long lines with a numerous screen in arrowhead formation, which was taken to be the Japanese main fleet. The sighting report brought nine army B-17 bombers from Midway, which delivered three high-level bombing attacks and claimed to have hit two battleships or heavy cruisers and two transports. But the enemy was in reality the Midway Occupation Force of transports and tankers, and no hits were scored on them until four amphibious Catalinas from Midway discovered them again in bright moonlight in the early hours of June 4 and succeeded in torpedoing a tanker. Damage was slight, however, and the tanker remained in formation.

More than 800 miles away to the east, Fletcher intercepted the reports of these encounters but from his detailed knowledge of the enemy's plan was able to identify the Occupation Force. Nagumo's carriers, he knew, were much closer, some 400 miles to the west of him, approaching their flying-off position from the north-west. During the night, therefore, Task Forces 16 and 17 steamed south-west for a position 200 miles

Mitsubishi A6M2 Zero fighter first saw service in 1940 over China. During the period of runaway Japanese victories in the Pacific this model performed outstandingly. **Max speed:** 331 mph at 16,000 feet. **Max range:** 1160 miles. **Armament:** 2×20-mm cannon; 2×7·7-mm machine-guns

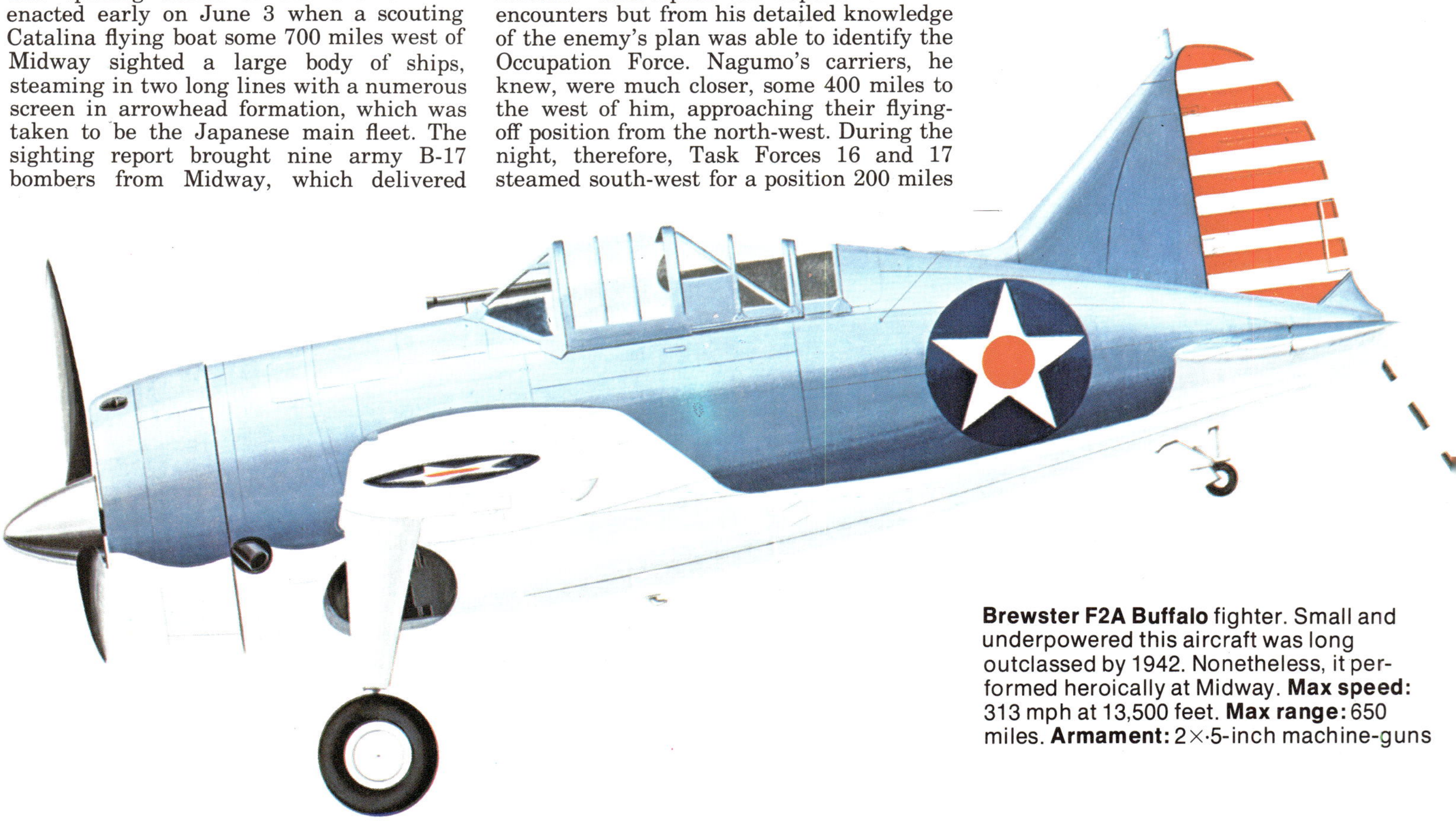

Brewster F2A Buffalo fighter. Small and underpowered this aircraft was long outclassed by 1942. Nonetheless, it performed heroically at Midway. **Max speed:** 313 mph at 13,500 feet. **Max range:** 650 miles. **Armament:** 2×·5-inch machine-guns

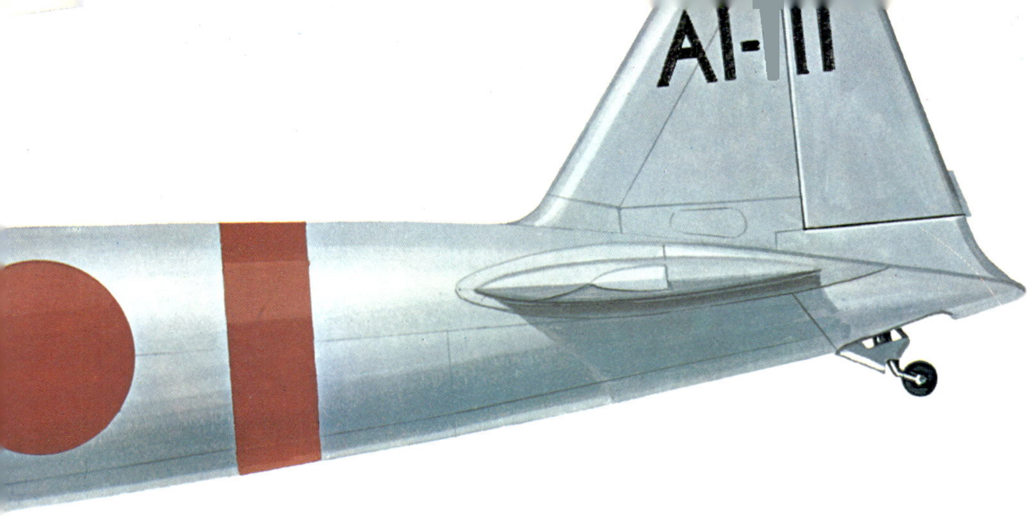

north of Midway which would place them at dawn within scouting range of the unsuspecting enemy. The scene was now set for what was to be one of the great decisive battles of history.

Deadly game of hide-and-seek

The last hour of darkness before sunrise on June 4 saw the familiar activity in both the carrier forces of ranging-up aircraft on the flight-deck for dawn operations. Aboard the *Yorktown*, whose turn it was to mount the first scouting flight of the day, there were Dauntless scout dive-bombers, ten of which were launched at 0430 hours for a search to a depth of 100 miles between west and east through north, a precaution against being taken by surprise while waiting for news from the scouting flying boats from Midway.

Reconnaissance aircraft were dispatched at the same moment from Nagumo's force. One each from the *Akagi* and *Kaga*, and two seaplanes each from the cruisers *Tone* and *Chikuma* were to search to a depth of 300 miles to the east and south. The seaplane carried in the battleship *Haruna*, being of an older type, was restricted to 150 miles. The main activity in Nagumo's carriers, however, was the preparation of the striking force to attack Midway—36 'Kate' torpedo-bombers each carrying a 1,770-pound bomb, 36 'Val' dive-bombers each with a single 550-pound bomb, and 36 Zero fighters as escort. Led by Lieutenant Joichi Tomonaga, this formidable force also took off at 0430.

By 0445 all these aircraft were on their way—with one notable exception. In the cruiser *Tone*, one of the catapults had given trouble, and it was not until 0500 that her second seaplane got away. This apparently minor dislocation of the schedule was to have vital consequences. Meanwhile, the carrier lifts were already hoisting up on deck an equally powerful second wave; but under the bellies of the 'Kates' were slung torpedoes, for these aircraft were to be ready to attack any enemy naval force which might be discovered by the scouts.

The lull in proceedings which followed the dawn fly-off from both carrier forces was broken with dramatic suddenness. At 0520, aboard Nagumo's flagship *Akagi*, the alarm was sounded. An enemy flying boat on reconnaissance had been sighted. Zeros roared off the deck in pursuit. A deadly game of hide-and-seek among the clouds developed, but the American naval fliers evaded their hunters. At 0534 Fletcher's radio office received the message 'Enemy carriers in sight', followed by another reporting many enemy aircraft heading for Midway; finally, at 0603, details were received of the position and composition of Nagumo's force, 200 miles west-south-west of the *Yorktown*. The time for action had arrived.

The *Yorktown*'s scouting aircraft were at once recalled and while she waited to gather them in, Fletcher ordered Spruance to proceed with his Task Force 16 'south-westerly and attack enemy carriers when definitely located'. *Enterprise* and *Hornet* with their screening cruisers and destroyers turned away, increasing to 25 knots, while hooters blared for 'General Quarters' and aircrews manned their planes to warm-up ready for take-off. Meanwhile, 240 miles to the south, Midway was preparing to meet the impending attack.

Radar had picked up the approaching aerial swarm at 0553 and seven minutes later every available aircraft on the island had taken off. Bombers and flying-boats were ordered to keep clear, but Marine Corps fighters in two groups clawed their way upwards, and at 0616 swooped in to the attack. But of the 26 planes, all but six were obsolescent Brewster Buffaloes, hopelessly outclassed by the highly manoeuvrable Zeros. Though they took their toll of Japanese bombers, they were in turn overwhelmed, 17 being shot down and seven others damaged beyond repair. The survivors of the Japanese squadrons pressed on to drop their bombs on power-plants, seaplane hangars, and oil tanks.

At the same time as the Marine fighters, ten torpedo-bombers had also taken off from Midway—six of the new Grumman Avengers (which were soon to supersede the unsatisfactory Devastator torpedo-bombers in American aircraft-carriers) and four Army Marauders. At 0710 they located and attacked the Japanese carriers; but with no fighter protection against the many Zeros sent up against them, half of them were shot down before they could reach a launching position. Those which broke through, armed with the slow and unreliable torpedoes which had earned Japanese contempt in the Coral Sea battle, failed to score any hits; greeted with a storm of gunfire, only one Avenger and two Marauders escaped to crash-land on Midway.

Unsuccessful as these attacks were, they had important consequences. From over Midway, Lieutenant Tomonaga, surveying the result of his attack, at 0700 signalled that a further strike was necessary to knock out the island's defences. The torpedo attacks seemed to Nagumo to bear this out, and, as no inkling of any enemy surface forces in the vicinity had yet come to him, he made the first of a train of fatal decisions. At 0715 he ordered the second wave of aircraft to stand by to attack Midway. The 'Kate' bombers, concentrated in the *Akagi* and *Kaga*, had to be struck down into the hangars to have their torpedoes replaced by bombs. Ground crews swarmed round to move them one by one to the lifts which took them below where mechanics set feverishly to work to make the exchange. It could not be a quick operation, however, and it had not been half completed when, at 0728, came a message which threw Nagumo into an agony of indecision.

The reconnaissance seaplane from the *Tone*—the one which had been launched 30 minutes behind schedule—was fated to be the one in whose search sector the American fleet was to be found; and now it sent back the signal—'Have sighted ten ships, apparently enemy, bearing 010 degrees, 240 miles away from Midway: Course 150 degrees, speed more than 20 knots.' For the next quarter of an hour Nagumo waited with mounting impatience for a further signal giving the composition of the enemy force.

Only if it included carriers was it any immediate menace at its range of 200 miles—but in that case it was vital to get a strike launched against it at once. At 0745 Nagumo ordered the re-arming of the 'Kates' to be suspended and all aircraft to prepare for an attack on ships, and two minutes later he signalled to the search plane: 'Ascertain ship types and maintain contact.' The response was a signal of 0758 reporting only a change of the enemy's course; but 12 minutes later came the report: 'Enemy ships are five cruisers and five destroyers.'

Nagumo's hopes crushed

This message was received with heartfelt relief by Nagumo and his staff; for at this moment his force came under attack first by 16 Marine Corps dive-bombers from Midway, followed by 15 Flying Fortresses, bombing from 20,000 feet, and finally 11 Marine Corps Vindicator scout-bombers. Every available Zero was sent aloft to deal with them, and not a single hit was scored by the bombers. But now, should Nagumo decide to launch an air strike, it would lack escort

Below: The doomed Japanese carrier *Akagi* evades US bombs at Midway

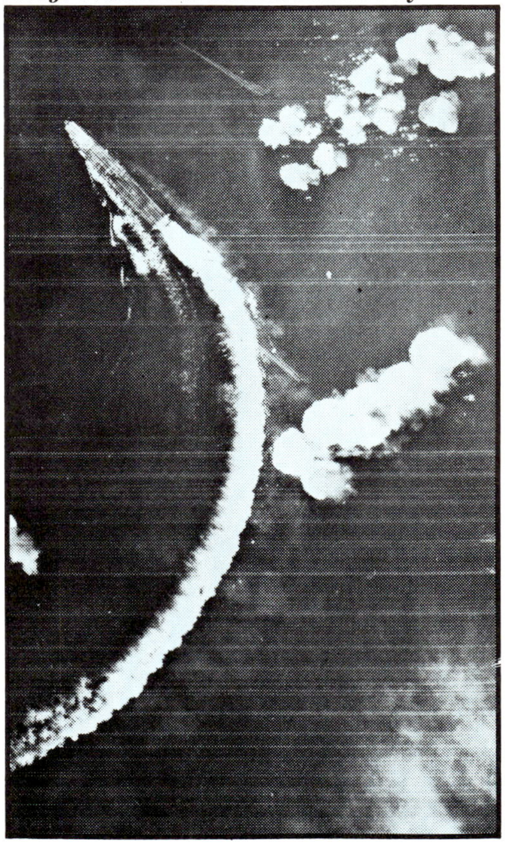

US Air Force

fighters until the Zeros had been recovered, refuelled, and re-armed. While the air attacks were in progress, further alarms occupied the attention of the battleship and cruiser screen when the US submarine *Nautilus*—one of 12 covering Midway—fired a torpedo at a battleship at 0825. But neither this nor the massive depth-charge attacks in retaliation were effective; and in the midst of the noise and confusion of the air attacks—at 0820—Nagumo received the message he dreaded to hear: 'Enemy force accompanied by what appears to be a carrier.'

The luckless Japanese admiral's dilemma, however, had been disastrously resolved for him by the return of the survivors of Tomonaga's Midway strike at 0830. With some damaged and all short of fuel, their recovery was urgent; and rejecting the advice of his subordinate carrier squadron commander—Rear-Admiral Yamaguchi, in the *Hiryu*—to launch his strike force, Nagumo issued the order to strike below all aircraft on deck and land the returning aircraft. By the time this was completed, it was 0918.

Refuelling, re-arming, and ranging-up a striking-force in all four carriers began at once, the force consisting of 36 'Val' dive-bombers and 54 'Kates', now again armed with torpedoes, with an escort of as many Zeros as could be spared from defensive patrol over the carriers. Thus it was at a carrier force's most vulnerable moment that—from his screening ships to the south—Nagumo received the report of an approaching swarm of aircraft. The earlier catapult defect in the *Tone*; the inefficient scouting of its aircraft's crew; Nagumo's own vacillation (perhaps induced by the confusion caused by the otherwise ineffective air attacks from Midway); but above all the fatal assumption that the Midway attack would be over long before any enemy aircraft-carriers could arrive in the area—all had combined to plunge Nagumo into a catastrophic situation. The pride and vainglory of the victorious carrier force had just one more hour to run.

When Task Force 16 had turned to the south-west, leaving the *Yorktown* to recover her reconnaissance aircraft, Nagumo's carriers were still too far away for Spruance's aircraft to reach him and return; and if the Japanese continued to steer towards Midway, it would be nearly 0900 before Spruance could launch his strike. When calculations showed that Nagumo would probably be occupied recovering his aircraft at about that time, however, Spruance had decided to accept the consequences of an earlier launching in order to catch him off balance. Every serviceable aircraft in his two carriers, with the exception of the fighters required for defensive patrol, was to be included, involving a double launching, taking a full hour to complete, during which the first aircraft off would have to orbit and wait, eating up precious fuel.

It was just 0702 when the first of the 67 Dauntless dive-bombers, 29 Devastator torpedo-bombers, and 20 Wildcat fighters, which formed Task Force 16's striking force, flew off. The torpedo squadrons had not yet taken the air when the sight of the *Tone*'s float plane, circling warily on the horizon, told Spruance that he could not afford to wait for his striking force to form up before dispatching them. The *Enterprise*'s dive-bombers led by Lieutenant-Commander McClusky, which had been the first to take off, were ordered to lead on without waiting for the torpedo-bombers or for the fighter escort whose primary task must be to protect the slow, lumbering Devastators. At 0752, McClusky took departure, steering to intercept Nagumo's force which was assumed to be steering south-east towards Midway. The remainder of the air groups followed at intervals, the dive-bombers and fighters up at 19,000 feet, the torpedo-bombers skimming low over the sea.

This distance between them, in which layers of broken cloud made maintenance of contact difficult, had calamitous consequences. The fighters from the *Enterprise*, led by Lieutenant Gray, took station above but did not make contact with Lieutenant-Commander Waldron's torpedo squadron from the *Hornet*, leaving the *Enterprise*'s torpedo squadron, led by Lieutenant-Commander Lindsey, unescorted. *Hornet*'s fighters never achieved contact with Waldron, and flew instead in company with their dive-bombers. Thus Task Force 16's air strike advanced in four separate, independent groups—McClusky's dive-bombers, the *Hornet*'s dive-bombers and fighters, and the two torpedo squadrons.

All steered initially for the estimated position of Nagumo, assuming he had maintained his south-easterly course for Midway. In fact, at 0918, having recovered Tomonaga's Midway striking force, he had altered course to north-east to close the distance between him and the enemy while his projected strike was being ranged up on deck. When the four air groups from TF 16 found nothing at the expected point of interception, therefore, they had various courses of action to choose between. The *Hornet*'s dive-bombers decided to search south-easterly where, of course, they found nothing. As fuel ran low, some of the bombers returned to the carrier, others made for Midway to refuel. The fighters were not so lucky: one by one they were forced to ditch as their engines spluttered and died.

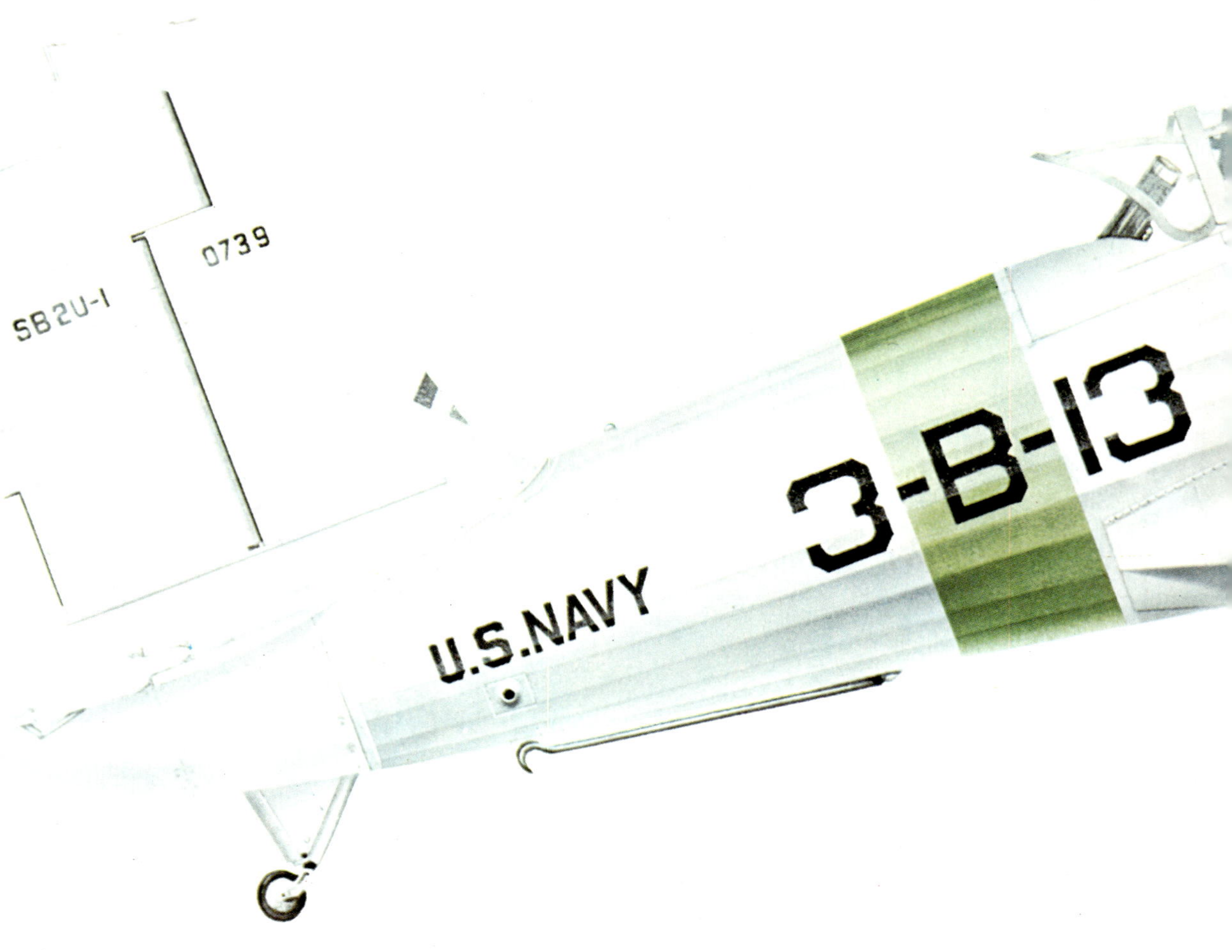

The two torpedo squadrons, on the other hand, low down over the water, sighted smoke on the northern horizon and, turning towards it, were rewarded with the sight of the Japanese carriers shortly after 0930. Though bereft of fighter protection, both promptly headed in to the attack. Neither Waldron nor Lindsey had any doubts of the suicidal nature of the task ahead of them. The former, in his last message to his squadron had written: 'My greatest hope is that we encounter a favourable tactical situation, but if we don't, and the worst comes to the worst, I want each of us to do his utmost to destroy our enemies. If there is only one plane left to make a final run in, I want that man to go in and get a hit. May God be with us all.'

His hopes for a favourable tactical situation were doomed. Fifty or more Zeros concentrated on his formation long before they reached a launching position. High overhead, Lieutenant Gray, leading the *Enterprise*'s fighter squadron, waited for a call for help as arranged with Lindsey, thinking that Waldron's planes were the torpedo squadron from his own ship – a call which never came. From the cruisers and destroyers of the screen came a withering fire. One by one the torpedo-bombers were shot down. A few managed to get their torpedoes away before crashing, but none hit the enemy. Only one of the pilots, Ensign George H. Gay, survived the massacre, clinging to a rubber seat cushion which floated away from his smashed aircraft, until dusk when he could inflate his life-raft without attracting strafing Zeros.

Five minutes later it was the turn of Lindsey's 14 Devastators from the *Enterprise*. Purely by chance, as he was making his attack on the starboard side of the *Kaga*, the torpedo squadron from the *Yorktown* came sweeping in from the other side, aiming to attack the *Soryu*, and drawing off some of the fighter opposition.

The *Yorktown*'s strike group of 17 dive-bombers led by Lieutenant-Commander Maxwell F. Leslie, with 12 torpedo-bombers of Lieutenant-Commander Lance E. Massey's squadron and an escort of six Wildcats, had taken departure from their carrier an hour and a quarter after the strike groups of Task Force 16. A more accurate assessment of probabilities by Leslie, however, had brought the whole of this force simultaneously over the enemy to deliver the co-ordinated, massed attack which alone could hope to swamp and break through the defences. In addition, at this same moment, McClusky's dive-bombers also arrived overhead. McClusky, after reaching the expected point of interception, had continued for a time on his south-westerly course and had then made a cast to the north-west. There he had sighted a destroyer steering north-east at high speed. This was the *Arashi*, which had been left behind to depth-charge the *Nautilus*. Turning to follow her, McClusky was led straight to his objective.

The simultaneous attack by the two torpedo squadrons brought no result of itself. Scores of Zeros swarmed about them, brushing aside the puny force of six Wildcats. The massacre of the clumsy Devastators was re-enacted. Lindsey and ten others of his force were shot down. Of Massey's squadron, only two survived. The few torpedoes launched were easily evaded.

The sacrifice of the torpedo-bombers had not been in vain, nevertheless. For, while every Japanese fighter plane was milling about low over the water, enjoying the easy prey offered to them there, high overhead there were gathering, all unseen and unmolested, the dive-bombers – McClusky's 18, and Leslie's 17. And now, like hawks swooping to their prey, they came plummeting down out of the sky.

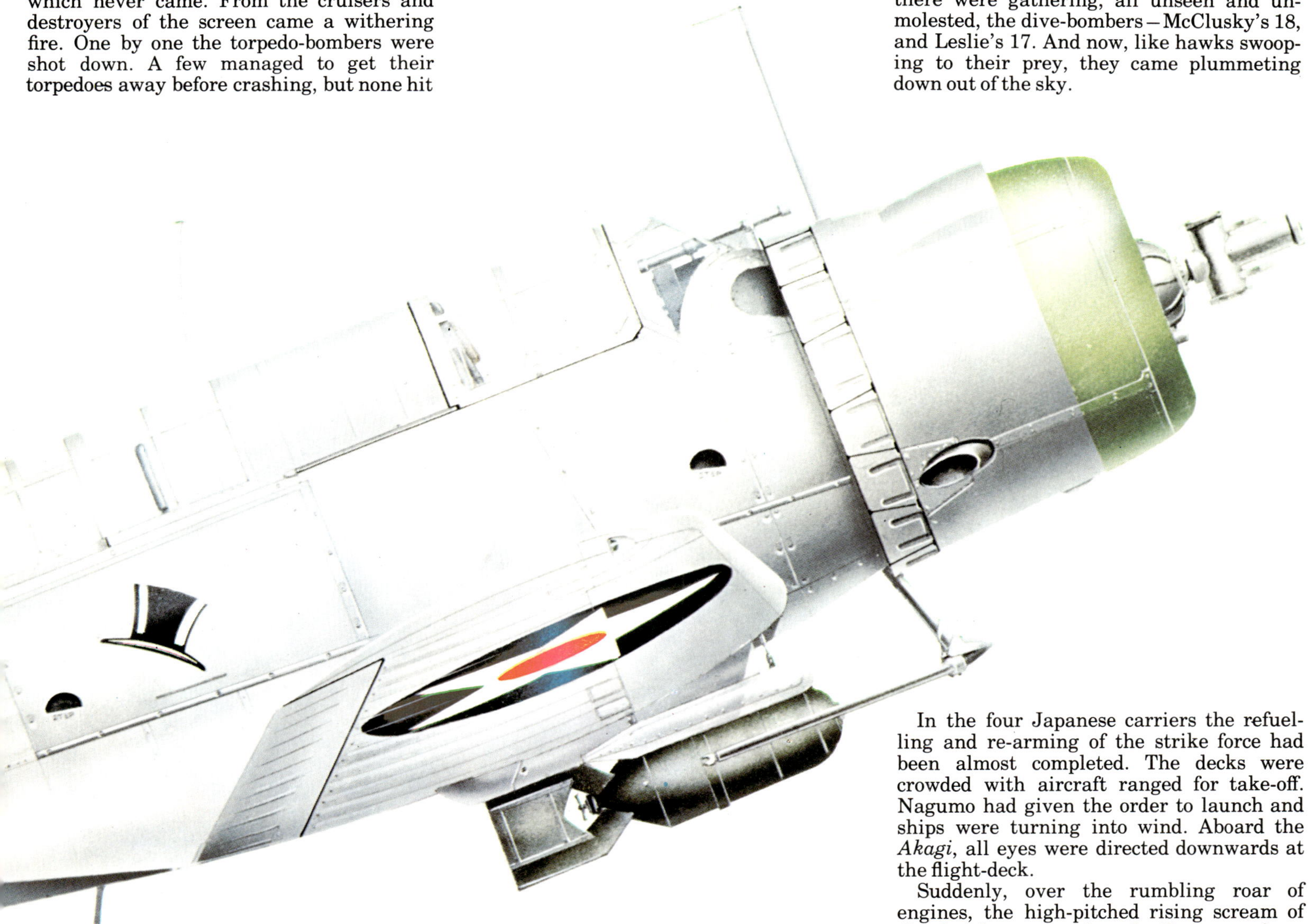

Vought-Sikorsky SB2U-1 Vindicator. Known as 'Vibrators' by their Marine crews, the SB2 was one of the US Navy's first monoplane types. Some were still in service at Midway. **Max speed:** 257 mph at 11,000 feet. **Max range:** 700 miles. **Armament:** 5 machine-guns and 1500-lb bombload

In the four Japanese carriers the refuelling and re-arming of the strike force had been almost completed. The decks were crowded with aircraft ranged for take-off. Nagumo had given the order to launch and ships were turning into wind. Aboard the *Akagi*, all eyes were directed downwards at the flight-deck.

Suddenly, over the rumbling roar of engines, the high-pitched rising scream of dive-bombers was heard. Even as faces swivelled upwards at the sound, the black dots which were 1,000-pound bombs were seen leaving three 'Hell-Divers' as they pulled out from their near-vertical dive. Fascinated eyes watched the bombs grow in size as they fell inexorably towards that most vulnerable of targets, a full deck load of armed and fuelled aircraft. One bomb struck the *Akagi* squarely amidships, opposite the bridge and just behind the aircraft lift, plunged down into the hangar and there exploded, detonating stored torpedoes, tearing up the flight deck, and destroying the lift. A second exploded in the midst of the 'Kates' on the after part of the deck, starting a tremendous conflagration to add to that in the hangar. In a matter of seconds Nagumo's proud flagship had been reduced to a blazing shambles. From time to time she was further shaken by internal explosions as the flames touched off petrol tanks, bombs, and torpedoes. Within a few minutes Captain Aoki knew that the damage and fires were beyond control. He persuaded the reluctant Nagumo that it was necessary to transfer his flag to a ship with radio communication intact. Admiral and staff picked their way through the flames to reach the forecastle whence they lowered themselves down ropes to a boat which took them to the light cruiser *Nagara* of the screen.

Imperial War Museum

Above: The major US casualty at Midway, the *Yorktown*, lies dead in the water.

Carnage in the Japanese carriers

Only three dive-bombers from the *Enterprise* had attacked the flagship. The remainder of the air group, 34 dive-bombers, all concentrated on the *Kaga*. Of four bombs which scored direct hits, the first burst just forward of the superstructure, blowing up a petrol truck which stood there, and the sheet of flame which swept the bridge killed everyone on it, including the captain. The other three bombs falling among the massed aircraft on the flight deck set the ship ablaze and started the same fatal train of fires and explosions as in the *Akagi*. Within a few minutes, the situation was so beyond control that the senior surviving officer ordered the transfer of the Emperor's portrait to an attendant destroyer – the custom obligatory when a ship was known to be doomed, and conducted with strict naval ceremony. The *Kaga* was to survive for several hours, nevertheless.

Simultaneously, with the *Akagi* and *Kaga*, the *Soryu* had also been reeling under a devastating attack. Leslie of the *Yorktown* was leading veterans of the Coral Sea battle, probably the most battle-experienced aviators in the American navy at that time. With deadly efficiency they dived in three waves in quick succession from the starboard bow, the starboard quarter, and the port quarter, released their bombs and climbed away without a single casualty. Out of the shower of 1,000-pound bombs, three hit. The first penetrated to the hangar deck and the explosion lifted the steel platform of the lift, folding it back against the bridge. The others landed among the massed aircraft, causing the whole ship to be engulfed in flames. It took Captain Ryusaku Yanaginoto only 20 minutes to decide to order 'Abandon Ship' to save his crew from being burnt alive, though the *Soryu*, like her sisters, was to survive for some hours yet.

Thus, in five brief, searing minutes, half of Japan's entire fleet carrier force, her naval *corps d'élite*, had been shattered. For the time being the *Hiryu*, some miles away, remained untouched. She was to avenge her sisters in some measure before the day was over; but before going on to tell of her part in the battle let us follow the remainder to their deaths in the blue Pacific waters.

On board the *Akagi*, though the bomb damage was confined at first to her flight and hangar decks and her machinery spaces remained intact, the fires fed by aviation petrol from aircraft and from fuel lines were beyond the capacity of the Japanese crew to master. They fought them for seven hours but by 1715 Captain Aoki had decided there was no hope of saving his ship. The Emperor's portrait was transferred to a destroyer and the ship was abandoned. Permission was asked of the C-in-C to hasten her end but it was not until nearly dawn on the following day – when Yamamoto at last fully understood the fullness of the Japanese defeat – that he gave his approval and the *Akagi* was sent to the bottom by torpedoes from a destroyer.

Petrol-fed fires similarly swept the *Kaga* and defeated all efforts to save her. Lying stopped and burning she became the target for three torpedoes from the *Nautilus* which, after her earlier adventure, had surfaced and chased after the Japanese carriers. Even the stationary target, however, was too much for the unreliable torpedoes with which the Americans were at that time equipped. Of three fired, two missed, and the third struck but failed to explode. At 1640 orders were given to abandon the *Kaga*, and at 1925 two great explosions tore her asunder and sent her to the bottom.

The *Soryu*'s story was a similar one, of intermittent internal explosions from within the great mass of flame and smoke which she had become. When Captain Yanaginoto gave the order 'Abandon Ship', he determined to immolate himself, dying in the flames or going down with her. A party of his men returning on board with the intention of persuading him or, if necessary, of forcing him to save himself, fell back abashed at the heroic, determined figure of their captain, standing sword in hand, facing forward, awaiting his end. They left him to his chosen fate. As they did so they heard him singing the Japanese national anthem. Yanaginoto's resolution held fast till 1913 hours when at last the *Soryu* and the bodies of 718 of her crew slid beneath the surface.

Much had taken place in the meantime before Nagumo's three aircraft-carriers suffered their death throes. The first survivors of the American strike groups to land back on their ships made it clear that one Japanese carrier had not yet been located. This was the *Hiryu* which, at the time of the attack, had become separated from the remainder. Admiral Fletcher therefore launched a ten-plane search from the *Yorktown*, and sent up a defensive patrol of a dozen Wildcats. It was none too soon. At a few minutes before noon, the *Yorktown*'s radar gave the warning of enemy planes coming in from the west.

These were the *Hiryu*'s attack group of 18 dive-bombers and six fighters, led by Lieutenant Michio Kobayashi, a veteran leader who had taken part in every operation of the Nagumo force. As soon as they had flown off, a further strike of ten torpedo-bombers and six Zeros, to be led by the redoubtable Tomonago, was ranged up. Kobayashi's force had followed some of the *Yorktown*'s attack planes back and now concentrated on Fletcher's flagship. Wildcats – for once outnumbering the escorting

Below: A crippling collision with another heavy cruiser, US bombs and engine-room

US Navy

It was later sunk by an enemy submarine

Zeros—broke through to get at the 'Vals', shooting down ten of them, including the leader. Of the eight which remained, two were knocked down by anti-aircraft fire from the cruiser screen.

The six survivors, however, showed that they had lost none of their skill as they screamed down on the carrier. One 'Val' broke up under anti-aircraft fire, but its bomb sped on to burst on the flight-deck, killing many men, and starting a hangar fire below. A second bomb plunged through the side of the funnel and burst inside, starting more fires. With three boiler uptakes smashed and the furnaces of five or six boilers extinguished, the carrier's speed fell away until, 20 minutes later, she came to a stop. A third bomb penetrated to the fourth deck where for a time a fire threatened the forward petrol tanks and magazines.

His flagship immobilised, her radio and radar knocked out, Admiral Fletcher transferred his flag to the cruiser *Astoria*, and ordered the *Portland* to take the aircraft-carrier in tow. The damage-control organization worked wonders, however. Before the towline had been passed, the *Yorktown* was under way again and working up to 20 knots, and the refuelling of the fighters was in progress. Prospects seemed bright. Then a cruiser's radar picked up Tomonaga's air group, 40 miles away and coming in fast. There was just time to launch eight of the refuelling Wildcats to join the four already in the air, but they were unable to get

explosions sank the *Mikuma* at Midway

through the screen of fighters to get at the 'Kates'—though they shot down three of the 'Zeros'. A tremendous screen of bursting shells spread itself in front of the attackers, while the cruisers raised a barrage of splashes with their main armament, a wall of water columns through which it seemed impossible that the skimming 'Kates' could fly.

Yorktown fatally damaged

Five 'Kates' were shot down, but the remainder, coming in from four different angles, displayed all their deadly skill, boring doggedly in to drop their torpedoes at the point-blank range of 500 yards. It was impossible for the carrier to avoid them all. Two hit on her port side, tearing open the double-bottom fuel tanks and causing flooding which soon had her listing at 26 degrees. All power was lost, so that counter-flooding was impossible. It seemed that the *Yorktown* was about to capsize. At 1500, Captain Buckmaster ordered 'Abandon Ship'.

Meanwhile, however, the dive-bombers from Spruance's Task Force 16, operating some 60 miles to the north-east of the *Yorktown*, had wreaked vengeance on the *Hiryu*. Twenty-four Dauntlesses, of which ten had been transferred from the *Yorktown*, arrived overhead undetected soon after the few survivors of *Hiryu*'s attack had been recovered. The aircraft carrier circled and swerved to avoid the bombs from the plummeting dive-bombers, but in vain. Four of them hit, one of which blew the forward lift bodily on to the bridge. The others started the inevitable fires and explosions, and the same prolonged death agonies as the *Hiryu*'s sisters were still suffering. By 2123 she had come to a stop. Desperate efforts to subdue the flames went on through the night; but at 0230 the following morning she was abandoned to be torpedoed by her attendant destroyers.

When the night of June 4 closed over the four smoking Japanese carriers and over the crippled *Yorktown*, the battle of Midway was, in the main, over. Neither of the opposing commanders yet knew it, however, and manoeuvres and skirmishes were to continue for two more days. The Japanese commanders, except Nagumo, were slow to realise that the shattering of their four fleet carriers signified defeat and the end of the Midway operation. Admiral Kondo, with his two fast battleships, four heavy cruisers, and the light carrier *Zuiho* had set off to the help of Nagumo at midday on June 4, and soon afterwards Yamamoto was signalling to all his scattered forces to concentrate and attack the enemy. He himself, with the main body of his fleet, was coming up fast from the west bringing the 18-inch guns of the giant *Yamato* and the 16-inch ones of the *Nagato* and *Mutsu* to throw in their weight. Still underestimating his opponent, he was dreaming of a night encounter in which his immensely powerful fleet would overwhelm the American task force and avenge the losses of the previous day. The great 'fleet action' with battleships in stately line hurling huge shells at each other was still his hope and aim.

Such a concept had been forcibly removed from American naval strategy by the shambles of Pearl Harbor. Raymond Spruance, one of the greatest admirals to come to the fore during the war, was not to be lured within range of Yamamoto's battleships, above all at night, when his carriers, at this time untrained for night-flying, would be at a tremendous disadvantage. At sunset he turned away eastwards, aiming to take up a position on the following day from which he could either 'follow up retreating enemy forces or break up a landing attack on Midway'.

The Japanese C-in-C refused to credit the completeness of the disaster that had overtaken his fleet and the Midway plan until early on June 5 when, at 0255, he ordered a general retirement. Thus, when Spruance, after prudently steering eastwards to keep his distance from the still overwhelmingly superior Japanese surface fleet, and reversing course at midnight so as to be within supporting distance of Midway at daylight, sent a strike of 58 dive-bombers from his two ships during the afternoon of the 5th to seek out Yamamoto's Main Body, his airmen encountered nothing but a lone destroyer sent to search for the *Hiryu*.

Two final incidents remain to be briefly recounted. When Yamamoto ordered his general retirement, the squadron of four heavy cruisers of Admiral Kurita's Support Force, the *Kumano, Suzuya, Mikuma,* and *Mogami,* was to the westward of Midway, steering through the night to deliver a bombardment at dawn. They now swung round to reverse course full in view of the American submarine *Tambor*. As they steadied on their retirement course, from the flagship the *Tambor* was sighted in the moonlight ahead. The signal for an emergency turn to port was flashed down the line but was not taken in by the rear ship, *Mogami*. Failing to turn with the remainder she collided with the *Mikuma*, suffering serious damage which reduced her speed to 12 knots. Leaving the *Mikuma* and two destroyers to escort the cripple, Kurita hurried on with the remainder.

News of this attractive target soon reached Midway. Twelve army Flying Fortresses took off but were unable to locate it; but 12 Marine Corps dive-bombers sighted the long oil slick being trailed by the *Mikuma*, followed it up—and at 0805 dived to the attack. Their bombs failed to achieve direct hits, but the plane of Captain Richard E. Fleming crashed on the after turret of the *Mikuma*. Petrol fumes were sucked down into the cruiser's starboard engine-room and exploded, killing the whole engine-room crew.

The two cruisers nevertheless continued to limp slowly away, until the following day when Spruance, having abandoned hope of delivering another blow on Yamamoto's Main Fleet, was able to direct his dive-bombers on to them. The *Mikuma* was smothered and sunk, but the *Mogami* miraculously survived, heavily damaged, to reach the Japanese base at Truk.

While these events were taking place, far to the east the abandoned *Yorktown* had drifted crewless through the night of June 4/5. She was still afloat at noon the next day and it became clear she had been prematurely abandoned. A salvage party boarded her and she was taken in tow. Hopes of getting her to port were high until the Japanese submarine *I-168*, sent by Yamamoto for the purpose, found her, penetrated her anti-submarine screen, and put two torpedoes into her. At 0600 on June 7 the *Yorktown* sank at last.

At sundown on the previous day Spruance had turned his force back eastwards to meet his supply tankers. That the Battle of Midway was over was finally clear to all.

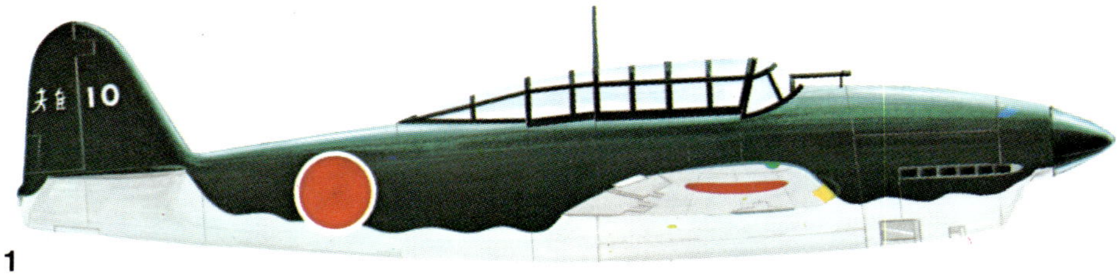

1

2

3

4

Japan's later warplanes

Japan's air forces went to war largely relying on the navy's Zero fighter, Kate torpedo-bomber, and Nell and Betty long-range bombers, and on the army's Oscar fighter and Sally bomber. Production of these machines was kept up to speed the 'Runaway Victory', and the newer designs were shelved. But after 18 months of the Pacific War the back of Japan's carrier fleet had been broken at Midway and her outermost conquests had already fallen to Allied 'island-hopping' offensives. Now the Japanese needed aircraft capable of operating more from shore bases than from aircraft-carriers, and the new aircraft were rushed ahead. The Zero was supplemented by the Jack, the Kate by the Jill and the Judy. For the army, the new single-engined Tony and the twin-engined Nick began to replace the ageing Oscar. A new long-range bomber—the Helen—was intended to replace the Sally, Nell, and Betty, but never did. Yet none of these aircraft, old or new, could halt the swelling flood of Lightnings, Thunderbolts, and Fortresses.

1. JUDY: Yokosuka D4Y-2 *Susei*
A navy carrier bomber, the Judy first saw service as a reconnaissance plane at Midway, was later used extensively, and finally—like most Japanese types—saw service as a Kamikaze. *Max speed:* 335 mph. *Range:* 1,320 miles. *Crew:* two. *Armament:* three 7·7-mm machine-guns; 1,100 lb of bombs

2. JACK: Mitsubishi J2M-3 *Raiden*
Designed as a single-seat shore-based interceptor fighter at the same time as the Zero, the Jack had so many teething troubles that it only entered service in small numbers. *Max speed:* 371 mph. *Range:* 650 miles. *Armament:* two 20-mm cannon, and two 7·1-mm machine-guns

5

6

7

8

3. MAVIS: Kawanishi H6K4-L Flying-boat
This was one of the more elderly Japanese long-range navy patrol bombers; it was an unarmed type, and the lessons learned from it resulted in the 'Emily', which was given five cannon and four MGs. Mavis was then relegated to transport duties. *Max speed:* 237 mph. *Range:* 4,000 miles. *Crew:* nine (plus 18 passengers)

4. IRVING: Nakajima JINI-S *Gekko*
Designed first as a fighter, then used by the navy in reconnaissance, then converted to a night fighter. It had a unique armament of two pairs of 20-mm cannon above and below the fuselage at an angle of 30°. *Max speed:* 315 mph. *Range:* 1,360 miles. *Crew:* two. *Armament:* four 20-mm cannon

5. TONY: Kawasaki Ki-61 *Hien*
When allied pilots first met Tony in action in 1943, it was thought to be a version of the German Me-109. Well armed and well protected, Tony was a formidable opponent; but its engine gave considerable trouble in service. *Max speed:* 348 mph. *Range:* 1,185 miles. *Armament:* two 20-mm cannon, and two 12·7-mm machine-guns

6. HELEN: Nakajima Ki-49 *Donryu*
Helen was an army heavy bomber, designed for use in the event of Japan going to war with Russia, but was first used in action in a raid on Darwin in 1943. It was never produced in great numbers. *Max speed:* 306 mph. *Range:* 1,490 miles. *Crew:* eight. *Armament:* one 20-mm cannon, five 7·7-mm machine-guns

7. JILL: Nakajima B6N-2 *Tenzan*
The Jill was the direct replacement for the Kate torpedo-bomber, and its first major action was the Battle of the Philippine Sea in June 1944. *Max speed:* 299 mph. *Range:* 1,600 miles. *Armament:* one 13-mm, one 7·9-mm machine-gun; one 1,764-lb torpedo OR six 220-lb bombs

8. NICK: Kawasaki Ki-45 *Toryu*
The Nick was the first twin-engined fighter to enter service with the Japanese army air force; the Allies first met it in action over New Guinea in 1943, and it was also used in home defence duties. *Max speed:* 340 mph. *Range:* 932 miles. *Crew:* two. *Armament:* varied, but a typical combination was: one 37-mm, two 20-mm cannon, and one 7·7-mm machine-gun

GUADALCANAL: JAPAN'S FIRST LAND DEFEAT

Imperial War Museum

A landing-craft brings in Marines to reinforce the US beach-head on Guadalcanal

At 0641 on the morning of August 7, 1942—eight months to the day after Pearl Harbor—the order to 'land the Marines' passed around the armada of transports and landing-craft gathered off the beaches of Guadalcanal. US land forces were, for the first time in the Pacific War, taking the offensive against the all-conquering might of the Rising Sun.

The object of the exercise, Guadalcanal, was a small, humid, hilly island in the Solomons group of the South Pacific, sitting astride the north-eastern approaches to Australia. Fever-ridden and almost uninhabitable, it was, nonetheless, a priceless possession for whichever side could hold it. And in early May, 1942, units of the Japanese army had occupied both Guadalcanal and the smaller neighbouring island of Tulagi, a fine anchorage from which to dominate the area. It was only in June, however, that coast-watchers reported up to 3,000 Japanese soldiers had moved from their base on Tulagi to begin building an airstrip on Guadalcanal.

Occupying one of the few patches of flat ground in the whole of the Solomons group, this airstrip at Henderson Field immediately presented a major strategic threat to the Allies. From there, enemy air forces would be able to dominate the skies on the approaches to Australia from America, thus isolating that continent as a base for future Allied operations in the Pacific. Clearly this situation could not long be tolerated, but Admiral King—the newly-appointed US naval chief—stressed that to merely destroy enemy installations and retire was not enough. Instead, he convinced Washington, the Solomons must be *denied* to the Japanese.

As a result, the 1st US Marine Division, reinforced by Marine Raider units and paratroop units, was chosen to do the job. Although nominally up to war strength, this Division was, in fact, made-up of thousands of raw recruits and a small core of seasoned veterans. Under its commander, Major-General Vandegrift, the Division left its North Carolina training base in late May, 1942; and it wasn't until June 25 that Vandegrift was actually informed that his men were destined for combat on August 1. By that time half his Division had not even arrived at its assembly-point in New Zealand.

Things were no better at sea. The cruiser force comprised the Australian ships *Hobart, Canberra* and *Australia,* and the US ships *Chicago* and *San Juan* backed up by nine destroyers under the command of Britain's Rear-Admiral Crutchley. Also present were Vice-Admiral Fletcher's US carriers *Saratoga, Wasp* and *Enterprise,* screened by the battleship *North Carolina.* These ships and Rear-Admiral Turner's South Pacific Amphibious Force of grey transports had never before worked together . . . and had no experience of amphibious landings.

Nonetheless, after postponements of D-Day first to the 4th and then the 7th, rehearsals of the assault went ahead off Koro in Fiji for four days from July 26. Bombing, bombardment, disembarkation, air-support, ship-to-shore and air-to-ground practices . . . all were chaotic. The whole rehearsal was described by senior officers as 'a fiasco'.

But there was no more time. On the morning of August 7, the Australian coastwatchers in their hill-top hide-outs saw the sea off Guadalcanal filled with the most powerful amphibious attack force at that time ever assembled. In 36-man boat teams, thousands of Marines arrived on the beaches in regulated waves.

Japanese resistance, amazingly, was non-existent. The invaders had achieved complete tactical surprise. Had they in fact met opposition in any force, the outcome of this first, hastily-planned Allied amphibious assault of the Pacific War might have been disastrously different.

Instead, by the evening of the 7th, troops had been landed, supplies had been piled high in chaotic heaps on the beaches, transport sections had moved off blindly into the jungle, and soldiers—exhausted by the tropic heat and often separated from their units—wandered around dazed and confused. The bitter, six-month struggle for Guadalcanal had begun amid a god-sent but ominous calm.

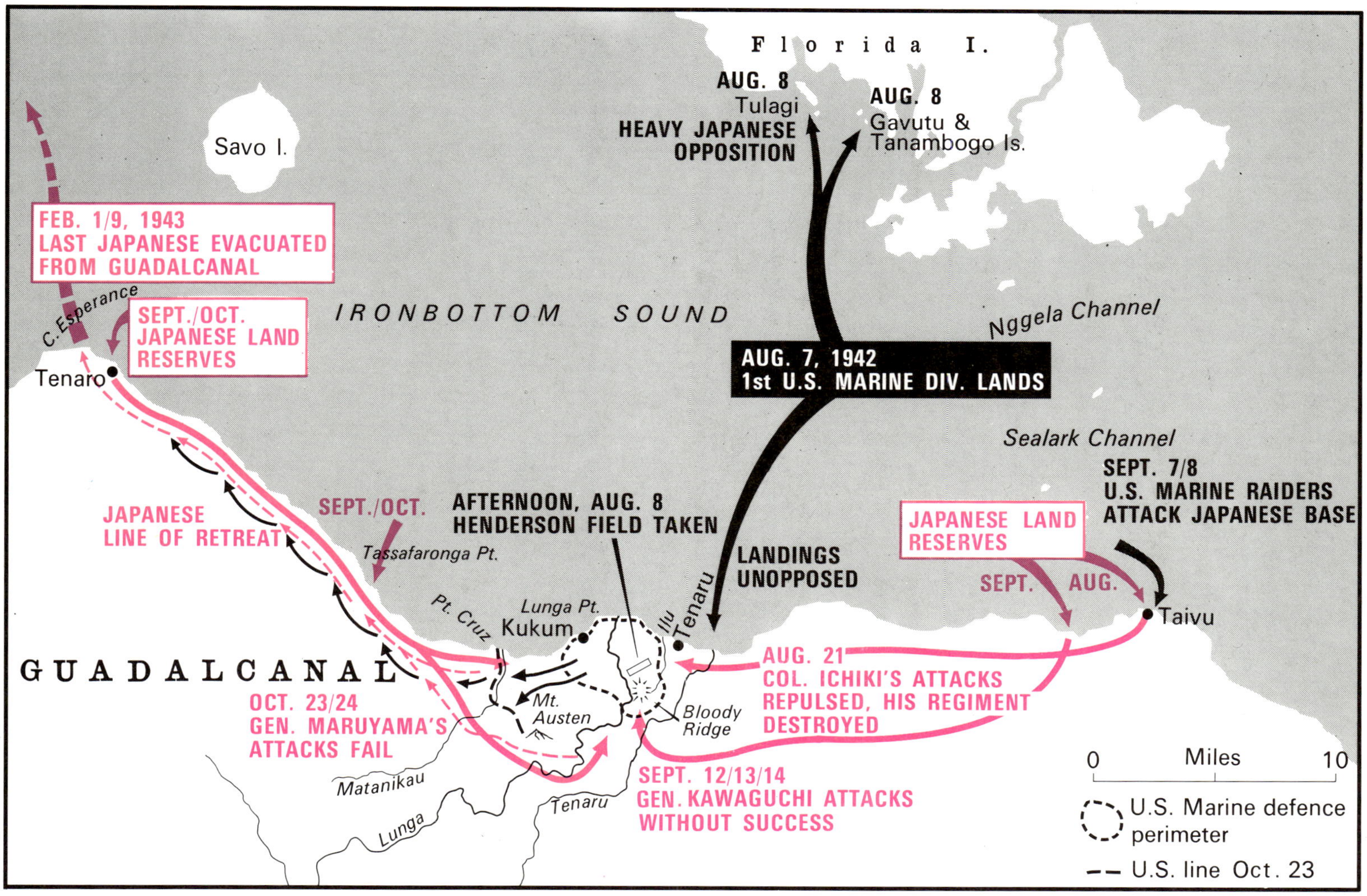

While there was no fighting on Guadalcanal in the first 24 hours, it was a different story on the neighbouring islands. On the larger island General Vandegrift had, as events had shown, picked as his point of disembarkation a spot where there were no Japanese and his men could go in unopposed. On the smaller islands he could expect no such bonus and it was therefore against these that he threw his more seasoned units led by officers with previous combat experience.

Colonel Merritt Edson, of 1st Marine Raiders, who was to seize Tulagi, ordered his men to strip down to minimum combat equipment – 'Don't worry about food,' he told them, 'Japs eat it too. All you have to do is get it.' Although their swift landing tactics got them established on the island before noon, stiff Japanese resistance made it impossible to capture the whole island before nightfall, and during the night the Japanese, liberally equipped with light mortars, grenade throwers, and heavy and light machine-guns, counterattacked. Four times they threw themselves against the Raiders and four times they were thrown back. Although most of the Japanese garrison died in these night attacks, it took the Raiders most of August 8 to eliminate the survivors.

The fighting was even tougher on the islet of Gavutu. The islet had been bombed from the air and shelled by ships' guns, but as the paratroops moved inshore, it became clear that the bombardment had had no effect on the defending Japanese in their reinforced dugouts and caves. The paratroops were met by a hail of fire. Their commanders asked for covering gunfire from the warships offshore, but because the waters around Gavutu were uncharted, none of the warships could move in close enough to give pin-point cover. Only after heavy losses did the paratroops secure a foothold.

On the neighbouring islet of Tanambogo, connected to Gavutu by a causeway, the story was grimmer still; the assault troops and their boats were shot to pieces by the defending Japanese before they touched land. Reinforcements were asked for and arrived on the morning of August 8. The Japanese were blasted and blown out of the caves and dugouts on Gavutu but there remained the problem of Tanambogo. Before crossing over from Gavutu, the American commander asked for two preliminary air-strikes to soften up Tanambogo's defenders, but neither air-strike made any impression. The heaviest casualties were suffered by the American assault troops poised on Gavutu, by bombs that fell short of their target. In despair their commander called on the US destroyer *Buchanan* to open fire on the Japanese in their caves and let go with everything she had. The bombardment was devastating and within minutes assault parties had captured Tanambogo.

On Guadalcanal the Americans had still encountered no Japanese but progress towards the airfield continued to be slow. Only as a result of General Vandegrift's unrelenting drive did the first American patrols eventually reach the airfield late in the afternoon of August 8. The Japanese construction teams and their Naval Landing Force protectors had fled into the jungle after the bombardment in the early hours of August 7. The Japanese had obviously been taken completely by surprise, for there were signs of panic everywhere – uniforms, shirts, caps, chopsticks, helmets, mosquito netting, rifles, teacups, and rice bowls, their contents half-consumed, littered the ground.

It had taken the Americans much longer to reach the airfield than General Vandegrift had hoped, and the speed and control of unloading at the main disembarkation point had shown up serious shortcomings. Moreover, the heavy casualties the Americans had suffered on Tulagi, Gavutu, and Tanambogo – in some cases higher than 20% – showed what tough and resourceful fighters the Japanese were in defence even when outmanned and outgunned.

Still the airfield on Guadalcanal and the islands in the immediate vicinity of the part of the coast of Guadalcanal where the airfield was situated, were in American hands. Despite delays, deficiencies, and mistakes the operation had achieved its objective of denying the Japanese a base from which to cut Allied supply lines and isolate Australia. There was immense relief in Australia, Washington, and London. But the feeling was not to last long. For, on the night of August 8/9, a Japanese cruiser force shattered the Allied naval forces under Admiral Crutchley, and the transports were forced to withdraw.

By the late afternoon of August 9, the last of Admiral Turner's ships had disappeared. The Marines were on their own.

Below: The six-month battle for Guadalcanal has since become a Marine legend

Camera Press

Could the Marines hold out?

The position facing General Vandegrift after Admiral Turner's departure was unenviable. He and his 1st Marine Division held an enclave consisting of a partially completed airfield surrounded by a few acres, on an island covered with dense, inhospitable jungle, in which lurked the remnants of the original Japanese construction and occupation forces. The waters around Guadalcanal were dominated by the Japanese navy. Indeed, in the days that followed, Japanese warships usually patrolled just off his enclave outside the range of his guns. On one occasion a Japanese submarine surfaced and in a leisurely fashion shelled the Marines' position on the beach and on another a Japanese cruiser landed a 200-

strong advance echelon and supplies along the coast in broad daylight. Moreover, constant Japanese bombing attacks on 'Henderson' (as the airfield came to be known) and the American-held area around it, never allowed General Vandegrift and his men to forget for long who was in control of the skies above Guadalcanal. Above all, the general knew that the Japanese were bound to try and annihilate his division sooner or later.

His main concern, therefore, was to build up his defences against assault both from the sea and from inland, and to complete the airfield so that it could be used by American aircraft to give him his own air cover. His difficulties in pursuing both these aims were immense, largely because so much essential equipment had sailed away in the holds of Admiral Turner's transports – only 18 spools of barbed wire had been landed; there were no anti-tank or anti-personnel mines, and no tools like axes, saws, shovels, machetes, or picks. Fortunately the equipment left behind by the Japanese – which included four heavy-duty tractors, six road-rollers, 12 trucks, and two petrol locomotives with hopper cars – made good these deficiences to some extent and within days the airfield was completed and work was begun on two subsidiary strips. On August 20 the first American aircraft – 19 Wildcat fighters and 12 Dauntless dive-bombers launched from an aircraft-carrier well to the south of Guadalcanal – landed on Henderson Field. A few hours later, shortly after midnight, before the aircraft could go into action, the Japanese attacked from the east.

Radio Tokyo had made no secret of its answer to the question of what fate had in store for the Marines on Guadalcanal. Admiral Mikawa (the area commander), it announced in triumph, had routed 'the remnants of Anglo-American naval strength in the Pacific and isolated Australia'. The Marines were like 'summer insects which have dropped into the fire by themselves'.

Such exaggerated claims may be excusable in propagandists intent on bolstering the morale of their own side and striking fear into the heart of the enemy. But what was astonishing in this instance was that these claims reflected the attitude of many senior Japanese staff officers. Men trained to assess every given situation coolly and without passion and then to lay their plans with care and attention to detail, refused to take the Marines on Guadalcanal seriously. It could, in their view, be no more than a reconnaissance in force, a manoeuvre to distract and annoy, and as such it was an insolent affront to the honour of Japanese arms which had to be washed away in blood without delay. No attempt was made to obtain an accurate picture of American strength and dispositions. Lieutenant-General Hyakutake, in command of XVII Army in the South Pacific area, was ordered to 'eliminate' the Americans, and he allocated the XXXV Infantry Brigade under Major-General Kawaguchi for the purpose but since the brigade had still to be assembled, it was decided to send in at once, in two echelons, the only units immediately available – Colonel Ichiki's regiment and a special naval landing force.

Colonel Ichiki landed with the first echelon on August 18. He was a distinguished officer who had fought in China in the 1930s, with

Imperial War Museum

Above: Marines embark for the beaches

LCI(L): landing-craft (infantry, large). With or without opening bows, these ocean-going craft were developed for use in the vast spaces of the Pacific. **Capacity:** 6 officers and 182 troops *or* 75 tons of cargo. **Range:** 4000 miles at 12 knots. **Armament:** 1×40-mm, 4×20-mm guns. **Displacement:** 280 tons (loaded)

The six-month battle for Guadalcanal

1942 August 7: US Marines land on Guadalcanal, meeting no opposition. But there is savage fighting on the neighbouring islands of Tulagi, Gavutu, and Tanambogo, before they are occupied.
August 8: American forces reach Henderson Field, to find that the Japanese have fled.
August 8/9: The Battle of Savo is fought at sea off Guadalcanal. Admiral Turner's transports are forced to retire, taking much of the Marines' equipment.
August 18: First Japanese reinforcements, Colonel Ichiki's regiment lands.
August 20: Henderson Field receives its first aircraft – 19 Wildcats and 12 Dauntlesses.
August 21/22: *Battle of the Tenaru:* Japanese forces attack across the Ilu and Tenaru rivers. They are driven back with heavy losses but continue to harass the Marines. General Vandegrift sends his reserve battalion around behind them, and the Japanese force is driven into the sea. Colonel Ichiki commits hara-kiri.
August 23/24: The Battle of the Eastern Solomons is fought at sea off Guadalcanal.
September 7: US Marine Raiders land at Taivu, capturing stores and equipment, and gaining intelligence about an impending Japanese attack.
September 12: Japanese bombers attack Henderson Field and the southern perimeter of the defences.
September 13: Japanese launch further heavy attacks, but they are driven back after losing 1,200 men.
September/October: Japanese II Division and the headquarters of XVII Army HQ are transferred to Guadalcanal. Meanwhile the US 7th Marines, the 164th Infantry Regiment, and other units reinforce the American forces.
October 9: The Battle of Cape Esperance is fought at sea off Guadalcanal.
October 23/24: Two major Japanese assaults are launched on the south of Henderson Field but lack of communication means that they are uncoordinated, and the Americans defeat them piecemeal. Battle of Santa Cruz is fought off Guadalcanal.
December 1/15: US 1st Marine Division is relieved by the 14th Army Corps.
December 31: Apalled by their mounting losses the Japanese begin to plan the withdrawal of XVII Army.

1943 February 1/9: The 'Tokyo Express' takes off the remnant of the once-proud Japanese XVII Army.

Behind the Allied victory

Even in the early days of the Pacific War, when the Japanese had the numerical advantage, they tended to split their forces and thus fall prey to the compact and well-deployed American task forces. But the American victory in the Pacific was due as much to her transports and replenishment craft as to the main arm of her sea power, her mighty aircraft-carriers. It was also due in no small measure to the spectacular losses inflicted by US submarines and surface raiders on Japanese transports, replenishment craft, and merchant shipping in general. Here we show two typical support ships—a transport and an oiler—an *Essex* class carrier, a chart showing the Allied success against Japanese tonnage, and a plan view of a typical task group (a component of a task force). It was these four elements—carrier superiority, huge logistic support, destruction of enemy shipping, and superior tactics—which helped to give the Americans the upper hand in the Pacific

A typical US task group, protected by a screen of destroyers and an inner ring of cruisers, contained at its heart its main striking force: the aircraft of the carriers, and the guns of the battleships

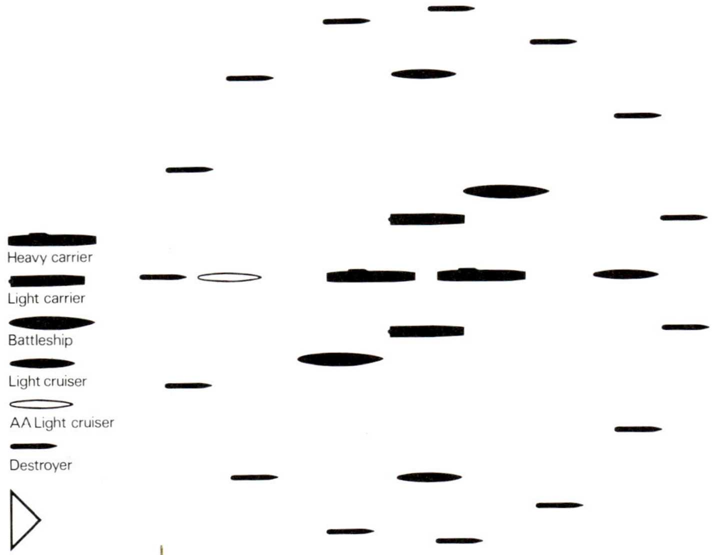

Trevor Wooldridge

Type C2-5-B1 Attack Cargo Ship. The attack cargo ship, essential for amphibious operations, could carry troops, their inshore landing craft, plus follow-up supplies, ammunition, spare parts, and so on. For operations in the Pacific, the US Navy had some 95 to 100 of these craft. *Length (overall):* 459 feet. *Beam:* 63 feet. *Armament:* one 5-inch gun, and eight 40-mm AA guns. *Crew (plus troops):* 404. *Displacement:* 6,556 tons

US Fleet Oiler T3-S2-A1. The huge distances involved in the Pacific War made some method of refuelling the fleet at sea indispensable. It also meant that the oiler, full, became an extremely important ship, and a much-prized target for submarine captains. *Length (overall):* 553 feet. *Beam:* 75 feet. *Armament:* four 5-inch guns, eight 40-mm guns. *Crew:* 304. *Displacement:* 7,356 tons.

The *Essex* class (the *Wasp* is shown here) became the standard US fleet carrier of the war and made up the core of the fast carrier forces. It introduced the outboard elevator on the port side. *Length:* 820 feet (waterline), 872 (overall). *Max Beam:* 147 feet. *Max Speed:* 32 knots. *Armament:* 12 5-inch guns, 44 to 68 40-mm AA guns, and 100 aircraft. *Crew:* 3,500. *Displacement:* 27,100 tons

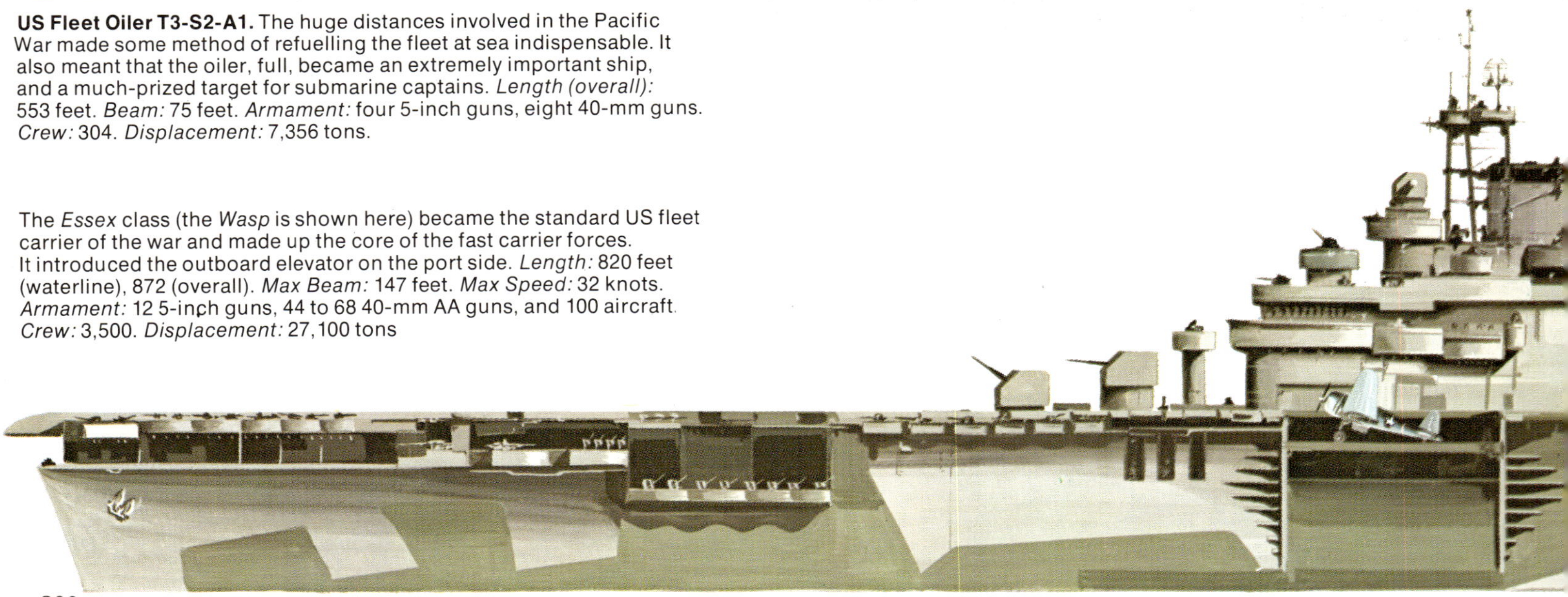

The Diminishing Asset: At the outbreak of war the Japanese had afloat some 6,000,000 tons of shipping, but by 1945 this had declined to 1,500,000 tons. With much Japanese shipping devoted to the hopeless task of maintaining their isolated island garrisons, the rate of sinkings by the Allies rose sharply to coincide with each major campaign. The result was a crescendo of destruction at a time when the Japanese could least afford it

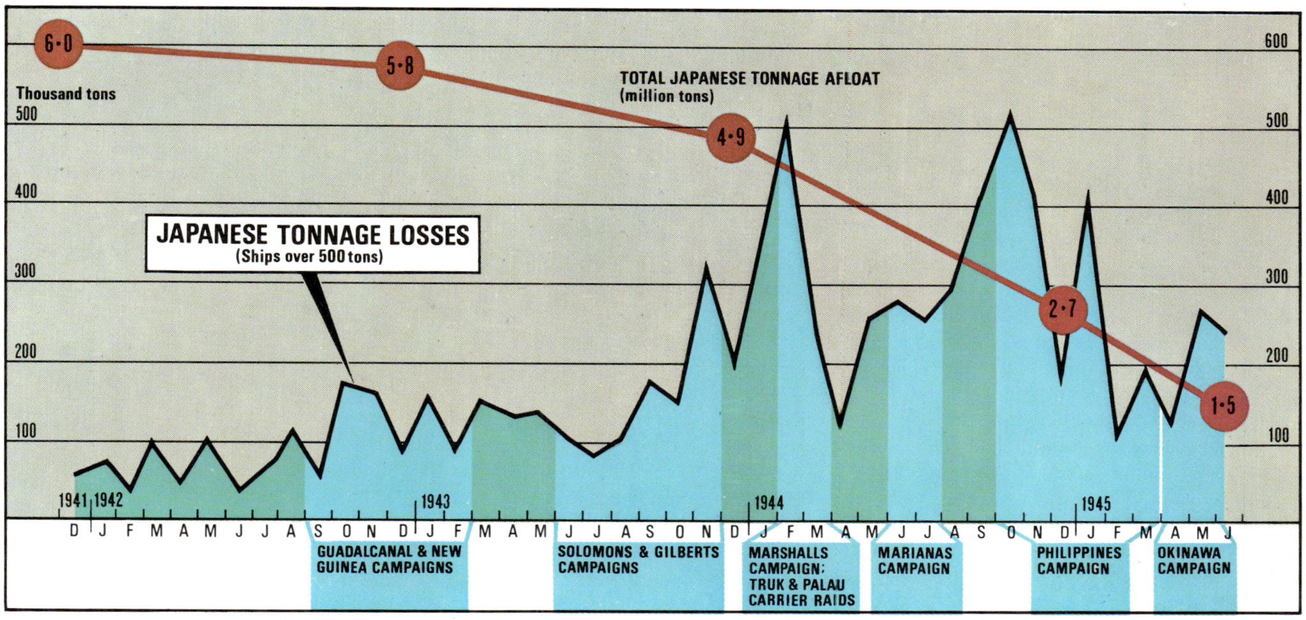

This cross-section view of an *Essex* class carrier, taken from the lift looking aft, shows many of the features of the improved design of this class. Two of them are the reinforced armour at and below the waterline, and the oil storage tanks well isolated from vulnerable spots

1. Lift
2. 20- & 40-mm AA guns
3. Two stacked lifeboats
4. Fan motors
5. Airframe workshop
6. Workshop deck & lift machinery
7. Ammo & aircraft stores
8. Air-conditioning plants
9. Main hangar (aft)
10. AA guns
11. AA guns
12. Servicing hangar
13. Aero engine stores
14. Engine servicing shop
15. Port ammunition stores
16. Emergency lighting plant
17. Engine-cooling motor
18. Steam pipes to turbines
19. Turbines
20. Fireproof coffer-dam
21. Aviation spirit tank
22. Oil fuel tanks

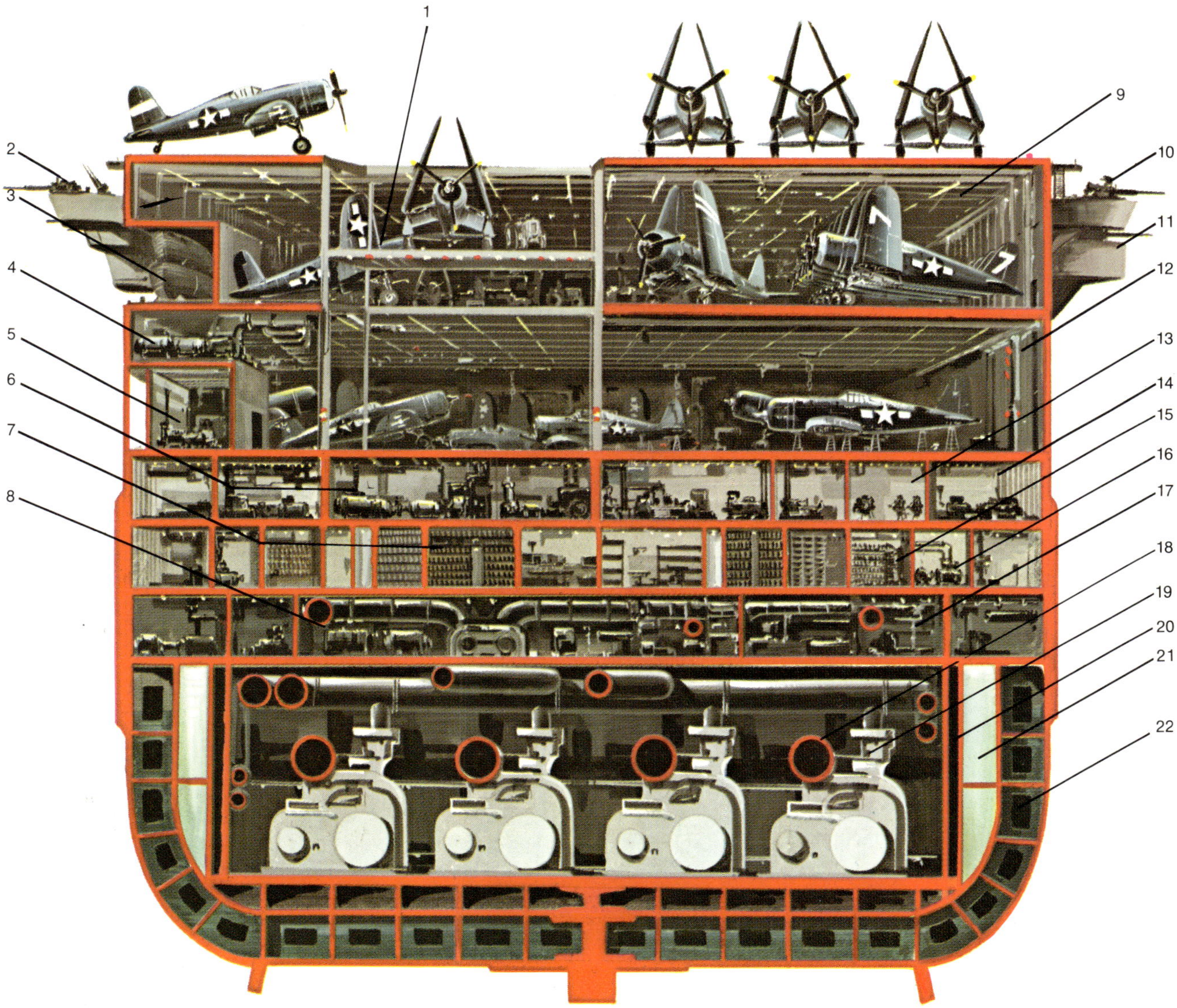

Paul Popper

Above: Japanese troops in the Shortland Islands embark to reinforce Guadalcanal

years of experience as a battalion and regimental commander, but on this occasion he disregarded all he had learned. Japanese Intelligence had told him that the Marines were no more than 2,000 strong and that their morale was low. In any case Colonel Ichiki was one of many Japanese officers who believed firmly that man for man the Japanese were infinitely superior to the Americans who were only effective when they had superior equipment. He therefore decided that he had no cause to wait even for his second echelon; he could wipe out this 'jungle beach-head' at one stroke.

In the early hours of August 21, after a brief preparatory mortar bombardment of the American positions on General Vandegrift's eastern perimeter, Colonel Ichiki's men who had waded across the Ilu and Tenaru rivers, threw themselves at the Marines in a bayonet charge. They were met and stopped by a deadly wall of fire from carefully sited positions, but somehow Ichiki managed to rally his men and launch a second bayonet charge, only to be stopped again. This time he decided to withdraw across the Ilu.

Only a crack formation like Ichiki's could have survived such a mauling without disintegrating, but the accurate and often telling fire to which the Marines were subjected from across the river on the following morning, told them that they were still facing a fighting unit that had to be reckoned with. General Vandegrift, who had had reports that further Japanese reinforcements were on the way, decided that Ichiki's men constituted too great a danger to be left where they were. He ordered one of his reserve battalions to cross the river and swing north in an enveloping movement.

By early afternoon Ichiki's men were encircled, and the final phase of what came to be known among the Marines as the 'Battle of the Tenaru' began. Bombed and strafed by the American aircraft that had landed at Henderson Field on the previous day, and bombarded at short range by artillery, the Japanese were pushed back slowly towards the sea from three sides. Finally, the few light tanks which had been landed with Vandegrift's division moved in, their steel treads mangling and crushing the living, the dying, and the dead. But still the Japanese refused to surrender. 'The rear of the tanks,' General Vandegrift wrote in his report, 'looked like meat grinders.' Even after organised fighting had ceased, the Japanese survivors did not allow themselves to be taken prisoner. 'The wounded will wait until men come up to examine them,' Vandegrift wrote, 'and blow themselves and the other fellow to pieces with a hand grenade.' At 'the Tenaru' the Marines learned what the Japanese meant by total resistance, resistance to the last breath of the last man.

Only a handful of men, led by Colonel Ichiki, got away to Taivu further along the coast to the east. There the Colonel ceremoniously tore up his regiment's colour, and committed *hara-kiri*.

The victory at the Tenaru lives on in the history of the US Marine Corps, but General Vandegrift knew that it did not answer the question of whether the Marines could hold out. It was merely the prelude to other stronger attempts by the Japanese. In fact, in the last ten days of August, a far more menacing force consisting of the late Colonel Ichiki's second echelon and General Kawaguchi's XXXV Brigade were waiting to be taken to Guadalcanal to finish the job. The main problem was how to get them there. Rear-Admiral Tanaka, who had been made commander of the Reinforcement Force with his base in the Shortlands to the north-west of Guadalcanal, understood the difficulties. The second echelon of Ichiki's detachment which he had been ordered to take to Guadalcanal in transports screened by a light cruiser and destroyers, had been spotted by aircraft from Henderson Field, bombed, and had had to turn back.

The arrival of the aircraft on Henderson Field had drastically altered the situation: the Japanese, Tanaka pointed out to General Kawaguchi, could only use the waters around Guadalcanal safely between dusk and dawn, and he therefore planned to move the Japanese army to Guadalcanal in a series of what were aptly named 'Rat runs', using fast destroyers as transports at night. Kawaguchi at first insisted on slower and more cumbersome barges being used as transport, and one barge 'run' that was organised against Tanaka's advice, ended in disaster. In the end Tanaka had his way and by the end of August, the 'Rat runs' were dashing back and forth with the precision of express trains, while the Marine positions were regularly bombarded from the sea.

General Vandegrift was aware of the gradual Japanese build-up to the east and west of his position. He brought Colonel Edson's crack Marine Raiders and the paratroops over from Tulagi and after dark on September 7 sent the Raiders by sea on a reconnaissance in force to Taivu, one of the main Japanese bases. Their foray was a complete success: they found only communications and headquarters personnel at the base who promptly fled into the jungle. They also found valuable stores and provisions which they brought back with

Type 99-1 7·7-mm Heavy Machine-Gun. This standard Japanese weapon was developed from the French Hotchkiss design. **Action:** gas-operated. **Coolant:** air. **Length:** 42·4 inches. **Ammunition:** 30-round clips. **Rate of fire:** 550 rpm

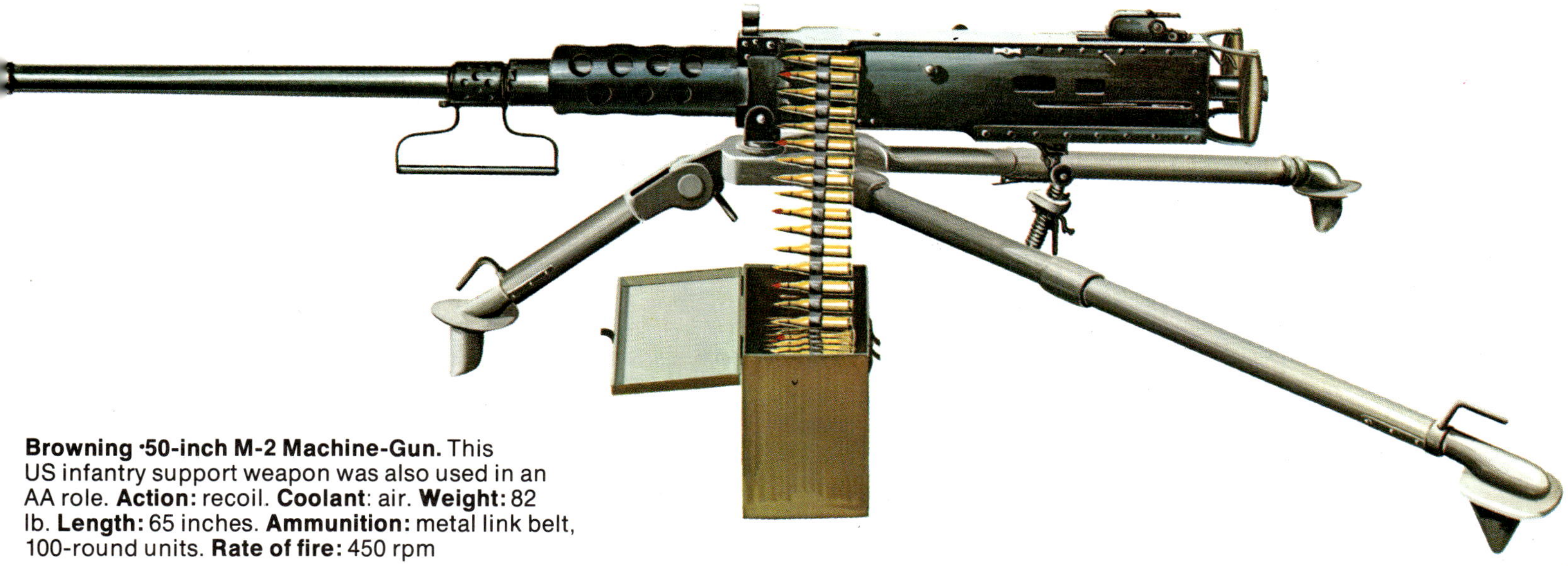

Browning ·50-inch M-2 Machine-Gun. This US infantry support weapon was also used in an AA role. **Action:** recoil. **Coolant**: air. **Weight:** 82 lb. **Length:** 65 inches. **Ammunition:** metal link belt, 100-round units. **Rate of fire:** 450 rpm

them. But the most valuable thing they brought back was information about the strength of the forces they would soon have to face and the news that General Kawaguchi had already moved off into the jungle with the bulk of his force. The second Japanese attack could not be long delayed, and General Vandegrift calculated that the main assault would be launched against the ridge to the south of Henderson Field. It was to this ridge that Vandegrift moved the Raiders and the paratroops, with his reserve – a Marine battalion – immediately behind them. He had no other uncommitted troops.

The Battle of Bloody Ridge

At noon on September 12, when Japanese bombers heavily bombed not Henderson Field, but the ridge south of the airfield, Vandegrift knew that his calculations about Japanese intentions had been correct. Shortly after darkness a Japanese cruiser and three destroyers started shelling the ridge, and when their gunfire ceased, Kawaguchi's troops began their probing. They cut off one Raider platoon but it fought back into the American lines.

When daylight came the Americans assumed that the Japanese had only been testing. They would have been heartened if they had known that Kawaguchi had intended his attack of the previous night to be decisive. His plan had been to attack the ridge with three battalions while his other units pinned down the Americans on the western and eastern flanks of his perimeter. But his long and arduous march had exhausted his troops, cut his communications with other units of his command, and deprived him of effective control. Despite these handicaps, however, he plunged ahead as recklessly as Ichiki had done before him and rigidly stuck to the order to attack on September 12.

At 2100 hours on September 13, Kawaguchi renewed his assault. As his two battalions – almost 2,000 men – rushed up the slopes of the ridge, Marine mortars sited in defilade poured shells into the assault waves as fast as loaders could slide them down the hot tubes. Marine artillery just to the rear of the Raiders pumped round after round into the attackers while seven Japanese destroyers shelled Henderson Field, which was illuminated by Japanese flares. On the ridge the Raiders' defences were bent but not broken, and eventually the Japanese fell back. Before long they returned in an assault as fierce as the first. Again the defences were dented but not broken; and again the Japanese fell back.

Two hours later, after a preparatory mortar bombardment which cut the Raiders' communications with Vandegrift and supporting artillery, the Japanese swept forward to within 1,000 yards of Henderson Field, only to be beaten back after some of the most ferocious fighting on Guadalcanal. They launched two more attacks before daybreak noticeably weaker than the first three, and when cannon-firing fighters from Henderson Field strafed the fringes of the jungle below the ridge, Kawaguchi decided to withdraw. He had over 1,200 officers and men killed, missing, and wounded. Hungry and plagued by disease the disorganised remnants of the XXXV Brigade, carrying only their rifles, clawed their way through the jungle for eight grim days to Point Cruz, west of Henderson Field.

The Raiders and the paratroops, too, had suffered heavily. Of slightly over 750 men who had landed on August 7, the Raiders had lost 234 casualties, and of 377 paratroops, 212 had been killed or wounded. But as far as the Marines were concerned, the question whether they could hold Guadalcanal, had been answered in the affirmative.

Imperial General Headquarters in Tokyo did not share the Marines' view. The XXXVIII Division, veterans of Hong Kong, Java, and Sumatra, were ordered to proceed to the South Pacific to join Lieutenant-General Hyakutake's XVII Army. In the meantime, the II Division under Lieutenant-General Maruyama, which was already in the area, was to be transported to Guadalcanal. Operations on

Below: A US Stuart light tank in action

Imperial War Museum

Below: Fighting in the jungles of Guadalcanal was necessarily at close quarters

Keystone

Associated Press

Above: By November, fatigue and strain were showing on the faces of the US Marines. Below: The object of the bloody exercise – Henderson Field airstrip

US Navy

New Guinea against Port Moresby were to be suspended so that all naval, air, and military resources could be concentrated on recapturing Guadalcanal, and General Hyakutake transferred XVII Army HQ to the island, to control a total force of some 20,000 men – including a regiment and three batteries of heavy artillery, a mortar battalion, and a tank company. In the next six weeks Admiral Tanaka's 'Rat run' or 'Tokyo Night Express' was busier than ever, and the Marines were bombarded every night from the sea.

Fortunately General Vandegrift, too, received reinforcements: the 7th Marines, an artillery battalion, motor transport companies, communications personnel, and later 164th Infantry Regiment, US Army – more than 6,000 men altogether, bringing his total strength to over 23,000. And equally vital the air force on Henderson Field was strengthened considerably. On paper Vandegrift's force looked impressive, in practice, it was less so. Although battle casualties had not yet reached 1,000, large numbers of Marines suffered from malnutrition, dysentery, virulent fungus infections, exposure, and plain exhaustion. Elsewhere, in fact, over a third of the men would have been unfit for combat.

On October 23 the Japanese II Division – consisting of some eight battalions totalling 5,600 troops, attacked the eastern perimeter in force with tanks across the Matanikau river. Concentrated artillery fire brought their advance to a bloody halt. Then, 24 hours later, General Maruyama attacked with the main force of more than 7,000 men from the south. For two days the Japanese flung themselves against the ridges to the south of Henderson Field – at one stage there was a Japanese enclave inside the perimeter – and then, like Kawaguchi's brigade, they sank back into the jungle, decimated and exhausted, having lost 3,500 men.

What had happened was that Japanese communications had broken down once again. Maruyama's approach march through the jungle – which had begun on October 16 – had been slower and more arduous than he had expected, and the artillery and mortars had had to be abandoned. Twice Maruyama had to postpone his offensive, and the second time, news of the postponement did not reach the Japanese commander on the Matanikau. Instead of being simultaneous, the two assaults took place 24 hours apart and General Vandegrift, operating on interior lines, was able to defeat each in turn.

General Vandegrift had now defeated three attempts by the Japanese to dislodge him, and both the Americans and the Japanese had to face the problem of what to do next. For Vandegrift and Admiral Halsey, who had recently replaced Admiral Ghormley as Area Commander, there was no doubt about the answer: it was time to go over to the offensive and drive what remained of the XVII Army out of Guadalcanal. It was equally obvious to both officers that the 1st Marine Division, after all it had been through, was not the ideal instrument for a long, harsh, and bitter offensive. Fresher and bigger units were required. And so after spending November in extending the perimeter and reducing threatening Japanese outposts around it in preparation for future offensive action, General Vandegrift and the 1st Marine Division were relieved at the beginning of December, and their place taken by the 25th Infantry Division, US Army, the 2nd Marine Division, and the America Division – all combined as 14th Corps under General Patch.

For the Japanese the problem was whether to go on trying to wrest Henderson Field and the shattered coconut groves around it from the Americans. Imperial General Headquarters refused to accept defeat; fresh divisions and brigades from distant parts of the Empire were allocated to XVII Army and Lieutenant-General Sano's XXVIII Division was ordered to Guadalcanal, in preparation for a fourth determined attempt to drive out the Americans to be launched about the middle of January 1943. But in mid-November 1942 a US naval squadron, despite crippling losses, stopped a Japanese squadron from bombarding Henderson Field, and neutralising its air force, and the Henderson Field aircraft, saved by this gallant action, pounced on a convoy of 11 transports in which the bulk of General Sano's division was being taken to Guadalcanal. Six transports were sunk, one was crippled, and four had to be beached. Only 2,000 men, most of them without equipment, reached Guadalcanal. The drain in men and resources, Imperial General Headquarters decided reluctantly after much argument, was too great to sustain any longer. Since August 7, the Japanese had lost 65 combat ships and more than 800 aircraft. On December 31, 1942, the Emperor gave his approval to the withdrawal of the XVII Army from Guadalcanal.

General Hyakutake accepted the order reluctantly. As he withdrew to the east, 14th Corps learned how tough and resourceful even starving and ill-equipped Japanese troops could be in defensive jungle warfare. At no time during January and early February were the Americans able to upset the pace and timing of the withdrawal, and between February 1 and 9 the destroyers of the 'Tokyo Night Express' took off what remained of the XVII Army – 11,000 men, only a fraction of those who had arrived to drive the Americans into the sea but still a fighting force destined to return to do battle another day.

For the Americans and their allies the successful seizure and defence of Guadalcanal brought immense advantages. Australia and New Zealand were safe, and Allied forces now stood on the flank of the Palau/Truk/Marshalls line, the outer cordon of the Japanese empire.

Below: Wary of enemy snipers, a Marine patrol advances beyond the defence zone

Central Press

GUADALCANAL: THE SEA BATTLES

The struggle of the Marines on Guadalcanal was accompanied by an equally bloody campaign at sea to intercept the 'Tokyo Express' and secure control of the approaches. In one disastrous action alone—the Battle of Savo Island—the Allied naval force was shattered; at the Battle of Santa Cruz on October 23/24 the large carriers on both sides were temporarily eliminated; and in a series of battles in November, Japanese ships scored notable victories over American cruisers and destroyers. In the end both sides lost 24 warships of roughly equal tonnage off Guadalcanal—but the Americans were able to accept such attrition far more easily than the Japanese . . .

A Japanese dive-bomber swoops on USS *Hornet* while a torpedo plane circles—Battle of Santa Cruz

Imperial War Museum

1. SAVO ISLAND—August 8/9, 1942

A Japanese cruiser force under Vice-Admiral Mikawa advances down 'The Slot' to attack the American transports unloading off Guadalcanal. An Allied cruiser force under Rear-Admiral Crutchley RN, divided into three squadrons, patrols the approaches around Savo Island. 0100 hours: The Japanese cruisers slip past the destroyers *Blue* and *Ralph Talbot*. 0138 hours: The cruisers *Canberra* and *Chicago* are sighted and disabled with accurate gunfire. When the *Vincennes*, *Quincy*, and *Astoria* intervene they too are disabled. The Japanese then retire damaging the *Ralph Talbot* as they go.

2. EASTERN SOLOMONS—August 23, 1942

An attempt to run supplies to the Japanese troops on Guadalcanal is supported by the aircraft-carriers *Shokaku*, *Zuikaku*, and *Ryujo*. Vice-Admiral Fletcher's Task Force 61, patrolling to the east of the Solomon Islands, sights the Japanese fleet. The Japanese reverse course, and avoid the American strike aircraft.

August 24: *Ryujo*, sailing ahead of the main Japanese fleet, is sighted by an American flying boat. An armed reconnaissance is flown off from *Enterprise*, and followed, at 1345 hours, by a strike force from *Saratoga*. *Ryujo* launches her aircraft to attack Henderson Field. Just as the American strike flies off, another reconnaissance aircraft sights *Shokaku* and *Zuikaku*, who have launched a massive striking force. An attempt to divert the US aircraft to the new target fails, but the *Ryujo* is sunk. *Enterprise* is hit three times by dive-bombers, but is able to continue recovering her aircraft.

3. CAPE ESPERANCE—October 11/12, 1942

American supply convoy sails for Guadalcanal. It is escorted by a cruiser squadron commanded by Rear-Admiral Scott, which is also to ambush any Japanese forces moving down the Slot.

October 11/12: A Japanese convoy, covered by Rear-Admiral Goto's cruiser squadron, moves down the Slot. Scott receives information of its approach, and steers to intercept it. 2325 hours: The cruiser *Helena*'s radar detects the Japanese at a range of 14 miles but she fails to inform Scott. At 2333 hours he decides to reverse course, but in the confusion the cohesion of his force is broken. Scott then learns of the enemy's approach. The destroyer *Duncan* attacks independently, and the *Helena* opens fire, followed by the other cruisers. An order to cease fire does not take effect until the *Aoba* and *Furutaka* have been severely damaged. The Japanese turn and retreat, and during the pursuit they damage the *Boise* and lose the destroyer *Fubuki*.

4. SANTA CRUZ—October 24/26, 1942

The Japanese Combined Fleet moves to the north of Guadalcanal, ready to fly aircraft in to Henderson Field as soon as it is captured.

October 24: US Task Force 16 *(Enterprise)* rejoins Task Force 17 *(Hornet)*, and is ordered to sweep in a wide circle around the Santa Cruz Islands to intercept any Japanese forces approaching Guadalcanal.

October 25: At noon an American flying boat sights two Japanese aircraft-carriers, but an American strike fails to make contact.

October 26: The Japanese fleet is again sighted and the *Enterprise* launches 16 dive-bombers to make an armed reconnaissance. At 0658 hours the Japanese aircraft-carriers *(Shokaku, Zuikaku, and Zuiho)* launch a first striking force. As a second force is being ranged up, two of the *Enterprise*'s dive-bombers attack *Zuiho* and put her out of action. 0730/0815 hours: *Enterprise* and *Hornet* launch three small strike forces. 0822 hours: *Shokaku* and *Zuikaku* launch their second strike. The main Japanese attack falls on *Hornet*, which is struck by two torpedoes and six bombs. Meanwhile *Shokaku* is seriously damaged by American dive-bombers. The second Japanese strike concentrates on the *Enterprise*: her forward lift is put permanently out of action, but her speed and manoeuvrability are unaffected. A third Japanese strike fails to achieve any results. The American forces then withdraw. *Hornet* is sunk by the Japanese when they find her burning hulk.

Grumman TBF-1 Avenger. With the defensive and strike capabilities of a twin-engined aircraft, the Avenger had the handling of a carrier aircraft and could carry bombs, depth charges or torpedoes. **Max speed:** 259 mph at 11,200 feet. **Max range:** 1000 miles loaded. **Armament:** 2×5-inch, 1×3-inch and 1×·5-inch machine-guns; 1×22-inch torpedo or 2000-lb bombload

Below: Santa Cruz. A Japanese Kate makes a torpedo run on the *South Dakota*

Below: Santa Cruz. The Japanese cruiser *Chikuma* evades an American attack

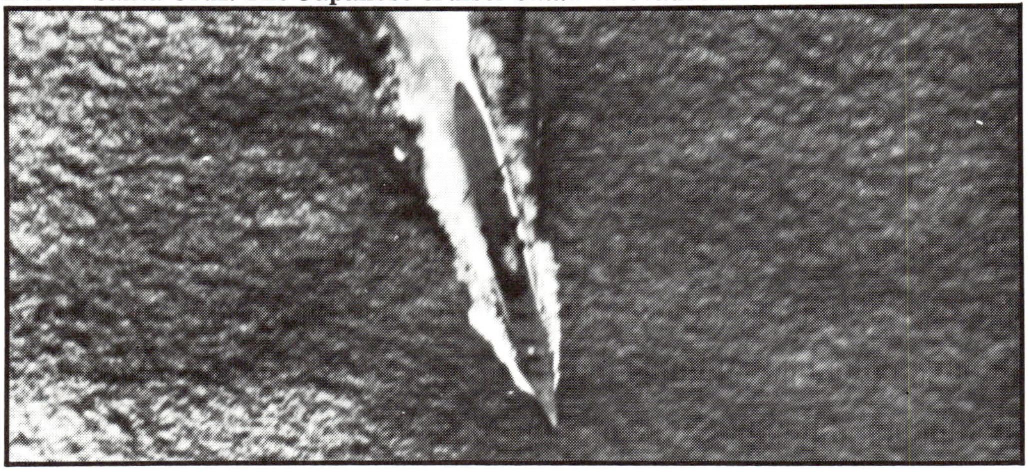

US Navy

Battle	US losses	Japanese losses
1. BATTLE OF SAVO ISLAND	Cruisers: Vincennes, Quincy, Astoria and Canberra	
2. BATTLE OF EASTERN SOLOMONS		Aircraft-carrier: Ryujo; Destroyer: Mutsuki
3. BATTLE OF CAPE ESPERANCE	Destroyer: Duncan	Destroyer: Fubuki; Cruiser: Furutaka
4. BATTLE OF SANTA CRUZ	Aircraft-carrier: Hornet	

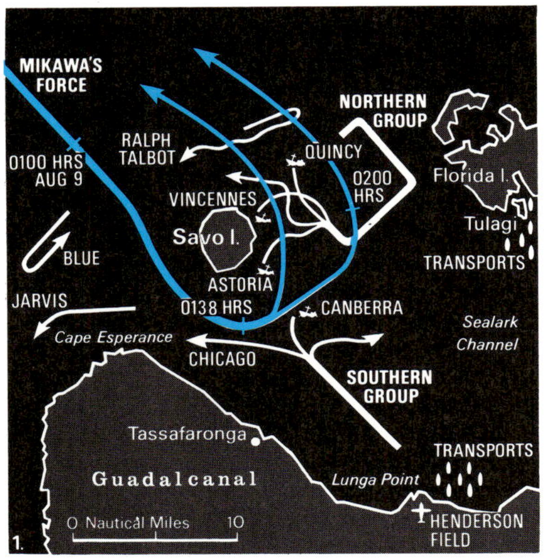

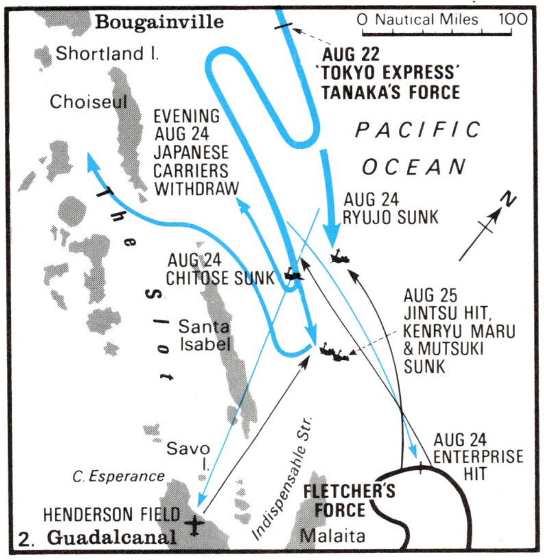

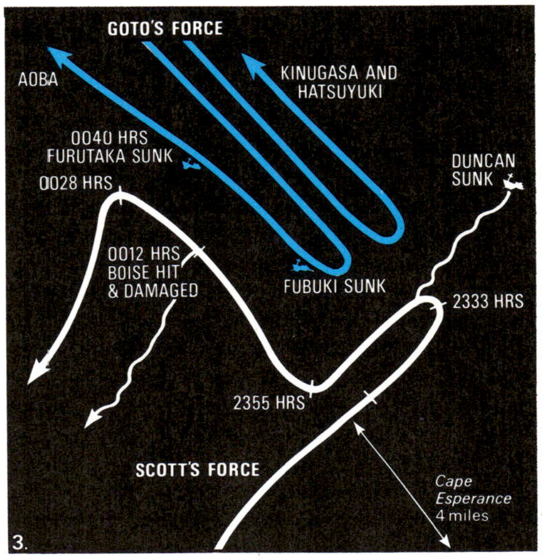

Below: The end of the US carrier *Wasp*, torpedoed by the Japanese submarine *I-19* while escorting a transport convoy

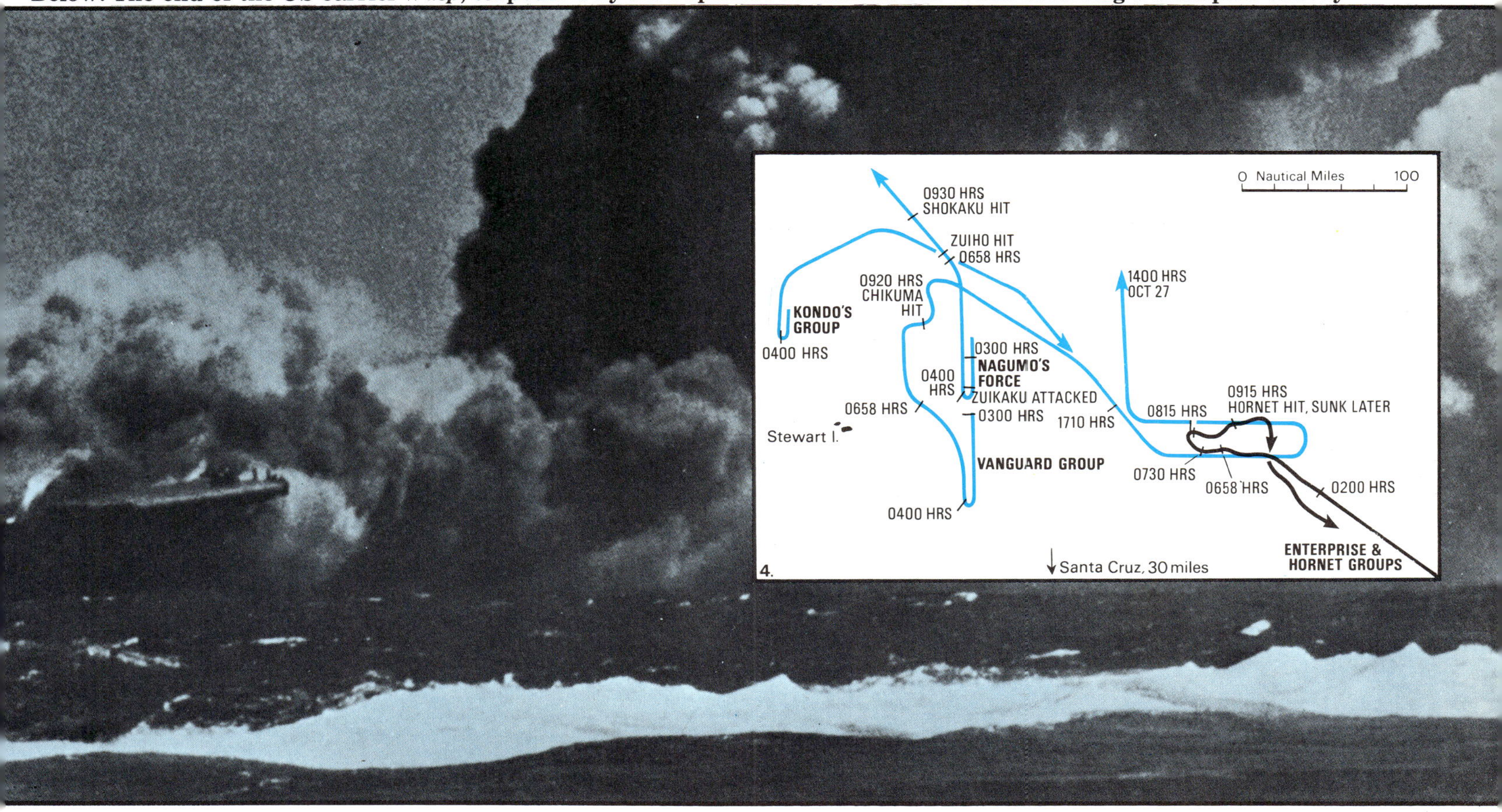

CRUISERS: KEY WARSHIPS IN TH

When the battle for Guadalcanal began in August 1942, the sea approaches to that vitally important island were dominated during the daylight hours by air power. And since two-thirds of the Japanese carrier fleet had been shattered at the Battle of Midway, and the Americans held the only air base in the Solomon Islands, air power was largely in American hands. No Japanese surface forces dared operate by day in those waters, but as darkness fell, the surface forces of both sides – particularly the cruisers and destroyers – moved in and clashed in savage combat in the narrow straits between the islands. In these skirmishes the Japanese showed themselves initially the masters. The Americans had radar, but the Japanese crews were trained to the highest pitch of night-fighting efficiency, and they had the superb 'Long Lance' torpedo – better than any torpedo in the American armoury. But the Americans had enormous reserves of ships and men to throw into the fight, whereas the Japanese ships and their crack crews, exhausted by battle after battle, were irreplaceable.

ALLIED LOSSES	JAPANESE LOSSES
1st BATTLE OF GUADALCANAL (November 12/13)	
Destroyers: **Cushing, Laffey, Barton and Monssen**	
Cruisers: **Atlanta and Juneau**	
2nd BATTLE OF GUADALCANAL (November 14/15)	
Destroyers: **Walke, Preston and Benham**	
BATTLE OF TASSAFARONGA (November 30)	
Cruiser: **Northampton**	

△ **Naval balance sheet for the last battles for Guadalcanal**

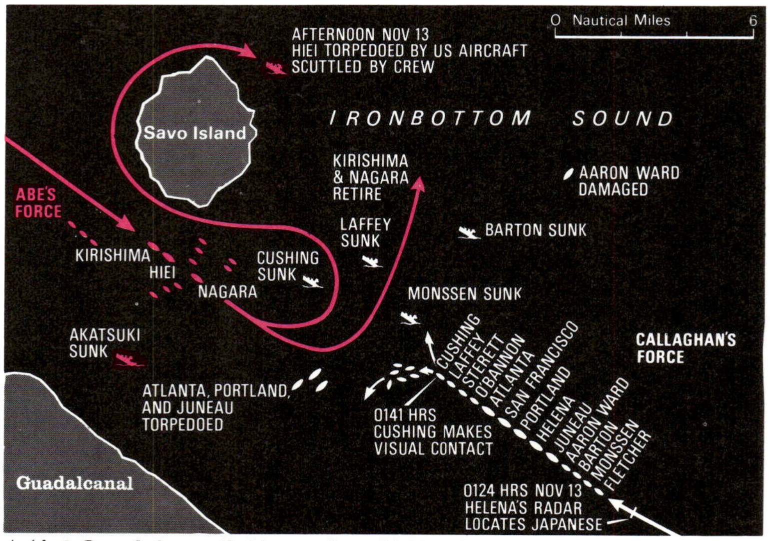

△ **'1st Guadalcanal', November 12/13. Callaghan's line of destroyers and cruisers was surprised by the Japanese, who smashed four destroyers and threw the US force into confusion – but *Hiei* was lost after US air attacks the following afternoon**

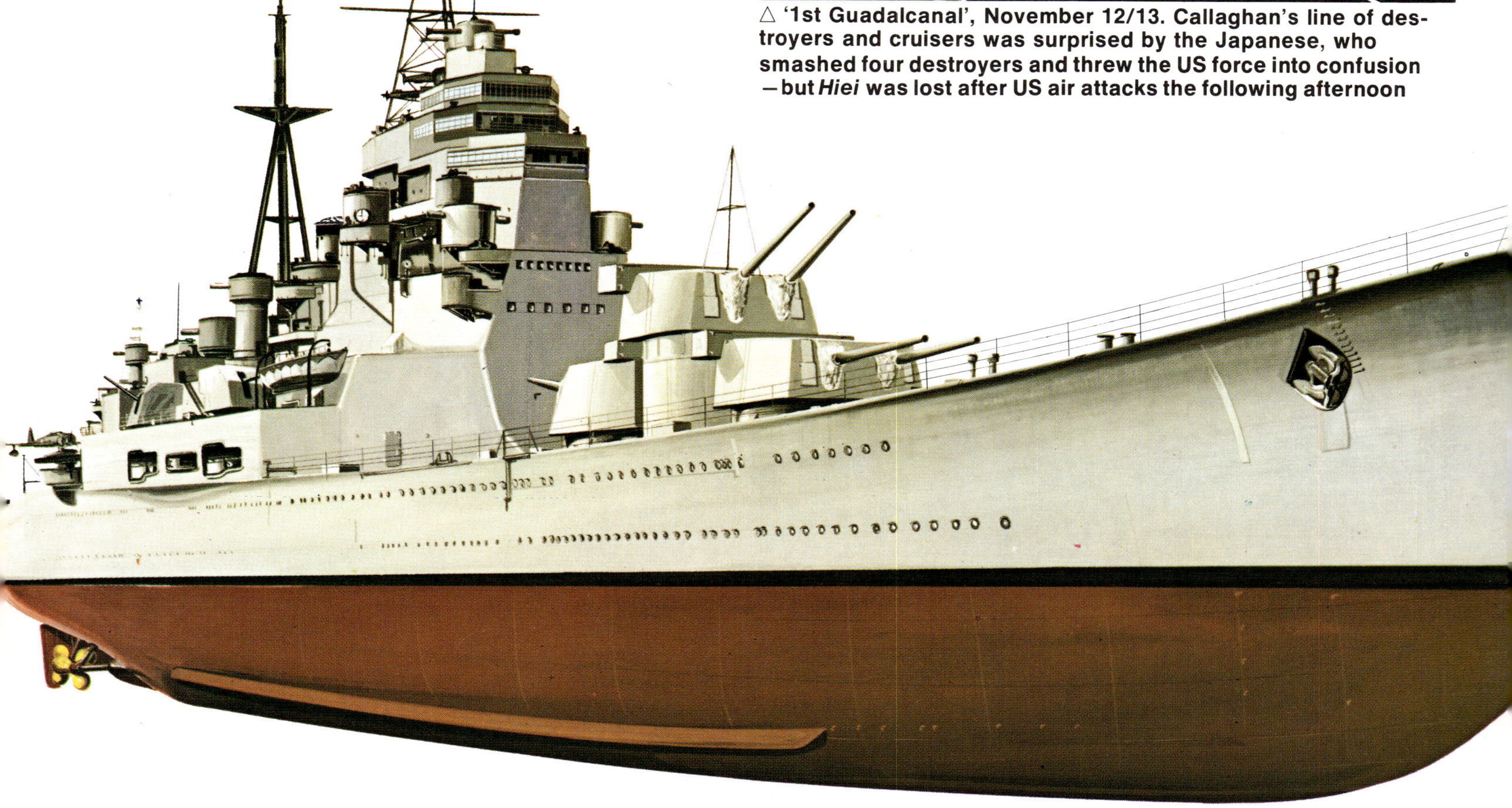

GUADALCANAL BATTLES

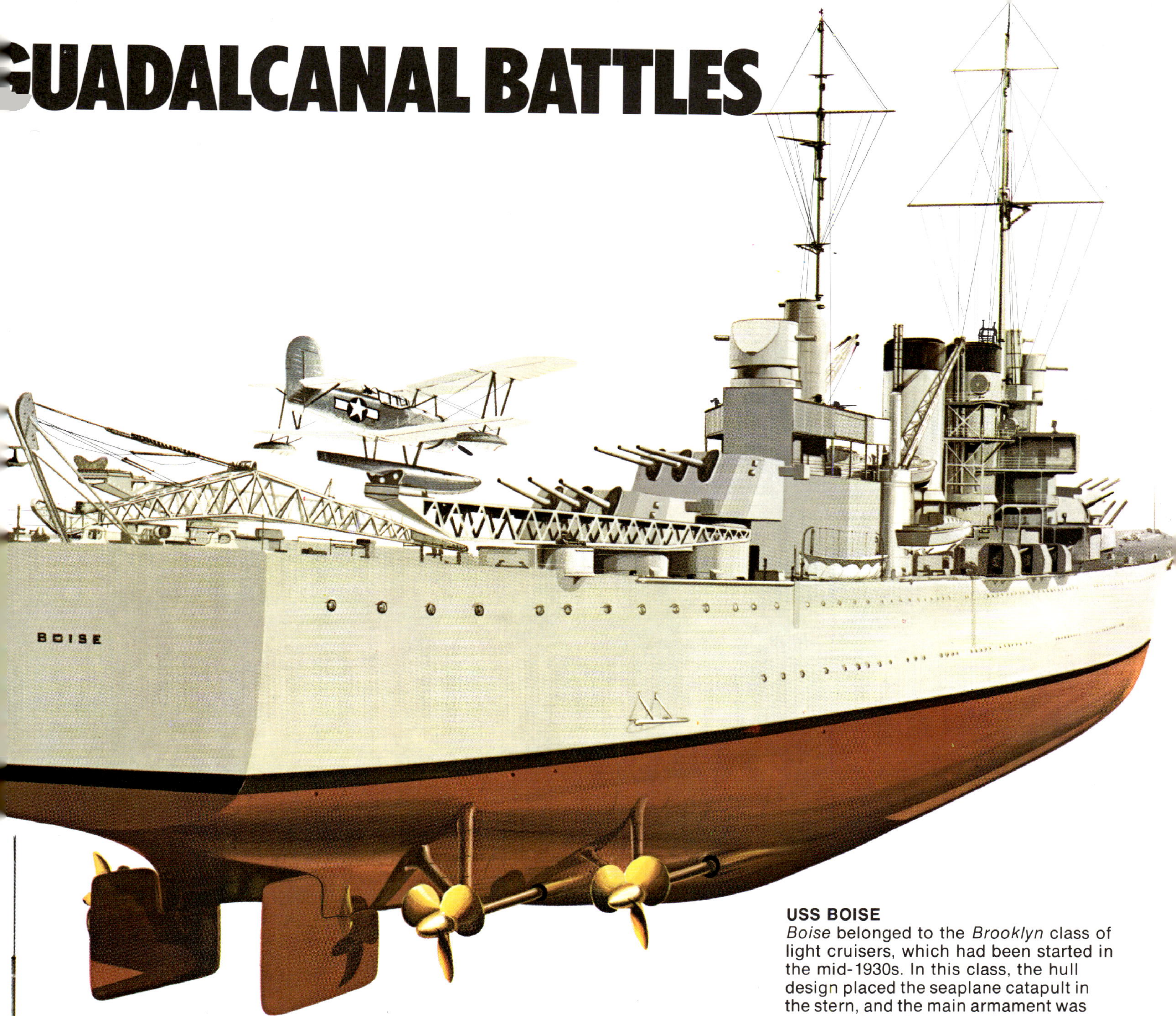

USS BOISE

Boise belonged to the *Brooklyn* class of light cruisers, which had been started in the mid-1930s. In this class, the hull design placed the seaplane catapult in the stern, and the main armament was mounted in triple turrets. *Boise* received heavy damage in the Battle of Cape Esperance on October 9, where she was part of Admiral Scott's squadron. **Length:** 608½ feet (overall). **Beam:** 61¾ feet. **Draught:** 19½ feet. **Max speed:** 34 knots. **Range:** 14,500 miles at 15 knots. **Armament:** 15 6-inch, eight 5-inch, four 3-pounder; multiple 20-mm AA guns. Four aircraft. **Complement:** 868

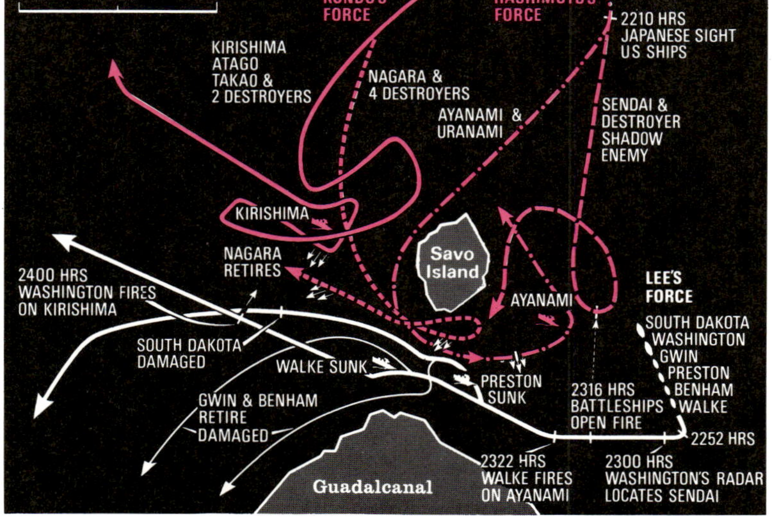

△ **'2nd Guadalcanal', November 14/15. Again the Japanese were able to exploit their mastery of night combat; but the superior gun-power of the US battleships recouped the initial losses and sank the battleship *Kirishima***

CHOKAI (far left)

Chokai belonged to the *Takao* class, which was launched in 1927/28, and which represented the 'second generation' of Japan's 10,000-ton cruisers. Main distinguishing features were the massive bridge structure and the high elevation of the main battery (up to 70° for AA use). *Chokai* was Admiral Mikawa's flagship in the Battle of Savo Island on the night of August 8/9, 1942. **Length:** 650 feet (overall). **Beam:** 62½ feet. **Draught:** 16⅔ feet. **Max speed:** 33 knots. **Range:** 14,000 miles at 15 knots. **Armament:** ten 8-inch guns, four 4·7-inch guns; eight 24-inch torpedo tubes. **Complement:** 692

BATTLESHIPS CLASH AT GUADALCANAL

The later naval battles off Guadalcanal saw the first direct clashes between battleships of the American and Japanese fleets – clashes that were disastrous for the Japanese battle fleet. In two successive battles, the Japanese lost first the *Hiei* and then the *Kirishima*; serious damage was caused to the USS *South Dakota*, but neither of the two American battleships in the actions was lost. Ship for ship, the Americans had all the advantages: superior manoeuvrability, superior hitting-power, and vastly superior protection; against these advantages, the Japanese superiority in speed proved of little value. But in the crews the story was different: the Japanese crews were the product of long training and were able to get the very best out of their ships. The Americans had only just managed to produce another Pacific battle fleet out of new crews and new ships.

South Dakota and ***Washington*** represented the first two classes of the US Navy's new fast battleships; they featured shorter length to improve manoeuvrability, a massive armour-belt, and 16-inch guns. **Specifications for *South Dakota*.** *Length:* 680 feet. *Beam:* 108 feet. *Draught:* 29 feet. *Speed:* 28 knots. *Max armour belt thickness:* 18 inches. *Armament:* nine 16-inch, 16 5-inch, 56 40-mm. AA. Three aircraft. *Complement:* 2,500

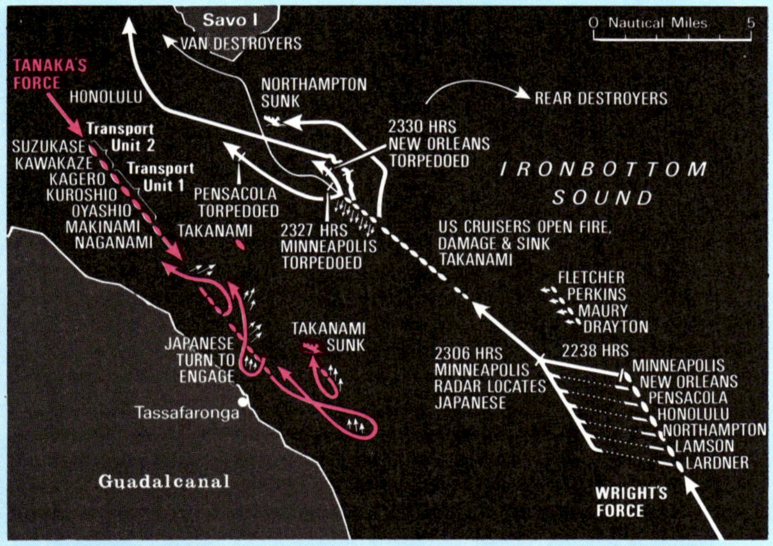

△ **'Battle of Tassafaronga', November 30. This was the last major clash before the Japanese pulled out of Guadalcanal. Tanaka repeated all the successful Japanese tactics, sinking one US cruiser and crippling four others which were towed back to Tulagi for repairs**

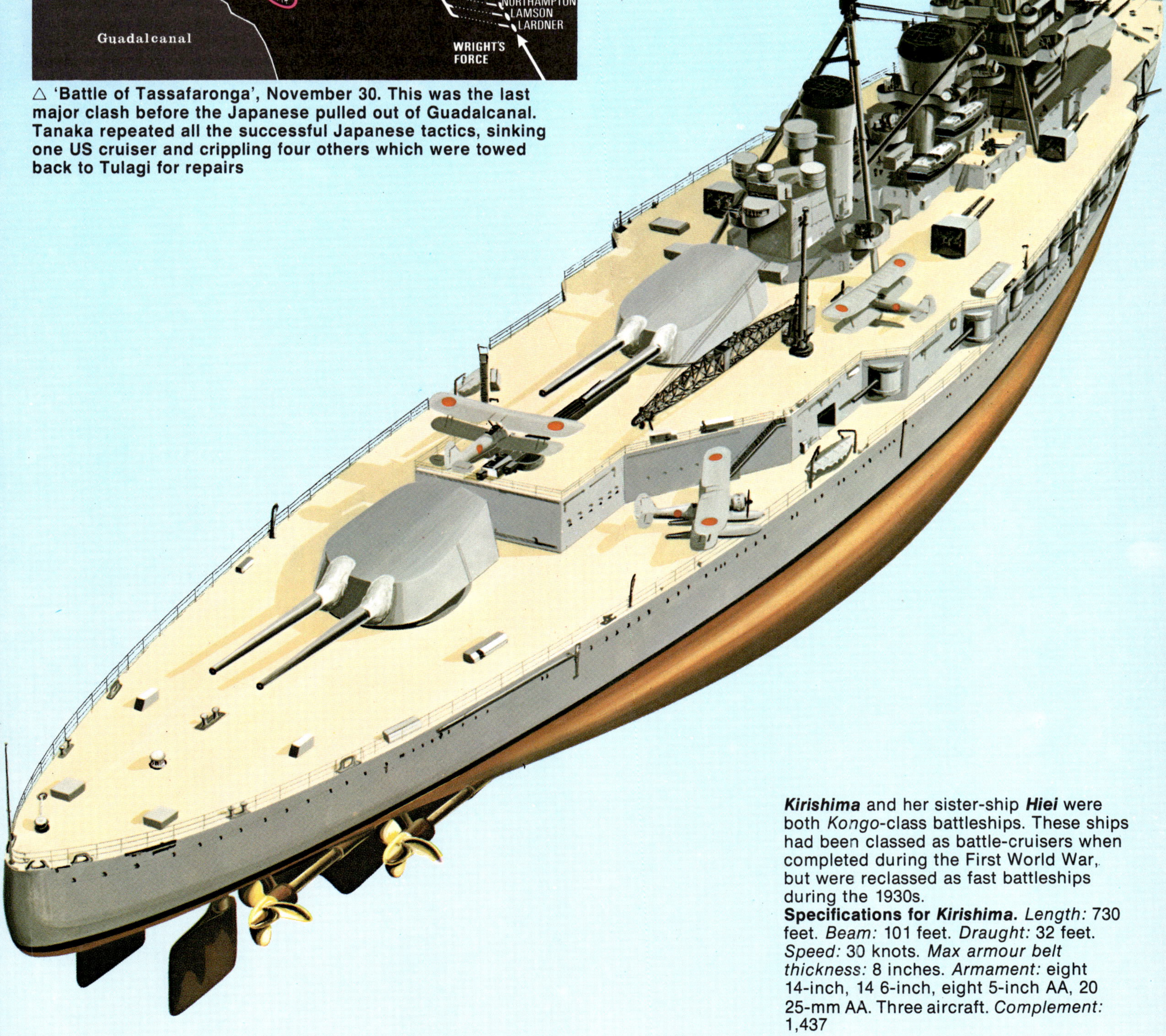

Kirishima and her sister-ship ***Hiei*** were both *Kongo*-class battleships. These ships had been classed as battle-cruisers when completed during the First World War, but were reclassed as fast battleships during the 1930s.
Specifications for *Kirishima*. *Length:* 730 feet. *Beam:* 101 feet. *Draught:* 32 feet. *Speed:* 30 knots. *Max armour belt thickness:* 8 inches. *Armament:* eight 14-inch, 14 6-inch, eight 5-inch AA, 20 25-mm AA. Three aircraft. *Complement:* 1,437

THE ROAD TO VICTORY....

In the early months of 1943, with renewed confidence following the six-month ordeal of Guadalcanal, American forces in the Pacific took the initiative. Using newly-developed techniques of amphibious warfare and the strategy of island-hopping to establish an overlapping system of controlled air-space, the bitterly-fought US offensive in New Georgia developed into a relentless advance through the Solomons towards Japan's massive strategic base of Rabaul in New Britain.

Meanwhile, in late 1942, Australian troops in New Guinea had shown that as a jungle fighter the Japanese soldier was not unbeatable. After months of bitter struggle along the Kokoda Trail a major enemy assault on Port Moresby – key to Australia and naval control of the South Pacific – had finally been crushed.

And then, in April, 1943, US fighters ambushed and shot down a plane carrying Admiral Yamamoto, undoubtedly Japan's outstanding naval strategist of the century. Everywhere the fortunes of the Rising Sun were waning. For the Allies, though, victories in the Solomons and New Guinea were just the beginning of a long, bloody campaign . . . one that would take them, island by island in the face of heroic enemy resistance, all the way to Okinawa.

US Marine Corps

Above: American soldiers struggle through Solomons swamps

Australian War Memorial

Above: Australian troops in New Guinea numbered 54,000

Buffalo. This armoured amphibious carrier was able to carry assault troops to the heart of enemy beach defences and proved invaluable during the Pacific War: **Speed:** 27 mph (land), 5·7 knots (sea). **Range:** 140 miles (land), 80 miles (sea). **Load:** 4·5 tons or 40 troops

GUADALCANAL TO OKINAWA

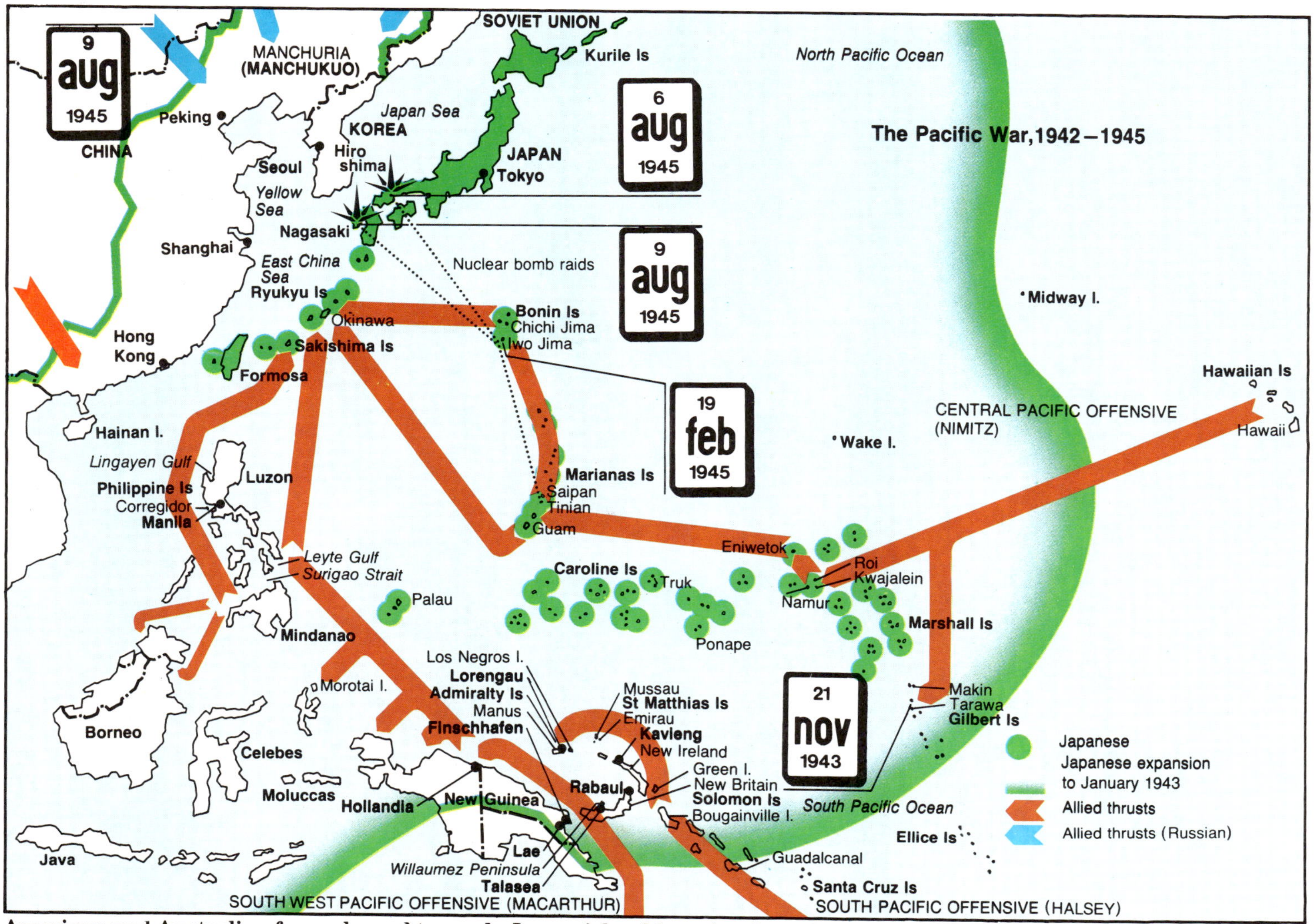

American and Australian forces bound towards Japan, island-hopping from Guadalcanal to Okinawa

CHI HA Type 97. This 1937-model Japanese medium tank was used extensively in Burma, China and on Guadalcanal. **Weight:** 15 tons. **Length:** 18 feet. **Armour:** 25-mm (max). **Crew:** 4. **Armament:** 1×57-mm gun; 2×7·7-mm machine-guns. **Speed:** 25 mph. **Range:** 120 miles

By December 1943, the situation in the Pacific was tense. In New Guinea, the Australian and American divisions under General MacArthur were closing in on the Huon Peninsular which was to fall that month. Further east, Admiral Nimitz's forces, with the Solomon Islands safely secured, had taken Tarawa Atoll in the Gilbert Islands in late November after a bitterly contested landing and were preparing for the next amphibious attack on the Marshall Islands in the central Pacific. As the two prongs of the Allied advance – MacArthur in New Guinea and Nimitz in the Solomons – had struggled forward in the summer of 1943, it had been thought necessary to capture Rabaul, the big Japanese naval airbase in New Britain. But as American air power began to overwhelm the Japanese, it was decided to bypass Rabaul and let it wither away through lack of supplies. During 1944 Nimitz's amphibious forces were to advance to the Marshalls, within bombing range of the great Japanese base at Truk which would be bypassed, and thence to Ponape in the Caroline Islands. Meanwhile MacArthur, supported by the 7th Fleet, was to work westward along the New Guinea coast, capturing Manus and its fine harbour in the Admiralty Islands en route. Thus by the end of 1944, the two prongs of the advance would meet for an attack on the Philippines which MacArthur was determined should be the next objective. But since Admiral King preferred that Nimitz's forces should swing north to the Marianas Islands and Formosa, no decision was taken at the time, and the argument eventually continued for many months.

THE MARSHALLS

On 1st February 1944, the 4th Marine Division landed on Kwajalein Atoll. The lesson of Tarawa had been well learned. Area bombardment which had failed to neutralize Japanese resistance there was replaced by close-range gunfire at selected targets. Small islands were captured to provide flank artillery support. Amphibious DUKWs were introduced for the first time in the Pacific. The results were good: the northern islands of Roi and Namur were taken on 2nd February by the marines and Kwajalein itself on 4th February by the army. Six weeks ahead of programme, Eniwetok Island was assaulted by the reserve which had not been required at Kwajalein and its capture was complete by the 23rd February.

THE MARIANAS

The next objective was now the Marianas Islands from which B-29 bombers would be able to reach the Japanese homeland. Saipan was to be attacked first on 15th June, followed by Tinian and Guam as soon as conditions allowed. Two vast assault forces, the northern comprising 71,000 troops for Saipan and Tinian and the southern of 56,000 men for Guam, were formed and the preliminary pounding from the air was allotted Task Force 58 of Admiral Spruance's 5th Fleet. This task force now contained no less than four separate aircraft-carrier groups and each had its own escort of battleships or cruisers

US Marine Corps

Above: Out of a 4836-man garrison, 4690 Japanese died in the battle for Tarawa. The two above committed *hara-kiri* in their bunker rather than surrender

Below: A Japanese dive-bomber crashes over the US Saipan invasion fleet

Ullstein

and destroyers and carried about 250 aircraft. On 11th June, the air attack started, the first targets being Guam, Saipan, and Tinian, with a diversion by two of the groups to neutralize Chichi Jima and Iwo Jima on the 12th. By 13th June, air supremacy was complete and on 15th June the first Americans landed in Saipan, supported by a bombarding group from Task Force 58.

THE PHILIPPINE SEA

But the Japanese had suspected that the Marianas or Palau in the western Carolines would be the next target and had prepared an elaborate plan to lure the American fleet within range of shore-based aircraft after which carrier aircraft from the Japanese main fleet would deliver the coup de grâce. The result was the Battle of the Philippine Sea on 19-20th June – the greatest carrier battle of history. Neither fleet sighted the other but during the action American air-strikes virtually destroyed remaining Japanese air strength at small loss. Although only two of the eight Japanese carriers were sunk (three were seriously damaged), there can be little doubt that the battle dealt the Japanese navy a blow from which it never recovered. The subsequent assaults were severe and long drawn out, but the issue was never in doubt. Saipan was secured by 9th July, Tinian by 1st August, and Guam by 15th August.

NEW BRITAIN

Attention must now turn to the left-hand prong. In the last weeks of December 1943, the 7th and 1st Marine Divisions, the latter a veteran of Guadalcanal which had been resting and re-training in Australia, landed on Cape Gloucester at the western end of New Britain and quickly established themselves ashore. Despite appalling terrain – the intelligence reports had been too optimistic – and bitter Japanese resistance, the airfield was captured on 1st January 1944, and thereafter the marines pushed steadily eastwards against a skilful and determined enemy retiring through easily defended jungle. The 5th Marine Division landed on

Willaumez Peninsula on 6th March, and the airfield at Talasea was quickly taken; the western part of the island was now secure and the straits between New Britain and New Guinea were safe. By the end of April an army division, the 45th, arrived to replace the marines who were released for further amphibious attacks. Meanwhile, on 29th February, units from the 1st Cavalry Division had made a reconnaissance in force on Los Negros Island in the Admiralties. MacArthur himself came ashore on the first day to assess the strength of the defences and it was soon evident that more forces would be needed. During the next two weeks, units from the 7th, 8th, and 12th Cavalry Divisions landed, both at Los Negros and on Manus Island itself near the airfield at Lorengau. By the end of March, the main resistance had ended, though sporadic fighting continued during May. A fine natural harbour was now available – it was used later by the British Pacific Fleet – and two large airfields were quickly constructed. The defence, as always, had been determined to the point of suicide and no Japanese prisoners were taken. A comparison of the American casualties – 329 killed and 1,189 wounded – with those of the Japanese – 3,280 killed – reflects the tenacity of the Japanese and the skill and weapon superiority of the Americans.

Concurrently, on 20th March, an unopposed landing by the 4th Marine Division on Emirau in the St Matthias Islands led to the speedy construction of a fine airfield. A glance at the map will show that both Rabaul and Kavieng, another Japanese base on New Ireland, were now surrounded by airfields at Manus, Emirau, Talasea, and Green Island, and the usefulness of the Japanese garrisons was rapidly nullified. Amphibious attacks were now unnecessary and both bases were 'mopped up' in 1945.

THE STRATEGIES

There were three important strategic possibilities – the first to defer the dispatch of the British fleet to join Nimitz in the central Pacific and to concentrate all available Commonwealth forces in South-East Asia with an object of completing the conquest of Burma, Sumatra, Malaya, and possibly Indo-China; the second to reduce the effort in South-East Asia and to form a British Commonwealth Task Force of all arms in the south-west Pacific under MacArthur. In this case, the British fleet could be detached to join Nimitz in the central Pacific if this was found desirable. The third possibility was to send the British fleet to the Pacific as soon as possible and to adopt a modified effort in S-E Asia.

Eventually it was decided at the Octagon Conference at Quebec in September 1944 to adopt the third course, with the addition of a bomber force of forty squadrons of Lancasters to join in the air attack on Japan when Germany had been defeated. President Roosevelt accepted this course in the face of a reluctant Admiral King, who would have preferred to finish off Japan unaided, and in the event, the coming of the *Kamikaze* suicide attacks made the contribution of the British fleet most welcome.

We must now return to the Pacific in the autumn of 1944. Admiral Halsey, with his 3rd Fleet (the Fleet was called the 3rd under Halsey and the 5th under Spruance; the ships were the same but the staff and command changed) was attacking the Philippines with his aircraft in mid-September, when, finding opposition unexpectedly light, he suggested that the invasion of Leyte Gulf be brought forward two months and that the operations against Yap, Palau, and Mindanao be abandoned. This was at once agreed by the Joint Chiefs of Staff, then meeting at Quebec, and so the shape of future strategy was decided. MacArthur's 'Philippines first' concept had won.

LEYTE GULF

The operations which then centred on Leyte Gulf involved the greatest number of warships ever engaged in battle at sea, while the land and air force units which took part were also very powerful. Again, the Japanese navy had planned to lure away the main American fleet, leaving the amphibious forces to be destroyed by two powerful surface forces attacking from the west. The plan at first succeeded admirably and on 24th October, Halsey with the whole of the 3rd Fleet, was drawn northwards by the Japanese aircraft carrier force under Ozawa. Ozawa had few aircraft in his carriers and his mission was suicidal; he lost all four carriers, but the beachhead in the Leyte Gulf was left very lightly defended – by a few escort-carriers and destroyers. However, the main Japanese surface force under Kurita, which had lost a battleship and two cruisers from air and submarine attacks en route, hesitated, and so reached the beachhead via the San Bernardino Straits too late. By then the second surface force under Nishima had already been destroyed in the Surigao Straits by Admiral Ollendorf's battleships, cruisers, and destroyers, and Kurita's nerve seemed to fail. He mistook the escort carriers and

Above: A painting by T. Ishikawa shows American and Japanese carrier-borne aircraft duelling over the South Pacific, an ocean where the skies ruled supreme

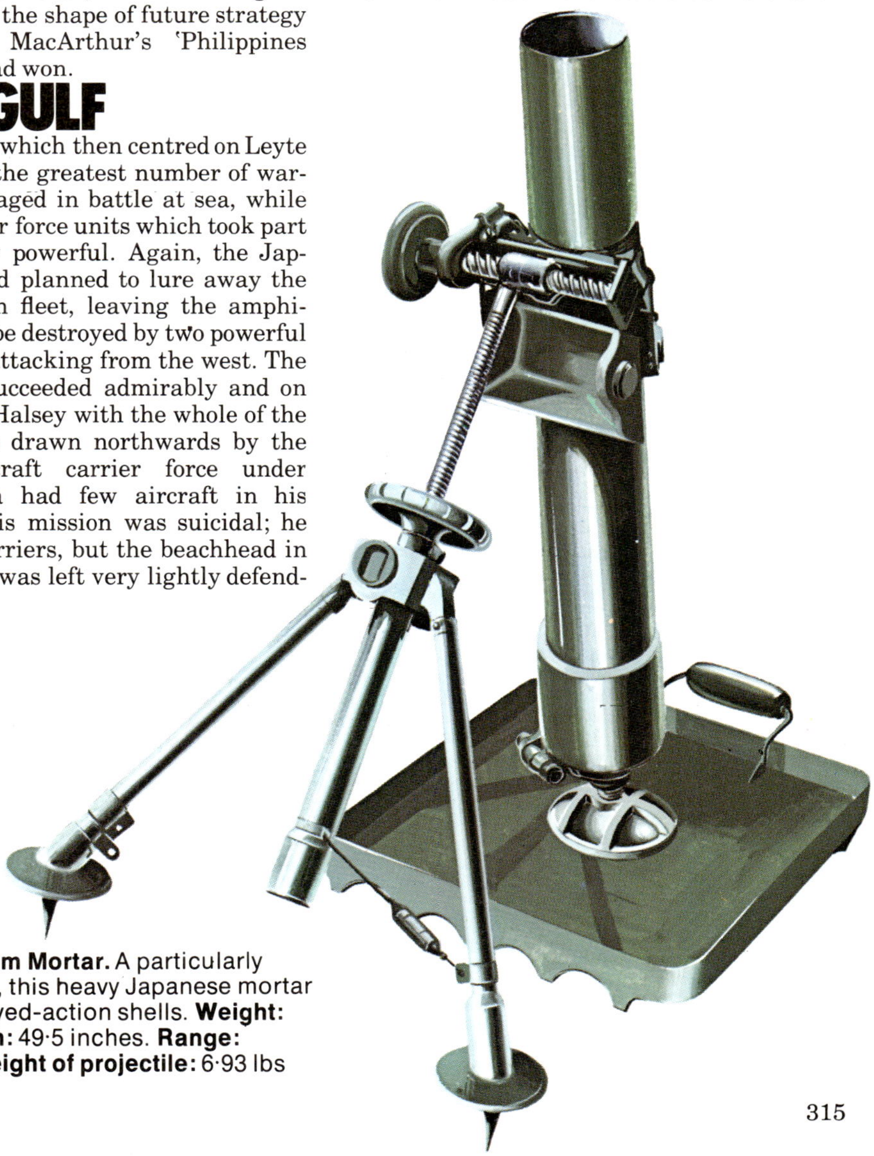

Model 97 81-mm Mortar. A particularly useful weapon, this heavy Japanese mortar could fire delayed-action shells. **Weight:** 145 lbs. **Length:** 49·5 inches. **Range:** 3100 yards. **Weight of projectile:** 6·93 lbs

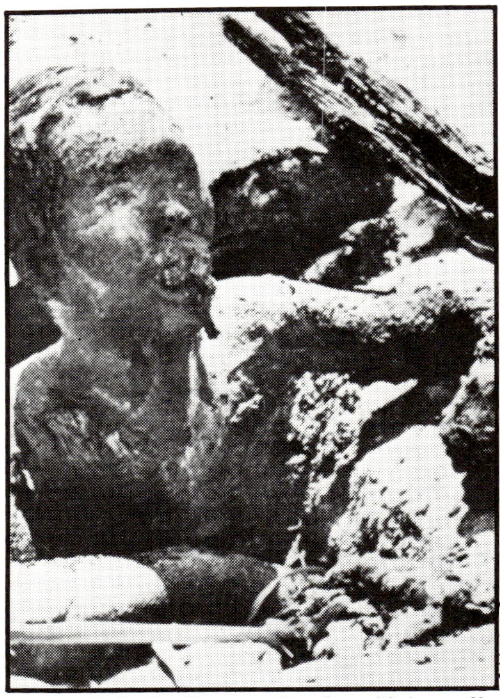

Alvin Coox

US Marine Corps

Above left: On Luzon, the horrifying effects of an American flame-thrower attack. Above centre: US Marines inching their

destroyers at the beachhead, which fought very bravely, for a 'gigantic task force', and after a short engagement he turned back, so losing a perfect opportunity of causing extensive damage to the assault forces. The Japanese navy had failed, and so ended its last great battle of the war for it never succeeded in getting into action again.

Ashore, the fighting was hard and there were delays in setting up the airfields, but after heavy losses Leyte Island was secured by 25th December.

LUZON & IWO JIMA

The next step was the invasion of Luzon which started on 9th January 1945. Again, the fighting was bitter and involved the largest scale land operations of the Pacific War. Admiral Kreuger's 6th army contained over 200,000 men, and the Japanese defenders over 250,000 men. The approach to Lingayan Gulf was made most disagreeable by the first *Kamikaze* air attacks, which succeeded in hitting several American and Australian ships, but the landing itself was unopposed and the serious fighting started well away from the beachhead. Corregidor, MacArthur's former headquarters, was taken on 21st February and Manila was secured by the end of March; after this the operation became that of 'mopping up' a desperate and fanatical enemy, but by April the main battle was over the the key points captured.

Almost at once, Nimitz took over the headlines by the attack on Iwo Jima, which was needed as an airbase for fighter planes to escort the bombers over Japan, and as a refuge for damaged aircraft. After several weeks of aerial bombardment from the Marianas and several days battering by ships, the 4th and 5th Marine Division landed on 19th February 1945. The 3rd Marine Division was in reserve, but was soon committed to the fight. Spruance's 5th Fleet was in support and made sure that no reinforcements reached Iwo Jima. The island was small—only eight square miles—but it had three airfield sites and the volcanic hills had been made into defensive warrens with many disguised weapon sites. Serious fortification did not start till December 1944, and the full plan was not completed by the day of the landing but the garrison had been reinforced to a total of 21,000 men. The initial landing was not strongly opposed and the Americans were first attacked when about 200 yards from the beach, when they met a murderous fire from the island's caves, pillboxes, and blockhouses. But they had been able to land much engineering equipment as well as tanks and guns and were well prepared for a tough battle. Co-operation with the bombarding ships and aircraft was excellent and gradually the most important defence positions were destroyed, but the honeycombs were difficult to subdue and the island was not declared secure until 18th March, while fighting continued spasmodically until 26th March. Even so, the first damaged B-29 landed safely on

Yamato
Displacement: 64,170 tons. **Dimensions:** 863×127×35 feet. **Armour:** *Main belt* 16 inches; *Deck* 7¾ inches; *Turrets* 20-25 inches. **Armament:** 9×18-inch, 12×6·1-inch AA, 24×25-mm AA, 4×13-mm guns, plus 6 aircraft. **Crew:** 3332. **Speed:** 27 knots

US Coast Guard

way up the beach on Iwo Jima. Above right: The scene on Okinawa beach in the early days after the massive US landings

4th March (the first of 850 emergency landings in three months) and on 7th April the first fighters left to escort a daylight bombing raid on Tokyo. The Americans lost about 7,000 marines and sailors.

OKINAWA

The next main operations quickly followed with the invasion of Okinawa by Buckner's 10th Army, which included three marine divisions for the intial landings. At this point the Royal Navy came into action in the Pacific with the task of neutralizing the airfields on the Sakishima Islands, through which the Japanese hoped to fly reinforcements to Okinawa.

After a bombardment of Palembang in Sumatra, the British fleet had arrived in Australia on 4th February 1945. By April, when Okinawa was attacked, its main elements were four aircraft-carriers, two battleships, four cruisers, eleven destroyers, and a large 'fleet train' of supply ships which enabled operations to continue for many weeks without putting in to harbour. Admiral Fraser was in overall command. Admiral Rawlings the commander at sea, and Admiral Vian in charge of the carriers. It is enough to say that the British force acquitted itself well and in particular that its armoured deck aircraft-carriers were able to survive the *Kamikaze* attacks whereas the lighter decked Americans had to retire when struck.

The attack on Okinawa was on an enormous scale. During the campaign, which lasted eighty-two days, over half a million Allied troops took part and the initial assault was carried out by 183,000 soldiers and marines. The ships at sea suffered severely from the *Kamikaze* attacks and many were sunk or damaged during their long ordeal. Again, the troops landed without opposition, but soon came up against a fanatical defence. The campaign was long and bitter but the island was finally secure by 21st June, by which time the Japanese had lost 110,000 men, while the Americans had suffered nearly 8,000 killed and the ships afloat nearly 5,000 – the latter almost all victims of *Kamikaze* attacks.

Although it was not known at the time, the last great operation of the Pacific War was over, though in July and August Halsey's 3rd Fleet, of which the British contingent formed part, cruised freely off Honshu, attacking the enemy with aircraft and bombarding him.

INSIDE JAPAN

It is now time to consider the internal situation in Japan. By the middle of 1944, a number of thoughtful politicians and serving officers had come to the conclusion that defeat was inevitable and that it was in the interest of the country to negotiate a settlement of the war as soon as possible. Otherwise, it was argued, Communism would follow the inevitable chaos.

After the fall of Saipan in July 1944, the government of General Tojo, who had been Prime Minister since 1941, fell and a

DEATH OF A BEHEMOTH

The *Yamato*, the greatest battleship ever built, had also the shortest active career of any capital ship in the Second World War. Intended originally to be the first of a 'super' battle fleet, she was the foundation of Japanese naval hopes of defeating the Americans at sea. She was believed to be absolutely superior in guns, speed, and armour to any other capital ship, as indeed she was – but without air cover these great assets were of no avail. The pointless loss of this ship in a 'special' attack on the Okinawa landings emphasises the straits to which the Japanese navy was reduced.

coalition took over with a mandate to continue to prosecute the war. Tojo had accumulated much power over the years and he ended up as his own Chief of the Army General Staff as well as being Prime Minister. He refused to consider the possibility of defeat and believed, like many of the Japanese generals, that honour demanded the destruction of the whole Japanese people rather than voluntary submission. By early 1945, the Emperor was extremely worried and he consulted many elder statesmen, most of whom advised the continuation of the war. Prince Konoye, a former Prime Minister, declared roundly, however, that the war had been lost and that peace must be made as soon as possible. The loss of Iwo Jima in April 1945 brought the fall of the coalition government: almost simultaneously the Russians announced that they would not renew the neutrality pact with Japan which was due to expire in April 1946. After much discussion, an elderly Admiral, Suzuki, was nominated as Prime Minister with a clear mandate to bring the war to an end as soon as possible. The shipping situation was disastrous, heavy air-raids were destroying Japanese cities one by one, and production of war materials was coming to an end. Suzuki's task was not easy – most of the generals were fanatically determined on resistance to the bitter end and the Japanese people had relapsed into fatalistic despair. After the end of the war in Europe, it was decided to ask the Russians for mediation and talks were held with the Russian ambassador to Japan Jacob Malik. But the Russians did not answer and it was not until 12th July that the Japanese ambassador in Moscow was ordered by cable to approach the Russian government. On 21st July he made a formal request for Soviet mediation to bring the war to an end. The Potsdam Conference was then in session, and Stalin informed Roosevelt and Churchill of this approach (of which the Americans were already aware through their reading of the Japanese cyphers), but nothing was done because the Japanese had not yet agreed to surrender unconditionally. Behind all these discussions loomed the atomic bomb, which was successfully tested during the conference. The first bomb was dropped on 6th August, and the second on 9th August, on the same day as the Russian invasion of Manchuria. On 15th August the Emperor broadcast his rescript which ended the war.

The Russian invasion was swift and successful and the whole of Manchuria and north Korea was in their hands by the end of August. Elsewhere, Hong Kong was reoccupied by British naval forces in early September, and in many Pacific islands surrenders were being arranged. On 2nd September a formal surrender ceremony was held aboard the American battleship *Missouri* in Tokyo Bay. General MacArthur signed as Supreme Commander of the Allied Powers, and he was followed by representatives of all the powers which had taken part in the war against Japan.

Thus, happily, the great invasion of the Japanese homeland, which had been planned during the summer of 1945, was unnecessary. 'Operation Olympic' against Kyusho was due to take place on 1st November, and the main operations against Honshu in March or April of 1946 ('Operation Coronet'). Both invasions would have been on an enormous scale. A British Commonwealth force of two or three divisions was planned to join Coronet and by then British bombers would also have been taking part in the air attack on Japan. While there can be no doubt as to the eventual outcome, the operations would have been tough and losses high. The Japanese armies were still intact and they had good supplies of ammunition, while the remaining aircraft would have been used in suicide attacks which could cause great damage. The American High Command was divided on the problem of whether the invasion would be ultimately necessary and some high officers believed that capitulation would come through the air and sea blockade alone. Historians are similarly divided, though the full knowledge of the underground work of the peace party in the summer of 1945 has only been widely known comparatively recently, and thus the evidence against invasion has been somewhat strengthened. It is too soon for a certain judgement to be made – the issue is still fogged by inter-service rivalry. Whatever the decision of history, however, nothing can alter the superb achievements of the American forces nor of the industry which worked miracles of production to support them. Nor can the story of the fanatical bravery and skill – however misguided – of the Japanese fighting men ever be diminished.

National Archives

Life Magazine

Above: A Japanese suicide plane *(Kamikaze)* approaches an American warship, explodes in a ball of fire, and leaves in its wake a serious danger to the ship and crew. Left: A small section of a fire-bombed Japanese city.

National Archives

ARTWORK INDEX